HITLER AND
THE POWER OF
AESTHETICS

HITLER AND THE POWER OF AESTHETICS

FREDERIC SPOTTS

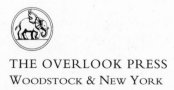

THE OVERLOOK PRESS
WOODSTOCK & NEW YORK

First published in paperback in the United States in 2004 by
The Overlook Press, Peter Mayer Publishers, Inc.
Woodstock & New York

WOODSTOCK:
One Overlook Drive
Woodstock, NY 12498
www.overlookpress.com
[for individual orders, bulk and special sales, contact our Woodstock office]

NEW YORK:
141 Wooster Street
New York, NY 10012

Library of Congress Cataloging-in-Publication Data

Spotts, Frederic.
Hitler and the power of aesthetics / Frederic Spotts
p. cm.
Includes bibliographical references and index.
1. Hitler, Adolf, 1889-1945—Biography. 2. National socialism and art.
3. Germany—Cultural policy. 4. Art and state—Germany—History—20th century.
5. Aesthetics, German—20th century. 6 Aesthetics, Austrian—20th century. I. Title
DD247.H5 S654 2002   943.086'092 B 21   2002066302

Manufactured in the United States of America
ISBN 1-58567-507-5
1 2 3 4 5 6 7 8 9 10

The fellow is a catastrophe. But that is no reason why we should not find him interesting, as a character and as an event.

THOMAS MANN, *Brother Hitler*

Contents

HITLER AND THE POWER OF AESTHETICS

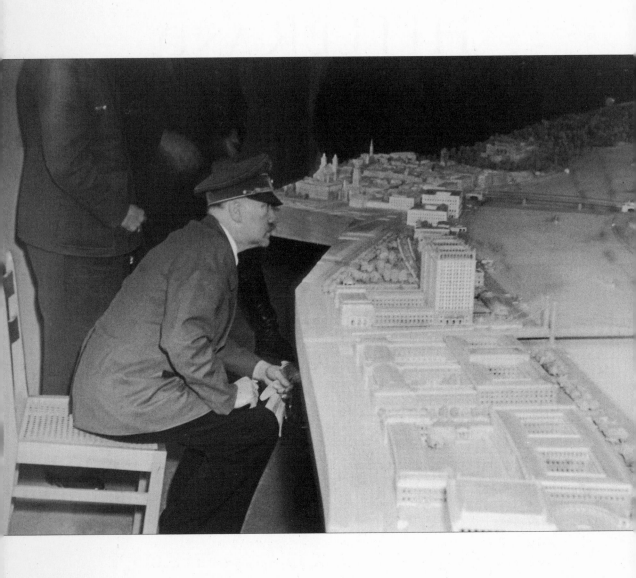

Preface

There he sits, deep in thought, studying a grand model of his home town of Linz. The model shows the city as it will look after being transformed into the culture centre of Europe. It had been delivered the day before and lighting arrangements were installed to enable him to envisage how the buildings would appear at various times of the day as well as by moonlight. The date is 13 February 1945. The place is the bunker under the Reich chancellery in Berlin. The Russians are at the Oder, a hundred miles away; the British and Americans are near the Rhine some 300 miles to the west. Yet Hitler spends hours absorbed in his model. He worries that the bell tower in the centre of town may be too tall; it must not eclipse the spire of the cathedral at Ulm further up the Danube since that would hurt the pride of the people living there. But it must be high enough to catch the first beams of the sun in the morning and the last in the evening. 'In the tower I want a carillon to play – not every day but on special days – a theme from Bruckner's Fourth, the Romantic Symphony,' he tells his architect. During the weeks and months to follow, the model will continue to offer him solace, even as his Reich – and it was his Reich – collapses around him.

This book is about the life of Adolf Hitler as epitomized in that scene – his aesthetic nature, his conviction that the ultimate objective of political effort should be artistic achievement and his dream of creating the greatest culture state since ancient times, or perhaps of all time. 'I became a politician against my will,' he said over and over. 'If someone else had been found, I would never have gone into politics; I would have become an artist or philosopher.' After being appointed chancellor in 1933 the first building he had erected was not a monument to his own triumph – comparable to Mussolini's Forum Mussolini or Franco's Valle de los Caidos – but a massive art gallery. Having failed to induce Churchill to drop out of the war in 1940, he complained to his field commanders, 'It is a pity that I have to wage war on account of that drunk instead of serving the works of peace.' A little later he commented, 'Military battles are eventually forgotten. Our buildings, however, will stand.' And, speaking of the cultural marvels he intended to create after his final victory, he assured his staff, 'The funds which I shall devote to these will vastly exceed the expenditures which we found necessary for the conduct of this war.'

Did he mean what he said? Are his words credible in light of the indescribable death and destruction he caused? Shortly after he launched his war in 1939, Albert Speer's secretary overheard him say, 'We must end this war quickly. We don't want war; we want to build.' Years later she asked herself, 'Are we to think that that was a lie too?' It was not a lie, as the following pages show, but it was a half-truth. He wanted both war *and* art. Once he had won his war and established an Aryan state that was a dominant world power, he intended to devote himself to the creation of cultural monuments that would change the face of Germany and immortalize himself. Destruction was to be the way to construction.

The Hitler of this book is someone for whom culture was not only the end to which power should aspire but also a means of achieving and keeping it. In *The Story of Art*, E. H. Gombrich observed that Expressionism sprang from the fear of 'that utter loneliness that would reign if art were to fail and each man remained immured in himself'. This fear was deeply felt by Hitler personally, even though he considered Expressionism the disease it sought to cure. Perceiving the anomie of twentieth-century life may have been his most precocious intuition. To replace the German feeling of defeat and isolation with self-confidence and pride was the aim he set for himself and a critical element in his political appeal. Culture, which historically defined German identity in the face of disunity and ambiguous borders, played a vital role.

It was Hitler's aesthetic talents that also help to explain his mysterious grip on the German people. What Stalin accomplished through terror, Hitler achieved through seduction. Using a new style of politics, mediated through symbols, myths, rites, spectacles and personal dramatics, he reached the masses as did no other leader of his time. Though he took away democratic government, he gave Germans what they clearly found a more meaningful sense of political participation, transforming them from spectators into participants in National Socialist theatre.

Yet for over fifty years books written about Hitler have ignored the centrality of the arts in his life and career. And for over fifty years studies of one or another aspect of cultural life in the Third Reich have left him out of the picture. Why? With a few notable exceptions in recent years, most art historians do not know or want to know about this embarrassing connection. Among biographers a strong preference for 'drum and trumpet history' is a large part of the explanation. History written during the last hundred years, as Fernand Braudel observed, is almost invariably *l'histoire événementielle*, political history focusing on the drama of 'great events' – in this case, what-Hitler-did-next. 'We failed to see,' George Mosse said on behalf of the liberal left, 'that the fascist aesthetic itself reflected the needs and hopes of contemporary society, that what we brushed aside as the so-called superstructure was in reality the means through which most people grasped the fascist message, transforming politics into a civic religion.' Only in the memoirs of Albert Speer is to be found some appreciation of the way Hitler applied his aesthetic talents to public life and only in the biography of Hitler by Speer's editor, Joachim Fest, is this trait touched on.

But even Fest and more recently Ian Kershaw have viewed Hitler as basically an 'unperson'. In comparison with Napoleon, Bismarck, Churchill and Kennedy, who were 'figures of substance outside their public lives', according to Kershaw, 'outside politics Hitler's life was largely a void'. This is as misleading about Napoleon, Bismarck, Churchill and especially Kennedy as it is about Hitler. Hitler's interest in the arts was as intense as his racism; to disregard the one is as profound a distortion as to pass over the other. But how is this side of Hitler to be reconciled with the all-too-familiar one? Carl J. Burckhardt, League of Nations Commissioner in Danzig, who met the dictator twice on the eve of the war in 1939, gave the only answer. The man had a dual personality, he concluded, 'the first being that of the rather gentle artist and the second that of the homicidal maniac'. For the last half-century and for obvious reasons writers have written about Hitler the homicidal maniac. Without in any way ignoring that Hitler, this book examines the other one.

Being neither biography nor a history of the arts in the Third Reich, the book treats biographical material and cultural developments only insofar as they are directly pertinent to an understanding of Hitler's aesthetic bent of mind and how that worked its way out in his personal and political life. Although Hitler enjoyed looking at movies, he had no interest in the film as an art form and left it to Joseph Goebbels to exploit cinema for propaganda purposes. Relatively fond of the theatre though he was, he paid little attention to it after becoming chancellor. Although in his youth he loved adventure stories – not just Karl May's Wild West fantasies, as is often thought, but also such works as *Robinson Crusoe*, *Gulliver's Travels*, *Uncle Tom's Cabin* and especially *Don Quixote* – serious literature held no interest for him. Therefore it has been possible to pass over these topics.

Sources

Half the world believes what the other half invents. Biographers and historians have not always distinguished themselves in their handling of secondary material about Hitler. Since there is little documentation about his personal life, especially in the early years, writers have relied on books written many years after the events described by persons whose backgrounds were often dubious. Some of their products are as fraudulent as the 'Hitler Diaries' of 1983, yet these fabulations have been taken up and recycled as hard fact. As a result, fake facts and invented quotations abound.

The most notorious example is August Kubizek's *Adolf Hitler, Mein Jugendfreund*, which has been used by writer after writer as the prime source of information on Hitler's youth. Between 1905 and 1908 Kubizek knew Hitler in both Linz and Vienna. The two men did not meet again until 1938 when, following the *Anschluß*, Hitler returned to Linz and invited Kubizek, then a town clerk in Eferding, for a chat. A short time later party officials requested Kubizek to write down his memories of life with his friend. Hagiography was predestined. As one official reported to party headquarters, Kubizek's insight into Hitler's mind was amazing. 'The greatness of the Führer that we all find so incredible was already evident in his youth.' Kubizek, though scarcely needing it, had his cue.

Contrary to claims that he had produced a manuscript in 1938 or 1939, Kubizek did not manage to put anything on paper for several years. Indeed, as he admitted in both the foreword and the text of his book, he was repeatedly prodded by Martin Bormann and other party officials to get down to work. Even Hitler found it necessary in July 1943 to authorize a one-time payment along with a monthly stipend to cajole him into producing a text. The mayor of Eferding also applied pressure and assigned him a secretary to help. Finally Kubizek started toiling away and at length drafted what he referred to as two *Büchel*, booklets, entitled 'Erinnerungen an die mit dem Führer gemeinsam verlebten Jünglingsjahre 1904–1908 in Linz und Wien' (Reminiscences of youthful years spent with the Führer in 1904–1908 in Linz and Vienna).

Completing them some time before the end of the war but never submitting them to the party, Kubizek hid the booklets in the wall of his house to prevent their being confiscated when American occupation forces arrived.

Interned after the war because of his friendship with Hitler, Kubizek was contacted in 1948 by Franz Jetzinger, librarian of the provincial archive in Linz, who had begun writing an account of Hitler's early life and sought out everyone who might provide first-hand information. Kubizek was only too happy to co-operate. He still idolized his old friend and lent his 'Reminiscences' to Jetzinger with a plea to turn them into a biography or drama that would, as he put it, 'destroy the caricature' of Hitler created by hostile writers. For nearly a year the two met and corresponded. To Jetzinger's probing questions, Kubizek wrote long answers, some of which were plausible but trivial and some of which aroused Jetzinger's strong scepticism, prompting a hurt Kubizek to ask, 'Why should I lie to you?' But he admitted that in contrast to Jetzinger's scholarly and factual approach, his fuzzy commentary was bound to sound like 'a tale, a short story or a novel'. Jetzinger, an anti-Nazi Social Democrat in the 1930s, was increasingly exasperated by Kubizek's undiminished admiration for Hitler, whom he variously described as 'above all a great idealist', 'one of the brightest nova stars of our age', 'a unique phenomenon in the history of the German people' and the like. Eventually relations were broken off.

In 1953 *Adolf Hitler, Mein Jugendfreund* came out and was heralded as a unique first-hand account of Hitler's early years. English-language translations followed, appearing in Britain as *Young Hitler: The Story of Our Friendship* and in America as *The Young Hitler I Knew*. The fact alone that nearly a half-century had elapsed between publication and the events described should have been sufficient warning to beware of the book. But desperate to account for Hitler's early life and having next to no solid information to go on, historians mined it as though it were biographic gold. For the British edition Hugh Trevor-Roper, who later authenticated the 'Hitler Diaries' with similar credulity, even wrote a gushing introduction, which itself contained errors.

Jetzinger responded in 1956 with his own book, *Hitlers Jugend*,★ which denounced Kubizek's work as 'at least ninety per cent lies and fantastic fairy

★ *Hitler's Youth*, purporting to be a straightforward translation of the book, is a poorly translated, drastically abridged and revised version of the original. The abridgement and revisions are acknowledged neither by the translator nor by Alan Bullock, who contributed a foreword in which he claimed that Kubizek's 'Reminiscences' had 'appeared' in 1938.

tales to glorify Hitler'. The characterization was true enough. But the greater truth is that the book cannot even have been written by Kubizek. As he stated in his letters to Jetzinger and as his contacts with Nazi authorities after 1938 confirm, Kubizek found writing an incubus – 'writing is a horrible burden; it is not something I can do'. Not only did he suffer writer's block, he also lacked, as is evident in the crude prose of the letters, a minimal ability to write. In fact, he himself remarked to Jetzinger that his own writings 'belong in the hands of a real writer [*ein Dichter*] if they are to be given the shape necessary to make them effective'. Moreover, what was eventually published contradicted the 'Reminiscences'. The latter were undoubtedly written to endear himself to Hitler and the Nazi party; the book was an obvious attempt to whitewash the late lamented dictator in the eyes of the post-war public. In the early text Hitler was already in 1907 viciously anti-Semitic; the Hitler of the published version was scarcely anti-Semitic at all. Hitler Mark I was quoted verbatim only twice and briefly; Hitler Mark II never stopped talking, pouring forth countless verbatim remarks in stilted language. In the book an entire chapter was devoted to Hitler's passion for a girl named Stephanie, possibly to demonstrate the man's sexual normality; in the memoir Stephanie's name was not mentioned. Other discrepancies abound.

It is therefore impossible to believe that in the course of a year or so someone who was unable to write adequate prose and who had needed nearly six years to produce two little booklets could have begotten an entirely new text of 350 printed pages, all smoothly written, with purple passages and literary flourishes. A claim by the Austrian writer Brigitte Hamann that he turned 'earlier drafts' over to his publisher, Stocker Verlag, where they were rewritten and padded out by an imaginative editor, is denied by the publisher. The director of the house has insisted that Kubizek 'provided a completed manuscript' and '*nothing was rewritten* by the publishing house (up to the present moment) so as to maintain its documentary value'. Whether a ghost-writer or an editorial assistant, Kubizek found his 'real writer' who produced a script concocted of shaky memories and invented stories with the intent of idealizing the late Führer. In accordance with a corollary of Gresham's law that bad books drive out good ones, Kubizek's bogus work was translated into various languages and continues to be cited as a credible source. Still readily available in German-language bookshops, it is now in its sixth edition.

Is Kubizek's testimony, then, worthless? The book, a mixture of the possibly true, the provably false and a ghost-writer's fancy, is no better than a historical novel and its verbatim quotations are outright inventions. The 'Reminiscences' are a slightly different story. Even the sceptical Jetzinger found some parts of them to be 'plausible', and that manuscript is on a few occasions cited here when the testimony appears to fall into that category.

A similar problem bedevils accounts of Hitler's later years in Vienna. Here, too, in the absence of solid information, some historians have compensated by drawing on accounts published in later decades by two rogues, Reinhold Hanisch and Josef Greiner. Greiner never met Hitler; articles under Hanisch's name were published posthumously in English in New York but the identity of the author is unknown, as is the relationship between what was published and what was actually written by Hanisch. Hanisch was a major forger of Hitler's paintings; many of his claims – such as Hitler's philo-Semitism – are almost certainly as fraudulent. These writings, too, are the stuff of the 'Hitler Diaries'.

Memoirs of Hitler after his entry into politics by such diverse characters as Hermann Rauschning, Hans Frank, Ernst Hanfstaengl (described by William Shirer as 'an immense, high-strung, incoherent clown'), Johannes von Müllern-Schönhausen, Henriette von Schirach, Heinz Heinz, Arno Breker and Friedelind Wagner fall in the category of interesting-if-true, where fact is often impossible to winnow out from demonstrable invention. Here these books are shunned except where a passage from them is consistent with other sources; the authorship is cited so the testimony can be appropriately evaluated. Albert Speer's two volumes of memoirs *Inside the Third Reich* and *Spandau: The Secret Diaries* present their own problems. Written with a compulsion to exculpate and puff up their author while disparaging almost everyone else, they routinely distort facts. Still, their account of Hitler's activities and comments in the cultural sphere is fully consistent with the testimony of primary material, such as Hitler's recorded monologues and Goebbels's diaries. The other of Hitler's major architects who left a memoir, Hermann Giesler, revered Hitler as much after 1945 as before, but his words on architectural matters appear generally trustworthy. Such is similarly the case with the reminiscences about the arts by Hans Severus Ziegler, who knew Hitler from 1924 on.

There is, however, another category of post-war memoirs, those by members of Hitler's entourage and officials of government who, unlike

Speer, focus their attention on Hitler rather than on themselves and, unlike Giesler and Ziegler, take a more distant – in some cases critical – attitude towards their subject. These include accounts by Otto Dietrich, Christa Schroeder, Baldur von Schirach, Lutz Schwerin von Krosigk, Nicolaus von Below, Heinrich Hoffmann, Fritz Wiedemann, Heinz Linge, Friedrich Christian zu Schaumburg-Lippe and even at times Alfred Rosenberg, for example. What they have written of relevance to this book are matters about which they had no motive to distort the record and which normally accord with other accounts. That is similarly the case with the voluminous diaries of Joseph Goebbels, including those portions found in Moscow in 1992, which have a great deal to say about Hitler's interest and activities in the arts.

Hitler's own expansive comments on culture and the arts are to be found in *Mein Kampf*, his speeches, his lengthy remarks at the cultural session of the party rallies and the so-called table talk or monologues. The standard English translation of *Mein Kampf* by Ralph Manheim is used here, although occasionally minor changes have been made to bring it closer to the original text. The record made of Hitler's mealtime and post-prandial remarks have been published in various versions; this book relies primarily on the edition edited by Werner Jochmann but also occasionally the 1976 edition by Henry Picker. Speer's comment is worth quoting: 'Almost all of what Picker puts into Hitler's mouth I likewise heard Hitler say in the same or similar phrases.' Hitler's statements as recorded in the monologues as well as by Goebbels, Speer, Schroeder and, more fragmentarily, by others of the inner entourage such as Hoffmann and Dietrich, are essentially identical, providing solid evidence of their mutual reliability.

This text draws on archival material held by the Oberösterreiches Landesarchiv in Linz ('Reminiscences' of August Kubizek and his correspondence with Franz Jetzinger); the Institut für Zeitgeschichte and Bayerisches Hauptstaatsarchiv in Munich; the Bundesarchiv in Berlin; the National Archives in Washington (Consolidated Interrogation Report No.4: Linz: Hitler's Museum and Library; OSS Report of 15 December 1945; Detailed Interrogation Report No. 12: Hermann Voss: OSS Report of 12 September 1945; Supplement of 15 January 1946 to Consolidated Interrogation Report No.4: Linz; and Detailed Interrogation Report No.1: Heinrich Hoffmann; OSS Report of 1 July 1945; Interrogation of Paula Wolf of 5 June 1946); the Germanisches Nationalmuseum in Nuremberg (Hans Posse's diaries); the American Army Military Museum in Washington (four of Hitler's watercolours) and the Richard Strauss Archive in Garmisch (Richard Strauss's correspondence with Winifred Wagner). The surviving documentation assembled by the Hauptarchiv der NSDAP was seized by the American Army in 1945 and, after being microfilmed by the Hoover Institution in 1964, was deposited in the Berlin Document Centre and now forms part of the Bundesarchiv in Berlin. The citations here are to the microfilms.

In the pages that follow Hitler himself is often quoted, sometimes at length. Confronting his own words and mode of expression makes it easier to imagine his authentic voice and to see his mind in action in a way that is not possible by summary and paraphrase. The source of these and other quotations and references in the text is cited at the end of the book by page number and initial phrase.

Acknowledgements

It is a pleasure to thank the persons and institutions without whose help this book would not have been possible. I am particularly beholden to Harry Kreisler, Executive Director of the Institute of International Studies, University of California at Berkeley for offering me a friendly academic home where I could work. Among the curators, librarians and archivists whose assistance was invaluable, I wish to single out Gerhart Marckhgott (Oberösterreisches Landesarchiv, Linz); Frfr. Andrian-Werburg (Germanisches Nationalmuseum, Nuremberg); Gabriele Strauss (Richard Strauss Archive, Garmisch); Frau Hufeland (Federal Archive, Berlin); Michael Fritthum (Vienna State Opera); Max Oppel (Wittelsbacher Ausgleichsfond, Munich); Sven Friedrich and Gudrun Föttinger (Richard Wagner Museum, Bayreuth); Raimund Wünsche (Staatliche Antikensammlungen, Munich); E. van de Wetering (Kunsthistorisch Instituut, Amsterdam); Margaret Sherry (Princeton University Library); James Spohrer and Kathryn Wayne (University of California, Berkeley library); Elena Danielson, Agnes Peterson and Linda Wheeler (the Hoover Institution); Atti Vihinen (Sibelius Hall, Lahti); Trish Hayes (BBC Archives Centre); Hannelore Koehler (German Information Service); Jane Kallir (The Galerie St Etienne, New York); Friedrich Mayrhofer (Archiv der Stadt Linz); Ursel Berger (Kolbe Museum, Berlin).

For additional help and illustrative material I am grateful to the Institut für Zeitgeschichte, Munich; the Institut für Zeitgeschichte, Vienna; Ilse Dvorak-Stocker, Stocker Verlag, Graz; National Archives, Library of Congress and the American Army Military Museum, Washington; Karen Tieth and Annette Samaras, Ullstein Bild, Berlin; Bayerisches Hauptstaatsarchiv, Munich; Angelika Obermeier, Bayerische StaatsBibliothek, Munich; Stadtarchiv Linz; Stadtarchiv Landeshauptstadt München, Munich; Oberösterreiches Landesarchiv, Linz; Norbert Ludwig, Bildarchiv preußischer Kulturbesitz, Berlin; B. Schäche, Landesarchiv Berlin; Deutsches Historisches Museum, Berlin; the Goethe Institute, New York and the Austrian Cultural Institute, New York.

Photocopies of Hitler's architectural sketchbook, Lieselotte Schmidt's stenographic record and letters, the record of Wilhelm Furtwängler's denazification trial along with a few other documents were provided by sources who requested anonymity.

Thanks are due to the following for permission to reproduce illustrations on the pages listed below:

Bayerische StaatsBibliothek, Munich (70, 78, 82, 83, 103, 105, 165, 166, 171, 179, 185, 331, 333, 336, 389)

Bildarchiv preußischer Kulturbesitz, Berlin (45, 46, 48, 57, 349)

Institut für Zeitgeschichte, Vienna (229, 297)

Richard Wagner Museum, Bayreuth (84, 85, 251, 254)

Landesarchiv, Berlin (357, 359)

Stadtarchiv, Munich (115, 116, 369)

Richard Strauss Archiv, Garmisch (299)

Ullstein Bilderdienst, Berlin (20, 157, 164, 231, 347, 394, 395, 396, 398)

Germanisches Nationalmuseum, Nuremberg (190)

Stadtarchiv Linz (213, 215, 375)

Bayerisches Hauptstaatsarchiv, Munich (214, 370)

I also wish to thank Hanns-Peter Frentz for permission to publish photographs by his father, Walter Frentz, on pages *x*, 93, 175, 181, 371, 372, 377 and 378.

My sincerest thanks go to Reinhold Brinkmann, Elizabeth Honig, Kathleen James, William Schaffer, Hermann Weiß, Theodor Wieser and Philip Wolfson for reading parts of the draft manuscript. My gratitude is due as well to those who answered enquiries or contributed in other ways: Barry Millington, Hans Hotter, Peter Selz, Klaus Harpprecht, Philipp Lichenthaler, Ulla Morris-Carter, Gesine Schaffer, Gordon Grant, Lindsay Newman, Roger Cardinal, Henri-Louis de la Grange, Anton Joachimsthaler, Paul Friedrich, Paul Jascot, Manfred Wagner and Ina Cooper.

Even with the assistance of those mentioned, this book would not have appeared in print without the help of my agent Anthea Morton-Saner and above all my editor at Hutchinson, Tony Whittome. For publication in the United States, I am indebted to Peter Mayer, publisher of the Overlook Press. To them all my heartiest thanks.

THE
RELUCTANT
DICTATOR

1 THE BOHEMIAN AESTHETE

NOT SURPRISINGLY IT WAS AN ARTIST – Thomas Mann – who was the first to point out that Adolf Hitler was himself essentially an artist and that it was his aesthetic nature that endowed him with a wizardry that left Germany and Europe seemingly helpless under its spell. 'Like it or not, how can we fail to recognize in this phenomenon a sign of artistry?' he asked in his 1938 essay, *Brother Hitler*. Fifteen years earlier Houston Stewart Chamberlain, the great evangelist of German anti-Semitism, had met Hitler in Bayreuth and immediately sensed a similar quality. Hitler was, Chamberlain found, 'not a fanatic but . . . the exact opposite of a fanatic', not a politician 'but the opposite of a politician'. His appeal was not to the head but to the heart, and the power he possessed over people was expressed through his eyes and hand movements. Indeed, Hitler's most perceptive biographer, Joachim Fest, repeatedly asks whether Hitler was anything but an artist. Did politics ever mean anything more to him than rhetoric, than the histrionics of processions, parades and party rallies or the spectacle aspects of war? The answer was an emphatic no, according to Albert Speer, who knew Hitler better than any other survivor of the Third Reich. After twenty years of thinking it over in Spandau prison, Speer came to the conclusion that for his entire life Hitler was always and with his whole heart basically an artist.

These remarks, even Mann's, would have delighted Hitler. In fact, his reaction to Chamberlain's comment was witnessed and recorded. As the joy of a child on receiving a treasured gift, is how it was described. Some detected this instinctively. Even the venerable President of Germany, Paul von Hindenburg – 'of rigid mind and slow reasoning' – often referred to Hitler as 'that bohemian corporal'. Although this was in the misapprehension that Hitler's birthplace was in Bohemia rather than Austria, it was also because Hindenburg sensed in him the romantic quality of an artist. It was this aesthetic spark, this artistic impulse that inspired Hitler and separated him from others – from his schoolmates at first, from the entire German political class later on and eventually from all the other European statesmen. Again and again over the years he insisted to friends, associates and even foreign officials that he thought of himself not as a politician but as an artist.

The origin of this aesthetic bent of mind is a mystery. It was certainly neither genetic nor environmental. The family was uncultured. His father, Alois, was a rough customs official; his mother, Klara, an uneducated hausfrau. His sole brush with culture occurred in the form of singing and piano lessons, and participation in the local church choir, all of it very brief. The school he attended in Linz was a good one – Ludwig Wittgenstein was a fellow student – but he did poorly, probably by rebellious intent. After his father's sudden death in 1903, Klara placed him in another school, but the results were just as dismal. Yet somehow there had taken root elements of what has been considered an artistic disposition – a love of drawing, a proclivity for fantasy, an independence of spirit, an aversion to disciplined work. According to his sister Paula, he developed an 'extraordinary interest' in 'architecture, painting and music'. At the age of twelve – in 1901 – he attended his first play, Schiller's *Wilhelm Tell*, and shortly afterwards his first opera, *Lohengrin*. The opera occasioned a transcendent aesthetic experience that left him Wagner's prisoner for life. By now he was determined to follow a career in the arts, declaring to family and schoolmates his intention of becoming a painter – not just a painter but a famous one.

A failure at school, he managed by the autumn of 1905, at the age of sixteen, to bully his mother into letting him drop out without getting a diploma. His dream of living the free life of an artist was now reality. He regularly attended the theatre and opera, joined a musical society, sketched, painted and read. The following spring his mother made arrangements for him to make his first visit to Vienna so that he could see the paintings in the great Habsburg collections. From the moment of arrival he was so bedazzled that he still raved about it nearly two decades later when he came to write *Mein Kampf*. What over-whelmed him even more than the famous canvases were the public buildings. 'For hours I could stand in front of the Opera,' he recalled, 'for hours I could gaze at the Parliament; the whole Ringstraße seemed to me like an enchantment out of the *Arabian Nights*.' His enthusiasm was such that he could not help sharing it with his one close friend in Linz, August Kubizek. In a number of postcards – the oldest surviving documents in Hitler's hand – he reported his first impressions, and these were of the operas he attended and the acoustics of the opera house itself. Not for this serious young man were the amusements of the Prater, the beer halls or the cafés.

So fascinated was he by what he had seen that on his return home he was prompted to try his hand at simple architectural sketches and even drew the exterior and floor plan of a villa which he promised some day to build for Kubizek. There also survive an ink drawing of a newly constructed villa, a watercolour of the Pöstlingberg restaurant and two sketches of the interior of a proposed opera house in Linz. During the following months he spent hours, accompanied by his friend, wandering about the town looking at the buildings and imagining how individual structures and whole areas might be reconstructed. The aesthetic urge was still not satisfied. He decided to write a play. Then he took piano lessons. Later he thought he might like to be a composer.

But it was as a painter that he saw his destiny and in 1907 he took a decisive step when he left home to seek entry to the Vienna Academy of Fine Arts. To his profound shock, he was rejected. What he did in the months that followed is not clear. Judging by his comments later in life, he passed much of the time sketching churches, street scenes and public buildings, and spent what little money he had on tickets to the opera. After a year he again applied to the Academy and was again turned down. He was devastated.

Biographic orthodoxy has it that Hitler now, even more than earlier in his life, was nothing more than a feckless wastrel who led 'a parasitical existence', 'a drone's life'. But in fact he differed scarcely at all from thousands of young people of artistic bent throughout history. Such aspiring artists spend years in a tormented struggle trying to realize themselves. Those who achieve success are praised for their perseverance, those who fail are considered lazy drifters. Hitler's problem – in a way his tragedy – was that he confused aesthetic drive with aesthetic talent. Although the difference must have begun to be apparent to him by 1908, he was determined to pursue his muse as best he could.

Next to nothing is known about his life during the following year or so beyond exiguous data in Viennese police files based on his residential registration forms. From these emerges a young man on the skids, sleeping in cafés, parks, cheap lodging houses and eventually various shelters for the homeless. 'This was the saddest period of my life,' he commented in *Mein Kampf*. It was also the moment when, by his own testimony, it rooted in him a deep cruelty which, as he remarked, 'kills all pity' and 'destroys our feeling for the misery of those who have remained behind'.

With no artistic training and limited talent, he could do no better than eke out a meagre existence by painting and selling scenes of Vienna. At times he had to barter one for a meal. But gradually his life took a turn for the better and, more adept at his trade, he turned out his works at a rate of five or six a week, earning a modest income. At the same time something more important was happening. In what time he could find, he continued his favourite pastime of reading – 'art history, cultural history, architectural history', he claimed. 'I had but one pleasure: my books,' he remarked of these years. Long afterwards his secretary Christa Schroeder recalled him saying that during his youth in Vienna he had devoured the entire 500 volumes of a city library. It is not known what books he saw – and historians have questioned how many he actually read and how much of them he absorbed – but he later insisted that there took shape during those years what he later styled 'the granite foundation of all my acts'.

Hitler came to hate Vienna and was happy to leave that disgusting 'Babylon of races', as he called it. He did not so much leave, however, as flee and not in May of 1912, as he claimed in *Mein Kampf*, but a full year later. The reason he gave – to fulfil an irrepressible longing to be united with the German fatherland – may have been true in a way. But there were other reasons. The most compelling was that he faced imprisonment for evading military service. Having received his share of his father's estate a month earlier, he found himself with funds to travel. And he may have hoped to have better career prospects in Germany. In any event, when he came to write *Mein Kampf* he had a lot of explaining to do if he was to avoid political ruin for having evaded military service. He pre-dated his entry into Germany by a full year, concealed the fact that he registered himself as stateless to leave no trace for the Austrian police and claimed he had left Austria for purely political reasons – 'inner revulsion for the Habsburg state'.

It is revealing that the place of refuge Hitler chose was Munich, with its reputation as a centre of culture. The life and atmosphere there delighted him. He was able both to paint and to while away his days in the cafés and restaurants of the artists' district of Schwabing. 'This period before the war,' he declared, 'was the happiest and by far the most contented of my life.' Ever after, Munich was his favourite city – 'I am more attached to this city than to any other spot of earth in this world' – and once in power he made it both 'Hauptstadt der Bewegung', capital of the National Socialist movement, and the cultural centre of Germany.

In Munich he went on painting, and though he did so with somewhat greater skill and eventually greater financial reward, life remained a struggle. It must have been obvious to him that he was not developing into the great painter of his dreams and was unlikely even to earn much of an income. The outbreak of war in 1914 therefore offered an exciting escape from a life at a dead end. He described it as 'a release', adding, 'I fell down on my knees and thanked heaven from an overflowing heart for granting me the good fortune of being permitted to live at this time.' Like most other young men of his age, he enthusiastically joined up. Although still an Austrian citizen, he successfully petitioned to enter a Bavarian infantry regiment and ably served as a courier on the Western front. He was wounded twice and decorated twice. In what time he could find, he sketched and painted war scenes.

After the war and into the early 1920s Hitler continued to describe himself as an artist, though the precise terminology varied from *Künstler* (artist) to *Maler* (painter), *Kunstmaler* (artistic painter), *Architektur Maler* (architectural painter) and at times *Schriftsteller* (writer). In fact, the end of the war found him completely adrift. On the one hand he could see no prospect in resuming a career as a painter. On the other he could think of no alternative, admitting in *Mein Kampf* that 'I, nameless as I was, did not possess the least basis for any useful action'. Consequently he stayed in the army and was eventually recruited by the paramilitary *Reichswehr* to join a group of 'education officers' whose role was to restore the morale of the troops by giving them stirring, nationalistic pep talks. Though apparently a fervent pan-German nationalist since his Vienna days, Hitler still showed no serious interest in a political career. But thanks to a remarkable intuitive skill in understanding and manipulating audiences, he soon discovered that his rabble-rousing speeches to the troops were quite a success. At last he had found himself. Politics had come to Hitler, not Hitler to politics.

So it was not as a man with a sense of ideological mission or a leader with a visionary programme that he entered public life but as an opportunistic mob orator for the army. A political career offered itself to Hitler at the moment he realized that his artistic career was going nowhere and provided him with a way out of a personal impasse. Yet even when he took his first step into politics – by joining the tiny German Workers' Party in 1920 – he still declared his occupation to be 'painter'. And, initially at least, he was motivated less by any concrete political goal than by the electric effect of that mesmeric charisma which the perceptive Chamberlain later recognized.

In no time his oratorical talents in denouncing Bolsheviks, Jews and the peace settlement of 1919 gained him attention, while his forceful manner propelled him into a position of authority. By the time of his discharge from the army in April 1920 he had progressed from an insignificant firebrand to a beer hall agitator on the far right of Bavarian politics. In short order he transformed a band of beer-drinking, anti-Semitic Bavarian chauvinists into the National Socialist Workers' Party, which in July 1921 he took over as leader. More a Mussolini than a Lenin, he realized fifty years earlier than democratic politicians that psychological manipulation can be more potent than reasoned argument or concrete programmes. Thanks no doubt to his artistic sensibility he was the first to intuit that the medium, in a later phrase, could itself be the message.

Not until his thirty-first year, then, did the person who was to turn Europe upside down and nearly destroy it enter politics. Taking that plunge he later characterized as 'by far the most difficult decision' he had ever made. Even so, as he commented to his staff years later,

> I became a politician against my will. For me politics are only a means to an end. There are people who believe that it will be difficult for me no longer to be active. No! It will be the most beautiful day of my life when I retire from political affairs and leave all the worries, troubles and vexations behind me . . . . If someone else had been found, I would never have gone into politics; I would have become an artist or a philosopher.

Repeatedly, throughout his career, Hitler complained about having to sacrifice his artistic interests to the burdens of governing. As the diplomatic crisis over Poland was reaching its height in early August 1939, Hitler summoned the League of Nations Commissioner in Danzig, Carl Burckhardt, to the Berghof, his Alpine retreat in the Obersalzberg near Berchtesgaden. After a heated discussion, Hitler took his guest to the great terrace to admire the sweeping view and said, 'Oh, how I wish I could stay here and work as an artist. I am after all an artist.' Two weeks later he met with Sir Nevile Henderson, British ambassador at Berlin. 'Among the various points mentioned by Herr Hitler were,' Henderson reported to London, 'that he was by nature an artist not a politician. . . .' And then, on completing final plans for his attack on Poland, he turned to the assembled military leaders and remarked, 'How I would like to stay here and paint.' The same urge overcame him again just a month after launching the invasion of the Soviet Union. As he sat with his closest associates in his field headquarters, he brought the conversation around to cultural matters and warmly reminisced about the delights of his state visit to Italy in 1938 which he remembered primarily for the thrilling sights of Rome, Florence and Naples.

'All I wished then,' he wistfully concluded, 'was that I might be able to wander around Italy as an unknown painter.'

This was not a momentary flight of fancy. In fact during that visit he had expressed the same sentiments to his Italian hosts. His Italian guide, the distinguished art historian Ranuccio Bianchi Bandinelli, recalled his saying that he dreamed of renting a villa on the outskirts of Rome and spending his days visiting museums without anyone taking notice of him. Bianchi Bandinelli added,

> When he spoke this way he left the impression that he might get up one morning and say, 'Enough! I have been fooling myself; I am no longer the Führer.' In the case of Mussolini such a thought was inconceivable . . . . But when Hitler spoke this way, he left the impression of being sincere.

Over the years Hitler had the same effect on others, who heard him insist again and again that it would be the happiest day of his life when he could take off his military uniform and devote himself solely to the arts.

How are these various statements to be understood? Hitler was not saying that he did not want war or Lebensraum in the East or to make Germany the dominant power of Europe. What he was saying was that after he had achieved his military and political ambitions, he would devote himself to what really interested him and what he considered of ultimate importance. This was to create a German culture state where the arts were supreme and where he could construct his buildings, hold art shows, stage operas, encourage artists and promote the music, painting and sculpture he loved. His seriousness of intent was evident in his devotion to the arts from the moment he was appointed chancellor. But whether he would ever have followed the example of Charles V and retired, while not in his case to a monastery but to an artist's studio, is another question. Speer said he had often asked himself what course Hitler would have followed had a wealthy patron offered to take him on as his architect. In the end he concluded that Hitler's sense of political mission and his architectural ambitions were inseparable and that only through political success could he have fulfilled himself artistically.

Hence the central enigma of Hitler's life and career – how could he combine a sincere devotion to the arts with totalitarian rule, warfare and racial genocide? Even Speer was slow to ponder the issue. Sitting in his cell one evening in 1963, after eighteen years of being locked up in Spandau, he finally asked himself how 'the regime's fascination with beauty, which in fact was very marked' could go hand in hand with its ruthlessness and inhumanity. Some claimed it was aesthetic camouflage, calculated to distract the attention of the oppressed masses. 'But that was not so,' he insisted. There was also a genuine, unselfish social impulse at work, a desire to reconcile the unavoidable ugliness of modern technology with familiar aesthetic forms, with beauty. Carl Burckhardt, based on his observations of the dictator at a critical moment, summed up the dichotomy more simply. Hitler was, he said, a case of 'a dual personality, the first being that of the rather gentle artist and the second that of the homicidal maniac'.

And so there had emerged in the course of the early 1920s Hitler the *Künstlerpolitiker*, artist-politician, that Chamberlain and Hindenburg sensed and that Mann clearly recognized. Devotion to culture is one that totalitarian leaders have always proclaimed and often demonstrated. All totalitarian leaders, Hitler no less than Stalin, departed from Marx, it has been pointed out, in believing that the control of culture was as important as that of the economy. On the one hand they realized that it offered respectability to themselves, contributed to a sense of national unity, helped to maintain morale at difficult times and provided the painted veil behind which they could commit whatever horrors they pleased. On the other they understood the potentially subversive effect of the arts. A state that executes people for writing poetry, as Osip Mandelstam observed, is a state that recognises its power. Though Hitler grasped these facts and acted on them, he was fundamentally different from Stalin as well as Lenin, Mussolini, Mao Tse-tung and their ilk. Unlike Lenin, who never set foot in an art gallery, or Stalin, whose art collection was pictures torn out of an illustrated magazine, or Mussolini, who despised the arts, he held a deep and genuine interest in music, painting, sculpture and architecture. He regarded politics not art as a means to an end, the end of which was art. Hence the paradox of a man who wanted to be an artist but lacked the talent, who hated politics but was a political genius.

Indeed, at no time did conventional politics – the interplay of institutions and people engaged in public policy – interest him. On the contrary. His career as a statesman was built on a rejection of everything that sort of politics involves – freedom, debate and compromise; parties, parliaments and the institutions of a pluralist society. As soon as he could, he abolished them all. What absorbed him was ruling, and ruling in his view followed the same evolutionary principles as culture. He made this point in a speech in January 1928 in which he asked how culture comes about.

> The process within a nation is thus: there is always the individual as creator; nothing comes from the mass of the people itself . . . . What we regard as culture does not come about through majority vote. No. It is the product of individuals, of creative acts of single persons. They have risen above the common crowd and followed the lead of the best minds.

Thus did he see a direct link between his notion of governing and his concept of artistic creativity.

The connection must not be overstated. Many of Hitler's key policies – such as racial genocide and the military domination of Europe – did not grow out of his aesthetic ideals. Hitler the ruler and Hitler the artist sometimes coincided, sometimes not. But at all times he used culture to buttress his power, while power opened the way for him to realize himself through grandiose cultural projects. To that extent power and art merged, and he could, as he repeatedly did, define his historic mission in artistic terms. Cultural interests were thus not simply a youthful passing phase that became merely the showy pretension of an artistic dilettante once he entered politics. He could have said with Schopenhauer, whose five-volume collected works he claimed to have carried in his knapsack throughout the war, that culture always occupied a pivotal place in his mental universe.

In this Hitler was heir to the Central European Romantic tradition. Typically, Romantics worshipped the artist and his achievement as the embodiment of the highest social aspirations of an age. At the same time they were lost in admiration for, as Isaiah Berlin said with Napoleon in mind, 'the sinister artist whose materials are men – the destroyer of old societies and the creator of new ones – no matter at what human cost: the superhuman leader who tortures and destroys in order to build on new foundations . . . .' Hitler was a Romantic in both senses.

During the best and worst years of his military campaigns, no matter how urgent the situation, he always found time to turn his mind to cultural affairs. Christa Schroeder noted that, except at military briefings, his conversation reverted more and more to topics about the arts. This is confirmed by the so-called table talk, remarks recorded without his knowledge at table and in the night afterwards. Goebbels's diaries also provide example after example. 'I cannot enumerate all the cultural issues that we discussed,' declares a typical entry. And indeed on most occasions when the two men met, up until the final months of the war, Hitler brought up questions about the arts. 'The intensity of the Führer's longing for music, theatre and cultural relaxation is enormous,' Goebbels reported after visiting him on the Eastern front in January 1942. 'He said he never speaks of this to others, but he could tell me that the life he is now leading is culturally empty and inconsequential, and therefore he has to fill his days with work and other activities. Once the war was over he would compensate for this by a dedication stronger than ever to the more beautiful sides of life.' Four months later, on the eve of what turned out to be the decisive military operation in Russia, the two men spent an entire afternoon discussing cultural affairs. An issue that was gripping Hitler's interest on the occasion was a proposed film about King Ludwig I of Bavaria. In the face of his other urgent obligations, he had made time to study the script of the film and now announced that he could not approve either the script or the intended principal actor and wanted a fresh start. Another topic he raised was the cultural competition among Vienna, Linz and Munich and how to bring them into balance. He went on to state that he had become better informed about recent musical developments thanks to new tape-recording technology which made it possible for him to hear the latest symphonic and operatic performances. He must have been listening to these with care, since he commented that he found the strings of the Berlin Philharmonic to be better – 'younger' – than those of the Vienna. He added that recordings had left him thrilled by the conducting at the Munich Opera. At the same time he found that a number of prominent singers were in vocal decline and reflected on who might succeed them. He also took the occasion to gossip about Richard Wagner and his descendants, to give explicit instructions that retired artists should receive generous stipends and to authorize the release of scarce foreign exchange to purchase a collection of rare stringed instruments available in Italy. Such were the highlights of a single discussion.

Six months after that conversation Goebbels journeyed to see Hitler at his military headquarters at Rastenberg in East Prussia. Although the battle of Stalingrad was now at its height, Goebbels noted that 'despite the gravity of the situation, the Führer remains as devoted as ever to the arts and cannot wait for the moment when he can devote more time to them'. On this occasion the conversation began with Hitler speaking of his pleasure in Bruckner's symphonies and concluded with his comparing the philosophies of Kant, Schopenhauer and Nietzsche. In early May of that year – when aerial bombing was shattering German cities, the *Wehrmacht* was in retreat in Russia and the German military had been thrown out of Africa – Hitler returned briefly to Berlin and met with Goebbels on four successive days, dealing on each occasion with 'a variety of cultural and artistic questions'. What was on his mind this time? In the visual arts, it was the need to encourage individuals to buy paintings for themselves and not leave it up to art museums to acquire them. He also wanted art galleries to be run by the community not the Reich. He went on to render his judgement about architects and sculptors. After discussing problems of the Berlin theatre, he turned to the world of music. He ordered that the Hamburg Symphony, the Gewandhaus Orchestra and the orchestra of the German Opera in Berlin should be given increased status and that a newly created Bruckner Orchestra in Linz was to be turned into one of the very best in the Reich. He scotched a proposal to increase the price of theatre and opera tickets. He lamented the lack of cultural sensibility on the part of local party leaders; for all their political competence, he complained, many were 'complete failures in the field of the arts'. He also fretted about Frederick the Great's coffin and decided that after the war it should be moved either to Sans Souci or a new mausoleum in Berlin. At their fourth meeting he discussed the philosophies of Kant, Hegel, Schopenhauer and Nietzsche. 'He looks forward to nothing so much as exchanging his grey [military] jacket for a brown [party] one.' His dream, Goebbels remarked, was to resume his cultural activities and never again have anything to do with generals.

A scarcely less remarkable conversation took place in September 1943. The military situation was worse than ever. British and American forces were on the Italian mainland, Italy had surrendered, the *Wehrmacht* was in retreat in the East and the bombing of German cities had reached a catastrophic level. Yet in the context of a long discussion of the possibility of negotiating a compromise peace settlement, Hitler could not refrain from dealing at length with artistic matters. This time these concerned operatic and theatrical life in Berlin and Munich, the political unreliability of artists, Göring's faulty concept of the arts, Frau Göring's unfortunate interference in the Berlin theatre and the quality of various opera companies. And on went such discussions at meeting after meeting. In the words of another typical entry – this one of 25 January 1944 – 'We then go on to discuss a thousand-and-one questions about cultural and artistic life which absolutely fascinate the Führer. I am amazed at how accurately informed he is about hundreds of details.'

Perhaps the most extraordinary of such conversations took place on the eve of D-Day in June 1944. Hitler was then at the Berghof, and at lunch that day had treated his guests to a long disquisition on the arts. 'We talked about problems of the theatre and opera, film, literature and heaven knows what else,' Goebbels noted. When the Propaganda Minister mentioned that he had recently read Schopenhauer's essay on writing, Hitler responded that he had once carefully studied it and had profited. At ten that night German intelligence officials began reporting that radio intercepts indicated that the Allied invasion would begin the following morning. Yet as Goebbels recorded, 'Later on we looked at the latest newsreels . . . and talk a lot about film, opera and theatre matters. . . . We then sit in front of the fireplace until 2 a.m. sharing memories. . . .'

Six months later, with the Third Reich now in incipient collapse, Hitler suddenly summoned Goebbels at midnight to the chancellery to talk for five and a half hours about his plans – military, political and cultural. 'Cultural life of course continues to engage his intense interest,' the Propaganda Minister remarked. Among the topics Hitler raised were films, the behaviour of prominent actors, Frau Göring's bad influence on the theatre, his plans for post-war operatic stage design and the like. One other entry – on 25 January 1945 – sounded for a final time the leitmotif that Hitler had periodically stated throughout the years of his political career:

> He laments the bitter irony that he, a man devoted to the arts, should be chosen by destiny itself to lead this most difficult of all wars for the Reich. But such was also the case with Frederick the Great. In reality he also was not cut out for a seven-year war but rather for the easy life, philosophy and flute-playing. Nonetheless he had no choice but to fulfil his historic mission.

By now the arts had acquired a different sort of meaning for Hitler. Ever since he had launched his attack against the Soviet Union he found he could sleep only after spending several hours looking at picture books about painting or architecture. As military catastrophe approached, and especially after the July assassination attempt when he increasingly withdrew into himself, they offered his only escape from the encircling doom. One visitor always welcome at his military headquarters was his favourite stage designer, Benno von Arent, who regaled him with the latest gossip in the art world. On bidding him farewell, Hitler would shake Arent's hand warmly and say, 'I am glad you seek me out from time to time in my loneliness. You are for me the bridge to a more beautiful world.' Even at the best of times Hitler had been wont to describe the arts as 'a truly stable pole in the flux of all other phenomena', 'an escape from confusion and distress', a source of 'the eternal, magic strength . . . to master confusion and restore a new order out of chaos'. At all times, in other words, they provided a refuge from harsh reality.

Although there were many traits conventionally associated with artists that he lacked, his aesthetic impulse was an essential element of his character, indelibly colouring both his personal life and his career. Portrayals of him as someone who cynically used the arts merely for their value as ideological propaganda therefore misunderstood him as much as those which made him out a nihilistic revolutionary with no aim except power for himself and as an end in itself. During the whole of his political career, whether imposing a totalitarian dictatorship on Germany, leading the world into war or engaging in mass genocide, he always thought of himself simultaneously as supreme ruler, supreme military commander and supreme cultural authority.

Thinking back on those years, Lutz Count Schwerin von Krosigk, Finance Minister from 1932 until the end, wrote in 1952 that he found it impossible to escape the impression that creating cultural monuments had been the overriding interest of Hitler's life. Some of those who worked near him, such as Arno Breker, Albert Speer and Hermann Giesler, as well as German biographers who studied his life, such as Joachim Fest and Werner Maser, all came to the conclusion that power was for Hitler ultimately an instrument for achieving his cultural ambitions.

2 A PHILOSOPHY OF CULTURE

I T IS DIFFICULT TO THINK OF ANY OTHER leader in history who attached such importance to culture and indeed talked so much about it. *Mein Kampf*, speeches at the party rallies and on other occasions, conversations with his inner circle and endless post-prandial chats were filled with it. In the manner of dictators – and everyday bores – he stated his views not as reasoned arguments but as dogmatic truths allowing of no debate. And he had an opinion on everything. Speer once said that if he had to sum him up in one phrase it would be, 'he was a genius of dilettantism'. In his memoirs Leonard Woolf related that after a big game hunt in the jungles of Ceylon, when the animals were slaughtered and the half-digested contents of their intestines spilled out, the sight invariably reminded him of the innards of a crazed colleague's mind. Hitler too ingested but never fully digested bits of literature, art, history, music, theatre, politics, philosophy and most everything between. And what spilled out in his conversations was an ill-digested jumble of fact, pseudo-fact and non-fact. Yet in the course of his cultural musings he also showed real sense and came to grips with some of the central issues concerning the relationship between culture and the state, the artist and society, art and politics. Out of this plethora of words emerged a set of ideas that amounts to a philosophy of culture. Race was the keystone, and it established an indivisible link between his cultural and political views.

Significantly, Hitler's theories on race, politics and culture were enunciated simultaneously and at the very outset of his political career – in Munich in 1920 in a speech appropriately entitled 'Why Are We Anti-Semites?' In this he took up the then fashionable challenge-and-response interpretation of history. During the earliest times people who lived in harsh, northern climes had been forced to work hard; these were the people, he said, who had developed into the strong and creative Aryan race. People in the south, where life was easy, had degenerated and become soft.

So the race we label Aryan was the inspirer of all the later great cultures

. . . We know that Egypt was raised to its cultural height by Aryan immigrants, similarly Persia and Greece. The immigrants were blond, blue-eyed Aryans, and we know that apart from these states no cultured states ever existed on earth . . . .

But culture was a product not of race alone; it also needed a dynamic political environment. And so,

. . . art flowers above all where a great political movement gives it the opportunity. We know that the arts in Greece reached their pinnacle after the young state triumphed over the Persian army. . . . Rome first became a city of culture after the Punic wars . . . . We know that art, as reflected, for example, in the beauty of our German cities, was always dependent on the political development of these cities . . . .

Where does 'the Jew' figure into this? he then asked. Not having engaged in the creative struggle of the Aryan, 'The Jew has never had his own art. Even his temples had to be built by foreigners, first the Assyrians and then in a later period by the Romans. He has left no art behind, nothing in the way of painting, no buildings, nothing.' On the contrary, his objective was to destroy a nation's culture, as could be seen in Modernist music, painting, sculpture and literature. For the Jew, the arts were mere objects of commerce, simply the means of making money, he concluded. A corollary of Hitler's racial notions was his conviction that national identity and cultural identity were different sides of the same coin. 'All great art is national,' he said in a speech in Nuremberg in January 1923. 'Great musicians, such as Beethoven, Mozart, Bach, created German music that was deeply rooted in the very core of the German spirit and the German mind . . . . That is equally true of German sculptors, painters, architects.' What truth there was in this contention he construed to mean that a nation's culture had therefore to exist in isolation. Consequently, 'international' art – here he singled out Cubism and Futurism – was essentially destructive and 'synonymous with kitsch'. Not only that, one glance sufficed to show that it sprang from 'a Jewish, foreign mentality'.

When he came to write *Mein Kampf* a year or so later, he took up another issue, one that had profound policy consequences once he became chancellor. Why, he asked, had twentieth-century culture suffered the same precipitate decline as politics and how could this be reversed? His response, in a chapter entitled 'Causes of the Collapse', argued that the downfall of Bismarck's Reich in 1918 resulted not from economic or military factors but from social ones. A 'moral plague' had polluted big cities and infected all the arts. Cubism and Dadaism, alias 'art Bolshevism', had emerged and threatened to drive people 'into the arms of spiritual madness'. Their perpetrators were 'lunatics or criminals' whose aim was to destroy the great works of the past. As a result the very foundations of Western civilization were decaying, and nowhere was this so evident as in the arts. 'For if the age of Pericles was embodied in the Parthenon,' he commented in one of his better lines, 'the Bolshevist present is embodied in a Cubist monstrosity.' The conclusion was inevitable, 'Theatre, art, literature, cinema, press, even posters and window displays must be cleansed of all manifestations of our rotting world and put in the service of a moral, political and cultural ideal.'

A further symptom of cultural decline that sent Hitler into a frenzy of despair was the transformation of cities from 'cultural sites' into 'mere human settlements' lacking both social cohesion and great architecture. In the past, monumental structures were not private but civic edifices, such as temples and cathedrals constructed for the pleasure and pride of the entire community. They lent a city its unique character and engendered civic pride. Contemporary buildings, by contrast, were constructed for private ostentation and evinced money rather than beauty and culture – visible in the late nineteenth-century architectural horrors of Berlin, Munich and other cities. 'If the fate of Rome should strike Berlin,' he remarked, 'future generations would some day admire the department stores of a few Jews as the mightiest works of our era and the hotels of a few corporations as characteristic examples of the culture of our times.' In earlier centuries the various German princes had been exemplary patrons of the arts; their successors were 'laughable'. The old imperial government had spent twice as much on a single battleship as in constructing the new Reichstag building, a structure meant to reflect the glory of the new Reich, he commented in disgust. This sort of crass materialism had destroyed the country's 'artistic state of mind'.

In another chapter, 'Nation and Race', Hitler elaborated his notion of the racial basis of the arts. The entire animal kingdom, he wrote, was divided into higher and lower forms; if the two mingled, the higher race was ruined – 'All mingling of Aryan blood with that of lower people results in the end of the cultured people.' He went on to divide mankind into three groups – founders of culture, bearers of culture and destroyers of culture. The Aryan was the founder – 'All human culture, all art, science and technology that we see today, is almost exclusively the creative product of the Aryan.' The Japanese were an example of bearers; they adapted the Aryans' achievements to their own uses.

In time, he said, 'all east Asia would possess a culture whose ultimate foundation is Hellenic in spirit and Germanic in technology'. Traditional culture
would continue to 'determine the colour of life', but day-to-day activities
would be grounded on 'the gigantic scientific-technical achievements of
Europe and America – that is, of Aryan people'. Were the Aryan influence to
dry up, Japan would be bound to regress since its people lacked an independent
creative impulse. As for the Jews, being a disorganized tribe without a territory,
they lacked 'the basis on which alone culture can arise'. As a consequence 'the
Jewish people, despite all apparent intellectual qualities, is without any true
culture, and especially without any culture of its own'. Certainly 'the two
queens of all the arts, architecture and music, owe nothing original to the Jews'.
Imitation, not creativity, was the Jewish métier and therefore the reason Jews
were eminent in the least original of the arts, acting.

This led to a second element in his theory of Jews and culture. Lacking
creativity and originality, 'What they do accomplish in the field of art is
either patchwork or intellectual theft.' For 'the Jew . . . is always and only a
parasite in the body of other peoples'. But – and this was Hitler's final point
– he does not just steal from the culture of others, '. . . he contaminates art,
literature, the theatre, makes a mockery of natural feeling, overthrows all
concepts of beauty and sublimity, of the noble and the good, and instead
drags men down into the sphere of his own base nature'. It was during his
Vienna years, he maintained, that he realized that Jews were responsible for
'nine-tenths of all literary filth, artistic trash, and theatrical idiocy'. Through
their control of the press, they promoted international, Modernist, Bolshevist
and cosmopolitan rather than German works of art.

In such terms had Hitler laid out his cultural philosophy by the mid-1920s
and his later speeches simply embroidered his views or made them more
specific. One of these – entitled 'National Socialism and Arts Policy', delivered
in Munich in January 1928 – discussed the social purpose of art and the cultural
role of the state in a way that hinted at specific policies he followed once in
power. After becoming chancellor, he used the Nuremberg party rallies as a
platform for an annual lecture on culture to the party and the nation. These
were of enormous importance to him and he convened a special session – the
Kulturtagung – for them. To composing these 'major oratorical flights', in
Speer's words, he devoted tremendous time and effort. Following a hefty dose
of Wagner at Bayreuth every August, he would withdraw in exaltation to the
Alpine grandeur of the Berghof and there set down his thoughts.

One of his favourite themes was that Western civilization had reached its finest flowering in the Mediterranean basin, in the civilizations of Egypt, Greece and Rome. His admiration of the Greeks, in particular, knew no bounds and in many respects his views bore an uncanny resemblance to those of the great Johann Joachim Winckelmann. There is no way of knowing whether Hitler, a notorious pickpocket in the market of ideas, actually took these notions from the pioneer art historian. But Winckelmann's dictum that 'the only way for us to become great . . . lies in the imitation of the Greeks' is one that Hitler repeated virtually word for word on various occasions. What he saw in their culture was a peerless aesthetic ideal. 'What makes the Greek concept of beauty a model is the wonderful combination of the most magnificent physical beauty with a brilliant mind and the noblest soul.' As a result the Greeks had achieved perfection in every field. He considered the Parthenon to be supreme and the architectural style he himself later endorsed was initially a pastiche of neo-Dorian. Greek sculpture had never been

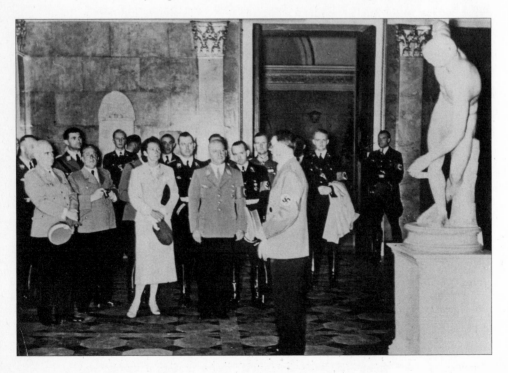

Hitler showing honoured guests his favourite sculpture, Myron's Discus Thrower, *at the Munich Glyptotek, July 1938. Among those looking on are Gerdy Troost and Arturo Marpicati, vice-secretary of the Italian Fascist Party. Considering them culturally challenged, Hitler declined to invite any of his own party officials.*

surpassed in his view and one of his most prized possessions was the best
surviving copy of Myron's *Discobolus, Discus Thrower*. He had acquired it in
1938 and on placing it on exhibition praised it as an aesthetic model for all
time. 'May you all then realize how glorious man already was back then in
his physical beauty,' he told his audience. 'We can speak of progress only if
we have attained like perfection or if we manage to surpass it.' He also
admired the Greeks for 'the excellence of their world of thought'. 'Our
technology alone is all they lacked,' he maintained. Despite his own non-
belief, he even admired Greek religion and his entourage must have found it
hard to trust their ears when they heard him say, 'We would not be in any
danger today to pray to Zeus.' The strength and serenity of pagan
iconography he contrasted to Christian imagery of suffering and pain – 'You
need only look at the head of Zeus or Athena and compare it to that of a
medieval crucifixion scene or of some saint.' The distinction was visible in
architecture as well. 'What a difference,' he said, 'between a dark cathedral
and a bright, open ancient temple.' All in all, Greek civilization represented
'a beauty that exceeds anything that is evident today'.

It was an enthusiasm he never lost. In 1941, after the *Wehrmacht* had
devastated Yugoslavia in its march through the Balkans and crossed the
Greek border, Hitler commented to Goebbels how much he admired the
bravery of the Greek army. 'Perhaps there is still some of the old Hellenic in
them.' The Führer, Goebbels further recorded, 'forbids any bombing of
Athens . . . . Rome and Athens are Meccas for him. He deeply regrets having
to fight the Greeks. Had the British not intervened, he would never have
hastened to help the Italians.' A few weeks later, he returned to find Hitler
'sad that he considered it at all necessary to fight in Greece. The Greeks
certainly did not deserve it. He intends to treat them as humanely as he
possibly can. We watch a newsreel of our entry into Athens. The Führer can
take absolutely no pleasure in it, so deeply saddened is he by Greece's fate.'

His esteem for the Romans was of a different order. He admired their
'grandeur', their 'world empire', their 'imperial might'. The age of Augustus
marked the zenith of Western civilization. 'Ancient Rome was a colossally
serious state. Great ideas inspired the Romans.' Above all, it was their
architecture and its enduring influence on Italy that he venerated. Years after
his state visit to Italy he was still in raptures: 'Rome moved me. And in
Naples, the courtyard of the royal palace, how splendid are its proportions,
one element balanced by another.' In Rome he was left in awe by the

magnitude of the great ruins, in particular the Colosseum and the Baths of Caracalla. But the Pantheon and Hadrian's tomb impressed him still more. As time passed it was less to the Greeks and more to the Romans, with their domes, vaults, arches and arcades, that he turned for architectural inspiration.

Hitler deplored the fall of the Roman Empire and, having often pondered the reasons for it, eventually came to the conclusion that 'Rome was broken by Christianity not by the Teutons and Huns'. He even appeared to justify the crucifixion of Jesus, commenting on the Oberammergau passion play, which he attended in 1930 and 1934, 'Rarely has the Jewish threat to the ancient Roman world been so graphically illustrated as in the person of Pontius Pilate in this play; he emerges as a Roman so racially and intellectually superior that he stands out like a rock amid the Jewish dung and rabble.' Had it not been for the Christians, he said on another occasion, Rome would have retained control of all Europe and its legions would have demolished the Hunic tribes. European history would have taken an entirely different course. 'It would be better,' he said, 'to speak of "Constantine the Traitor" and "Julian the Steadfast" instead of calling the one "the Great" and the other "the Apostate".'

Hitler's mention of the Huns was made in the presence of Heinrich Himmler – whom Hitler enjoyed taunting – and was no doubt an intentional barb. An even more primitive racist than his Führer, Himmler glorified the old Germanic tribes and sponsored excavations of their prehistoric sites. This evoked Hitler's open contempt and Speer recorded him once saying:

> Why do we call the whole world's attention to the fact that we have no past? It isn't enough that the Romans were erecting great buildings when our forefathers were still living in mud huts; now Himmler is starting to dig up these villages of mud huts and goes into raptures over every potsherd and stone axe he finds. All we prove by that is that we were still throwing stone hatchets and crouching around open fires when Greece and Rome had already reached the highest stage of culture. We really should do our best to keep quiet about this past. Instead Himmler makes a great fuss about it all. The present-day Romans must be having a laugh at these discoveries.

But how did Hitler reconcile the cultural ascendancy of the Mediterranean peoples with the notion of Aryan supremacy, the bedrock of everything he believed? Picking up on his old theory of northern peoples dominating southern peoples, he expounded the view – itself historically respectable – that the Dorians were northern barbarians who had invaded Greece in the post-Minoan *Völkerwanderung*. He accordingly argued that Germanic tribes had fallen into two types, a seafaring group which migrated south where it produced 'one eternal art – Greek Nordic art' and a group that stayed behind in its mud huts: 'The Teuton must go to a sunny climate to develop his capacities. It was first in Greece and Rome that the Teutonic spirit really flowered. . . . The Teutons who remained in Holstein were still boorish after 2000 years while their brothers who migrated to Greece rose to culture.'

In contrast to the great classical model stood the culture of his own time. Hitler was not alone in arguing that the barbarians – the Modernists – were already inside the gates. In an era of collapsing values, economic crisis and political bewilderment – Oswald Spengler's 1920s international best-seller *Decline of the West* well caught the widespread sense of doom – the Modernist movement reflected and reinforced a popular mood of cynicism and anxiety. Much of Hitler's popular appeal lay in his promise of order, security and protection from modern life and its discontents. In speech after speech he urged resistance to the cultural decay of the time. 'He expressed, in a crude and brutal fashion,' it has been well said, 'the fears and hatreds of those who were uncomfortable in the modern world, who were haunted by the idea of decadence and decline, and who believed that it was possible by an act of will to reassert control over what they saw as an errant European history.'

So while Hitler was speaking from his own heart, he was also speaking to the hearts of many others. Modernism had engendered animosity everywhere, from New York and London to Budapest and St Petersburg. Everywhere there were those who regarded it as a form of madness being propagated by a sinister underworld of anarchist deviants. But only in Germany was the phenomenon transformed from a matter of aesthetic taste into an ideological dispute and from that into an issue of outright political warfare. This was literally a *Kulturkampf*, part of the titanic struggle between conservatives and modernizers that had followed unification in 1871. In the cultural sphere the dispute had been openly joined in 1893 when Max Nordau, a pioneer Zionist, published his widely read book, *Degeneration*, which applied the concept of biological degeneration to cultural decline. According to this, societies were living organisms, subject to the ordinary human process of birth, development, decay and death. By the same token, degenerate painting was the product of biologically degenerate painters, who suffered from, among other ailments, brain debilitation and optical disease. Impressionists, for example, were victims of disorders of the nervous system and the retina. Such degenerates were enemies of society, 'anti-social vermin' who must be 'mercilessly crush[ed]'. Nordau proposed that they should be tried as criminals or committed to insane asylums. Picking up on such ideas, the popular writer Julius Langbehn maintained that the arts reflected a society's health; changes of style and fashions in art were not only anti-artistic but antisocial. Both Nordau and Langbehn were reincarnated in the architect and art historian Paul Schultze-Naumburg who in the years of the Weimar Republic synthesized their views into a cultural-political creed. 'A life-and-death struggle is taking place in art, just as it is in the realm of politics,' he wrote in his appropriately named *Kampf um die Kunst* (*Battle over Art*). In 1928 he published *Kunst und Rasse* (*Art and Race*),which expanded Nordau's notion of artistic degeneracy. Expressionism, for instance, was a pathological symptom, an illness. To spread the word he went on a national tour in the early 1930s and showed slides juxtaposing clinical photos of deformities with photos of works by such artists as Barlach, Kirchner and Nolde.

In Hitler's speeches, as in his private remarks, the concepts and vocabulary of Nordau, Langbehn and Schultze-Naumburg can be heard. Side by side with a humane and enlightened Germany, there was a Germany that after unification in 1871 idolized blood and iron, prized irrationality and intuition, rejected Enlightenment ideals, breathed chauvinism and anti-Semitism. Hitler exploited this sentiment and took it directly into everyday politics, and from there into opera houses, concert halls and art museums. Modernist art forms were slandered in political terms, as 'cultural Bolshevism', 'art Bolshevism' and 'music Bolshevism'. What was conveyed by these widely used expressions and the full extent of the innuendo have never been better articulated than by the publicist Carl von Ossietzky in *Weltbühne* in April 1931:

> When a conductor takes his tempi differently from his colleague Furtwängler, when a painter gives a sunset a different colour from that seen in Lower Pomerania even in broad daylight, when someone favours birth control or builds a house with a flat roof, all that is cultural Bolshevism just as much as the depiction of a Caesarian birth in a film. Cultural Bolshevism is promoted by the actor Chaplin, and when the physicist Einstein asserts that the principle of the constant speed of light applies only when there is no gravitation that is also cultural Bolshevism and a personal favour to Stalin. Cultural Bolshevism is the democracy of the Mann brothers; cultural Bolshevism is a composition by Hindemith or Weill and to be placed in the same category as the revolutionary demands of a crazy person who advocates a law that would permit marrying one's own grandmother. All those things are services for Moscow, either paid for or given for free.

Ossietzky's words exposed the state of mind of Hitler and countless other Germans who were convinced that Western culture was being destroyed by – the terms were equivalent – Modernists, liberals, internationalists, Bolshevists and Jews. Political degeneration and cultural decay walked hand in hand.

Hitler spelled this out publicly in an emotional speech at the cultural session of the 1935 party rally. In a rhetorically violent prologue, he exposed his long-pent-up rage at modern political and cultural life. Boasting that the institutions of the pre-Nazi era had been 'crushed', 'broken', 'beaten and pursued', 'annihilated' and 'extinguished', he threatened similar consequences in the art world. The perpetrators of Modernism were 'criminals of world culture', 'destroyers of our art', 'facile smearers of paint', 'fools or knaves', 'imbecile degenerates' deserving the 'prison or the madhouse', 'incompetents, cheats and madmen' not to be let loose on the public, 'pitiable unfortunates who clearly suffer from defects of vision' and who should be turned over to the police or the criminal court. Their works had been 'crimes', 'creations of a diseased imagination', 'Jewish-Bolshevistic mockery of art', 'Bolshevist madness' and such. Modernist culture, he thundered, was a perversion. It distorted nature and truth; its sights and sounds were ugly, incoherent, incomprehensible, shocking, depressing, bizarre. The style and substance of great art was rooted in 'historical realities' and followed 'eternal principles'. But by deliberately breaking with the past, by always venturing into new territory and by constantly trying to discover new ways of interpreting the world, Modernism was at once frivolous and revolutionary. Above all, great art should bring people together, not divide them. Modernism, however, was no more than 'a subject of conversation among consumptive aesthetes'. Such 'dadaistic artistic activity' had not merely been rejected but ignored by almost everyone. As a result, culture and society had grown apart.

Having thus vented, Hitler calmed down and devoted the major portion of his oration to what was really on his mind at the time: culture versus money. Here he addressed – now, for a change, in a moment of cogency – a problem facing every government, even a dictatorship. What is the justification for government devoting public funds to high culture? In this case even the dictator found it necessary to explain why, when Germany was just beginning to recover from a devastating war, catastrophic inflation and a worldwide economic crisis, he should devote huge sums to the arts and grandiose public building projects. Therefore he asked,

Is it right to undertake monumental works of engineering and building instead of restricting ourselves exclusively to what is practical and absolutely necessary at the moment? . . . . Can we permit sacrifices to be made in the interests of art at such a time as this when we find ourselves surrounded with poverty, distress, misery and discontent? In the last analysis isn't art the luxury of a small minority? What has that to do with supplying bread to the masses?

In response, he made four points. One was that artistic activity dare not be suspended, even temporarily. No more was it feasible to pension off artists in difficult times than to pension off mathematicians and physicists. Doing so would damage not just one sector of society but the whole nation.

Let us take an instance. Opera may be looked upon as one of the most characteristic creations of the neoclassical theatre. Now, if the activities involved in operatic production were to be suspended for a longer or shorter period – even though only temporarily, with the intention of restoring opera once again in its old brilliance – what would be the consequence? Training and other preparations necessary for operatic production would be suspended. But the consequences would not end there. They would extend to the general public. In a manner similar to the performers themselves, the public needs to have its faculties for appreciating opera constantly developed and trained, requiring opera to be always available.

The arts, indeed all creative endeavours, are interrelated, he went on. The artist inspired the public; the public produced the atmosphere in which creative forces could unfold.

That led to his second point. Since the state of the arts and the state of society are directly linked, it is precisely when people are 'oppressed with cares and troubles' that they need the ennobling inspiration of culture to reassure them of their national greatness. 'Art is the great mainstay of a people, because it raises them above the petty cares of the moment and shows them that, after all, their individual woes are not of such great importance.' And from this followed his next argument, that some poverty had always existed and spending money on the arts would not alter that fact. 'Does anybody think that if the Greeks had not built the Acropolis there would have been no poverty or misery in Athens at that time? Or would there have been no human distress in the Middle Ages if they had renounced the idea of building their cathedrals? . . . Were there no poor and needy people in Bavaria before Ludwig [I] began to carry out his great building plans?' The notion that commerce should prevail over aesthetics was to him anathema.

Finally, he turned to the charge that art was a luxury for the elite. Such an objection, he maintained, might just as easily and erroneously be raised against activities in other fields. Nobody could say that the masses of the people appreciate the theoretical developments in chemistry and physics or any other scientific or intellectual pursuit. In fact, he insisted, the arts have a far broader appeal than the sciences. 'Art is the clearest and most immediate reflection of the spiritual life of a people. It exercises the greatest conscious and unconscious influence on the masses of the people. . . . In its thousandfold manifestations and influences it benefits the nation as a whole. . . .'

These were strong arguments, though coming from a dictator it mattered little whether they persuaded anyone. But even a dictator could not alter the fact that by ignoring the huge and widening gap between high culture and mass culture they suffered a serious flaw. Radio, phonograph, photography, illustrated magazines and cinema had created new art forms with a vast and varied audience. Two cultures had evolved – highbrow and lowbrow, elitist and popular. Hitler looked back admiringly on a pre-twentieth-century world when high culture was effectively the predominant art form and when cultivated patrons and a cultural elite dictated taste. By the 1930s those days had passed forever. This he could not accept. Consequently a great contradiction lay at the heart of his cultural policies. On the one hand he admonished artists to make their art accessible to the public. On the other he wanted the public to enjoy the sort of art he himself enjoyed. And so for the remainder of his life it was his aesthetic ideals and taste that he sought to impose on the German people, whether or not they shared them.

3 THE GRAND PARADOX

ONFRONTED BY MODERNISM, art Bolshevism, cultural degeneracy and Jewish corruption of the arts, Hitler regarded himself not merely as saviour of Hans Sachs's *heil'ge deutsche Kunst* but also, indeed, as the very guardian of Western civilization. Not simply guardian but also guide. 'For me politics is only the means to an end,' he told his intimates on more than one occasion. And that end had already been spelled out in *Mein Kampf*. 'I am convinced,' he had written there, 'that the work of great statesmen and military leaders always lies in the field of art.' And since he further believed that the ultimate worth of a society and an era was to be judged by its cultural achievement, his mission was plain. By his accomplishments in the arts, he believed, would history judge him. Such was the lesson of the ancient world.

One of his foremost objectives was therefore to create a Germany in which culture was supreme and German culture a model for the world. It might be thought he did not have far to go. In no other country in the world – not even in France or Italy – was there such popular respect for the arts and so broad a participation in them. This was not Hitler's view. The old Reich, he contended, had been so immersed in domestic and foreign affairs that it had completely ignored artists and their work. Its leaders were pitiable. 'Wilhelm I had no taste at all. Bismarck was totally philistine. Wilhelm II had a lot of taste but it was absolutely terrible.' As for the leaders of the Weimar Republic, they and their laissez-faire attitude towards the arts were beneath contempt. For him political power was an elixir to be used to produce great cultural works. When his friend Heinrich Hoffmann asked him why he had not become an architect instead of a politician, he responded that he preferred to be the master builder of the Third Reich, in that way combining the role of ruler and artist. The notion that Europe had reached the end of its civilizing mission and that that role had now passed to the United States and the Soviet Union was one that he bitterly contested. As he said in a speech in 1938: 'The world will come to Germany and convince itself that Germany has become the guardian of European culture and civilization. When I read of other countries, and particularly of democratic countries, that they are called upon to protect culture, I say, "First build up a little more culture yourselves and then you can protect it." '

Hence the colossal paradox. The man responsible for more death and destruction than anyone else in modern times wished to forge a state whose cultural achievements would rival those of the greatest civilizations of the past. And inside that paradox lay another. The warlord who built up the greatest land army since Napoleon regretted having to spend money on weapons that could have been devoted to the arts. In 1937, as German rearmament was getting into high gear, he admonished his party comrades at the party rally to keep in mind that 'the armament of a nation is morally justified only when it serves as a shield and sword of a higher mission'. On another occasion around the same time, when warned of the immense cost of a gigantic stadium planned for Nuremberg, he responded defiantly, 'That is less than two battleships of the *Bismarck* class. How quickly a warship can be destroyed, and if not, it is scrap-iron anyhow in ten years. But this building will stand for centuries.' Once the war was well under way, he uttered perhaps his choicest comment: 'It is a pity that I have to wage war on account of that drunk [Churchill] instead of serving the works of peace.'

Early in the Russian campaign, when German armies were in sight of Moscow and the war appeared close to a victorious end, he remarked on how quickly wars are forgotten. 'By the time of the War of the Spanish Succession no one remembered the Thirty Years War; the battles around 1700 were forgotten after Frederick the Great's wars; Sedan replaced the Battle of Leipzig; Tannenberg as well as our campaigns in Poland and the West will fade after the current one in the East. One day this will also be forgotten. Our buildings, however, will stand.' The whole point of power, he went on to say, was to produce 'cultural wonders'. And he promised that after winning his war the funds he would devote to these 'will vastly exceed the expenditures which we found necessary for the conduct of this war'. In this sense he considered war a step towards his final goal of founding a culture-state. Looking back over his career, he commented in October 1941, 'If I were to assess my work, I would first emphasize that in the face of an uncomprehending world I succeeded in making the racial idea the basis of life, and second that I made culture the driving force in German greatness.'

No single statement ever summed up so openly and concisely his two supreme goals of racial genocide and the establishment of a state in which the arts were supreme. That he made it in the privacy of his field headquarters to a group of generals and did so at the moment when – with German armies ranged from the English Channel to the outskirts of both Moscow and Cairo – he was the military master of Europe and North Africa underscores that he was not speaking for effect but as a triumphant leader.

On coming to power, Hitler lost no time in working towards his Aryan culture state. His first step was to eliminate Jewish and Modernist traces in art. The intention had been spelled out in *Mein Kampf* and was repeated almost verbatim in what was in effect his inaugural address as chancellor – his Reichstag speech on 23 March 1933 – when he left no doubt about what was to come.

> Simultaneously with the political purification of our public life, the government of the Reich will undertake a thorough moral purging of the collective body of the nation. The entire educational system, the theatre, cinema, literature, press and radio – all these will be used as means to this end . . . . Blood and race will once more become the source of artistic intuition.

Thus it was that *Säuberung* – cleansing or purification – became a hallmark, political and cultural, of the Nazi state. In the cultural field Goebbels led the way and by mid-March he had already purged key officials throughout the country. 'All important posts are being filled with impeccable National Socialists,' he recorded by mid-May. On 7 April the first law stemming directly from an objective announced in *Mein Kampf* was enacted. This 'Law for the Restoration of the Civil Service' provided the Nazis a free hand to discharge any member of the civil service, and in Germany this included persons in the arts since most cultural institutions – opera houses, theatres, museums, conservatories, orchestras, art academies and so on – were state institutions. In November government control was extended over unorganized artists through the establishment of a Reich Culture Chamber. No one was legally permitted to practise his profession unless he was a member of this body, and to become a member one was subject to rigorous racial and ideological standards.

The consequences were disastrous. Jews, Communists, Social Democrats and liberals from every area of the arts were summarily dismissed. Some others fled of their own will within the year. Around 250 notable writers and professors left within the first few weeks. Certain eminent persons – such as Lion

Feuchtwanger, Alfred Kerr, Heinrich and Thomas Mann, Theodor Plievier, Anna Seghers, Erich Maria Remarque and Albert Einstein – were later stripped of their citizenship. Of those who remained, some were prohibited from practising their profession while others were eventually driven to suicide or were sent to concentration camps where they perished. Already by the end of 1933 there was not an opera house or concert hall, museum or academic institution that had not been purged; by then forty-nine of the eighty-five heads of opera houses had been sacked. Musical works and books were banned, paintings and sculptures confiscated, the theatrical repertory was purged. On 10 May some 20,000 books were burned in public squares in Berlin and other university cities. By December 1933 more than 1000 titles had been banned, while in the course of the following year some 4000 publications were closed down.

Hitler had started as he meant to go on. In the years that followed he set guidelines which subordinates implemented. Goebbels took the lead, using his Reich Culture Chamber as his instrument. Nothing gave him greater pleasure than tracking down and expelling Jews. For a time he was stymied since it was not entirely certain who counted as a Jew until the Nuremberg race laws were promulgated in 1935, and even then there were ambiguities. By the summer of 1936 he was going full out, but a year later had to admit less than total success. Especially difficult was determining how to deal with artists who were only partly Jewish or who were married to Jews – a relatively large number in the cultural world. 'Ridding Jews from the Chamber goes ahead. I shall have no peace until it is completely *judenrein* [cleansed of Jews],' he wrote in his diary. At times he was even more royal than the king. On asking Hitler what action to take against female Aryan artists who maintained a 'racially disgraceful relationship' with Jewish males, the answer was, 'Führer decrees: nothing.' Eventually, in late 1938 he claimed that his goal had been achieved. Roughly 3000 'Jews and Jewish comrades' had been removed from German artistic life, a figure that did not include those who had fled.

Germany had also to be cleansed of art criticism. Such a ban was both more and less than a token gesture. On the one hand it could have little practical effect since all the notable critics had either left Germany or had muzzled themselves or had gone over to the Nazis. On the other it translated Hitler's personal hatred of what he considered the 'tyranny' of art criticism into government policy. All dictators consider cultural commentary a serious matter. In Hitler's case it was one of his oldest bugbears, going back to the early 1920s, if not before. He associated it with critical approval of Modernism, which in turn was linked to Jewish influence in the arts. He railed against it in some of his earliest speeches and was still doing so near the end of his life. Not only had Jews promoted the avant-garde, he exploded one evening in September 1942 – he was then in his field headquarters on the Russian front – but they had also disparaged his favourite painters. 'The filthy Jews labelled as kitsch almost everything that is healthy . . . .' By the autumn of 1936 he decided to ban it outright. What prompted the timing of the decision is not known. In an entry in his diary in October, Goebbels commented merely that criticism had sooner or later to be done away with. 'Only reporting is permissible. Just as in politics. The stupid must not criticize the clever.' Late the following month he drafted a decree which, following the Führer's revisions, he read to the Reich Culture Chamber on 27 November. Four years had been allowed for critics to adjust to the New Order, the minister intoned, but they had failed to do so. Cultural criticism was henceforth to be replaced with straightforward reporting and positive evaluation.

Purifying the arts also meant starkly limiting foreign influences. Hitler encouraged German painters and sculptors to exhibit and orchestras and opera companies to perform abroad. That would demonstrate the high achievement of German, Aryan culture. But artists from outside the borders were invited only when it suited his political aims. Cultural frontiers were closed, and art became a national affair. In this way Hitler's desire to promote a cultural renaissance in Germany was undermined by his own policies. Through ideology, racism, purges, persecution and cultural autarky, he provoked the greatest migration of creative figures in history and brought to an end some of the most exciting artistic work of the century.

But *Säuberung* was only the negative side of Hitler's grand cultural design. His higher ambition was to alter the cultural face of his Greater German Reich in positive ways. He envisaged the construction of stupendous public edifices, opera houses, theatres and museums. He gave lavish financial support to artists and artistic institutions, commissioned works of music, painting, sculpture and architecture; he made plans to redistribute cultural capital, to remodel cities and even build entirely new ones, to construct autobahns and bridges. The entire Reich was to be given a new cultural shape. Even small towns were to have at least one art gallery and those without a concert hall or opera house were to have visits from travelling orchestras and opera companies. Big cities were to be lavishly endowed; Munich was to become 'the capital of German art'.

In the triumphalist mood induced by his great military victory in the West in 1940, Hitler developed his ideas further, now planning to establish regional cultural centres. In the east, Königsberg was to be the major site. It would have a fine new opera house, theatres, a library and museums to house all the artistic loot from Eastern Europe and the Soviet Union – including the 40,000 works of art taken from the czars' palaces outside Leningrad. In the west, Strasbourg was to be denuded of any French traits and its cathedral made a monument to German culture. In the south, the cultural infrastructure of Munich was to be enhanced with another opera house and additional theatres and museums. Linz was to have the greatest art gallery in the world. In the far north, in a project especially dear to his heart, he planned an entirely new city in Norway, near Trondheim. Originally to be called Nordstern (polar star) and then renamed Drondheim, it was to be wholly German with a population of 250,000 – three times larger than Trondheim at the time. It would have an opera, theatres, libraries, a large art gallery – for exclusively German masters – and other cultural requisites. Hitler himself chose the specific site and by 1945 planning was at an advanced stage.

One city was to be massively diminished. Vienna, the city of his youthful aspirations, became the object of his vengeance. Immediately after the annexation of Austria in March 1938 he returned for the first time since 1913 and in the tumultuous reception undoubtedly savoured a special sense of triumph. But he could never forget or forgive the years of humiliation. Given its historic place in Europe and its cultural eminence, he reckoned that the city would not be easily reconciled to its much diminished status inside the Greater German Reich. His intention was to deprive it of any political influence but allow it a rich cultural life. To carry this off he sent Baldur von Schirach to Vienna as governor in 1940. Schirach, erstwhile head of the Hitler Youth, was a man who thought of himself as National Socialist poet laureate; he had great cultural pretensions but no political ambitions.

Schirach's mission was like that of a symphony conductor under instructions to conduct *con tempo giusto ma non troppo* – that is, do the right thing but not too well. Hitler gave him exceptional latitude – administrative autonomy from Berlin and a huge budget – and for a time things went well. But difficulties were inherent in the situation. One was personal. Schirach was a cultural peacock, not for nothing known as 'Madame Pompadour of Vienna'. Hitler, who had been friendly with him and his wife for many years, began accusing him of having been nobbled – 'poisoned' was the word he used – by the

Viennese. The imputations varied. Schirach affected an American accent; he rolled his Rs like an actor; he 'only ever spoke in a Hugo von Hofmannsthal style'; he spent too much time with artists and was more suited to diplomacy than governing. He was not even a good Nazi. The barbs of course delighted the Führer's entourage who did their best to feed Hitler's suspicions.

The more fundamental problem was that Schirach's activities and Hitler's intentions increasingly diverged. Entries in Goebbels's diaries show that the dictator's loathing of the city steadily grew. 'The Führer gave vent to his extraordinary dislike of Vienna,' reads a typical passage. 'Under no circumstances must anything be given to Vienna; rather, whatever can be taken away, should be taken away.' 'He wants absolutely nothing to be done with Vienna,' reads another. 'Hitler has decided to destroy Vienna's cultural hegemony . . . .' runs still another. The animosity eventually became so obsessive that Goebbels's diary contains a virtual litany of how Hitler planned to punish the city. On a visit to the Berghof in 1943, Schirach listened in appalled silence as Hitler poured out his 'unlimited hatred' of the city and its people.

Not surprisingly, it was Schirach's success that got him into trouble. On taking over he had been determined to make the city and himself glitter, announcing that Vienna was no longer to be a 'cultural cemetery' but the greatest artistic centre in the Reich, with the best theatre and music. With the help of a cultural adviser, Walter Thomas, he enticed stage directors, actors and singers, particularly Austrian ones, to return to Vienna from Berlin and Munich, and concluded long-term contracts with the leading conductors of the time – Hans Knappertsbusch, Wilhelm Furtwängler, Clemens Krauss and Karl Böhm. A large part of the attraction of Vienna was the tolerant artistic atmosphere which he created. This was one reason why Richard Strauss moved himself and his family from Garmisch to Vienna and lent his own support to Schirach. To the Viennese, Schirach's cultural programmes were a welcome form of resistance to 'Prussian colonialism'. To Hitler, they fed the very sense of rivalry to Berlin that he would not tolerate. Goebbels recorded a meeting in May 1942 in which Hitler again swore to destroy Vienna's cultural status. 'He does not want two capitals competing with one another. Nor should Vienna occupy a hegemonic position within Austria. Vienna is simply a big city like Hamburg, nothing more. Schirach is therefore following an entirely wrong course.'

What brought Schirach down was that very artistic liberalism that made Vienna attractive to artists. Sailing ever closer to the ideological wind, he authorized performances of *Parsifal*, banned elsewhere in the Reich after the war began, as well as works of Tchaikovsky and Chekhov during the war with the Soviet Union. In October 1941 he proposed to mount an exhibition of French Impressionist paintings belonging to the Berlin National Gallery. As soon as Hitler heard of it, he forbade the show and denounced Impressionism as 'incompatible with our [German] character'. A year later Schirach arranged a 'Gerhart Hauptmann Week' and an eightieth birthday ceremony, even though the dramatist-novelist was no longer in good odour with the Führer. Despite a dressing down from Berlin as a result, he later held an ostentatious celebration of Strauss's eightieth birthday, even though the composer had by then also fallen into Hitler's disfavour.

In January 1943 he finally went too far when he sponsored an art exhibition, 'Junge Kunst im Dritten Reich' (Young Art in the Third Reich), which included works considered Modernist. An outraged Hitler closed the show and summoned the miscreant to the Berghof and accused him of artistic sabotage. Opening a copy of the Hitler Youth publication, he pointed to a photo taken from the exhibit. 'Look at that picture – a green dog! . . . That is not youth education, it is education in opposition.' The next day the atmosphere between the two men became colder still until Hitler, his face contorted in fury, finally burst out: 'It was my mistake to have sent you to Vienna. It was a mistake that I ever brought these Viennese into the Greater German Reich. I know these people. In my youth I lived among them. They are the enemies of Germany.'

Schirach felt he had no alternative but to resign on the spot. 'That is not your decision,' Hitler responded. 'You stay where you are.' After the war Schirach excused Hitler's ill temper on the ground that the *Wehrmacht* had just been crushed at Stalingrad. More remarkable perhaps was that at a moment of military debacle, the commander-in-chief was worrying about a minor art exhibit.

Even after this episode Hitler continued to fret about Vienna. In a long monologue in June 1943, when the war had by now turned against him on all fronts, he spent an evening unburdening himself to his staff. Since his feelings towards Vienna were such common knowledge, he was moved to comment defensively:

I am certainly not prejudiced against Vienna; that is entirely erroneous. I also criticize whatever I do not like in Berlin. But my concerns go far beyond the issue of Vienna versus Berlin . . . . I must already think of what may happen when I am no longer here. It would be dangerous if Vienna should dominate the Austrian cultural scene. That is why I am already trying to prevent such a situation by developing other cultural centres. Vienna already has too great a cultural attraction. That leads to an increase in political attraction, and this must not be allowed . . . .

Then, turning to Schirach, who was present, he added, 'It is your job to make certain that Vienna does not go into cultural decline. My job is to protect the interests of the Reich.' Hitler never really forgave the Governor of Vienna for his cultural policies, however, and told Goebbels that he meant to get rid of him as soon as he could find a replacement.

After the heavy bombing of the city started in November 1944, Schirach repeatedly appealed to Hitler to augment anti-aircraft units. Hitler responded that it would be well for the city to have the experience of aerial bombardment and refused. In the last weeks of the war, when Vienna was flooded with refugees and wounded soldiers, Schirach pleaded with Hitler to declare Vienna an open city. The Führer's response – 'his last message to Vienna' – was instead to order that his collection of antique armour should be sent to safety at the Berghof. To him the city was, as he told Henriette von Schirach, 'racially completely worthless'. What befell it was of no concern to him.

The Vienna episode highlighted the stark contradictions inherent in Hitler's cultural policies. Artistic life in the Nazi Reich was to flourish, but it was to bloom in a harshly regulated garden. Since the only point in being a dictator was to dictate, Hitler took enormous pleasure in pontificating about the arts and in laying down the law about what artists were to produce – and even what the public was to enjoy. The arts were to enrich the lives of the public as his own life had been enriched. The Strength through Joy organization, for example, was established not only to organize mass vacation activities but also to bring culture to the masses – or rather, the masses to culture, whether they liked it or not. Groups were taken to music festivals, shown travelling art exhibits, treated to free concerts and the like. 'I remember Strength through Joy weekends,' Alfred Rosenberg observed in his memoirs, 'when the Ninth Symphony was played in the morning, a museum was visited in the afternoon, and *Tristan* was performed at night.' As early as 1934 Strength through Joy sponsored no fewer than 120 art exhibits in factories alone, a figure that increased nearly six-fold within three years. Arrangements were also made for artists themselves to give talks, perform, paint or sculpt in public.

As with the end-users, so the producers. They were to provide clean and simple lines in architecture, 'beauty' rather than 'daubs' in painting and harmonious melodies rather than atonality or jazz rhythms in music. But the arts, as the ultimate form of independent creativity, demand unhindered expression. You cannot write poems about trees, Brecht pointed out, if the forest is filled with policemen. This Hitler never understood. 'The artist does not create for the artist,' he declared in a speech in July 1937 on opening the House of German Art in Munich, 'he creates for the people, and we will see to it that from now on the people will be called upon to judge its art.' It was to be expected, he commented on another occasion, that in periods of rapid revolutionary change, the arts needed guidance from above 'even at the risk of the most rigorous intervention'.

Here Hitler encountered any number of problems. The most obvious was the one that confronts all totalitarian leaders – how to regulate free spirits like artists. It was one thing to crush trade unions and political parties, and even to restrain the churches, but entirely another to regulate creative individuals working independently. How were the hands of painters, composers, sculptors, writers and architects to be guided and to what end? Hitler did not begin to have it worked out. In fact, nothing was apparent except that Jews, liberals and Bolsheviks were to be excluded from artistic institutions and forbidden to practise their art. The uncertainty and confusion at the very top was duplicated right down the ranks to artists and local party leaders who debated, often ferociously, what styles of painting, music, architecture, sculpture and literature expressed National Socialist ideology. Years passed and they still did not know where they stood. In the end nothing counted except the judgement of the Führer and, unless this materialized, everyone was left to divine what it might be. What was a mystery to party leaders was a total enigma to artists, museum directors, opera managers, conductors and anyone else engaged in the arts. The dilemma was never resolved.

Hitler never wavered from what he saw as his great civilizing mission. After launching war in 1939, he amazed everyone by ordering cultural activities to go on as before. In contrast to Britain where all theatres were closed – Covent Garden Opera became a dance hall – German theatres, concert halls, opera houses and museums, instead of terminating or drastically curtailing their programmes, maintained their normal routine. In part Hitler feared, as he told Goebbels, that the quality of artistic life would otherwise be seriously damaged. In part he also wanted to advertise that the Third Reich remained the world's great culture state and that culture was an essential element in what it was fighting for. In addition he wanted to show that Germany could conduct a full-scale war without any disruption of normal social life and victory was just around the corner. 'It must be our principle to make the war as easy as possible for the population,' Goebbels echoed. This was picked up by the German press which trumpeted the theme that 'thanks to the protection offered by Germany's glorious weapons', German cultural life could go on undisturbed. Unlike the Louvre and the National Gallery, which had evacuated their collections in fear of destruction, German museums remained open, the director of the Berlin museums pointed out, 'to do their duty by serving the nation while waiting for victory'. It was a good line and it was valid for several years. As Howard K. Smith, the Berlin correspondent of an American newspaper at the time, wrote:

> It was heartbreaking, but it seemed true, when a German officer, at whose side I was strolling down Unter den Linden in the first spring of the war, told me: 'Look around you, Herr Smith. Nowhere a sign of war. Not the slightest difference from two years ago . . . .' How, under these circumstances, could the horror of war ever be brought home to the German people? War wasn't so bad. It was not a struggle of life and death.

When the *Wehrmacht* failed to deal Soviet forces a fatal blow by the end of 1941, Hitler regarded a thriving cultural life to be crucial in preventing the collapse of public morale that had occurred in 1918. After a meeting with him at the end of November, Goebbels commented in his diary, 'Cultural life is an effective way of encouraging perseverance in the hard struggles which we survived and have yet to survive.' By and large, accounts of morale in those years bore out Hitler's policy. People saw in it evidence of his confidence in victory and, until that was achieved, an escape from the horrors of the war. They flocked to the opera, theatre, museums and cinema as never before. The worse the military situation, the more they craved a cultural outlet. As the war ground on and aerial bombing on the home front intensified, however, Goebbels urged Hitler to channel all the nation's resources into the war effort. Hitler responded by admonishing him 'under all circumstances to maintain cultural activities during the entire length of the war'. After the defeat at Stalingrad, Goebbels, Speer and Bormann implored him to declare 'total war' and put a stop to cultural diversions. He refused to hear of it. By the summer of 1944 Goebbels once more risked taking issue with Hitler, again without success. 'He is of the opinion, despite my objections, that the Great German Art Exhibition must be opened as usual in Munich,' Goebbels noted in his diary. 'I consider this mistaken.' The exhibition was held.

Not until August 1944, in light of the military situation and the shock of the attempt on his life a month earlier, was Hitler gradually worn down. '[Bormann] calls for a total liquidation of our cultural life, the closure of theatre, opera and cabarets,' Goebbels noted. He went on:

> At first the Führer fiercely resisted the proposal to close the operas, theatres and stage shows. He is above all afraid that once theatres and opera houses are closed, we would not be able to open them again as long as the war lasts; once people accustomed themselves to the lack of opera and theatre, that could become a permanent state of affairs. And should the war go on for years, the nation would lose any memory of theatre and opera and content themselves with radio and film, as is already largely the case in America.

Eventually Goebbels managed to persuade him that his fears were overdrawn and assured him that symphony orchestras would remain intact, performing now on radio. Stopping the publication of arts journals so pained him, however, that he agreed only when paper supplies were no longer available from Finland. Even then, after an appeal from Heinrich Hoffmann, he reversed his order. Nor would he countenance any disruption of the performances of the Berlin Philharmonic or the Munich Opera. As late as December 1944 he was still planning to have the Bayreuth Festival take place as usual the following summer. After one of his final conversations with Hitler about cultural affairs, Goebbels recorded, 'I can easily foresee that once the war is over he will once again devote himself with the most passionate enthusiasm to such matters.'

THE
ARTFUL LEADER

4 THE ARTIST AS POLITICIAN

'HIS CREATIVITY IS THAT OF THE GENUINE ARTIST, no matter in what field he may be working,' boasted Goebbels. And indeed, Hitler regarded governing itself as not merely having art as an ingredient; it *was* art. Political leadership, he said at his 1924 treason trial, should be regarded not as *Staatswissenschaft* but as *Staatskunst* – not political science but statecraft. It was an intuitive art and, like every art, a product of genius. In notes he made for one of his early speeches, he scrawled: 'You cannot educate for politics – Politics is not science – but – art – Ten thousand "educated democrats" – A single Bismar[c]k is born. . . .' A true mastery of *Staatskunst* was thus an innate gift; one was either born with it or never had it. General Ludendorff had botched his political chances in the early 1920s, he told Alfred Rosenberg, precisely because he lacked this vital talent. Only an artistically sensitive figure, he explained, 'could feel the vibrations of a people's soul' and so know how to lead. Like Bismarck, he – as he was never reluctant to assert – possessed this gift.

In fact, Hitler took the practice of politics-as-an-art vastly beyond anything imagined by the Iron Chancellor – to the extent, indeed, where he could, in an unguarded moment, style himself 'the greatest actor in Europe'. With no immodesty he might have added that he was also the greatest theatrical impresario, the most daring playwright and the cleverest stage manager on the inter-war political scene. And those skills were only one of his talents. Combined with his artistry was an ice-cold, calculating realism. Together the two traits fused into a skill which enabled him to master Germany and go on to set the course of world history.

Reason is the slave of the passions – Hume's dictum was the underlying premise of Hitler's *Staatskunst*. He was convinced that historical change resulted not from social forces or philosophical writings but from the work of 'agitators led by demagogues in the grand style'. It was Lenin not Marx who had ignited the Russian revolution. The trick was to know how to stir the passions of the public. As George Orwell pointed out, 'Hitler, because in his own joyless mind he feels it with exceptional strength, knows that human beings *don't* only want comfort, safety, short working hours . . . and, in general, common sense; they also, at least intermittently, want struggle and self-sacrifice, not to mention drums, flags and loyalty parades.' From the outset of his political career Hitler therefore pitched his appeal not to the mind but to the senses, to emotion rather than reason. Psychological manipulation, not political logic was the essence of his technique. By demonstrating that people care less for their material interests than for some ideological nostrum and are moved less by rational choice than by irrational forces, he challenged the very basis of Western democracy.

In this he claimed little originality, making a point in *Mein Kampf* of attributing his inspiration primarily to British wartime propaganda and post-war Communist agit-prop activities. His model was Lloyd George, whom he praised for his 'psychological masterpieces in the art of mass propaganda' which had 'made his people serve his will completely'. Revealingly he credited the British prime minister's success to 'the primitiveness of his language, the primordiality of its forms of expression, and the use of easily intelligible examples of the simplest sort'. Therein lay 'the proof of the towering political ability of this Englishman', he claimed. Similarly, he traced Lenin's achievement to the effect not of his political pamphlets but of his 'hate-fomenting oratorical activity'. In this way he came to the conclusion that all 'the great religious and political avalanches in history' had been touched off by 'the magic power of the spoken word' or, in an even more vivid metaphor, 'the torch of the spoken word hurled into the masses'.

Hitler's speeches – or, better, his public performances – were the most potent expression of his artistic talents and the key to his rise to power. In *Mein Kampf* he described his first public speech, which took place in 1919 in a small room in the Munich Hofbräuhaus. 'I spoke for thirty minutes, and what before I had simply felt within me, without in any way knowing it, now proved to be real. I could speak!' And speak he could! Like a religious evangelist, he could convert crowds and he could convert individuals. Rosenberg confessed that he had been thoroughly unimpressed at their first encounter but then attended a speech. 'That was what drew me to Adolf Hitler in the first fifteen minutes.' Another of Hitler's addresses had the same effect on Kurt Lüdecke, a well-connected, right-wing wheeler-dealer. 'My critical faculty was swept away. . . . I experienced an exaltation that could only be likened to religious conversion . . . . I had found myself, my leader, and my cause.' And on hearing him at a Berlin Sports Palace rally in 1932, Leni

Riefenstahl found herself nearly blown away by an almost apocalyptic vision. 'It seemed as if the earth's surface were spreading out in front of me . . . spewing out an enormous jet of water, so powerful that it touched the sky and shook the earth. I felt quite paralysed.' A few names stand for many. And so, with no money and no following, Hitler realized that giving speeches was his sole way to power. In the years that ensued they were not only what launched him on this political career but also what most obviously distinguished him from other German politicians, what caught international attention and what helped him to keep the German people in his grip. What was it about them?

It was not just a remarkable rhetorical ability. It was not just his movements and mannerisms. It was not just his voice and the way he used it. It was all those, but it was something more important, a psychic ability to connect with an audience and mesmerize it. What resulted was not a mere speech, it was a *Gesamtkunstwerk*, a total artwork. Hitler ravished his audiences. He sensed what his listeners felt, not what they thought, but what they felt – frustration, anger, paranoia, xenophobia. Then he told them what to think. His secretary Christa Schroeder, having observed him for fifteen years, concluded that he possessed the 'gift of a rare magnetic power to reach people', 'a sixth sense and a clairvoyant intuition'. He could 'in some mysterious way foretell the subconscious reactions of the masses and in some inexplicable manner mesmerize his interlocutors'. He possessed, she said, 'the receptivity of a medium and at the same time the magnetism of a hypnotist'. Many others observed these same qualities. After seeing him in action for several years, French ambassador André François-Poncet found that Hitler

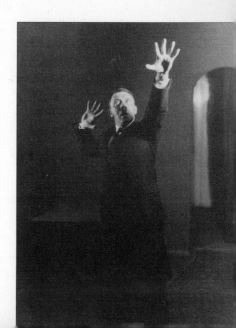

Hitler claimed it took him two years of practice to perfect his oratorical skills. In that time he learned how to transform himself, like Fafner in Wagner's Siegfried, *from a pathetic worm into a fearsome dragon which spewed fire and poison. His dramatics combined a mad sort of rhetorical logic with a hypnotic sort of theatrical fanaticism – a delirium which both speaker and audience shared.*

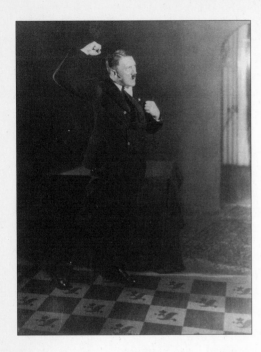

'His technique resembled the thrusts and parries of a fencer, or the perfect balance of a tightrope-walker.' (Ernst Hanfstaengl)

seemed almost to possess psychic antennae telling him exactly what the crowds wanted or feared, approved or hated, believed or disbelieved and that he played on these emotions to perfection.

Combined with this was his peculiar manner of delivery. Whether or not you agreed with him, whether or not you liked him, he left the impression of someone who had guts, who would unhesitatingly go to the stake for his convictions. In no other of his repertory of theatrical personae was he quite so much in his element. His aim was less to deal with concrete issues – those

'Our notion of genius has always been shrouded in a superstitious haze. But I question whether today the haze is thick enough to prevent our calling this man a genius . . . . The phenomenon of the great man has after all been most often an aesthetic, not an ethical phenomenon.' (Thomas Mann)

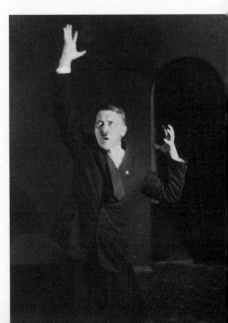

he invented or twisted as he pleased – but to create an emotional impact through his posture, movements, demeanour and facial expressions. Nothing was spontaneous. Early in his career he practised and rehearsed gestures while standing in front of a mirror, and photographs survive, taken by Heinrich Hoffmann in 1926, showing his various poses. Ernst Hanfstaengl, one of his early hangers-on, witnessed these gestures during his speeches and commented that they put him in mind of 'the thrusts and parries of a fencer', 'the perfect balance of a tightrope-walker', 'a skilled violinist', 'a really great orchestral conductor who instead of just hammering out the downbeat, suggests the existence of hidden rhythms and meaning with the upward flick of his baton'.

Nothing was left to chance. According to Goebbels, he rehearsed entire passages as if he were an actor going on stage. Every gesture was calculated with the utmost precision. He ordered equipment to be installed in the speaker's podium allowing him to alter the lighting and to signal precisely when cameras should photograph him. So as not to compromise his simple appearance by being seen to wear glasses, his notes or texts had to be typed in large print. The meeting site itself was selected with great care as to its size, shape, acoustics, location and appearance. Care was taken to see that the hall was always over-filled. A speech was only the pièce de résistance, the public's appetite having been whetted beforehand by bands, marches, banners, singing – in short, a festival atmosphere. 'All these histrionic elements built up the suspense and made the speech seem like an annunciation,' Joachim Fest has written. At length, rising to speak, he would begin by not speaking at all. For a time – seemingly endless – he would stand mute, contemplative, and then begin quietly, even hesitantly, and gradually the dramatic torrent of words would flow forth, eventually reaching a tremendous crescendo with shrieking in a high-pitched voice. It is small wonder that his performances were likened to a symphonic work. Yet Hitler's technique has routinely been characterized as little more than rabble-rousing, hysterical, scarcely grammatical ranting, and some post-war film clips have been doctored to heighten this impression. In fact, it was all utterly controlled. 'Hitler was not an emotional orator, as so many people (especially among his opponents) believed,' the one-time Gauleiter of Hamburg commented. 'He constructed his speeches systematically, and always knew exactly what he was saying and what effect he intended with his words.'

He was invariably his own speechwriter. When chancellor, he threw away government department drafts or at most used their statistical data. He struggled over his texts, redrafting them over and over. 'He spoke very proudly of the fact that he corrected his speeches and proclamations three,

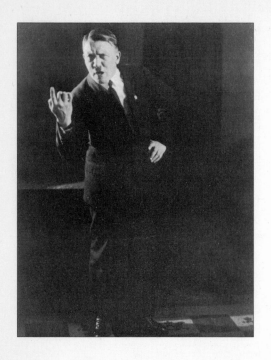

'Threatening and beseeching, with small, pleading hands and flamboyant, steel-blue eyes, he had the look of a fanatic.' (Kurt Lüdecke)

four, five times,' Goebbels noted. 'That is something he shares with the best stylists of the German language.' For all his occasional shrillness, even the harshest of critics credited him with a good command of the finer nuances of the German language. Hitler was tremendously proud of his orations and invariably refused to change the text for publication.

And the substance itself? The stock themes – the evil of the Versailles Treaty, the threat of Bolshevism, the wickedness of Jews, liberals and the

'He engages in angry abuse in the manner of a Homeric hero, he rages, he intimates he can barely hold himself back from grabbing his opponent by the throat, he challenges him by name, he makes fun of him. The listener is captivated, sharing the speaker's sense of triumph and believing what he believes.' (Bert Brecht)

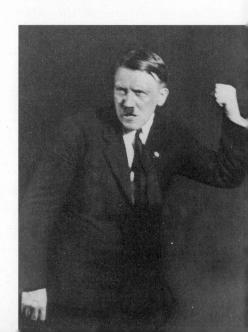

Weimar Republic – mattered little. 'Not a single one began with a statement of subject,' Otto Dietrich, his press spokesman, noted. But by the time he reached the conclusion, he had 'so overwhelmed the audience that serious political controversy and a real clarification of the problem no longer seemed necessary'. The emptiness of his message must not be overdone. The seed would not have flourished had it not fallen on fertile ground. At another time, in another place, the oratory would not have worked. But in the 1920s many Germans were looking for a saviour, Hitler was looking for a following, and they found one another. Hitler's critics likened his artistry to that of a magician whose oratorical prestidigitation left his listeners spellbound without understanding why. They noted that he did not make an attempt to persuade through logical argument but rather induced a mood akin to inebriation which unleashed primitive passions. Some traced his technique to the Catholicism of his youth, from which he learned the effectiveness of repeating rote phrases to instil a trance-like mood. Another trait sometimes remarked upon was a perceived sexual undertone both in the speeches and in the response of the audience. Hitler himself regarded an audience as a feminine organism. 'Like the woman whose psychic state is determined less by grounds of abstract reason than by an indefinable longing,' he wrote in *Mein Kampf*, 'the masses love a commander more than a petitioner.' And then there was his messianic appeal. After meeting Hitler in Weimar in 1932, Nietzsche's sister Elisabeth spoke for many others in saying that he left her with the impression not of being a politician but of being a religious figure. The American journalist William L. Shirer commented how shocked he was on first seeing the faces of women when Hitler appeared briefly on the balcony of his hotel in Nuremberg at the time of the 1934 party rally:

> They reminded me of the crazed expressions I once saw in the back country of Louisiana on the faces of some Holy Rollers who were about to hit the trail. They looked up at him as if he were a Messiah, their faces transformed into something positively inhuman. If he had remained in sight for more than a few moments, I think many of the women would have swooned from excitement.

Others found a sado-masochistic undertone in Hitler's relationship with his audiences. Still others sensed an aesthetic, even musical quality to his oratory. Many eminent German exiles – Heinrich, Thomas and Klaus Mann, Emil Ludwig, Ludwig Marcuse and Bert Brecht, for example – claimed there was something Wagnerian about it. 'What he learned from Wagner he inserted in his speeches – the pompous and the nebulous, brutality and innocence; these are what give his speeches such resonance for Germans,' Ludwig wrote.

Through his aesthetic sensibility Hitler also had an instinctive understanding of the emotive power of symbols – flags, uniforms, standards and so on – and applied this in designing the party's iconography. None of the basic ideas originated with him. His genius lay in knowing which symbols to choose and how to present them in an arresting way. The central symbol, the swastika, had been around for some time in Austria and southern Germany as an emblem of right-wing politics and anti-Semitism. Although not the first to propose it as a party sign, he secured its adoption and turned it into a pre-eminent icon of anti-Semitism. It was he who determined that it should face right rather than left and who ordained its colours. Colour, an art critic has observed, has a hot line to instinct. As such it can be used to demagogic effect, and so it was in his stark use of black, white and red. The red, which had to be blood red, was, he said, 'to speak to the working masses' – in other words he hijacked it from the left. As he later wrote in *Mein Kampf*, 'In *red*

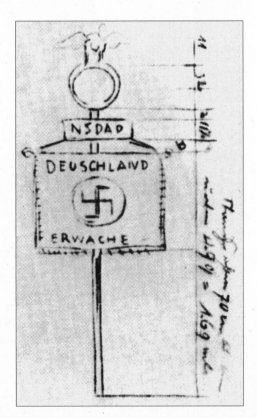

Hitler's sketch of a party standard, specifying its precise measurements. The inception of the standard has been termed 'Caesar by way of Mussolini'.

we see the social idea of the movement, in *white* the nationalistic idea, in the swastika . . . the victory of the Aryan man, and, by the same token, the victory of creative work, which as such has always been and will always be anti-Semitic.' The black swastika inside a white disc against a red background was not only eye-catching but also had a potent subconscious effect. 'An uncanny power emanated from the mysterious sign,' wrote one biographer; it radiated 'psychological magic', according to another.

With these elements Hitler fashioned a party flag. When it was first flown in the summer of 1920, he himself discovered that it 'had the effect of a burning torch'. He also devised a party badge, party stationery, the masthead of the party newspaper and even the official rubber stamp, all bearing an eagle with a swastika in its talons. Such was the importance he attached to these symbols that he spent hours poring over old art publications and books on heraldry to find a model for the eagle. Eventually he discovered what he

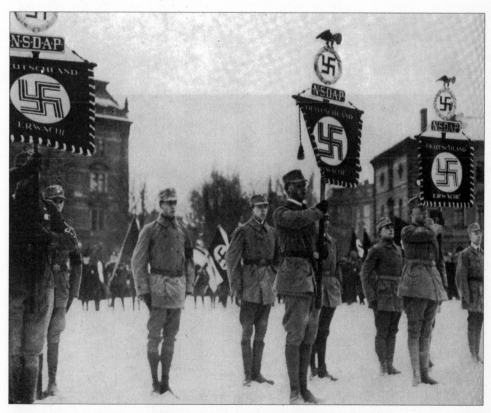

The first public display of the party standard. The consecration took place on 28 February 1923 at the Marsfeld in Munich.

wanted in an anti-Semitic lexicon where the fowl was characterized as the Aryan of the animal kingdom. He then asked a jeweller to design a model, but when this proved too feeble, he invented his own – a menacing eagle which appeared about to take flight. Impressed by the neo-Roman emblems of Italian fascists, he also devised the elaborate standard that became the insignia of mass meetings and parades. His definitive sketch has survived and shows that he worked out every measurement and detail.

He borrowed and adapted other visual symbols. The brown shirts worn by party activists were modelled on the blackshirts of Italian fascists, just as the raised arm greeting was a variant of Mussolini's Roman salute, though he

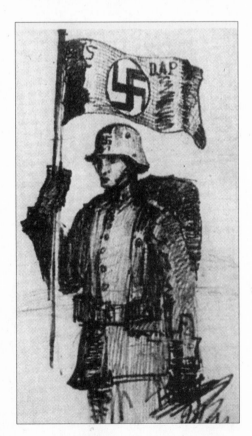

Hitler's sketch of party flag and Storm Trooper uniform.

Swastikas on our helmets
Armbands red, black and white
Storm Detachment Hitler
Ready for the fight!

(Storm Trooper song)

insisted he took it from medieval German practice. Uniforms were of enormous importance, obliterating individuality and the hierarchic order of society while manifesting the encompassing power of the party and state. In the rank order of uniforms, those of the SS – black, svelte, decorated with Germanic runes and the death's-head badge and complemented with heavy black leather boots – were the most aesthetically suggestive. These were clearly men who were not only supremely violent but also supremely beautiful. Hitler also developed a repertory of aural symbols – such as the 'Sieg Heil', which had old German roots, and its variant, 'Heil Hitler'. The first Nazi song was the musical setting of Dietrich Eckart's poem 'Sturm, Sturm, Sturm' with its climax 'Deutschland Erwache!' (Germany Wake Up!). He personally rehearsed it before authorizing its use at a party rally in Munich in 1923. In all this, Hitler knew no rival but had one counterpart and he, too, was an artist-politician and a fascist, Gabriele D'Annunzio.

It was in his spectacular public meetings that Hitler's application of aesthetics to mass politics reached its zenith. These were such a feature of his rule that 'theatrocracy', in Jacob Burckhardt's neologism, could almost be one of the aliases of the Third Reich. Inspired by the street demonstrations of leftist parties after the war, he developed ceremonies, rhetoric and ritual in a way to seduce the subconscious of an audience. In fact, during his earliest years in politics he conducted experiments in crowd reaction and found that the key element lay in the circumstances of the occasion – the time and place.

> The same lecture, the same speaker, the same theme have an entirely different effect at ten o'clock in the morning, at three o'clock in the afternoon, or at night. [By the same token] there are halls which leave people cold for reasons that are hard to discern, but which somehow arouse the most violent resistance to any creation of mood.

At issue was a contest of wills or, as he said, 'a wrestling bout' between a speaker and his audience. During the day, people's will power was strong enough to withstand new ideas. 'At night, however, they succumb more easily to the dominating force of a stronger will.' This instinctive feeling for what Thomas Mann called 'the quintessentially Romantic glorification of the night' is another aspect of Hitler's link to Romanticism. Night is the realm of the senses rather than reason, intuition rather than logic. German Romantics revelled in this notion, which received its fullest expression in Novalis's *Hymnen an die Nacht* (Hymns to Night). While there is no reason to think that Hitler was aware of such writings, he intuitively recognized the potent psychological effect of darkness and made a point of staging his greatest visual events at a time when he could play with controlled lighting effects. The flickering of torches, the rolling of drums and the fanfares of trumpets drew the participants into a mystical realm in which the individual surrendered himself totally.

To entice people into his phantasmal world, Hitler worked out a vast panoply of artistic techniques – extravagant and imaginative use of lighting, colour, sound and such simple tricks as heightening tension by making a crowd wait for several hours until he appeared. As producer, director and stage manager, he appealed to all but one of the senses. Whether decorating cities with gigantic banners or deploying Storm Troopers and other party units in their black, brown or red-brown uniforms, he blended and contrasted colour as though he were still a painter. Through bands and mass choruses he created moods as though a composer. He arranged regimented blocks of human beings in geometric formations as though he were an architect. He made over a hundred thousand men stand motionless and at the snap of his fingers had them turn, march, sing, shout or raise their arms in the party salute as though a choreographer or stage director. In such ways he demonstrated the unity of the nation, his supreme power and the desire of the masses to obey his will without hesitation. 'Never before,' it has been remarked, 'was the relation of masters and slaves so consciously aestheticized.'

Once in power he made all Germany his stage. He began practising his art only hours after being appointed chancellor with a huge torchlight parade of Storm Troops through the centre of Berlin. Soon afterwards he organized the famous 'Potsdam Day', when he, along with President Hindenburg and the other fossils of the old *Kaiserreich*, met in Potsdam's Garrison Church in a ceremony that formally inaugurated the new government. The place and date were symbolic. The site was a hallowed one to the kings and army of Prussia, the place where Frederick the Great himself was interred. And the timing – 21 March – was the anniversary of Bismarck's inauguration of the first Reichstag in 1871. All the top military brass along with the ex-Crown Prince and a few other members of the Hohenzollern family attended the event which culminated in Hitler's dramatic – and much photographed – handshake with the aged head of state. At the conclusion of the event Hitler, in morning coat and top hat, descended to the vault of the church to pay his respects at the tomb of the old king. The ceremony was brilliantly staged to leave the impression that Hitler and his party venerated the glorious Prussian tradition going back to 'old Fritz', and that Germany's destiny was safe in the new chancellor's hands. Hitler described Potsdam Day as signifying that 'the marriage has been consummated between the symbols of the old greatness and the new strength'. The event marked the first example of Hitler's transformation of statecraft into stagecraft.

In fact, the drama of that day had just begun. When the Reichstag itself later convened, the members found themselves in a hall decorated with an enormous version of the Nazi eagle and swastika that Hitler had designed a decade earlier. Though still a parliamentary minority, the Nazi party had visually taken over the assembly. And so it continued in the weeks and months that followed. In August Hitler led a national pilgrimage to the site of the German army's victory over the Russians at Tannenberg in 1914 and once again hauled out the icon of German tradition, President Hindenburg, to participate. This bogus obeisance to Prussian tradition was rerun a year later after the old president had died. Following a grand memorial ceremony in Berlin, an even grander interment was enacted in the courtyard of the Tannenberg monument. Since Hitler could not imagine even a funeral without suggestive stage props, he instructed Speer to rush to East Prussia to decorate the site. The obsequies lasted several days and culminated in Hitler's apostrophic Wagnerian valediction, 'Dead warlord, now enter Valhalla.'

As at Potsdam, the impresario used the ceremony not just to evoke nationalistic sentiment and associate National Socialism with German military glory but also to put a gloss on a deadly political purpose, in this case the abolition of the office of president and thereby the removal of any institutional limit on his power. With Hindenburg scarcely cold in his grave, he announced that the offices of chief of state and head of government were joined in his own person as Führer. To secure his position further he also made himself supreme military commander by requiring a formal oath of allegiance from the top military leaders and, in ceremonies repeated throughout Germany the next day, from every member of the German armed forces.

In subsequent years Hitler employed a quite different form of dramatics, his celebrated diplomatic surprises which were contrived to startle the world. These *coups de théâtre* were usually sprung on Saturdays, catching other governments off guard and drawing double press coverage, first in the weekend press and then again in the regular Monday newspapers. An early example was his transformation of a decree abrogating the Versailles Treaty's limits on German armament into a gala of frenzied nationalism. The announcement was issued on Saturday, 16 March 1934. Not by chance, this was the day before the traditional commemoration of those who had fallen in war. What in another country would have been a terse government announcement explaining away, with decent embarrassment, its violation of a major international obligation was turned into a brazen celebration. Shirer described the theatrical effects:

I went to the ceremony at noon at the State Opera House and there witnessed a scene which Germany had not seen since 1914. The entire lower floor was a sea of military uniforms, the faded gray uniforms and spiked helmets of the old Imperial Army mingling with the attire of the new Army, including the sky-blue uniforms of the Luftwaffe, which few had seen before. At Hitler's side was Field Marshal von Mackensen, the last surviving field marshal of the Kaiser's Army, colourfully attired in the uniform of the Death's Head Hussars. Strong lights played on the stage, where young officers stood like marble statues holding upright the nation's war flags. Behind them on an enormous curtain hung an immense silver-and-black Iron Cross.

Spectacles on a far grander scale became a constant feature of public life in the Third Reich. 'Hitler was one of the first great rock stars,' the rock star David Bowie declared after he and Mick Jagger had seen *Triumph of the Will*, Leni Riefenstahl's film of the 1934 Nuremberg rally, fifteen times. 'He was no politician, he was a great media artist. How he worked his audience! He made women hot and sweaty and guys all wished they were the ones who were up there. The world will never see anything like that again. He made an entire country a stage show.' In manipulating and mobilizing public opinion Hitler was well ahead of his time. A media figure before the notion of media figure had arrived, he exercised a psychological power that was without precedent and that made him the pre-eminent charismatic leader of the century. He made Nazism seem sexy.

Even those who despised him most, the exiled German artists and intellectuals, admitted that he had a genius for pushing highly emotive buttons. No less a playwright than Bertolt Brecht expressed downright awe of Hitler's native theatrical sense. It was not just the skilled use of lighting, music and so on in his productions but also his '*Politik des Bluffs und Theatercoups*' in international politics. That, Brecht freely admitted, was '*sehr interessantes Theater*'. The playwright was clearly envious of someone whose stage was the entire country, while he was confined to the interior of a theatre. He was even moved to write a poem to the effect that Hitler's sole achievement was theatrical, three lines of which ran:

. . . his virtuoso use of lighting
is no different from
his virtuoso use of the truncheon.

The transparently theatrical nature of public life was divulged in 1936 when

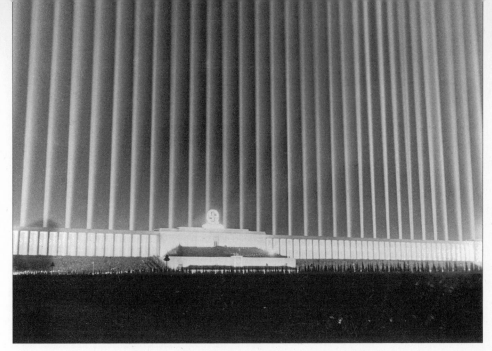

*To create a 'cathedral of light', Speer placed 130 flak searchlights
(almost the entire Luftwaffe reserve), at intervals of forty feet, to shoot beams into the
sky to a height of 25,000 ft. 'The actual effect far surpassed anything
I had imagined,' he said.*

Hitler established the position of Reich Stage Designer and appointed to it a theatrical producer, Benno von Arent. Arent's function was to create scenery not only for operas but entire cities and great state events.

Others saw Hitler's talents as essentially Wagnerian. Endless parades, continuous music, oaths of loyalty, praise of heroism – 'all this fulfilled the German dream of obedience and music, discipline and worship, a combination of *Lohengrin* and the Brigade of Guards'. Such was the comment of the historian Emil Ludwig who, like most other exiles, admitted that at the simplest level Hitler was providing the sort of excitement and pageantry that was totally lacking in the Weimar Republic and that, however irrational the means, he succeeded in his objective of arousing a deep sense of national pride. More important still, his pageantry and rites provided the populace, now deprived of debate and elections, with a stronger sense of political participation than ever before.

In staging his events, Hitler had a talent, deriving from his rich operatic experience, for mood creation through illumination. Although Speer claimed to have invented independently the fantastic lighting effects at the party rallies, the original inspiration probably came from Hitler, who was ruminating about atmospheric lighting when Speer was a mere child. So impressed had he been by the staging and lighting of Alfred Roller's famous 1903 production of *Tristan und Isolde* in Vienna, which he attended in 1906, that he included among the drawings in his 1925 sketchbook his rendering of the second and third acts. Similarly the *Parsifal* performance he saw at Bayreuth in 1923 had left him awestruck by the 'mysterious magic' of the darkened atmosphere of the opera house. From such experiences he learned that light could make the black wall of night even blacker and that darkness could make the outer world vanish. The psychological intent was to cause the participants to feel drawn together in mystical communion.

Another of Hitler's favourite devices was fire, which made figures, banners and flags shimmer in an eerie glow. Fire was a key element in the scenography of the commemorative ceremonies that gave him such pleasure. Torches, bonfires, Bengal lights, fireworks, flares, pyres, flames rising out of enormous braziers all produced a wondrous spell. It was for the sake of such fiery effects and the impact of nocturnal lighting that he saved his favourite ceremonies for night-time. His intent, he declared in *Mein Kampf*, was to destroy the 'freedom of will' of his audience and induce a state comparable to religious exaltation.

Hitler also calculated the effect of sounds and availed himself not just of music but of sirens, cannon salutes, rifle shots, fanfares, church bells and even the tread of boots and aircraft fly-pasts. With these he could create various moods – usually solemn, often heroic and exciting, sometimes martial, occasionally jubilant. He arranged the build-up to his own appearances with the skill of a composer. His arrivals, accompanied by an approaching swell of cheers as he progressed along the way, were evocative of the Swan Chorus in *Lohengrin*. His oratory also imitated music – by turn *piano*, *crescendo*, *fortissimo*, *appassionato*, often *agitato*, occasionally *scherzando* though never *dolce* or *affetuoso*.

At times theatrics assumed such importance that Hitler appeared to be lost in the art itself, more absorbed in the sheer extravaganza than its ideological intent. Max Reinhardt, Edward Gordon Craig and Cecil B. de Mille might have done things differently but not with as much panache. Big, sculpted scenic effects were Hitler's forte and in the course of every year he furnished his audience – the German public – with an elaborate programme of parades, festivals, dedications, commemorations, salutes, torchlight processions and the like. He himself was producer, director, stage designer and lead actor – literally. No operatic or theatrical performance was prepared with greater care, and he gave every detail his personal attention.

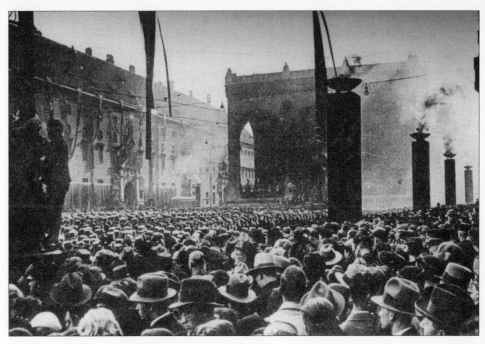

Banners and fiery, smoking braziers lend a pagan atmosphere to the annual commemoration of the Beer Hall Putsch at the Feldherrnhalle. The loggia, originally a Bavarian military monument, was converted by Hitler into 'the Altar of the Movement'.

The overwhelming visual and aural effects – the sheer colour of thousands upon thousands of flags, standards, pennants, streamers and banners; the excitement of illuminations, searchlights, torchlight processions; the thrill of regiments of bands and singers; the exhilaration of fanfares, sirens, salvoes and aerial fly-pasts – all this pummelled the participants nearly senseless. The entire German nation was turned into supernumeraries in Hitler's National Socialist theatre.

In planning his mass meetings, Hitler's architectural skills gave him a sophisticated appreciation of the importance of the physical ambience of a site. His principles were strict. The space itself was ideally to be rectangular. It was to be isolated from the outside world. The participants were to be formed with military exactitude into solid blocks. Attention was to be continuously focused on the leader, with nothing else in the sight lines. Practical details followed from that. To be plainly visible and the centre of attention, the tribune for Hitler was elevated above the rest of the site at one end of the narrow side of the space. Behind it, to emphasize its visual primacy still further, would stand a forest of flags and banners and behind them a huge replica of the party symbol, the eagle and swastika. The axis connecting the entrance to the tribune formed a corridor exclusively for Hitler and the few who might accompany him. The architecture and decoration of the space along with other visual and acoustical features were designed to heighten the impact of Hitler's movements and voice. It added up to a message that could not have been more inescapable. The Führer is all, the individual exists only in the mass.

In addition to Hitler the dramaturge and Hitler the architect, there was Hitler the Catholic. By his own word, the idea of casting a spell on audiences originated in his childhood religious experience. 'The same purpose, after all, is served by the artificial and yet mysterious twilight in Catholic churches, the burning of lamps, incense, censers, etc.,' he had written in *Mein Kampf*. And so he invented an array of ceremonies, each with its rituals and symbols, references and terminology. Processions, banners, smoke and fire, holy flame, sacred relics, catechismal oaths and symbolic rites gave National Socialism the character of a religion akin to Catholicism and its pagan antecedent. This was evident to both supporters and opponents. Of the 1934 Nuremberg party rally Shirer commented,

> I'm beginning to comprehend, I think, some of the reasons for Hitler's astounding success. Borrowing a chapter from the Roman church, he is restoring pageantry and colour and mysticism to the drab lives of twentieth-century Germans. This morning's opening meeting in the Luitpold Hall on the outskirts of Nuremberg was more than a gorgeous show; it also had something of the mysticism and religious fervour of an Easter or Christmas Mass in a great Gothic cathedral . . . . You have to go through one of these to understand Hitler's hold on the people.

Insiders were equally impressed by Hitler's techniques. 'With its boundless mystical magic,' Goebbels wrote admiringly of the 1937 rally, 'it was almost a religious ceremony.' Not surprisingly, Hitler succeeded in arousing a religious-like fervour even in those who were devout Christians.

But for all their insight, Brecht, Bowie and Shirer never quite grasped the deeper significance of Hitler's theatrics. Ultimately the purpose of these spectacles was to fill a void at the centre of National Socialism. Nazi ideology was, in Karl Dietrich Bracher's words, essentially 'an eclectic conglomeration of ideas and ways of thinking, concepts and hopes, emotions of various origins that was welded together only through the manipulation of a radical political movement at a time of crisis'. In other words, unlike Marxism, it offered little that was concrete enough to get hold of. What Hitler provided was ritual in place of belief, or ritual *as* belief. Ritual inculcates obedience. It involves loyalty rather than conviction, blind faith rather than reasoned understanding. In ceremonies adapted from Catholic practices, ritual was not so much an outward expression of belief as a mode of producing it. Hitler's rituals, even those without oath-taking ceremonies, created commitment and established bonds; they provided certitude precisely because they were beyond reason and doubt. Such theatrocacy was participatory ideology. His ceremonies were a throwback to a pre-Homeric primitive, even savage, rite in which totem, taboo and ritual reinforced the unity of the tribe.

Linked to this was Hitler's own near deification. On examining one of Hitler's speeches at the 1936 rally, J. P. Stern discovered passage after passage of sheer pastiche of texts from the Christian Gospels – 'blessed are they that have not seen, yet have believed', for example, became 'Once you heard the voice of a man . . . and you followed this voice'. 'A little while, and ye shall not see me: and again a little while, and ye shall see me' was echoed in 'Not everyone of you sees me, and I do not see everyone of you. But I feel *you*, and you feel *me*.' Hitler himself once remarked that the hundreds of thousands who attended these occasions 'often gained the impression that they were no longer at a political meeting but in the grip of a deep sense of prayer'. His belief in his own near divinity – the notion of being the instrument of providence, as he repeatedly put it – increased as his political and diplomatic successes multiplied. It was following the 1938 party rally that Speer acknowledged waking up to the shocking realization that 'all these formations, processions, dedications' were less a clever propagandistic revue than 'almost like the rites of the founding of a church'. Hitler, he said, had deliberately restrained his rhetorical powers so as to downplay his status as a celebrated popular hero and gain the far greater position of founder of a religion. And, in fact, Hitler had at that time begun to order the centre of dozens of German cities to be reconstructed to create mammoth meeting places – in Berlin a space for a million people – to celebrate his appearances – that is, to worship him. In such ways he had progressed in the course of his life, as has been said, 'from "artist" to "God-man" '.

Hitler's talents as artist as well as his status as God-man were most obvious in the party rallies. Held every September, they have been recorded in numerous photographs and in 1934 immortalized in Riefenstahl's *Triumph of the Will*. There were ten such meetings in all, the first convoked by Hitler in 1923 in Munich. The next, in 1926 when he was still banned from speaking publicly in Bavaria following his putsch attempt, had to be held in Weimar. After that he decided they should always take place in Nuremberg, and they were held there in 1927, 1929 and from 1933 through 1938. Lasting for four days in the first years, they were eventually stretched out to twice as long. Attendance also expanded from several thousand in the earliest days to a quarter of a million from 1933 on, with plans for an eventual 400,000. To highlight their all-inclusive character, Hitler summoned groups from all major sectors of society and every area of the country. Some 500 trains transported them to a specially constructed railroad station at the site. These assemblies were undoubtedly the most powerful ideological 'durbars' ever held. No stage performance could have been prepared more fastidiously and Hitler himself arranged every feature – the schedule of events, march routes, speakers, choreography of the ceremonies, selection of musical works and conductors, and even the seating arrangements for official guests. His attention to detail is evident in a surviving sketch in his own hand, showing his design for the lighting and decorations at the 1935 rally.

The choice of archetypical German Nuremberg – 'the most German of all German cities', in the words of its Nazi mayor – was highly symbolic. Hitler's aim was to reinforce the impression that the Third Reich was rooted in the oldest, most authentic German tradition going back to the First Reich of the Middle Ages. This was not the 'soulless modern city' that Hitler so derided but one of the best-preserved medieval sites in Europe. He regarded it, he said at the 1929 session, as Germany's great old '*Reichstadt*' and 'an outstanding shrine of German art and German culture'. Following the annexation of Austria in 1938, he removed from Vienna the ancient ensigns and coronation regalia of the Holy Roman Empire – two fourteenth-century sceptres, one silver and one gold, and the twelfth-century orb – that had been taken there following Napoleon's dissolution of the old Empire in 1806. He sought to show the world, he said, that 'more than half a millennium prior to the discovery of the new world, a gigantic Germanic-German Reich stood on this ground'. With these symbols Hitler and his movement were meant to be linked to the glory of the First Reich, while the Third Reich was to appear more authentically German than any of the intermediate German states. The symbolic significance was openly stated at the presentation ceremony: 'It is as though the Third Reich has finally and completely merged into the stream of history, from the first appearance of Germans in the dawn of history down to the present day . . . . The myth of the First Reich lives in this Imperial treasure.'

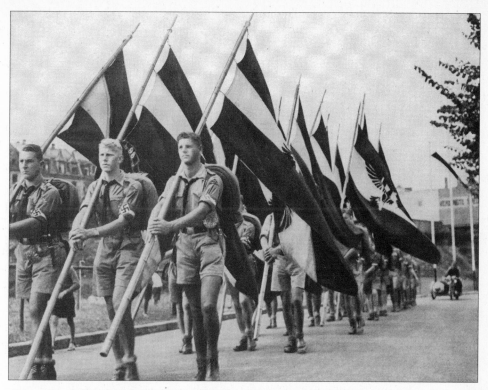

*Fifty thousand members of the Hitler Youth and German Girls' League participated
in the party rallies, the boys bearing red and white banners, the girls carrying
black banners decorated with a silver eagle. Concluding the festive ceremony,
eighteen-year-olds were sworn in as candidate members of the party.*

The proceedings hardened into a rite, which varied little from year to
year. Hitler's arrival was the first drama. In 1934 he arrived by air, as though
a god from the heavens. In later years he came by train and was met by all
the party leaders in a solemn welcoming ceremony. After being driven in his
open car through flag-bedecked streets, amid wildly cheering crowds and the
joyous tolling of church bells, he was formally received by the mayor at the
city hall in a large assembly room which was kept in 'magical half-darkness'
so as to create a sense of cultic sacrament. To crown the day Hitler hosted a
gala performance of *Die Meistersinger von Nürnberg* in the city's opera house to
which he issued a personal invitation to party officials and honoured guests.

The next day began with a march-past by Hitler Youth, which the Führer
viewed from the balcony of his hotel. Around 2000 of these – out of a total
of roughly 50,000 who attended – had walked several thousand kilometres

on an 'Adolf Hitler march' to reach the city. After that the rally was officially convened in the assembly room of the Luitpold Hall. The ceremony combined features of stage production with religious liturgy. The walls of the great hall were lined with white silk, the seats for the guests, orchestra and chorus were upholstered in deep red and the entire space was dominated by a gigantic swastika encircled by a sparkling gold wreath against a black background. Greeted with dramatic fanfares and the *Badenweiler March*, Hitler entered the hall to ecstatic cheers. To intensify the dramatic moment still further, Hitler indulged his passion for music. First came the *Nibelung March* which accompanied the presentation of the party standards and the party's most holy relic, the *Blutfahne*, or blood flag, the swastika banner that had been carried in the 1923 putsch attempt on which had allegedly been spilled the blood of the 'martyrs' shot down on that occasion. Then two principal themes from the overture to Wagner's *Rienzi* were played, followed by further musical selections, including a choral rendering of the Dutch *Dankgebet*. Rudolf Hess, as the Führer's deputy, opened the session with the party's sacred ritual, the *Totenehrung*, or homage to the dead. This was the Nazi 'catechism', a recitation of the names of party martyrs and 'heroes' who had 'sealed their loyalty to the Führer and nation with their heart's blood'. Hess went on to deliver his address, a fugue on the theme of unquestioning obedience to Hitler because, he declared, 'The German people know that everything the Führer does is right.' A party official then read Hitler's 'sermon', which was a declamation of the party's achievements during the previous year. The session concluded with the singing of a Beethoven hymn.

The evening was devoted to the event dear to Hitler's heart, the cultural session. Here Hitler presented himself not as the Great Leader but as the Great Teacher and addressed not the party thugs but leading figures from German cultural and intellectual life along with a few party officials with cultural pretensions. He also forwent the mass party antics of the other meetings, confining himself to philosophical ruminations on the state of Western culture. These occasions were of such importance to him that he ordered a special *Kulturhalle* to be built for them and drew his own sketches of the exterior and floor plan of the structure. Until then the meetings were held in the Nuremberg opera house. These opened with all or part of a Bruckner symphony, after which Hitler expatiated endlessly – sometimes for at least three hours – about the state of the arts.

The third day was dedicated to the Labour Service, the organization that had replaced the unions. It began with a parade, reviewed by Hitler, of

50,000 Service members, marching with shovels over their shoulders like soldiers with rifles – in fact, they were called 'soldiers of peace'. The participants, all bronzed, strong, clean, healthy and obviously Aryan, were a very model of the new German worker. After a greeting by Hitler, the participants broke into a rendering of the 'Song of the Labour Service', which praised the value of work and 'loyalty to the Führer if necessary to the death'. There followed a horrifying litany of chants and responses. 'The fulfilment of duty for us is not serfdom,' went the verse of one. 'The Führer wants to give the world peace,' ran another. 'Wherever he leads, we follow,' was the response. Then came more songs, a demonstration of mass calisthenics, the requisite homage to the party martyrs, a speech by Hitler and yet another song. In the afternoon the entire Labour Service group marched through the city.

A 'Day of the Community' followed. This began with speeches by heads

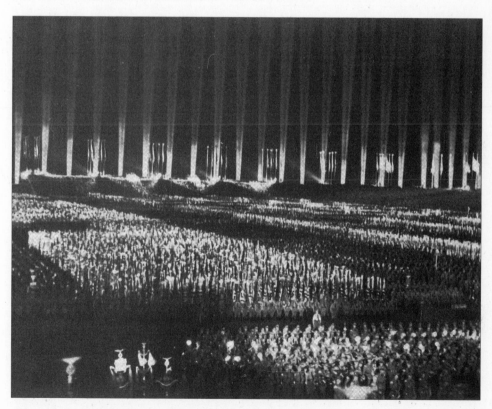

An angler in the lake of darkness, Hitler staged his most important ceremonies at night, as here at the 1936 Nuremberg rally. Civilization, said Freud, requires repression of aggressive, brutish instincts. The intent of the rallies was to release those repressions.

of various party organizations, went on to sports events and concluded with a torchlight parade through the city, which the Führer observed while standing for hours, arm raised as though paralysed in the party salute. The fifth day was the 'Day of the Political Leaders' and from 1936 this event culminated in the dramatic high point of the rallies. After sundown 110,000 men marched on to the review field while 100,000 spectators took their places on the stands. At a signal, once darkness fell, the space was suddenly encircled by a ring of light, with 30,000 flags and standards glistening in the illumination. Spotlights would focus on the main gate, as distant cheers announced the Führer's approach. At the instant he entered, 150 powerful searchlights would shoot into the sky to produce a gigantic, shimmering 'cathedral of light', as it was called. More vividly, the British ambassador famously described it as 'solemn and beautiful . . . like being inside a cathedral of ice'. In either case 'cathedral' was the apt term since the essence of the ceremony was one of sacramental dedication to Führer and party. Encased in a circle of light and dark, the participants were transported into a vast phantasmagoria. Striding through the group formations – along a *via triumphalis* of living bodies, in Goebbels's phrase – Hitler reached his place and at that moment, as his personal standard was raised, there cascaded on to the field a wave of some 30,000 flag bearers, the silver tips and fringes of their flags glittering in the searchlights, creating the impression of 'a great tide of crimson seeping through the lanes between the solid blocs of brown', in the words of the *New York Times*. Then the beams of lower searchlights would light up the gilded eagles of the party standards and tinge the flood of red with flecks of gold. The overall effect was described by the journalist as 'indescribably beautiful' and by the British ambassador as 'indescribably picturesque'. 'I had spent six years in St Petersburg before the war in the best days of the old Russian ballet,' the ambassador commented in his memoirs, 'but in grandiose beauty I have never seen a ballet to compare with it.' Once the Führer delivered himself of a brief speech, the voices of a quarter of a million men would join in Nazi hymns.

The sixth day belonged largely to the Hitler Youth. It was an occasion for German youth to be indoctrinated with the idea that they belonged not to the German state or the Nazi party but to Hitler personally. 'Heil, my youth,' he shouted on arrival. 'Heil, my Führer,' the 50,000 young people cried back. There was much music and singing along with speeches by Hitler, Hess and Baldur von Schirach, the Hitler Youth leader. The crowning moment occurred when the assembly swore a solemn pledge: 'I swear by God this sacred oath – I shall at all times be loyal and obedient to my Führer, Adolf Hitler.'

The Day of the Storm Troops, the seventh day, was one of the most evocative. On his arrival Hitler would greet the 100,000 troopers deployed in the stadium with 'Heil, my men,' to which they would reply with one voice, 'Heil, my Führer.' Hitler would stand, motionless and bareheaded, as the men, to the sound of a steady drumbeat, formed squads on either side of 'the street of the Führer'. As the flags dipped in respect and reverential music softly sounded, Hitler would walk through the massed formations to a memorial monument where, facing the party's sacred blood flag, he would lay a large wreath. Then he would pause in lonely meditation. 'With a raised right hand,' in the words of an official report, 'he honoured the dead heroes who, in loyalty and belief in him and, through him, in the entire German people, had sacrificed their lives.' In total silence he would return, followed by the bearer of the blood flag. Twenty-four rows of SS troops, forming a solid black block, would then march across the field, the tread of their heavy boots reverberating on the granite paving. To the sound of the national anthem and the 'Horst Wessel Song', Hitler would walk along the endless ranks of new party standards and consecrate each by touching it with an edge of the sacred blood flag, as a rifle salute sounded each time. The event concluded with the party hymn, ending with the words 'Germany wake up!'. Afterwards, in the city itself, 120,000 Storm Troops paraded for five hours in never-ending lines through the festively decorated streets.

The eighth and final day was the 'Day of the Armed Forces'. Hitler's intent was both to link the military with the party and in later years to demonstrate the growing power of the country's military machine. Older military officers are said to have viewed these occasions with acute distaste. To them the exercises had more to do with circus than war and they disliked playing the role of clowns.

By the end of each rally Hitler was nearly wiped out. He once complained to his staff that he found that week 'the worst time of the year' and had thought of spreading the event over ten days to relieve the terrible strain. 'Most demanding is having to stand for hours at the march-pasts,' he said. 'Several times I nearly fainted. You can have no conception of how painful it is to have to stand with your knees locked for such a long time.' Standing was only part of the ordeal. Between ceremonial entries and exits, unending rituals and march-pasts, he bathed his audiences in an unending cascade of words – as many as eighteen or twenty speeches, each carefully prepared. Though exhausted, Hitler was enraptured, and the participants were in a state of inebriation – sometimes literally as a result of the widespread boozing after the official events.

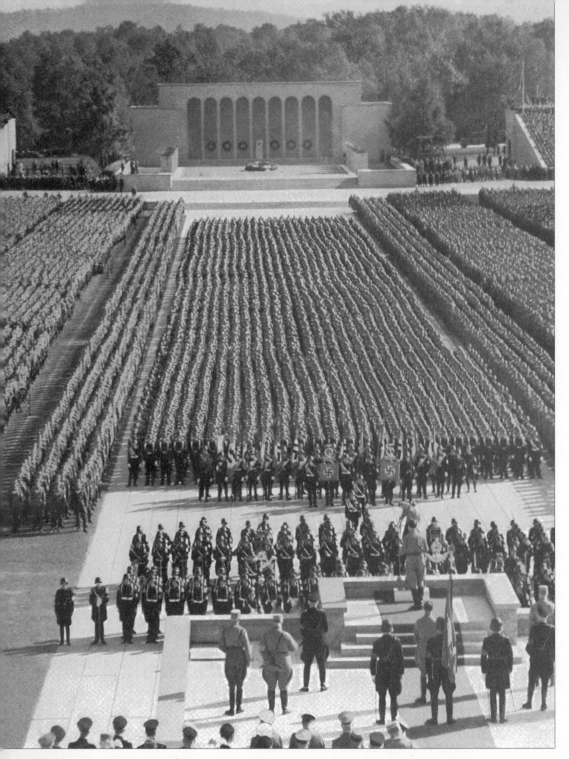

*SA and SS at 1936 party rally. 'I had long thought that all these formations, processions,
dedications were part of a clever propagandistic revue. Now I finally understood that for
Hitler they were almost like rites of the founding of a church.'*

(Albert Speer)

With his rallies Hitler brought to a height his genius for psychological manipulation through spectacle. Outsiders were no less awed. François-Poncet was putting it mildly when he declared that the experience at Nuremberg was so hypnotic that 'many returned home seduced and conquered, ready to collaborate, failing to perceive the sinister reality hidden behind the false pomp'. One of these victims was the young Philip Johnson, not yet launched on his architectural career, who said of the 1938 rally, 'Like the *Ring* [*des Nibelungen*], even if you were at first indifferent, you were at last overcome, and if you were a believer to begin with, the effect was even more staggering. Even the Americans who were there – no special friends of the Nazis – were carried away by it all.'

The sinister reality was that Hitler made the dramatic arts a technique of mental manipulation and mind control. By merging into the mass, the individual felt he had gained his sense of identity. In the party rallies the German people symbolically enacted their willingness to be used by Hitler at his will. In his well-known aphorism, Walter Benjamin observed that fascism aestheticized politics. In fact, Hitler's fascism anaesthetized politics. The rallies were a microcosm of Hitler's ideal world: a people reduced to unthinking automatons subject to the control not of the state, not even of the party but of him personally – and that unto death. Never before was there a clearer example of aesthetics used to promote enslavement and heroic death.

This was reflected in the architecture of the site. If the participants in Hitler's shows were the actors and the activities the drama, the meeting place represented the stage and auditorium. Hitler oversaw each aspect of the design, spatial arrangements and building materials of the complex. These expressed the same twin themes – absolute obedience to the Führer and loyalty to him unto death. Accordingly Hitler had constantly to be at the visual centre. 'The eye-to-eye position of the Führer with his people is always the underlying principle,' wrote an architecture critic in 1938. 'The elevation of the Führer is an expression of his position, a man who with all his deeds is always the leader of his people.' The death cult also was visible in a number of ways. An already existing necropolis was incorporated into the site. The new structures, particularly the Zeppelin Field platform, which was a grotesquely hypertrophied version of the ancient sacrificial altar at Pergamum, bore an obvious sepulchral character, augmented by such funereal features as huge braziers at critical places. Hitler's walk to the site of the martyr's memorial was his *Opfergang*, the path of sacrifice. The forests of flags and banners, the solemn music and flaming braziers all added to the

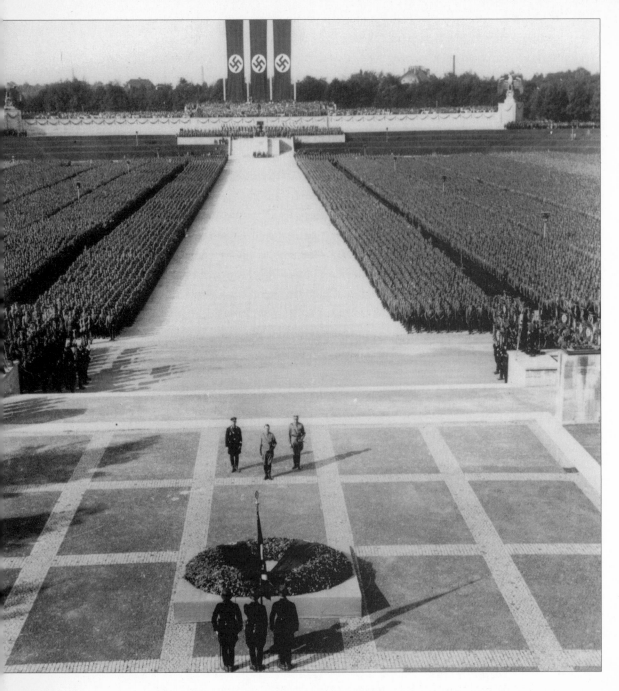

Caesar-Führer-God-man – Hitler salutes the blood flag in the Luitpold Arena, while the heads of
the SS (Heinrich Himmler) and SA (Viktor Lutze) stand several respectful paces behind.
In a scene of almost pagan ritual, animal sacrifice has been replaced by the prospective human
sacrifice of wars to come.

necromantic mood. Thus did ideology, melodrama and architecture complement one another in the self-sacrifice of the nation.

The rally area exhibited Hitler's political-psychological intent in still other ways. A broad avenue, paved in granite, extended from the March Field – alias Field of Mars, god of war – to the eleventh-century Nuremberg castle, symbolically linking the party with Germany's past. Even the building materials were selected for their ideological effect. Granite, limestone and marble were used to suggest tradition, hardness, indestructibility. German oak, a mythical symbol of Germanness, embellished interiors and there was to be a plantation of oaks in the area. The overall impression, reinforced by the lack of ornamentation, was one of cold impersonality. But above all, the desire to overwhelm, to bludgeon the mind, was manifest in sheer magnitude. The complex, covering more than ten square miles (16.5 square kilometres), would be, as Hitler boasted at the 1936 rally, 'by far the largest such site under construction in the world today'. Each of the major structures was similarly bloated. Speer reconstructed the existing Luitpold arena for 200,000 people. The newly constructed Zeppelin Field stadium provided a marching area for 250,000 and seating for 70,000. The planned German Stadium was to accommodate 405,000 spectators, while the March Field was to be a parade ground for 500,000 soldiers. In addition to a Culture Hall, a Congress Hall would have an auditorium for an audience of 60,000 and a stage able to accommodate 2400. Giganticism of this nature inevitably reflected glory on its primogenitor and at the same time demonstrated 'the power and greatness of the [National Socialist] movement in the context of the heroic spirit of the time', as Hitler's press spokesman phrased it at the 1935 session. 'This sacred site with its unique concepts of architecture and use of space,' he went on to say, 'will be the highest symbol of National Socialist life and National Socialist culture; in it the unique style of National Socialism will find its strongest expression.'

Hitler had begun thinking about a rally site even before he was in power. His initial concept was a modest one that flowed harmoniously into the local landscape. A plan for a large Congress Hall already existed, and in 1933 he instructed its designer, Ludwig Ruff, to carry it out. By 1934 he had far grander ideas, however, and to realize them turned to Albert Speer, thus initiating their long and close collaboration. In *Inside the Third Reich* Speer claimed to be the father of various designs but blamed their magnification on Hitler, entitling his chapter on the subject 'Architectural Megalomania'. In fact, something like the reverse was the case. Hitler's initial rough sketches of the major rally sites were in a restrained, neoclassicist style. In Speer's hands these were transmogrified into a gigantic ideological message in stone. The architect said he saw his brief as one of providing 'a monumental backdrop' for the rally activities. Monumentalism, however, quickly gained priority over backdrop and almost became an end in itself. Caught up in the enthusiasm, Hitler eagerly supported Speer's concept. It was not only the buildings that were gargantuan but also the costs. Hitler used a good deal of legerdemain to conceal these from the German public and indeed even from the Finance Ministry. It was in this context that he defensively compared the expense of this 'lasting monument' with the wasteful extravagance of two evanescent battleships.

'Lasting' was indeed the counterpart to monumentalism. These structures were being built for a Reich that was to last 1000 years. 'I can still see him in Nuremberg standing in front of the model of the new Congress Hall,' Fritz Wiedemann, his personal adjutant, recalled. 'As I stood there . . . I observed him contemplating the model and thinking over every detail – where the musicians and the standard bearers were to have their place, how and from which side the flags should come in. And then he said, "We must also consider where the Führer – not the one in the immediate future but the one in eight hundred years from now – should enter. We are building not for our time but for eternity." '

5 THE POLITICIAN AS ARTIST

WHICH WAS PASTIME, WHICH WAS WORK; which personal, which official – art or governing? It was not always easy to know. After an evening spent with Hitler in July 1926, Goebbels noted in his diary, 'He talks about the future architectural image of the country and is thoroughly the architect. After that he paints a picture of a new German constitution and then is entirely the political artist.' Nearly five years later, with the party nearing the threshold of power, Goebbels found that what was on Hitler's mind, and the only thing on his mind at the time, was the reconstruction of the party's headquarters in Munich. And the year after that, while campaigning against Hindenburg in the presidential election, he spent his free moments worrying about plans for the architectural redevelopment of Berlin. Then, on the very evening after being appointed chancellor, one of the subjects he raised with his assembled friends was the derisory size and shabby condition of the Reich chancellery. 'He was deeply excited and agitated,' witnesses reported. 'The most diverse thoughts crossed his mind. The Reich chancellor's office did not suit him at all. That would be the first thing he would change; it was nothing more than "a mere cigar box", absolutely worthless for representational purposes.'

During the following weeks and months – the critical period when the Nazis fastened their grip on the German state – Hitler let nothing interfere with his personal cultural pleasures, always seeming to find time for an opera, play or art exhibition. 'Art will always remain the expression and reflection of the longings and the realities of an era,' he declared in his inaugural address to the Reichstag in March. This blandest of statements was in fact a signal that as chancellor he intended to turn the state itself into a patron of the arts beyond anything previously seen. To mark the moment he ordered the construction of the first great building of the Nazi state, an art gallery in Munich, which he named the House of German Art. Upon its completion in 1937, he proclaimed that had he accomplished nothing more in his life than the construction of that one structure, he would have done more for German art than anyone else in the century.

Beyond that, however, Hitler had neither a programme for the arts nor any interest in directing them day-to-day. With no leadership and a party apparatus run by ideologues lacking administrative experience, cultural affairs were in a state of chaos. Several local party bosses, having personal scores to settle, took actions that in some cases greatly embarrassed the national leaders. These in turn all detested one another and were from the start engaged in cut-throat and never-ending power struggles. Each party baron had his own army (his bureaucracy) and his own territory (his ministerial remit). Since Hitler deliberately left the frontiers between the bureaucratic fiefdoms ill-defined and ever changing, the battles were ceaseless. Adding to the war-like atmosphere, the serfs – the artists – were scarcely more loving among themselves and only too happy to seek advantage at a colleague's expense.

There were six primary combatants. Bernhard Rust, Minister of Science, Education and Culture, held formal authority over museums, art academies, music conservatories and similar institutions. Robert Ley, the labour boss, controlled artists' professional associations as well as Strength through Joy, which sponsored cultural activitites. To Hermann Göring, as Minister-President of Prussia, belonged the opera houses and theatres of the Prussian state theatre system. And Baldur von Schirach reigned autonomously in his satrapy of Vienna. Rust and Ley were primarily concerned to protect their bureaucratic authority. Göring and Schirach were prima donnas, concerned with personal prestige and therefore artistic quality rather than with party doctrine.

The chief contenders were Alfred Rosenberg and Joseph Goebbels. Rosenberg, born in Estonia and educated in pre-revolutionary Russia, was a fanatical German nationalist, anti-Semite and anti-Communist. Before coming to power, Hitler found him useful as a vitriolic enemy of the Weimar Republic and made him editor of the party daily, *Völkischer Beobachter*. He also saw his potential as a mouthpiece of cultural invective and in 1927 appointed him head of the so-called Fighting League for German Culture. But for the man himself, he had little more than contempt. His great work, *The Myth of the 20th Century*, Hitler dismissed as 'stuff nobody can understand'. By the time he was appointed chancellor, he considered Rosenberg and his followers right-wing romantics and the Fighting League an ideological nuisance. His concept of the New Order was anything but Rosenberg's fantasy of a state embodying archaic Teutonic ideals. Consequently he refused to give 'the narrow-minded Balt', as he was often referred to, a government position. 'He sharply criticizes Rosenberg, because he accomplishes everything and nothing,' Goebbels commented in July 1933. Rosenberg himself described in his memoirs how hurt he was that in the evenings after dinner the Führer often invited his favourites for a long talk by the fireplace and sadly admitted he did not know what they discussed 'because I was never asked'. At the party rally the next year, though not mentioning his name, Hitler brutally denounced Rosenberg's reactionary ideology. Nonetheless as editor of the *Völkischer Beobachter* and the monthly journal *Die Kunst im Dritten* – later, *Deutschen – Reich* (Art in the Third – German – Reich) and as head of the Fighting League, Rosenberg remained the leading cultural spokesman of the hard right. He made a lot of noise and for a time could not be entirely ignored.

Joseph Goebbels came from a Rhineland Catholic family and, like Hitler, easily exchanged religious for political dogma when, as a failed writer, he found a career in the Nazi movement. Hitler was attracted by his political shrewdness and his effectiveness as an orator. Ideologically on the left of the party and not entirely closed-minded to Modernism in the arts, Goebbels initially viewed Hitler askance. But he had, as one of his biographers has written, no convictions at all and by 1930 was motivated by no greater desire than to please his Führer. Like the other party leaders, he was Hitler's creature and nothing more. Clever, power-hungry and without principle, he was the consummate bureaucrat and outsmarted his rival at every turn. Although scarcely unbiased, Rosenberg did not exaggerate when he asserted that 'Goebbels never spoke a single original, creative word about the arts'. What the doctrinaire Rosenberg did not give him credit for was his tactical skill. Viewing everything for its propagandistic effect, he was often disposed to compromise with certain artists and certain works of art in the interests of the country's cultural prestige. He did his best to keep such potential defectors as Wilhelm Furtwängler in Germany and tried to lure back figures like Thomas Mann and Marlene Dietrich.

Goebbels and Rosenberg had begun loathing one another in the 1920s, and as soon as the Nazi party came to power open warfare ensued. Always on his toes, Goebbels swiftly moved to get control over cultural affairs by establishing a Reich Culture Chamber, which everyone in the art world was required to join. In approving the move, Hitler signalled that he sided with Goebbels. Rosenberg responded by notifying Hitler that he intended to bow out of the picture. Three days later he withdrew his threat. Hitler paid no attention to either message and in later years could not be bothered to reply to his memoranda. 'Hitler knew very well, of course, that I understood art and culture much more deeply than Goebbels, who could hardly look beyond the mere surface,' Rosenberg wrote in 1945; but Goebbels played up to Hitler's cultural interests in a way that 'I was never able to manage'.

Hitler considered it impolitic completely to ignore the party's dogmatic right wing, however, and in January 1934 he endowed Rosenberg with the florid title 'Representative of the Führer for the Overall Philosophical and Intellectual Training and Education of the National Socialist Party'. This appeared to grant authority over everything but, as a party and not a government position, in practice it gave him control over nothing. In 1935 Hitler approved his suggestion of setting up a Cultural Senate but then reversed himself and instead authorized Goebbels to do so. 'Cultural leadership clearly lies with me,' Goebbels gloated. When the Fighting League was transformed into the larger National Socialist Cultural Community in 1934, it appeared to offer Rosenberg a greater role. But in practice the organization had no influence and was dissolved in 1937. In the end Rosenberg was reduced to trying to exert influence through his art journal, *Die Kunst im Dritten Reich*. By 1939 even Goebbels was moved to remark that his rival did not deserve to have fallen so low.

So Goebbels came to be, under Hitler's aegis, cultural overseer of the Third Reich. His own position was, however, far from impregnable. Formal authority rested on his status as Propaganda Minister and head of the Reich Culture Chamber. But lacking a power base in the party – and being universally detested – he was in reality a general without an army. Consequently his actual influence depended entirely on his relationship to the commander-in-chief. 'I have few friends in the party. Practically only Hitler,' he once confided to his diary. And in fact it was only the handles of power that Goebbels held; his formal title, 'Executor of the Führer and Reich Chancellor for Art and Cultural Life', said it all. His diaries leave no doubt that he never took an important decision without Hitler's knowledge and that until 1943 he was not really sure that he enjoyed the dictator's full confidence. Even his speeches were submitted to Hitler for approval – and correction. What he then said was usually little more than an echo of the Führer's own words on some previous occasion. Nor did he ever get his hands on some of the most important cultural institutions. A number of leading opera houses and theatres were under Göring's control; the Bayreuth Festival belonged to Winifred Wagner, wife of the composer's son, Siegfried; cultural activities in Vienna were in von Schirach's hands; the Great German Art Exhibitions and the Munich Opera came under Hitler's own purview while the operas in Hamburg and Dresden were controlled by the local party boss. Conservatories and art galleries fell to Rust. In addition there was an even more basic restriction. Hitler may well have rejected Rosenberg's reactionary dogmatism, but he had even less sympathy with Goebbels's flirt with Modernism.

Quando due litigano, gode il terzo. In the conditions of the Third Reich, the old Italian saying perfectly summed up Hitler's recipe for dictatorial power – when everyone fights everyone else, only one person comes out on top. With his subordinates in checkmate, the Führer remained Führer. The organizational anarchy and absence of an arts policy was so marked that a 1938 secret police report could not forbear giving testimony:

> Despite the large number of cultural organizations there is no coherent planning. The Education Ministry, Interior Ministry, Propaganda Ministry, Rosenberg's office, the cultural administrations of the Länder and provinces, the cultural agencies of the party, the Reich Culture Chamber and its individual chambers, the Strength through Joy organization, the Professors' Federation, the Student Federation, the scientific and research agencies of the army, similar agencies of science and industry and so on are all individually seeking to promote a National Socialist cultural policy but have never succeeded in organizing these forces into a coherent, mutually supporting and forward-looking policy in the cultural sphere.

Consequently, instead of a policy there were a series of arbitrary decisions, reached case by case, or incident by incident. Conceivably this, too, was what Hitler wanted. Despotism is most effective when everyone but the despot is left guessing what is permitted.

The formal instrument of control over the arts was the Reich Culture Chamber, with its subordinate chambers for literature, radio, theatre, music, film, visual arts and press. All artists had to join, and to apply for membership it was necessary to answer a questionnaire about the applicant's racial and political background. If the responses were unsuitable, the applicant excluded himself. To regulate cultural activities at the local level Goebbels further organized a network of propaganda officers to keep an eye on performances, exhibitions, publications and so on. In this way the Reich Culture Chamber imposed severe constraints over artists while conning them into believing it promoted their interests.

To drive home the point that state and culture were now inseparably linked, Hitler made a great to-do over the Chamber's inaugural ceremony. Held in the Berlin Philharmonic Hall on 15 November 1933, it was attended by the entire cabinet, regional cultural officials, prominent artists and even the diplomatic corps. Furtwängler and the Berlin Philharmonic opened the session with Beethoven's *Egmont Overture*; Heinrich Schlusnus sang Schubert, Wolf and Strauss lieder, followed by Strauss himself conducting his own *Festival Prelude*. Goebbels then spoke, assuring artists that the new government wanted 'nothing more than to be the patron saint of German art and culture in all areas' but making plain that changes were on the way. The event concluded, appropriately enough, with the 'Wach auf!' chorus from *Die Meistersinger*. Its opening line, 'Awake! Full soon will dawn the day', was a poetic warning that artists would do well to wake up to the fact that a new day was dawning for their world.

Most did not need the hint. The overwhelming majority of artists and professionals in the field – critics, writers and academics – could scarcely wait to associate themselves with the New Order. 'During the early months, when the regime was courting recognition and decorative names, testimoni-

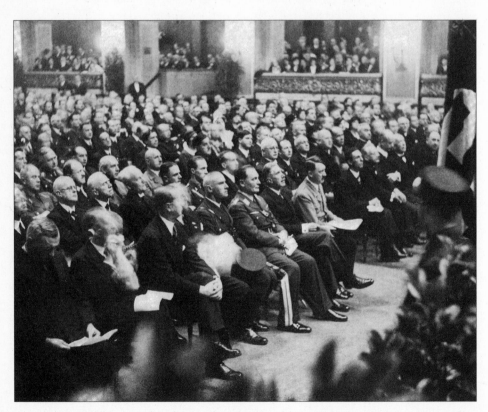

Attending an elaborate ceremony to inaugurate the Reich Culture Chamber are (from left) *Interior Minister Frick, Göring, Vice-Chancellor von Papen, Hitler, Goebbels, Hans Pfitzner, Wilhelm Furtwängler, Richard Strauss and Walther Funk, Goebbels's deputy at the time.*

als of loyalty rained down upon it unrequested,' as Fest has written. Painters volunteered a statement declaring that they 'expect from now on only one guiding principle will be permitted' and that one was to be anchored 'in the blood and history of the people and the state'. It went on, 'They expect that materialism, Marxism and Communism will not only be tracked down, forbidden and exterminated but that this cultural struggle will be taken over by the nation as a whole and will bring about the complete destruction of Bolshevist un-art and unculture . . . .' Eminent literary figures signed a 'Pledge of Loyalty by German Writers to the People's Chancellor, Adolf Hitler'. Equally noted figures in music and the visual arts announced in a public letter to Hitler, 'The artists and musicians of the Prussian Academy want to assure you of their devotion and gratitude for your memorable words in Nuremberg and Munich. They underscore the importance of the arts for the nation and the state.' Other luminaries who announced their individual confidence in the new government included Gerhart Hauptmann, Nobel Prize laureate for literature, Ernst Bertram, the poet and essayist, and Gottfried Benn, the Expressionist poet. Noted composers and conductors gladly accepted official positions. The recalcitrant were easily neutralized; some were forced to resign, some retired, a few worked more or less in secret. Those who could not stomach the New Order fled, sometimes to live in poverty. Although their defection caused embarrassment, Hitler considered himself well rid of troublemakers. In short, he found that getting control of the artistic community was easy.

In subsequent years blandishments were sufficient to keep artists compliant. 'If German artists knew what I intend to do for them,' Hitler had said before coming to power – and Goebbels liked to repeat once he had – 'they would all stand by me.' His hard times in Vienna and Munich were burned into his memory cells. When someone questioned the extent of his generosity, he responded, 'My artists should live like princes and not have to inhabit attic rooms, as you seem to envisage from your romantic notion of an artist's existence.' And like princes is how his favourites lived.

He took enormous pleasure in bestowing commissions, grants, awards, honorariums, pensions, tax abatements, scholarships, gifts, titles, professorships, studios and even houses, some of them confiscated from Jews. Conductors like Furtwängler and Clemens Krauss, actors like Hans Albers and Emil Jannings, stage designers like Benno von Arent and Caspar Neher, photographers like Heinrich Hoffmann and Leni Riefenstahl, sculptors like Arno Breker and Josef Thorak, architects like Speer and Giesler became wealthy. In 1938 Hitler approved an initial list of 773 names of artists in all fields whose income taxes were to be cut by as much as 40 per cent. In the music field this included the most noted singers of the day, such as Rudolf Bockelmann, Josef von Manowarda, Helge Roswaenge, Erna Berger, Maria Müller and Margarete Slezak. Probably none did so well as Breker and Thorak. Thorak received lucrative commissions and a gigantic studio, Breker a country house with ample grounds and a studio. Hitler further arranged that Breker, then earning 1 million marks a year, should not have to pay tax of more than 15 per cent on his income. He also gave Speer a studio as well as honorariums of 7 million marks for planning the reconstruction of Berlin. The painter Sepp Hilz received a personal gift of 100,000 marks for a studio and Gerdy Troost, the widow of Hitler's favourite architect and interior decorator, received an equal amount in each of three years. Even in their retirement, he made certain artists were cared for. 'The Führer gives me an explicit instruction,' Goebbels noted, 'to provide the most generous funding to retired [artists] so that their final years can be spent in comfort.' As late as the end of 1944 Hitler privately financed the renovation of the residence and studio of a minor Austrian painter whose works had struck his fancy. 'No royal patron was ever so generous to artists as he,' Goebbels could say without exaggeration. With some justice Hitler himself claimed to be the successor to those great Bavarian patrons of the arts, Ludwig I and Ludwig II.

It also gave Hitler pleasure to confer titles and honours, and indeed he arrogated to himself sole legal right to do so. He established the most honorific, the National Prize for Art and Science, in 1937 after the Nobel Peace Prize had been awarded to Carl von Ossietzky, an anti-Nazi then languishing in a concentration camp. Angered by the affront, Hitler decreed that no German might thereafter accept a Nobel award and founded the alternative which he conferred at his own fancy – and after long deliberation – on that sacred occasion, the Nuremberg party rally. His selections were often based less on objective achievement than on personal admiration or sense of obligation. In 1937 the winners included Gerdy Troost, on her husband's behalf, and Ferdinand Sauerbruch, a noted surgeon. In 1938 he gave it to four figures important to German rearmament, Ernst Heinkel, Willy Messerschmitt, Ferdinand Porsche and Fritz Todt. Hitler also continued to award the Goethe Medal, a pre-Third Reich honour to distinguished figures in the humanities. In earlier years winners had included writers such as Thomas Mann, André Gide and Paul Valéry. From 1933 on it was given to painters, writers, publishers, museum directors and academics known for their support for the Nazi state. In 1935 it was awarded to Jan Sibelius; though the composer had no known Nazi sympathies, he suited Nazi ideological purposes. Candidates were normally proposed, vetted and approved by Goebbels himself, but Hitler's personal views influenced the process at every stage. In some cases an award was a booby prize for being excluded from a position of importance. In giving the National Prize to Rosenberg in 1937, for example, Hitler frankly acknowledged to Goebbels that the gesture was actually 'a bandage for a wound to unrequited ambition'. Such was no doubt similarly the case with Paul Schultze-Naumburg, who received the Adlersschild (eagle's shield), established in 1922 to honour persons for services to the state.

Another of Hitler's pleasures was dispensing honorary professorships. These he bestowed upon such artists as Breker and Thorak, Speer and Giesler, Willy Kriegel and Sepp Hilz as well as upon such pseudo-artistic figures as Gerdy Troost, Heinrich Hoffmann and Benno von Arent. The inflation of state flattery reached its comic height in 1935 when Hitler authorized Goebbels to set up the Cultural Senate. The conductors Wilhelm Furtwängler and Clemens Krauss, the composer Hans Pfitzner, the director of the Bayreuth Festival Heinz Tietjen, the actor Gustaf Gründgens and Benno von Arent were among its members. In practice, a Cultural Senator's sole prerogative was the right to claim two good seats at any public performance of opera, concert or theatre.

And then there were Hitler's subsidies to the arts. Never had such monies flowed into cultural institutions or the pockets of individual artists. Even Goebbels was eventually moved to complain about the 'excess of unrestrained spending'. The funds at Hitler's personal disposal were enormous, though impossible fully to calculate since the surviving documentation is incomplete. They came from a variety of sources, legal and semi-legal, ethical and corrupt, all of it tax-exempt. Most straightforward were royalties from *Mein Kampf*. With nearly every German family owning a copy, these amounted to roughly 1.5 to 2 million marks annually during the Third Reich years. Hitler earmarked these monies for museums, foundations and construction projects in favoured cities. Another source was the so-called Cultural Fund, which he instituted in 1937. This was largely financed by a scheme – dreamed up by Heinrich Hoffmann and the Postal Minister Wilhelm Ohnesorge – to pay Hitler a royalty on every stamp with his picture on it. This wheeze raised no less than 75 million marks over the years. The Cultural Fund also received sizeable transfers arranged by Goebbels from the film industry and a variety

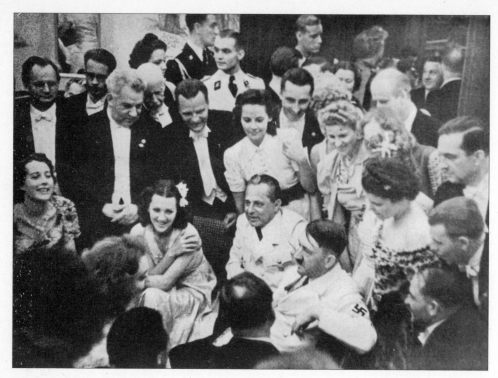

Hitler surrounded by adoring artists during a reception at the opening of the House of German Art in 1937.

of other sources. It was this income that Hitler drew on to bestow his benefactions to artists, to make his own art purchases and to contribute to his building projects. Another rich source was the Adolf Hitler Charity, bankrolled by German industrialists through quarterly contributions. Estimates of this ever-replenished fund range from 300 million to a billion marks, though how much of this Hitler devoted to cultural works is not known. He apparently tapped, too, into proceeds from the sale of property confiscated from Jews. These monies largely went to purchase artworks.

It was also in his everyday life and in large ways and small that Hitler's aesthetic nature was evident. Just being in a vaguely artistic environment gave him pleasure. His favourite Munich restaurant, the Osteria Bavaria, for example, was an artists' hang-out and, even when chancellor, he went there whenever possible. Then, at his most genial and relaxed, he never tired of hearing stories that Hoffmann told about the goings-on of the Schwabing painters whom he knew. But it was being in the company of artists themselves, as the memoirs of his intimates all concur, that made him happiest.

according to Christa Schroeder, that 'he felt, with his whole heart and soul, most contented'. Such occasions were 'undoubtedly the most light-hearted and relaxed' and the only ones when 'Hitler's inapproachability was destroyed', according to Fritz Wiedemann. 'Like a proud father he would sit on a sofa surrounded by women from the world of film and ballet.' Most adept at playing up to Hitler's bohemian revels was Goebbels. He would take 'beautiful and gifted artists and great actresses to the Führer', Rosenberg enviously commented. 'He told him stories about life among the artists. He fed the theatrical element in his nature with gorgeously mounted products of the lighter muses. . . .' Hitler held an annual gala reception for artists at the chancellery and almost always after attending a theatrical or operatic performance invited the actors or singers to join him at receptions that often went on till dawn. Supreme among these were the parties at the Bayreuth Festival. One of the singers he met there and came to like was Josef von Manowarda. The esteemed bass died in December 1942 and when this fact was not reported with banner headlines on the front page of the country's

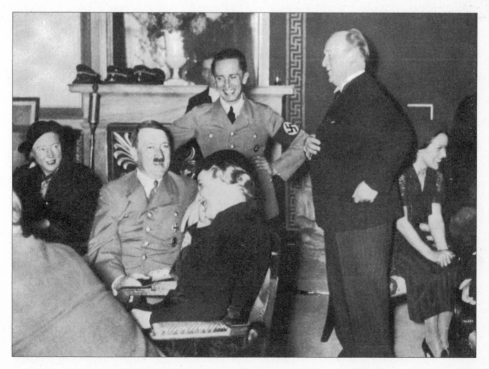

Like most dictators, Hitler seldom smiled. With artists he relaxed. Here with Käthe Dorsch, the film actress, Wilhelm Rode, singer and director of the German Opera, Joseph and Magda Goebbels.

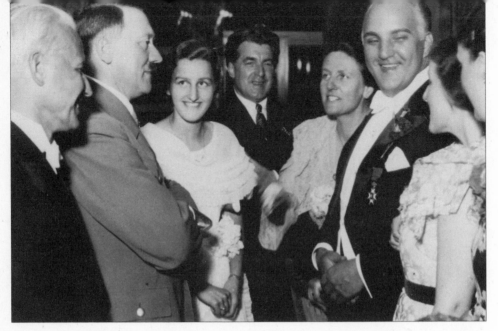

A reception at Wahnfried during the 1936 Festival (from left) *Franz von Hößlin, Hitler, Verena Wagner, Fritz Deiß (member of Festival chorus), Winifred Wagner, Max Lorenz and Friedelind Wagner.*

newspapers Hitler fell into a frenzy of rage which lasted for hours and left him literally unable to work for the rest of the day. Although the *Wehrmacht* was then engaged at Stalingrad, Hitler took time to ensure that the singer had a state funeral and that Göring and Goebbels attended the ceremony.

Even a few Jewish artists received Hitler's grudging recognition. Most remarkable was his esteem for two whose artistry he knew firsthand, Gustav Mahler and Max Reinhardt – Mahler for his conducting at the Vienna Opera and Reinhardt for his directing in the Berlin theatre. 'He spoke favourably of such phenomena as Mahler and Max Reinhardt, whose abilities and achievements he did not deny,' Goebbels noted in his diary. 'When it came to reproducing the arts, the Jew often had something to contribute.' He was not always impeccably doctrinaire in his personal treatment of artists who were Jewish or partly Jewish. The opera singer Margarete Slezak, despite Jewish grandparents, was such a favourite that he promoted her career at the German Opera in Berlin after 1933 and often invited her to official receptions at the chancellery. One of his art dealers, Maria Almas Dietrich, had a Jewish father, bore a love child to a Jewish lover and was married for many years to a Turkish Jew. Under Gerdy Troost's prodding he reinstated a Jewish composer, Arthur Piechler, at the Augsburg conservatory. And he was friendly towards artists with Jewish relatives, such as Franz Lehár, the tenor Max Lorenz, the soprano Frida Leider and the conductor Franz von Hößlin, all of whom had Jewish spouses. These were exceptional cases, however, and the vast mass of Jewish artists found no mercy.

Crime itself was forgivable in Hitler's eyes if committed by an artist. Informed on one occasion that a painter of his acquaintance had swindled a bank out of more than 1 million marks, he responded: 'The man is an artist – I am also an artist. Artists understand nothing of financial affairs. I forbid any action being taken against the man.' Such was also the case with the crime of homosexuality. Convinced that it was rampant in the Catholic clergy, he had no reluctance to have members of monastic orders jailed. In the case of artists his policy was 'don't ask, don't tell'. Consequently actors such as Gustaf Gründgens continued to act and singers such as Max Lorenz and Herbert Janssen went on singing. Most extraordinary of all, however, was Henriette von Schirach's interesting – if true – story that after his final victory he intended to imprison all the enemy leaders with the exception of the British prime minister. He admired him, he purportedly said, because he was an artist, just as

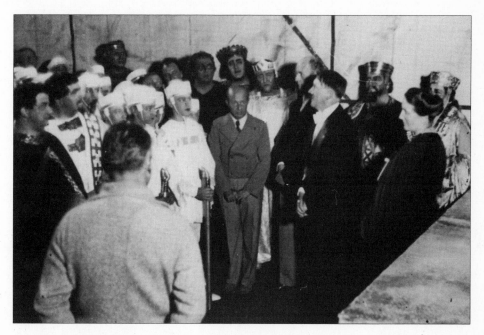

One of Hitler's greatest pleasures was to slip behind stage after an opera. Here, following a 1936 performance of Lohengrin *at Bayreuth, he chats with (from left)* Heinz Tietjen, members of the chorus, Emil Preetorius, Wilhelm Furtwängler, Josef von Manowarda *and* Winifred Wagner.

he himself had been in his youth. 'Churchill will live comfortably in a fortress where I shall make it possible for him to write his memoirs and paint.'

To keep the arts going and forestall artists being killed in combat, Hitler decided on the eve of his attack on Poland in 1939 to exempt artists from military service, a privilege enjoyed by members of no other profession, even scientists. According to Speer, Hitler personally tore up the conscription papers of everyone whose name appeared on lists that Goebbels had given him. These lists had been prepared on Hitler's instructions by the Propaganda Ministry and the final selection was an amalgam of Hitler's personal preferences and *raison d'état*. Those on list A were officially considered 'property of supreme importance' and were excused from all wartime obligations. Among the twenty-one such figures – nicknamed 'the divine' or 'the immortal' – were six from the field of literature (including Hans Carossa and Gerhart Hauptmann), twelve from the visual arts (including Arno Breker, Josef Thorak and Hermann Giesler) and three from the music world (Richard Strauss, Hans Pfitzner and Wilhelm Furtwängler). Four persons from the theatre were later added. List B, of somewhat less exalted artists, included the names of seventy-three painters, thirty-four sculptors, fifty architects, twenty-three industrial designers, fifteen conductors, eighteen composers, seventeen pianists, eighty-eight actors, numerous singers, one hundred and fifty persons from film and radio, countless instrumental players and all the members of nine symphony orchestras. In all, there were at least 20,000 exemptions, and the names of up-and-coming artists were continually added to the lists.

As the war got bloodier, these exemptions became increasingly unpopular on the home front and even more with the military. But when the generals told Hitler in early 1942 that an additional 800,000 men had to be found if operations in the East were to be resumed later that year and pressed for a reduction in the number of artists' exemptions to help fill the gap, Hitler would not hear of it. 'If we gradually wind down cultural activities, the home front will slip into a mood of resignation and after that into a mood of pessimism,' he responded. When Ulrich Roller, the son of the noted stage designer Alfred Roller, fell in Russia in 1942, Hitler was enraged and stormed, 'What is served by sending an artist to war? Some Russian idiot simply shoots down such a man! . . . A man of his sort is irreplaceable.' A year later, after the defeat at Stalingrad, when Speer was pressing for total mobilization at home, Goebbels – in an almost unique case of open disagreement with Hitler – proposed reducing artists' exemptions by 3500. Even now Hitler was unbending. As Goebbels noted,

Instead he took the position that precisely now, when the nation is called upon to make such tremendous efforts and such great sacrifices, something at least must remain intact so that people do not fall into bleak hopelessness. And so the Führer once again gives me the strict instruction not to touch opera, theatre, concert and film. The number of men would in any case make up only a regiment. But this regiment can accomplish much more at home or with the troops than if they were in active combat.

Three months later he forbade certain Berlin artists from voluntarily enlisting in the military. Only after incessant nagging by Speer and Goebbels was a compromise finally reached. He assented to a reduction in the number of exemptions, and Goebbels agreed to draw up what he called 'a list of the so-called "divine" – approximately 300 to 400 genuinely outstanding artists of lasting importance who should remain exempted from military or civilian service'. As a consequence of Hitler's obstinacy, major orchestras and operas continued, as recordings demonstrate, to proffer outstanding performances right to the end. It was near the end that the Berlin Philharmonic was involved in what must rank as the most grotesque episode in musical history. There was apparently a general understanding that when the Philharmonic's programme included Bruckner's Fourth Symphony that would be a signal that the final days of the Third Reich had come. The concert of 13 April included the work. As everyone left the hall they encountered uniformed members of the Hitler Youth at the exits passing out free cyanide capsules.

Loyal as he was to 'his' artists, Hitler felt personally betrayed by any sign of ingratitude. During the war, when conductors and singers avoided performing in Berlin and other large cities to escape the danger from bombing, he was deeply angered. Similarly, on learning that one of the more skilled Third Reich painters, Constantin Gerhardinger, had refused to show his works in the 1943 Great German Art Exhibition in Munich for fear that they could be destroyed in an air raid, Hitler was beside himself. Before 1933 the artist had been totally unknown and often near starvation; to make his life and work easier, he blustered, he had seen to it that Gerhardinger, like other painters, had received high prices for his works and had become rich. In revenge Hitler revoked all the artist's privileges, annulled his honorary professorship, forbade him to exhibit and gave orders that the press should never again mention his name. By the same token he was deeply gratified when Furtwängler in the later years of the war refused to leave Berlin and, to protect him, ordered Speer to construct a special air raid shelter for him and his family.

The supreme irony is that Hitler looked upon artists with good-natured contempt. He considered them, in Heinrich Hoffmann's words, 'too unsettled, too independent and too undisciplined'. Speer put it more bluntly: 'He regarded them one and all as politically feeble-minded.' Under his genial benevolence, they enjoyed their *Narrenfreiheit*, the freedom of fools to do what they wished and be what they were. He was normally indifferent to their political views. 'I have no intention of forcing anyone into National Socialism,' he said. Some artists who joined the party or were sincere Nazi supporters – such as Emil Nolde – he treated brutally; some who had nothing to do with the party retained his artistic respect and their artistic freedom. Speer witnessed Hitler's reaction on being informed that Josef Thorak had signed a Communist proclamation as late as January 1933:

> Oh, you know I don't take any of that seriously. We should never judge artists by their political views. The imagination they need for their work deprives them of the ability to think in realistic terms. Let's keep Thorak on. Artists are simple-hearted souls. Today they sign this, tomorrow that; they don't even look to see what it is, so long as it seems to them well meaning.

More remarkable still was the case of Adolf Ziegler, a prominent Third Reich painter and head of the Reich Chamber of Visual Arts. Convinced by the summer of 1943 that the war was lost, he committed the treasonable act of – according to the most colourful of several accounts – participating in discussions looking towards a negotiated peace in which Randolph Churchill was to be the middleman. He was arrested, sent to a concentration camp and faced trial before a war tribunal, which would almost certainly have sentenced him to death. Although usually ruthless in dealing with cases of 'defeatism', Hitler commented mildly, 'Ziegler is not only a bad painter but also a bad politician,' adding that artists are 'like children' when it comes to politics. He ordered the painter to be released and did no more than dismiss him as head of the Reich Chamber of Visual Arts. But what Hitler tolerated at times in artists, he refused to condone in others, as is evident in successive entries in Goebbels's diaries in the same year:

> 23 September. The Führer tells me not to worry much about the political views of film people, although treason and outright opposition to the war could not be permitted. Otherwise it is best to be tolerant. Artists could not be taken seriously when it came to political affairs.

> 25 September. A series of death sentences have been passed on Catholic

and Protestant clergy. In the most perfidious way they undermined German military power.

The further irony is that when it came to party and government officials, Hitler was anything but indifferent to their artistic sensibilities. A feeling for the arts was crucial if one were to enjoy his respect and it was a bitter frustration to him that he failed to find this quality in those around him. To be sure, some of Hitler's inner circle had once aspired to an artistic career. In his youth Goebbels had written plays and a novel; Alfred Rosenberg had studied architecture and considered himself a philosopher and writer; Hermann Göring had an interest in the visual arts or at least in collecting them; Baldur von Schirach, a person of some cultivation, wrote flamboyant Nazi poetry and was a music patron; Hans Frank was an aspiring poet and fancied himself a patron of the arts; Bernhard Rust had been a schoolteacher; Wilhelm Frick was a music lover; Walther Funk regarded himself a musician; Robert Ley married into artistic circles and Heinrich Hoffmann was a photographer and art collector. But Hitler had no illusions about the cultural level of any of these failed and pseudo-artists. He condemned Göring's 'concept of painting' and lamented that most gauleiters were 'complete failures in the field of the arts'.

For their part Nazi officials quickly caught on to the fact that the royal road to Hitler's respect was to demonstrate at least slight interest in one of the arts. And since winning his favour was an obsessive preoccupation, cultural pretension was a professional requisite. To arrange a tête-à-tête with the Führer, they knew it was enough to offer to show him photos of the stage settings of some new opera or operetta. The sham never really fooled Hitler, who despaired of ever finding anyone who shared his interests. 'My entourage is certainly not very musical,' he grumbled to Gertraud Junge, who had joined his secretarial staff in 1943. 'When I go to a gala, I have to keep my eye on all the people who accompany me to make sure they do not go to sleep.' When his *Luftwaffe* attaché Nicolaus von Below volunteered to accompany him to a performance of *La Bohème* at the German Opera in 1937, he was amazed to find someone in his entourage who liked opera and even knew the Puccini work. So delighted was he that he invited Below and his wife to attend the next Bayreuth Festival and, as Below recorded, 'from this moment on we were part of his private circle'.

Lack of artistic appreciation could, by contrast, have fatal professional consequences. In Speer's words, 'criticism, especially of a man's aesthetic judgement, could sometimes spell an end to a career'. Such was the case even at the very top echelon when it came to the all-important question of the succession. None of the leading contenders was the artistic type that Hitler envisaged. Rudolf Hess, the original number two, had been ruled out years before his flight to Scotland. After seeing Hess's newly decorated house outside Munich, Hitler was so revolted he told his press secretary, Otto Dietrich, that Hess would never do as his successor. The wretched man fell into still further disgrace when the Führer visited his new Berlin headquarters. Its austere furnishings and a stairwell painted fiery red left Hitler utterly appalled. He denounced his deputy as 'totally inartistic' and swore 'never to let him build anything new ... because he is completely ignorant on such matters'. It was a short time later that he appointed Göring, who at least was an art collector, as his successor. Considering Göring unreliable and corrupt, however, he was never content with his choice and gave continuous thought to an alternative. Heinrich Himmler, the SS chief, and Martin Bormann, his chief of staff, he knew to be cretins, and he regarded Goebbels as a philistine. Speer was at one point considered a suitable candidate. 'He is an artist; we are twin souls,' Christa Schroeder recalled Hitler's saying. 'I have the warmest human relationship to him because I understand him so well. Like me, he is an architect; intelligent, discreet and not a military blockhead.'

By 1945 the succession issue grew into an obsession. Schroeder recalled an afternoon in March of that year when Hitler arrived for lunch in a mood as furious as Wotan's in the third act of *Die Walküre*. 'If something happens to me, Germany is lost,' he stormed, 'because I have no successor. Hess went crazy, Göring has forfeited the sympathy of the German people and Himmler is rejected by the party.' When Schroeder took exception to the remark about Himmler, he brushed aside her objection with his ultimate anathema, 'Himmler is completely inartistic.' He left her in no doubt that he found it deeply offensive that she could think that he and the Gestapo chief were on the same cultural level.

So concerned was Hitler about cultural life after his retirement or death that he even planned to take this into account in his territorial reconstruction of the Reich. The final objective of his war, he had told Goebbels in November 1939, was to redraw the map of Europe by liquidating the Treaty of Westphalia of 1648. Within Germany itself both Prussia and Bavaria were to be dissolved and subdivided into historic provinces. The point was to put in place institutional arrangements ensuring that the arts would receive sufficient financial and political support to continue to flourish. As Goebbels noted, 'The Führer has no guarantee that when he is no longer alive, his successor will have the same interest in cultural problems and requirements or will have the same open and liberal hand.' By June of 1942 Hitler decided to leave Bavaria intact. On the one hand, Munich posed no threat to the unity of the Reich since it had never had 'the vanity' to challenge Berlin's leadership in the Reich, he reasoned. And on the other 'a city of the arts like Munich' could only maintain itself if it had an economic hinterland. 'Circumstances might arise,' Hitler went on, 'in which there would be a financial crisis in the Reich prompting the finance minister to put an end to subsidies for cultural programmes in Munich.' Preserving the city's cultural status was vital. 'A gauleiter of Munich must have an interest in culture,' he insisted, 'and must have the ambition to make Munich the German Florence in contrast to Berlin, which is to become a city like Rome.'

Another trait of Hitler's artistic nature, described over and over, was his chaotic work habits and indecisiveness. During the critical years of the struggle for power these left his colleagues exasperated. 'Hitler himself works too little. It simply cannot go on like this. And he lacks the courage to take decisions. He no longer leads.' Thus Goebbels noted in his diary in January 1930. A year later he fretted about Hitler's obsession with remodelling the party's Munich headquarters, rather than with running the party. As chancellor, although at times efficient and hard-working, he normally hated reading reports, seeing officials, attending meetings. At first he maintained at least a minimum of office routine, seeing ministers from ten until one or two, and, after lunch, meeting with military or foreign policy advisers. But this began to break down in less than a year. Late in 1933 President Hindenburg, in failing health, retired to his estate at Neudeck in East Prussia. 'That was the end of Hitler's workaday schedule,' according to Dietrich. 'He once more returned to his habit of rising at noon and during the day entered his offices only for important receptions. All other work was dealt with in his apartment as he stalked about his rooms, dropping a word here and a word there, settling important matters in the most casual fashion.' Otherwise his time was given over to his infamous monologues, in which he harangued his entourage for hour upon hour with his views – always the same – on anything and everything but often about his early life and his opinions on the arts. At night there was invariably a film, often American. As the years passed he squandered more and more of his time. He might spend days in a near trance-like state, as Joachim Fest wrote, dozing like a crocodile in the mud of the Nile, and then suddenly erupt in frenetic activity. Dietrich described this sort of governing as 'the greatest confusion that has ever existed in a civilized state'.

At the Berghof he rarely did any work. He appeared around two, had lunch, took a long walk and gave the evenings over to the inevitable film and the equally inevitable monologue. On occasion his staff found it nearly impossible to get his signature on state documents and even urgent correspondence. From 1938 he held no further meetings of the cabinet and sometimes made individual ministers wait literally several years before seeing them. Even high party officials, such as Göring, were put off for days, weeks or even months. Once the war started, however, and particularly after making himself field commander in December 1941, he worked very hard. Even so, lunch and dinner lasted for several hours and in the evenings he refused to attend to any disagreeable business because it would disturb his sleep. And always there was time to see one of his artists – Speer, Giesler or another architect to discuss his grand construction projects, Clemens Krauss or another conductor to discuss music, Benno von Arent to hear about new stage designs or Heinrich Hoffmann just to gossip.

Everyone around Hitler knew the reason. 'In the bohemian manner of the artist he despised discipline and could not or would not force himself to work regularly.' The words were Speer's but they could have been those of any other member of his personal staff. This sort of Austrian *Schlamperei* drove those around him to despair. Again Goebbels's diaries are testimony. 'Act! Not look and observe. And sit in a café! Poor Hitler!' The Propaganda Minister defended him, however, by reason of his aesthetic nature. 'The genius has a right to be and live differently from others.' The feminine side of his character, labeled 'bohemian', 'intuitive' and 'artistic', was obvious to those who knew him. Otto Dietrich put it this way: 'By nature Hitler was a bohemian. He allowed himself to be guided almost exclusively by emotional considerations. . . . He often said that a single brilliant idea was more valuable than a whole lifetime of conscientious office work.'

Even the uncritical Below had to admit being befuddled by his Führer's manifest contradictions. In his opinion Hitler was victim of two conflicting drives. On the one hand he was an artist, with the artist's love of freedom and his reliance on intuition and inspiration. On the other he believed, like Rienzi, that he had no choice but to sacrifice himself to save his fatherland. The aesthetic impulse, Below maintained, could never be reconciled with the demands of state. Fritz Wiedemann put it less poetically. Hitler, he said, liked to believe that 'problems resolve themselves', and he therefore simply

'He says that Hitler is the most profoundly feminine man that he has ever met, and that there are moments when he becomes almost effeminate. He imitates the movements of his white flabby hands.' (Harold Nicolson's diary entry on a conversation with Carl Burckhardt)

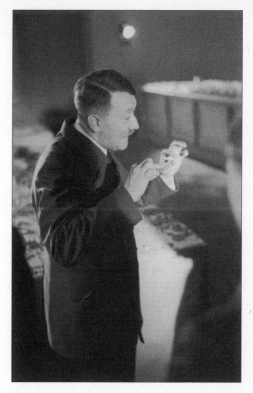

let troublesome matters slide. In any case with the passage of time these various characteristics became more pronounced. 'The surer Hitler felt in the possession of power,' according to Fest, 'the more conspicuously his old bohemian traits came to the fore, his lapses into torpor, his moodiness.' The point was repeatedly confirmed in Goebbels's diaries. Far from being the invariably firm, decisive dictator that he appeared publicly to be, Hitler could often be a dilatory and wavering leader.

Yet Hitler was anything but a dreamy aesthete with his head in the clouds. He was shrewd and highly intelligent and enjoyed an extraordinary memory. According to his Finance Minister he was able to 'recall statistical data about the most arcane topics with amazing precision' and could 'get right to the heart of a problem, to draw concise conclusions from long discussions and to throw new light on a matter that had been the object of lengthy deliberation'. One of the rare foreigners to know him personally and professionally, André François-Poncet, found Hitler 'an ice-cold realist, a profoundly calculating person'. Admittedly, the ambassador went on, he was lazy, incapable of tying himself down to any sort of regular work routine and hated to read documents. But he insisted on being orally informed of everything that went on and took an interest in the smallest details. There was nothing that happened in the Reich of which he was unaware, including actions taken by his officials whom he allowed broad administrative autonomy. It was this solid realism in politics, domestic and foreign, that contributed to Hitler's greatest successes. At the same time it was the other side of his nature, his artistic sensibility, that took him into a private world of illusion – of such illusion that he could find himself in childlike absorption in a model of a reconstructed Linz when the real world around him was literally collapsing.

Hitler's devotion to the arts left him largely indifferent to science. Dietrich noted that the idea of future technological advance troubled him. Occasionally he would remark that modern developments in aviation – symbolizing the domination of soulless, inanimate forces – were depersonalizing human life. In such a world, he would declare, life no longer seemed to him worth living. Here, again, was Hitler the Romantic and it emerged in any number of ways. Not only did he dislike flying, he had a psychological aversion to the whole idea of aviation. By contrast, battleships held a strange fascination for him – his 1925 sketchbook included careful drawings of several. But he had no appreciation of ships as a fighting instrument and thought them a waste of money. True, as field commander in Russia, he had a keen interest in advanced army weaponry. But even here, as Speer observed, when he inspected new weapons systems he always took note of their aesthetic qualities as well.

It was his own intuitive leaps of imagination, over the rational objections of his generals, that led to the successful reoccupation of the Rhineland and the annexation of Austria and Czechoslovakia. The amazing blitzkrieg in the West in 1940 was in part the result of novel strategic concepts that historians credit Hitler with having grasped and supported against military orthodoxy. Similar qualities marked his command in the attack on the Soviet Union the following year. 'His ability to gauge the feeling of the common soldier and to inspire him is unquestioned,' a writer has commented. 'And in the early months of the war his élan, his propensity to take risks, his "intuition", had reaped a tremendous harvest.' It is possible to see in these victories the triumph of impulse over experience, will over reason, creativity over orthodoxy – and metaphorically the triumph of the failed painter over the artistic pedants of the Vienna Academy of Fine Arts.

THE
ARTIST OF
DESTRUCTION

6 THE NEW GERMANY AND THE NEW GERMAN

'WHO IS THIS HITLER AND WHAT DOES HE WANT?' asked the puzzled lady in a James Thurber cartoon in the *New Yorker* in April 1940. It was very late in the day even for someone in isolated and isolationist America to be posing such a question. In any case had the woman been a reader of *Kladderadatsch* she would have had a good idea of the answer. For within a year of Hitler's coming to power that German

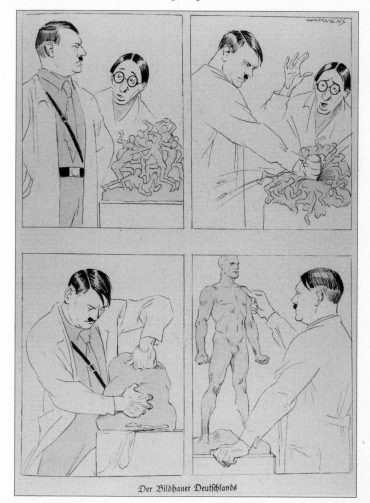

Germany's Sculptor by O. Garvens, Kladderadatsch, 3 December 1933.

Der Bildhauer Deutschlands

satirical magazine had published a four-part cartoon which accurately illustrated how Hitler regarded his mission. In the first panel the new chancellor confronts a small sculpture of a quarrelling mob, a symbol of the chaotic state of German politics in the Weimar Republic. Next, with one blow of his firm fist, he smashes the jumbled mess. Out of the raw material he then creates a new man – a strong, potent, clench-fisted Aryan German. The sculptor of the original statuette, a caricature Jew, at first looks on in dismay as his work is demolished but by the end has vanished. Hitler, in party uniform under a sculptor's smock, stands proudly as an artist-politician. Appropriately, the cartoon was entitled 'Germany's sculptor'.

In no time the metaphor took shape in reality. By 1936 Goebbels could claim that of the many great works of art created after the Nazi party came to power, the greatest of all was Hitler's own. Out of the most primitive material, he had formed a nation. And the inspiration, Goebbels boasted, 'grew out of his artistic fantasy'. Indeed, it was true that Hitler had transformed a nation suffering a crippling psychological depression – as a result of the defeat of 1918, the territorial and economic terms of the Versailles Treaty and its war guilt clause, the occupation of the Ruhr by the French, a catastrophic inflation, domestic political disorder and massive unemployment – into one that had regained its self-esteem, was economically on the mend and enjoyed a central role in European affairs.

Such was the 'work of art' which Goebbels had praised; the 'artistic fantasy' that had inspired it was Hitler's conviction that a flourishing culture was the key element in Germany's identity and repute. He therefore saw his mission as much an artistic as a political one and told the party rally in 1935, the task of National Socialism – meaning the task of Adolf Hitler – was

> to convince the nation of its higher mission through its supreme cultural achievements. He who would educate a people to be proud of itself must give visible reason for pride. The work and sacrifices which went into building the Parthenon occurred only once but the pride of Greece never ended. The modern German state that I and my associates have established has produced the conditions for a new, vigorous flowering of the arts.

What Hitler-the-artist also realized was that of all the arts, architecture had throughout history been a primary mode of expressing a sense of national greatness. Of course monomaniacal leaders always used monumental structures to enhance and perpetuate the glory of their state and their person. Even

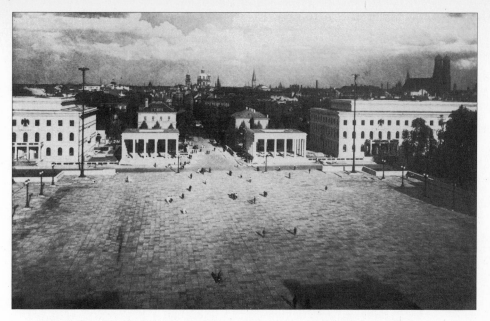

Königsplatz, Munich, laid out by Ludwig I in 1816, was converted by Hitler into the most sacred Nazi site, an Acropolis Germanae. Far left, the Führer Building, Hitler's offices and site of the 1938 Munich Conference; far right, Nazi party administrative headquarters; between, Temples of Honour; behind, the Brown House.

modern democratic states have constructed grand buildings as a way to demonstrate civic pride. In Hitler's case, however, the construction of monuments became an obsession, the visible manifestation of his rule. No sooner had he been appointed chancellor than he initiated a massive programme for the construction of civic edifices. These structures, he declared again and again, would redress the feelings of inferiority of the German people and prove that, in his phrase, the German nation had at last acquired its Germanic Reich. To initiate the process, one of his first actions was to have Munich's ceremonial square, the Königsplatz, paved with 24,000 square feet of granite slabs that had been quarried from every corner of Germany. At the same time he started work on the autobahns, which were, in Speer's words, 'uniformly designed so that they would compellingly express the concept of a unified Reich'. Emphasizing the bond between his cultural and political aims, Hitler told the 1937 party rally:

> It is precisely these buildings which will help to unify our people politically more closely than ever and strengthen them; these buildings will inspire German society with a proud consciousness that each and all belong together; they will prove how ridiculous in our social life are all earthly differences in the face of these mighty, gigantic witnesses to the life which we share as a community. They will fill our people with a limitless self-

confidence as they remember that they are German. These mighty works will at the same time provide the most sublime evidence of the political strength of the German nation.

Decoded, the words meant that National Socialism was to take form in stone and express what National Socialism was – monolithic, irresistible, massive, triumphant.

Hitler also used his aesthetic imagination in less tangible ways to create a sense of national unity and collective submission to the Nazi state. Almost any occurrence – a funeral, a state visit, the laying of a cornerstone, the dedication of a building, the opening of an art exhibition, the signature or abrogation of a treaty – offered a pretext to stage public spectacles designed to overwhelm the public with a desire to surrender to a greater power. The most significant celebrations, ascribed by some to his Catholic past, were a series of events that evolved into a calendar of hallowed rites. He even set up a government agency, the Bureau of Festivals, Leisure and Celebrations, to organize the solemnities and institutionalize them so firmly that they would remain forever unalterable. 'Perhaps future leaders of the Reich will not be able to achieve the effects I can, but this framework will support them and lend them authority,' he said to Speer on one occasion.

On coming to power, Hitler abolished all but three traditional state anniversaries and these three were altered to his own purposes. One of them, the long-established 'Day of National Mourning' in remembrance of the fallen in war, became 'Heroes' Day'. As time passed it was further changed into a celebration of German military might, marked throughout the country with parades, torchlight processions and chauvinistic speeches. He also took advantage of these occasions to announce important political decisions – the abrogation of the Versailles Treaty's limits on German armament in 1934, the introduction of compulsory military service in 1935, the reoccupation of the Rhineland in 1936 and the annexation of Austria in 1938. As time passed, the event was made increasingly festive and even in the final years of the war it was staged not as a commemoration of those who fell in combat but a celebration of the ideal of military heroism.

Stagecraft was also employed in absorbing the powerful trade union movement into the Nazi German Workers' Front. Instead of abolishing the traditional workers' May Day celebration, as Rosenberg had proposed, Hitler made it a 'Day of National Brotherhood'. Mammoth demonstrations were staged throughout Germany as out-and-out Nazi events. After a few years the original purpose of the holiday was completely subverted. The event was renamed the 'National Festival of the German People' and turned into a German tribal festival of the May, with May trees, May kings and queens, flower garlands and other storybook paraphernalia. The point of it all, as officially stated, was to celebrate 'the unity of the people based on blood and soil and history'. Apparently it succeeded. François-Poncet found that the effect of observing the festivities and listening to the speeches was to leave 'Germans and foreigners with the impression that the wind of reconciliation and unity blew over the Third Reich'.

The third of the state holidays was a Nazified version of the traditional autumn harvest festival. Hitler had no interest whatever in agriculture but regarded this 'Rally in Honour of German Farmers' as an opportunity to foster the party's 'blood and soil' ideology. The principal event took place in the Lower Saxon town of Bückeburg, to which hundreds of special trains hauled the participants – 500,000 in 1933, a figure that rose to well over 1 million by 1937. The occasion was more genuinely festive than the other anniversaries. Bands played, choral groups sang, dance groups danced. Swastika flags festooned every possible space – including the sky, some pulled across the heavens by aeroplanes and dirigibles. The optical focus of the event was the 'harvest altar' which, at the climax of the festival, Hitler approached through a half-mile-long path lined by peasants in the colourful costumes of their locality. His address was followed by fireworks, illuminations and a military tattoo.

In addition to these state occasions there were fourteen Nazi party observances, of which the most important was Hitler's birthday on 20 April. On the eve of the anniversary, solemn rites were held when all newly appointed party functionaries formally professed their obedience to him. In other ceremonies, mass inductions of ten-year-olds into the Hitler Youth were convened for the same purpose. Although these events were held throughout Germany, the principal oath-taking ceremony was held on the Königsplatz in Munich. In Hitler's presence, the party officials and Hitler Youth novitiates swore an oath of unqualified loyalty to their Führer. Held at night to increase the mystical atmosphere, the ceremonies were meant to associate the participants indissolubly with the party's martyrs and, by extension, Hitler, if necessary unto death.

The day itself was increasingly turned into an orgy of osculation, with hundreds of individuals and organizations paying homage and presenting gifts. Even the opera houses were mobilized; from 1934 on, by decree of the Reich Culture Chamber, a Wagnerian opera was to be performed for the occasion.

The celebrations always concluded with a military parade, which Hitler viewed from the balcony of the chancellery. To emphasize his position as commander-in-chief, Hitler stood three paces in front of his generals and for hours reviewed *his* troops. At the end there was a torchlight parade by party members and a tattoo by the armed forces. Once again theatrics were used for a variety of political purposes – not just puffing up the Führer cult still further but also forcing the military to demonstrate its collective subordination.

Obeisance reached its zenith on the occasion of his fiftieth birthday in 1939. A high point of the celebration was the greatest military parade in Berlin's history, a four-hour march-past in which Hitler displayed for the first time – and to the astonishment, it was said, of foreign military attachés – tanks and artillery whose existence had up to then been kept secret. No less demonstrative were the gifts showered upon him from countless individuals and institutions – rare books, carpets, tapestries, statues, old etchings and prints, paintings (such as works of Titian, Cranach, Defregger, Spitzweg, Thoma and Lenbach), historical documents (including a letter of Frederick the Great), original musical scores (including many of Wagner's), first editions (among them Schopenhauer's complete works), ancient German antiquities, old weapons, Bismarck's field mess kit, Bohemian cut glass, a long-case clock that played a different folk song on each hour as well as arts and crafts peculiar to every area of Germany. Speer sneered at the gifts as 'pretty much a collection of kitsch'. In his opinion the only worthy present was his own thirteen-foot-high model of the arch of triumph that was planned for the centre of Berlin. This, he maintained with characteristic self-effacement, made Hitler's day. 'That night he returned to look at the model several times.' The model and other gifts were for the most part lost either in the bombing and sacking of the chancellery in 1945 or in the bonfires of his personal property that he himself ordered in his final days.

Among the other party anniversaries, the three most important were commemorations of key events in National Socialist history. One was the celebration of the founding of the party, which had taken place on 24 February 1920 in a room at the Hofbräuhaus in Munich. For a time the event was re-enacted there in the presence of the *alte Kämpfer*, the early Nazi activists. The main feature was a sentimental speech by Hitler on location in which he spoke of the party's rough road to success. A second event marked the anniversary of Hitler's appointment as chancellor on 30 January 1933. The original torchlight parade through the Brandenburg Gate was restaged every year until 1940 when fear that the RAF might crash the party and drop bombs on the site forced the

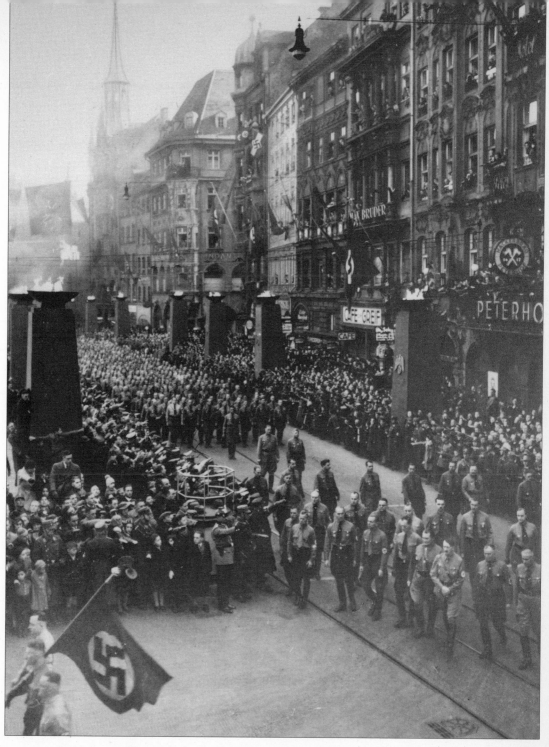

Hitler, the stage designer. Behind the blood flag he marches with Göring and other putschists in this 1936 commemorative march. To heighten the effects of these annual dramas he decorated the streets with vivid splashes of blood red and Stygian black, broadcast rousing music and employed such evocative props as flaming, smoking braziers.

celebration indoors. Hitler used some of these occasions for a political purpose – in 1934 to abolish provincial governments; in 1935 to abolish the provinces themselves; in 1937 to extend his dictatorial powers for another four years and in 1939 to inaugurate the first Reichstag of the Greater German Reich, as Germany with its expanded borders was now officially called.

The third and supreme anniversary commemorated the so-called Beer Hall Putsch – Hitler's attempt in 1923 to spark a national revolution by seizing power in Bavaria and then, in imitation of Mussolini's march on Rome the year before, take power in Berlin. The plot collapsed ignominiously when the police fired on the motley band, killing sixteen of them. Despite the fiasco, Hitler perceived the dramatic possibilities and, ever the stage director, turned what had been a burlesque into a sacred celebration of heroism and the birth of National Socialist Germany. The event was memorialized from 1926 on and, once Hitler was in power, it was solemnly played out again on the streets of Munich. A 'Bureau for 8–9 November' was formed to organize the ceremony and provide garb, modelled on that of 1923, for the *alte Kämpfer* to wear in the march. The participants would gather at the beer hall the night before and the next day march along the route that the putschists had followed to the Feldherrnhalle, a military memorial near the site of the bloodshed. In 1935 Hitler transformed the ceremony into a melodramatic sacrament of fidelity to himself. Now, exactly a dozen years after the putsch, the coffins of the sixteen 'martyrs' were carried in total silence along darkened streets lit only by torches to the Feldherrnhalle where they were illuminated by the flickering flames of huge braziers. Hitler arrived at midnight, approaching the site standing in an open car, his long route lit by mounted flares. At a certain point 60,000 Storm Troopers carrying torches on either side of his way formed two moving lines of fire down the length of the avenue. 'What a great moment!' Goebbels wrote in his diary. 'Never was anything so well and effectively done.' Of the next year's ceremony he commented, 'An overpowering display of strange mysticism.'

The following day the march of the putschists was re-enacted along a route that was flanked by hundreds of pylons draped in blood-red banners, crowned with smoking braziers and emblazoned with the names of party heroes. Loudspeakers along the streets amplified the 'Horst Wessel Song' and repeated over and over the names of the dead heroes. When the procession reached the Feldherrnhalle a sixteen-gun salute was sounded. In total silence Hitler placed an enormous wreath at the site, as thousands of swastika flags dipped in respect. The coffins were then carried to the Königsplatz. There, in another elaborate ceremony, the name of each of the sixteen was called out, to which the formations of party members responded each time with a loud 'Here!' Finally the remains were placed in sarcophagi that lay inside the two neo-Greek 'Temples of Honour' that had just been erected on the Königsplatz. There, under permanent SS guard and lit by the flickering flames of great braziers, the martyrs remained on 'eternal watch for Germany'. The ritual was repeated every year, and each time Hitler appeared at midnight and, standing in front of the sacred temples, administered the SS Life Guards' oath of fealty. So sacred did he consider the event that even during the difficult days of the war, when he almost never appeared in public or addressed the German people, he made a point of attending the ceremony. It was there in 1942 that he declared defiantly, 'I am in Stalingrad, and I shall remain in Stalingrad.' And it was on that occasion the following year, with the *Wehrmacht* in general retreat and many German cities in ruins, that he issued a message of uncompromising resistance.

The ceremony evolved into a cult of the 'martyrs of the movement' which had its own anthem, *The March to the Feldherrnhalle*, and its own relics, in particular the blood flag. The religious parallels were evident, whether as the Stations of the Cross commemorating the suffering, death and resurrection at Easter or in Corpus Christi processions. The sixteen heroes were venerated as saints of the movement. The vocabulary of the speeches and press reports

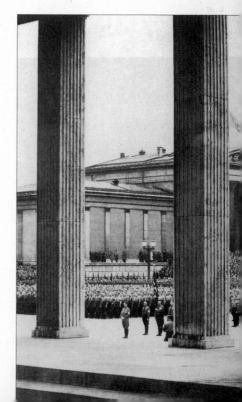

Hitler, the actor. One of his favourite roles was that of the lonely leader. In this 1935 ceremony, he remains motionless in silent homage at the Temples of Honour before the coffins of the 'Martyrs of the Movement' who stand 'eternal watch' for Germany.

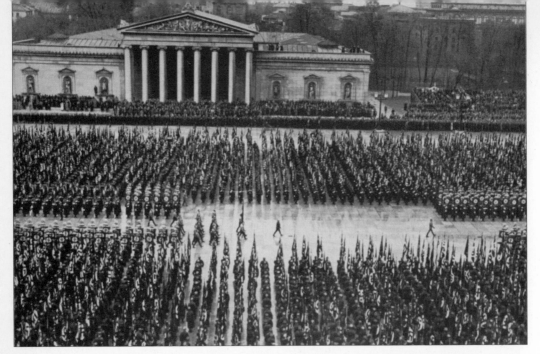

Hitler, the choreographer. With a cast of 60,000 Storm Troopers as his corps de ballet and the Königsplatz as his stage, he designed one of the most imposing scenes in the entire commemorative pageant.

about the event – 'martyr', 'resurrection', 'sacrifice', 'holy place of pilgrimage', 'hero', 'death' – were religious as well. It all added up to a simple message: sacrifice of oneself to the party and its Führer as a sacred duty, if necessary with the shedding of blood – that is, to the death. The point of these celebrations was not simply to overwhelm the senses but to transform the minds of those who participated and as far as possible those who listened on the radio or watched on newsreel film. The aspects of religion – conversion, hope, devotion, communion, solace, salvation and above all unity in the faith – were all implicit in the event. It was by such constant rallying of the masses to ever-renewed acts of faith in their Führer that Hitler's political artistry sought to replace a sense of individuality with a conviction of belonging to himself. As a statement typical of the time had it, 'People are no longer a mass of individuals – a formless, artless mass. Now they form a union, moved by a will and a communal feeling. They learn to move in formations or to stand still, as if moulded by an invisible hand.'

It is hardly surprising that Hitler grew increasingly opposed to the revival of ancient Germanic cults that Rosenberg, Himmler and hard-right Nazis were fostering. Their efforts to establish a Wotan cult and to replace Christian ceremonies with Nordic rituals ran directly counter to his own intention of making National Socialism the religion of the Third Reich and himself the object of unique veneration. Such was similarly the case with the so-called Thing movement, which performed cultic dramas in Germanic-style open-air theatres – or Things. More than forty Thing theatres were built in the early years of the Third Reich. By 1938, however, Hitler had had enough of such Teutonic tomfoolery and denounced it at the party rally that year. 'We therefore have no cultic assembly areas but only Halls of the People, no cultic sites but meeting places and marching areas. Hence the National Socialist movement will not tolerate subversion by superstitious mystics in search of an afterlife.' That was the end of the Thing movement and the Wotan cult.

In such ways did Hitler use ceremonies and ritual to create his ideal state – a Germany incorporating the racial purity and martial discipline of Sparta, the aesthetic ideals of Athens and the imperial power of the Romans. It was this admiration for the Roman Empire which underlay his respect for the British Empire, an attitude that verged for a time on Anglophilia. What he liked were not the qualities which that other Austrian Anglophile Sigmund Freud esteemed – industriousness, concern for public well-being, devotion to justice and an empirical and rationalist frame of mind. Instead it was the bravery of British soldiers in battle, personally witnessed in the First World War. It was the 'brutality' of British governments in building their empire along with their 'ruthlessness' in defending it. And it was the shrewdness and success of British statesmen in pursuing not world peace but British domination of the world. After Churchill refused to do a deal with him in 1940, however, he reacted like a jilted lover and peppered his conversations with petulant complaints about the shortcomings of the British, particularly in the cultural sphere.

'Nonetheless,' as he hastened to add, 'I find an Englishman a thousand times preferable to an American. . . . I feel the deepest hatred and repulsion towards anything American. In its whole outlook America is a half-Jewish, half-Negroid society.' While he long worried about the political and economic power of the 'upsurging American continent', he ridiculed Americans for their low cultural standards. 'The German Reich has 270 opera houses and a richer cultural life than is known there. Basically Americans live like pigs in a well-tiled sty.' Unable to 'see beyond the waves of skyscrapers', they lacked the Germans' feeling for nature and were completely bereft of any sense of Romanticism. 'Indian lore is the only source of Romanticism the North American has. And it is interesting that the best portrayer of this is none other than a German,' he remarked with reference to the novelist Karl May. For that matter he did not like his Japanese ally either. He was angered by Japan's entry into the war in 1941 and, no doubt for racial reasons, felt completely estranged

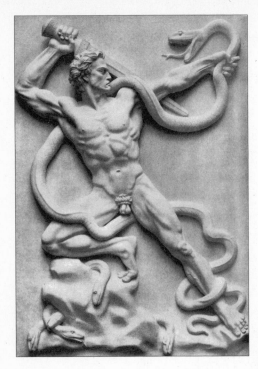

Hitler greatly admired bas-reliefs – another influence of ancient Greece and Rome – and commissioned some 150 of them to adorn sites in Berlin and Munich. In 1925 he had drawn a rough frieze for a Berlin Arch of Triumph and in 1938 instructed Arno Breker to design it. There were to be sixty human figures and fifteen horses. Here are three of Breker's models: Avenger, Guardian and Warrior's Departure. Avenger was shown at the Munich exhibitions in 1940 and 1941.

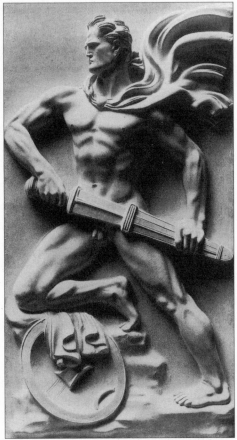

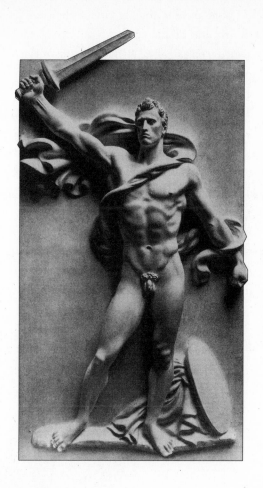

from that country. 'To the Japanese we have no real link. They are too foreign to us in culture and way of life,' he commented a month after their attack on Pearl Harbor. In the months that followed, much as he admired their military successes, even more did he worry about their 'forcing the white man into retreat'.

Another side of Hitler's utopian vision was the evolution of the 'new man' to inhabit his ideal state. National Socialism, he was wont to say, 'is more than a religion, it is the determination to create a new man'. He would be 'slender and supple, swift as a greyhound, tough as leather and hard as Krupp steel', as the Führer characterized him to the Hitler Youth. The supreme physical model was Myron's *Discus Thrower*, and undoubtedly this is why he was so determined to acquire the statue. The work, he said, epitomized 'the sanctity of beauty' and 'offered a glimpse of the divine in the human'. The athlete's physical structure and bearing testified to his racial superiority while the self-control of his posture and the virility of his muscles symbolized both the dynamism and the discipline that was central to National Socialism. Hitler had selected *Triumph of the Will* as the title of Riefenstahl's film of the party rally, and it is not unlikely he suggested making the statue an opening image in her film of the 1936 Olympics. 'We see a new type of man developing around us,' Hitler asserted at the party rally following the games. 'This type is a symbol for a new age,' he reiterated at the next year's rally. 'We watched as it appeared in its shining, proud physical strength and beauty, in front of the whole world at last year's Olympic games.'

The athletic ideal fascinated Hitler both ideologically and aesthetically. To him, race, beauty, art and athletics were intertwined. Future Olympics were therefore of great importance. He would allow them to be held one more time – as scheduled in Tokyo in 1940 – according to the traditional rules. After that, as leader of a triumphant Reich, he would assert the right to convene them forever more in Nuremberg. That was part of the reason

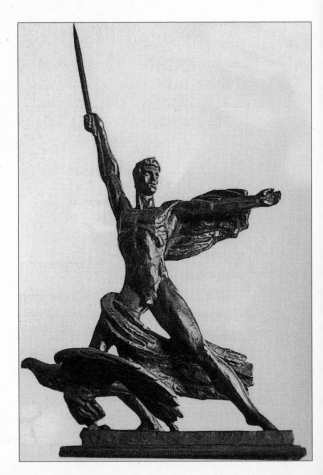

Adolf Wamper created ideologically-oriented statues suitable for state and party buildings. His Genius of Victory of 1940 accentuates two favourite Third Reich symbols, the sword and the eagle.

for his gigantic stadium there. When it was pointed out that the planned field would vastly exceed Olympic norms, he responded that in the future he himself would decide the rules and every aspect of the games.

The naked virile male was a prominent National Socialist image. The formal invitation to the 1934 party rally pictured half-naked men carrying the party standard. The official symbol of the first Great German Art Exhibition was Richard Klein's *Awakening*, depicting a reclining nude man. Even the SS often represented itself symbolically as an idealized semi-nude male. This prototypical Nordic Aryan was corporealized in German sculpture of the time. He was almost always holding a sword, as in Breker's *Readiness*, Georg Kolbe's *Commemorative Sculpture* and Adolf Wamper's *Genius of Victory*. Leaving aside the phallic undertones, the works made plain that the new man was someone willing to fight and die for state and Führer.

'It is surprising,' a writer on Third Reich art commented, 'that a puritanical regime, which put homosexuals into concentration camps, would celebrate the nude male body to such an extent.' Actually it is anything but surprising. Manliness and virility, camaraderie and male bonding, the beautiful body and youthful energy were not only central elements of the Nazi self-image, they were also homoerotic ideals. Writing about Heinrich Himmler, George Mosse pointed out, 'If he emphasized the contrast between homosexuality and manliness, it was because of his fear that the one could easily turn into the other.' Such is what happened, and for a time the party held a reputation for tolerating homosexuality, even on the part of some high officials. Not only did anti-Nazis use this against the party, but certain party members also turned it against their enemies inside the party. For years Hitler was indifferent, considering the matter a personal, private one. Of Ernst Röhm, head of the Storm Troops and a major target of press attack already in the 1920s, Hitler commented to Hoffmann, 'His private life does not interest me as long as he maintains the necessary discretion.' In early 1931 he again defended the Storm Troops with the argument that their sexual recreation was 'purely in the private sphere' and that these units were not a 'moral establishment' but 'a band of rough fighters'. But many in the party considered it a disgrace, an exasperated Goebbels commenting in his diary at the time, 'Hitler pays too little attention to it.' When Hitler finally purged Röhm and his men in 1934, their homosexuality was not the real motive, although used as such. Even so, there continued to be a homoerotic undertone at party functions, as some were quick to detect. 'There is a virile male voluptuousness which courses everywhere,' a French writer, himself homosexual, commented of the 1935 party rally. Two years later the SS journal, *Das Schwarze Korps*, considered it necessary to criticize the way illustrations 'of Nordic racial types' were being used as a pretext for titillating the baser senses. The 'racial beauty cult' was being exploited for sensationalist ends by publications 'which previously promoted concealed and unconcealed vice'. By 1942 homosexual acts in the SS reached such a level that Hitler decreed they must be punished by death.

7 PURIFICATION BY DEATH

BEFORE THE NEW GERMANY COULD BE CREATED, the old Germany had to be ideologically cleansed. The ensuing purge resulted in the dismissal of thousands of officials, the suppression of hundreds of organizations and the exclusion of Jews, liberals, Social Democrats, Communists and many others from the life of the nation. Cleansing also took the form of fire, in magic and religion the great medium of purification and historically a mythic means of destroying evil influences. So it was in the Third Reich, with book burnings, the torching of synagogues and other Jewish property on Kristallnacht, the incineration of some 5000 banned works of art on the eve of the war and eventually the cremation of human beings. As Frazer pointed out in *The Golden Bough*, fire was 'purificatory in intention, being designed to burn up and destroy all harmful influences. . . .'

Fire was not just a medium. To Hitler it was sacred. Prometheus, who in Greek mythology brought fire to earth, he regarded as the great symbol of the Aryan race. Fire also held great psychological potency, fascinating and moving him. On one occasion, as his darkened train moved slowly through the Ruhr at night, he is said to have become so enraptured at the sight of the glow and sparks of fire of the vast steelworks that he was rendered speechless for an hour. Years later Speer was prompted to reflect on the association of individuals with a specific natural element and concluded that he would unhesitatingly say that fire was Hitler's proper element. In Speer's view what attracted Hitler was not its Promethean association but its destructive force. He was ecstatic watching documentary films of London and Warsaw being consumed in a sea of flames caused by German air raids. 'Above all he was deeply impressed by photos of London burning,' Goebbels noted. On another occasion, while imagining New York being consumed in a hurricane of fire – 'skyscrapers being turned into gigantic burning torches, collapsing upon one another, the glow of the exploding city illuminating the dark sky' – he worked himself into a delirium of joy.

Not far removed from apocalypse and conflagration was another element of Hitler's imagery, blood. Blood meant, of course, race, but it also meant battle and killing. The National Socialist party itself was drenched in blood. Literally it was spilled in the 1923 putsch attempt and street battles of the early years, in the Röhm purge and the slaughter of war. The concept fascinated him, and he referred to it again and again in *Mein Kampf* and his speeches, with such expressions as 'aryan blood', 'the infection of impure blood', 'a nation's blood-worth', 'blood ownership', 'blood and soil', 'blood-guilt', 'heroes' blood', 'blood witnesses', 'the blood martyrs of the movement'. He put blood-red in the swastika flag, ordered blood-red banners to festoon march routes, created the Medal of the Blood Order (worn on a blood-red band) and invented the myth of the blood flag that was venerated as the party's most sacred relic. Referring to the party's violent beginnings, he described the blood of the 1923 putsch as 'baptismal water for the Reich'. Speer recalled an occasion at the Berghof in late August 1939 when there was a rare and spectacular aurora borealis, which bathed everything in red light. Hitler was deeply moved and remarked, 'Looks like a great deal of blood', and then, thinking of his impending attack on Poland, added, 'This time we won't bring it off without violence.'

Who sheds blood – that is, whose blood is shed for Führer and party? The hero. The hero would unquestioningly kill for the party and willingly lay down his life for the Führer. As Hitler declared at the 1929 Nuremberg rally, 'The hero says, what is the value of my life if I can save the community?' Commemorations of dead heroes were a central part of every great party occasion. Always to the sound of solemn music, the Führer would stride through the massed ranks of thousands of uniformed men to pay his tribute. With Hitler's encouragement these events, in particular the 1923 putsch, were memorialized for eternity in works of art – the painting of Paul Hermann, the poetasty of Schirach and the architecture of Troost. Far more than commemorations, these events were iconic exhibitions of Hitler's personal fascination with death and the artistic expressions of it that he revelled in. But Hitlerite death was not death in its tragic reality, it was death ritualized and without feeling, aestheticized and without horror. No painting gave Hitler a greater thrill than Hans Makart's *The Plague in Florence* with its yellow-green corpses. His favourite operatic scene was said to be the finale of *Götterdämmerung* with its apocalyptic end of the world. His ultimate architectural objective was skeletons of great buildings in a state of mellow ruin. The music he wished to hear at the moment of his death was the

'Liebestod' of *Tristan und Isolde* in which Isolde experiences death as 'to drown, unconscious, the greatest bliss'. Here is death as the glory and joy of which Siegfried and Brünnhilde sing – 'laughing let us be destroyed; laughing let us perish . . . let night descend, the night of annihilation . . . laughing death . . . laughing death'. Death abounds in drama and opera, but normally as tragedy. In Wagner and the German Romantic tradition, however, it promises triumph or redemption – or sometimes nothing. 'I want only one thing yet,' cries Wotan in the second act of *Die Walküre*, 'the end, the end.' Despair, reconciled to life through beauty, was a Greek concept; life reconciled to death through beauty was the nineteenth-century German Romantic notion. Death as a heroic act in obedience to Hitler was a central part of the ethos of the Third Reich. Orwell saw it as part of Hitler's appeal. 'Whereas Socialism, and even capitalism in a more grudging way, have said to people "I offer you a good time", Hitler has said to them "I offer you struggle, danger and death", and as a result a whole nation flings itself at his feet.' Better an end with horror than a horror without end, summed up Hitler's message.

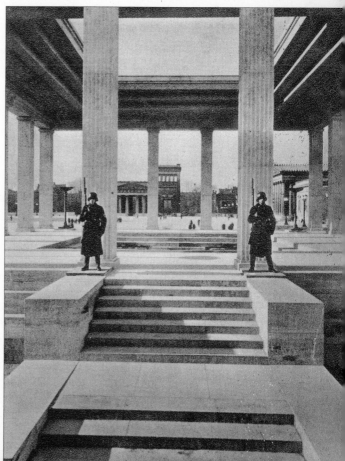

'The Eternal Guard' at the Temples of Honour in Munich. The structures were designed by Paul Ludwig Troost in 1933, dedicated in 1935 and demolished in January 1947 by order of the Four Power Control Council as 'buildings of National Socialist character'.

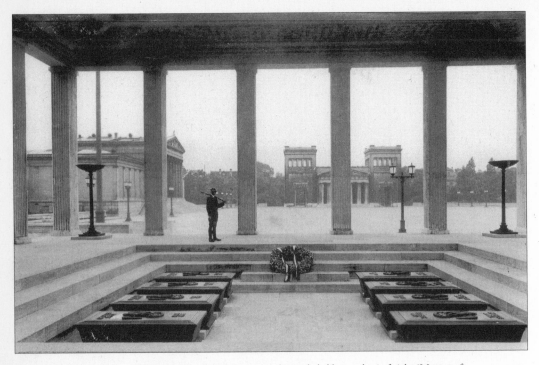

Framed by twenty pillars of yellow limestone, each temple held sarcophagi of eight 'Martyrs of the Movement', men killed in the 1923 putsch attempt. After the war the sarcophagi were melted down and the coffins reburied at their original sites.

Viewing love and death as ideals and linking the two was typical of the Romantic outlook. And in Hitler's mind as well, the means and ends of his vision were somehow contingent. To adapt a phrase of Walter Benjamin, Hitler's self-alienation reached such a degree that he experienced destruction – his own and others' – as an aesthetic pleasure. To some extent this, too, harked back to the Romantic tradition where sacrifice for a cause, rather than the cause itself, was the ideal – indeed, the sacrifice validated the cause. An early architectural expression was Leo von Klenze's 1841 neoclassical temple, the Valhalla at Regensburg. Hitler, however, transformed this reverence for the dead into a necrophilic cult that he initiated as soon as he reached power. First he commissioned the Königsplatz tombs for the party martyrs. Then he drew up plans for a gigantic Soldiers' Hall in the centre of Berlin, to honour dead heroes. In addition there was to be a mausoleum and two 'cemeteries of honour'. More dramatic still were the gigantic *Totenburgen*, citadels for the dead. He envisaged a network of these huge stone structures to girdle his empire, from the Atlantic to the Urals, from Norway to North Africa. They

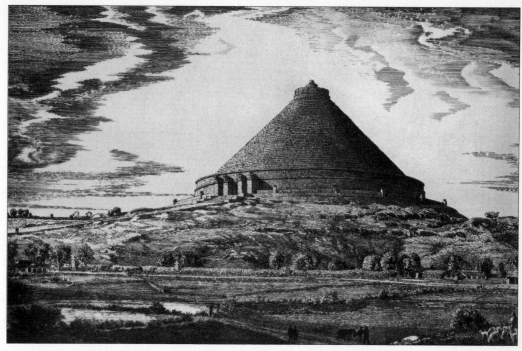

Envisaging masses of dead soldiers from his wars, Hitler commissioned Wilhelm Kreis to design Totenburgen — Citadels of the Dead — for key battle sites. Imitating ancient tumuli, Kreis designed several models to Hitler's satisfaction. This one, sketched in 1941, was to stand along the Dnieper River.

were to glorify war, honour its dead heroes and symbolize the impregnable power of the German race.

Heroism, blood, death, fire – in both their literal and mythic forms – added up to the supreme paradox of Hitler's rule: the conscious pursuit of antithetical ideals – culture and vandalism, creativity and destruction, beauty and horror, life and death. Everyone and everything was drawn into Hitler's grand dream. Art, creativity, beauty and life were indissolubly linked to their opposites not just by party and government officials but by conductors, singers, instrumentalists and actors who performed in support of the regime and its war effort, by art connoisseurs and museum curators who plundered and destroyed artworks, by impresarios who disbanded orchestras and opera companies in occupied countries, by the heads of concentration camps who savoured chamber music played by Jewish inmates before executing them. The combining of culture and barbarism was of the essence of Hitler's Reich. It is the conundrum that Hitler himself epitomized.

Can it be made at all comprehensible? It is possible to catch just a glimpse of the way Hitler's mind worked. Conversations were recorded – without his knowledge – in which the Jekyll and Hyde in his character can be witnessed directly contending with one another. On one occasion, while in his military headquarters shortly after the German attack on the Soviet Union, he warmly reminisced about his past travels. The fond memories of his state visit to Italy came flooding back, and what he recalled were not the political discussions with Mussolini but rather the beauty of Italian cities and Italian art. At one point he worried about the possibility of their being damaged in the war. 'Each palazzo in Florence or Rome,' he said, 'is worth more than all of Windsor Castle. It would be a crime if the British destroy anything in Florence or Rome. It would not be a shame . . . in the case of Berlin.' And when the time came in November 1943, as German forces were being prised out of Italy, he agreed to alter German military plans and instructed that Florence should not be defended. 'Florence is too beautiful a city to destroy,' he told the German ambassador in Italy, adding, 'Do what you can to protect it: you have my permission and assistance.'

How to explain the mechanics of a mind that admired the treasures of Italy on the one hand but that was indifferent to the destruction, even of his own capital, caused by his wars on the other? 'I must be cruel, only to be kind,' he might have said with Hamlet. In fact, speaking to his staff as the *Wehrmacht* was rapidly advancing towards Moscow and Leningrad in September 1941, he himself addressed the issue this way:

> I can imagine that some people today might ask in amazement – 'How can the Führer possibly destroy a city like Petersburg!' To be sure, I am by upbringing perhaps of an entirely different way of thinking. I do not want to see anyone suffer or to hurt anyone; but when I perceive that the species itself is in danger, ice-cold reason replaces feelings. I can only see the sacrifices to be suffered in the future if there is no sacrifice today.

Several weeks after that, he commented,

> To save the old city of culture, we limited our air attacks on Paris to the airfields on the periphery. . . . It would really have bothered me to attack a city like Laon with its cathedral . . . .

Then in the same breath he said,

> . . . I do not feel a thing about levelling Kiev, Moscow and Petersburg to the ground. . . . In comparison with Russia even Poland is a cultured country.

Later he juxtaposed this thought:

> . . . Mankind has a natural drive to discover beauty. How rich the world will be for him who uses his senses. Furthermore, nature has instilled in everyone the desire to share with others everything beautiful that one encounters. The beautiful should reign over humans; the beautiful itself wants to retain its power.

with another:

> The life of the individual should not be given such a high value. A fly lays a million eggs; they all die. But flies survive.

Hitler's lack of feeling for humans, even for fanatical party members, was already evident at the Nuremberg rallies and other spectacles when his 'architecturalizing' of the participants and his deployment of them in geometrical patterns reduced them to noctambulent creatures. It was most horrifyingly manifested in his wars and extermination camps. 'Really outstanding geniuses,' he believed, 'permit themselves no concern for normal human beings.' Their deeper insight, their higher mission justified any cruelty. Compared with them, individuals were mere 'planetary bacilli'.

The mission of the new Germany was to bring about the salvation of the world from the infection of impure blood and subversive ideas through the creation of an Aryan state based on National Socialist concepts and dedicated to high culture. 'A state which in this age of racial poisoning dedicates itself to the care of its best racial elements,' the penultimate sentence of *Mein Kampf* declared, 'must some day become lord of the earth.' In his speech to the party rally in 1929 he went further and declared, 'If a million children were born annually in Germany and seven to eight hundred thousand of the weakest were eliminated, the end result might even be an increase in strength.' It is the healthy members of a society, he went on to say, who enable a nation to achieve 'heroic deeds' and 'a high human culture'. And it was thus that 'our history will become world history'.

Like Kant's inquisitor, Hitler believed he was acting in obedience to moral duty. And like the inquisitor he believed that his 'mission' allowed him to violate Kant's imperative of treating people as ends not means. He would have agreed with Stalin, that one death could be a tragedy – as Ulrich Roller's – but a million deaths were a mere statistic. It might appear that his brutal social Darwinism – human beings are no different from flies and both are helpless victims of the cruel laws of nature – led him simply to disconnect mass murder from the world of cultural beauty. In fact, the horrors of the war that he had unleashed upon Europe did not trouble him. In a revealing statement that he made on several occasions, he said, 'Wars come and go; cultural achievements alone survive.' War, like genocide, was simply the means to a higher end – a new man, a new Germany and a new world, freed of impure blood, dedicated to beauty in all things, with the arts enthroned at the spiritual apex of the New Order. To adapt Voltaire's epigram about the court of Frederick the Great – Sparta in the morning, Athens in the afternoon – Hitler's Reich was Carthage by day, Florence by night.

Who, then, was this Hitler and what did he want? *Who* he was remains difficult to answer. Christa Schroeder spoke for others in his inner circle when she stated after the war that she never ceased trying to make sense of the man she thought she knew. In the end she confessed that it was impossible to discover his '*wahre Gesicht*', his true face. He had, she realised, too many faces. There was no one Hitler. *What* he wanted, however, is all too clear. It was a world purified of everyone he regarded as degenerate and corrupting – beginning with Jews, Communists, democrats, liberals, Freemasons, Modernists, Poles, Slavs, cripples, the mentally retarded and extending ever further until finally a cleansed world emerged similar to the one longed for by Hugo von Hofmannsthal's mythological princess, Ariadne:

> *Es gibt ein Reich, wo alles rein ist:*
> *Es hat auch einen Namen:*
> *Totenreich.*

> There is a land where all is pure:
> And it has a name:
> Land of the dead.

THE
FAILED PAINTER

8 THE STRUGGLING
WATERCOLOURIST

AT THE AGE OF TWELVE HITLER DECIDED on a career. 'How it happened, I myself do not know, but one day it became clear to me that I would become a painter, an artist.' His father, having taken it for granted that the boy would follow him into the civil service, reacted with incredulity. ' "Painter? Artist?" ' When that had no effect, he tried brutal rejection. ' "Artist, no, never as long as I live." ' But neither the father's pleas nor his threats could shake the boy. 'I wanted to become a painter and no power in the world could make me a civil servant.' Although some historians have questioned whether this harsh Oedipal struggle as recounted in *Mein Kampf* actually took place, the balance of testimony leaves little doubt that Alois at times treated his son tyrannically – giving him a 'sound thrashing every day', according to his sister, Paula. In the end the disagreement hardly mattered. Alois died a few years later and the emollient Klara allowed her son to decide his future for himself.

The lad's interest in painting was deep and sincere. At school he loved to sketch – a subject in which he earned good grades – and in later years relatives and friends recalled how insistent he was that he would some day be not just a painter but a famous painter. 'He spent his days doing practically nothing but paint and draw,' a neighbour said years later. In the autumn of 1905 Hitler dropped out of school and, according to one of his earliest biographers, went to Munich for several months to study drawing at a private art academy. While this is certainly false, his mother did in fact arrange for him to spend the following May in Vienna to see the paintings in the great Habsburg collections. That experience left him more determined than ever in his choice of a career. Early in September of 1907, now eighteen, he left home for Vienna to enrol in the Academy of Fine Arts, which he regarded as the essential step to an artistic career. 'I set out with a pile of drawings, convinced that it would be child's play to pass the examination,' he wrote in *Mein Kampf*. 'At school I had been by far the best in my class in drawing, and since then my ability had developed amazingly.'

Before a candidate qualified to sit for the examination, a sample of his work had first to be found satisfactory. Although nearly a third of the 113 candidates were dismissed from the competition at this stage, Hitler's works passed and he was admitted to the examination. To prepare himself he took lessons at a noted art studio run by a sculptor, Rudolf Panholzer. The test itself took place on 1 and 2 October, with morning and afternoon sessions of three hours each. In this time a candidate was required to produce a number of freehand sketches from a list of specified subjects, such as 'the hunt', 'autumn', 'joy', 'the good Samaritan', 'night'. The examiners found Hitler's drawings unsatisfactory, giving as their reason the lack of figures, or, as the record tersely stated, 'test draw[ings] unsatisfactory' – 'few heads'.

Although this was hardly a disgrace – only twenty-eight candidates passed – Hitler was mortified. 'I was so convinced that I would be successful that when I received my rejection, it struck me as a bolt from the blue.' He could not bear to admit the failure to anyone. Only when he came to write *Mein Kampf* seventeen years later did he finally acknowledge it. Then he maintained that he had sought out the rector of the Academy who said that while the sketches showed talent for someone wanting to be an architect, they demonstrated no aptitude at all for painting. Years afterwards, in one of his nocturnal monologues, Hitler elaborated: 'The professor asked me what architecture school I had attended. What? I never went to any architecture school! But you must have gone to some architecture school. You have an obvious talent for architecture. That was devastating to me, because on the one hand I wanted to go into painting classes but on the other I realized that, yes, he was right.'

What Hitler to the end of his life passed over in silence was that he continued to pin all his hopes on studying at the Academy. On being offered a job in the post office, following the death of his mother in December 1907, he rejected it out of hand. When family friends warned that he had neither the money nor the connections to pursue a painting career, he is said to have brushed aside their objections with the comment, 'Makart and Rubens also worked their way up from poor circumstances.' And so, setting off with a new set of works in September 1908, he made a second attempt to enter the Academy. This time his submission was not found adequate for him even to sit for the exam. The rejection was such a crushing humiliation that he went wild with fury and despair. Making a clean break with the past and with the world, he fled his lodgings without a forwarding address and severed contact with his sisters as well as his friend and roommate, Kubizek. On registering his new address with the police, he now gave his occupation not as 'artist' but as 'student'.

The two rejections tormented him to the end of his life. Passages in *Mein Kampf* that follow mention of his failure are deeply bitter. At one moment he blames it on inadequate schooling and at another on destiny for forcing 'the sons of poor parents to stagnate in misery and obscurity'. Years later Christa Schroeder recalled, 'Every time he spoke of this painful rejection, he became sombre and ill-tempered. Then he went on to complain of the injustice of destiny.' The experience taught him a lesson he never forgot and instilled in him a resentment he never got over. Forever more he despised authorities and experts, had only contempt for rules and established institutions, scornfully brushed aside advice and views differing from his own. He withdrew into himself, took solace from the example of the unappreciated artist he saw in the young Wagner and, like Hagen in the composer's *Götterdämmerung*, learned to hate. 'I owe it to that period that I grew hard and am still capable of being hard.' And 'hard' is the word he always used once in power in justifying what he himself acknowledged were acts of heartless brutality. From now on all that mattered was his own indomitable 'will' – another term, along with 'defiance' and 'determination to resist', that repeatedly appears in *Mein Kampf*. Eventually 'my will to resistance grew, and in the end this will was victorious', he wrote. So he persevered in his resolve to be a painter. And in persevering there revealed itself that cast of mind which led on to his later successes and defeats. For him, will, destiny, dreams were reality.

In painting, as in everything else he took up, Hitler was an autodidact. He had a modicum of talent – at least in sketching buildings – but what technique he learned he picked up on his own. Like most amateurs, he began by painting simple landscapes. With neither innate originality nor professional training, he went on to imitate the watercolours and prints of the south German school and the postcard scenes – everyday urban views – that were popular at the time. Cityscapes also coincided with his interest in architecture while other subjects suggested nostalgia for the simple, bucolic life of an imagined youth. Such works, handled realistically, required none of the skill necessary for a Romantic dreamscape, a portrait or a genre scene with people. Moreover, he had to paint the sort of thing that an unknown and untalented amateur might be able to sell, and that was inexpensive reproductions of familiar places. He once said as much to an acquaintance when he remarked, 'I paint what people want.' He was, after all, leading a hand-to-mouth existence. This is probably why he painted with watercolours, which were quicker to do and cheaper than oils and canvas.

In his early years Hitler looked for inspiration to the works of Carl

Schütz, a late eighteenth-century watercolourist, and Rudolf von Alt, the outstanding Central European watercolourist of the following century. Their speciality was highly accomplished, near-photographic reproductions of street scenes and nostalgic views of old Vienna. Such straightforward realism, architectural subject matter, scrupulous attention to detail and conventionality of treatment suited Hitler's interest and ability. With craftsmanlike precision he did his best to emulate these works down to the last decorative feature. Some of these paintings can be matched to Schütz's and Alt's originals, demonstrating Hitler's respectable effort at duplication. Others lacked such a pedigree, however, and were evidently reproductions of prints, picture postcards and photographs of well-known sites. Subjects ranged from concrete, realistic scenes of urban settings – in particular the churches and great public buildings of Vienna – to soft, dreamy country landscapes. The style was always simple and naturalistic. Fascination with detail, especially architectural, spoke through everything. Equally striking is that his was a world largely devoid of people. Although all his life he enjoyed drawing caricatures of faces, like many other topographical artists, even good ones, he was hopeless at painting figures, and in most of his watercolours avoided them entirely.

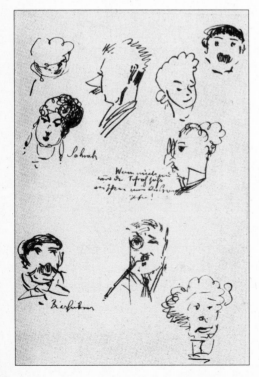

Hitler was a compulsive sketcher-doodler and his secretaries had always to keep a ready supply of paper on his writing table. Here is a rare surviving page of faces.

Hitler apparently did not often go outdoors with easel and paints but worked in a corner of the reading room at the men's hostel where he lived. The one firsthand account of his routine was recorded in a memoir written by Karl Honisch, a denizen of the same homeless shelter who came to know Hitler briefly in 1913:

> As a rule he did one painting a day. In the morning he sketched it out; after lunch he coloured it. Most pictures were roughly 35 x 45 cm [14in. x 16in.] and were almost invariably Viennese scenes. Most often it was the Charles Church that he drew or scenes from old Vienna and the old Vienna Naschmarkt. I recall that he would often do especially saleable subjects a dozen times, one after the other.
>
> Whether these pictures can be regarded as works of art, I do not know. . . . When a picture was finished and we all said how much we admired it, he would often say disparagingly that he was only a dilettante and that he had yet to learn to paint. But his works could not have been bad because otherwise they would never have sold as well as they did since dealers were even then not in the charity business.

When he bestirred himself – and Honisch contended that he was 'very hard-working' – he could turn out as many as six or seven watercolours a week. Years later Hitler estimated that he had painted between 700 and 800 pictures during the Vienna years. Some scenes he painted so often, he later told friends, he was able to do them from memory.

The subject and style of Hitler's paintings catered to an unsophisticated clientele who could not afford anything better. 'These were the cheapest things we ever sold,' the daughter of one art dealer commented years later. 'The only people who had any interest in them were tourists who were looking for inexpensive souvenirs of Vienna.' Actually, there were other buyers as well. Some were residents of the neighbourhood who wanted a local scene to decorate a wall in their home. Others were frame and glass dealers who took them simply to fill an empty frame for display in a shop window. Once in a while he received a commission. The most substantial was for a series of landscapes of the countryside around Salzburg done for the frame maker Samuel Morgenstern. Since he rarely got more than three or four krone★ for a picture, Hitler's earnings were for a long time meagre. It is said he sometimes bartered a painting for a meal from a restaurant owner. But

★ roughly the equivalent of £7 or $10–12 today

claims that he was reduced to drawing posters and advertising graphics for shoe polish, tobacco, wash soap, cosmetics, shoes, women's underwear and an antiperspirant powder called 'Teddy' are in all likelihood false. Most, if not all, of the drawings on which the stories are based are bogus, either forgeries or inventions of detractors such as Josef Greiner. In testimony to the Vienna police in 1936, Otto Kallir, a Vienna art dealer, declared that posters brought to his attention were fabrications.

Evidently lacking confidence in his work, Hitler was at first diffident about personally marketing his paintings. 'I had the impression that he had previously been ashamed of having to sell his paintings,' Jakob Altenberg, one of his dealers, recalled. But in early 1910 he found a collaborator in another resident of the homeless shelter. Reinhold Hanisch had been making and selling silhouettes when he learned of Hitler's interest in painting. He proposed a deal. Hitler would paint, he would sell and they would divide the take. For a time the arrangement worked. Hitler produced his watercolours and Hanisch made the rounds of taverns, frame makers and small-time dealers. After a few months, in August 1910, they quarrelled. Hitler went to the police, claiming he had been swindled out of his share of the proceeds of two paintings. Hanisch was arrested and sentenced to a week in jail, though not as a result of Hitler's charge but because he had registered with the police under a false name.

After that, two other men whom Hitler met at the hostel, Josef Neumann and Siegfried Löffner, helped to sell his works until Hitler gradually overcame his shyness. Neumann and Löffner were Jews, as were his principal dealers, Altenberg and Morgenstern. They not only gave him as good a price as anyone else but also were willing to take his works without having a ready customer. The most helpful was Morgenstern, who later stated that Hitler had appeared in his shop in 1911 or 1912 to offer him three paintings in the style of von Alt. According to Peter Jahn, a Viennese art dealer who later had responsibility for tracing Hitler's works for the Nazi party, 'Morgenstern was the first person to offer a good price for his pictures, and that is how the commercial relationship began.' As Jahn commented, 'Morgenstern's shop was at that time Hitler's major source of income, and the dealer was very fair to him. Hitler himself later told me that Morgenstern had been his "saviour" and had given him many important commissions.' The dealer maintained a card file with the names of purchasers and from this it was known that most of the customers for Hitler's watercolours were Jews who lived in the area. One, a lawyer named

Josef Feingold, liked Hitler's work so much he bought a series of paintings which Morgenstern framed.★

Such considerations would appear to contradict occasional speculation that Hitler's anti-Semitism was in some way related to his work as a painter. Yet there is no more obvious characteristic of his hatred of Jews than that it had nothing whatever to do with objective fact. Indeed, his sister Paula, interviewed by American army officials after the war, remarked that in her view it was possible 'that the hard years during his youth in Vienna caused his anti-Jewish attitude. He was starving severely in Vienna,' she said, 'and he believed that his failure in painting was only due to the fact that trade in works of art was in Jewish hands.' Her comment is not only consistent with Kubizek's 'Reminiscences', for what they are worth, but, more important, with Hitler's repeated insistence that Jews controlled the art trade as well as his claim in *Mein Kampf* that Jewish corruption of the arts was an important element in his conversion to anti-Semitism.

Despite his two failures, Hitler made a third attempt to gain entry to the Academy of Fine Arts. In August 1910 he called on a curator of the Court Museum, Professor Ritschel, and showed him a substantial portfolio of drawings and watercolours of buildings of old Vienna, all with his usual attention to detail. 'Hitler's works had an architectural quality and were done with such painstaking care that they almost gave the impression of being a photograph,' one of Ritschel's assistants later recorded. Hitler presumably hoped that on the basis of these he would be reconsidered for admission to the Academy. For whatever reason nothing came of the venture and there could now be no prospect of ever receiving professional training in Vienna. This may have strengthened a determination to leave. Karl Honisch commented years later, 'I believe that Hitler was the only one among us with a definite long-term plan in mind. He had often told us of his future intentions. He wanted to live in Munich so that he could attend the art academy there and improve his artistic abilities.' And so in May of 1913 he left Vienna for the Bavarian capital. With him must have gone his early sketchbook of some forty small watercolours as well as a few other paintings – works that were found in the Berlin bunker at the end of his life.

On arriving in Munich, Hitler gave his occupation to police authorities as *Kunstmaler*, artistic painter, and went on as before, painting the same sort

---

★ Following the *Anschluß*, Feingold fled to France. Altenberg lost his shop and means of income but survived thanks to having an Aryan wife. Morgenstern appealed to Hitler for help but the letter never reached him, and the dealer and his wife were deported.

of subjects in the same naturalistic style. At first he found it difficult to get established. According to people who knew him at the time, he would paint for several days and then make the rounds of the cafés, beer halls and small dealers. One of his early customers, a doctor named Hans Schirmer, provided a first-hand account of how he went about it. Schirmer was sitting in the garden of the Hofbräuhaus in the summer of 1913 when Hitler entered:

> Around eight o'clock I noticed a very unassuming, quite shabby-looking young man, whom I took for an impoverished student, pass by my table offering to sell a small oil painting. Around ten o'clock I observed that he had still not managed to sell his painting. . . . At length I met his price. It was a mood piece, called Evening. As soon as the painter left me I noticed that he went to the buffet and bought a piece of bread and two Vienna sausages. He ate this alone, without any beer.

Although Schirmer himself was not well-off, he felt sorry for the young painter and asked him to paint two further small oils, which were promptly produced. 'I could see that life was a hard struggle for him but that he was too proud to take charity.'

Rudolf Häusler, a friend from the men's hostel who had accompanied him to Munich and shared a small room, did his best to sell the paintings but met with little success. Once in a while Hitler had a stroke of luck, as when a justice of a Bavarian court commissioned an oil painting for the dining room of his home. But at times, according to Häusler, the two had to do odd jobs to earn a little money and even then occasionally went hungry. To make matters worse, disaster threatened in January 1914 when Austrian authorities succeeded in tracking Hitler down and ordered him to account for his failure to have done his military service. In an effort to exculpate himself he wrote a letter giving a woeful impression of his life at this time:

> The fact is I earn my living as a free-lance painter but, since I am without private means (my father was a civil servant), this is only to finance my further training. . . . My income is really very modest, just enough for me to get by on.

> As evidence of this I enclose my tax document. . . . This shows my income to be 1200 marks,* too much rather than too little, but this should not be taken to mean that I earn exactly 100 marks a month. Oh no. My monthly

---

* roughly the equivalent of £500 or $800 today.

income varies greatly, but at the moment it is really small, since art sales in Munich at this time of year are in winter's sleep, and there are three thousand artists who live or try to live here.

In the end Austrian officials took pity and declared him unfit to serve.

A short time later his career took a turn for the better. As he made the rounds with his paintings, he found an increasing number of ready customers. Some considered the works attractive; some felt sorry for the strange young man; some bought them for both reasons. 'I liked the picture,' one purchaser recalled. 'The young artist aroused my pity, so I bought it.' A baker said, 'I just wanted to help the young man. He always looked so hungry.' For some the watercolours had a genuine appeal; having bought one, they ordered more. One customer, a jeweller, took no fewer than twenty-one of them in the course of six months. Gradually he found a steady outlet for his works.

Over and over Hitler painted popular scenes – the Asam House and St John's Church, the Hofbräuhaus, the opera house and similar sites. 'I looked at two of his paintings,' remarked a customer, 'one of the old city hall with a view of the Marienplatz and the other of the old royal palace. I bought both because I really liked the fresh representation of Munich's architectural beauty.' If his best-seller in Vienna had been his rendering of the Charles Church, in Munich it was no doubt the Munich marriage register office. He produced it in quantities – later saying it was so familiar he could do it in his sleep – and sold them to newlywed couples as they left the ceremony. One of Hitler's own favourites was the courtyard of the Old Residenz. He must have done a good many of these as well, and presented one to Heinrich Hoffmann for his fiftieth birthday in 1935. To Hoffmann's daughter, Henriette von Schirach, he once commented that he had often washed out his paintbrushes in the courtyard fountain there – a remark implying that he was now painting from nature.

Commercially he was prospering. In the beginning he had asked five marks a painting but in the course of 1914 was sometimes charging as much as twenty.* Even if he sold only ten a month, he was earning at least as much as the average worker. Hence, since he lived abstemiously and paid only twenty marks a month room rent, he had achieved a measure of financial security. Beyond that, however, his career was going nowhere. There is no evidence that he took any concrete step to gain entry into an art academy.

---

* roughly the equivalent of £50 or $80 today.

Hope of ever becoming the great painter of his dreams must have come to seem impossibly remote and at one point he altered his residence registration with the police to give his occupation as 'writer'. In *Mein Kampf* he declared that at this time he was painting to live rather than living to paint.

Small wonder that he greeted the outbreak of war in 1914 with a sense of exhilaration. He immediately volunteered for military service and arrived at the front on 29 October, to find his unit engaged in the first battle of Ypres, in the course of which most of the regiment was wiped out. However, a few weeks later, at Wychaete, a village in Flanders, he began painting, and a watercolour of a battlefield scene survives. Sometime after that his regiment moved to winter quarters near the village of Messines, and there he turned out a number of works. In all, at least a dozen watercolours, nine pencil sketches and five pen-and-ink drawings are known to have come through the war, including a few sketches done in

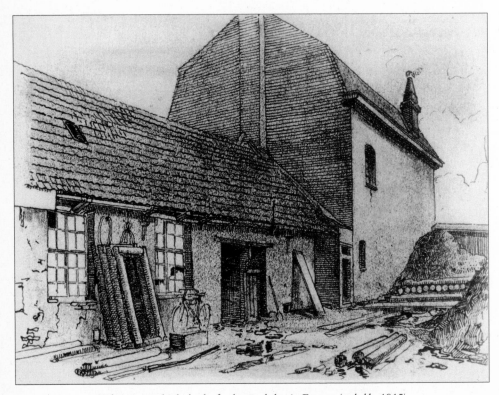

Hitler's pen-and-ink sketch of a dugout shelter in Fournes (probably 1915).
He later tinted it in several pastels.

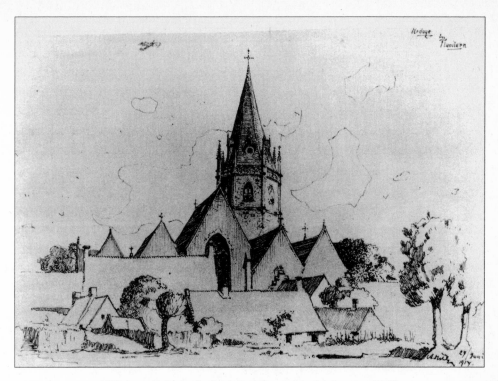

Hitler's pencil sketch of a church in Ardoye in Flanders (summer 1917).

the summer of 1915 of men in his unit. One of these men, Karl Lippert, recalled: 'On calm days at the front at Fromelles or Fournes Hitler spent his time drawing and reading. He sketched almost every man on the regimental staff, some in caricatures. Unfortunately I do not have the comic things that I had kept for years in my knapsack but which eventually disintegrated in the wind and rain.' Some months later when Hitler was sketching a courtyard gate and the ruins of a church, just across the front line a British officer, by remarkable coincidence, was painting the ruins of a farmyard and a village under enemy shelling. Winston Churchill, then doing a period of military service, had just taken up what was to become the great pastime of his later life.

There is no way of knowing whether Hitler viewed his wartime works as a continuation of his career or a diversion from the war. Probably he himself did not know. Yet there can be no doubt that his pleasure in art was unabated. On the two occasions when given leave, he headed straight for Berlin to visit the galleries. 'At last I have an opportunity to study the museums somewhat better,' he wrote on a postcard to an army comrade,

Ernst Schmidt, who was also a painter. After the armistice in 1918, Hitler returned to Munich and apparently discussed with Schmidt the idea of studying painting, possibly realizing his old dream of entering an art academy. A number of regimental friends are said to have encouraged him and he showed some of his recent works to two professional painters, Max Zaeper and Ferdinand Staeger, who were supposedly impressed. But he allowed matters to drift, and drifting they eventually took him into politics.

In the course of his career as a watercolourist Hitler had gradually achieved a modest competence at his craft. But his was a technical ability that any reasonably skilled art student could learn. What was remarkable was that he taught himself without anyone's help, much less any professional training. His style was rooted in the naturalistic German tradition – concrete and identifiable subjects, clean lines and attention to detail. His handling of the material was at times laboured and clumsy, at other times technically competent and visually attractive. His repertory was narrow. In his early youth he mostly painted simple, even primitive, landscapes, as is evident in his watercolour sketchbook. Afterwards his subject was almost exclusively the exterior of buildings. Paintings of interiors and still lifes were extremely rare. His forte was the craftsmanlike precision that he learned to instil in his treatment of architectural subjects. Through his repeated portraiture of well-known Vienna and Munich buildings he developed the near-professional eye of an architect. But he did not begin to find an interpretive technique of his own and, as far as can be judged, neither embellished nor altered what he copied. As a result he rarely gave his scenes life or feeling. Nor did he even begin to deal with the problems of light and shadow. With little or no imagination, much less daring, these were timid works. Their most marked failing lay in the figures. Those he inserted looked like mannequins and cast a mood of artificiality, not to say crudity, over the whole work. All in all, the impression left by his watercolours is one of a static and emotionally empty depiction of scenes aspiring to photograph-like quality.

That is not the whole story, however. What is intriguing is that a number of paintings – all of them almost certainly authentic – demonstrate a respectable mastery of the medium. Works such as *Weissenkirchen in the Wachau* of 1910, *Old Vienna Courtyard near St Ulrich's Church* of 1911–12, *The Main River Gate* of 1913 along with two unfinished wartime works – *Haubourdin* and *The Seminar Church in Haubourdin* – manifest a remarkable technical leap. Possibly when he did not try to imitate and instead let himself go and worked from nature, he developed a certain innate skill. Alfred

Rosenberg, whose post-war memoirs were openly critical of Hitler's taste in painting and aptitude in drawing, acknowledged finding in his war paintings 'a natural gift, a feeling for the essential and a pronounced pictorial talent'.

Yet even with training it seems unlikely that Hitler would ever have been more than a skilled Sunday afternoon amateur. As an artist he was impotent, unable to do what he later did in politics and architecture – create a world instead of merely copying one. The possibility of probing the paintings for insight into Hitler's character is diminished by the fact that most of them are formulaic works. However, the fact that they are copies – and copies of a certain type – may say something. They disclose a basic conventionality of outlook, a longing for a world of order, a narrow idea of beauty and an interest in buildings rather than people. Otherwise there is no overt ideology in his works. They are of interest solely because of who painted them.

That is similarly the case with those of the other noted statesman-painter, Winston Churchill, though in style and subject the works of the two could not be less alike and more revealing of their differing characters. Churchill's were weak in drawing and composition but dramatic in colour and atmosphere. The mechanical treatment of the impersonal cityscapes in Hitler's watercolours contrasts with the warmth and brightness of Churchill's handling of landscapes and still lifes in oils. The one's literal Naturalism is a world away from the other's dreamy Impressionism. Unlike Hitler, Churchill mostly painted broad vistas and, after struggling with the effects of light and shade on water and trees, produced such delightful works as *The Loup River*, now in the Tate. Churchill's painterly creation was a P. G. Wodehouse universe of sunshine, gardens, flowers, fish ponds, trees and streams – the English aristocrat's dream of a rural land of peace and contentment.

Hitler's surviving watercolours and sketches are scattered, individually or in collections, around the world. At the war's end Hitler's retainers in Munich and at the Berghof made away with some of them and they were later sold, given away or lost. The watercolour sketchbook of his youth and a few paintings – as well as a uniform and other items taken by the Russian army from the bunker under the chancellery – are now in the State Special Trophy Archives in Moscow. Paintings that had been collected by the Nazi party's Hauptarchiv have vanished, though much documentation survived and was seized by the American army. It is now deposited in the Federal Archive in Berlin. Individual American soldiers carried away those works they got their hands on. A packet of twenty paintings collected by party authorities in the 1930s was taken by Martin Bormann's wife to northern

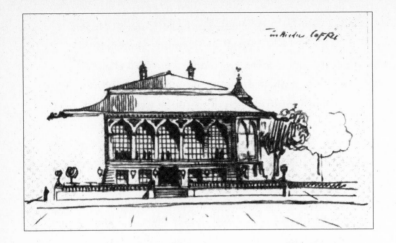

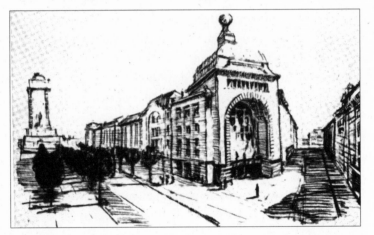

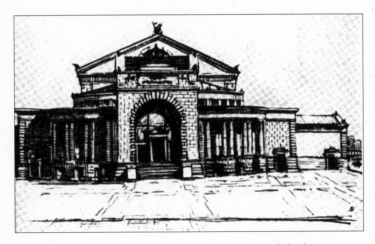

Three of Hitler's earliest architectural sketches.

Italy in the last days of the war. Before her death in March 1946 Gerda Bormann gave the paintings to Rodolfo Siviero, an Italian official in charge of art restitution. The works, at least eighteen of which are authentic, were exhibited in Florence in 1984. Nine years later, after their export was prohibited by the Italian government, the paintings were sold to a private Italian collector. Four watercolours belonging to Heinrich Hoffmann were seized by the American army and are held by the Museum Division of the Center of Military History in Washington. Two paintings of Viennese scenes which Hitler gave to the Iranian ambassador at Berlin, Hassan Esfandiari, are now held by the Bonyad Montazana Foundation in Teheran. Although some collectors decline to be identified or permit the works to be seen, it is known that important collections are held by Fritz Stiefel, Wolfgang von Mertschinsky, the sixth Marquess of Bath and Billy F. Price.

Hitler's architectural and other sketches are also widely dispersed. Included in the documentation of the Hauptarchiv are several sketches of buildings, undated but probably of the early 1920s, and scribbled caricatures of faces. In April 1945 at the Berghof Christa Schroeder walked off with a hundred drawings – out of as many as 250 – to prevent their being burned in a bonfire of Hitler's private papers. Upon her internment, these were taken from her by Alfred Zoller, a French army officer serving as an interrogator for American forces in Germany. Zoller returned only fifty of them, and these she later sold or gave away. The remaining fifty are said to be in the possession of Zoller's family. Fifty-three architectural sketches relating to Hitler's construction projects with Hermann Giesler are held by the Bayerisches Hauptstaatsarchiv in Munich.

9 FORGERS AND COLLECTORS

THE GENERAL PUBLIC KNOWS NOTHING OF Hitler's career as a painter or at most vaguely recalls wartime propaganda depicting him as a house painter or wallpaper hanger. Only on rare occasions – such as in Florence in 1984 and Moscow in 2000 – have even a few of his works been shown publicly. Occasionally one comes to light and is reproduced in the press before being sold at auction. In 1983 what purported to be an authoritative *catalogue raisonné* of some 750 of Hitler's watercolours, oils and sketches was published in Switzerland under the title *Adolf Hitler als Maler und Zeichner* (Adolf Hitler as Painter and Draftsman). Assembled and edited by August Priesack, and financed and published by Billy F. Price, a Texas businessman and collector of Hitler's paintings, the book was banned in Germany. Offered in translation after some textual bowdlerization to several New York publishing houses, it was rejected on the grounds that it risked making Hitler appear human. The book was printed privately in 1984 under the title, *Adolf Hitler: The Unknown Artist*, but received almost no notice.

Otherwise nothing has been written about Hitler's paintings beyond a few exiguous references by writers who have ridiculed them, usually sight unseen. Hitler himself has been dismissed as 'nothing more than a postcard copyist' – though postcard copying was famously done by such artists as Utrillo and Picasso. The works themselves have been derided as postcard-type paintings – though their actual size averaged at least 28.5 x 38 cm (11 in. x 15 in.). Even the vocabulary on the subject is slanted. Hitler did not 'sell' his paintings, he 'peddled' or 'hawked' them. According to Konrad Heiden, his first biographer, Hitler's rendering of people was 'a total failure'. 'They stand like tiny stuffed sacks,' he said. William L. Shirer found the paintings 'crude little pictures' and 'pitiful pieces' which were 'stilted and lifeless' and whose human figures were 'so bad as to remind one of a comic strip'. In Joachim Fest's view, Hitler was a 'modest postcard copyist' whose 'pedantic brushwork showed his secret craving for wholeness and idealized

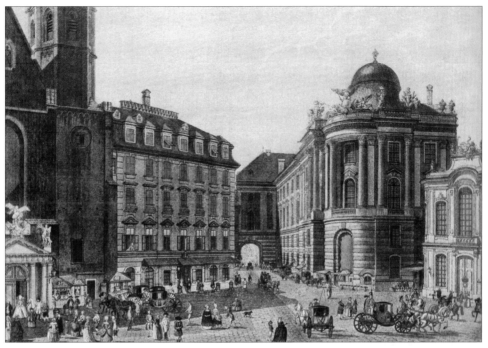

Although based on Carl Schütz's Michaelerplatz (above), Hitler's Old Burg Theatre avoids simple imitation by shifting perspective. The weakness of his figures is evident.

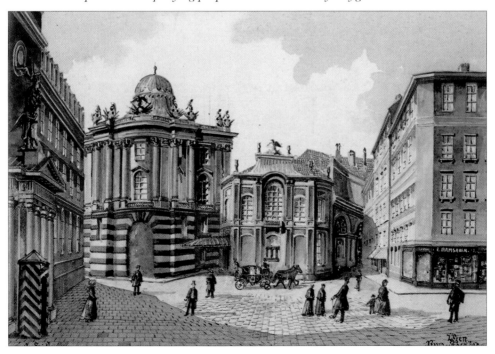

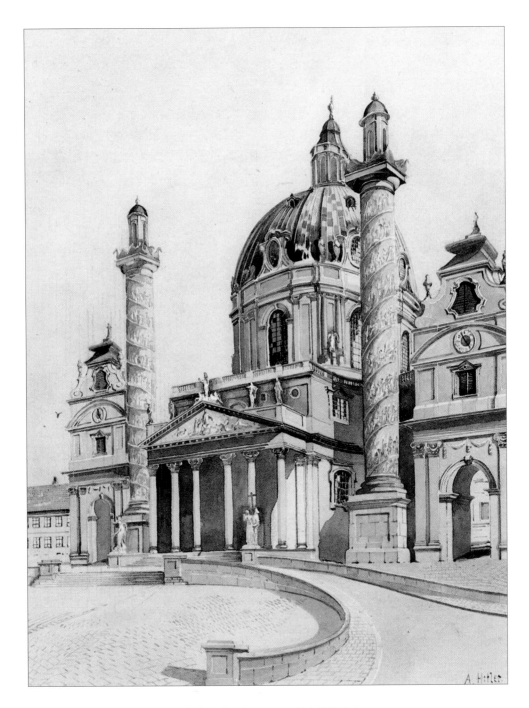

Charles Church, Vienna (Adolf Hitler)

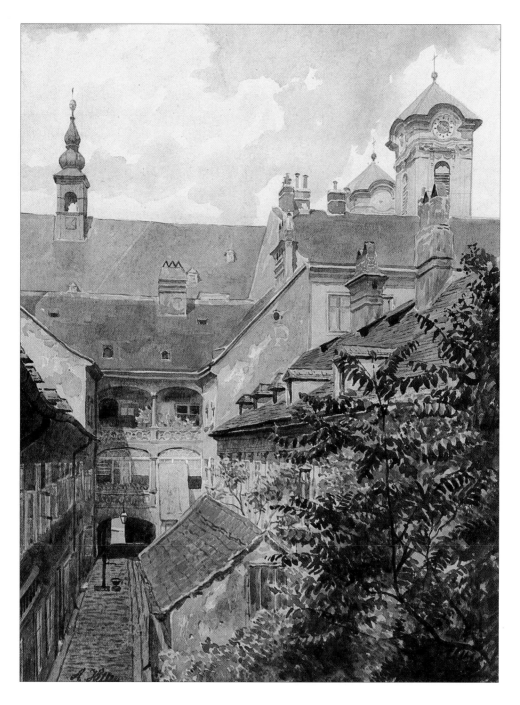

Old Vienna Courtyard (Adolf Hitler, 1911–12)

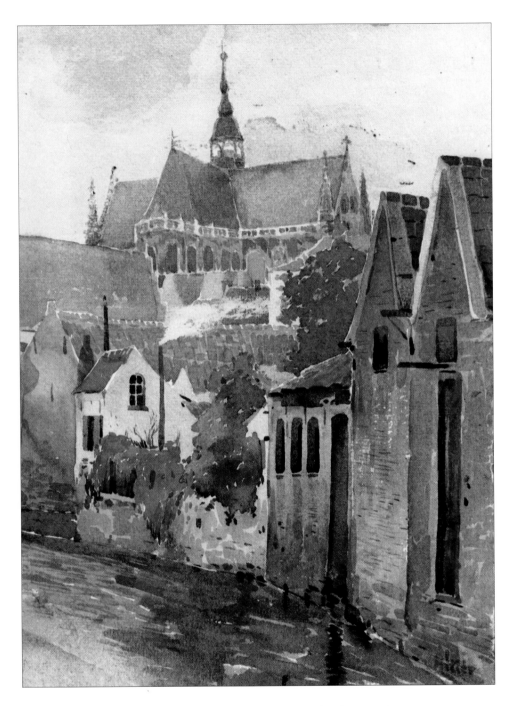

Haubourdin, The Seminar Church (Adolf Hitler, 1916)

beauty'. Alan Bullock passed off his works as 'drawings' which were 'mostly stiff, lifeless copies of buildings'.

It is not just Hitler's works that have been ridiculed but the whole artistic tradition in which they were rooted. Heiden made great fun of Hitler for aspiring to be a painter like Makart and Lenbach, artists whom Heiden derided as 'by now half forgotten in their own country'. For Fest, Hitler's love of the nineteenth-century German school was simply another aspect of 'that phenomenon of early rigidity which characterizes all his mental and imaginative processes'. What appealed to Hitler was the 'pompous decadence' of a Feuerbach and Makart as well as the 'sentimental genre painting' of a Grützner and the 'folksy idyll' of a Spitzweg. According to Peter Adam, it was the 'empty and pompous theatricality' of such paintings that suited Hitler's taste. Leaving aside the fact that German painting of that period included many works of the highest quality, these were not the works that Hitler copied. A brooding Friedrich canvas, a Lenbach portrait or Makart scene of a historic event, or a Spitzweg depiction of Biedermeier social life were, even to imitate, worlds beyond him. At the same time Hitler has been reproached for having been, as it is phrased, aesthetically immune to the artistic revolution swirling around him in Vienna and Munich. Why, he might have sat in the same cafés with Klimt and Schiele or Klee and Kandinsky! Yet both the Vienna Secession and the Blaue Reiter, it is said, passed him by. The reality is that the avant-garde passed by the overwhelming majority of painters, even some notable ones, especially in artistically conservative Vienna and Munich. In any case the Modernist mode of painting was not such that an untrained beginner could have begun to emulate.

Hitler himself was ambivalent about his paintings. In later years they undoubtedly held deep emotional significance. Physical reminders of the dreams of greatness that danced in his head while he painted, they were precious relics of his years of struggle, tangible memorials of how far he had come. The fact that he kept the watercolour sketchbook of his youth with him all his life and that it was – along with his Iron Cross from the First World War – among the items he took with him when he moved permanently into the bunker in early 1945 shows how important his paintings were to him. When, as chancellor, he wished to bestow a token of special esteem, he would present the person with one of his works. Yet Hitler knew enough about painting to have no illusions about his own efforts. Already in 1924 when he came to write *Mein Kampf* he claimed to have been no more than a '*kleiner Maler*', a minor painter. As his political career progressed, he sought to rewrite the biographical script by creating the impression that painting had been no more than a means of earning a little money rather than a would-be profession and that architecture had always been his true interest. Suddenly the man who had been obsessed with getting into the Academy of Fine Arts became the man who never took painting seriously.

After becoming chancellor, Hitler tried to quell public interest in his paintings. On an exceptional basis he had permitted Heinrich Hoffmann in 1935 to issue a limited edition of a portfolio of seven wartime works. Why and why then is not known. Publication, coinciding with the introduction of military conscription in Germany, may have been intended to highlight his own wartime service. A similar portfolio was later circulated among Hitler Youth groups. Four of these wartime paintings and one of the courtyard of the Old Residenz in Munich were included in a propaganda publication issued in 1936, *Adolf Hitler: Pictures from the Life of the Führer, 1931–1935*. Similar articles were published in two American publications, *Esquire* in 1936 and *Collier's* two years later. But that was the end of it. In June 1937 publishing any comment on his works was outlawed and several months later exhibiting them was banned. When Martin Bormann informed Hitler that a number of Nazi party newspapers and journals planned to publish colour reproductions of seven wartime paintings along with a number of other works in special issues on the occasion of his fiftieth birthday in April 1939, Hitler emphatically forbade it. In January 1942 his paintings were declared to be 'valuable national cultural property' and as such had to be registered with authorities and might not be sold outside Germany.

But there are limits even on dictators' ability to dictate. Once Hitler was in power, his paintings became collectors' items. In Vienna some people came to realize – to their amazement – that the new German chancellor was none other than that diffident young man from whom they had bought a watercolour or two several decades earlier. Prices soared. Quickest to take advantage of the situation was Reinhold Hanisch. With his knowledge of the paintings and those who had bought them, he spotted a golden opportunity to cash in by buying and reselling them at a profit. Altenberg still held two – one of St Ruprecht's Church and one of the Church at Ober St Veit – but Hanisch could not meet his price. Such paintings were already fetching relatively large sums, and Altenberg later sold the two to a dealer in Munich for 1100 marks. Hanisch therefore took the direct approach of manufacturing them himself. One purchaser was Franz Feiler, a young tram conductor from Innsbruck. Dubious about the work's authenticity he took it to Hitler, who was spending Easter at the Berghof. Hitler denied the watercolour was his and encouraged Feiler to take legal action. Although police files register that Hanisch had already served five jail sentences for a variety of minor crimes, they make no mention of this case.

Hanisch was a torment to Hitler in other ways. In the words of the Vienna police, he 'pursued him with implacable hatred'. Although the two had been acquainted for only a matter of months, Hanisch claimed to have known him quite well. He spread dark stories that Hitler had led a scruffy life as a tramp, had refused to work, was filthy about his person, had Jewish forebears and so on. Maintaining that he was the prime mover in Hitler's career as a painter, Hanisch claimed his friend was too lazy to turn out paintings fast enough and so relations were broken off. Such titbits as these were passed on to various journalists for money and became raw material for two of the earliest Hitler biographies, those by Rudolf Olden and Konrad Heiden, and then for others down to the present. They were also the basis of a pamphlet published in Bratislava in 1933, entitled 'Hitler, wie er wirklich ist' (Hitler as he really is), and two subsequent pieces, 'Adolf Hitlers Weggenosse in Wien erzählt' (Adolf Hitler's companion in Vienna speaks out) and 'Meine Begegnung mit Adolf Hitler' (My encounter with Adolf Hitler), that could not find a publisher despite Hanisch's best efforts. Eventually this material was turned into a three-part article, written in claudicate English, possibly by Heiden, and posthumously published in April 1939 in the *New Republic* under the title 'I Was Hitler's Buddy'. While some of the text rings true, the comments on Hitler's work as a painter were largely defamatory. They hammered at two main themes. One was his alleged idleness – he was 'a very slow worker', 'never an ardent worker', 'impossible to make him work', 'neglecting his work', 'more engaged in debate than in painting' and so on. The other was the putative meanness of his work – 'of very poor quality', 'not the work of artists but of daubers', 'he had daubed for more than eight days', 'shoddy trash done with very little love for work'. The watercolours themselves were passed off as little postcards copied from other postcards but never from nature.

Failing to earn anything from his foray into journalism, Hanisch went on forging paintings, not just Hitler's but even Old Masters. With the help of a middleman named Jacques Weiss, he sold his bogus products throughout Europe. By now Hitler was horrified, fearing that his own modest works and the even more modest forgeries would be held up to public derision. He, the great Führer, would look ridiculous. 'Hitler's fear of appearing foolish,' Christa Schroeder observed, 'reached the point of illness.' He therefore took action to have Hanisch's operation closed down. In November 1936 the

Vienna police 'were made confidentially aware' of Hanisch's activities. They placed him in detention and began an immediate investigation. Within days they fanned out through Vienna to question anyone they could trace who had sold or bought suspected forgeries.

One person was Jakob Altenberg, who had purchased some twenty-five works from Hitler. Shown a number of paintings that Hanisch had passed off as genuine, the dealer declared 'with absolute certainty' that the signature, size, style and subject demonstrated they were bogus. 'Hitler never painted still lifes (of fruit) [and] these still lifes are not in the style of Hitler's paintings; they are primitive concoctions. Such smearings would have been impossible to sell.' Another dealer, Otto Kallir, had begun acquiring Hitler material in 1935 from and through Hanisch, who had briefly been an employee. He testified that Hanisch had tried to sell him two posters, including the antiperspirant advertisement, that turned out to be fake. Kallir further reported that he had recently purchased a number of watercolours, three of which were later shown to Hitler, who declared them to be crude fabrications.

Under interrogation, Hanisch flatly denied ever having produced or sold forgeries. But the evidence against him was overwhelming. In his rooms the police found watercolours, paper, postcards of old Vienna scenes and a material for ageing paper. They determined that the paintings he sold were larger than any of Hitler's and, unlike the neat, clean and detailed work of the real article, his were sloppy. The subjects included still lifes such as Hitler never painted. And the signatures were plainly false. In case any doubt remained, the police also found letters from Jacques Weiss, who in the meantime had been jailed in Brussels for forgery and bribery, which detailed their collaboration. On 3 February of the following year, while awaiting trial, Hanisch 'suddenly died in his cell', in the words of the police report. The report eluded early biographers, who assumed foul play and maintained, to cite Fest's version, that after Austria's incorporation in the Reich in March 1938, Hitler 'had Hanisch tracked down and killed'. While this is obviously false, it is difficult to escape a suspicion that his death – recorded as a heart attack – was the result of Hitler's machinations. However, the case against Hanisch was so solid that he was bound to be sentenced. More exculpatory still, Nazi party authorities were long unaware of his death and as late as February 1944 Martin Bormann mentioned in an internal party document having learned that 'Hanisch hanged himself after the takeover of Austria'.

In the meantime Hitler had been doing his utmost to get physical control of as many paintings as possible. Responsibility for tracing them was given to the Hauptarchiv der NSDAP, the central party archive, which had been set up in Munich in 1934 under the aegis of Rudolf Hess as deputy of the Führer. Its purpose was to collect – and often confiscate – documents concerning Hitler's past so as to prevent anything embarrassing from reaching the public. In tracking down Hitler's paintings, the agency tried to persuade owners to sell them to the Hauptarchiv or at least to permit them to be authenticated, photographed and catalogued. As they went about their duties, archival officials also interviewed anyone who had known Hitler in his early years – thus acquiring the testimonies about Hitler's youthful aspirations to be 'a great painter'. The operation was directed by Ernst Schulte-Strathaus, who delegated the practical work of collecting, authenticating and cataloguing to Wilhelm Dammann and August Priesack.

Finding the paintings was obviously far from easy. Vienna was the main target. Before 1938 it was a responsibility of Otto von Stein, counsellor of the German legation in Vienna, to acquire those he could locate. Within days of the *Anschluß*, German and Austrian security officials scoured the city. Although Morgenstern and Altenberg had maintained some records, most works were scattered without a trace. Even when they were found, some owners refused to give them up. 'As a member of the party, he declined to sell the pictures by his beloved Führer and complained that he had had more than enough trouble with the Gestapo precisely because of the paintings,' read one report. The problem was further complicated by the fact that party officials liked to have a Hitler or two on their walls at home or at the office. Eventually the Hauptarchiv had to pay large sums – as much as 8000 marks★ – for those that could be located. When Heinrich Hoffmann proudly showed Hitler a watercolour he had just purchased – this was in 1944 – Hitler commented, 'These things should not go for more than one hundred and fifty or two hundred marks today. It is insane to pay more than that.' But the insanity went on and he was the cause, having certainly authorized the payments. In the end archival officials were able to account for fewer than fifty paintings, of which photocopies of only thirty-four survive. Forgeries along with genuine but badly done works were destroyed as they surfaced. Identifying forgeries was often difficult; Hitler himself, when shown a questionable painting, was sometimes uncertain whether it was his. Once the war began, the operation petered out and a projected catalogue was never issued. But up to the end of the Third Reich, as party and government files

---

★ roughly equivalent to £10,000 or $15,000 in today's terms.

show, Hitler remained perturbed about Hanisch's forgeries and resolute about hunting them down. As late as 1942 he instructed Himmler to destroy three of Hanisch's forgeries that had just been discovered.

The most curious and sinister aspect of the forgery story occurred after 1945. In response to the high prices commanded for Nazi memorabilia, any number of bogus paintings and sketches came on the market. Adding to the confusion, one of the authenticators of Hitler's works, Peter Jahn, fell under suspicion of trading in them. But the chief culprit was Konrad Kujau, a graphics artist, born in 1938 in East Germany, who became famous in 1983 as author of the 'Hitler Diaries'. Always better as a forger – at an early age fabricating autographs of East German leaders – than as an artist, Kujau – alias 'Konrad Fischer', 'Peter Fischer', 'Professor Fischer' and simply 'Conny' – fled to the Federal Republic in 1957 and eventually made a business of manufacturing and selling Nazi memorabilia. In contact with neo-Nazi circles and some of the Führer's surviving cronies, he engaged in an effort, some think a plot, to rehabilitate Hitler. Drawing on a variety of sources, Kujau fabricated as many as 300 paintings and sketches, not to mention poems, letters, autographs, notes, articles, orders, decrees and memoranda in which were buried neo-Nazi propaganda.

In the manner of stories and paintings about the lives of the saints, these documented critical events leading to Hitler's eventual apotheosis as Führer. Kujau's Hitler was a deeply human person – serious and humorous, kindly

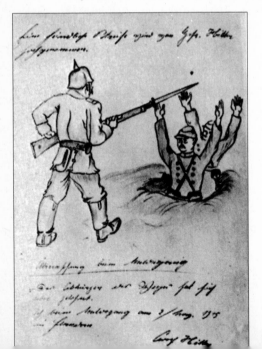

This and the three pictures that follow are Konrad Kujau's forgeries of Hitler's works. A sketch of Hitler taking British prisoners in the First World War; a sketch of Geli Raubal, Hitler's niece; a painting of a rural scene and a painting of flowers at a window.

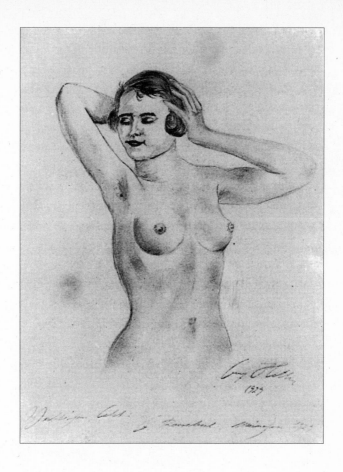

and firm, a lover of nature and the arts, a simple man rooted in German soil. For Hitler-the-struggling-artist, he produced early sketches and the Vienna examination drawings. For Hitler-the-courageous-soldier, he invented dozens of sketches illustrating deeds of heroism, kindness and humour. To represent Hitler-the-precocious-party-leader, he devised Nazi emblems, flags and uniforms as well as nationalistic and anti-Semitic posters. Hitler-the-Landsberg-inmate was commemorated with drawings of his prison room, a caricature of the public prosecutor who had him consigned there and portraits of the others sentenced with him. To each of these precious sketches was appended an inflammatory political comment in Hitler's hand. Portraits of dogs and female nudes were presumably intended to demonstrate his affection for each. Kujau even fabricated historic events by chronicling the course of Hitler's artistic career in letters to his sister Paula, his half-sister Angela and various friends. The propaganda became ever more overt. On the

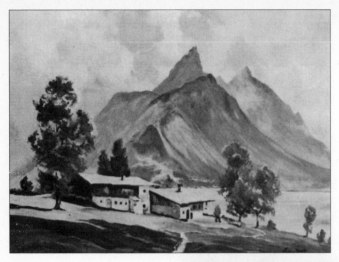

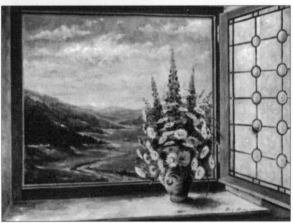

back of a bogus painting of an Alpine farm, supposedly done in 1931, was written in Hitler's hand, 'I was often a guest here and could see how the German farmer clung to the soil, despite the hardness of the work. Farmers in the Alps are especially bound to their poor soil.' Such messages were a warm-up for the later diaries. Although the artistic quality of these works was as crude as the political intent, they found ready buyers.

In fact, Kujau's technical ability as a forger was vastly outstripped by his imagination as a swindler. Not content to manufacture phoney paintings and sketches, he invented an event – an exhibition in Linz in 1936 at which Hitler's paintings as well as autographs and artefacts related to his career up to then had been placed on display. To add interest to the exhibit, Kujau manufactured letters by officials such as Himmler to go with the paintings and then, in a final touch, produced documentation for each work declaring that it had been 'loaned for the 1936 exhibition'. As time went on Kujau did not stop at fabricating paintings but added to their allure by dreaming up a variety of authentications. Certain works were alleged to have been presented by Hitler to one or another Nazi leader with an endorsement intended to show what a thoughtful Führer he could be. 'I extend my best wishes to you, my dear Goebbels, on your 36th birthday. Your Adolf Hitler, 23 October 1933', Hitler had purportedly written on the frame of a painting of flowers. Adding a further grace note, Kujau faked a document stating that Goebbels had permitted it to be shown in the Linz exhibition. Göring also received a painting on his birthday and he, too, graciously permitted it to be shown in Linz. Since Hitler never wrote on his paintings, such appended texts were in fact a gratuitous sign of forgery. Kujau also inadvertently revealed his handiwork by dating some works after 1918 and signing many of them 'Adolf Hitler', ignorant of the fact that Hitler is not known to have painted after the war and usually signed his works either 'A. H.' or 'A. Hitler'. One of Kujau's promoters was August Priesack, the primary editor of the original German edition of Price's book – he of the Nazi central party archive. Whether he was an accomplice or a credulous bystander is not clear.

Kujau's inventiveness was matched by the gullibility of collectors and historians. The supposedly definitive edition of Hitler's early holographs and documents, *Sämtliche Aufzeichnungen 1905–1924*, was filled with forged texts. A 1993 film, *Degenerate Art*, produced by the Los Angeles County Museum of Art and David Grubin Productions for the American Public Broadcasting Service, included a dozen works attributed to Hitler; all but two were Kujaus. Probably two-thirds of the paintings and sketches in Price's book are also forgeries, most of them by Kujau. It was only upon being unmasked as the fabricator of the 'Hitler Diaries' that Kujau admitted having forged these works. He then confused matters by claiming that certain of the paintings he had sold were genuine. Whether he was covering up some deeper swindle or had himself been taken in by a forger cleverer than he is not known.

THE
ART DICTATOR

10 THE MODERNIST ENEMY

ONE OF THE FAMILIAR CHAPTERS IN THE HISTORY of the Third Reich is the tragic destruction of Modernist works of art. That Hitler personally loathed Modernism but for four years did nothing about it and then, after holding it up to public mockery, exterminated it is all too well known. Less understood is why he hated it and why he felt he had no choice but to root it out. Was it primarily an affront to his personal taste? Or was it incompatible with his ideology? Did it have anything to do with anti-Semitism? How much of it had he ever seen? Why did he wait for four years to suppress it?

Hitler's aesthetic starting point was simple enough. The nineteenth century was the golden age of German cultural and intellectual achievement. It was the era, as he said many times, that had produced the greatest music composers of all time, the most outstanding poets and thinkers, the best architects, sculptors and painters. Then suddenly a broad cultural degeneration had set in; artists, instead of building on what had been achieved, broke violently with it. Although wavering on precisely when this had begun, he finally settled on the first decade of the century. 'Up to 1910 we displayed an extraordinarily high level in our artistic achievement,' he said. 'After that unfortunately everything went ever more precipitously downhill.'

That year marked an arbitrary but as good a dividing line in the evolution of the arts as any, and a remarkably diverse variety of artists likewise singled it out as the juncture when the old gave way to the new. 'In or about December, 1910,' Virginia Woolf famously wrote, 'human character changed.' In the visual arts it was the year when Kandinsky painted the first abstract and published *On the Spiritual in Art*, when Chagall arrived in Paris, when the 'Technical Manifesto of Futurist Painting' was issued, when Roger Fry's first post-Impressionist show took place in London. These events were no doubt well beyond Hitler's ken, however, and he never suggested why he fastened on to that date. But he clearly recognized that in the arts, as in the sciences, the world was undergoing revolutionary changes, finding radical new directions, techniques, ideas. It was this bewildering development that he was determined to halt and reverse.

Nor did he ever divulge when he made the acquaintance of the avant-garde. Munich was anything but a hotbed of Modernism. The Blaue Reiter group existed only briefly and made no local impact. But whether by seeing actual canvases or only published photographs, he must have had a vague impression by 1920 since he started haranguing against it in his earliest speeches. At first his message was simple. Modernist art was corrupting society; Jews were behind Modernist art; therefore society was being corrupted by Jews. In an article published in January 1921 entitled 'Stupidity or Crime', he argued that the German people were being intellectually poisoned and among the poisoners were painters. The value of their works, he jested, 'stands in inverse relation to the length of the perpetrators' hair'. To the average man in the street, he went on, it was incomprehensible not just that artists could produce such things but also that 'the manufacturers of such monstrosities lived in ateliers rather than insane asylums'. By 1923 he was identifying the perpetrators as Bolshevists, Cubists and Futurists but still ventured no opinion of their specific works. Even in *Mein Kampf* he referred to avant-garde painting simply as 'the products of spiritual degenerates or slimy swindlers' and 'the hallucinations of lunatics or criminals'. He took personal affront at the notion that anyone who did not like Modernism was 'a backward philistine' unable to understand products of an 'inner experience'. The reaction is interesting in revealing that he was at least aware of the Modernist concept of artistic perception as, in Paul Klee's phrase, 'a synthesis of external vision and inner contemplation' or Mondrian's notion of re-creating nature 'according to spirit'.

Such fugitive remarks barely conveyed thought content, much less a policy. The styles he mocked – Cubism, Dadaism, Futurism and Impressionism – were not, strictly speaking, those of the German avant-garde. Expressionism, Abstraction and other terms that did apply were none he ever used. 'Schwabing Decadent' – conceivably a reference to the Blaue Reiter – was the closest he came. And he had never so much as uttered the name of any Modernist painter. So when he came to power in January 1933 no one had any idea what he intended to do about Modernist painting. Obviously it was in trouble. But which artists were Modernists? What were the qualities that made a painting or a sculpture unacceptable? Was an artist's whole oeuvre in question or only certain of his works? No one knew, because Hitler had not said and did not know himself.

Nazi hotheads were a different story. They had been agitating against the avant-garde back in the 1920s. On the first occasion when they got into government – in the provincial administration of Thuringia in 1930 – they lost no time in removing from the Schloß Museum in Weimar works of such painters as Klee, Nolde, Kokoschka and Feininger. In Dessau they notoriously destroyed Oskar Schlemmer's frescoes in the Bauhaus stairwell. The National Socialist revolution, they proclaimed, was not just political but cultural; indeed, cultural above all. Once the party gained power nationally, that cultural-political revolution swept the country. In no time local party officials dismissed museum directors and curators – twenty in 1933 alone – along with art professors and art scholars. They were replaced by people known for their party rather than their artistic qualifications. The more fanatical administrators immediately removed avant-garde works from display and in some cases arranged exhibitions designed to hold them up to public ridicule. Such shows, advertised under rubrics such as 'Chamber of Art Horrors', 'Abomination Exhibitions', 'Images of Cultural Bolshevism' and so on were held in Stuttgart, Karlsruhe, Chemnitz, Dresden, Nuremberg, Breslau, Mannheim and nine other cities. In the following several years many galleries either stored their Modernist works or sold them abroad or closed entirely. Yet, attesting to the muddle of those early years, a few museums managed to preserve their collections and, with discretion, to exhibit and even add to them. Noted dealers in various cities also continued to show avant-garde works. As late as 1937 the Ferdinand Möller Gallery in Berlin had the audacity to hold a major exhibition of Nolde's works in celebration of the artist's seventieth birthday.

The predicament of the museum world was paralleled by dissension within the party at the national level. Abstract, non-objective painting and abstract, non-naturalistic sculpture were universally condemned, along with most post-1850 works by non-Germans. The disagreement largely arose over Expressionism in general and this or that individual artist in particular. There was a small movement in the party that defended Expressionism as an inherently Germanic art movement, heir to German Gothic, part of the national patrimony, the artistic counterpart to the National Socialist political revolution. Gottfried Benn, the eminent poet who became an early supporter of the New Order, argued that Expressionism represented 'Europe's last great artistic renaissance'. Echoing this view, the National Socialist Student Federation at Berlin University went so far in July of 1933 as to hold an exhibition under the title 'Thirty German Artists' which included works by Barlach, Heckel, Lehmbruck, Macke, Marc, Nolde, Rohlfs and Schmidt-Rottluff as well as younger, lesser-known painters. But that was going too far for the vast majority in the party, and the show was closed after three days. Confusion was worse confounded in March 1934 when Italian Futurists, led by Marinetti himself, put on an exhibition in Berlin. Hitler detested Futurism but permitted it because he was cultivating Marinetti's friend Mussolini. Göring, Goebbels and Rust had agreed to be members of the sponsoring committee but then found it prudent not to put in an appearance. A few party stalwarts argued that the exhibition demonstrated that good modern art could be good fascist art, but Rosenberg blasted it in the *Völkische Beobachter* as gross foreign interference. Nonetheless the battle to have Expressionist art accepted as National Socialist art went on right into 1935.

No less confused were painters and sculptors themselves. A good Nazi like Nolde expected to be honoured and was incredulous when he was not. Non-Nazis such as Barlach, Hofer, Schlemmer, Kandinsky and Kirchner tried to be accepted by the Nazi state and believed it was the result of a terrible mis-understanding that they were not. Some – Beckmann, Belling, Campendonk, Ernst, Feininger, Grosz, Klee, Kandinsky, Kirchner, Kokoschka, Schwitters and perhaps two dozen others – fled. Those who remained withdrew into a state of inner emigration and virtually disappeared from public life. They lost their positions in art academies, were not permitted to teach, to exhibit or sell their works and in most cases were forbidden to paint, forcing most of them into desperate financial straits. Pechstein fished, to have food to eat. Schlemmer went into shepherding and farming, later joining a number of other painters who worked in a lacquer factory in Wuppertal. Nolde withdrew to Frisia and surreptitiously produced his tiny 'unpainted pictures', as he called them. Barlach lost the home he had built. His sculptures and monuments were destroyed, and he with them. Their careers and lives ruined, a few, such as Kirchner, committed suicide. At least one painter was consigned to a con-centration camp. Two Jewish painters – Otto Freundlich and Felix Nussbaum – fled, but after German armies swept over Western Europe, they were found and sent to concentration camps, where they perished.

For years Hitler laid down no policy. As nature abhors a vacuum, however, so power abhors a void. With the exception of Göring and to a lesser extent Goebbels, Nazi leaders personally had little or no genuine feeling for the visual arts and, apart from Rosenberg, they had little or no interest in cultural ideology. Their passion was bureaucratic power. Rust claimed formal juris-diction over museums and art academies. Ley, as head of the Labour Front, controlled artists' professional organizations. Rosenberg had his grand title and the backing of various right-wing cultural groups. Goebbels's authority came both from his position as Propaganda Minister and head of the Reich Culture Chamber. Göring, engrossed in amassing a private art collection, was usually above these rivalries. Compounding the confusion, those who had Hitler's ear and whose artistic judgement Hitler valued were all from outside the hierarchy of party and government – Heinrich Hoffmann, Gerdy Troost, Arno Breker, Benno von Arent and, later, his art adviser, Hans Posse.

Plotting against bureaucratic rivals became almost an end in itself. Although Rust occasionally asserted himself, the main contenders were as always Goebbels and Rosenberg. Rosenberg wanted to wipe out Modernism; Goebbels wanted to encourage it. In fact, had Hitler read the latter's diaries, he would have been appalled. An entry in August 1924 praised Slevogt, van Gogh – 'marvellous, spare characterization' – Nolde – 'Wonderful colours' – and above all Barlach – 'the very essence of Expressionism'. His taste for the latter two artists never diminished, even to the point of keeping one of Barlach's statues in his office until 1937. Indeed, as chief propagandist he believed it would add to the lustre of the Third Reich as a culture state if they, along with Heckel, Schmidt-Rottluff and Munch, were sponsored as exemplars of Aryan, Nordic art. To Rosenberg's fury, he sent Munch a congratulatory telegram on his seventieth birthday in December 1933, praising him and his work for its Nordic spirit. He also planned to appoint Hans Weidemann, a young protégé of Nolde, Vice-President of the Reich Chamber of Visual Arts.

The contest was a curious one. Bureaucratically Rosenberg was doomed from the start, given Hitler's low opinion. Yet even though Goebbels had his chief's ear and was the more cunning, ideologically he did not stand a chance. The first indication came in a casual way as early as the summer of 1933 when Hitler visited Goebbels's new Berlin home. After remodelling the house, Speer hung several Nolde watercolours borrowed from the Berlin National Gallery. Goebbels and his wife were delighted. But when Hitler visited and saw them he was horrified. 'The pictures have to go at once,' the minister then told Speer, 'they are simply impossible.' In short, all the hand-wringing over whether this or that painter was an Expressionist and whether Expressionism was in essence Nordic and Nazi was pointless. What Benn or Rosenberg or Goebbels or anyone else said or thought was of no account. All that mattered was what Hitler thought. He hated Nolde's work and that was that. He further instructed Goebbels to get rid of Weidemann.

An incident does not amount to a policy and Hitler was unwilling to go further than to set vague guidelines. In the first of his annual speeches on culture at the Nuremberg rally in September 1933 he firmly rejected the notion that any type of Modernism might be acceptable: 'We must not permit incompetents and charlatans suddenly to change sides and enlist under the banner of the new state as if nothing had happened. . . .' That closed the door to the Kirchners and others who wanted to be accepted in the Nazi Reich. When dissension continued, he took the occasion of the following year's rally to go further. The party, he said, faced two dangers. On the one hand there were the 'Cubists, Futurists, Dadaists and others'. They were 'saboteurs of art', 'either imbeciles or shrewd impostors', 'sensationalists', 'plasterers' and 'canvas smearers'. Once the National Socialist movement had dealt with them, 'it would be as though they had never existed'. On the other hand there were those who were 'backward-looking' and had a 'quaintly olde-German' notion of art. They lived in some 'laughable Germanic dream world' and lacked the slightest idea of what the National Socialist revolution was all about. 'So, today, they propose railway stations in original German renaissance style, street signs and typewriting in old Gothic letters, song texts in the manner of Walther von der Vogelweide, dress fashions in the style of Gretchen and Faust . . . and shields and crossbows as weapons of defence.' These people had no role to play and should give up the illusion they had, he concluded. Thus did Hitler cut both Goebbels and Rosenberg down to size while ensuring they remained rivals.

During his first four years in power, Hitler took only one concrete action regarding the visual arts. In June 1933 he received a group of anti-Modernists, including Paul Schultze-Naumburg, who showed him photos of the collection in the Kronprinzen-Palais, a branch of the National Gallery. With some 500 Modernist works, this was the world's premier museum of the avant-garde. Hitler was suitably outraged and gave orders for the director, Ludwig Justi, to be sacked and the paintings to be removed from display, though 'not destroyed but preserved in special rooms as monuments of a period of German degeneration'. With equal amounts of optimism and naïvete, gallery officials thought they might get by if they exhibited only the very best of their Modernist works. To do the deed they called in the director of the Halle municipal museum, Alois Schardt, in the hope that his reputation as a promoter of 'Nordic art' might appease Nazi critics. Schardt made his choices and, to minimize provocation, tucked them away on the top floor while installing works by Caspar David Friedrich and some of Hitler's other favourite Romantics on the floors below. The ploy failed. Rust forbade the public to view the collection and fired Schardt, who fled to America. Still adamant, museum officials passed the poisoned cup to Eberhard Hanfstaengl, head of the municipal art collection in Munich. Since he came from conservative southern Germany and was therefore no friend of Modernism, it was hoped that he could offer cover. The new director consigned fifty important paintings to storage but reopened the galleries with a limited selection, still demurely installed in the upper rooms. On this basis the museum continued for several years to exhibit and even to acquire contemporary works.

Strange to say, Hitler visited the collection and even stranger to say did nothing about it. The episode occurred in early 1934 when he went to the museum to see a special exhibition of works by Karl Leipold, a protégé of Rudolf Hess. After putting in an appearance there, he insisted on visiting the rest of the museum and eventually came upon the gallery's avant-garde works.

Hitler at a 'Chamber of Horrors' exhibition in Dresden in August 1935.
The show, mostly works from the Dresden City Museum, was organized by
the head of the Dresden Art Academy. The larger portrait was by Erich Heckel,
the smaller by Lea Grundig.

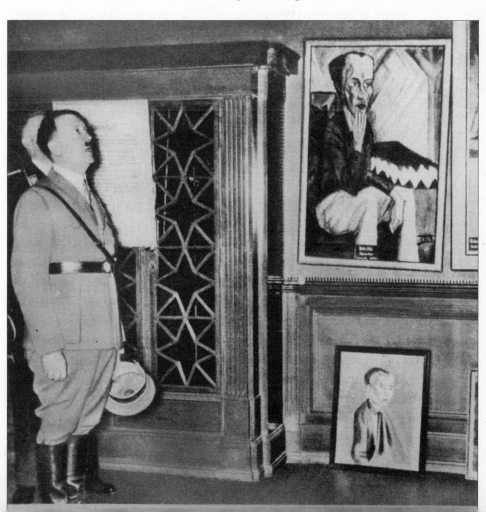

He winced but said nothing. In fact, the visit turned out to be more an architectural field trip. What excited him and provoked his only comment was the vista, visible from the windows of the upper galleries, of Schinkel's great classical buildings in the centre of Berlin. It was not until nearly two years later that Hitler again raised the subject of the Kronprinzen-Palais collection when at lunch one day he spoke of 'cleaning out all that rubbish'. But again nothing came of it.

Hitler apparently had his first really good look at Modernist canvases during a visit to Dresden in August 1935 when he toured the local 'Images of Decadence in Art' exhibition that had been put together two years earlier. He found the show such an exemplary display of Modernist horrors that he ordered it to tour the country. Several weeks later it went to Nuremberg and was shown in connection with that year's party rally. The event, along with the subsequent opening of the House of German Art, offered Hitler platforms at last to spell out what he so detested in this 'cultural perfume'. One trait was its sheer 'ugliness': 'It is not the function of art to wallow in dirt for dirt's sake, never its task to paint men only in a state of decomposition, to draw cretins as the symbol of motherhood, to picture hunch-backed idiots as representatives of manly strength.' Linked to this was the perversion of naturalism: 'There really are men who in principle feel meadows to be blue, the heavens green, clouds sulphur-yellow – or as they prefer to say "experience" them in this way.' Still another fault was its primitivism: 'It is either impudent effrontery or incomprehensible stupidity publicly to exhibit today works which ten or twenty thousand years ago might have been made by a man of the Stone Age. They talk of primitive art, but they forget it is not the function of art to go backward . . . .' Its style was contemptible: 'Theirs is a small art – small in form and substance – and at the same time intolerant of the masters of the past and the rivals of the present.'

To make matters worse, changes of style were never-ending: 'Just as in fashions one must wear "modern" clothes whether beautiful or not, so the great masters of the past have been decried. These facile daubers of paint are but the products of a day; yesterday, non-existent; today, modern; tomorrow, out of date.' Additionally, Modernism lacked national character: '. . . Art was said to be "an international experience", and so its intimate association with the nation has been stifled; it was said that there was no such thing as the art of a nation or of a race – there was only the art of a certain period.' And it was elitist, without meaning for the general public: 'An art which cannot count on the readiest and most heartfelt agreement of the great mass of the people, an art which must rely upon the support of small cliques, is intolerable.'

Leaving aside personal taste and racism, Hitler spoke true – truer than he knew – in analysing Modernism and its place in the cultural crisis of the time. Modernists differed significantly in their artistic intentions; avant-garde painters did not always work in the same direction as their counterparts in music, literature or architecture. But by and large Modernists were guilty as charged, even if the prosecution's case was as exaggerated and contorted as it accused Modernist paintings themselves of being.

Modernists were indeed revolutionaries. They rejected the notion that art must be rooted in a nation's history, and they deliberately sought change and experimentation. 'To every age its own art' was the founding principle of the Vienna Secession in 1897. It was permissible for art to be 'ugly' and to emulate the blunt energy of 'primitivism'. They were more concerned for truth and doubts than for beauty and certainties, more interested in questions than in answers, more anxious to communicate feelings – Hitler's 'inner experience' – than to portray visual reality. In the face of the Germans' consuming passion for order, Modernists celebrated disorder and uncertainty. Far from shunning the epithet of elitist, they raised it to a high principle that artists were independent of society and that culture was a sphere unto itself. The gulf that had opened between Modernists and the public was not their fault; it was the public that had lost its aesthetic sense and gone its own way. Nothing could have been more foreign to the Modernists than the idea that they had an obligation to society. Inculcating national pride or providing the public with security, beauty and joy, not to mention a refuge from life's travails, was not what they had in mind.

In seeking to obliterate Modernist art forms, Hitler was obviously imposing a personal artistic preference. The straightforward realism of most of the nineteenth-century German school was what he admired and what he believed to be the culmination of everything worthwhile in the visual arts. In its simplest form it was the style he had painted in. It was the style that he could understand and that the mass of the public could grasp. But why did the 'ugliness' of a Modernist canvas trouble him? Why did the exuberant play with colour grate? Why was the raw power of primitive art disturbing? Why did he see obscenity in irony? Simply to ask the questions is to make the answers obvious and leads to the very heart of his hatred of the avant-garde. For him Modernism was intolerable because it was thought-provoking, unconventional, uncomfortable, shocking, abstract, pessimistic, distorted, cynical, enigmatic, disorderly, freakish. It was exactly what you do not want if what you want for yourself – and for your nation – is an escape into a world of security, conventional beauty, conformity, simplicity, reassurance. He did not put it that way. What he said was '*Deutsch sein heißt klar sein*' – to be German means to be clear – a gnomic aphorism referring 'not only to subject matter but also to the clarity of rendering sentiments'. Paradoxically it was the very realism of Modernism – not in the manner of his nineteenth-century favourites but in the metaphorical representation of the unease and terror of modern life – that made it unbearable to him. He wanted art to provide escape from pain, not confrontation with it. Ultimately the issue was not simply one of artistic taste but even more of social eschatology. He had no *political* choice but to oppose it. Hitler knew, as Plato knew, that art and society are moved by similar forces and that art not only reflects but promotes social upheaval.

Sad to say, Hitler's antipathy to Modernist painting was broadly shared in time and space, and even his very terms of abuse were common currency. Roger Fry's post-Impressionist exhibition in London had been variously likened by British critics to 'another Gunpowder Plot, an attempt to plant a bomb under the institutions of art', 'a widespread plot to destroy the whole fabric of European painting', 'the exact analogue to the anarchical movements in the political world', 'another form of madness'. The art critic of *The Times* explicitly labelled it 'degenerate'. But in Germany, where politics and culture were historically intertwined, Modernism was denounced not just by some critics but also by authorities of the state. In 1901, after ordering the director of the Berlin National Gallery to be discharged for buying a large number of Modernist paintings, the head of the Second Reich – Wilhelm II – declared, in words strikingly similar to those later uttered by the leader of the Third: 'Art is not art if it transgresses the laws and barriers laid down by me. The word "liberty" is often misused and can lead to licence and presumption. . . . Art which merely portrays misery is a sin against the German people. . . .'

A great irony of the attack on Modernism by the Kaiser and the Führer is that it was provoked precisely by the fact that Germany was in its vanguard. Not only were there more Modernist painters of note in Germany than elsewhere, there were more art museums collecting avant-garde works. In 1897 Berlin's National Gallery was the first museum anywhere to buy a Cézanne; the Folkwang Museum in Essen was one of the earliest promoters of Gauguin and van Gogh; some fifty other museums followed their lead. Through the inter-war period, while British and French galleries refused Modernist works, even when offered as gifts, on the ground that such works, as the director of the Tate said, 'might exercise a disturbing and even deleterious influence upon our younger painters', German museums were steadily expanding their collections. Their holdings were consequently the foremost in the world, supplemented by a number of extremely important private collections. The total number of Modernist works in Germany probably reached an impressive 18,000.

Hitler was only speaking the truth when he insisted that, as a result of being captured by Modernism, the arts had lost their mass appeal and culture had been detached from the experience of all but a small minority. Popular response to the avant-garde ran the gamut from indifference and incomprehension to hostility. The great majority of German painters and sculptors themselves were traditionalists to whom any form of Modernism was foreign in every sense of the word. This was particularly true in southern Germany, as reflected in the annual summer exhibitions in Munich's Glass Palace. Of nearly a thousand painters who showed there in 1930, for instance, only a dozen or so could be considered Modernists.

Hitler's antipathy, however, had two unique elements. One was the centrality of anti-Semitism. The association of Jews with Modernism had no basis in fact. Chagall apart, there were no Jewish painters of note and only five or six minor ones, none the equivalent in painting to Schoenberg in music or Erich Mendelsohn in architecture. In truth, he tacitly recognized this fact. His speeches condemned not Jewish painters but Jewish influence on painting, which had made itself felt through art commentary in the Jewish-controlled press. He once explained to Christa Schroeder what he was driving at. Jews knew very well, he said, that Modernist painting was worthless and decadent. But they bought it and made a tremendous fuss about it; as a result prices were inflated and they then sold it and made huge profits. With these they acquired valuable Old Masters for themselves. He believed this was borne out when private Jewish art collections began being seized in the late 1930s. 'What is so remarkable,' he told Goebbels, 'is that Jews – as is now becoming evident from the confiscation of Jewish property – spent all the money that they swindled from people for [Modernist] kitsch on outstandingly good and valuable pictures.'

The other noteworthy element was the depth of his hatred and the strength of his resolve to obliterate it. Stalin banned and burned art he disliked but remained personally aloof and rarely, if ever, spoke of it. Hitler could not stop railing against it. The 'manufacturers of this nuisance', he told the party rally in 1935, were 'incompetents, cheats and madmen', adding that 'in the Third Reich we have no intention of letting them loose on the people'. Their activities were criminal, suiting them for a mental asylum or

prison. Two years later, in an address at the opening of the House of German
Art, he appeared to threaten a somewhat different alternative – imprisonment
if not sterilization:

> . . . In the name of the German people it is my duty to prevent these
> pitiable unfortunates, who plainly suffer from defects of vision, from
> attempting to persuade others by their chatter that these faults of
> observation are indeed realities and from presenting them as 'art'. There
> are only two possibilities. Either these 'artists' really do see things this way
> and believe what they paint – in which case one has to ask how the
> defective vision arose and, if it is hereditary, leave it to the Interior
> Minister to prevent such a ghastly defect from perpetuating itself. Or, if
> they do *not* believe in the reality of such impressions but are seeking to
> impose their notions through humbug, then it is a matter for a criminal
> court.

In delivering this speech, according to Paul Rave, acting director of the
Berlin National Gallery, 'his manner of speaking became more agitated, to a
degree that had never been heard even in a political tirade. He foamed with
rage as though out of his mind, his mouth slavering, so that even his
entourage stared at him in horror.'

What is puzzling is that for all his volcanic anger Hitler shrank from
doing anything about it. When he did eventually act, it was at the
prompting of others. So it was not until October 1936, with all the foreign
visitors to the Olympic games gone, that he at last agreed to Rust's proposal
to close the Modernist galleries at the Kronprinzen-Palais. And not until the
middle of the following year did he at last take action on the national level.
Even then, he followed the lead of Goebbels. In a reversal remarkable even
for such a cynical opportunist, this closet Modernist resolved to goad the
Führer into action. Although the reason for the minister's volte-face is
uncertain – none of his biographers has provided an explanation – it is
generally assumed that Goebbels feared being outflanked by Rust.
Consequently he went to Hitler with a suggestion not just to ban Modernist
art but to make a grand public spectacle of it. His diary entry for 5 June
reads: 'Horrible examples of art Bolshevism have been brought to my
attention. Now I am going to take action . . . . I want to arrange an exhibit
in Berlin of art from the period of degeneracy. So that people can see and
learn to recognize it.' Up to then, exhibitions of objectionable art had been
local affairs, arranged by gallery officials. Here was a proposal by a
government minister to drag it out of all the country's museums and, in a

great public display and with the sanction of the state, to hold it up to the derision of the crowds.

Hitler, always regarded as the evil genius behind the notorious degenerate art exhibition, was thus a passive figure. In fact, he reacted cautiously to Goebbels's proposal and did not go along with it for several weeks. Then an idea occurred to him. By holding the exhibition in Munich rather than in Berlin and mounting it concurrently with the opening of the long-planned Great German Art Exhibition in the new House of German Art, he could produce the most dramatic confrontation in history between conflicting styles of art. He therefore approved the proposal and on 30 June signed a decree authorizing Goebbels to help himself to all 'German degenerate art since 1910, both painting and sculpture', which was held in public collections anywhere in Germany. Degenerate art was defined as works that 'insult German feeling, or destroy or confuse natural form or simply reveal an absence of adequate manual and artistic skill'. The wording of the decree was pure Hitler – 1910 was the year he considered the critical artistic turning point and the definition of degeneracy echoed the words of his public denunciations. The confiscations themselves were left to Adolf Ziegler, the newly appointed head of the Reich Chamber of Visual Arts and a painter of svelte asexual female nudes. Ziegler and his assistants – termed by an art historian as 'five ignorant fanatics' – threw themselves into their job with such enthusiasm that they could not restrain themselves from going beyond their mandate and gathered up works prior to 1910 as well as paintings by Picasso, Matisse and other non-Germans.

To his amazement, Goebbels found that his project aroused widespread hostility. Speer, who had initially offered to help, turned against him, as did even a few members of his own staff. 'Opposition on all sides,' the Propaganda Minister admitted. 'In the face of all the animosity, the Führer stands solidly behind me,' he commented on another occasion. Actually, the Führer wavered and not until the very last minute did he allow the exhibition to go ahead. Preparations were consequently haphazard and frenetic. In a mere two weeks between 600 and 700 works from around Germany were seized, dispatched to Munich and hung. The show opened on 19 July 1937 with some 650 works by 112 'art stutterers' from thirty-two public museums on display. It included examples from all the major schools of German painting and sculpture – Expressionism, Verism, Abstraction, Bauhaus, Dada, New Objectivity – and all the major artists. Although he had inspected the collection beforehand, Hitler did not deign to put in a public appearance once the exhibition opened. But he inaugurated it vicariously the day before in a raging speech. '. . . The

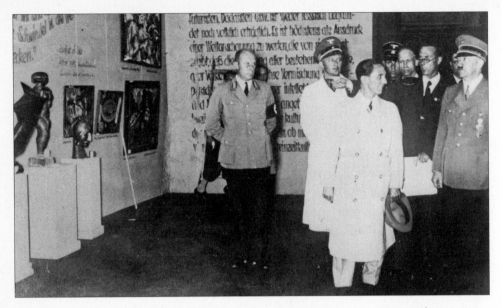

A pleased Goebbels leads a po-faced Hitler through the 'degenerate art' show in Munich on 17 July 1937. Even among the organizers, the show was controversial up to the very last, with ferocious disagreements over which paintings to include – a debate that went on beyond the opening.

end of madness in German art and, with it, the cultural destruction of our people has begun,' he proclaimed. 'From this moment we shall conduct a merciless war against the remnants of our cultural disintegration.' On he sputtered, reviling 'the cliques of chatterboxes, dilettantes and art swindlers'.

Like enemy prisoners being thrown to the lions in the Colosseum, the victims were to be seen and mocked by the crowd before being consumed. The show was designed to demonstrate that Modernist art was not simply ugly, indecent and deranged but that it also directly assaulted traditional social mores by disparaging motherhood, military heroism, religion and whatever was healthy, clean and chaste. Hitler's criteria – post-1910 German works – were generally followed, though stretched to include such adoptive Germans as Chagall and Jawlensky, and two non-Germans, Mondrian and Munch. The work by the good Nordic Munch caused such ideological indigestion that after a few days the room where it hung was closed. The paintings, presented in a way to heighten ridicule, were not so much displayed as plastered helter-skelter on the walls, though this may have resulted partly from the haste with which the show was assembled. To leave no doubt about their iniquity, the works were labelled with such propagandistic slogans as 'madness becomes a method', 'nature as seen by sick minds' and 'an insult to

German womanhood'. Ensuring that no one could have the slightest doubt about the iniquity of the works, it is said that actors were sent to the exhibit to make raucous fun of what they saw.

It was the biggest blockbuster art show of all time. Hitler ordered that entry should be without charge and encouraged the public to attend. And attend it did. One million people went in the first six weeks alone and more than two million in the remaining six months in Munich. Another million or so saw the exhibition when it travelled to twelve other cities between February 1938 and April 1941. By all accounts spectators went to bury, not to praise. 'It became increasingly obvious to me that most people had come to see the exhibition with the intention of disliking everything,' it was later commented. Some non-Nazis, some non-Germans also applauded. A Boston art critic commented, 'There are probably plenty of people – art lovers – in Boston, who will side with Hitler in this particular purge.' The Führer was enormously pleased with the popular response. It appeared to prove his point that Modernism was an elitist phenomenon that had lost meaning for the great mass of the public. It further seemed to support his belief in 'the people as the judge of art'. So gratified was he, in fact, that at his direction a pamphlet with illustrations of the works accompanied by hostile commentary was published and widely circulated. He had achieved his purpose. The event was a stunning demonstration of his power to crush what he opposed. In so doing, he brought to an end the most exciting school of painting and sculpture in modern German history.

In his pre-exhibition stroll through the rooms of the Archaeological Institute where the works were displayed, Hitler professed outrage at what he saw. It

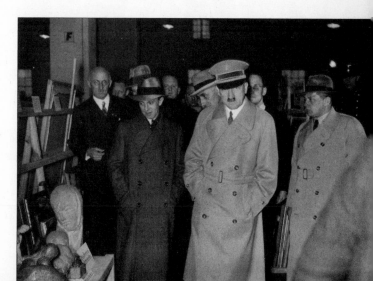

Hitler at the Köpenicker Straße storage site in Berlin on 13 January 1938 to inspect confiscated, 'degenerate' artworks. From left, *Franz Hofmann, an assistant to Goebbels, Goebbels, Hitler and Heinrich Hoffmann.* On the foreground left is *Wilhelm Lehmbruck's statue,* Mother and Child.

may be that up to then he had no good idea of the full gamut of Modernist painting or the extent of the holdings of German museums. Ziegler's hasty and haphazard round of confiscations still left dozens of galleries filled with Modernist works. Now that the public had demonstrated its disgust, Hitler must have concluded he could exploit its sentiment and finish the job. 'In this hour I affirm my unalterable resolve in this, as in the realm of political confusion, to remove all the claptrap from artistic life in Germany,' he declared a few days later. Within the week he issued an order through Goebbels which authorized Ziegler to remove 'all those products of the age of decadence' from every museum in the country.

And so, 'between the months of August and September 1937', an

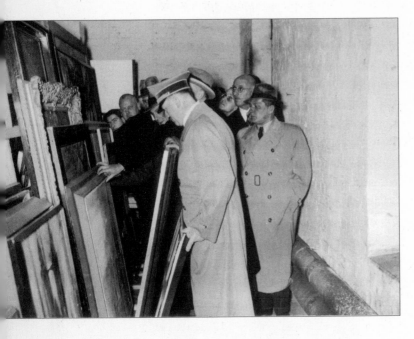

Early in 1939 the Köpenicker Straße depot was turned into a storage site for grain. Remaining works were either returned to previous owners and museums, sold, incinerated or transferred to a castle at Niederschönhausen outside Berlin. In 1943 the remnants were moved to the basement of the Propaganda Ministry and eventually disappeared.

art historian has written, 'German museums were despoiled of their entire holdings of modern art.' By the time the confiscation committees finished, they had impounded almost 5000 paintings and 12,000 drawings, prints and sculptures – the works of some 1400 artists, among them Barlach, Beckmann, Campendonk, Corinth, Dix, Feininger, Grosz, Heckel, Hofer, Kandinsky, Kirchner, Klee, Kokoschka, Kollwitz, Kubin, Lehmbruck, Marc, Marcks, Nolde, Pechstein, Rohlfs, Schmidt-Rottluff and a few works of the Austrians Klimt and Schiele as well. Every museum lost all its Modernist works. By March of 1938 the confiscation committees were able to declare that the purge of Germany's galleries was complete. Although some private collections were ransacked by local Nazi officials, except in the case of Jews these were generally left untouched.

While some foreign museum directors and art critics looked on in helpless dismay, the outside world took relatively little note of this cultural catastrophe. But there was one response that left Hitler enraged. In the summer of 1938 Herbert Read and a number of other art critics organized an exhibition at the New Burlington Galleries in London of some 270 works by artists proscribed in Germany. Under the rubric '20th-Century German Art' and with such sponsors as Picasso and Le Corbusier, the show was opened by Augustus John and addressed in a notable speech, 'My Theory of Painting', by Max Beckmann, who defended the German avant-garde while implicitly deriding the sort of painting produced in the Third Reich. The event was reported to Berlin by the German embassy and so incensed Hitler that he responded twice. At the opening of the second Great German Art Exhibition a short time later, he poured scorn on works of these exiled 'tribes of the Dada and Cubi' and insisted that there was no place for such 'Neanderthal men of art' in Germany. A few weeks afterwards at the annual Nuremberg rally, he followed a different tack, condemning what he labelled 'Jewish, Marxist, democratic, internationalist circles' for their criticism:

> Naturally it is not important what attitude, if any, foreigners take towards our cultural achievements since we have no doubt that creative cultural works cannot be understood, much less appreciated, by individuals or races unrelated to ourselves. Therefore we do not seek to make German art and culture suit the tastes of international Jewry.

Despite the defiant words, Hitler had been wounded. Even he could not believe that the Third Reich was a cultural model for the world.

Inevitably the question had to be resolved of what to do with the confiscated works, which had been stowed at a depot in the Köpenickerstraße in Berlin. In the company of Goebbels and his assistant, Franz Hofmann, Hitler spent two hours inspecting them in January 1938. 'The result is devastating,' Goebbels recorded. 'Not a single work finds favour. The Führer also wants confiscation without compensation. We want to exchange some of them abroad for decent Old Masters.' At Hitler's instruction a committee was set up under the Propaganda Minister's direction to dispose of the works. A short time later it occurred to Göring not simply to exchange but to sell some of the paintings abroad and buy Old Masters with the proceeds – precisely what Hitler had accused Jewish dealers of having conspired to do. Since Germany badly needed hard currency, Hitler authorized straightforward sales. 'We hope to be able to earn some money from this garbage,' Goebbels noted in his diary. Hitler lost no time in trading works of Corinth, Liebermann and others for Italian works, later remarking that he 'was royally pleased to have come into possession of some Old Masters so cheaply'. Göring grabbed for himself a number of the paintings – works of van Gogh, Munch, Marc, Cézanne, Gauguin and Signac – which he sold for his own benefit. He also used his international connections to sell and barter others he did not want.

Even though earning foreign exchange was the motive for sales, some works were disposed of for almost literally nothing just to get them out of the country – one Beckmann canvas went for $20 and another for a single Swiss franc. In the same spirit Hitler authorized the auction of some of the best paintings, 125 of which went on the block in Lucerne in June 1939 in the notorious sale by the Galerie Fischer. These, too, sold at absurd prices – one of Matisse's finest works for SFr9100 and van Gogh's self-portrait for SFr175,000. Goebbels later claimed that the purchasers did not really like the stuff, having bought it only to spite Hitler. In America, he claimed, these paintings 'were being sold by the kilo and were going for ten cents a kilo'. In reality foreign collectors were reluctant to participate in what they saw as a sacrilege.

Much of the total residue – 1004 paintings and sculptures and 3825 watercolours, drawings and prints – was said to have been incinerated in the courtyard of Berlin's central fire station in March 1939. In his final report to Hitler on 4 July, Goebbels stated that almost all the 16,000 confiscated artworks had been destroyed, stored, traded or sold, with sales bringing in £10,000, $45,000 and SFr 80,000, and trades accounting for Old Masters worth more than 130,000 marks. 'Degenerate art has brought us a lot of foreign exchange,' he gloated. 'It will go into the pot for war expenses, and after the war will be devoted to the purchase of art.' Some sales and trades went on until mid-1941, realizing a total of about 1 million marks. When it was over at least 5000 works had been lost.

11 THE FAILURE OF NATIONAL SOCIALIST REALISM

SIMULTANEOUSLY AND ACROSS THE STREET FROM the degenerate show – a hundred yards away and a hundred years behind – the works of the first of the annual Great German Art Exhibitions were displayed in the House of German Art. As rival to the degenerate exhibit, it was to expose the best of Third Reich painting and sculpture, and so demonstrate the triumph of true German art over the odious works of the Modernists. As Hitler said in his speech formally inaugurating the event, 'When we celebrated the laying of the cornerstone of this building four years ago, we were all aware that we had to lay not only the cornerstone of a new home but also the foundation of a new and genuine German art.'

The two exhibitions of July 1937 were intended to mark a high point in Hitler's cultural programme. Their precise juxtaposition, physically and chronologically, was to reveal Hitler's didactic purpose to perfection. Germany and the world were to see and compare good and bad art, and to imbibe Hitler's aesthetic judgements. The annual official exhibitions would teach visitors to admire the painting and sculpture that Hitler admired. 'When people pass through these galleries they will recognize in me their own spokesman and counsellor,' he said at the opening ceremony. 'They will draw a sigh of relief and express their joyous agreement with this purification of art.' Such words, along with Hitler's ostentatious promotion of the exhibitions, gave rise to two assumptions that have been commonly held from that day to this – that the art of the Third Reich was 'Nazi art' and that Hitler liked it. In reality neither was true. From the start, Hitler considered the shows a fiasco.

Originally Hitler had intended the House of German Art to exhibit works of an entire millennium – '1000 Years of German Painting and Sculpture', it was to be called. But by 1937 he had decided to establish that museum elsewhere and to restrict the Munich exhibition to contemporary works. His aim was not simply to put them on show but to make possible their purchase by middle income families. In that way he would enrich painters while taking

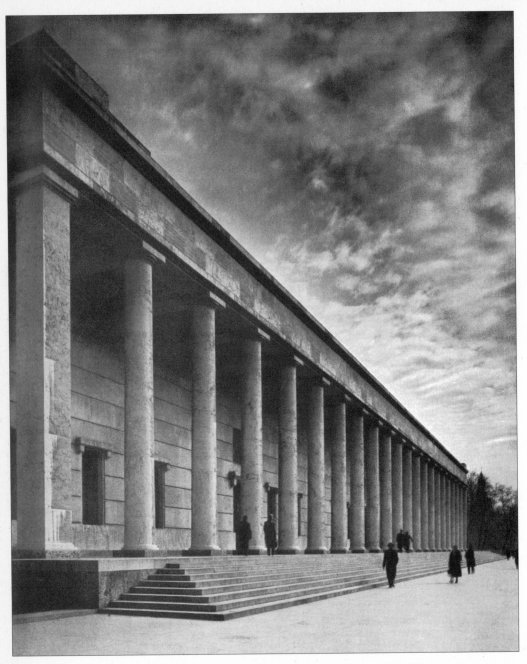

The House of German Art was described by Hitler as 'the first beautiful building
of the new Reich' and 'a temple for genuine and eternal German art'. In designing the structure in 1933,
Hitler already revealed his plan for eventual war by providing for an air raid shelter in the basement.
Irreverent locals nicknamed the building 'the Athens railway station' and 'a sausage stand'.

his ideal of artistic beauty into the average German home. Contributions had been solicited from any artist of German nationality including, at the Führer's express direction, persons of German ancestry living abroad. The response was staggering, with an outpouring of more than 15,000 entries. A jury of pseudo-professionals, including Adolf Ziegler and Gerdy Troost, selected some 900 of these for exhibition and invited the Führer to a preview. Hitler went, he saw, he exploded. Of the many descriptions of the lurid scene, Goebbels's was the least colourful but the most concise:

> The sculptures are all right but some paintings are a downright catastrophe. Pieces were hung that made one positively cringe. . . . The Führer was beside himself in rage. Frau Prof. Troost fought with the courage of a lioness but made no impact at all on the Führer.

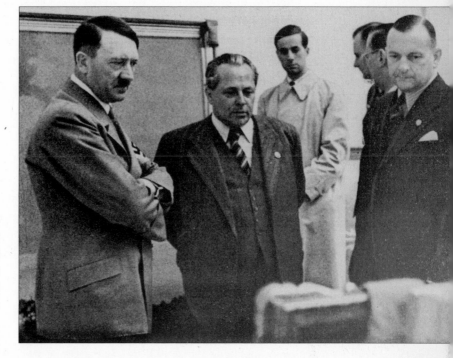

Hitler and Heinrich Hoffmann choosing paintings for the Great German Art Exhibition. Karl Kolb, Director of the House of German Art, looks on.

Years later Gerdy Troost maintained that the selection had angered Hitler not only because it included works with slightly Modernist qualities but also because it excluded anything he liked. The lioness would have nothing to do with those he picked out of the refusés. 'These are grey. They have already been refused by our grandmothers,' she told him. When he questioned a reject, she replied, 'It's impossible. Too sweet for our exhibition.' Unwilling to alter her judgement, she went on to say, 'And since you can't approve our selection and have a completely different opinion, I resign this moment as a member of the jury.'

The real cause of Hitler's fury went far deeper than acceptances and rejections. It was now all too obvious that, contrary to his confident prediction, National Socialism had failed to inspire great painting. So disappointed and humiliated did he feel that he saw no alternative except to cancel the show. 'These paintings demonstrate,' he fumed, 'that we in Germany have no artists whose works are worthy of being hung in this splendid building.' But when his old crony Heinrich Hoffmann interjected that among all the submissions there had to be a goodly number of acceptable works, he relented and allowed him to try to put together an acceptable exhibit. 'But I don't like any sloppy paintings where you cannot tell which is top or bottom. . . .' Thereupon he dismissed the selection panel, placed Hoffmann in charge and stomped off to the Berghof. Hoffmann made his choices, which Hitler then reviewed, reinstating some that had been excluded while 'furiously rejecting' eighty others, commenting in disgust that he would not tolerate 'unfinished paintings' – coincidentally the precise phrase that had been used a century earlier in Paris to condemn the first Impressionist works. The appointment of Hoffmann, an alcoholic and a cretin who knew little more about painting than did the average plumber, had appalled the artistic community. 'But,' as Hoffmann said in his own defence, 'I knew Hitler's wishes and I knew what would appeal to him.' His selections, according to Goebbels, left Gerdy Troost 'in tears'.

Under these circumstances – with the museum built and the exhibition already arranged with great fanfare – Hitler decided to grit his teeth and let the show go on. But his disillusionment was so great, according to Otto Dietrich, that he could only reluctantly acknowledge it even to his intimates and 'jealously guarded it from the ears of the public'. By the time of the following year's exhibition he could restrain himself no longer and at the opening ceremony publicly confessed that he had been so shocked by the character of the paintings the year before that he had considered giving up the whole idea of ever holding an annual art show. 'In the case of many pictures it was obvious that the artist had confused the two exhibitions, the 1937 exhibition of German art and the concurrent one of degenerate art,' he declared. Of the current year's show, the best he could say was the most damning of faint praise: 'A decent general average of achievement had been secured.' As for painters, he admitted there did not seem to be any 'genius of permanent significance'. His disappointment was such that he was still ranting about it to his staff in March 1942, even while otherwise preoccupied with the Russian campaign.

Later exhibitions took place without serious problems, though Hitler always took care to see the collection before it was opened to the public. Submissions were first reviewed by Hoffmann who, arbitrarily and with a mere glance – though without any regard for the artist's political views or party membership – culled those he considered worthy to be looked upon by the Führer. These were then provisionally hung in the galleries for Hitler to inspect. Dietrich described the scene as '. . . Hitler, going the rounds for hours, would let fall one personal opinion after the next upon the paintings, thereby deciding the fate of the artists. . . . He had in effect nominated himself as the pope of art. The things he liked would be exhibited; what he rejected was second-rate, and therefore the artist was also second-rate. The works that were not shown to Hitler at all were not even considered art.' That summed it up. It was strictly a Hitler, not a Nazi party, affair. It is revealing of the extent to which he kept decisions about the arts out of the hands of party leaders that Göring, Goebbels, Rust, Rosenberg and Ley had no role in these shows except to put in an appearance at the opening ceremony. Hitler would have been as contemptuous of their praise as, if they had dared, of their criticism.

Whatever his disappointments, Hitler made the event a grand spectacle, a veritable cultural mardi gras, liberally financed by money from his personal cultural fund. He opened the annual 'Day of German Art' with an inevitable address on the arts and then inaugurated a monumental parade-pageant dedicated to the theme of '2000 Years of German Culture', which had reached its culmination in the Third Reich. More than 6000 marchers, half of them clad in Nordic costumes, accompanied or drew twenty-six gigantic floats, many of them iconic representations of Nordic tradition. Some 500 'Nordic' animals – horses, dogs and even falcons – participated as well. At the end, to remind spectators that lyre and sword belonged together in National Socialist Germany, there was a march-past of military units.

Although the exhibition travelled each year to Berlin and other cities, the Munich opening was the highlight. It was held every summer through 1944 and drew a sizeable audience – 600,000 in 1937 and, after dropping off in later years, rising during the war to 847,000 in 1942. Hitler attended at least the preview and every year he bought paintings – 202 in 1937; 372 in 1938; 264 in 1939; 202 in 1940; 121 in 1941; 48 in 1943 and an undetermined number in 1942 and 1944. He usually ignored paintings glorifying National Socialism in favour of simple landscapes and works Speer described as 'conventionally beautiful'. Each year as many as 150 portraits of himself were submitted; with a single exception – Knirr's painting of him in military uniform – these were done from photographs. He permitted only one to be included in any year and selected it himself. 'Armoured Adolf', as Hubert Lanzinger's well-known portrait of Hitler in a suit of armour was impiously called, was his choice for 1938. He bought on a grand scale, spending nearly 600,000 marks in 1937 and by 1942 more than a million. Financially and in every other sense he was the great patron of Third Reich art. And yet he disliked the lot. In Christa Schroeder's words, 'He did not really care for contemporary German artists. Even though he did not like them, he nonetheless bought a large number of their paintings simply to encourage artists in their work. "Our artists today," he said, "will never show the care and patience which was the case with painters in the great artistic eras."' What had gone wrong?

Hitler had fallen victim to his belief that his New Order, in destroying 'Modernist, Bolshevist, Jewish influences', would produce an atmosphere in which great art inevitably emerged. 'I am convinced that, after a few years under National Socialist leadership of the state and nation, the Germans will produce much more and greater work in the cultural domain than has been accomplished during the recent decades of the Jewish regime.' So he assured the party at the 1935 Nuremberg rally. Given the very nature of creativity, however, there was no possibility that 'art made tongue-tied by authority', in the Bard's phrase, could flourish. The spontaneous, inventive, questing spirit – Keats's magic hand of chance – which is of the essence of art is forbidden to the artist in a totalitarian state. Like other dictators, Hitler found this to be not just an aesthetic theory but a pragmatic fact.

Hitler also erred in thinking that by getting control over artists, he was getting a grip on the arts. If he, the political artist, could transform the German state within a matter of months, he believed they should be able to do the same in their fields within a few years. Like the *Kladderadatsch* artist-statesman, he supposed he could take the clay of the German nation and mould it into exactly what he wanted. 'I have no doubt you will be moved by the same feelings that moved me when I first saw this unparalleled testimony to eternal beauty and achievement,' he assured his audience in placing the *Discus Thrower* on exhibition in 1938. However, he soon learned that even totalitarian power has its limits. It can ban and burn art, and imprison and kill artists, but it cannot incubate talent. Even his henchmen knew this. 'You cannot manufacture an artist,' said Goebbels. 'It is always easier over time to make a decent National Socialist out of an artist than to make a great artist out of a minor party member,' Göring admitted. Why was

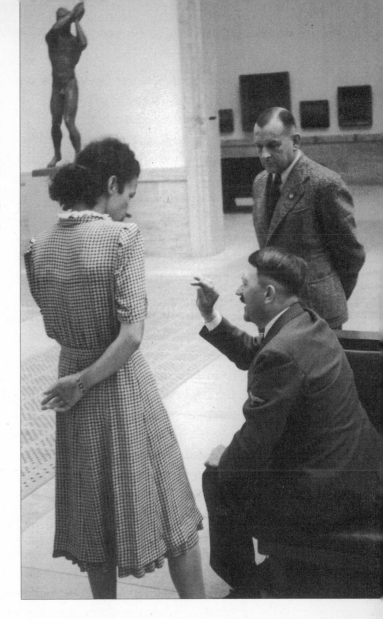

By 1940 Gerdy Troost was back as advisor to the Great German Art Exhibition. Here she, Hitler and Kolb discuss arrangement for that summer's show. In 1937 884 works had been exhibited, in later years an average of 1200. Since prices were modest – oils for as little as 250 marks and drawings for half as much – most were sold.

Hitler-the-artist not the first to recognize this? The answer may lie in his own artistry. His epigonous paintings were so removed from the creative process, so divorced from the painterly muse, that he may have believed art emerged less from talent than from iron will.

Although Hitler had no difficulty identifying bad art, he never succeeded in defining what he considered good. In *Mein Kampf* he had declared great art to be Aryan and specified the works of Moritz von Schwind and Arnold Böcklin as examples. Later on, in his cultural speeches to the party at Nuremberg, he was scarcely more specific. In 1934 he laid down the parameters of acceptable art – no Modernism on the one hand and no throwback to a distant Germanic past on the other. 'The National Socialist state must defend itself from those backward-looking people who seek to tie the National Socialist revolution to a "Teutonic art" concocted from a dreamy world of their own romantic visions,' he warned. In other speeches he tried to identify the attributes of good painting – 'serves a social purpose', 'draws a true picture of life', is 'clear and simple in style and subject', is 'healthy and beautiful', 'solid and decent' and, of course, German rather than 'international'. Again, the German Romantics were held up as models.

What emerged was essentially imitative, a variant of some past style that had been recycled into a new-old work. Roughly eighty per cent of the painters of note in the Third Reich were middle-class, academy artists from the conservative Munich school of the turn of the century. Commercial producers of conventional works, they had exhibited in Munich before 1933 and went on depicting their usual subjects – landscapes, flowers, animals, family scenes, portraits – in their usual way. Indeed, some exhibited works had been painted long before Hitler was in power, a few as far back as the previous century. Much of it did not differ from conventional works elsewhere – would have looked at home at the Royal Academy or in American exhibitions – and what was painted before and after. Most painters lacked the imagination even to try to develop a 'Nazi style'. The best they could do was to add an ideological title to give a work topicality. Werner Peiner called a scene of a farmer ploughing his field *German Soil*. He could as easily have called it 'Russian soil' or 'Kansas soil' – indeed it was not dissimilar to Grant Wood's *Fall Plowing*. Sometimes a bit of Nazi iconography was added. Paul Mathias Padua's *The Führer Speaks* pictures a family group listening to a Hitler speech on a 'people's radio' that the party promoted. Remove the radio and the picture of Hitler on the wall, and it becomes straightforward naturalism without a political twist. Few paintings portrayed Nazi party scenes or were explicitly ideological – Hitler despised political art – and next to none was anti-Semitic. At the first exhibition approximately forty per cent of the works were landscapes, fifteen per cent figures and ten per cent animals. With the passage of time a slightly larger proportion took on a political tinge, especially after 1939 when a new genre developed – war art that glorified fighting, depicted heroism and idealized sacrifice. Even so, landscapes and other eirenic subjects continued to prevail. By 1943 hardly any war paintings were on view. The predominant mood of the shows was now downright escapist, no one wanting to be reminded of war or the politics that led to it.

Contrary to the impression left by art historians and most books on the topic – which single out extreme examples of ideological works – there was no uniquely National Socialist style and very little that could be considered Nazi subject matter. Of course self-censorship governed both subject and style. Urban scenes were shunned; nature, simple people, rural life were common subjects. Nudes, usually female, were idealized, wooden and unerotic, often with references to classical mythology. 'Beauty without sensuality', the mode was aptly labelled. Faces were always expressionless; *never* was a smile to be seen. If a single theme predominated, it was the grimness of life. Here was narcotic art that never asked questions or provoked thought. This was primarily the fault of Hoffmann, who chose works by south German painters rather than the more experimental northern ones. When Hitler offered Arno Breker the presidency of the Reich Chamber of Visual Arts, the sculptor accepted on the understanding that he could have a free hand to 'clean out the Munich crowd' and get rid of the 'sweet postcard type of painting' they promoted. Since this would have required dumping Heinrich Hoffmann and Karl Kolb, director of the House of German Art, Hitler refused. Consequently, the Great German Art Exhibitions continued to be dominated by what a disgusted Goebbels labelled 'Munich-school kitsch'.

Disappointed as he was in the exhibitions, Hitler changed their primary purpose from one of showing off German art to one of educating painters to create it. Woe unto those who failed the lesson, as Hitler warned:

> By standing foursquare on the principle that someone who considers himself a painter but submits some kind of garbage is either a swindler, therefore belonging in prison, or a buffoon, therefore suited for an insane asylum, or, if his mental state is confused, a concentration camp to be re-educated, the exhibition will be a real terror for the incompetent.

Alternating with such gentle pedagogic methods, Hitler applied equally subtle cajolery in the form of honorariums, lifetime annuities, tax abatements and various other gratuities. He authorized nearly 2 million marks for the renovation of the Munich Künstlerhaus, an artists' club, and a further 10,000 marks a month to pay for accommodation and meals for young painters. He later established a similar institution in Berlin. In April 1939 alone he authorized 80,000 marks for stipends for promising young artists and in 1940 donated funds for scholarships to the Albrecht Dürer Foundation in Nuremberg. These figures, a German scholar has calculated, represent only the smallest portion of his philanthropy that can be reconstructed from surviving records. Money was not his only largesse. After 1939, he issued the famous list – list A, the 'immortals' – identifying artists to be exempted from any form of military service. These were ones who enjoyed his particular favour: Hermann Gradl, Arthur Kampf, Willy Kriegel, Werner Peiner, generally known for their landscapes and other pacific subjects. Among them were not, interestingly enough, bloodthirsty painters like Elk Eber, war artists like Claus Bergen or even the head of the Chamber for Visual Arts, Adolf Ziegler, often incorrectly identified as the Führer's favourite painter.

The Great German Art Exhibitions may have been the highlight but they were by no means the totality of the German art scene. In 1938 alone there were some 170 artistic competitions, offering substantial prize monies. As late as 1941, even as the war was beginning to take its toll, more than 1000 art shows took place. By then, however, some painters had become so affronted by the capricious method of selection for the Munich exhibitions that – to Hitler's fury – they boycotted them and showed their works privately. Others painted and sculpted but did not exhibit at all. In fact an art underground developed, surfacing briefly in Vienna in January 1943. This was the 'Junge Kunst im Dritten Reich' exhibition – the show that had nearly cost Schirach his job. Some 173 artists from all over the Reich submitted works that they had up to then kept hidden in fear of the authorities. Although none of these was at all revolutionary – nothing as daring as Barlach or Nolde – the exhibition as a whole marked a sharp contrast with the suffocating banality of the usual stuff on show in Munich. Arno Breker, who happened to attend the opening, regarded the paintings as degenerate, however, and immediately appealed to Hitler to close the show. Later, when both were inmates at Spandau, Speer told Schirach what had transpired in Berlin at the time.

> I remembered the dinner in the chancellery, to which Goebbels had come with the catalogue of the exhibition in his raised hand, remarking smugly, 'Degenerate art under the sponsorship of the Reich and the party.' . . . Hitler had leafed through the catalogue and with increasing irritation had exclaimed, 'The title alone is all wrong. "Young Art"! Why these are all old men, idiots from the day before yesterday who are still painting this way.'

To get a firsthand assessment, Benno von Arent was dispatched to Vienna. When he reported that the works were '*liberalistische Schweinerei*' – liberalistic slop – Hitler ordered the show to be closed and summoned Schirach to the Berghof. It was on this occasion that Hitler accused him of artistic sabotage and unleashed a tirade against the Viennese. But the confusion in the art world could not have been more open than it became a month later when an even more risky exhibition, 'Deutsche Zeichnungen der Jahrhundertwende' (German Drawings of the Turn of the Century), including works by Kollwitz and Schiele, was scheduled a short distance away in the Albertina. Not long after that, possibly as a replacement for the suppressed 'Junge Kunst' show, the largest retrospective of Klimt's works ever held, before or since, took place.

In the end Hitler gave up. Lavish rewards, brutish threats and an annual art extravaganza to educate artists only brought forth paintings that left him despondent. Most works were purchased by state and party officials and hung in office buildings. Hitler's own purchases were intended to keep the show going, to encourage young painters and to dole out what were in effect welfare payments. Destiny had failed to give the Third Reich any great painters. The nation would have to fall back on the cultural achievements of the past. He consoled himself with the thought that, as he told his party comrades, 'This nation has works of such enduring value in those spheres of art where we lack great master spirits today that for the time being we can be content with what we already possess in such spheres.' It was a bitter admission of failure.

He could not even bear to have the paintings around him. At his two private residences, the Berghof and the Prinzregentenplatz apartment in Munich, there were none. In his Munich headquarters, the so-called Führer Building, Adolf Ziegler's *The Four Elements* hung over the fireplace of

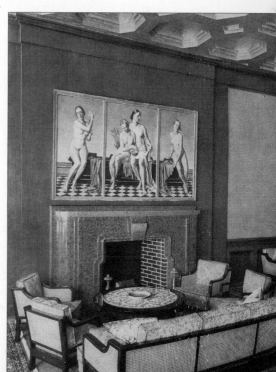

Dominating Hitler's salon in the Führer Building was Adolf Ziegler's The Four Elements. *The French ambassador said it should have been called 'The Four Senses' — since taste was lacking. After Ziegler disgraced himself in 1943 by recommending peace negotiations, the painting was removed.*

Hitler's salon, and it is said that one other contemporary work was in his study in the same building. In the new Reich chancellery the only such works were six landscapes – essentially wallpaper – which Hitler commissioned from Hermann Gradl for the grand dining room. Of the 5000 or so paintings which Hitler collected for his Linz Museum, at most two dozen were contemporary German ones. And these, a German scholar has calculated on the basis of documents in the German Federal Archive, were almost exclusively works that meant something to Hitler personally, such as individual portraits of the sixteen comrades killed in the Beer Hall Putsch, and several paintings by Paul Ludwig Troost. Otherwise he surrounded himself with works by his favourite nineteenth-century German painters.*

As time passed Hitler's interest consequently shifted to sculpture, and it was an open secret that he came to regard this as the central attraction of the Munich exhibitions. Statistics tell the tale; 200 sculptures were on exhibition in 1939, over 400 in later years. His ideal being the masterpieces of Greece and Rome, styles straying far from that model were not tolerated. Expressionist works by Ernst Barlach, Gerhard Marcks, Käthe Kollwitz, Wilhelm Lehmbruck and Rudolf Belling were removed from buildings and public squares and in most cases destroyed. Even books about such sculptures were confiscated. Barlach, one of the most powerful German sculptors since Riemenschneider, believed his unflinching naturalism – as Nolde considered the clangorous contrasts of colour in his paintings – to be in the best Nordic tradition; like the painter, he could not comprehend why his works in Kiel, Magdeburg and the famous *Hovering Angel* in Güstrow cathedral were demolished soon after the Nazis came to power.

Hitler responded to Modernist sculpture as he did its equivalent in painting. When the art purges got under way in 1937, 116 of Lehmbruck's

---

* Seven hundred paintings and sculptures exhibited in the Great German Art Exhibitions, mostly Hitler's purchases, have survived and since 1998 have been held by the German Historical Museum in Berlin. Nearly 9000 pieces of war art and works considered of National Socialist character were confiscated by the American army between 1945 and 1950 and deposited in Washington. Between 1950 and 1986 most were returned to German authorities, the American army retaining around 450 paintings – portraits of Nazi leaders and works considered propagandist in nature – along with four of Hitler's watercolours that had belonged to Heinrich Hoffmann. Most of these works are now in the Bavarian Army Museum in Ingolstadt. What became of the Grützners, Spitzwegs and other paintings that formed Hitler's personal collection cannot be established.

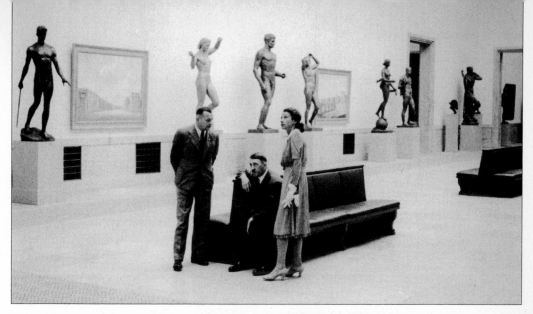

Hitler's intense interest in sculpture was evident at the 1940 Munich art show. The classical style was the hallmark of sculpture in the Third Reich and exemplified Hitler's new Germany – 'in form and condition not seen and scarcely even dreamed of for more than a thousand years', he claimed.

sculptures, 381 of Barlach's and 86 of Marcks's were confiscated and some were included in the degenerate art exhibition. Belling was the artist who had the distinction of being held up to ridicule with two works in that show and at the same time of being honoured for another, a bust of the boxer Max Schmeling, in the Great German Art Exhibition. Modernist sculptors were forbidden to exhibit even privately. Marcks, dismissed from his teaching position both for his style and his support for Jewish colleagues, fled to Italy in 1935. Barlach died a broken man in 1938. Others stopped practising their art.

In contrast to painters, however, there were a number of notable sculptors of the Weimar period – Georg Kolbe, Fritz Klimsch, Richard Scheibe among them – whose neoclassical and realistic works provoked little controversy. They accepted the New Order, and the New Order accepted them. Hitler allowed them to work without interference and even on occasion awarded them important commissions. Some sculpted as before, some fell in with the monumentalism of the day. Scheibe continued to produce nudes in a realistic style, sometimes with and sometimes without ideological intent. Kolbe bent least to Nazi ideals and increasingly fell out of favour. By contrast Hitler found Klimsch 'ever greater and more significant', and in time almost every German town had at least one of his nudes on display. On the whole these artists brought Third Reich sculpture to a level distinctly higher than that achieved in painting.

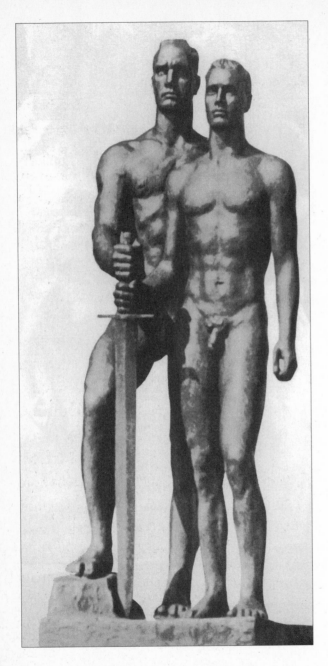

Two men hold the iconic sword of the German warrior. Yet Kolbe's war memorial at Stralsund (1935) avoids the usual heroic and aggressive character of other Third Reich sculpture. As such it stands as a monument to the ambiguities of German art at the time.

In addition there were a number of somewhat younger men whose competence was of a high order and who used it in the service of National Socialism. Josef Wackerle, one of Hitler's favourites, produced monumental works for the Olympic stadium and official buildings as well as smaller ones for the Berghof compound. Kurt Schmid-Ehmen gained note as a designer of the Nazi insignias – eagle and swastika – that adorned important buildings in Berlin, Munich and Nuremberg. For the Zeppelin Field he sculpted four figures symbolizing Nazi virtues – *Loyalty*, *Battle*, *Sacrifice* and *Victory*. Karl Albiker did several huge works for the Olympic stadium. Adolf Wamper fashioned large heroic statues such as *Icarus* and *Genius of Victory* for party buildings. Bernhard Bleeker was known for his busts of Nazi hierarchs; Willy Meller contributed heroic figures for the Olympic stadium and the Ordensburg, or party school, at Vogelsang. Although male figures lent themselves to Hitler's heroic, bellicose ideal, female nudes were also used to convey other National Socialist principles. 'The iconography was always the same,' it has been written, 'the representation of woman made by and for man, determined by her biological function.'

Far and away Hitler's supreme favourites were Josef Thorak and Arno Breker. Both were sculptors of outstanding skill. And both effortlessly sold

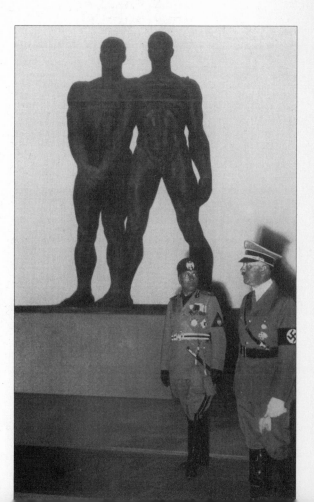

During Mussolini's visit to Germany in 1937, Hitler took his comrade to see Josef Thorak's recently completed Comradeship. *Created for exhibition at the 1937 Paris World's Fair, the work went missing after the war.*

out to the new ideology to design works as hypertrophied in proportions and as Nazified in intent as the buildings of Speer and Giesler which they were to adorn. The first to gain the Führer's attention was Thorak, in the Weimar era a leading sculptor of Impressionist style, many of whose patrons were Jews. His muscular and hunky males greatly appealed to Hitler. When the Olympic Committee was acquainted with this fact in 1935, they obligingly invited Thorak to contribute, and he obligingly complied by producing several huge nude male athletes. The following year he sculpted gigantic statues, *The Family* and *Comradeship*, for the German pavilion at the Paris World's Fair. 'Thorak is our strongest sculptural talent. We must give him commissions,' Goebbels remarked in February 1937. Hitler provided him with an atelier, said to be the world's largest, where he created his enormous works. These included two mammoth horses for the garden entrance to the new chancellery.

Breker came to Hitler's attention after winning a silver medal from the Olympic Committee for two statues, *Decathlete* and *Victor*. Quickly rising to be the Führer's preferred artist, he was commissioned to make the most important sculptural contributions to Hitler's building projects in Berlin,

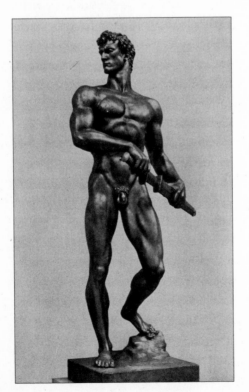

Breker's Readiness, *a quintessential work of Third Reich art, was exhibited in the 1939 Great German Art Exhibition. It was intended for a Nuremberg party rally site.*

Nuremberg and Weimar. Those in Berlin included massive bronzes clebrating the twin bases of Hitler's power – *The Party* and *The Military* – which stood in the court of honour of the new chancellery. Hitler declared them to be 'among the most beautiful ever created in Germany'. Some of his other works were highlights of the Great German Art Exhibitions – *Readiness* in 1939, and *Torchbearer* and *Comrades* a year later. 'The Führer highly praises the most recent models of Breker, whom he considers the greatest sculptor of our time. Thorak by contrast fades away,' Goebbels observed in February 1940. Breker also did busts of prominent Third Reich figures such as Speer and the Führer himself, as well as one of Richard Wagner, which adorned a central position in the grand salon of the Berghof. Breker's Wagner was arrogant, cold and contemptuous – Wagner a Nazi, Wagner a Hitlerite. Such qualities permeated his other works. In his younger years Breker, like Thorak, had been influenced by the restrained neoclassicist style of Aristide Maillol. But, like Thorak, he heard Hitler's call and responded.

Hitler considered Myron's *Discus Thrower* to be the platonic ideal of the male athlete, the supreme Olympic figure and the 'new man' emerging from the Third Reich. Breker's starting point was the same, the Greek nude, and he used notable German athletes as his models. But while Greek sculptors idealized the body and glorified sport, Breker idealized the Aryan man and glorified National Socialist ideals. Because he was a powerful artist, he was able to convey his images with great intensity. To compare the *Discus Thrower* with, say, *Readiness*, is to see that the one is natural and human, the other stilted and brutish. 'Each muscle, each tendon, had to express strength and force,' it has been observed of Breker's nudes. 'In their disciplined, steel-like bodies they were representatives of a disciplined, steely nation.' As such they perfectly reflected the Führer's belief that the step from athlete to warrior was a tiny one. These works expressed the ideals of camaraderie, discipline, heroism, will to do battle, readiness to die. Their very titles, *Comrades*, *Avenger*, *Victor*, *Readiness*, *Domination*, *Sacrifice*, *Destruction*, *Wounded* and so on, left no doubt.

Breker perverted the classical ideal of sculpture to produce caricatures of virility. Ignoring Greek principles of moderation in structure, simplicity in expression and proportion in the parts, he produced works that owed everything to size and exaggeration – shoulders too broad, hips too narrow, muscles too pronounced, stance too mannered. Such torsos, crowned with faces that were grim, arrogant and ruthless, were icons of brutality and perhaps sexual fantasy. Their apparent homoerotic, if not sado-masochistic, quality raises question about the subconscious impulses behind Nazi ideals of comradeship, heroism, discipline and submission. National Socialist sculpture may have been more revealing of itself than it knew. It is also revealing of their innate character that Breker's statues are used today by some American Aryan groups as ideological symbols, while Thorak's *Comradeship* is now an icon of male camaraderie among German gay groups.

12 THE ART COLLECTOR

MEPHISTOPHELES COULD NOT HAVE FOUND a more willing Faust. On 20 June 1939, Hitler summoned Hans Posse, director of the noted Dresden Picture Gallery, to the Berghof and offered to place him in charge of the greatest art acquisition project in history. He explained, as Posse recorded in his diary, that he intended to establish a museum in his home town of Linz which would hold 'only the best of all periods from the prehistoric beginnings of art . . . to the nineteenth century and recent times'. The collection was to be formed not just of purchases but also, he was frank to state, of confiscated works. The aim was to make Linz a cultural centre and to undo the past when Vienna had 'selfishly gobbled up everything'. 'I shall give you all necessary legal documentation and authority,' he concluded. 'You are moreover to deal only with me. I shall make the decisions.' Six days after this meeting Hitler issued a formal decree charging Posse 'with the establishment of a new art museum for the city of Linz' and ordering all party and government authorities to give him full assistance.

The origin of this extraordinary project went back to Hitler's earlier years. His 1925 sketchbook included a meticulously drafted design which he entitled 'Sketch of a German Museum for Berlin (National Gallery)'. The unusual shape of his imagined building suggests that it may have been inspired by the Kaiser Friedrich Museum, which he knew from his visit to Berlin while on army leave in 1917. His sketch divided the gallery into two sections, of twenty-eight and thirty rooms each. One section was devoted to his favourite painters at the time. He wrote their names on the side of the sketch and specified room by room where their works were to be displayed, and even indicated by line and arrow the path that imagined visitors were to follow through the gallery. His ideas evolved further in June 1931 when the old Glass Palace in Munich was destroyed by fire. Before city officials could build a replacement, he was in power and in one of his first acts ordered the construction of the House of German Art, which he intended to fill with German paintings from the early Renaissance up to the twentieth century.

But in 1937 the impending prospect of annexing Austria gave him another idea. The exhibitions in the House of German Art, he decided, would be limited to shows of contemporary German painting and sculpture. The grand museum of his dreams was now to be elsewhere. It could not be in Berlin or Munich or Vienna, where it would be overshadowed by existing institutions; it must stand alone and house a collection shaped entirely by himself. It was to be a Hitler gallery and what more appropriate place for it than his home town. A few weeks after the *Anschluß*, on 8 April, Hitler went to Linz and visited the Provincial Museum that he had known in his youth. There he met

Hitler's 1925 sketchbook included the plan of a proposed German National Museum. In the margin are the names of his favourite artists and the room number where their works were to be displayed. A line is visible showing how visitors were to tour the galleries.

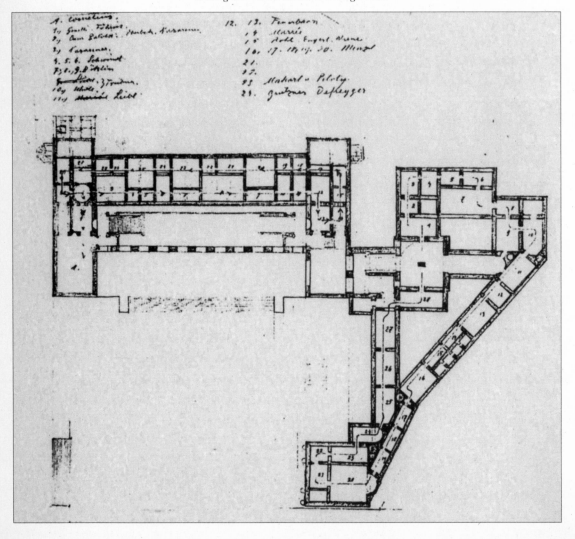

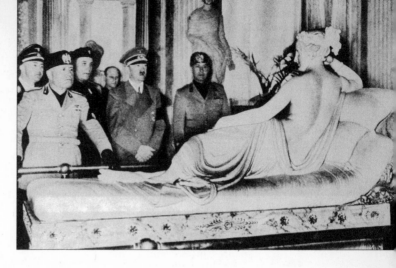

During his state visit to Italy in May 1938 Hitler spent every available minute visiting museums and cultural sites. Here at the Villa Borghese he views Canova's marble statue of Pauline Borghese Bonaparte. With him (from left) are Heinrich Himmler, Mussolini and Bianchi Bandinelli.

its director, Theodor Kerschner, and, though no protocol exists of what was discussed, it has been supposed that Hitler broadly outlined his scheme.

It was in May of the same year, following the state visit to Italy, that the Linz project took final form. Hitler was far from the first German in history to fall in love with the land where the lemons blossom. But few others could have had their narrow aesthetic horizons broadened so abruptly, in this case through visits to the Borghese Gallery in Rome and the Uffizi in Florence. For years afterwards, Christa Schroeder said, 'He never stopped expressing his joy that the visits to Rome and Florence had made it possible to admire immortal masterpieces that he had previously known only from photographs.' So deeply, in fact, did he admire a particular Titian at the Uffizi that for one chilling instant his guide feared Mussolini would take it off the wall and present it to his guest. The visit was enough to leave Hitler determined to establish a museum of similar distinction in Germany both as a personal indulgence and as a memorial to himself. Thus it was that the original notion of a gallery for German nineteenth-century painting evolved into a plan for a museum with the greatest works of all major European schools and periods up to the twentieth century. It was to be one of the world's greatest galleries, if not the greatest. Hans Posse was to bring it off.

Appointed director of the Dresden Gallery in 1910 at the remarkable age of thirty-one, Posse was a protégé of the distinguished art historian, Wilhelm von Bode. His publications included works on the collections at the Kaiser Friedrich Museum and the Dresden Gallery as well as studies on Lucas Cranach, the seventeenth-century Roman painter Andrea Sacchi and Robert Sterl, a second generation – and second-rate – German Impressionist. As early as 1919 Posse began introducing German Expressionists into the museum's collection and his continued acquisitions sparked an ever more irate conservative backlash. He held to his guns until Hitler came to power, when he beat a hasty retreat. He promptly closed the museum's Modernist collection and distanced himself from it, arguing that of the 2850 works in the gallery, only 310 had been acquired during his time, and of those a mere thirty-three were post-1910 works, most of them gifts and loans. He had taken them in, he insisted, merely to encourage local artists. In May 1933 he applied for membership in the Nazi party, which his wife had joined the year before. In June 1934, for reasons unrecorded in party records, his application was rejected. Making matters more difficult, an art hack named Walter Gasch wanted his job and accused him of having promoted degenerate art and of

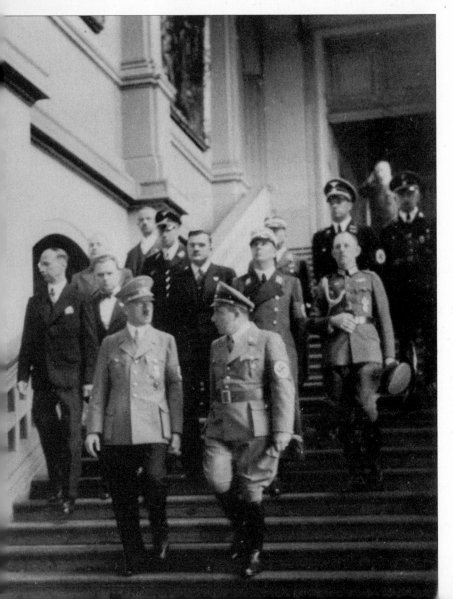

Dictator descending a staircase. Hitler at the Dresden Picture Gallery on 18 June 1938. On his far right is Hans Posse, on his left Martin Bormann.

being partly Jewish. Asked to resign in March 1938, Posse stood firm, taking a leave of absence instead. Shortly afterwards he was discharged.

Suddenly, at Hitler's command, he was reinstated. The most convincing of the various explanations is that it came about through collusion between Posse and Karl Haberstock, a Berlin art dealer who had been selling paintings for several years both to Hitler for his private collection and to Posse for the Dresden Gallery. Posse's diary records almost daily telephone conversations between the two at the time. While no mention is made of the subject discussed, Frau Posse no doubt gave the answer in 1945 when she told American occupation officials, 'Through him, my husband brought his situation to the attention of the Führer.' It is therefore possible to surmise it was at Haberstock's suggestion that Hitler went to Dresden on 18 June to size him up under the pretext of attending an exhibition of German and Dutch paintings. On the occasion Hitler summoned the ex-director, whose diary records their exchange:

> HITLER   You have resigned? Why?
> POSSE   Because it was desired and also because the Provincial Governor
> is said to have requested it. As a result I felt I had no choice.
> HITLER (*aside*)   You are said to have purchased such horrible pictures.

Later, again in Frau Posse's words, 'He asked to see all the documents [regarding Posse's acquisitions] and after examining them, he decided that my husband should have back his old job.' Thus did Hitler have Posse in position for the Linz job the following year.

For everyone concerned the arrangement was perfect. Hitler, ever willing to overlook an artist's errant past, found the sort of collaborator he liked – a professional of absolute loyalty and anxious to do as bidden. Posse, the opportunist willing to renounce, if not denounce, the very Modernist painters he had once collected, was overjoyed at an opportunity never before offered any museum director – unlimited authority and boundless funds to buy or confiscate whatever he wanted. And Haberstock now had two grateful patrons to whom he could sell great paintings, providing him with substantial profits and prestige. In years to come he was Posse's preferred agent, eventually selling him over a hundred works for Linz.

Posse worked with such devotion that when he died of cancer in December 1942 Hitler arranged a state funeral to which directors of all German museums were invited and at which Goebbels gave the eulogy. Hitler turned to Hermann Voss as his successor. The appointment evoked surprise since Voss, despite his secure reputation as a scholar and museum curator, was a known anti-Nazi. Charged with 'cosmopolitan and democratic tendencies, and friendship with many Jewish colleagues', he had lost his position as director of the Kaiser Friedrich Museum shortly after Hitler came to power. He tried to emigrate to England but was unable to find a position and in 1935 settled for the directorship of the small Nassau Provincial Museum in Wiesbaden. He continued to travel outside Germany at frequent intervals, lecturing at the Courtauld Institute in London, often visiting Paris and making an extensive lecture tour of the United States. How to understand this mysterious appointment? Some said Hoffmann engineered it to dislodge Haberstock, whom Voss was known to dislike – and, in fact, Voss never bought anything from the dealer. Frau Posse later told Voss that her husband had recommended him, and a memorandum was found after the war in which Bormann stated that Posse had once vaguely mentioned Voss as a possible successor. The document went on to make the more telling point that he was both an expert in early German painting and a noted specialist in Italian Renaissance and baroque art.

Voss's writings included on the one hand *Der Ursprung des Donaustils* (The Origin of the Danube Style) and *Albrech Altdorfer und Wolf Huber* and on the other *Die Malerei der Spätrenaissance in Rom und Florenz* (Painting of the Late Renaissance in Rome and Florence) and *Die Malerei des Barock in Rom* (Baroque Painting in Rome), both of which achieved international note. His appeal for Hitler lay no doubt in his simultaneous expertise in Italian painting and his strong background in German, especially south German, art. His political proclivities, however unfortunate, would have been of little concern. On meeting him, Hitler was satisfied with what he saw and, after monologising for an hour on the new museum, he appointed him to both the Dresden and Linz positions.

To organize the work Hitler established a small staff under his personal supervision, called *Sonderauftrag Linz*, Special Commission Linz. Chief of staff was Bormann; finance was handled by Hans Lammers, head of the Reich chancellery; administration was in the hands of Bormann's assistant, Kurt Hanssen and later Helmut von Hummel, described by an American official as 'a particularly vicious Nazi'. Others were responsible for cataloguing, restoration and storage – in all, some twenty persons. At the centre was Posse, with the titles of Director of the Dresden Picture Gallery and Special Commissioner of the Führer. To assist, he had a curator for books and autographs, Friedrich Wolffhard; later on there were also curators for armour, Leopold Rupprecht, and for coins, Fritz Dworschak. Although Posse reported to Hitler through Bormann, his letters were forwarded promptly and received unstinting attention. The Führer had full confidence in Posse and, though setting the general guidelines, gave him a free hand in what he acquired and as much money as he wanted. In a gesture of personal esteem, he awarded Posse the title of professor in April 1940.

Voss did not enjoy Hitler's trust to the same extent and was not given authority over the library or the armour and coin collections. The two men met on only three or four occasions, and it was later rumoured that Voss had complained to others, 'He's even worse than I thought.' Relations had become so strained by the end of 1943 that Voss thought it wise to take the occasion of the Führer's birthday the following year to send him a handsome gift – a Greek gold headband, a Greek silver wreath with gold leaves and a gold medallion decorated with a Silenus head, all of the fifth century BC. Along with them went a list of his acquisitions during his first year in office. Voss could not forbear pointing out that in comparison with the previous reporting period – that is, Posse's last year – when only 122 paintings had been added to the pool, he had acquired fully 881 works. Unlike his predecessor, Voss rarely travelled but instead sent out agents to search for paintings and had dealers bring their wares to him. Until the final months of the war, when Bormann and Lammers drastically reduced his budget, Voss bought far more freely than Posse. When interrogated by American authorities after the war, he claimed he had procured three times as many paintings.

Although some museum directors caught wind of it, the existence of the Linz project was kept from the public. The works themselves were hidden away and, with but two exceptions, never exhibited. Presumably Hitler felt that massive spending on what might be regarded as a self-indulgent cultural enterprise would be unpopular when the nation was making drastic sacrifices in war. Thus a decree Hitler signed in October 1942 formally endowing the entire Linz cultural institution to the nation was not made public. The project was not even mentioned at Posse's ostentatious funeral, the very purpose of which was to honour his devotion to it. Not until April 1943, on the occasion of Hitler's birthday, was the veil finally lifted with the publication of a special edition of Hoffmann's art magazine *Kunst dem Volk*. The text, carefully vetted by the Führer himself, had an obvious propaganda intent at a moment when the *Wehrmacht* was in retreat and German cities were being heavily bombed. The Führer was giving thought, the text said, to the post-war beautification of the country and chief among his plans was a great art gallery in Linz. What in other cases had taken centuries to collect, it went on, he had accomplished in a few years through 'acquisitions' – at Hitler's instruction no mention was made of confiscations – from 'private collections'. The major artists were named, and there were large colour plates of Rembrandt's *Hendrickje Stoffels*, Leonardo's *Leda*, Brueghel's *Hay Harvest*, Makart's *The Plague in Florence* and eleven other works, including his German favourites. Vermeer's *Artist in his Studio* graced the cover. Hitler had given the German people a gift it could never forget, the text concluded, and the people would never be able to repay 'its debt of gratitude to its Führer'. Decoded, the article said that, even in the travails of the moment, the Great Leader was selflessly devoted to the cultural betterment of the nation.

The *Kunst dem Volk* article was also of interest for a quite different reason – its tacit disclosure of how Hitler's taste had changed over time. His earliest preferences were graphically evident in his 1925 sketch of his National Gallery. In this imaginary museum he had only nineteenth-century German painters. Five rooms were allotted to Menzel, three to both Schwind and Böcklin and one each to Cornelius, Genelli, Führich, Leibl, Feuerbach, Marées and the so-called Nazarenes. Rooms were to be shared by Uhde and Trübner, Makart and Piloty, Grützner and Defregger as well as Rottmann, Engerth and Werner. Theirs were the works he had collected once *Mein Kampf* began earning royalties. With Hoffmann as his agent, he gradually assembled some twenty works of Friedrich Stahl, a dozen of Karl Leipold, thirty Grützners and, he claimed, the world's finest collection of Spitzwegs. 'He . . . takes great pleasure in having been able to acquire so many pictures,' Goebbels noted in his diary. Some of these works were soft, cosy Biedermeier genre scenes (Spitzweg), some were humorous and sentimental (Grützner), some were strange and allegorical (von Stuck) and some were flamboyant and colourful (Makart).

Given such differences in style, subject and mood, it is difficult to know what it was that appealed to him. Presumably they touched different sides of his character. Whatever, he enjoyed having them around him and loved to show them off. Many hung in his private apartment in Munich, along with Feuerbach's *Park Landscape*, Stuck's *The Sin*, a Lenbach portrait of Bismarck and a Zügel. In his office in the Führer Building in Munich hung Menzel's *Frederick the Great Travelling*, a gift from Himmler, and Spitzweg's *The Serenade*, which had been purchased for him in Prague in 1937. And of those at the Berghof in later years, Otto Dietrich left this description:

The walls around the room glowed with the rich colours of classical paintings by German and Italian masters. Over the massive mantel a Madonna by an unknown Italian looked down upon the company. On the left was Feuerbach's Nana and a portrait of King Henry . . . on the right a female nude by Botticelli and the sea-nymphs from Böcklin's *Play of the Waves*.

Speer identified a few others in the room, among them a Bordone, a Titian and a Pannini or two.

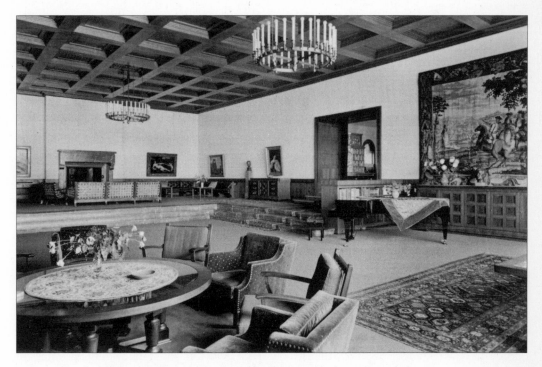

Welcoming, warm and cosy do not describe the grand salon at the Berghof nor do stately, imposing and well proportioned. The coffered ceiling, oriental carpets, tapestries and paintings are pure Hitler; the furniture and interior decoration are the work of Gerdy Troost.

Hitler's selections for the state rooms were similar. In the dining room of the old Reich chancellery he had hung Kaulbach's *Entry of the Sun Goddess* and Schwind's *Bacchus Festival*. For the new Reich chancellery he selected several paintings of the late eighteenth and nineteenth centuries, including a Füger, a Lenbach portrait of Bismarck and a work of Angelica Kauffmann, a painter whom he considered much underrated. In the reception room, the cabinet room and his own office in the new Reich chancellery he hung works of the sixteenth, seventeenth and eighteenth centuries on loan from Vienna and Berlin galleries. Without ever losing his predilection for late nineteenth-century German genre works, he came to like Cranach on the one hand and the Romantics on the other. 'The Führer is a great admirer of Romantic landscape painting and has a particularly high regard for Caspar David Friedrich,' Goebbels once commented. Occasionally he took an impulsive liking to a painter whose work was new to him. Again Goebbels: 'He told me that all of a sudden he had come to appreciate Blechen's landscapes; it had happened recently with a simple glance at a painting he had just bought.'

Hitler loved his nineteenth-century German painters, but he loved them alone. They had no appeal to Göring. Goebbels could not stand them. 'Yesterday morning at the National Gallery,' he recorded in 1929. 'Böcklin, Feuerbach, Cornelius – unbearable for our own time. These painters only paint colours but no mood, no atmosphere. However, today we look at things entirely differently. . . . A collection of nineteenth-century paintings brings to mind a chamber of the dead.' Even Troost and Rosenberg found his taste an embarrassment.

Though his acquaintance with painting slowly broadened from the pleasant if trivial Grützner to encompass the yearning, mysterious Friedrich, it was outside influences that caused the most drastic change in his knowledge and taste. Above all, his tours of the Borghese Gallery and the Uffizi left him in awe of the world of the Italian high Renaissance. This broadening influence was reinforced by Posse. His efforts to mould Hitler's judgement and guide the selections for Linz were witnessed by Speer on the occasion of Posse's appointment in 1939. 'Hitler went on about his favourite paintings in his usual way,' Speer noted, 'but Posse refused to be overwhelmed either by Hitler's position or by his engaging amiability.' On being shown some of the Führer's favourites, the director was said to have commented, 'Scarcely useful', or 'Not in keeping with the stature of the gallery as I conceive it'. Hitler accepted the criticisms without demur. Another influence on Hitler came paradoxically from confiscated Jewish collections, especially those of the Rothschilds. As he became acquainted with them, he increasingly admired not just the Italian, Spanish, Dutch, Flemish and French paintings but also the furniture, armour, coins and books.

As an experienced museum director, Posse well knew that money could buy a lot but not everything and that developing a balanced collection, even within Hitler's guidelines of pre-twentieth-century European art, would take some doing. In normal times it would have been slow and difficult, but the times were anything but normal and windfall after windfall came his way. By the time he took up his duties, Austria had been annexed and Czechoslovakia invaded. A few months later German armies began sweeping through Europe. In Eastern Europe everything was liable to confiscation and Posse could take his pick. In Western Europe public collections were left untouched, but private collections were an entirely different story.

The main cause of the dislocation of art treasures that lasts to this day was the massive confiscation of holdings that were categorized as *staatsfeindliches Vermögen*, property of enemies of the state. This meant primarily property of Jews but also of anyone who had fled or whom Nazi authorities considered undesirable. Art collections of such persons were the object of extortion or, more often, outright brutal theft. These actions were outlawed by the Hague Convention of 1907, which protects private property in conditions of war. With their fine sense of legal propriety, Nazi authorities did not ignore the regulation, they declared it inoperative with respect to Jews, Freemasons and anyone who had fled. Euphemism was another legal nicety. Items were often not confiscated but initially 'safeguarded'. Forced sale effected by blackmail was another means. This is the saga of roughly 220,000 works of art, valued at the equivalent of $25 billion in contemporary terms. Half these works are reported to be still missing or the object of dispute.

It is an appalling and heartbreaking story, and it began in Vienna. The looting started the moment German troops arrived in March 1938. Virtually no Jew, rich or poor, escaped its fury. In some ways it resembled the sacking of Rome by the Goths in 411, and Gibbon's description of that event in the third volume of *The Decline and Fall* echoes in such accounts of the ransacking of the property of Viennese Jews as William L. Shirer's, about when he turned into the garden of Baron Louis Rothschild's residence in Prinz-Eugen-Straße: 'As we entered we almost collided with some SS officers who were carting up silver and other loot from the basement. One had a gold-framed picture under his arm. One was the commandant. His arms were loaded with silver knives and forks, but he was not embarrassed.'

Reports like these did not greatly trouble the outside world and during the following months the Gestapo went on to seize some 10,000 works of art, primarily from Louis and Alphonse Rothschild and Rudolf Gutmann, but also from the rich collections of the Thorsch, Goldmann, Haas, Kornfeld and other Jewish families. At first no one had any idea about what was to become of the booty. Museum officials in Vienna as well as foreign dealers – Duveen in London and Fischer in Lucerne – had their eyes on the treasure. But the confiscations were not legalized until November, and a settlement with the Rothschilds was reached only in May 1939. When the gauleiter of Vienna then ventured to hint that he might like to have some of the works, Bormann immediately let him know that Hitler alone had first refusal on everything – a rule that eventually applied everywhere and came to be known as the 'Führer-reserve'.

The first concrete step towards establishing the Linz museum was taken in July 1939 when Hitler instructed Posse to go to Vienna to inspect the loot. After a further visit in October Posse reported that he had identified 270 paintings of merit and recommended that they should be treated as a single collection. Linz was to have the best of them, with the remainder going to other important Austrian museums. 'The best' – most of it Rothschild property – comprised 122 works, with another sixty held in reserve for possible later inclusion. Among these were some of the outstanding works for Linz – including paintings of Holbein (*Portrait of a Man*), Cranach (*Portrait of Melanchthon*), van Dyck (*Bolingbroke Family* and *Portrait of a Man with a Sword*), Rembrandt (*Portrait of Anthonia Coopal*), Hals (*Portrait of a Man* and *Portrait of a Woman*), van Ruysdael, Steen, Cuyp, van Ostade, Hobbema, Ter Borch, Metsu, Tintoretto, Guardi (*Piazza San Marco* and *Fire in Venice*), Tiepolo, Fragonard, Boucher and Romney (*Portrait of Lady Forbes*). Unaware of Hitler's antipathy to Vienna, Posse further suggested that the Kunsthistorisches Museum should have forty-four of the remaining works, including a noted life-size portrait of Madame de Pompadour by Boucher. Except for the Boucher portrait, Hitler turned him down cold. 'Vienna already has enough works of art, and it is entirely unnecessary to expand these collections,' he was told.

Posse also acquired in Vienna some highly important works through purchase – albeit purchase at times facilitated by threats. The main prize was one of the very few of the thirty-five authentic Vermeers owned privately, *The Artist in His Studio*, the property of the Czernin family. Over the years various bids had been made for it, including a substantial one by Andrew Mellon, but export had always been prohibited. Only after long negotiations did the Czernin brothers agree in October 1940 to sell the work at a price Hitler was willing to pay – 1,625,000 marks. Other works included Titian's *Toilet of Venus*, Canova's *Polyhymnia* and two Rembrandts. Through Haberstock,

Posse also obtained two further Rembrandts, a late self-portrait and a *Portrait of Hendrickje Stoffels*.★ They had been put up for sale in December 1941 along with a Rubens, a Guardi, a Degas and a Manet by 'a not entirely Aryan woman living in Italy', as it was phrased in a report at the time. She was, in fact, Giuletta Gordigiam-Mendelssohn, who resided in Rome. Initially she asked 500,000 marks for the self-portrait and 600,000 marks for the other. By the time Posse laid claim to them, she had been persuaded by her dealer to double the price on *Hendrickje Stoffels* and raise the price on the self-portrait to 850,000 marks. Hitler, strangely enough, agreed to pay 750,000 marks for the latter and 850,000 for the former, a fifty per cent increase over the original asking price. But why did he pay anything at all when the paintings could have been confiscated as Jewish property? Who, indeed, was the actual owner or owners and how did the paintings find their way in late 1941 to Vienna?

Another oddity. Nothing appears to have gone to Linz from collections inside Germany itself. As early as 1935 anyone who emigrated, Jewish or not, had to surrender his property or sell it at minimal prices or take whatever was offered at auction. When the Rhineland industrialist, Fritz Thyssen, fled, for example, his artworks were confiscated and divided among museums in the area. After pillaging Jewish collections in Austria with no noticeable international reaction, Nazi authorities turned to Germany proper. Following the infamous Kristallnacht, the systematic confiscation of the property of every Jewish family began. Posse's diary is silent about what may have been seized for Linz and it appears that, at Hitler's direction, almost all of it went to local museums. Posse did, however, purchase nearly 200 works which Jewish collectors had succeeded in moving into Switzerland during the early years of the Third Reich.

Hitler's hatred of the Czechs went back to his Viennese youth and when Czechoslovakia was seized in 1939 he imposed no restraints. Every work of art, whether or not belonging to Jews and whether or not public or private, was liable to confiscation. Such was the extent of the rapacity that even a German official complained of 'plundering expeditions that are reducing Prague to the status of a German village'. Hitler's contempt went so far that, after spending the night at the Prague castle in March 1939, he thought nothing of walking off the next morning with several valuable tapestries, rolled up and furtively stuffed into the back of his car, it has been written, like some hotel guest surreptitiously stealing the establishment's bath towels

★ The *Portrait of Hendrickje Stoffels* has since been downgraded to 'a product of the Rembrandt workshop'.

before checking out. Brazen larceny typified Posse's activities as well. One of his most important bags was the famous collection of Prince Lobkovic, which included, as he reported to Hitler, '. . . armour and objets d'art and *very valuable* German, Italian, French and Dutch paintings (including the *Hay Harvest* by Pieter Brueghel the Elder). . . .' Even religious establishments did not escape and Posse's most important seizure in Czechoslovakia was an invaluable altarpiece from the monastery at Hohenfurth, which he described to Hitler as 'nine panels of the Hohenfurth Master, which count among the oldest and best achievements of fourteenth-century German panel painting'.

Even so, the victimization of Czechoslovakia was nothing compared with what befell Poland. Reaching Warsaw in late November 1939, Posse found German officials behaving like savages, ripping apart the Royal Palace and sending off its furnishings and interior decoration to the new capital, Cracow. What artworks he saw, he reported to Hitler, were not of a quality suitable for Linz except for Raphael's *Portrait of a Gentleman,* Leonardo's *Lady with the Ermine* and Rembrandt's *Landscape with the Good Samaritan.* Nonetheless a catalogue of 521 items – tapestries, armour, furniture, coins and rare manuscripts – was compiled from which Hitler was to make his selections. He chose the three Old Masters, but Hans Frank, the Governor of Poland, eventually spirited them away to his private residence in southern Bavaria. By the time American forces arrived there in May 1945 the Raphael had vanished for good. Of all the Polish treasure, only thirty Dürer drawings came to Hitler. These gave him such pleasure that he kept them with him at his military headquarters and presumably in the bunker at the end.

In the early spring of 1940 unimagined possibilities suddenly unfolded for Posse and, appropriately enough, he was in Hitler's presence as they were set in train. Summoned to the chancellery on 9 April, he learned that the *Wehrmacht* had just initiated the campaign in Western Europe that ended with complete success a few months later. Of that day Posse wrote in his diary: 'Meeting with the Führer in presence of Bormann concerning [Prince] Johann Georg's collection [of notable drawings]. Wonderful mood despite the historical events of such profound significance; in spite of continuous discussions with government and military officials, the keenest interest in these cultural matters.' In the wake of the military advance, the Gestapo and the SS moved in to seize state archives as well as artworks – and anything else – belonging to Jews.

'The acquisition of riches served only to stimulate the avarice of the rapacious barbarians, who proceeded, by threats, by blows, and by tortures, to force from their prisoners the confession of hidden treasure.' So Gibbon, again. And thus it was in the Netherlands. The ransacking of the country began the day after Dutch forces surrendered on 15 May. Responsibility for confiscating Jewish property was delegated by German authorities to an Amsterdam bank, Lippmann, Rosenthal & Co. To extract art from the mass of loot, an agency was established under Kajetan Mühlmann, an SS colonel and former plunderer-in-chief of Poland. But what to look for and where to find it? Neither Mühlmann nor the dozens of German art fortune hunters, alias dealers, who now overran the country had any idea. Thus developed the anomalous situation in which the pillagers had to seek the help of Dutch dealers and art experts, and some of the most important of these were Jewish.

Threats, blows and torture were not always necessary. Dutch art dealers and anyone else with a painting to sell had no reluctance to appease the avarice of the rapacious barbarians. Pieter de Boer, a prominent dealer – and one with a Jewish wife – sold them over 300 paintings at considerable profit. The renowned Koenigs collection of drawings, bought just before the German invasion by a Dutch collector D. G. van Beuningen for 1 million guilders, was offered to Posse shortly afterwards for 5 million. Posse's most important Dutch dealer, Nathan Katz, bargained his services in return for permission for himself and some twenty-five members of his extended family to leave the country. Occasionally Jews were able to save their lives by bartering paintings for safe passage into neutral countries. A Brueghel went to Linz in this way. Several Jews also served as expert advisers to German dealers. Posse's chief agent, Erhard Göpel, recruited a Russian Jewish dealer in The Hague, Vitale Bloch. In return for first refusal on everything Bloch found, Göpel secured his exemption from anti-Semitic regulations. Max Friedländer, a septuagenarian Berlin art historian, was released from a concentration camp to serve as a consultant for the agents of Göring and others. There were non-Jewish consultants as well. One was a Berlin specialist, Edouard Plietzsch, who was not only an expert adviser but also an expert sleuth. He tracked down the paintings of a Berlin Jewish collector, Alfons Jaffe, that had been hidden in a Leiden museum. Jaffe was one of a number of Jews who had succeeded in fleeing before the invader arrived. Such collections were routinely confiscated.

Within days of the *Wehrmacht*'s victory in the West, German dealers mounted a second invasion and engaged in a buying frenzy that was described after the war as 'the most elaborate purchasing expedition in the history of art dealing'. They were loaded with cash and sellers were eager to take advantage of rapidly rising prices. The art market boomed as never before. German dealers consorted freely with autochthonous ones, who, it has been well said, saw 'no reason to forgo the enormous profits at the expense of the enemy'. It was a situation out of *Catch 22*, in which everyone traded with everyone else – buyer and seller, friend and foe – and everyone appeared to benefit.

When Posse arrived in late June he was appalled at the sight of German dealers taking everything they could get their hands on. Prices were soaring, he reported to Hitler, and the ultimate beneficiaries were 'the big Jewish art dealers'. But when he appealed in February 1941 for a ban on the wild spending sprees by dealers, chief of them Heinrich Hoffmann, Hitler turned him down. In spite of everything, Posse did well in the Netherlands. Apart from works seized from Austrian and French Rothschilds, he acquired more there than anywhere else. He was finicky, though. In August 1940, after examining seventy-five paintings that had been transported from the Netherlands to Munich for consideration, he informed Hitler that only two – 'a very beautiful Momper and an outstanding Teniers' – qualified for possible purchase. He was also underwhelmed by the collection of Jacques Goudstikker, a high-living Jewish dealer who managed to flee. Göring helped himself to no fewer than 600 of his paintings and a dealer named Alois Miedl took the remainder. Some of these went to Adolf Weinmüller who put them up for sale at his auction house in Munich. Hitler instructed Posse to have a look. 'They were mostly well-known old Dutch things from the art dealer Goudstikker (Miedl) and the rest . . . [are] what many people call "the rubbish of the Netherlands",' he informed Hitler. But, he added, 'I took the best – specifically six paintings, among them a very handsome, if somewhat cleaned-up, portrait by Paolo Veronese, a Verspronck, Parmigianino, Palamedez, Maes and Guercino.'

By December 1940 Posse was able to send Hitler five albums of photos of paintings so far acquired. These included Brueghel's *Carrying of the Cross*, Rubens's *Elizabeth of Valois* and *Gregory and Domitilla*, Engelbrechtsen's *Crucifixion*, Dou's *Portrait of Rembrandt's Father*, van Goyen's *Village Landscape* and Netscher's *Lady Making Music*. Nonetheless Hitler was impatient. According to Frau Posse, he told her husband, 'Buy! Buy! What we cannot use for Linz can go to the small museums.' To which Posse was said to have responded, 'My Führer, I cannot do that; up to now every work is a jewel.' Spurning his adviser's professional scruples, Hitler turned to his dealers. From his old crony Hoffmann he took 155 paintings for Linz. Another source was Hoffmann's protégé, Maria Almas Dietrich, who was reputed to share with her patron 'a considerable ignorance of the art of painting' but also a keen understanding of the Führer's taste. Despite a Jewish father, a Jewish husband (whom she divorced) and the adoption of the Jewish religion (which she renounced), Hitler was fond of her – it could not have hurt that Eva Braun was a friend of her daughter – and obtained no fewer than 270 paintings from her, without consulting Posse or Voss. She had begun selling to Hitler in 1938 and in that year her income rose more than ten times – from 47,000 to 483,000 marks – and later reached even higher levels. Her profits on sales just to Linz exceeded 600,000 marks. Honest in her dealings but credulous in her purchases, she did not have an expert eye and bought any number of fakes. Bormann once took her to task for accepting a von Alt watercolour that Hitler found an obvious forgery. She was admonished 'in the future to study old paintings *very carefully*'. Few, if any, of her pictures were of the first rank.

Posse went on his own careful way, searching for works from important Dutch collections. One unwilling donor was Frits Lugt, who fled to the United States leaving behind twenty-four paintings, including canvasses by Ter Borch, Brueghel, van Goyen, van Ostade, Kalf, Lastman, Steen, van de Velde and more than a dozen other good Dutch masters. Franz Koenigs's collection of Old Master drawings was one of the world's finest – 2700 works, among them twenty-four Dürers and forty Rembrandts. Posse took 527 of the best for 1.4 million guilders. He also secured Hitler's approval to purchase an Italian Renaissance collection then on loan to the Rijksmuseum. The items, which included paintings, furniture, sculptures and objets d'art, had been the property of Otto Lanz, late Swiss consul in Amsterdam. From D.G. van Beuningen, Posse acquired Watteau's *L'Indiscret*, Goya's *Maja Clothed*, Lucas van Leyden's *Lot and His Daughters* and several other fine works.

The biggest prize was a collection belonging, as Posse phrased it, 'to the refugee finance Jew F. Mannheimer'. It was one of the finest private collections in Europe and everyone wanted it. Fritz Mannheimer, a German banker resident in the Netherlands, had used his considerable wealth to amass a great number of artworks, many from private and public collections in Moscow and St Petersburg. By the time of his suicide in 1939, he was effectively bankrupt, however, and the collection fell to his Amsterdam bank. After threats and haggling over the price, Posse got the entire collection including twenty-seven works that Mannheimer's wife had taken with her to France. The Dutch portion included Rembrandt's *Portrait of Efraim Bonos*, Steen's *Village Marriage*, van Ruysdael's *View of Haarlem* and *The Ferry*, van der Heyden's *Keyersgracht in Amsterdam* and van Ostade's *River Landscape in Winter*. Among the works in France were Guardi's *Santa Maria della Salute*, Chardin's *Soap Bubbles*, Fragonard's *Young Woman Reading* and five other of his works, Ingres's *Portrait of a Woman*, van Ruysdael's *The Ferryman*, drawings of Watteau and Canaletto, Molenaer's *The Concert* and *The Young Musicians* and, most valuable of all, Crivelli's *Maria Magdalena*, once held by the Kaiser Friedrich Museum. The works were photographed and catalogued, and produced in a sumptuous three-volume edition, bound in pigskin, which was sent to Hitler for his pleasure.

Although Posse found little in Belgium, the country lost three great national treasures, the van Eyck *Adoration of the Lamb* from Ghent, the Dirk Bouts *Last Supper* from Louvain and Michelangelo's early *Madonna and Child* from Bruges. Two panels of the van Eyck altarpiece had belonged to the Berlin National Gallery and were turned over to Belgium in 1919 in keeping with the reparation terms of the Versailles Treaty. In July 1942 Hitler ordered the removal of the entire altarpiece from France, where it had been unsuccessfully concealed, and its transport to Germany. The other two were taken away late in the war, purportedly to save them from possible destruction in combat. Whether Hitler knew of the action and intended the works for the Linz museum is not known.

In July 1940, one year after taking up his duties, Posse presented Hitler with the first definitive list of paintings for the Linz museum. The inventory comprised 324 works, with another 150 held in reserve. All those in reserve and roughly two-thirds of the major works came from the Rothschild and other confiscated Jewish collections. Most of the remainder were Hitler's own nineteenth-century Germans. Posse divided the paintings into eight categories – fourteen works were German of the fifteenth and sixteenth centuries; twenty-one German of the seventeenth and eighteenth centuries; 114 German of the nineteenth and twentieth centuries (predominantly from Hitler's own collection); six Dutch of the fifteenth and sixteenth centuries; ninety-eight Dutch of the seventeenth century; thirty-five Italian; thirty-four French and two English. Chief among them, in addition to the Rothschilds' works provisionally identified a year earlier, were paintings by Dosso Dossi, Tintoretto, Lotto, Tiepolo, Guardi, Magnasco, Le Nain, Fragonard, Boucher, Nattier, van der Velde, Ruysdael, Ter Borch, Hals, Teniers, van Dyck and Rubens. These formed the keystone of the Linz collection.

Posse was fly enough to realize that Hitler's fondness for German Romantics had to be appeased, even though he intended to counterbalance them with other schools. But Hitler was wary, and he warned Posse not to neglect his favourites. In a striking resurrection of his 1925 sketch of a National Gallery, he instructed that these works were not to be displayed collectively; each painter was to have a separate room. If, as a result, the planned gallery proved to be too small, a second building would have to be constructed. Then, as though he knew Posse did not share his taste, he went on to say he was convinced 'that in fifty or a hundred years the painters of the Munich School will be accorded a significance vastly outstripping the contemporary assessment'.

It was with the occupation of France in June 1940 that there fell into Hitler's hands some of the world's outstanding private art collections, many of them the property of Jews, in particular the Rothschilds – Edouard, Robert and Maurice. To forestall any transfer of ownership that would legally place artworks beyond German control, Hitler's first step after the armistice was to issue a decree declaring that 'in addition to artworks of the French state, private artworks and antiquities, especially those belonging to Jews, should be taken into provisional custody by the occupation forces to prevent their removal or concealment . . . . This is not confiscation but guardianship of property to be used as collateral in peace negotiations.' In reality, outright vandalizing began immediately. Otto Abetz, German ambassador in Paris, set up special teams to seize the property of Jews who had fled. They were joined by a new organization, the Einsatzstab (Operations Staff) Reichsleiter Rosenberg, which Hitler had authorized in July 1940. This organization was an outgrowth of the Institute for the Investigation of the Jewish Question which Rosenberg had established a year earlier, with authority to confiscate libraries, archives and other property belonging to Jews, Freemasons and other enemies of National Socialism. In September 1940 it extended its mission into one of wholesale plundering of cultural property both in France and the Low Countries. Hitler gave Rosenberg his personal authority to seize any cultural objects considered of value and to ship them to Germany where he, Hitler, would decide what to do with them.

The Einsatzstab, the Gestapo and other agencies pillaged at will from the homes, businesses and bank vaults of Jews and anyone considered objectionable. The loot was taken to the Jeu de Paume, a pavilion built by Napoleon III on the site of an old real-tennis court. As the scene has been described:

> Truckload after truckload would appear at the door of the Jeu de Paume
> and be dumped there, often without any indication of provenance. There
> were clocks, statues, paintings, jewellery, and furniture from banks, storage
> warehouses and abandoned apartments. Soon the whole ground floor was
> full. More and more now came from the many Rothschild country houses.
> Twenty-two chests containing their jewellery were brought in from a
> bank vault and presented to Göring . . . .

Accounts of this sort could go on for page after sickening page. In toto the Einsatzstab seized 21,903 objects from 203 collections. The largest portion, 5009 items, had belonged to the Rothschilds; 2009 works came from the David-Weill collection and 1202 from that of Alphonse Kann. Among these treasures were 10,890 paintings, engravings, drawings, watercolours and miniatures, 583 sculptures, 2477 items of furniture as well as tapestries, carpets, ceramics, jewellery, coins, woodcarvings, ivories and antiquities.

All the while Posse was notable for his absence. In spite of unlimited funds and unlimited authority, he was uncharacteristically reluctant to participate in the looting. To avoid confronting Göring and Rosenberg? Shamed by the artistic rape of France? It is impossible to know. What others did with bare fists, Posse did with gloved hands. He never inspected the raw pillage of the Rosenberg operation as it was being assembled at the Jeu de Paume but selected from it once it arrived at Neuschwanstein and other storage sites in Germany. He did not purchase works himself but worked through German dealers. Not until October 1940 did he even venture to Paris and then only for a day in response to orders from Hitler. He was accompanied by Haberstock, whom he then unleashed on the French art market. Not just a dealer but a wheeler-dealer with a reputation of being shifty and unscrupulous, Haberstock – working through eighty-two French agents – got the goods. In 1942 he brokered a purchase of two outstanding Rembrandts – *Landscape with Castle* and *Portrait of Titus* – sold on behalf of a French wine merchant, Etienne Nicholas, who had bought them from Wildenstein, who had sold them for Gulbenkian who had acquired them from the Hermitage after the Russian revolution. A partial list of his acquisitions for Linz – sixty-two items – included works of Lorrain, Poussin (*The Finding of Moses*), Rembrandt, van Ostade, Brueghel, Pannini, Longhi, Veronese (*Leda and Swan*), Boucher (*Mlle Murphy Reclining*), Guardi, Rubens (*Pan and Syrinx*), a large number of Dutch masters and any number of Hitler's nineteenth-century German favourites. Haberstock also procured Watteau's *The Dance* from August Wilhelm, the German Crown Prince, Böcklin's *Italian Villa* from the Duke of Oldenburg as well as the two Gordigiam-Mendelssohn Rembrandts. Posse turned to other dealers too. Out of a total of 320 works purchased in Paris by Dietrich, Posse took eighty paintings. Through Hildebrandt Gurlitt, he made one of his most expensive purchases, four Beauvais tapestries as well as an important work of Lorenzo di Credi, and drawings by Claude, Boucher and Poussin.

Despite Göring's notorious greed, many of the best works that went to

Hitler from Paris were those the Reich Marshal selected for him. After taking 600 items from the pile for himself, he chose fifty-three masterpieces for Linz, almost all from Rothschild collections. Although the most notable was Vermeer's *Astronomer*, others included works by Hals (*Portrait of a Woman*), Rembrandt (*Portrait of a Man*), Boucher (*Portrait of Madame de Pompadour*, *Fountain with Water Nymphs* and *Shepherd Couple*), Fragonard, Pannini, Goya (*Portrait of a Boy* and *Portrait of Clara de Soria at Age Six*), Rubens (*Portrait of Helene Fourment* and *Portrait of a Family*), Gainsborough (*Portrait of Lady Hibbert*), and Dutch Old Masters, along with tapestries and six eighteenth-century commodes.

A serendipitous purchase appealing to Hitler's fascination with theatrical staging was the personal archive of the great theatrical reformer, Edward Gordon Craig. Nearly impoverished, Craig had for years been hoping to sell his archive, which was stored in Paris. By chance, German agents learned of the collection; Posse was informed and, undoubtedly at Hitler's instruction, purchased it for nearly 2.4 million francs – six times what he had paid for Guardi's *Santa Maria della Salute* and three times what he had given for Chardin's *Soap Bubbles*. The archive included letters, books, designs and drawings, diaries and daybooks, manuscripts, marionettes and masks, notebooks, opuscules and scrapbooks.

A significant acquisition came into Hitler's hands after Posse's death, although he had been angling for it for over a year. This was a collection of some 335 works, largely minor Dutch paintings of the seventeenth century, most of them signed and dated, belonging to a French collector, Adolphe Schloss. The paintings had been concealed in a chateau near Limoges, and to track them down French and German authorities arrested members of the family in April 1943 and forced them to reveal the hiding place. According to an agreement between the authorities, the French had first choice and selected forty-nine works for the Louvre, most of the remainder, 262 works, going to Hitler. The Führer was greatly vexed by the fact that the Louvre got the best and held Voss to account. Voss did his best to make amends by sending Hitler his first annual report showing that he had amassed no fewer than 881 paintings in his first year. To drive the point home, he itemized them:

Old German masters (up to 1800)	45
German painters after 1800	92
German painters after 1800 (Austrians)	50
Old Dutch (up to 1600)	30
Flemish (17th and 18th centuries)	88

Dutch (17th and 18th centuries)	395
Dutch (19th century)	54
Italian	72
French	42
Spanish	5
English	5
Swiss	3

in addition:

136 drawings and watercolours

174 prints, including the entire works
  of Marious Bauere and Otto Greiner

8 pastels and miniatures

10 sculptures

39 objets d'art and items of furniture

In all, the Linz museum acquired 2293 paintings, prints, tapestries and items of furniture from France, more than seventy per cent of it confiscated from Jewish collections.

Even Germany's sole European ally was not exempt from Hitler's attentions. Of all his acquisitions for Linz, no other meant so much to him as Myron's *Discobolus*. This second-century Roman marble copy of a Greek bronze original was one of the best surviving statues of the ancient world. Discovered in Rome in 1781, it belonged to the Lancellotti family on whose property it had been found. Although Ludwig I of Bavaria had tried to purchase it early in the nineteenth century, it was not until 1937 that it went up for sale. The Metropolitan Museum tried to get it for New York, the Berlin State Museums wanted it for Berlin and Prince Philipp of Hesse had his eye on it for Hitler. Prince Philipp was turned down, and, when the Metropolitan could not raise the money, Berlin acquired it for the then hefty sum of $327,000. Or rather, Berlin paid for it but never acquired it. At Hitler's order, the marble athlete was off-loaded in Munich and placed in the Glyptothek there. If the director of the Glyptothek felt embarrassed by his unexpected windfall, the director of the Berlin museum felt swindled by his unexpected loss.

What had happened has been an object of speculation, but there can be no doubt that Hitler, far from arbitrarily kidnapping the work, had always intended to have it for himself and used the unwitting State Museums as his agent. The funds for the statue came from the government and were certainly authorized by him. By permitting museum officials to conclude the deal, he was able, as was his wont, to conceal his artistic extravagance at taxpayer's expense. However, the State Museums faced the problem of securing Italian export approval. It was precisely during these discussions that Hitler made his state visit to Italy. A few days after his arrival, he took Mussolini to inspect the statue and presumably appealed to the Duce to let him have it. Two weeks after that Foreign Minister Ciano informed Italian officials that the export had been authorized 'in view of the personal interest of the Reich chancellor'.

To a tremendous ballyhoo, Hitler placed the *Discus Thrower* on exhibition in the Glyptothek coincident with the opening of the Great German Art Exhibition that summer. Though he could not prevent foreign newspapers from revealing the purchase price, he muzzled the German press and told the German public that the statue was a gift from Mussolini, a dividend of the Rome-Berlin axis. And to disguise the fact that it was intended for Linz, he declared that he was donating it to the German people. It remained in the Glyptothek until the war, when it was removed to a secure place.★

Various other works came to Hitler from Italy. One of Pannini's *Ruins* was a gift from Mussolini and hung at the Berghof. For his birthday in 1943 Göring gave him two views of Rome by the same painter. Over time Posse and his agents acquired so many of Pannini's canvases of ancient ruins – which combined Hitler's love of Rome and the Romantic style – that a gallery might almost have been set up for them alone. After the *Discus Thrower*, probably no work secured from Italy meant so much to Hitler as Makart's twelve-foot-long triptych *The Plague in Florence* which he had wanted for years. It belonged to the Landau-Finaly family, relatives of the Paris Rothschilds, and hung in their villa near Florence. Despite appeals by Posse and Haberstock, the family refused to sell, especially to Hitler. Determined to have it, Hitler appealed to Mussolini, who compliantly ordered the villa and its contents to be seized. A month later, when Hitler briefly visited Mussolini in Florence, the Duce handed over the strange painting on the railway station platform, and it accompanied Hitler on his train back to Munich. There it was exhibited twice that same year and identified as a gift from the Duce – as, in a sense, it was. So proud was Hitler of Makart's masterpiece that it and the Myron statue were the only two works intended for Linz that he permitted to be shown to the public.

★ In 1948 American occupation authorities in Germany ordered the transfer of the statue to the Italian government, despite its having been legitimately purchased and exported. The American decision, over vigorous German protest, was guided by a desire to influence the outcome of the Italian general election that year in favour of the ruling Christian Democrats.

Not until 1941, with occupied Europe robbed of its treasure, did Posse himself turn to Italy. He made three shopping expeditions, with Prince Philipp of Hesse as his guide. Philipp, related to the Prussian royal family and through it to Queen Victoria, had lived in Italy since 1922. He was a supporter of Mussolini and an early member of the Nazi party and the Storm Troops. In 1925 he had married Princess Mafalda, second daughter of the king and queen of Italy, and with that connection enjoyed incomparable entrée to aristocratic circles. '. . . I was in Rome (twice), Naples, Florence (twice), Turin and Genoa,' Posse reported to Hitler about a junket in early March 1941, 'and was able to buy nearly twenty-five paintings – among them an unknown but important *Portrait of a Man* by Titian, a stupendous double portrait by Tintoretto (dated 1562), as well as works by Moroni, Salviati, Filippo Mazzola, Macerino d'Alba (large altarpiece), Pontormo, several pieces by Strozzi, Maratti, Castiliglione, Amigoni and an early life-size portrait by Waldmüller of the wife of the composer Rossini, full length in an interior (about 1831).' In no time Posse and Prince Philipp procured some ninety pictures for Linz. In addition to those mentioned in the letter to Hitler were Parmigianino's *Portrait of a Bearded Man*, Tintoretto's *Entombment of Christ* and two portraits, Leonardo's *Leda*, two portraits by Lotto, Longhi's *Portrait of Giovanni Grassi* and another portrait, a landscape by Canaletto, two mythical scenes by Tiepolo, Veronese's *Portrait of a Man in Armour*, the bust of a woman by Jacopo della Quercia, an equestrian portrait by Rubens, two religious scenes with the attribution 'Raphael (Pinturicchio?)' and five Etruscan bronzes. At times Prince Philipp acted on his own, and it was he who bought from Prince Corsini perhaps the grandest prize, Memling's *Portrait of a Man in a Black Cap*.

German acquisition of such artworks, even by purchase from willing sellers, touched a raw nerve among Italians. Historically, Italians compensated for their diminished sense of nationalistic feeling with a deep pride in their nation's cultural patrimony. In art circles every work lost caused pain. A problem that had existed for a century now became acute as Hitler's acquisitiveness was matched by Mussolini's connivance. The Duce's philistine disdain for art was notorious. 'I have little faith in our race,' he once said. 'At the first bombardment that might destroy a famous campanile or a painting by Giotto, the Italians would go into a fit of artistic sentimentality and raise their hands in surrender.' Even Hitler was forced to admit, 'Where art is concerned, the man's a fathead!' Members of the Italian government were horrified by their leader's willingness to squander the country's heritage. Following lunch with Ciano in July 1941, the Minister for Education and Culture, Giuseppe Bottai, recorded in his diary:

> He speaks of the theft of artworks that the Germans – and he names Göring and Hitler – are carrying out in Italy, with the approval of Mussolini, who has said he is disposed to give them 'some hundreds of square kilometres of paintings, in order to get some oil'. I, who have tried from time to time to resist, confess my repugnance. 'I would prefer,' I say, 'not to be the minister who underwrites this.'
> 'You are right,' Galleazzo [Ciano] responds, 'but prepare yourself for worse.'
> 'What?' I ask.
> 'If one day the Germans ask us for Alto Adige.'

In fact, Hitler had already claimed title to cultural property in Alto Adige, or South Tyrol, a part of the Austrian empire that had been ceded to Italy after the First World War. The area was culturally and linguistically German, and by an agreement between Hitler and Mussolini in October 1939, Germany was permitted to remove from private and public collections any paintings, archives or monuments that were historically Germanic. Responsible for the transfer was Himmler's *Ahnenerbe*, a unit established to repatriate such items wherever found in Europe. But as Himmler and Posse soon found, the Italians repeatedly agreed in principle but stonewalled again and again in practice. Reporting to Hitler in March 1941, Posse wrote that he had just spent two days in Bolzano 'to discuss with the gentlemen of the *Ahnenerbe* the outstanding question of the return of German works of art. The difficulties raised in this connection by the Italian side are enormous.' In the end Italian negotiators, with a national flair for agreeing without agreeing, never gave up anything, though some works were looted late in the war as the *Wehrmacht* retreated.

With his love of books, it is not surprising that Hitler had always planned to have a library as a pendant to his art gallery. Originally envisaging a modest collection of around 250,000 volumes, he probably wanted a depository for his personal collection at the Reich chancellery, augmented by acquisitions on such subjects of interest to him as painting, architecture and music. But his horizons later expanded and, paradoxically, Jews were again partly responsible. After having a look at the libraries confiscated from the Vienna Rothschilds and Rudolf Gutmann, Posse was so impressed he recommended integrating them into the Linz library. The Gutmann collection, for example, included valuable seventeenth- and eighteenth-century French books and what were labelled 'especially rare items' of various origins. In approving Posse's proposal, Hitler drastically broadened the nature of the library. And since this development coincided with an ever-growing passion for the biggest of everything, he then determined that his should be the largest library in Europe.

Development was placed in the hands of Friedrich Wolffhardt, a devout and practising Nazi and SS officer. He was a ruthless despoiler of private collections, and after the war American investigators noted that his correspondence was 'crowded with allusions to confiscations' and he himself 'was enthusiastic and tenacious in tracking down every possibility of this sort'. He had carte blanche to spend as much as he wanted not only on books and incunabula but also on manuscripts, journals and music items, which became an ever more important part of the collection. He and his agents roamed throughout the Reich and the occupied countries buying whole libraries, the contents of antiquarian bookshops, manuscript collections, music books and musical instruments. Hitler himself lent a hand in building up the library by ordering the Austrian National Library in Vienna to turn over all its duplicates, a practice to be followed by other large institutions elsewhere in the Reich.

In the course of time – or rather, in the course of confiscations – Hitler decided to establish two additional collections, one for coins and the other for arms and armour. It is doubtful that he had much personal interest in these but rather regarded them as a way of helping to create the world's largest museum. Again, both were originally inspired by confiscations of Rothschild property. On first seeing the holdings of armour, Posse was so impressed that he recommended that 170 items of the 190-piece collection should go to Linz. Hitler unhesitatingly agreed. Posse then appointed Leopold Ruprecht, curator of armour at the Kunsthistorisches Museum, to develop the collection. This Ruprecht did with a vengeance. His main victims were several aristocratic families resident in Czechoslovakia – Prince Lobkowitz, Prince Schwartzenberg, Count Coloredo and Archduke Franz Ferdinand. In short order he assembled no fewer than 1294 pieces. With that, Hitler decided to construct a separate armour hall which he later planned to turn into a war museum, with a variety of exhibits and models to impress young people.

Collections confiscated from Louis Rothschild and Leo Fürst in Vienna, as well as from several Polish holders, formed the foundation of the coin and medal collection that Hitler decided upon in September 1942. But the main source was the outright theft of collections held by thirteen Austrian religious foundations, most notably that of Klosterneuburg. The curator of the Linz collection was Fritz Dworschak, who had been appointed by Schirach to be director of the Kunsthistorisches Museum. At the end of the war the items were scattered in a variety of sites, although the major part, thirty-two cases of coins along with a numismatic library, was found intact.

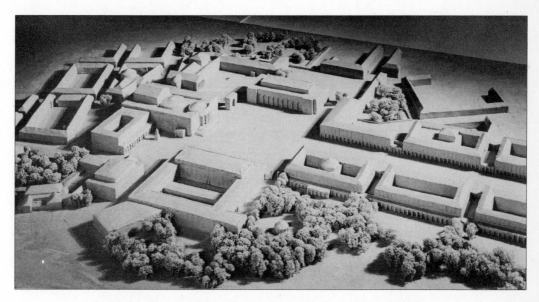

Model of the European Culture Centre at Linz, with Opera Plaza and (right)
In den Lauben, a boulevard of flower arcades (Lauben). On left of Opera Plaza
is the opera house with its convex front; the art gallery is below right; to its left
the Bruckner concert hall. Across from the art gallery is the library,
left of which is the operetta house.

In these ways Hitler's original plan for a museum and library expanded into a fine arts centre with a complex of galleries, a library, an opera house, an operetta house, a cinema, a concert hall, a music hall and a theatre. As it evolved, the Linz museum project became caught up in Hitler's mania to outdo everything comparable anywhere in the world and developed into a culture centre that was no longer to be merely the greatest in the German Reich but one of the grandest anywhere. This European Culture Centre, as it came to be called, was to be sited in the middle of the city. That the railway station had to be moved as a result did not trouble Hitler, for whom the arts not commerce should be at the heart of every city. He himself sketched the rough outlines of the sort of buildings he wanted and turned them over to his coterie of architects. The opera house project was assigned to Paul

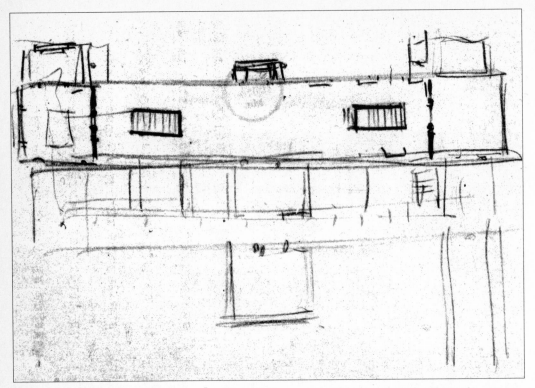

Hitler's rough sketch of the Linz art gallery envisaged a colonnaded façade of 150 metres (450 feet)
without any central accent, similar to the House of German Art. To those who criticized the design as
unsuitable, the architect, Roderich Fick, responded he had no choice but to follow Hitler's plan.

Baumgarten, the library to his old friend Leonhard Gall and the gallery for weapons and armour to Wilhelm Kreis. Roderich Fick was charged with the main art gallery. Contrary to some accounts, Speer had no role in Linz, despite desperate attempts to insert himself.

As aerial bombing of Germany intensified in early 1943, Hitler worried about the safety of the various castles and monasteries storing works intended for his museum. At his instructions strenuous, if unsuccessful, efforts were made to camouflage the Kremsmünster monastery to look like a farm complex. Neuschwanstein, he feared, was a sitting duck for air attack. In reality, as an American military officer later wrote, 'Not by the widest stretch of the imagination would any of the repositories have been subjected to air attack . . . . Yet the hysteria in the Reich chancellery had become so intense by the end of 1943 that Hitler ordered a wholesale evacuation of the repositories in favor of a still safer refuge.' After a search, it was agreed that the ancient Steinberg salt mine at Alt Aussee in Upper Austria would be ideal. With considerable effort the site was readied – walls and ceiling sealed and covered, wooden floors laid, storage racks built and electricity installed – so that by early January 1944 shipments could be received. Access was extremely difficult, however, since the road traversed two high passes which were closed at height of winter. Even in clement weather oxen and tanks were needed to haul the crates. The mine itself was a labyrinth with a single entry opening into a tunnel scarcely more than six feet high. The passage extended two kilometres horizontally into the mountain and led to eleven huge galleries from which salt had for centuries been mined. Somehow thousands of artworks, almost all of them for Linz, were brought there safely. The last delivery was made only a few weeks before the end of hostilities.

In an oft-told tale, the works stored in the mine were nearly destroyed when August Eigruber, gauleiter of Upper Austria, ordered the galleries to be filled with demolition charges and set off when Allied troops neared the site. Hitler countermanded the order but Eigruber ignored this and threatened to execute the caretakers if they failed to obey his command. At the last minute Eigruber fled and workmen did not set off the charges. Less happy was the denouement at the Führer Building in Munich, where 723 works, including the 262 paintings from the Schloss collection, were still stored. In the chaos just before American troops entered the city, the building was broken into by a mob that made off with most of the paintings.

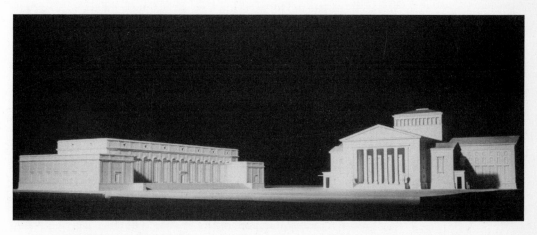

This 1938–9 model shows the Linz art gallery and the opera house, designed by Paul Baumgarten.
Hitler later altered the traditional shape of the opera theatre with its flat façade and gave it a convex front.

American soldiers apparently helped themselves to what remained. Only 148 pictures, including twenty-two from the Schloss collection, were recovered.

There is no secure figure for the total number of artworks that were confiscated or purchased for the Linz museum. The highest accession number recorded at the Führer Building, where all paintings were to be catalogued, was 3922 but this did not include works that arrived there after January 1945 or that were sent direct from France and the Netherlands to other storage sites. At Alt Aussee a handwritten 'Summary of deposits in the salt mine Altaussee according to my knowledge', compiled by Karl Sieber, the person in charge of the depository, recorded 4353 works. Obviously this inventory also excluded what was held elsewhere, such as the Mannheimer collection at Hohenfurth, the 1732 paintings and forty-nine sculptures, tapestries and furniture items at Kremsmünster, the Koenigs collection at Weesenstein and the 262 works from the Schloss collection along with others arriving at the Führer Building in Munich in the last months of the war. These numbers suggest that a total of roughly 7000 works had been specifically acquired for Linz. The Art Looting Investigation Unit confirmed that figure, a calculation based on records discovered which listed 6755 paintings stored at Alt Aussee of which 5350 were earmarked for Linz, along with twenty-one contemporary German paintings, 230 drawings and watercolours, 1039 prints, ninety-five tapestries, sixty-eight sculptures, thirty-two cases of coins and a numismatic library, 128 weapons and pieces of armour, sixty-four pieces of antique furniture, 237 cases of books and the Gordon Craig theatre archive.

Also at Alt Aussee in Hitler's name were 209 paintings intended for a castle at Posen which Hitler wanted as a private residence, as well as 534 paintings, nine tapestries and sixteen sculptures designated for the Berghof compound. In addition there was a gigantic pile of loot from the Soviet Union in storage in Berlin. The so-called Special Command Künsberg had removed some 305,000 works, a high percentage of which were books, maps and other printed material. Only one painting was formally earmarked for Linz, and it was an oddity: Frans Francken's *The Battle of the Amalekites*. It portrayed the victory of Israelites over the Amalekite tribe. Posse made few enquiries about art collections in Russia, and neither he nor Voss ever visited there, possibly as a result of Hitler's pathological antipathy towards everything Russian.

The precise figure is unimportant. As of 1945, Hitler's collection was, it might be said, *in posse* but not yet *in esse*. The number of works merely hints at the extent of the plundering up to then and gives no idea of the eventual size of the Linz museum. Acquisition stopped only when the military situation prevented further collecting. Even so, the mountains of art objects stored at Neuschwanstein – to say nothing of the loot from Eastern Europe and scattered about the Reich – had yet to be sorted through. The best things were to go to Linz and the remainder were to be given to smaller museums throughout the Reich. And had he won his war, Hitler would presumably have helped himself to the holdings of European public galleries as one of the terms of a peace settlement.

Similarly, the various estimates of the amount Hitler spent on his collection convey little meaning today, when a single Picasso can fetch £31 ($48) million, a van Gogh £52 ($81) million, a Renoir £50 ($78) million. But even for the time, the figures offer no accurate idea. Many sales were made under duress at absurdly low prices. Moreover, the claim by the Art Looting Investigation Unit that 'most of the several thousands of objects which formed the Führer collections were acquired by purchase' is highly misleading. It is impossible to make a firm distinction between paintings bought and paintings confiscated since many purchases were of works seized and later sold by dealers or at auction. Every work registered for Linz was assigned a bookkeeping price, but this was often vastly below the true value. The price attached to the Rothschilds' Vermeer was 100,000 marks; Hitler had paid 1,650,000 marks for the one purchased from the Czernin brothers, a painting sold for less than it was probably worth. Artworks of the Viennese Rothschilds were sold at auction in London in 1999 for about £35 ($54) million, a figure that may offer some rough notion of their monetary value.

Hitler could have spent as much as he wished on his Linz collection. Since the main source of his personal funds was donations by German industry and royalties from postage stamps with his picture, art expenditures in no sense came out of his own pocket. Yet he was a careful spender, at times haggling to get the price down or passing up a work because of its cost. During an encounter at Spandau, Schirach commented to Speer, 'Hitler had spent all his money on artistic purposes. Göring on the other hand had . . . amassed huge funds solely to satisfy his lust for luxury. In personal matters . . . Hitler had had a rather ascetic bent right to the end, but Göring had been a good-for-nothing spendthrift.'

What sort of collection had Hitler amassed by 1945? The most striking feature is the least unexpected – the hypertrophy of nineteenth-century German-Austrian painters. Among them were seventy-five Lenbachs (at least a dozen of them portraits of Bismarck), fifty-eight Stucks, fifty-eight Kaulbachs, fifty-five Waldmüllers, fifty-two Menzels, forty-six Grützners and forty-four Spitzwegs. To that extent Hitler ended where he began in 1925 in his sketchbook list of artists for his National Gallery. 'Anyone who wants to study nineteenth-century painting,' he remarked to his staff in 1942, 'will sooner or later find it necessary to go to the Linz gallery, because only there will it be possible to find complete collections.'

All the same, Hitler's collection of Old Masters was far from unimpressive. It included at least fifteen Rembrandts, twenty-three Brueghels, two Vermeers, fifteen Canalettos, fifteen Tintorettos, eight Tiepolos, four Titians, Leonardo's *Lady with the Ermine* and *Leda with the Swan*, as well as works by Botticelli, Guardi, Pannini and Veronese. In addition to Hals, Holbein, Cranach, van Dyck and Rubens, every significant Dutch painter was well represented with outstanding examples. There were also works of Chardin, Poussin, Boucher, Fragonard, Watteau and Nattier. But even just as a European collection, it suffered from yawning gaps. Only a dozen English works, all portraits except for one Constable. Apart from several Goyas, little or nothing else from the Spanish school. The Italian portion lacked anything by Correggio, Caravaggio, Mantegna, Signorelli, Bellini or Giorgione, to mention a few names. Painful for Posse and his patron was the paucity of works from the Northern Renaissance – no paintings by Dürer, van Eyck, Bosch or Grünewald. This gap was almost inevitable since, as Posse pointed out to Hitler, few such were ever available. It was for this reason that he did not hesitate to steal the great altar from the monastery at Hohenfurth as well as the Altdorfers from St Florian and other monasteries. And it was in the hope of finding similar early works that he followed developments in the South Tyrol with such interest. Similarly, when Göring got his hands on Hans Baldung's *Venus*, Hitler made him give it up – a unique case of his pulling rank on the Reich Marshal for a painting. However, nothing could prise a Holbein *Madonna* from the Grand Duke of Hesse-Darmstadt. '. . . We must once again inform you,' his Grace's secretary declared in a letter to Haberstock, one of the Madonna's persistent suitors, 'that we have absolutely no intention of selling the Holbein *Madonna*. All enquiries of this sort are pointless, and we beg you to inform your prospective purchaser accordingly. Heil Hitler!'★

★ The Grim Reaper eventually succeeded where the Führer failed. In 2002 *The Darmstadt Madonna*, one of the most important works of the German Renaissance, had to be sold in settlement of death duties following the demise of Princess Margaret of Hesse.

No doubt the strangest feature of Hitler's art collecting was the inclusion of at least seven paintings with Jewish subjects or references. Most blatant was Tintoretto's *Finding of Moses*, which Hitler hung in the cabinet room of the Reich chancellery. Among works for Linz were a Poussin of the same subject, Francken's *Battle of the Amalekites*, a fifteenth-century German *Flight from Egypt* as well as two Rembrandts – the *Portrait of Ephraim Bonos*, a Jewish doctor, and *Jew in a Fur Cap*. And on the wall of the room depicted in Vermeer's *Astronomer* hung a painting of the founder of Judaism.

The most Hitler ever saw of his paintings were brief viewings in the Führer Building and photos bound in albums that were periodically sent to him as the pictures were acquired. Nonetheless, as Christa Schroeder recalled, 'The Linz museum was one of his favourite conversation topics at late afternoon tea.' And in the course of these conversations the artist manqué even described the precise conditions in which he wanted his paintings to be displayed. They were not to be hung close together as in the Louvre where, in his words, 'one overwhelms the other'. Rather, each was to be allowed a generous space, similar to the way he exhibited works at the House of German Art. He further wanted each school to be presented in period rooms, with furniture, panelling, draperies and even window frames typical of the historical milieu – and therefore reflecting the social atmosphere – in which the works were executed. His concern for detail even extended to the way light was to fall on the paintings.

How much did they mean to him? Typical of all autocrats in history, he undoubtedly regarded them as trophies of power and wealth. At the same time he was enough of a painter to appreciate them as precious objects in themselves. Even Bianchi Bandinelli, his sceptical Italian guide at the Borghese Gallery and the Uffizi, credited him with 'admiring, even if he did not understand, the subject [of a painting] as well as the painter's technical ability, the use of colour and the psychological elements'. His addiction to German genre and urban scenes of the von Alt school never wavered. Dutch Old Masters as well as works of Pannini, Guardi and Canaletto or Chardin – with their literal and realistic renderings of rural and urban scenes or of Roman ruins – were bound to have great appeal. Although he had no time for early Italian painting, he developed an admiration for Titian, Tintoretto and their school.

At the very end of his life, the Linz museum was one of the matters uppermost in Hitler's mind, so much so that in his so-called private will, written just before his suicide, he declared, 'I never bought the paintings that are in the collections that I built up over the years for my own benefit but only for the establishment of a gallery in my home town of Linz.' True enough, though the ultimate purpose of the gallery was to glorify its founder and perpetuate his memory as one of the great cultural benefactors of history.

After the war the disposition of Hitler's Linz collection occasioned an unseemly grab by national authorities and museum directors for as much as they could get their hands on. Alt Aussee being in Austria, the Austrians wanted it all. The Italians demanded everything of Italian provenance and the Dutch of Dutch provenance, even when legitimately purchased and willingly sold, sometimes at exorbitant prices. The American army, which held everything, was instructed to return works to the country of origin, whether looted, confiscated or purchased at fair market value. Their further disposition was left to authorities of each country. Thus the Dutch portion of the Mannheimer collection was sent back to the Netherlands. There it was declared to have been confiscated by the Germans, and the works were either given to the Rijksmuseum or sold. The French part of the collection was sent to France, where Mme Mannheimer was permitted to have back a few paintings – which she then sold a second time. Most private owners got nothing back from their government. The 527 drawings purchased from the Koenigs collection were found by the Russians and dispatched to Moscow as reparations, though a few were later sent to the Netherlands. Some works purchased in the Greater German Reich – over 1000 paintings, including *Hendrickje Stoffels* – were turned over to German authorities; some – including the Czernin Vermeer – went to Austria.

THE
PERFECT WAGNERITE

13 HITLER'S WAGNER OR WAGNER'S HITLER?

THE MOST MOMENTOUS NON-EVENT OF THE CENTURY occurred in February of 1908. And it occurred in Vienna to Alfred Roller. Today Roller is not so much underestimated as unknown, at least outside a small circle of opera devotees. Yet in 1908 he was one of the most important figures on the Viennese artistic scene. He was a painter who, along with Gustav Klimt, organized the Vienna Secession. He was also professor of fine arts and soon to be appointed director of the School of Applied Arts. But above all he was a stage designer of great distinction. In 1903, on the twentieth anniversary of Wagner's death, he and Gustav Mahler initiated a cycle of the composer's works in fresh musical and visual interpretations. The *Tristan und Isolde* of that year marked the first break with the Bayreuth tradition. That production and those that followed – in particular the première of *Der Rosenkavalier* in 1911 – made him the world's most talked-about operatic producer.

In that first week of February, Roller received a letter from a friend declaring that a young man of her acquaintance was a great admirer of his. The lad was an aspiring painter and loved opera; he would give anything, she wrote, to meet Roller to discuss his professional prospects, either in painting or in stage design. Despite his heavy commitments, Roller generously agreed to meet him, take a look at some of his work and advise him on a career. The young man was overjoyed and a short time later, with Roller's reply and a portfolio of his works in hand, went to the opera house. On reaching the entrance, so he later said, he got cold feet and left. A short time later he summoned up his courage, returned and this time made it as far as the grand staircase, when he again took fright. On a third occasion he was well on his way to Roller's office when an opera house attendant asked his business. At that, he turned on his heels and fled for good. But he never forgot the gesture and, when he finally met Roller in 1934, he told him the story. The young man was now chancellor of Germany.

If only, history sighs, Roller and Hitler had met in 1908 and Hitler had been taken on as an assistant at the opera or enrolled at the School of Applied Arts! As Hitler himself remarked to his personal staff in 1942:

> Without a recommendation it was impossible to get anywhere in Austria. When I came to Vienna I had a recommendation to Roller. But I never made use of it. If I had gone to him with it, he would have taken me right off. But I do not know whether that would have been better for me. Certainly everything would have been much easier.

And much different. In any event Hitler never lost his admiration of Roller. When Winifred Wagner decided in 1933 to stage a new production of *Parsifal* at Bayreuth — the first since the original of 1882 — Hitler proposed Roller to do it and she agreed.

Hitler's love affair with Wagnerian opera had begun in Linz in 1901 when at the age of twelve he attended his first opera. The performance was of *Lohengrin* and, as he later wrote in *Mein Kampf*, 'I was captivated at once. My youthful enthusiasm for the Master of Bayreuth knew no bounds. Again and again I was drawn to his works. . . .' From that moment the lad found himself addicted, literally so, to Wagner's operas. The composer's musical and intellectual influence in Central Europe was then at its zenith, and Hitler embraced the cult as devoutly as anyone. During the years following the ecstasy of that first *Lohengrin* performance, Hitler returned to the Linz opera house night after night. It was there that he eventually met another opera enthusiast, August Kubizek. The slightly older August, although training to follow in the footsteps of his father as an upholsterer, was a serious amateur musician, able to play several stringed and brass instruments. In a short time he became the sole friend of Hitler's youth. It was not simply the mutual interest in opera that drew them together but the compliant Kubizek's willingness — an absolute requisite for everyone else later as well — to listen in tacit agreement or at least silence as the domineering Adolf expatiated on whatever caught his fancy.

According to Hitler's comments to Speer, the two young men spent hours wandering through the streets of Linz as he rambled on about music, architecture and the importance of the arts. On visiting Vienna for the first time in 1906, it was to Kubizek that he wrote. 'Tomorrow I am going to the opera, *Tristan*, and the day after *Flying Dutchman*, etc.,' he reported soon after arriving. Later the same day he dispatched a second postcard of the opera house on which he had written grandiloquently:

The interior of the edifice is not exciting. If the exterior is mighty majesty, lending the building the seriousness of an artistic monument, one feels in the interior admiration rather than dignity. Only when the mighty sound waves flow through the auditorium and when the whisperings of the wind give way to the terrible roaring of the sound waves does one feel the grandeur and forget the surfeit of gold and velvet covering the interior.

On settling in Vienna the following year, he persuaded Kubizek, who had been admitted to the Music Conservatory, to join him there. The two lived together until 1908 when Hitler, following the humiliation of his second rejection by the Academy of Fine Arts, suddenly vanished from his companion's life.

Beyond his Wagnermania next to nothing is known for certain about Hitler's youthful activities. He sang in a church choir but found that he had a bad voice and gave it up. On leaving school, he joined a music club and took piano lessons from October 1906 until the end of the following January from a man named Josef Prawratsky. He soon quit, whether out of boredom with the routine of exercises or for lack of money as a result of the expense of his mother's cancer treatments. However, his sister Paula recalled him 'sitting for hours at the beautiful Heitzmann grand piano my mother had given him'. In later years he occasionally played – according to Winifred Wagner fairly well – but what he played remains a mystery.

Kubizek's 1954 book, *Young Hitler*, and the recycling of its stories by later writers has produced an impression of Hitler's musical background that is widely accepted but almost completely false. The claim that Hitler was devoted to the works of Haydn, Mozart and Beethoven as well as Bruckner, Weber, Schubert, Mendelssohn, Schumann and Grieg, that he was especially fond of Mozart and of Beethoven's violin and piano concertos along with Mendelssohn's violin concerto and above all Schumann's piano concerto, lacks any basis in fact and is contrary to everything that is known or that his entourage ever said about his musical taste. Even the account of Hitler's Wagnerism is laughable. That the two of them attended *Parsifal* cannot be true since the opera was not performed in Vienna until 1914, long after they had parted. The assertion that Hitler read Wagner's prose writings and everything else he could get his hands on by or about Wagner is contradicted by Kubizek's own 'Reminiscences' as well as his statement to Franz Jetzinger, librarian at the Linz archive, that Hitler did no serious reading at all at the time. And while the young Hitler was undoubtedly enthralled by Wagner's music, the flamboyantly purple prose of the book claiming that Hitler was

> . . . transported into that extraordinary state which Wagner's music produced in him, that trance, that escape into a mystical dream-world . . .
>
> . . . a changed man; his violence left him, he became quiet, yielding and tractable.
>
> . . . intoxicated and bewitched . . .
>
> . . . willing to let himself be carried away into a mystical universe . . .
>
> . . . from the stale, musty prison of his back room, transported into the blissful regions of Germanic antiquity . . .

is the pure whimsy of a ghost-writer rather than anything that could have come from Kubizek's pen.

According to another oft-repeated legend, Hitler wrote an opera, based on a prose sketch which Wagner had developed but abandoned, entitled *Wieland der Schmied* (Wieland the Blacksmith). An entire chapter is devoted to the story and tells how the young Hitler worked out leitmotifs, a cast of characters, a plot, a dramatic structure and a rough score. Even after the passage of forty-five years, Kubizek claimed to be able to recall the specific names, all old-Teutonic, of the characters. None of this appeared in the 'Reminiscences'. There he said that within three days of conceiving the idea of the opera, Hitler had already composed an overture – in Wagnerian style – which he played for his friend on the piano in their completely darkened room. 'Eventually there was produced a very serious sketch for a music drama with Adolf Hitler as its composer.' But even this account was contradicted by a still earlier version, given in December 1938 to a party official. At that time Kubizek said that Hitler had written not an opera but a *play* called *Wieland der Schmied*. Another of Kubizek's yarns claimed that Hitler dreamed up the idea of a 'Mobile Reichs Orchestra' – called in the 'Reminiscences' a Reich Symphony Orchestra – which was to tour German provinces and perform without charge. In 1928 an orchestra dedicated to promoting Nazi ideals was organized and in 1931 it became, with Hitler's approval, a travelling National Socialist Symphony Orchestra. In a history of the orchestra published in 1940 there was no suggestion that Hitler had so much as heard of the band before becoming its patron.

By far the best known of Kubizek's stories was a political parable. Following a performance at the Linz Opera of Wagner's *Rienzi*, so it went, Hitler ascended to a high place – the Freinberg hill overlooking the city – where he experienced an ideological epiphany. Inspired by the hero of the opera, a simple man driven by a sense of mission to restore greatness to Rome, Hitler fell into a state of 'complete ecstasy and rapture' and declared that he too was destined to lead his people to greatness. Kubizek went on to say that he mentioned the episode to Hitler when they met in Bayreuth in 1939 and found that he recalled it. 'In that hour it began,' the Führer supposedly commented. Provocative in itself, Kubizek's account offered the added titillation of willy-nilly associating Wagner with the launching of Hitler's political career – a link strengthened by the fact that the Nuremberg party rally opened with themes from the prelude to the opera.

Even biographers relatively credulous of Kubizek's memoirs have found the *Rienzi* story too much to swallow. Yet, paradoxically, it is one story – albeit minus the book's overwrought verbiage – that is anchored in fact. One fact is that the opera was actually performed at the local opera house beginning in January 1905. Another is that this is a rare case where the book and the 'Reminiscences' are consistent, although the latter refers merely to 'that memorable night after the *Rienzi* performance at the Linz Opera in the dark, cold and foggy streets of Linz'. When a sceptical Jetzinger read that passage and challenged it, Kubizek responded in evident dudgeon, 'The experience after *Rienzi* really happened.' But most telling is Hitler's own testimony to Speer in 1938, a full year before Kubizek raised the topic at Bayreuth. Explaining why the party rallies opened with the overture to the opera, he said it was not simply because of the impressiveness of the music but also because it had great personal significance. 'Listening to this blessed music as a young man in the opera at Linz, I had the vision that I too must some day succeed in uniting the German empire and making it great once more.' Upon the annexation of Austria, Hitler publicly expressed identical sentiments, without the personal reference to *Rienzi*, telling an audience in Vienna, 'I believe it was God's will to send a youth from here into the Reich, to let him grow up, to raise him to be the leader of the nation so as to enable him to lead his homeland back into the Reich'. In some sense, then, the *Rienzi* experience marked the primal scene of his political career. The central force behind Hitler's later actions was his deepening conviction of being a tool of destiny; the opera, he later came to believe, marked the providential Annunciation.

Hitler's love of music was intense, fanatical even. But as in painting, his taste was limited to a specific type. Wilhelm Furtwängler learned this to his shock at a long meeting with the Führer in August 1933. Music, Hitler left him in no doubt, meant opera, and opera meant Wagner and Puccini. Symphonies held little interest and chamber music none at all. There is no record of his ever having attended a chamber concert or a lieder recital. His attendance at symphony concerts was increasingly rare as time passed and, when chancellor, he seldom appeared except on ceremonial occasions. He wanted music to be readily available, however, and after 1933 built up a large collection of phonograph recordings at the chancellery in Berlin, at the Berghof, on his train and, later on, at his military headquarters on the Eastern front. According to all accounts, these were outstanding in quality and quantity, and the playing equipment was excellent. In the evenings he enjoyed hearing short excerpts and dramatic highlights of favourite pieces. 'He would then sit back,' according to Christa Schroeder,

> and listen with his eyes closed. It was always the same recordings that were played and usually the guests knew the number of the record by heart. When Hitler said, for example, 'Aida, last act: The fatal stone upon me now is closing', then one of the guests would shout the catalogue number to a member of the household staff: 'Record number one-hundred-whatever.'

'Before long,' according to Speer, 'the order of the records became virtually fixed. First he wanted a few bravura selections from Wagnerian operas, to be followed promptly with operettas.' All the while he would try to guess the names of the singers and, as Speer remarked, 'was pleased when he guessed right, as he frequently did'.

Hitler was not genuinely fond of Beethoven and, as time passed, his attendance at performances of his symphonies was usually confined to official events. This was awkward. Traditionally Germans looked upon Beethoven along with Goethe, Rembrandt and Shakespeare as the supreme figures of modern Western culture. Unlike the others, however, Beethoven was never just a cultural figure but also an ideological symbol, invoked by every political movement. Nazi fanatics, Rosenberg in particular, claimed the composer as an Aryan hero – an 'artistic Führer' – and his music as an elixir that would contribute to the nation's renewal. In his speeches Hitler consequently felt obliged to give the composer his due, but his praise rarely rose above the perfunctory. So if Hitler had his Wagner, the party had its Beethoven. When Hitler 'entertained' on state occasions, Wagner was performed; when the party 'entertained' on party occasions Beethoven was played. And played he was, more often than any other symphonic composer. His works, above all the Ninth Symphony, were the pre-eminent musical set pieces for important occasions. When Hitler wanted to impress state visitors, he hauled them off to a gala performance of a Wagnerian opera. In 1938, anxious to gain Hungarian support for his impending dismemberment of

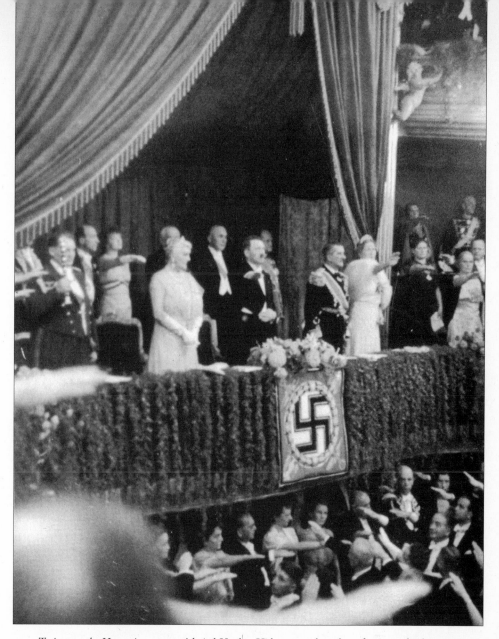

To impress the Hungarian regent, Admiral Horthy, Hitler arranged a gala performance of Lohengrin *at the Berlin State Opera on 25 August 1938. Heinz Tietjen conducted a sublime Bayreuth production, supported by the Berlin and Vienna opera choruses. (From left) Göring, Mme Horthy, Hitler, Admiral Horthy and Emmy Göring.*

Czechoslovakia, he invited the Regent, Admiral Horthy, to make a state visit. The social high point of the occasion was a stunning performance of *Lohengrin* – a rather tactless choice considering the opera opens with a call to arms to defend Germany from the Hungarian invader. The following year Prince Paul, Prince Regent of Yugoslavia, was invited to Berlin for similar reasons, in this case the imminent invasion of Poland. He was treated to the happier *Meistersinger von Nürnberg*. Hitler apparently believed that outstanding musical performances – like his magnificent works of architecture – would leave foreign leaders in awe of the greatness of the Third Reich and incline them to support his policies.

Brahms he did not like. Hitler's admirers, such as Hans Severus Ziegler and Furtwängler, traced his antipathy to the old rivalry between the Brahms and Bruckner camps in Vienna. In an attempt to have him overlook history and concentrate on the music, they persuaded him to attend a concert of the Berlin Philharmonic, which included the composer's Fourth Symphony. But when he blithely commented afterwards, 'Well, Furtwängler is *such* a good conductor that under such a baton even Brahms is impressive,' they admitted defeat.

Unfortunately the record is silent on what Hitler thought of Strauss's operas or even which ones he knew. The story that Hitler begged money from relatives to attend the Austrian première of *Salome* in Graz in May 1906, an event that also drew most of the eminent composers of the day, is apocryphal. Not until after the *Anschluß* in 1938 did he even visit the city. Hitler liked the best-known operas of Verdi and Puccini. In fact, a performance of *Madama Butterfly* at the Berlin Volksoper in 1937 left him so delighted that he decided then and there to donate 100,000 marks a year to the opera company. Even so, when once attending a performance of *La Bohème*, what he talked about during the intermissions was Wagner and Bayreuth. Otherwise there were few if any non-German composers whose works he could abide. According to Heinrich Hoffmann, he especially disliked Stravinsky and Prokofiev, and when Hoffmann's daughter, Henriette von Schirach, presented him with a recording of Tchaikovsky's Sixth Symphony, he brusquely refused to listen to it. In music, as in painting, his taste never developed beyond late German Romanticism. He liked his music to be melodic, euphonious and accessible.

Hitler's taste underwent several significant changes, however. During most of his life, Bruckner held little appeal. Hoffmann did not so much as mention the composer's name when once identifying Hitler's favourites. Even after becoming chancellor, Speer noted, his interest 'never seemed very marked'. The composer had, however, symbolic importance to him, both as a 'home town boy' and as a rival to Brahms, so beloved in Vienna. It was a fixed part of the Nuremberg rallies for the cultural session to open with a movement of one of his symphonies. In June 1937 he was famously photographed paying his respects to the composer, standing in mute homage

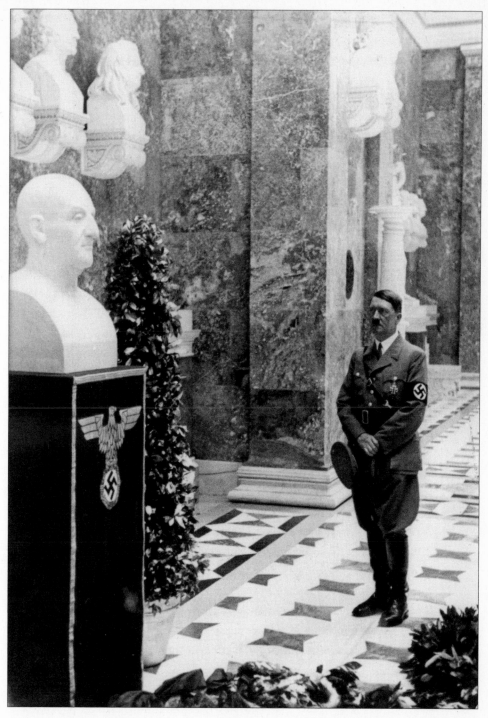

At a propaganda spectacle at the Regensburg Valhalla on 6 June 1937 Hitler National-Socialized Anton Bruckner, a composer whose music he did not greatly care for at the time.

before a monument at the 'Valhalla hall of fame' near Regensburg as Siegmund von Hausegger and the Munich Philharmonic played the adagio of the Seventh Symphony. The ceremony was a graphic example of the painstaking artifice of totalitarian theatrics – comparable with Mussolini's grotesque reburial of Garibaldi or Lenin's being pickled and displayed on Red Square – in which a national figure is used as a symbol for some ulterior purpose. The hypocrisy of the event was epitomized in the fact that the main address was given by Goebbels, who was anything but an admirer of the composer. 'I do not really like Bruckner,' he later confided to his diary, 'he cannot be considered among the great symphonic composers.' And his only comment on the ceremony itself was a cynical: 'We should promote him more.' Even then he did not take his own advice and Bruckner's symphonies were performed less frequently in the Third Reich than they had been in the Weimar period.

Why Hitler staged that event is not known. Speculation has ranged from the theory that it was intended as a cultural precursor of the annexation of Austria the following year to the notion that it was out of nostalgia for his 'beautiful time as a choirboy' with its Bruckner associations. Undoubtedly the dictator felt a personal kinship. Both had come from small Austrian towns, grew up in modest circumstances, had fathers who died at an early age, were autodidacts and made their way in life despite great obstacles. On a number of occasions he contrasted the Austrian Catholic Bruckner, whom the Viennese shunned, to the north German Protestant Brahms, whom they idolized. But suddenly in 1940 he developed a passion for Bruckner's symphonies. He even began mentioning him in the same breath with Wagner. 'He told me,' Goebbels noted in his diary, '. . . that it was only now during the war, that he had learned to like him at all.' The enthusiasm steadily grew. By 1942 he placed Bruckner on a level with Beethoven and categorized the former's Seventh Symphony as 'one of the most splendid manifestations of German musical creativity, the equivalent of Beethoven's Ninth'. His feelings about Bruckner, man and composer, are best conveyed by remarks he made after listening to a recording of the first movement of the Seventh at his military headquarters in January 1942:

[Those are] pure popular melodies from Upper Austria, nothing taken over literally but piece for piece ländler and so on that I know from my youth. What the man made out of this primitive material! In this case it was a priest who deserves well for having supported a great master. The bishop of Linz sat for hours alone in the cathedral when Bruckner, the greatest organist of his time, played the organ. One can imagine how difficult it was for a small peasant lad when he went to Vienna, that urbanized, debauched society. A remark by him about Brahms, which a newspaper recently carried, brought him closer to me: Brahms's music is quite lovely, but he preferred his own. That is the healthy self-confidence of a peasant who is modest but when it came down to it knew how to promote a cause when it was his own. That critic Hanslick made his life in Vienna hell. But when he could no longer be ignored, he was given honours and awards. But what could he do with those? It was his creative activity that should have been made easier.

Brahms was praised to the heavens by Jewry, a creature of salons, a theatrical figure with his flowing beard and hair and his hands raised above the keyboard. Bruckner on the other hand, a shrunken little man, would perhaps have been too shy even to play in such society.

From then on Hitler did everything possible to promote Bruckner and to enlist him in his vendetta against Vienna. St Florian, where the composer's career had begun, was to be turned into a pilgrimage site in the manner of Bayreuth. 'He wants to establish a new cultural centre here,' Goebbels noted. 'Simply as a counterweight to Vienna, which must gradually be shoved aside. . . . He intends to renovate St Florian at his own expense.' Accordingly, Hitler financed a centre of Bruckner studies there, had the famous organ repaired and augmented the composer's library. He even designed a monument in his honour to stand in Linz and endowed a Bruckner Orchestra which he was determined to make one of the world's best. The publication of the Haas edition of the composer's original scores was subsidized from his own funds. And he dreamed of constructing a bell tower in Linz with a carillon that would play a theme from the Fourth Symphony.

An even more startling transformation in Hitler's musical taste was a growing passion for operetta, in particular Franz Lehár's *The Merry Widow*. There was a remarkable irony in this. Although Hitler almost always avoided mentioning the names of contemporary composers and their works, in speeches in 1920 and 1922 he singled out *The Merry Widow* as a pre-eminent example of artistic kitsch. There is no way of knowing when he changed his mind. But some time in the 1930s that very opera became one of his favourites. He never missed a new production of either that or Johann Strauss's *Fledermaus* and drew large sums from his private account for lavish new stagings. Speer even claimed that he considered these works, as well as Carl Zeller's *Der Vogelhändler* and Strauss's *Der Zigeunerbaron*, as sacred parts of the German cultural heritage and the equal of Wagner's.

Eventually Hitler came to revere Lehár as one of the greatest of composers, despite his Jewish wife and his various librettists, all of whom were Jewish. So thrilled was he upon meeting the composer in 1936 at a session of the Reich Culture Chamber that he talked about the experience for days afterwards. The importance of Lehár's music in the last years of his life was evident when he celebrated his birthday in 1943 by treating himself and his guests to a recording of *The Merry Widow*. Making a tremendous to-do over whether it should be a Munich performance or a Berlin performance which Lehár had conducted for him, he launched into a flood of memories and comparisons, finally concluding that the Munich version was, after all, ten per cent better.

Clearly Hitler had a keen ear, but how much did he actually know about music? He possessed a powerful memory, and in fields that interested him – battle fleets and military ordnance, architecture and automobiles – he often befuddled specialists with his detailed, even expert, knowledge. In fact, confounding professionals and showing off to his entourage gave him wicked pleasure, and those around him occasionally suspected that he boned up on a topic only to bring the conversation round to it so that he could exhibit his 'extraordinary knowledge'. After the Viennese première of Richard Strauss's *Friedenstag*, Hitler gave a reception for the artists at which, according to one account, 'He showed an astonishing array of musical knowledge, and was able, for example, to remind Hans Hotter of what he had been singing ten years previously: "Isn't Scarpia too high for you? That G-flat in Act II?"' While confirming the story, Hotter commented that it was difficult to draw much of a conclusion from it. 'Hitler had an exceptionally good memory. According to the nature of an event – in this case music – he would prepare himself by reading relevant literature and surprise everybody by his insider's knowledge.'

Most accounts of his musical expertise relate to his knowledge of Wagnerian opera. Typical was a comment of Winifred Wagner who, as her secretary recorded, 'could not stop raving about what an attentive listener he is and how well he knows the works, above all musically'. In the same vein, Heinz Tietjen remarked that he was 'amazed' at how well the Führer knew Wagner's scores, citing as an example Hitler's comment after a performance that the oboe had not played quite in tune. 'And I had to acknowledge he was right,' the impresario said. More convincing are the comments of Baldur von Schirach. Writing after he had served twenty years in Spandau, he cannot be suspected of gilding the lily. He recalled a performance of *Die Walküre*, which Hitler had attended in Weimar in 1925. Schirach's father was managing director of the opera house and, after the performance, Hitler was introduced to him and went on at great length about what he had seen and heard in a way that demonstrated he really knew his Wagner. He compared the production with those he had attended in Vienna as a young man, naming singers and conductors, and so impressed the elder Schirach that he was invited home to tea. After he left, Schirach *père* was said to have commented: 'In all my life I never met a layman who understood so much about music, Wagner's in particular.' To this account, Speer added that at his fiftieth birthday celebration in 1939 Hitler had been particularly excited by a gift of some of Wagner's original scores and, as he leafed through that of *Götterdämmerung*, 'showed sheet after sheet to the assembled guests, making knowledgeable comments'.

Which were his favourite operas? Despite the poverty of his Vienna years, he managed to attend *Tristan und Isolde* alone thirty or forty times, and in the course of his life heard it and *Die Meistersinger* probably a hundred times. According to his press chief, Otto Dietrich, he knew *Die Meistersinger* by heart and could hum or whistle all its themes. *Lohengrin* no doubt held a special place in his heart. According to Fest, Hitler considered the final scene of *Götterdämmerung* to be 'the summit of all opera'. He further cites Speer as having told him, 'In Bayreuth, whenever the citadel of the gods collapsed in flames amid the musical uproar, in the darkness of the loge he would take the hand of Frau Wagner, sitting next to him, and in deep emotion bestow a kiss upon it.'

Be that as it may, it was *Tristan und Isolde* that meant most to him. After listening one evening in 1942 to a recording of the Prelude and Liebestod, he commented, 'Well, *Tristan* was his greatest work.' According to Christa Schroeder, the Liebestod moved him so deeply that he said he wished to hear it at the time of his death. And in a letter from Landsberg prison in 1924 he wrote that he often 'dreamed of *Tristan*'. At a 1938 Bayreuth performance Winifred observed, 'He is overjoyed at each beautiful passage that he especially loves; then his face just shines.' There is no way of knowing whether it was the eroticism, the sense of longing, the triumph of sensuality over reason that – in contrast to his own repressed and unfulfilled sexual instincts – appealed to him. Possibly it was the cult of the night or the tragic end. Maybe just the music.

Tannhäuser engaged him less, and he was long familiar only with the composer's earliest score, the so-called Dresden version. At some point in the 1930s he heard the later Paris version and was so taken with it that he ordered Goebbels and Göring to permit only that score to be performed. *Parsifal* aroused grave misgivings. Whatever he thought of the music, he could not have liked the story. His anti-clericalism and active detestation of priests and monks – to say nothing of such notions as penitence, redemption and compassion – made it intolerable. Since the plot could not be altered, however, he wanted the opera at least to be performed in a way that secularized it. This was the reason he wanted Roller to restage it at Bayreuth. And this elucidates Hans Frank's story that, while riding on his train through the Rhineland in 1936, Hitler asked to have played for him a recording of Karl Muck's performance of the Prelude to the opera. Afterwards, in a deeply contemplative mood, he purportedly remarked, 'Out of *Parsifal* I shall make for myself a religion, religious service in solemn form without theological disputation.' He went on to say that it – presumably both the opera and his new religion – was to be stripped of all its sacred aspects. Once the war began permission to stage the opera was, except in Vienna, rarely given.

The religious symbolism in the opera continued to nag at Hitler even during the war. Returning briefly to Berlin from the Russian front in November 1941, he raised the subject during a meeting with Goebbels. After the war, he declared, he would see to it either that religion was banished from *Parsifal* or that *Parsifal* was banished from the stage. He recalled that the Vienna opera archive held sketches of Roller's 1914 production and he commended these as models for producers. Not waiting for the final victory, Goebbels passed on the word to his ministerial officials with instructions to have photographs of the Roller sketches circulated to every opera house. Managers were informed that any future staging of the work was to follow the Roller model and 'was no longer to be done in the Byzantine-sacred style that was common up to then'.

It has sometimes been assumed that Hitler was attracted to Wagner's works because of the plots, with their classic conflict between the outsider and a rigid social order, their lonely heroes and dark villains, their Nordic myths and Germanic legends. However, there is no record of any comment on how he interpreted the works or whether he saw in them any ideological message – much less whether he envisaged himself as Lohengrin, Siegmund, Siegfried, Wotan or any other Wagnerian character. It was the music that moved him. 'When I hear Wagner it seems to me like the rhythms of the primeval world,' he said. 'And I could imagine that science will one day find measures of creation in the proportions of the physically perceptible vibrations of the *Rheingold* music.' Perhaps he was trying to say what Thomas Mann wrote in *Dr Faustus* – that the elements of music are the first and simplest materials of the world and make music one with the world, that 'the beginning of all things had its music'. Through Wagner's works Hitler probably came to experience a bliss that was as close to spirituality as he ever reached. Christa Schroeder recalled his saying that 'Wagner's musical language sounded in his ear like a revelation of the divine'. The vocabulary suggests that the feelings conjured by the operas may have filled the void left by the religious belief he lost or never really had. In one of his earliest speeches he made the revealing comment that in their way Wagner's works were holy, that they offered 'exaltation and liberation from all the wretchedness and misery as well as all the decadence that prevails' and that they lift one 'up into the pure air'. If escape and purification were part of the appeal, the operas also responded to that proclivity for the overwhelming, the oceanic, the romantic, the orgasmic that was evident in his public rallies, parades and spectacles.

Like Wagner himself, Hitler believed that music fully realized itself only when it fused with other arts in visible form on stage. And, like Wagner, his interest extended to virtually every aspect of operatic production, down to the fabric and design of the theatre itself. He was fascinated by backstage operations, including the functioning of stage machinery. During his visit to Weimar in 1925, he asked to go behind the stage at the National Theatre. Schirach was with him at the time and later remarked, 'He was familiar with all sorts of lighting systems and could discourse in detail on the proper illumination for certain scenes.' Hans Severus Ziegler recalled taking a walk with Hitler one night at the Berghof when the moon suddenly appeared from behind a cloud and lit the surrounding meadow. Hitler stopped in his tracks and launched into a discussion of the colour of light necessary to achieve verisimilitude for moonlight on a stage, as in the concluding scene of the second act of *Die Meistersinger*. He was insistent that it should be white; but 'it is often greenish or blueish and that is wrong', he complained. 'That is just Romantic kitsch.'

Already in his youth Hitler had made sketches of Wagnerian stage sets that he imagined or actually saw. Although a drawing of Siegfried holding a raised sword is a Kujau forgery, several authentic sketches survive. Among them is one of the second act of *Lohengrin*; others include his rendering of the second and third acts of the famous 1903 Mahler-Roller production of *Tristan und Isolde*, which he had attended in Vienna. This interest in stage design increased after he became chancellor and reached such an eccentric level that it was common knowledge that the best way to get an appointment with him, which otherwise might take months, was to let him know that you had photos of a new staging of an operetta or opera, particularly Wagnerian. An invitation was almost certain to follow, and then Hitler would spend

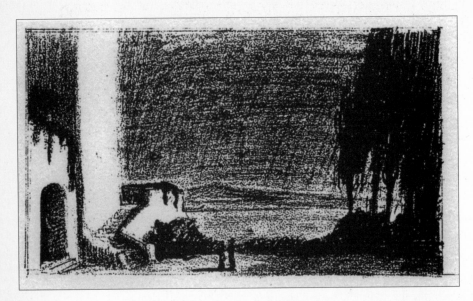

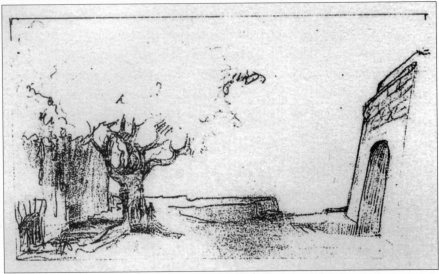

Hitler's 1925 sketchbook included sketches of the staging of Acts II and III of Tristan und Isolde, *based on Alfred Roller's 1903 production.*

countless hours studying the pictures. Most of all he relished working with Benno von Arent, and together they designed several productions that he commissioned and paid for with his private funds – among them, *Lohengrin* in 1935 at the German Opera in Berlin, *Rienzi* in 1939 at the Dietrich Eckart Open Air Theatre in Berlin and *Die Meistersinger* in 1934 and later years at

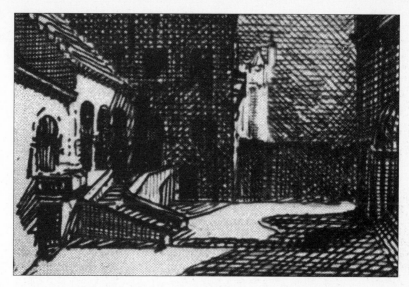

One of Hitler's early opera sketches is of the second act of Lohengrin.

the Nuremberg opera in connection with the party rally. Speer recalled:

> At the chancellery Hitler once sent up to his bedroom for neatly executed
> stage designs, coloured with crayons, for all the acts of Tristan und Isolde;
> these were to be given to Arent to serve as an inspiration. Another time he
> gave Arent a series of sketches for all the scenes of Der Ring des
> Nibelungen. At lunch he told us with great satisfaction that for three weeks
> he had sat up over these, night after night. This surprised me the more
> because at this particular time Hitler's daily schedule was unusually heavy
> with visitors, speeches, sightseeing and other public activities.

Undoubtedly, Arent's work reflected Hitler's taste. His setting for the
second act of *Tristan*, for example, was a vulgar pastiche of Roller's Vienna
staging that Hitler adored. The main trait of the Hitler–Arent style was, as
Speer phrased it, 'smashing effects', and Arent's productions were smashing.
Gigantic choruses and parades, huge casts of extras and glitzy costumes
characterized *Lohengrin* and *Rienzi*. But the Hitler–Arent chef-d'oeuvre was
their 1934 joint production of *Die Meistersinger*. This culminated in a third-
act meadow scene staged in the manner of a Nuremberg party rally, with
massed banners and martial chorus. No detail of the production escaped
Hitler's eye. He fretted over the moonlight scene in the second act and went
into ecstasies over the brilliant colours he wanted for the final scene on the
mastersingers' meadow and over the romantic look of the little gabled houses
opposite Hans Sachs's cobbler's shop. In any case what Hitler imposed on the

opera was more his personal taste than his ideology, with the result that the production was memorable more for its vulgarity than its politics. So proud of it was he that he sent it on tour – from Nuremberg to the German Opera in Berlin in 1935, then to Munich in 1936, Danzig in 1938, Weimar in 1939 and Linz in 1941. It even enjoyed a measure of resurrection after the war when the costumes were used in 1951 at the Bayreuth Festival, then too impoverished to afford to make its own.

Hitler's adulation of Wagner-the-composer probably developed into veneration of Wagner-the-man rather quickly. Except for Frederick the Great and Bismarck, on no other person did he lavish such repeated and fulsome praise. 'I must be frank to say that Richard Wagner's personality meant more to me than Goethe's,' he remarked on one occasion. 'The Führer talks to me of Richard Wagner, he reveres him and knows of no one like him,' Goebbels once recorded. He even managed to drag Wagner's name into his 1923 putsch attempt, telling the court at his trial that he had been partly inspired by the composer's example of preferring deeds to words.

> When I stood at Wagner's grave for the first time my heart just overflowed with pride that here rested a man who would not permit the inscription on his tombstone: 'Here lies Privy Counsellor, Music Director, His Excellency Baron Richard von Wagner'. I was proud that this man, like many men in German history, was content to leave his name to posterity not a title.

From these crumbs some writers have cooked a banquet. Already in the early 1930s it was being argued that Wagner did not simply enchant Hitler with his music and inspire his anti-Semitism, stagecraft and political ideas but also that he helped to create the very ideological atmosphere that put him in power. 'Of all German creative figures, Wagner has been the most dangerous, having contributed more than anyone else to the confusion of the present time. He is the real father of the current German state of mind,' wrote Emil Ludwig. It was not by chance, he went on, that Hitler was a Wagnerian. The two men were personally alike – 'genuine fanatics and at the same time consummate actors'. Moreover, they worked the same material. The composer took the German sagas just as they were. 'In them there was no freedom or loyalty but only power, betrayal and sex.' Such were the ideals that Wagner proffered the German people. But it was not just the stories and the 'impenetrable fog of musical sound' that created a mood of 'mystical rapture' but also his twisting of the German language. 'Only Hitler's prose could compete with his,' the historian complained.

Dangerous morals, dangerous music, dangerous language. These were themes developed in later years by Thomas Mann. The novelist was scarcely less smitten by Wagner than was Hitler himself. He too as a youth had haunted his local opera house and *Lohengrin* had also been the first of the Master's operas he had attended. Mann spoke of the composer as his '*stärkstes, bestimmendes Erlebnis*', his strongest and most formative experience. From the beginning to the end of his life he was enthralled by the music and bewitched by the man. Wagner was the subject or important theme of nearly a dozen essays, any number of letters and countless diary entries. But while Hitler uncritically admired everything he knew about the composer's life, character, ideology and musical creation, Mann was ambivalent about them all. 'Questionable' and 'dubious' were adjectives he used over and over. At one point he insisted that a choice had to be made between Goethe and Wagner, at another that the spirit of both was embedded in the German mind. Not only was Mann's attitude ambivalent and contradictory, it constantly changed. 'I can write about him today like this and tomorrow like that,' he confessed late in life.

Mann's most important commentary on Wagner was an address to the Goethe Society of Munich in February 1933 on the fiftieth anniversary of the composer's death. Entitled *The Sufferings and Greatness of Richard Wagner*, it was a deeply searching and astute treatment of Wagner's place in European culture. The fruit of years of thought, it placed the composer among the greatest of artistic figures without overlooking his weaknesses of character. The talk concluded with a warning – inserted after Hitler's rise to power some days earlier – that Wagner's works would be traduced were they turned to chauvinist effect. 'It is thoroughly inadmissible to ascribe a contemporary meaning to Wagner's nationalist gestures and speeches. To do so is to falsify and abuse them, to sully their Romantic purity.'

Despite its praise and its silence about Wagner's anti-Semitism, omitted as inappropriate to the occasion, Mann's speech occasioned a furious reaction on the part of Hans Knappertsbusch. The arch-conservative and nationalistic conductor circulated an open letter, signed by Richard Strauss and Hans Pfitzner among others, condemning Mann for his 'aestheticizing snobbery' and for having 'insulted' the composer for his 'dilettantism'. Knappertsbusch was a great hater, and this gratuitous attack may have offered a way of indirectly settling accounts with Bruno Walter via his friend, Thomas Mann. Or it may have been an effort to ingratiate himself with the new Führer who by then had already made Wagner the cultural hero of the new Reich. Whether Hitler himself was aware of the episode is not known, though the letter was signed by his close friend and the publisher of *Mein Kampf*, Max Amann. In any event the letter created a climate so vicious that Mann was forced into exile.

In the course of the 1930s, as he witnessed Europe in a trance-like state succumbing to the evil arts of a political magician, Mann examined Hitler's character and the more he looked the more he saw Wagner. By 1938 this prompted him to remark in his first out-and-out anti-Nazi essay, *Bruder Hitler* (Brother Hitler), that the 'Hitler phenomenon' was 'Wagnerian, albeit in a perverted way. One had long noticed it and recognizes the reasonable though somewhat illicit adoration which the political miracle-worker devotes to that artistic enchanter of Europe whom Gottfried Keller once called "hairdresser and charlatan".'

Yet it was less the composer than the compositions that increasingly troubled him. The music he had always found deeply unsettling. In 1901, at the very time Hitler was making his first acquaintance with *Lohengrin*, Mann was drafting a passage in *Buddenbrooks* about the reaction of Herr Pfühl, an organist and Buddenbrook family friend, upon first hearing a few bars of *Tristan* on the piano: 'This is demagogy, blasphemy, insanity, madness! It is a perfumed fog, shot through with lightning. It is the end of all honesty in art.' It would, he claimed, utterly corrupt a person's soul. Eventually, however, Pfühl succumbed and 'with an expression of shamefaced pleasure, he would glide into the weaving harmonies of the leitmotiv'. This passage was, in fact, autobiographical and Herr Pfühl's comments illustrate how Mann himself had been converted but never lost the feeling that the operas were intoxicating but dangerous – indeed, dangerous because they were intoxicating – and appealed to the irrational side of the mind. On the same day in October 1937 Mann noted in his diary on the one hand that he found 'elements of a frighteningly Hitleresque quality' in a poem Wagner had written for Cosima and on the other that he had listened to a recording of *Die Walküre* 'with admiration'. A month earlier he had heard a broadcast of a performance of his much loved *Lohengrin*, and this had provoked another diary comment, '*furchtbare Hitlerei*' – dreadful Hitlerism.

Not until 1940 did he confess his confusions publicly. In a letter to a New York monthly publication, *Common Sense*, he wrote:

I find an element of Nazism not only in Wagner's questionable literature; I find it also in his 'music', in his work. . . . This work, created and directed 'against civilization', against the entire culture and society dominant since the Renaissance, emerges from the bourgeois-humanist epoch in the same manner as does Hitlerism. With its Wagalaweia and its alliteration, its mixture of roots-in-the-soil and eyes-towards-the-future, its appeal for a classless society, its mythical-reactionary revolutionism – with all these, it is the exact spiritual forerunner of the 'metapolitical' movement today terrorizing the world.

Here was Mann at his most emotional and opaque, Mann indulging in the tortured philosophical musings of the civilized German of his day in the desperate search for some explanation of what Germany had come to. But even looking back from the relative tranquillity of 1949, he still saw similarities in the character of the two men. 'There is, in Wagner's bragging, endless ranting, domineering monologue, and above all having a say about everything, an unspeakable arrogance that prefigures Hitler – certainly there is much "Hitler" in Wagner. . . .'

Those were trivial traits to lead to such an awesome conclusion. But in his final comment on the subject, in 1951, he returned to where he had started. Despite Hitler's defilement of it, he praised *Die Meistersinger* as 'a splendid work, a festival drama if ever there was one, a poetic work in which wisdom and daring, the worthy and revolutionary, tradition and the future are wedded together in a gloriously serene manner that arouses a deep-seated enthusiasm for life and for art'.

The case for the prosecution received fresh impetus with the publication both of Theodor Adorno's *Versuch über Wagner* (In Search of Wagner), which deprecated the composer from a musicologist's point of view, and of Joachim Fest's searching biography, which was more broadly accusatory. According to Fest, the youthful Hitler

succumbed to the music of Richard Wagner. . . . The charged emotionality of this music seemed to have served him as a means for self-hypnosis, while he found in its lush air of bourgeois luxury the necessary ingredients for escapist fantasy . . . .

Hitler himself in fact later declared that with the exception of Richard Wagner he had 'no forerunners', and by Wagner he meant not only the composer but Wagner the personality, 'the greatest prophetic figure the German people has had' . . . . The points of contact between the two temperaments – all the more marked because the young postcard painter consciously modelled himself after his hero – produce a curious sense of family resemblance . . . .

The style of public ceremonies in the Third Reich is inconceivable without [Wagner's] operatic tradition, without the essentially demagogical art of Richard Wagner. . . . [Hitler and Wagner] were masters of the art of brilliant fraudulence, of inspired swindling . . . .

For the Master of Bayreuth was not only Hitler's great exemplar, he was also the young man's ideological mentor. Wagner's political writings were Hitler's favourite reading, and the sprawling pomposity of his style unmistakably influenced Hitler's own grammar and syntax. Those political writings, together with the operas, form the entire framework for Hitler's ideology. . . . Here he found the 'granite foundations' for his view of the world.

Nothing could have symbolized the association more provocatively than the opening scene of Hans Jürgen Syberberg's 1977 film, *Hitler*, in which the dictator rises ectoplasmically out of Wagner's Bayreuth grave. As attacks on the composer's anti-Semitism became an obsession in some circles in the 1980s and 1990s, Hitler almost became a mere accessory after the fact to the point that the dictator was eventually portrayed as a passive creature of the wicked composer. It was 'Wagner's Hitler', as one writer entitled his book, rather than 'Hitler's Wagner'.

Such are the allegations. What are the facts? One is that what Hitler admired in the composer was what he admired in his other heroes, courage. In a speech in 1923 he defined the vital quality of human greatness as 'the heroic' and attributed it to three men: Luther, Frederick the Great and Wagner – the reformer because he possessed the courage to stand alone against the world, the king because he never lost courage when his lot appeared hopeless and the composer because he had the courage to struggle in solitude. Each had fought, had fought alone and had fought 'like a titan'. As a desperately lonely and friendless figure in his early days, Hitler must have seen his own situation mirrored in such struggles. Wagner was thus a symbol or, better, a model of someone who believed in his destiny and let nothing deter him from it. It was no doubt in this sense that he considered the composer, in the oft-cited phrase, his only forebear. Once he had started his wars, however, it was Frederick the Great's example to which he turned and it was the king's portrait, not Wagner's, that he carried with him to his military headquarters and into the Berlin bunker at the end.

Another is that Hitler never ascribed any of his views to Wagner, not in *Mein Kampf*, his speeches, articles or recorded private conversations. He made occasional references to him – as to other artists, such as Schiller,

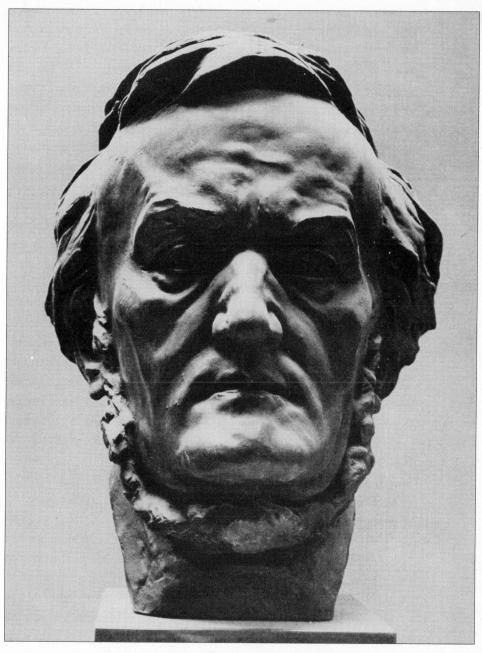

In 1940 Breker sculpted a bust of Hitler and one of Wagner. Hitler disliked the one of himself but was delighted with the Wagner work. He told Goebbels it achieved the sculptural ideal of avoiding both 'photography and phantasy' while expressing 'the characteristic and the enduring'.

Goethe and Beethoven – but none were of a substantive nature. It is easy to read *Mein Kampf* and the speeches, and then search Wagner's writings to find coincidences. But this is a game that can be played with countless other figures. True, there are certain obvious parallels in outlook – a demented anti-Semitism, Hellenism, the belief that culture was the *summum bonum* of a civilization, the notion that the arts should never be hostage to commerce and the like. But these ideas might just as easily have been picked up from others. Certainly Wagner's pamphlet *Judentum in der Musik* (Jewishness in Music) resonates in Hitler's claim that Jews lack artistic creativity. But it is remarkable that at no time did he ever trace his anti-Semitism to the composer, not even in his 1920 speech '*Warum sind wir Antisemiten?*' (Why are We Anti-Semites?), in which he expounded his views for the first time in public.

Indeed, there is no evidence that Hitler ever read Wagner's collected writings, much less that they were 'his favourite reading'. The origin of the myth is probably Kubizek's book, where the youthful Hitler was said to have read every biography, letter, essay, diary and other scrap by and about his hero that he could lay his hands on. But Kubizek himself contradicted that story in his 'Reminiscences'. In any case, Hitler himself never made such a claim. A large hall would be necessary to accommodate all the persons from whom Hitler picked up his ideas. To single out in the crowd the short man with a large nose and prominent chin as the one and only or even the most important one betrays a lack of knowledge of intellectual history. In short, to hold Wagner responsible for Hitler is as far-fetched as to make Marx responsible for Lenin and Stalin, the starvation of the kulaks and the great purges. Wagner's Hitler does not exist. 'Hitler's Wagner' was an opera composer, not a political mentor.

14 'Führer of the Bayreuth Republic'

WAGNER-THE-COMPOSER AND WAGNER-THE-MAN both inevitably drew Hitler to Bayreuth. To attend the Festival, he once wrote to the composer's son Siegfried, was a dream that had possessed him since the age of thirteen when he went to his first Wagnerian opera. However, it was neither opera nor homage to the composer that first took him there on 30 September 1923 but an engagement to speak at a National Socialist rally. After his speech, Hitler took the occasion to call upon Houston Stewart Chamberlain, author of the best-selling racist book *The Foundations of the Nineteenth Century* and a man whom Hitler admired. Chamberlain, an Englishman who had taken up German citizenship in 1914, was also a devotee of Wagner and had married his younger daughter Eva. Although crippled and able to communicate only through his wife, Chamberlain was convinced by the end of their meeting that he was in the presence of Germany's saviour. A short time later he said as much in a widely publicized letter, a pronouncement that gave Hitler his first endorsement by a noted national figure. Issued at a time when the party and its leader seemed headed nowhere, Chamberlain's words came, Fest has written, 'as the answer to his doubts, as a benediction from the Bayreuth Master himself'.

Following his meeting with Chamberlain, Hitler attended a reception at the Anker Hotel hosted by Edwin Bechstein, the piano manufacturer, and his wife Helene. Winifred Wagner was also present and, impressed by the young man's devotion to Wagner, invited him to come the next day to visit Wahnfried, the villa that the composer constructed for himself in 1874. On his arrival the Wagners found him nervous, pale and badly dressed. As they conducted him through the house, he was silent and thoughtful. Nothing escaped his awed attention. This was holy ground and so moved was he that twenty years later he was still reminiscing about it. Eventually they directed him to the Master's grave, where he stood alone for a long time in silent homage. On leaving, he remarked that since first hearing *Lohengrin* as a boy, he had regarded the composer as one of the greatest figures in German history. He promised that if he ever, as he put it, 'came to exert influence on Germany's destiny', he would honour Wagner's wish that *Parsifal* – out of copyright since 1913 – should be performed only in Bayreuth.

The visit inaugurated a personal relationship between Hitler and the Wagner family, above all with Winifred, that lasted for the rest of his life. Dramatic proof of the friendship came five weeks later in connection with the Beer Hall Putsch. The day after the coup attempt, Siegfried was in Innsbruck for a concert engagement and, learning that the wounded Hermann Göring had fled there, visited him in the hospital to pay his respects and, according to rumour, his medical bills as well. In Bayreuth, Winifred issued an open letter to the press giving the family's full endorsement to Hitler, who was now in prison. According to a story invented years later by her daughter Friedelind, she also sent him a gift package which included writing paper – and this was the very paper on which Hitler wrote *Mein Kampf*! In fact Hitler did not scribble out the text of his book, he dictated it to Rudolf Hess and others, and it is not known what they wrote on. The claim is irrelevant in any case, since the only point the story can have is the foolish one that Hitler would never have written *Mein Kampf* had Winifred not sent him paper.

What genuinely meant something to Hitler was Winifred's having actively campaigned on behalf of his party in the local election in April of the following year. Afterwards a deeply gratified Hitler sent Siegfried an effusive letter highlighting Bayreuth's significance for his political movement. Nothing could have given him greater satisfaction, he wrote, than the election success in Bayreuth, the very place 'where first the Master and then Chamberlain forged the spiritual sword with which we fight today'. The town, he continued, lay on the 'march route to Berlin'. He had wanted to thank Chamberlain for his 'wonderfully gracious letter', but the failure of his political action had made that impossible. He went on to express his deepest thanks for the way he and especially Winifred had identified themselves with his movement and 'the love that you have shown me in the face of all the hatred and calumny heaped on me'.

From this point on the Wagners became increasingly identified with the hard right in German politics. Siegfried was never a Nazi, but he was a naïve, arch-conservative who idolized General Ludendorff and fêted him as guest of honour at the 1924 Festival. Later he and Winifred lent their names to various Nazi-front organizations. Hitler never forgot their loyalty. 'It was not just the others but Siegfried Wagner as well who stood by me at the time when things were at their worst for me,' he remarked years later. But when he proposed to visit Wahnfried on leaving prison, Siegfried realized it would be embarrassing to have an ex-jailbird hanging around the house and turned him down. To allay hurt feelings, Winifred travelled to Munich to see Hitler and happened to find herself at the very meeting at which the Nazi party was refounded following the disastrous coup attempt. She persuaded her friend to accompany her to a performance of one of her husband's operas being held at Plauen in Saxony. En route they stopped in Bayreuth and Hitler spent his first night at Wahnfried. With this, the friendship between the two was sealed.

The following summer the Bechsteins invited Hitler to be their guest and to attend the Festival. 'I did not really want to go,' he later said, 'thinking to myself that the difficulties would be even greater for Siegfried – he was somewhat in the hands of the Jews.' But he went and was overjoyed. 'During the day I wore lederhosen, but to the Festival a dinner jacket or morning coat. The free days between performances were always wonderful. . . . When I went to the Eule [restaurant], I had no difficulty meeting singers. On the other hand I was not so famous that I did not have peace.' The *Ring* performances shocked him, however, to the point where he was still raving about it years later. 'That the Jew [Friedrich] Schorr sang Wotan just infuriated me – for me that was a racial outrage.' But that was the only cloud. 'It was a sunny time. . . . I was in seventh heaven,' he later said. He once told Schirach that he liked Bayreuth so much he could imagine spending the last years of his life in that 'culturally pre-eminent little town so impregnated with the spirit of Richard Wagner'.

But a man who had mounted a putsch, been convicted of treason, was banned from public speaking in Bavaria and had a reputation as an anti-Semitic rabble-rouser was not an adornment to the Festival and Hitler realized that his presence was an embarrassment. As he later remarked,

> Then for years I did not attend, which made me very sad. Frau Wagner was terribly upset, wrote to me a dozen times, telephoned me two dozen times. I very often went through Bayreuth, however, and then I stayed with them. Frau Wagner – and that is her historic service – linked Bayreuth to National Socialism. Although Siegfried was personally a friend, he was politically passive. The Jews would have wrung his neck; he could not do anything else.

In fact Jews, far from wringing Siegfried's neck, attended the Festival in goodly numbers and some – such as Thomas Mann's in-laws, the Pringsheims – were important patrons. What had actually nearly destroyed

Siegfried was Siegfried himself. His homosexual affairs, as Hitler well knew, had so risked scandal that his marriage to Winifred in 1915 had to be hastily arranged to forestall disaster for the institution. Hitler was entirely untroubled by the Wagner dynasty's sexual foibles and sometimes gossiped about them, once discussing the rumour that the noted Bayreuth conductor, Karl Muck, was the composer's son.

In the years before becoming chancellor Hitler often stopped in Bayreuth on his travels between Munich and Berlin, and stayed with Winifred and the children in clandestine nocturnal visits. He loved Wahnfried – it 'radiates life', he said – and preferred it to the Goethe-Haus which gave 'the impression of an absolute and utter deadness'. Both before and after 1933 it was a place of refuge for him. He was never taken to see Cosima, who was by then blind and lived, as her first biographer wrote, 'between dreaming and waking'. But the children – Wieland, Friedelind, Wolfgang and Verena – were his great pleasure. 'Sometimes Hitler's car crept up the drive after midnight and he would steal secretly into the house,' Friedelind recalled. 'Late as it was he never failed to come into the nursery and tell us gruesome tales of his adventures. We all sat up among the pillows in the half-light and listened while he made our flesh creep. . . .' They were among the very few permitted to use his nickname 'Wolf'. He called her 'Wini' and the children by their nicknames.

Winifred and her four children were as much of a family as he ever had, and the warm, familial atmosphere must have been of enormous emotional importance. Wahnfried was the home he had not known since childhood, Winifred was the woman he never married and the children were the offspring he lacked. That they were Wagners may have been the key to their allure, but they brought out a side of his character as no one else could do. In January 1942 while in his headquarters on the Russian front he could still rhapsodize about them. 'We used the familiar "*du*" in speaking to one another. I love these people and Wahnfried.' If the man had a heart, it was here, if anywhere, that it was touched.

There was nothing else in his life like this. At Wahnfried more than at the Berghof he could put aside the burdens of office and escape the thuggish party hacks who surrounded him. Everyone in his entourage noticed that Hitler was a changed person during his days at Wahnfried. 'With no other family did he maintain such a deep friendship,' Below recalled. After Siegfried's death in 1930 Hitler revelled in his role as paterfamilias and, when in Bayreuth, could not bear to have a meal unless at least one family member was present. Speer described his mood:

On these Festival days Hitler seemed more relaxed than usual. He obviously felt at ease in the Wagner family and free of the compulsion to represent power, which he sometimes thought himself obliged to do even with the evening group in the chancellery. He was gay, paternal to the children, friendly and solicitous towards Winifred Wagner. . . . As patron of the Festival and as the friend of the Wagner family, Hitler was no doubt realizing a dream which even in his youth he perhaps never quite dared to dream.

'The ten Bayreuth days were always my pleasantest time,' Hitler himself said, 'and how happy I was every time we arrived there again.' And when the Festival came to an end, he went on, 'it is something so sad, just as when the decorations are taken off the Christmas tree'.

One of the Führer's great pleasures were the annual receptions held at Wahnfried for performers. These generally went on through the night. He would expatiate almost nonstop on whatever caught his fancy at the

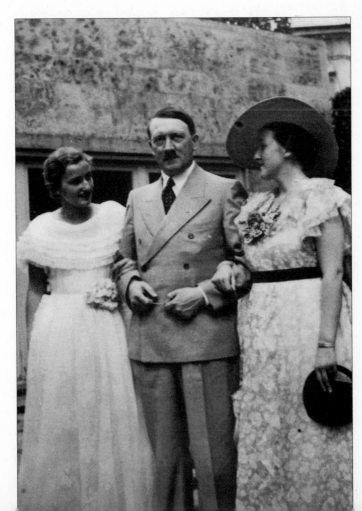

Hitler with Verena (left) and Friedelind Wagner

moment and everyone else listened enthralled without daring to interject a comment or ask a question. A minor singer who attended the 1937 levee wrote down a reverential record of the event, which typically dwelt more on Hitler's mode of speaking and the famous laser-beam effect of his eyes than on the content of his remarks. 'He did not so much speak as words simply flowed from him,' the soloist rhapsodized. 'His gaze seemed to come not from his body but from his entire being, without any physical limit.' Friedelind Wagner gave a similar though less venerative account. Hitler, she said, could never endure a normal exchange for more than five minutes. Instead, he would turn any conversation into a two-hour oration on world or artistic affairs. The effect, she went on, left his listeners 'purple in the face as though they were under the effect of a drug'. But when asked what he had said, 'they couldn't tell us; they . . . had been carried away by their emotions'.

The relationship between Hitler and Winifred was personal, not political. She held no party position and he never awarded her the highest party honour, the golden party badge. Though Hitler rarely corresponded, seven letters and notes to Winifred are known to survive. They convey a cordiality that was quite exceptional in his relationships. The earliest, of 30 December 1927, reads:

My dear Wini,

You simply cannot imagine what a great surprise your Christmas gift was to me. You really have outdone yourself. I have no idea how I can ever thank you.

I now look to the future. And as the end of this year arrives, I think happily of you. I remain convinced that destiny will take me where four years ago I hoped it would. Then the moment will come when your pride in your friend will be the thanks that I cannot today provide.

So heartiest greetings, and accept my best wishes for the coming year.
from your Wolf

Another, on a black-edged correspondence card dated 30 December 1931, thanked her for a Christmas gift and continued in a bleak vein:

These have been very sad days. I must overcome this sense of loneliness. On Christmas day I drove to Berneck and wanted to go on the next day to Berlin. But ice forced me to return to Munich. I passed through Bayreuth but could not bring myself to look you up. Why should one deprive others of their joy just because one is personally so sad? . . .

The most remarkable, written on 8 January 1933, just three weeks before he was appointed chancellor, stated,

> For weeks I have been bogged down by difficult and hard work. One worry after another! I do not know whether you will even understand me any longer. . . . For the past two years Christmas for me has been nothing more than a festival of sorrow. I can no longer manage to be what I was before. . . . I believe the time will certainly come when I can demonstrate my grateful devotion not with words but with deeds. Unfortunately there are always new mountains to be conquered. Today I understand why in my youth it was Wagner and his destiny that spoke to me more than many other great Germans. It was the same ordeal, the eternal struggle against hatred, envy and incomprehension.★ The worries are the same. Perhaps destiny will yet permit me to contribute something.

Hitler's friendship with Winifred aroused gossip, even rumours of romance and possible marriage. Whatever her feelings, Hitler had no intention of marrying anyone and occasionally had a good laugh at the notion that they might wed. The relationship cooled following a dreadful scandal provoked by Friedelind in 1940. Independent-minded, a bit of a rebel and troublemaker, she adored the anti-fascist Toscanini and was close to the soprano Frida Leider, herself married to a Jew. Through such friendships she had come to find Bayreuth and Germany intolerable and in 1938 went to Paris and on to Switzerland. She later claimed that Hitler sent Winifred there to warn that she would be 'destroyed and exterminated' unless she returned, though notations in her diary and correspondence with her mother at the time leave a different impression. In any event, she fled to London in March of 1940, just missing the *Wehrmacht*'s sweep through Western Europe. There, beginning in early May, she published in the *Daily Sketch* a series of twelve articles mocking Hitler and the Nazi leadership. These were immediately picked up by German authorities and passed on to Goebbels and Hitler himself. 'The fat, little Wagner girl divulges revelations about the Führer in London. What a little beast! This could possibly be somewhat embarrassing,' Goebbels confided to his diary when the series was advertised with such headlines as 'The Real Hitler', 'The Truth about this Man' and 'The Young Girl Who Declared War Against the Gods of Berchtesgaden'. Short on facts but long on purported quotes of the Führer and revelations

★ The original title of *Mein Kampf* was 'A Four-and-a-Half-Year Struggle Against Lies, Stupidity and Cowardice'.

about the atmosphere of his court, the articles portrayed Hitler as a bumbling fool who easily worked himself up into hysterics, 'rolling his eyes like some demented fanatic' and referred in other passages to 'his blue eyes now unmistakably those of a madman' and as someone who 'looked as though he were possessed by a demon'. He was, she assured her British readers, 'the greatest liar who ever lived'.

Even though no breath of this exposé ever reached the German public, Hitler, a man almost insanely concerned about his image, was devastated. What hostile articles and books had appeared up to then were all by outspoken anti-Nazis and dealt with Hitler's policies, not his personal life. Here were revelations from a social insider, one of only five persons in Germany – the others being her mother, brothers and sister – on whom he had lavished the most remarkable attention and, in his way, affection. That she should at a time of war go over to the enemy and betray and seek to hurt and humiliate him was a staggering blow. And that some of the factual titbits must originally have come from Winifred, intimating that she considered him socially awkward, doubtless undermined his relations with her.

It was of little importance that the contents were mostly harmless gossip and hearsay. What mattered was that they came from a friend. As one article

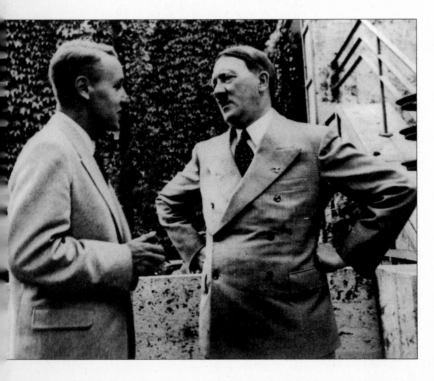

Hitler and Wieland Wagner at Bayreuth.

followed another, the Propaganda Minister became increasingly concerned and even accused her of high treason. 'The Führer has told Wieland Wagner about his sweet little sister. It is really a terrible scandal that this stupid bumpkin is causing.' Now, at the very moment of his greatest military triumph, he was being made fun of before the British public by a young woman with whom he had been so uncharacteristically close. 'He is deeply shaken by Friedelind Wagner's mean-spiritedness,' Goebbels noted. 'A traitor to her country.'

Despite his mortification, Hitler retained his interest in the family and the Festival to the end. Wieland, the eldest of the children and heir presumptive to the Festival, was the one on whom Hitler had always doted. He revered the boy as the corporeal descendant of the composer and spoiled him as a son. He showered him with favours, even inviting him to Munich to present him with a Mercedes as a reward for successfully completing secondary school. He gave Wieland sole permission to take and market photographs of himself in Bayreuth, an arrangement the lad turned to a handy profit. In 1936, when Wieland found life in compulsory labour service physically too demanding, Hitler moved him to an easier camp and ordered that he should be left free to work at the Festival. Once the war began, Hitler did him the greatest kindness by exempting him from military service. While other men his age were off fighting, Wieland spent the war years largely in Munich studying music and painting. Hitler continued to follow his career with interest and had Goebbels put him in charge of production at the opera company in the Saxon town of Altenburg, where he remained until all theatres in Germany were closed in August 1944.

From the moment of his appointment as chancellor, Hitler claimed for himself the Wagnerian legacy. 'After coming to power, my first thought was to erect a grandiose monument in memory of Richard Wagner . . . a monument that would symbolize the immense importance of this genius for German music,' he told Arno Breker. The project occasioned the first artistic competition tendered by the new government. Two weeks later he took advantage of the fiftieth anniversary of the composer's death on 13 February to stage a glittering memorial ceremony. To Leipzig, the composer's birthplace, he summoned the entire cabinet, the diplomatic corps, leading cultural figures as well as Winifred and Wieland. That evening he went on to Weimar and attended a gala performance of *Tristan und Isolde*. A month later, the ceremony in Potsdam formally inaugurating the Third Reich concluded with a performance at the Berlin State Opera of *Die Meistersinger*, a work from then on performed for official state visitors, at the annual party rally and at other important events. In March of 1934 he laid the cornerstone for the 'Richard Wagner National Monument of the German People', a vast sculpture park in the composer's honour in Leipzig. On the occasion of Wagner's 125th birthday in May 1938 he founded the Richard Wagner Memorial Centre in Bayreuth, a research institute devoted to the composer's life and work. Hitler placed the institution under his own aegis rather than the authority of the Propaganda Ministry and instructed that its first order of business should be to investigate the controversial question of whether the composer and his wife had Jewish antecedents.

Few, if any, personal possessions were so prized as his collection of the original scores of Wagner's operas that the composer had given Ludwig II – the autograph scores of *Die Feen*, *Das Liebesverbot* and *Rienzi*, the clean copies of *Das Rheingold* and *Die Walküre*, the original duplicate of the orchestral sketch of the third act of *Siegfried* and a copy of the orchestral sketch of *Götterdämmerung*. At Winifred Wagner's instigation the House of Wittelsbach was persuaded, under some duress, to sell the manuscripts for 800,000 marks to the Reich Economic Chamber, which presented them to the Führer on his fiftieth birthday in 1939. The gesture had a disastrous consequence. As aerial bombing of Berlin intensified and Russian troops neared the capital, Winifred repeatedly appealed to Hitler to send the scores to Bayreuth for safekeeping. Hitler adamantly refused to give them up, insisting they were secure. Whether they were deliberately incinerated in the bonfires that Hitler later ordered of the contents of his safes in Berlin and at the Berghof in his last days or whether they were destroyed by bombs or were carried off with other of his personal effects by the Russians is not known.

Hitler's passion for Wagner aroused great anguish inside the party where it was considered, as Winifred said, 'downright batty'. 'Most leading National Socialist figures were hostile to R[ichard] W[agner] and his art,' Winifred insisted in her memorandum to the denazification tribunal in 1946. Members of Hitler's inner circle, such as Speer, Hoffmann and Dietrich, confirmed this. The point has been so misunderstood and misrepresented since 1945 that a memorandum by Heinz Tietjen merits quotation:

> In reality leading party officials throughout the Reich were hostile to Wagner. . . . Top party officials came to Bayreuth only when ordered and then only a few of them and no more than once. . . . Once a year though

they all pretended to be Wagner fanatics but, even so, not at Bayreuth but after the Festival at the party rally in Nuremberg where they all pretended to like Die Meistersinger. I never attended but I understand that every year after each act more and more of the audience vanished and men in brown and black uniforms had to be rounded up from the streets to fill the auditorium. But the propaganda was always about Bayreuth. Germany believed and still believes in a 'Hitler Bayreuth' that never was. The party tolerated Hitler's Wagner enthusiasm, but fought against those who, like me, were devoted to his works – the people around Rosenberg openly, those around Goebbels covertly . . . .

Tietjen had put his finger on the problem. What most ostentatiously linked Hitler and Wagner in the public mind was the dictator's attendance at the Bayreuth Festival every summer from 1933 to 1940. Even before coming to power, he had several times intervened on the Festival's behalf. In 1930 he had offered his support in surmounting the artistic difficulties facing Bayreuth following Siegfried's death that summer. Two years later, when Wilhelm Furtwängler had a falling-out with Winifred and resigned, he tried to mediate. But it was when he became chancellor that his help was crucial. Ironically, the problem was the very result of his coming to power. Within weeks Winifred found to her horror that Nazi officials were cultural barbarians who deprecated Bayreuth as a musical playground for an international elite. The local party chief let it be known that he intended to 'smoke out that international crowd at Wahnfried'.

A frightened Winifred appealed to Hitler, who invited her to lunch at the chancellery two months after taking office. As cordial as ever, he acknowledged the animus against Wagner and Bayreuth within his party and promised that as long as he was alive the Festival could count on his protection. He said he could best counter the party's hostility by showing up there every summer. While his assurances removed her political worries, it did not solve her financial problems. Because of the international economic crisis and the domestic political situation, ticket sales that year were so meagre that the Festival faced bankruptcy. She returned to Berlin to plead for help, which Hitler promised without hesitation. He instructed party officials from then on to book large blocks of seats – sometimes entire performances – and further authorized a significant grant to fund new productions. He had once maintained he could imagine nothing finer than to be a cultural philanthropist. This was his first act of philanthropy and he relished it to the full. At a memorial event for Wagner held that summer at Ludwig II's castle at Neuschwanstein, he declared that he saw it as his mission to complete what the monarch, Wagner's great patron, had begun. By guaranteeing the Festival's finances for the first time in its history, Hitler did in fact give reality to the composer's dream of a Bayreuth recognized by the state as an 'obligation of the nation'.

Hitler's involvement with Bayreuth also had disadvantages. Foreigners and Jews, naturally enough, lost their taste for the Festival, and some singers declined to perform there. Most dramatically, Toscanini refused to conduct in 1933. Appalled at the treatment of a number of German conductors such as Bruno Walter, who had been prevented from conducting in Leipzig and Berlin that spring, Toscanini cancelled his engagement. It was a sensational public affront to the new chancellor and a great blow to the Festival where the conductor was popular with audiences and admired by critics. Toscanini joined Walter at the Salzburg Festival and their presence turned the long artistic rivalry between Bayreuth and Salzburg into open political confrontation. Hitler responded by requesting artists, such as Furtwängler and Strauss, to withdraw from Salzburg – they compliantly obeyed – and levied an exit tax at the German border so large as to make it impossible for the German public to attend.

The paradoxical effect of Hitler's patronage was to make the Festival the only cultural institution in the Third Reich independent of Nazi control. Since no party official dared interfere, Winifred and her team went on with their work, neither hiring nor firing anyone for political reasons. She retained Heinz Tietjen as her general manager and Emil Preetorius as her stage designer, even though neither was personally, politically or artistically in good odour with Hitler. Efforts by Rosenberg, whom she considered implacably hostile to Wagnerian opera, to merge all Wagner Societies into one organization under himself she scotched. She even managed to fend off the biggest predator of all, Goebbels. Tormented by the Festival's independence of his ministry and Hitler's closeness to the Wagner family, he tried again and again to get his hands on the institution or at least to force Winifred to join his Reich Theatre Chamber. He came to detest Winifred and Wieland, and disparaged the Festival as a 'family and clique affair' that should be taken out of their hands. But his efforts to poison Hitler's mind – by portraying the Festival as a hotbed of homosexuality, for example – all failed. The propaganda wizard had to content himself with venting his frustration to his diary: 'With a woman in charge, poor Bayreuth! The Führer is her greatest protector.'

'. . . You know that nothing happens in Bayreuth that is not at the Führer's initiative or in keeping with his explicit approval. . . .' Thus Winifred in a letter to Strauss in June 1935. 'Hitler never interfered with any artistic questions concerning the Festival but on the opposite backed any of my decisions which might not agree with the party programme.' Thus Winifred in a memorandum she wrote in English for American military authorities shortly after the war. Which statement is correct? Until all of Winifred's correspondence is made public – in any case many of their exchanges were by phone – there can be no conclusive answer.

Given his devotion to Wagner and fascination with operatic staging, Hitler must have been tempted to exert some influence on what went on. His request, soon after becoming chancellor, to have Roller do an entirely new production of *Parsifal* was evidence enough. Not long thereafter, as Richard Strauss's son wrote to a member of the Wagner family, 'The Führer told my dad that he has a lot of projects in mind for Bayreuth, but they are still up in the air.' Winifred herself mentioned in her 1975 television interview that after a performance she and Hitler returned to Wahnfried and discussed it long into the night. The Führer is said to have expressed strong opinions on these occasions, though it is unclear whether about the singing, conducting or staging. According to Friedelind Wagner, he made occasional suggestions about staging and would have liked a second act of *Tristan* similar

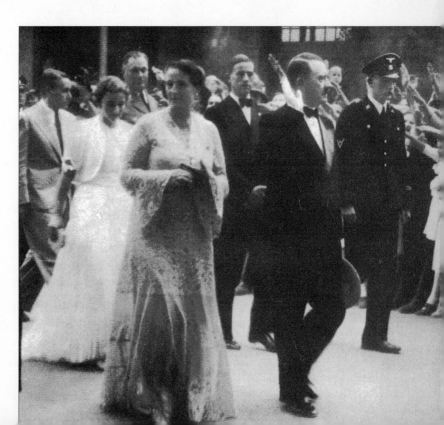

Hitler at his annual pilgrimage to the Bayreuth Festival. (From left) Wieland Wagner, Verena Wagner, Wilhelm Bruckner (an adjutant), Winifred Wagner, Karl Brandt (Hitler's physician) and Julius Schaub (an adjutant).

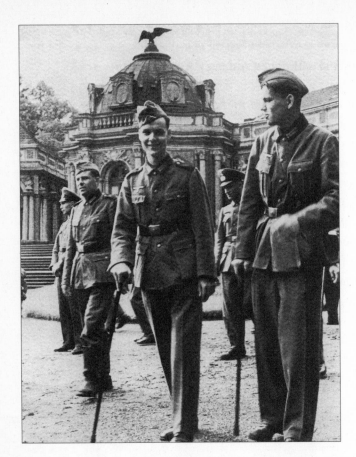

Hitler could think of no greater treat for his warriors than to give them a free performance of a Wagner opera at Bayreuth. Here some of them are enjoying a free morning at the Eremitage, a nearby margraviate country house.

to Roller's 1903 version in Vienna – with a romantic moon and countless stars – a drawing of which he had made in his 1925 sketchbook. Other ideas, if Friedelind is to be believed, were to have the Flower Maidens dance around Parsifal naked and the Norns sit on the top of a globe representing the world.

Both out of personal friendship and financial dependence – to say nothing of political realities – Winifred had little option but to take Hitler's views seriously. Judging by her later correspondence, she discussed with him the selection of conductors and major soloists – matters on which he had strong opinions. But while he more or less imposed Furtwängler on her in 1936, he allowed her to sack him the next year. All in all, Winifred ran the Festival as she saw fit. She protected gay singers – Max Lorenz and Herbert Janssen – and engaged Franz von Hößlin to conduct when, because of his Jewish wife, he was unwelcome at other German opera houses. There is no evidence, the Roller case apart, that Hitler interfered with staging or directing. To be sure, with his love of 'smashing effects', he found Bayreuth productions staid and pressed Winifred to bring in the dazzling Benno von Arent. Winifred stood firm, however, and, according to Speer, whenever the subject arose, 'she pretended not to know what Hitler was driving at'. After the war Heinz Tietjen declared flatly that 'Hitler himself never expressed any demands or wishes'.

He did interfere massively, however, by proposing to replace the composer's great opera theatre with a vast new edifice. His idea of impressive opera houses was Charles Garnier's ornate edifice in Paris and Gottfried Semper's imposing one in Dresden. Although eventually persuaded to retain Wagner's original auditorium because of its outstanding acoustics, he wanted it to be encased in a rambling building of typically neoclassical architecture designed by Rudolf Emil Mewis. The monstrous pile was to be inaugurated at a gala 'Peace Festival' celebrating Hitler's final military victory. Construction was initiated in 1939 but stopped after the war got under way.

For all the ideological agnosticism of what took place on stage, the Festival itself was almost as big a Nazi cultural jamboree as the Great German Art Exhibitions. With the town swathed in swastika banners, the cafés and restaurants filled with Hitler's retainers and party workers and shops selling not Richard Wagner but Adolf Hitler mementoes, what had been a Wagner festival became a Hitler festival. In the manner of a medieval monarch Hitler was followed to Bayreuth by a vast entourage of officials, attendants, courtiers, hangers-on and just about anybody who was anybody. Occasionally he invited several top party leaders to accompany him in the hope that the experience would be civilizing. But most of them hated it. After enduring one act in the oven heat of the Festspielhaus – where they had to be nudged in the ribs by their neighbours to stop snoring as they dozed – they would steal away and flee to the nearby countryside.

The association between Hitler and the Festival was so intimate and

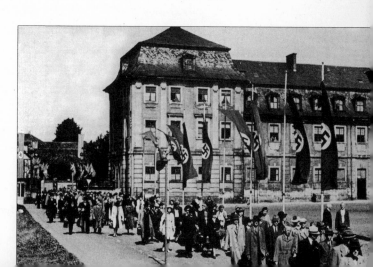

Workers from armaments factories were also 'Guests of the Führer' at Bayreuth. Here a group arrives for a performance of Die Meistersinger *during the 1943 War Festival.*

symbolic as to prompt Thomas Mann to style Bayreuth 'Hitler's court theatre' and a more lighthearted Bertolt Brecht to refer to Hitler as 'Führer of the Bayreuth Republic'. Hitler spent ten days there every summer, living in the small house where Siegfried had retreated during the day to work on his operas. Seated in the very loge where Wagner and King Ludwig had witnessed the original *Ring* production in 1876, he attended every performance of the first cycle of operas and later returned for another dose of *Götterdämmerung* and sometimes several other works as well. Even in the summer of 1939, while engrossed in final plans for the invasion of Poland and the negotiation of a non-aggression pact with the Soviet Union, he did not miss a performance. On returning from France in 1940, following his military success in the West, Hitler ordered his train to be diverted to Bayreuth so that he could take in a performance of *Götterdämmerung*. It was the last musical event he ever attended.

The outbreak of the war, far from causing a suspension in the Festival as had occurred in 1914, gave Hitler, ever the Wagnerian evangelist, an opportunity to use the institution for his own purposes. Unable himself to think of anything more wonderful than attending a Wagner opera at Bayreuth, he decided to 'reward' military personnel and workers in war industries by giving them a day at the opera, free of charge. Beginning in 1940 and going on through the summer of 1944, he instituted a 'War Festival' to which the deserving were taken, willingly or not. In the course of the five War Festivals there were a total of seventy-four performances attended by no fewer than 142,000 'guests of the Führer', as attendees were known. Hitler was terribly proud, saying to his staff in January 1942, 'I consider it a particular joy to have been able to keep Bayreuth going at a time when it faced economic collapse. And now, during the war, I have been able to realize what Wagner had wished: to enable selected persons from the general population, soldiers and workers to attend the Festival without charge.'

In the mood of the time, Bayreuth was even promoted as having miraculous curative powers for burned-out warriors. One of the popular films of those years, *Stukas*, told the story of a squadron of the eponymous German dive-bombers. In the first half, the handsome hero had the time of his life dive-bombing everything and everyone he could find in Poland and France. But with the defeat of France and the hiatus in active hostilities, he lost all interest in life and lay nearly comatose in a clinic. When no medical or psychological treatment could revive him, a nurse took him as a last resort to Bayreuth for a performance of *Götterdämmerung*. To the music of

Siegfried's 'Rhine Journey', the thrill and pleasure of bombing and killing was restored. Reborn, he enthusiastically returned to his unit just in time to join the first wave of planes to blitz London.

Despite the crushing burden of his military campaigns, Hitler took a keen interest in these War Festivals. From Winifred's correspondence it is clear that she consulted him on every major artistic decision of what was now in effect a wartime enterprise. The main problem was deciding on a suitable repertory. As the war turned against Germany, it seemed wise to replace *Götterdämmerung* with something more appropriate. As she wrote to Hitler, *Tristan und Isolde* had to be ruled out because of the long third act narrative by the wounded and dying Tristan about his suffering, loneliness and impending death. She feared that this would be, as she put it, 'too much of a burden' for wounded soldiers to handle. Hitler went along with her alternate suggestion of *Die Meistersinger*, even though he planned to have it performed following his final military victory at a triumphant 'Peace Festival'. That opera alone was then performed in the final two years of the War Festivals.

So enamoured was Hitler with his War Festivals that he decided he would continue this 'people's Bayreuth' after the war. The old Festival was to be done away with and replaced by a *Volksfest*, a popular festival for loyal party workers and other favoured groups. Thus would Bayreuth become a National Socialist pilgrimage site, and thus would the Nazi party and German public be 'Wagnerized'.

The final and most curious aspect of Hitler's Wagnermania was that after the German army's disaster at Stalingrad, he could no longer bear to listen to the operas. Before then he would still sometimes hold 'recording evenings', as he had in the good old days. But as the military situation worsened, hope vanished, memories were melancholy and dreams faded. Now an odd thing happened. After Stalingrad all he wanted to hear was Lehár. His valet, Heinz Linge, noted an occasion when Hitler was left deeply depressed by a military briefing. Afterwards he turned to him and asked, 'Linge, what music recordings do you have there?' The valet, who evidently never travelled anywhere without them, replied, 'Wagner and several operettas.' The choice fell immediately on Lehár. Marlene Exner, his cook at the military headquarters, recalled that *The Merry Widow* was all she ever heard him listen to from then on. So, in the course of his life, there were Wagner, Bruckner and Lehár, these three; but at the end, the greatest of these was Lehár.

THE
MUSIC MASTER

15 The Rape of Euterpe

O F ALL THE ARTS, MUSIC AROUSED HITLER'S DEEPEST anxiety during the years when he was scrabbling for power. In his speeches during the 1920s he spoke over and over of cultural decline, and it was usually contemporary music that he had most in mind. Because music meant so much to him, his heart ached at its parlous state. It was, he felt, thoroughly corrupted and wholly symptomatic of a sick society. With Jews, Modernists, internationalists and moneygrubbers on the loose, 'the result is not, for example, a *Maria Stuart* [by Schiller] but a *Merry Widow* [by Lehár]'. (This was of course in 1920 when he considered operetta trash.) Even his beloved Weimar, a city of the highest cultural standing, had been desecrated by the 'cultural poisoners of the German people' with their 'nigger-jazz' – possibly a reference to performances there at the time of Ernst Křenek's popular jazz opera *Jonny spielt auf!* The situation had so degenerated that the public was confusing culture with kitsch. Was it not beyond belief that anyone could seriously think that Křenek and 'his comrades' were genuine artists? For himself, he preferred 'a single German military march to all the garbage of a Modernist composer. The one is music, the other is no better than vomit. It is up to us to get rid of this muck.' That was the warning of a speech in January 1928.

Behind Hitler's plaint lay the fact that during the brief life of the Weimar Republic the bitterest battles in the cultural sphere had been waged over Modernism in music. Pressure had been building for some years and with the collapse of the old political order in 1918 an intellectual dam had broken. In opera overtly critical music theatre independent of the existing social order became possible. Romantic escapism was succeeded by raw social commentary – *Rosenkavalier* by *Wozzeck*. Musical life in those years – in terms of the sheer number of new works and their innovative qualities – was dazzling. It was also more and more politically committed, however, and the commitment was to the left. Polyhymnia and Thalia, in H. H. Stuckenschmidt's phrase, followed the red flag. Composers such as Hanns Eisler and Kurt Weill followed it in the belief that music would change the world. That was precisely what conservatives feared and their response extended from rejection on aesthetic grounds to repudiation on political ones. Hitler denounced contemporary music on both, seeing in it an artistic degeneration paralleling the country's political decay. So while antipathy to the works of Weill and Eisler as well as Křenek, Arnold Schoenberg and Alban Berg did not originate with him or his party, it was taken up and led by them. Atonality, dissonance, social chaos, Bolshevism, internationalism and Jews were regarded as ingredients of one unholy brew that was fatally poisoning German culture.

Just as much an anathema were the stage designs of both new and traditional operas, in particular those of Wagner, when these strayed in the slightest from the path of nineteenth-century convention. The innovative approach to staging, directing and acting that had been introduced by artists like Leopold Jeßner, Jürgen Fehling, Caspar Neher, Oskar Strnad and Ewald Dühlberg provoked outrage. Hitler himself was said to have been infuriated by a performance at the Kroll Opera in Berlin in 1929 of Hindemith's *Neues vom Tage* in which a seemingly naked soprano sang in her bath about the wonders of modern plumbing. In the same year, also at the Kroll, a production of *Der Fliegende Holländer* conducted by Otto Klemperer, directed by Fehling and staged by Dühlberg in the minimalist style known as New Objectivity, ended as more a political scandal than an operatic event.

No sooner did Hitler become chancellor than that sort of 'cultural Bolshevism' was throttled. Dismissals, threats, bullying and terror tactics swept out of concert halls and opera houses most Modernist music and Modernist scenography. Such notable Expressionist productions as Fehling's of *Tannhäuser* at the Berlin State Opera and Neher's of *Der fliegende Holländer* at the Berlin Municipal Opera were cancelled within days of Hitler's rise to power. Performances of works by Kurt Weill, Berthold Goldschmidt, Hanns Eisler, Ernst Křenek, Manfred Gurlitt, Franz Schreker and Alexander Zemlinsky were halted only weeks afterwards. Weill's *Der Silbersee*, which had opened simultaneously in Leipzig, Erfurt and Magdeburg on 18 February, was closed down a short time later, and rehearsals of the work at Max Reinhardt's Deutsches Theatre in Berlin were abandoned. Weill and Reinhardt soon fled. By then works by Arnold Schoenberg, Alban Berg, Paul Hindemith, Anton von Webern and some other composers were being excluded from concert programmes. Compositions by Jewish composers of an older vintage – Mendelssohn, Meyerbeer, Halévy, Offenbach and Mahler – also gradually vanished. In time works by foreign Jewish composers, such as Irving Berlin, were banned as well.

Swept away with the music were its agents. Conductors, instrumentalists, singers, opera managers, stage designers and directors were subjected to a racial and political purge. At the Berlin Municipal Opera Carl Ebert was immediately ousted as general manager; in early March Fritz Busch was harried from his position as chief conductor of the Dresden opera. Neither man was Jewish but both were labelled with a term that now became a pejorative buzzword, *untragbar* – unacceptable. In mid-March Bruno Walter was prevented from conducting in Leipzig and Berlin; Otto Klemperer was dismissed as conductor at the Berlin State Opera a few weeks later. Both were of Jewish background, as were some of the others forced out at that time, such as Fritz Stiedry, Jascha Horenstein, Joseph Rosenstock and Wilhelm Steinberg. All of them went into exile, followed by a number of singers as well as the soloists Adolf Busch, Fritz Schnabel, Fritz Kreisler and Simon Goldberg. Others who were removed from their positions included the managers of the operas at Baden-Baden, Bielefeld, Breslau, Chemnitz, Cologne, Darmstadt, Dresden, Erfurt, Frankfurt, Hamburg, Karlsruhe, Kassel, Königsberg, Leipzig, Mannheim, Munich, Münster, Schwerin and Stettin, as well as principal conductors in Berlin, Cologne, Dresden, Düsseldorf, Frankfurt, Magdeburg, Mannheim and more than a dozen other cities.

Racially or politically unacceptable teaching staff in conservatories and universities along with music critics in the press lost their positions. With their departure musicology, music history and music criticism were progressively Nazified. Schoenberg, Eisler, Ernst Toch and Weill were among the composers quickly hounded out of the country. A few non-Jewish Modernists, most notably Hindemith and Křenek, also left sooner or later. Jeßner fled, but most other stage designers and directors stayed and quickly learned to conform to the reactionary taste of party officials. Some artists married to Jews were able to pursue their profession by divorcing their spouses – such as Hans Schmidt-Isserstedt – or by settling them outside the country as did Lehár, Frida Leider and Franz von Hößlin.

The initial rampage of sackings was largely the spontaneous and uncoordinated action of local Nazis. Hitler himself complained about the way Busch had been forced out. 'It really is a shame that we do not have a gauleiter in Dresden who knows anything about the arts. . . . Busch would have been the best German conductor. But [Gauleiter] Mutschmann wanted to put old party comrades in the orchestra so as to introduce the National Socialist spirit.' The situation Hitler described was one that prevailed throughout Germany. Where he differed from the hotheaded Mutschmanns was in being less doctrinaire about a musician's political background. And he certainly did not want to lose talent unnecessarily. Yet those early excesses by no means ran counter to his long-term intentions.

Hitler wanted music to occupy the position in Germany that he imagined it had held in ancient Greece. There it was not as an art valid in itself but an instrument of social purpose and that purpose was to exalt the aesthetic feelings of the general public. He therefore saw it as the duty of the modern state to make music available to the entire population, just as it was the duty of composers to produce music aesthetically accessible to everyone. Should this organic relationship break down – as he believed it had in Weimar Germany – both music and the state were bound to suffer. Inevitably what followed was the corrupting and cheapening effect of commercialism. Again he cited the example of Schiller and Lehár. The great dramatist had had to be content with 346 thaler for *Maria Stuart*, while Lehár received 3 ½ million marks for *The Merry Widow*, a work he referred to as 'the most appalling kitsch'.

Controlling its content by placing music under the authority of the state was standard totalitarian doctrine going back to Plato. Unique to Hitler was his injection of anti-Semitism. On the one hand Germany was being poisoned by 'the complete judification of music', he argued. On the other Jews were unable to accomplish anything original or creative in music and therefore fell back on bragging about their Jewish conductors. But these had, in fact, achieved their fame only because they had been puffed up by the reviews of Jewish critics in the Jewish-controlled press. And on and on in that vein he went.

The other subversive element was Modernism, not always clearly defined and usually, but not invariably, linked to Jews and Bolsheviks. Although there is no way of knowing how much Modernist music he actually ever heard, he knew enough to realize that it was unacceptable. Atonality, like Cubism and Expressionism, was ugly and incomprehensible. Dissonance, like Nolde's green sky or blue meadows, was a perversion of reality. In both art forms these qualities were the equivalent of anarchism in politics. In its association with jazz and novel rhythms, Modernist music was 'internationalist' and when music ceased to be national, it became kitsch. The public did not want this new 'junk' and considered it an insult to the ears. Modernist music was also objectionable for another reason – it was elitist. Content to compose for a small minority, Modernist composers had refused to recognize that, culture being the bond holding society together, music had to appeal to everyone. In any case there was no need for new music. 'When the Modernists come along and unleash their dissonance on us, we tell them: our people do not even know older music.' It was the cornerstone of his aesthetic that great music, like great painting, had reached its final flowering around the turn of the century. This did not worry him, however. 'We need not create any new art; if we cannot achieve anything great then let us concentrate on what is already there, which is immortal.' What he found intolerable was that the fine music of the past was being replaced by the 'most appalling junk in opera and concert'.

Once he was in power his policies followed naturally. First and foremost, all Jews in the music profession – instrumentalists, composers, librettists, teachers, managers, stage designers, directors, agents, critics – had to be removed from public life and all musical works by Jews banned. Later on Jews were forbidden even to enter concert halls and opera houses to attend performances. At the same time Modernism was to be eliminated not only from music but also from directing and staging. Finally, music was to provide cultural and political credibility for his New Order. In its early days the new government desperately needed respectability. Music, Germany's greatest cultural achievement, was to be used to deflect attention from the terrorism that was being used to establish the totalitarian state. A rich musical life was intended to give the impression that everything in Germany was basically normal and that the Third Reich was not a terror state but a culture state. To this extent music for Hitler was not the subject but the object of policy.

The scope for political intervention was vast. There were an extraordinary number of orchestras (around 180), opera houses (nearly 90), career musicians (some 94,000), choral groups, conservatories and music publications. Since most orchestras and operas were state institutions, musicians, singers and so on were civil servants and therefore in the grip of government authorities. The immediate victims were persons of Jewish descent. They may have accounted for only two per cent of the professional music population, but they were vastly more important in music than in any of the other arts – eminent as conductors, soloists and instrumentalists and composers. With them went whole swaths of music, vanishing as quickly as the institutions of Weimar democracy. Within a short time it was as though works by Jewish and Modernist composers had never existed. Mendelssohn was the most difficult to dispatch since his violin concerto and *Midsummer Night's Dream* incidental music were highly popular. But after performances of the incidental music on two occasions in 1934 and of the concerto twice in 1935, they too disappeared.★

★ At a performance by the London Philharmonic Orchestra in Hitler's presence in Berlin in late 1936, Sir Thomas Beecham deferred to Hitler's request and withdrew Mendelssohn's *Scottish Symphony* from the program.

It is remarkable how easily Hitler was able to impose his policies on a nation that was musically more sophisticated and that had a deeper musical tradition than any other. In fact, less repression was necessary than in the other arts. While painters, architects and writers, including many of the most eminent, fled, even though they were not Jewish, very few Gentile musicians went into voluntary exile. It was not only that Germany was considered the only place for anyone in the music field to live, musicians saw in Hitler's New Order something for themselves. Few formally belonged to the party. Of 110 players in the Berlin Philharmonic, for example, only eight held party cards; of the entire staff of the Berlin State Opera, only seventeen were party members even a year after Hitler came to power. Similarly, only a few important conductors – Max von Schillings, Hans Schmidt-Isserstedt, Hausegger and von Karajan – joined. But most fell for the new government's promises. Despite numerous trivial acts of resistance, what was prescribed – or proscribed – was followed with scarcely a murmur. In no time, the richest musical scene in the world had been corrupted.

Hitler could therefore pursue the role he loved, patron of the arts. He selected conductors for the major opera houses and symphony orchestras and further reserved to himself the exclusive right to award the titles of professor of music, general music director, kapellmeister, chamber singer and the like. Grants for musical institutions, opera houses, operatic productions and individual artists required his personal approval. And in the case of artists who, though part-Jewish or married to a Jew, wished to be permitted to perform, he was the final court of appeal. Occasionally he laid down the law – literally, in ordaining the 'Badenweiler March' to be performed only in his presence and the 'Nibelungen March' solely on formal party occasions. He also decreed the metronome speed for the 'Horst Wessel Song' and the 'Deutschlandlied', the national anthem.

Beyond that he left musical affairs in the hands of his subordinates. These were the usual suspects. Bernhard Rust, as Education Minister, was in charge of music conservatories and other educational institutions. Robert Ley, as head of the Labour Front, controlled musicians' professional organizations. Rosenberg thought of himself as guarantor of ideological purity. Göring's satrapy included the Berlin State Opera as well as the operas of Wiesbaden, Kassel and Hanover. Baldur von Schirach claimed sovereignty over musical life in Vienna. And Goebbels, with his Propaganda Ministry and Reich Music Chamber, occupied a powerful bureaucratic bastion. He further strengthened his position once Strauss agreed to be president and Furtwängler vice-president of the Music Chamber.

The bureaucratic competition and doctrinal discord among them left policy in a shambolic state. Instead of coherent direction there was a continuously evolving series of actions based on a mixture of ideology, power plays and, always in the end if the issue engaged his interest, Hitler's arbitrary decision. But since the dictator declined to dictate except in matters of personal importance, confusion, uncertainty, indecision and inconsistency prevailed. Goebbels might proclaim in a speech in 1935, as recorded in the stenographic record: 'We do not intend to tell a conductor how he should conduct a score. But we do claim the sovereign right to decide [the speaker pounded repeatedly on the podium] *what* is played and *what* conforms to the spirit of *our* time [applause]. Therefore a conductor cannot say: I decide what is music.' but the fact was, party bosses could not do so either. Music should be German, they said, but no one was sure what that was. It should be *volksverbunden*, linked to the nation, but what did that mean? Compositions were to express *die deutsche Seele*, the German soul; but were these to be dreamy musical ruminations about the German spirit or xenophobic affirmations of German racial superiority? They pondered whether one key or another was Nordic and whether there was a specific Jewish quality in Schoenberg's music. They wanted neither a simple return to nineteenth-century Romanticism nor a continuation of Weimar avant-garde but also no experimentation.

Even some existing works left them scratching their heads in consternation. What to do about operetta, since many of its composers and librettists were Jews? Banning it was easy, and that was done along with works by Offenbach, Gershwin and Irving Berlin. But the convolutions the Nazi bureaucrats went through in cases such as Lehár's were themselves the stuff of operetta. The issue was not one of suppressing Hitler's hostile remarks about the composer in the 1920s, which no one presumably was aware of. Rather it was his background and works. His bloodlines – Hungarian, French and German – were a mess; he was a Hungarian citizen; his wife was Jewish, as were all his librettists. An investigation by Rosenberg's office discovered that he had written a waltz dedicated to France, had maintained contact with Jews and had on occasion criticized the Third Reich. The investigators also evaluated his music and found it to be kitsch and lacking any German sensibility. In some places his compositions were for a time withdrawn from the repertory. As Hitler's fondness for Lehár's operettas grew, however, all these sins had to be waved aside. His works were then widely performed and filmed, while new productions of *The Merry Widow* were richly subsidized by the Führer personally. On the occasion of his seventieth birthday in 1940, he awarded Lehár the Goethe Medal.

Party bureaucrats suffered a similar humiliation in the case of the partly Jewish Johann Strauss. Again, Hitler so much enjoyed his works that they, too, were performed without hindrance. When the composer's Jewish ancestry came to light in 1938, scandal loomed. An agitated Goebbels was provoked into what would have deserved entry in a National Socialist Dictionary of Quotations had there been one: 'I forbid that this should come to the knowledge of the public. First, it is not proven and second I have no desire to allow the German cultural heritage to be gradually impoverished. In the end only Widukind, Henry the Lion and Rosenberg would remain in our history. And that is rather too few.' Jazz caused still another headache. It was tainted not only ideologically and musically but also racially. It was so popular, however, that efforts to suppress it were unending and never entirely successful.

Then there was the problem of how to handle the libretti of Mozart's operas by the Jewish Da Ponte – and of Hermann Levi's German translations of them – as well as those of Richard Strauss's operas by the partly Jewish Hugo von Hofmannsthal. And what was to be done about such works as Handel's oratorios based on Old Testament texts or Schubert's and Schumann's settings of poems by Heine? Also troublesome were operas with religious scenes or Christian references – *Tiefland*, *Carmen*, *Tosca*, *Cavalleria rusticana*, *Faust*, *Der Freischütz* and even *Lohengrin* and *Tannhäuser*. *The Magic Flute* ran into difficulty because of its Masonic ceremony. Some fanatics went so far as to perform Mozart's *Requiem* with a new text – 'Deus in Sion' became 'Deus in coelis', for example, while 'in Jerusalem' was replaced by 'hic in terra'. When it came to scores, the only rule was that there was no firm rule. Although works by such composers as Berg, Webern and Křenek were forbidden, performances of operas using twelve-tone technique by Paul von Klenau and Winfried Zillig – both of them pupils of Schoenberg – were approved. Other exceptions were sometimes made either out of uncertainty or in response to some higher party objective. This offered composers and conductors a little room for manoeuvre. Yet the fact remains that the repertory of concert halls and opera houses was largely the good old standard works and anything else was rare.

Hitler himself was far less rigid than Rosenberg and the other sans-culottes of the music world. He squelched opposition not only to works of Lehár and Johann Strauss, but also to those of Mozart, Richard Strauss, Eugen d'Albert and others. So irritated was he by party officials who found the Masonic theme of *The Magic Flute* ideologically unacceptable that he addressed the matter at the Nuremberg rally in 1937. 'Only a person lacking respect for his own nationality,' he said, 'would condemn Mozart's *Magic Flute* because its text may be ideologically opposed to his own outlook.' Some years later he reiterated to Goebbels that he did not want the opera's content to be altered, though adding that he would like to see it performed more as a fairy tale than as a Masonic rite. In reality, he said, 'It is a great Mozart *revue*.'

Still more striking was his anger at authorities who wanted to ban Christian religious music. 'This belongs,' he told Goebbels, 'to the German cultural patrimony. It is impossible simply to erase two thousand years of German artistic and cultural development because we National Socialists hold a religious viewpoint that differs from these two thousand years.' On learning in 1943 that some party officials had prohibited operas such as *Carmen, Tosca* and even *Lohengrin*, and had 'Aryanized' certain operatic texts, he instructed the chancellery to send out a circular memorandum denouncing such activities as 'grotesque'. 'They arise from a primitive ideological vigilance that is insupportable.' The memorandum went on to state that once the war had been won, the Führer himself would decide what, if any, textual changes were necessary.

Foreign policy considerations at times compromised Hitler's policy of cultural autarky. Italian opera continued to be freely staged along with works by Modernist Italian composers, such as Ferruccio Busoni. In the interests of German-Hungarian relations, works of Zoltán Kodály were performed and occasionally even those of the anti-Nazi Bartók. Some pre-Bolshevik Russians – Tchaikovsky, Mussorgsky and Rimsky-Korsakov – remained in the repertory in the early years of the Third Reich. Stravinsky fell in and out of favour, though during the brief alliance between the Soviet Union and Germany, he, Prokofiev, Borodin and even Shostakovich were permitted. Another example of how foreign policy drove music policy was the case of Sibelius. For Hitler, anxious to include Finland in the greater National Socialist cultural Reich, the composer was perfect. A Nordic Aryan, strongly Germanophile, politically conservative and anti-Bolshevist, he was an exemplar of Nordic art and of Finnish resistance to the Soviet Union. Hitler is not known to have uttered an opinion on his music, though its conservative, even reactionary, quality would have pleased him. In 1934 Strauss appointed him a vice-president of the Permanent Council for the International Co-operation of Composers. The following year Hitler both awarded him the Goethe Prize and also sent a congratulatory letter on the occasion of his seventieth birthday. Taking the cue, his German publisher, Breitkopf and Härtel, did its bit by promoting his works. The composer was equally useful to the Finnish government in maintaining its ties with Germany. 'The Finns ask us to do more for Sibelius,' Goebbels noted in

1942. 'I have given my approval for the founding of a Sibelius Society.' Under the circumstances it is hardly surprising that Sibelius's music came to be more often performed than that of any other foreign composer.

To reduce confusion, lists were compiled identifying which compositions were to be encouraged and which forbidden. In June 1935 Strauss, as head of the Reich Music Chamber, approved a register of three categories of permissible operas. Several months later a list of 108 works 'under no circumstances to be performed' was drawn up. That was followed by a blacklist compiled by the Berlin Radio with the names of ninety-nine forbidden composers. Like many subsequent rosters and directories, these were tainted by gross errors and omissions – Schoenberg, Meyerbeer, Schreker and Halévy were not originally mentioned – and had to be corrected and amplified. In an effort to frame a more coherent music policy, Goebbels transferred the Music Chamber's powers to his ministry and in 1937 established the Reich Music Censorship Board to oversee music programming, broadcasting, recording and publication. Over the years it, too, catalogued works that were 'unacceptable' for German ears. In 1938 Hans Severus Ziegler did his bit to identify evil music by staging in Düsseldorf a Degenerate Music Exhibition, in imitation of Hitler's Degenerate Art Exhibition. In reality the show was less the intended exposure of 'cultural Bolshevism ... and the triumph of arrogant Jewish impudence' than of Ziegler's petty vindictiveness and reactionary musical taste. At the same time an annual Reich Music Festival was inaugurated, also an imitation – in this case of the Munich Great German Art Exhibition. What is interesting is that Hitler ostentatiously declined to endorse or even attend these events, much less organize an extravaganza of the sort that opened the visual arts exhibitions. Once the war began, he ordered the festival to be cancelled.

It is evident that Hitler did not act with anything like the ferocity in the music sphere that he did in painting and sculpture. Partly this was for the obvious reason that he could ban but not physically destroy music. And partly it was because, once in power, Hitler was relatively indifferent to music he did not know or like. Nor did he ever threaten composers with consignment to a concentration camp. With a few exceptions – Richard Mohaupt was one – composers who were ideologically suspect were permitted to compose and even at times have their works performed; reprobate painters were forbidden to practise and had their materials confiscated. Although he damaged the lives and careers of composers who were forced to flee and stifled the Modernist movement, Hitler did less harm to music than to painting and sculpture.

16 The Music Patron

Having rid the German music world of Jews and Modernists, Hitler believed that he had created an atmosphere in which great new music would inevitably emerge. In a sense he was right. No sooner was he in power than a wave of ideologically inspired compositions celebrating the New Order flowed forth. They arrived at the chancellery and Nazi party offices in such volume that within nine months Goebbels had to enjoin composers to send their creations directly to music publishers. In 1933 alone, fifty-eight works bearing Hitler's name were submitted; by 1935 the Führer had to put a stop to any further works being dedicated to him. The flood never ceased, however. Patriotic marches, Nazi fighting songs, Führer cantatas, songs for Christmas without Jesus, songs for German minorities in the Saar, Sudetenland and Poland and, later on, songs for the military along with hundreds of operas, choral works and the like surged in an endless stream.

Among the more notable offerings was Friedrich Jung's B-flat major symphony. With movements entitled 'Germany 1918', 'heroes' memorial', 'parliamentary death dance' and 'Germany 1933', it offered an unabashed musical history of Hitler's ascent to power. Another enthusiast was Gottfried Müller, who consciously attempted to compose works in a National Socialist spirit. He was but nineteen in 1933 and Hitler regarded him for a time as the great hope for German music. In 1934 he composed a *Deutsches Heldenrequiem* (German Heroes' Requiem), which he dedicated to the Führer. Three years later Hitler attended a rehearsal of it at the Philharmonic and was so impressed he commanded the work to be performed on May Day. The occasion was a great success and Hitler continued to see promise. But a choral work based on a theme from Hitler's final speech at the 1936 Nuremberg party rally was disappointing when finally performed in 1944.

In fact he had long since despaired, openly admitting at the 1935 party rally that 'fate' had not produced any worthwhile composers. So much for Egk and Orff, and other aspiring young composers, not to mention Strauss and Pfitzner and other old-timers. But he did his best to provide guidance that might yet inspire the sort of music he wanted. As one who demanded discipline, order and purity in politics and who insisted on paintings that were 'finished' and 'beautiful', he naturally required music to be 'healthy', 'right' and 'genuine'. Since he had to admit he did not understand what animated such music, however, he was reduced to stipulating what he could *not* accept. On the one hand he described this as music that employed a 'confusion of sounds' or that might bewilder a listener. Repeatedly he stressed that music, like the other arts, must be accessible to the general public. That Modernist music was beyond the ken of the average person was an argument he regularly used against it. On the other hand he ruled out compositions purporting to express political ideas. Such was neither music's function nor its ability. As Goebbels noted, 'The Führer does not like the newly composed music for the party rally. How much greater by contrast is Bruckner!'

What, then, did he see as music's nature and function? Basically he argued that in one way or another all music tells a story. That is why, in a performance, even the great symphonic conductors could not dispense with *sprachlich fixierte Anhaltspunkte*, musical language that elucidated an underlying concept. Music did not create a plot but was part of the plot – a *Zeitgemälde*, a picture of a moment. Music therefore achieved its greatest effectiveness when it served to illustrate visible action, and no one accomplished this better than Richard Wagner. In this tortuous way did Hitler justify his preference for opera over other types of music and his reason for making opera the favoured form of music in the Third Reich. He spelled out his ideas in a speech to the Nuremberg party rally in 1938. It was the most extensive statement he ever made on how he regarded music. A few excerpts convey the essence.

> Music as an absolute art follows laws that are unknown to us today. What produces beautiful sound and what causes dissonance we do not exactly know at present. Clearly music can claim to be the greatest animator of feelings and sensibilities that move the mind; yet it seems to be the least able to satisfy the intellect. . . . A world of feelings and moods that is difficult to describe in words is revealed in music. . . . The more music tends towards pure illustration, the more important it is to make visible its underlying action. The genius of the artist permits him to give additional meaning through the music, which rises above the treatment itself to achieve an overall mood and therefore an effect that can be achieved only

through music. This type of expression . . . reached its absolute summit in the works of the great Bayreuth Master.

. . . It is impossible to express or emphasize specific intellectual or political ideas or political insights in music. Therefore there is no musical party history or musical ideology just as there is no musical illustration or interpretation of philosophical principles. Only language can do that . . . . However, music must follow the broad rules of national life and therefore produce not a confusion of sounds that will bewilder a perplexed listener but instead move the heart through the beauty of sound. Our musicians should be motivated not by intellect but by an overflowing musical mind . . . .

Whether in architecture, or music, or sculpture or painting, one fundamental principle should never be overlooked: every true art must in its expression bear the stamp of beauty. The ideal for all of us lies in the cultivation of what is healthy. Only what is healthy is right and natural, and what is right and natural is therefore beautiful.

No doubt Hitler thought of himself as Hans Sachs explaining to uncertain but promising Walther von Stolzings how to produce good music. In fact, he left composers no better off than sailors adrift at sea with no idea how to tack through shifting winds to a destination that might or might not be the right one. Naturally enough, they went off in various directions. Some drew on styles of previous decades and developed attenuated forms of Modernism; some reverted to nineteenth-century Romanticism while others tried to combine a variety of modes to create a uniquely 'Third Reich music'. In the end the vaunted National Socialist musical revolution came down to nothing more than a purge of Jews and a ban on most Modernist and non-German music, except for Italian opera. Endorsing the 'treasures of the past' on the one hand and vaguely Modernist styles of a less distant past on the other, the revolution in music was essentially a counterrevolution.

Though hoping that fine new works might some day emerge, Hitler believed that by the turn of the century music had effectively reached the end of its development. He was not greatly troubled by this, since his taste in music, as in painting, was largely limited to products of the latter half of the nineteenth century. Of this sort of music he felt there was enough. But therein lay another great disappointment. The German public did not agree with him, or at least not fully. In particular, they refused to share his passion for Wagner. The number of performances of Wagnerian opera continued the steady decline that began as long back as 1914 to the point where by 1939–40 Verdi replaced him as the most performed operatic composer. And while programmes continued to favour German works, Mozart also lost ground to Verdi and Puccini. As time passed, and particularly as the war dragged on, operas with escapist themes, such as those of Strauss and Orff, gained in popularity. The former's *Arabella* led all contemporary works with 848 performances in ten seasons.

And so, giving up expectation that great new music was forthcoming, Hitler turned his attention to improving the existing repertory by raising the quality of performances. Since it was opera he loved, this was uppermost in his mind. The problems that nag every opera house impresario today were also those that concerned Hitler – how to achieve the highest artistic standards; how to ensure financing; how to devise a repertory and fix ticket prices so as to appeal to a broad audience; how to destroy the notion of opera as an art form of social privilege; how to encourage a community to regard its opera house as an object of civic pride.

Of all these issues, none was more important to him than the last. 'An opera house is the standard by which the culture of a city or civilization is measured,' was how he once put it to Speer. This was a conviction that originated in his youth, as is evident in his postcard to Kubizek from Vienna in 1906. A year after that he had nerve enough to enter a competition to design a new opera house for Linz and struggled for months over the plans.

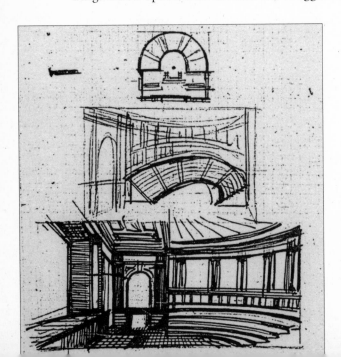

One of Hitler's earliest sketches of an opera house.

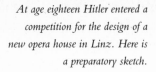

At age eighteen Hitler entered a competition for the design of a new opera house in Linz. Here is a preparatory sketch.

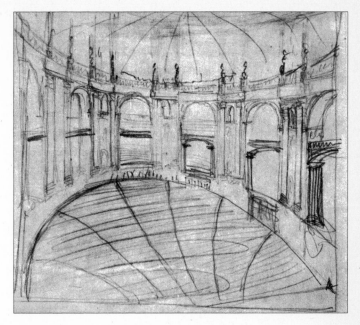

He scribbled two crude sketches and they survive. One is of the auditorium – a typical baroque horseshoe-shaped proscenium theatre – and the other a crude illustration of the imagined flow of the sound waves. Though testimony to his enthusiasm rather than any precocious expertise, the drawings show that he was trying to think through the problems of design and acoustics in a way that was not discreditable in an uneducated schoolboy. He later dreamed of studying architecture for several years and then working as a draughtsman for a well-known Munich construction firm. As he told the story long afterwards:

> . . . I would enter the first competition that was held and, I said to myself, people would see what this fellow could do. In fact, I participated on my own in competitions at the time, and as the proposed designs for a new Berlin opera house were published my heart was beating, because I had to say to myself 'they are much worse than what you designed'. I specialized, you see, in the theatrical area.

Some biographers have ridiculed this statement as one more far-fetched pipe dream, another sign of Hitler's divorce from reality. But like so many others, this pipe dream eventually became reality.

The fascination never waned. Of the various drawings in his 1925 sketch-book, one-quarter were of opera houses and during the remainder of his life he continued to produce such sketches. One of his first acts after becoming chancellor was to order the renovation of the Nuremberg opera house. Over the years Hitler had accumulated an expert of knowledge of opera house architecture. He was a prodigious reader of books on the subject, one of which was known to be Edwin Sachs's classic three-volume *Modern Opera Houses and Theatres* of 1897–8. Thanks to a near-photographic memory, he was familiar with the architecture of every important opera house in the world. According to Heinrich Hoffmann, he knew so much about the Dresden house he might have written a doctoral thesis about it. When Hans Severus Ziegler told him about a planned visit to Lille, Hitler commented, 'The theatre there . . . is architecturally quite impressive. The foyer is monumental in its way, in the manner of the Paris opera, although admittedly a lot of it is faux.' That despite his never having set foot in the building. Similarly, on once encountering the mayor of Nuremberg, who mentioned having just attended a performance at the Graz opera, Hitler complained that the transition from the auditorium to the stage had been botched. Again, he had not seen it himself. When Hugh Trevor-Roper inspected Hitler's bunker in September 1945 he found a room filled with illustrated books on opera house architecture. These meant so much to him that they were among the few things he took with him when he abandoned his apartments in the chancellery early in 1945.

But it was not just that he considered an opera house a city's most emblematic building. Equally, he wanted opera to be readily available to everyone, whatever their income and wherever they lived. People needed illusion to get through the struggles of life, he said over and over. The illusions provided by public spectacles – the party rallies and other annual celebrations – were only episodic. Opera was always to be available. For these reasons he planned a massive programme of opera house construction. And so perfectly did this ambition match his love of opera with his love of architecture that it developed into what both Speer and Goebbels labelled 'a maniacal passion'. The extent of this mania can be gauged from the fact that even when the stress of domestic and foreign affairs was nearly overwhelming, he always found time for his opera house projects. In early 1939, during the days leading up to the seizure of Czechoslovakia and onwards to the invasion of Poland, Goebbels recorded that Hitler insisted on talking about 'various theatre construction plans, especially in Linz. Opera house matters are certainly of the greatest interest to him. They are one of his passions.' Again and again he returned to the subject.

Hitler's concept of opera's role dictated the main elements of his construction programme. His opera houses were to be huge. Form was to follow function and function was to be guided by purpose. Accessibility was always a key factor. 'Big enough for a mass public, doing away with the aristocratic and bourgeois character of opera. New spaces – much greater in dimensions – new librettists, new works to attract the nation, not something for the upper classes.' Such was his social concept. Everyone was meant to enjoy opera as much as he did and – no doubt remembering his youth – everyone was to be able to attend, including the impecunious. From the earliest days of the Third Reich, therefore, members of Strength through Joy, Hitler Youth and similar organizations were entitled to purchase tickets for next to nothing, and in some cases blocks of tickets were given away to party groups. In fact, by 1935 the number of operagoers had already increased significantly and, according to contemporary records, many had attended a performance for the first time. That large numbers of workers and peasants became ardent opera fans is very doubtful. But if Hitler did not succeed in making high culture mass culture, he certainly made it freely available.

Since opera was to be available to everyone, it followed that there should be a greater number of houses – greater, indeed, than the ninety existing ones. Each city of importance was to have at least two; Berlin was to have four or five in addition to the two it already had and Munich one more in addition to its existing three. He also renovated or intended to renovate any number of fine older houses that he admired, such as those in Weimar and Augsburg. In addition to the huge opera complex at Bayreuth, the Festspielhaus at Salzburg was to be reconstructed and enlarged. New houses were planned for such cities as Königsberg, Wilhelmshafen, Saarbrücken, Reichenberg, Strasbourg, Düsseldorf, Linz, Graz, Kehl am Rhein and even Prague. The funds Hitler was prepared to devote to these projects were appropriately enormous. He defended his extravagance by arguing that existing houses had been constructed in the nineteenth century and in the meantime the population of urban centres had at least trebled. But he was insistent that opera houses 'must also be built in small cities so as to offer places for the general masses. Opera belongs to the people and must therefore be available to the people. Prices should accordingly be kept down. Performances must be "illusion" for the masses. The little man knows enough of the difficulty of life. . . . Opera must also be accessible to youth.'

When it was suggested that there might not be enough opera lovers to fill all the new buildings, he responded that when the first autobahn had been laid down, sceptics had claimed there were too few cars to use it. They had been proved wrong, and that, he said, 'is how it will be with opera houses'. Having a larger number of houses would also have the advantage, he maintained, of calling forth a larger number of singers. This new talent would correct what he termed the 'disastrous' shortage of Wagnerian tenors.

And so Hitler intended to cover the Reich with *his* opera houses – that is, to his design and for his purposes. Apart from the Paris opera, there were only two edifices – those in Vienna and Dresden – that he liked and did not intend to replace. Neither the Berlin State Opera, built at the time of Frederick the

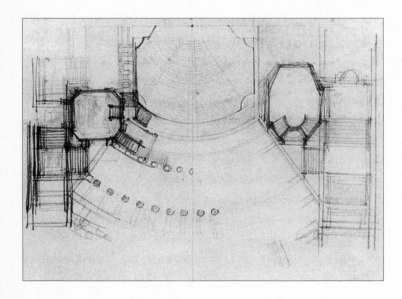

Among the drawings in Hitler's 1925 sketchbook is one of a proposed 'National Opera in Berlin'.

Great, nor the Munich Opera nor the Prince Regent's Theatre in Munich appealed to him. Berlin was therefore to have a monumental 'Reich Opera House' which would be 'the best and most beautiful imaginable' while Munich was to have the world's largest.

Over the years he spent hours making rough sketches of opera house floor plans and occasionally exteriors. Many of these still exist and show how his ideas evolved. His basic floor plan, despite frequent refinements, remained fundamentally unchanged. It was evidently based on a simulated Greco-Roman auditorium with a single row of loges at the rear. The basic exterior design, with its convex front façade, bore the influence of Gottfried Semper's Dresden Opera and Burg Theatre in Vienna. Greatly though he admired Semper's work, however, Hitler rigorously shunned his ornate decoration and overwrought entrances and adopted a style that was increasingly severe. Since he constantly revised his own designs, initial plans submitted by his architects inevitably failed to suit him. The very first project – Paul Schultze-Naumburg's reconstruction of the Nuremberg opera house in 1933–4 – left him so dissatisfied that he discharged the architect on the spot and selected another, Paul Baumgarten, to be his principal opera house architect. But when he also sometimes proved wanting, Hitler brought in others.

Although he sketched rough plans for any number of opera houses, the sole project to be fully worked out was the one for Munich, which he

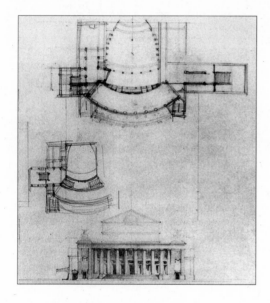

Hitler's 1925 sketchbook contained a number of freehand drawings of opera houses.

intended to serve as a model for others. To be the world's largest, it would seat an audience of between 4000 and 5000. When Baumgarten produced his designs in 1936, Hitler demanded revisions and drew sketches himself to guide him. 'Examined plans for new Munich opera,' Goebbels commented in his diary. 'They follow the Führer's own ideas. Now they make sense and have shape.' But Hitler continued to fret, changing the site, altering the design and scaling back the size to 3000 seats. Eventually he turned the project over to Waldemar Brinkmann, who produced a model that was put on exhibition at the second German Architecture Show in 1938. This displayed a sleek, windowless structure with a rounded front decorated with double columns of green marble. Arcades linked the structure to a restaurant on one side and a hotel on the other – features of all Hitler's opera house plans. It fascinated and delighted him but never got beyond the model stage.

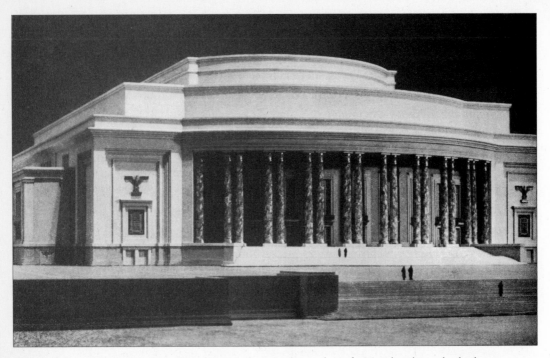

Hitler sketched the outlines of a new and mammoth opera house for Munich and gave the sketches to Waldemar Brinkmann to carry out. The 1938 model went through significant alterations. The convex front became a defining trait of all Hitler's planned opera theatres.

Despite all the plans and models only two new opera houses were ever built. Although both were constructed for political reasons, neither was Hitler's personal project. That he took no serious interest in them is apparent from their *sui generis* design. The coldly neoclassical one in Dessau, the former home of the Bauhaus, was purportedly to demonstrate that Modernism had been defeated and replaced by a 'German architectural monumentalism', as it was phrased. The other, in Saarbrücken, was 'a gift of the Führer' to celebrate the 1935 plebiscite that reunited the Saar with Germany. With its gabled roof, it was an architectural throwback to the principles of Schultze-Naumburg.

Hitler's passion for opera houses never diminished, even when the military situation turned disastrous. 'The bombing of an opera house,' Speer recalled, 'pained him more than the destruction of whole residential quarters.' Whenever this occurred – in Berlin with the State Opera in 1941 and the German Opera in 1943, in Mainz and Saarbrücken in 1942 and in Munich in 1943 – he ordered their immediate reconstruction. To Goebbels's argument that this would not be popular in light of the catastrophic housing shortage resulting from air raids, Hitler responded, '. . . the theatre is not merely a communal achievement but the one structure that belongs exclusively to the community. From this point of view, reconstructing housing would not achieve as much as reconstructing opera houses and theatres. . . . Of course, all this opera house construction means a loss of material for war production; but so be it.'

After becoming Minister for Armaments, Speer joined the fray and, as Goebbels witnessed, 'fought tooth and nail' against rebuilding the Munich structure. However, Goebbels had to record that the Führer 'believes that it would be irresponsible to leave such a historic structure in ruins. I go over all the reasons against reconstruction; nonetheless the Führer could not be persuaded.' A little later Hitler was just as stubborn about rebuilding the bombed-out Schiller Theatre and German Opera in Berlin.

Given his fascination with spectacle, it is hardly surprising that another of Hitler's ambitions was to influence operatic staging. So impressed had he been by Benno von Arent's decors for Wagner's operas that he created for him the position of Reich Stage Designer. By providing model designs, including those he and the Führer had done together, Arent was to give a cue to opera managers throughout Germany. Accordingly, in 1938 he published *Das deutsche Bühnenbild 1933–1936*, a large-format volume with reproductions of over a hundred stage and costume designs produced by himself and others during the first four years of the Third Reich – along with several old ones of Alfred Roller, presumably as a bow to Hitler. In his preface, Arent observed that the National Socialist revolution had reorientated German stage design and that its purpose had become one of serving German art 'as envisaged by the Führer'. The overall result, judging by the work of the forty-five stage designers illustrated in Arent's book, was one of crushing banality.

In the end the most immediate way Hitler influenced musical life was by raising the quality of performances to the highest possible standard. His primary means was through liberal financing of orchestras, soloists, instrumentalists and opera producers. His munificence put him on a level with some of the great patrons of history. He undoubtedly had an excellent ear for conducting talent – he considered Busch, Furtwängler and Clemens Krauss the best of their time – and selected conductors with as much care as he chose military commanders. Though disgusted by their childish vanity, he largely ignored personal and political considerations in deciding appointments. He

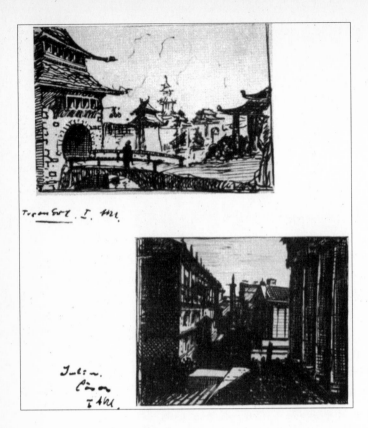

A stage designer manqué, Hitler tried his hand at sketching decors for plays and operas. Only a few of the early, less ambitious design ideas survive. Here are those for Puccini's Turandot *and Shakespeare's* Julius Caesar.

disliked Knappertsbusch, who was politically reactionary, admired Fritz Busch, who was on the left, and promoted Krauss despite his not belonging to the party or Nazi organizations. His concern was to match his favourite conductors with the orchestras and operas that were of the greatest interest to him. After Berlin, these were Dresden, Bayreuth, Munich and, following the incorporation of Austria in the Reich, Vienna. He also watched over the careers of concertmasters and the quality of orchestral playing, constantly comparing the Vienna and Berlin Philharmonics based on newly developed tape recordings. He was apparently a good judge of voice and did not allow his judgement to be swayed by politics or personal feelings. When he felt that Bockelmann, von Manowarda and Rode – good friends and good Nazis all – had passed their prime, he wanted them to retire. At the same time he was shrewd in perceiving future talent. In 1942 he predicted that 'the coming great baritone' was the then thirty-two-year-old Hans Hotter. 'We'll probably have to get him to Bayreuth some time,' he added.

17 CONDUCTORS AND COMPOSERS

NO FIGURE IN THE MUSIC WORLD WAS as important to Hitler personally as Wilhelm Furtwängler. One of the most prestigious conductors of his day, he was, more to the point, the Führer's favourite. The two men first met in the summer of 1932 following newspaper reports that the conductor had resigned as music director at Bayreuth. Furtwängler had demanded full artistic control over the Festival; Winifred Wagner had insisted that final word had to lie with her. Hitler, no doubt at Winifred's prompting, tried to mediate. At their encounter the conductor learned for the first but by no means the last time that his interlocutor was not a good listener. Instead of an exchange of views, the man who hoped to be chancellor launched into a monologue about the important role the Festival would have – and Furtwängler with it – once he came to power. In the end Hitler sided with Winifred and the conductor stayed away. But the point at issue – Furtwängler's insistence on total artistic autonomy – was precisely what the two men were to quarrel about in the years that followed.

Within months of this meeting Hitler had been appointed chancellor. In the wake of the racial purge that immediately followed, Furtwängler found himself under pressure to sack the non-Aryans in the Berlin Philharmonic – the six Jewish and two partly Jewish musicians. He refused. The function of art was to unite, not to divide, he wrote to Goebbels, and the only artistic distinction he recognized was that between good and bad. Men of Jewish background, like Klemperer and Walter, deserved to 'have a place in the future Germany'. However, the letter also included passages – omitted by the conductor's later biographers – that accepted the legitimacy of anti-Semitism itself: 'If the battle against Jews is directed primarily against those artists – themselves rootless and destructive – who seek to promote kitsch, empty virtuosity etc., then that is quite all right. The battle against them and the spirit they embody cannot be conducted strenuously and thoroughly enough.' In other words just as there were good and bad musicians so were there good and bad Jews. The Propaganda Minister responded with a masterpiece of double-talk which promised to support those artists of real ability as long as they respected the 'norms of the state'. Since one of the norms of the state was the exclusion of Jews from public life, the response conceded nothing.

In those early months of the new Reich, when he was anxious to cultivate an aura of cultural respectability, Hitler did not force the issue. But he drew Furtwängler ever further into the Nazi orbit. The conductor accepted appointment to a commission to vet music programmes, agreed to be vice-president of the Reich Music Chamber and was awarded the title of State Counsellor. Hitler wanted a politically compliant conductor; Furtwängler wanted recognition as the Third Reich's paramount cultural figure with, as he put it, 'responsibility for setting the whole standard of Germany's musical life'. He craved the Führer's approbation and repeatedly begged to meet him for a discussion. When his requests were denied, he was reduced to sending memoranda. An appeal to save the Philharmonic from bankruptcy Hitler readily agreed to. The conductor's views on 'how to fight the Jews in music' – repeating the good Jew-bad Jew argument while urging that eminent Jews in the music field should be permitted to keep their positions – received no response.

Not until August did Hitler finally agree to see the conductor. To prepare for the session, Furtwängler set down a list of the points he wished to raise. First of these was that he supported the Nazi party even though he was not a member of it. Second, the purge of Jews in the music field was too drastic, removing talented people and damaging Germany's reputation abroad. 'Insofar as the Jew is an intellectual enemy he must be fought with intellectual weapons. Written guidelines on how to fight Jews must be abandoned. . . .' Third, the Berlin Philharmonic should, on an exceptional basis, be permitted to retain its Jewish musicians. The orchestra, he noted, 'is at the present time the only institution to export culture and to serve as a propaganda tool for the German spirit which is still in demand abroad'.

Hitler must have found it an impertinence to be lectured on how to treat Jews and the meeting went badly. Furtwängler later told his secretary that he and Hitler had simply 'shouted at each other for about two hours'. In the months that followed the conductor continued to protest his loyalty to the new government – joining other artists in signing an open letter in August 1934 endorsing Hitler's succession to President Hindenburg as chief of state – while resisting pressure to get rid of his Jewish musicians and his Jewish secretary, the formidable Berta Geissmar. The problem eventually resolved itself as one by one each left the orchestra and Germany. In the meantime Furtwängler, who could have given Parsifal lessons in pure foolery, took it upon himself to espouse the cause of the most controversial composer of the moment, Paul Hindemith.

Promoting Hindemith was in itself sheer provocation, since the young composer was a noted Modernist whose music Hitler was known to dislike. Setting foot where any savvy angel would fear to tread, the conductor secured an appointment with Hitler to talk him into authorizing a performance of the composer's new opera, *Mathis der Maler.* Prior to the meeting, however, he wrote an article for a Berlin newspaper which stressed that Hindemith was a good Aryan, that his opera reflected this fact and that his emigration would be a misfortune. In the face of such an affront, an infuriated Hitler cancelled the meeting and decided to make an example of the conductor that would be terrifyingly clear to all German artists. Either they would toe the Nazi line, or they would pay the penalty. Furtwängler was given a choice of resigning all his positions or being summarily dismissed. In December 1934 he resigned as vice-president of the Reich Music Chamber, as head of the Berlin Philharmonic and as conductor of the Berlin State Opera. To leave no doubt that bridges had been burned, Göring replaced him at the State Opera with Clemens Krauss, whom he gave a ten-year contract. The lesson was obvious, though Furtwängler and most other German artists refused to learn it. In the Third Reich there was no purely artistic act; everything was ultimately political.

There was now no possibility, if there had ever been, of Hitler permitting Hindemith's opera to be performed. In several ways this was paradoxical. The new work marked a stylistic retreat from his earlier Modernism, which was a reason why Furtwängler had been emboldened to plead his case. Moreover, the composer was regarded by Goebbels, among others, as the most promising young Aryan composer in Germany and therefore the potential successor to the aged Strauss that they were looking for. These hopes were now dashed. Hindemith and party friends continued to work for an accommodation. But by 1938 the composer reluctantly concluded he had no prospects in the Third Reich and emigrated to the United States. His works were never formally banned and some scores continued to be published in Germany. However, this must have been without Hitler's knowledge. For the Führer, Hindemith's music was intolerable. In June 1943 – when it might be thought there were more urgent matters to concern him – he happened to notice in a Linz newspaper that a closed concert of Hindemith's works had been held in the city. 'The Führer is furious,' Bormann reported to the local gauleiter, 'that his instructions have been impertinently disregarded and the degenerate music of Hindemith had been performed in his home town of all places.' The person responsible lost his job and very nearly landed in a concentration camp.

The Furtwängler–Hindemith episode had the desired effect. Hitler demonstrated that he alone determined what was acceptable art. Musicians had either to conform or emigrate. Goebbels told Furtwängler he was free to leave Germany but could not return. The conductor responded that he had made up his mind to remain but, ever naïve, did not wish to be used as an instrument of political propaganda. The two agreed on a public statement in which Furtwängler apologized for his intervention in the Hindemith case and acknowledged that cultural policy was solely a matter for the determination of the Führer and his officials. The meeting was the critical moment in Furtwängler's relationship with the Third Reich. Although he continued to fret, he had subordinated himself to the Nazi order. Even Berta Geissmar was appalled, commenting that Furtwängler's capitulation was deplored not only outside Germany but inside where 'countless Germans, too, were aghast that this man on whom so many had relied . . . had given in at last'. One of those countless Germans was the liberal writer and theatre director Erich Ebermayer. 'I feel despondent that this successful master conductor has after all backed down like this,' he noted in his diary. 'A great moral success for us,' Goebbels crowed.

After that the relationship between the conductor and the Führer improved. Though still without permission to resume conducting in Germany, Furtwängler had signed contracts for concerts in Vienna, Budapest, Paris and London, which forced him to the indignity of another craven appeal. Invoking his 'declaration of loyalty to you which I gave to Dr Goebbels', he wrote to Hitler in early April 1935 asking to be allowed to honour his commitments. The two men met a short time later and permission was given. Not long afterwards it was announced that Furtwängler would conduct at the 1936 Bayreuth Festival. This was the year of the Olympics and Hitler was determined to impress foreign visitors with the splendours of German cultural life. He forced Bayreuth on Furtwängler and Furtwängler on Bayreuth, as Winifred's correspondence at the time made plain. The conductor was also permitted to return to the Berlin Philharmonic and did so on 24 April at a concert that was repeated on 3 May in the presence – as recorded in a widely published photo – of Hitler, Göring and Goebbels. The following September at Hitler's request he conducted *Die Meistersinger* at the opening of the annual Nuremberg Nazi party rally.

On Furtwängler's fiftieth birthday in January 1936, Hitler sent him an autographed photo of himself and instructed high officials to deliver other gifts to his home in Potsdam. The conductor, supposing this implied that he had been fully rehabilitated, sought to see Hitler to discuss his return to the Berlin State Opera. Before the meeting took place, however, there were reports that Furtwängler had agreed to conduct in New York. So angered was Hitler that the distraught conductor thought it best to send him another cringing letter. Not until April did Hitler consent to a meeting and, after keeping the conductor waiting for an hour, lectured him on modern music. A point of principle was involved, he said. Just as he would have nothing to do with a Jewish woman, however attractive, he could have nothing to do with modern music – presumably however beautiful. What else he said is not known, but the upshot was that Furtwängler agreed to withdraw from regular conducting for the time being, though agreeing to honour his engagement at Bayreuth. He was now thoroughly tamed. Goebbels, whom Furtwängler saw at the end of the 1936, well summed up the situation in his diary: 'He is now entirely on our side. He appreciates our great achievements. He still has some small requests, primarily to do with [press] criticism and Hindemith. Otherwise he is in line.' And being in line, he lent himself increasingly to Hitler's purposes. He conducted a concert for the Nazi charity, Winter Relief Work, a gala attended by the usual party cultural triarchy, Hitler, Göring and Goebbels. He joined the Fellowship of German Artists, an association which took 'National Socialism's philosophy as its defining principle'. In April 1937 he conducted Beethoven's Ninth Symphony in honour of Hitler's birthday, and the following September he took his orchestra to a propagandistic German Culture Week in Paris.

By the end of the 1937 Bayreuth season, the conductor and Winifred Wagner found themselves once more at odds. Yet again Furtwängler sought to raise the matter with Hitler and yet again was turned down. 'He is one of the most unpleasant persons I know,' the Führer was overheard to say. What Furt-wängler did not know was that Winifred and Hitler had already discussed the problem on the phone and had agreed that the conductor should, as her secretary phrased it, 'be booted out'. 'That way we will be rid of an antagonistic and troublesome element,' she added. Furtwängler was so astonished by the contumely of this upstart woman that he sent her an embittered letter, with a copy to Hitler. He had wanted to use Bayreuth to set an international standard for Wagnerian performance, he contended, and she had made this impossible. To this, Hitler responded by telephoning Winifred to say she enjoyed his full confidence and should not be unsettled by Furtwängler's outburst. When the conductor expressed a desire a year later to conduct Wagner at Salzburg, Hitler forbade it. Salzburg was not to benefit from Bayreuth's loss.

Furtwängler's Wagner tantrum was followed by a Tietjen outburst. The manager's remit at the Berlin State Opera had been expanded to comprise overall artistic authority. With this, Furtwängler realized that, in Berlin as in Bayreuth, he was to be a mere conductor rather than artistic supremo. He withdrew in high dudgeon and wrote to Göring saying he wished to have nothing further to do with the State Opera. In response the Reich Marshal complained that the conductor caused difficulties wherever he went and whatever he did and that 'the clockwork regularity of a Furtwängler case every year at the State Opera' left him exasperated.

Despite all this, the conductor remained loyal. In February 1938 he conducted the Berlin Philharmonic at a concert for the Hitler Youth. Some weeks later he withdrew from the Salzburg Festival on the grounds that he wished 'to avoid even the shadow of a "collision" of my interests with those of the Führer'. He publicly supported the annexation of Austria in the plebiscite that followed. And he conducted a performance of *Die Meistersinger* in celebration of Hitler's birthday that year and again at the party rally in Nuremberg. But he could not stop picking at the scabs of his own anxieties. The roster of those whom he feared and hated steadily grew – Tietjen, Winifred Wagner, Göring, Clemens Krauss, Richard Strauss, any number of lesser government officials and, most vexing of all, an upstart youth named Herbert von Karajan. More than ever he longed for reassurance from Hitler and several times asked to see him. The Führer, now in the final stage of his preparations for war, declined the appeals. In fact, they never again met.

As German forces overran Europe, Furtwängler's torment of himself and others gave way to a deep sense of patriotism. 'We can use him,' Goebbels commented gratefully, 'and he is at the moment very willing.' Some months later he added, 'He is very willing and volunteers to conduct the Berlin Philharmonic during my visit to Prague. This will be the culmination of our pacification work.' Thus it was that Furtwängler conducted in Prague not only in May 1940 but again in November, in Goebbels's programme to celebrate the German extinction of Czechoslovakia, and then returned in March 1944 to conduct at a concert for wounded German soldiers to commemorate the fifth anniversary of the German seizure of the country. Over and over Goebbels praised the conductor's services to the Reich. 'Once again he has done us excellent work abroad,' reads one diary entry. According to another, 'We can certainly use him, and he is also very willing.' Hitler was 'particularly pleased by

Furtwängler's activities', states a third. Upon the fall of France, Goebbels commented, 'He has become an out-and-out chauvinist.' In February 1942, after conducting the Berlin Philharmonic in Denmark and Sweden, he returned to Germany 'practically bursting with nationalistic enthusiasm [and] most willing to place himself at my disposal for any of my activities'. He also took his orchestra on tours to Norway, Switzerland and Hungary, and conducted a concert to celebrate Hitler's birthday in 1942. He even conducted, no doubt gritting his teeth, at the War Festivals in Bayreuth in 1943 and 1944.

'I am pleased that I succeeded in making Furtwängler so positive to the state and the Reich,' Goebbels wrote in his diary. 'It cost a lot of effort but he is on our side and I prefer a Furtwängler who causes me trouble but is a

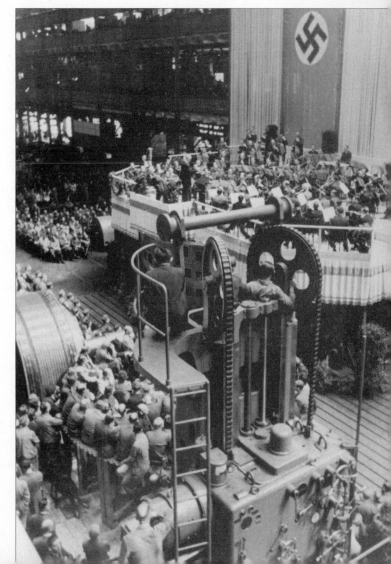

Hitler encouraged taking art and artists into factories. After 1939 the purpose of workers' concerts was to keep morale up and the war going. Here Furtwängler conducts a lunchtime concert at a Berlin armaments factory in October 1943.

citizen of the Reich to a Toscanini who no longer causes me trouble but lives abroad as an emigrant and can be used against Italy.' A deeply gratified Hitler instructed Goebbels to tell the conductor that his loyal behaviour 'would never be forgotten in the future'. And so on right to the end, when Goebbels noted, 'The Führer has the highest regard for Furtwängler. On national issues he has behaved impeccably; we will not forget that after the war.' Questioned about his behaviour at his denazification trial in 1946, Furtwängler refused to acknowledge that he had erred politically or morally and even claimed he had refused to conduct in any German-occupied country. When challenged, he responded feebly that 'Czechoslovakia was not actually conquered in the war' and that Denmark was not 'under occupation' but 'under protection'.

Next to Furtwängler, Clemens Krauss was the conductor of greatest interest to Hitler. He permitted Göring to put him in Furtwängler's place at the Berlin State Opera in December 1934 and already at that time had him in mind as the man to help build up Munich as the cultural capital of the Third Reich. To open the way, he ordered Knappertsbusch to be removed and transferred Krauss, unhappy in Berlin, to the Bavarian capital in 1937. There his conducting convinced Hitler he was the greatest of German opera conductors. He gave him and his artists an increase in salary, guaranteed him an enormous operating budget and forbore no artistic wish the conductor made. But Krauss longed to return home to Vienna and, seizing on Austria's incorporation in the Reich as a pretext, asked Hitler to appoint him director of the Vienna as well as the Munich operas. Hitler would not hear of it. A little later the conductor set his eye on the Salzburg Festival. Again the answer was no. In Munich Krauss remained to the end of the Third Reich.

Otherwise there were few conductors whom Hitler admired. Knappertsbusch he positively disliked. Appointed to the Munich State Opera in 1922 to succeed Bruno Walter, 'Kna' was popular with his conservative Bavarian audiences. An old-fashioned nationalist and anti-Semite, as well as a man of deep and lasting personal hatreds – Bruno Walter, Thomas Mann and Clemens Krauss were among his targets – Knappertsbusch greatly irritated Hitler with his manner of conducting, described as 'any number of jerky hand movements'. The dictator certainly did not want this 'military band leader', as he is said to have called him, to conduct in a city he intended to make a cultural centre. In 1935 Hitler ordered him to be pensioned off, although only forty-seven years old, and temporarily banned him from conducting in Germany. Knappertsbusch removed himself to Vienna where he was permanent guest conductor at the State Opera until replaced by Karl Böhm. Well-regarded in

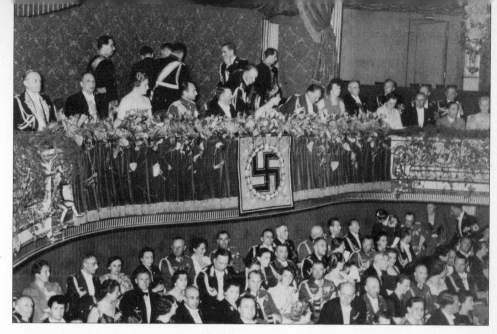

To entertain the Yugoslav Prince Regent, Hitler arranged a gala performance of Die Meistersinger *at the Berlin State Opera on 2 June 1939. The rising young star Herbert von Karajan conducted. (From left)* Foreign Minister Ribbentrop, Foreign Minister Cincar-Markovic, Emmy Göring, Prince Paul, the Führer, Princess Olga, Göring, Annelies Ribbentrop. *As usual, Goebbels,* far right, *was below the salt.*

party circles both for his conducting and his Nordic appearance, in later years he developed into one of the regime's leading conductors at party rallies, celebrations of Hitler's birthday and concerts in occupied countries. Only slowly did Hitler relent, as is evident in a passage in Goebbels's diary in 1944: 'I try to break a lance for Knappertsbusch. The Führer now at least finds him tolerable as a symphony conductor but worthless as an opera conductor.'

The young, up-and-coming conductors left Hitler cold. Böhm he termed 'second-rate'. He had authorized the conductor's release from his contract at the Hamburg opera in 1934 so he could replace Busch in Dresden. Mutschmann, the gauleiter there, wanted a musician loyal to the spirit of the Nazi order, and in the young Austrian he found him. Always at pains to ingratiate himself with party leaders, Böhm conducted *Die Meistersinger* on several occasions at the opening ritual of the Nuremberg party rallies and at celebrations of the Führer's birthday, signed public statements in favour of the Nazi state and the like. The Nazi spirit did not entirely corrupt his artistic work, however, and he was one of several conductors who included occasional modern works in his concerts. After six years Böhm found himself bored in Dresden and sought bigger things, namely Vienna. Schirach was in favour of the move and appealed to Hitler. However, the Führer had by now taken against the conductor, not so much for his musical taste as his conducting style, particularly in opera: 'Exactly like Knappertsbusch, Böhm uses a huge orchestra in an attempt to achieve massive effects and as a result ends up destroying the best vocal material.' He also felt the conductor failed completely in cultivating and coaching singers. Only in the summer of 1942 did he relent and permit him to move to Vienna.

One of the candidates to replace him in Dresden was Herbert von Karajan. Brought to Berlin from Aachen in 1938 by Tietjen, who was looking for someone to succeed Krauss and be a counterweight to Furtwängler, the young conductor shot into prominence with a performance of *Tristan und Isolde* which was regarded by some as a sensation. But the meteoric rise of 'the young magician' was followed by an almost equally precipitate fall. In June 1939 he was entrusted with conducting a gala performance of *Die Meistersinger* at the Berlin State Opera during the state visit of the Yugoslav prince regent, an occasion of political importance to Hitler. Something went wrong with the performance – stories differed – and an embarrassed and irate Hitler blamed the error on Karajan's practice of conducting from memory rather than with a score. 'That was extremely inconsiderate to the public as well as the singers,' he is reported to have commented. Karajan himself later told a biographer that Hitler was so angered that he swore 'he would never set foot in any event where I conducted. I was not a true representative of a "German conductor"'. And, indeed, Hitler never forgave the incident. 'He has a very derogatory opinion of Karajan and his way of conducting,' Goebbels noted a year later. Yet Karajan was never completely cast out and continued to conduct occasionally in Berlin and was a guest conductor of the Bruckner Orchestra in Linz. The Führer seems to have valued his conducting on propaganda tours outside Germany where he was a popular success. But when it came to an appointment to Dresden, Hitler passed over him in favour of Karl Elmendorff, Principal Conductor of the Berlin State Opera.

Along with Furtwängler, Richard Strauss was the most important figure in German musical life and someone whose prestige Hitler was equally anxious to exploit. For his part the composer, whose politics were as much of the late nineteenth century as most of his compositions, welcomed the advent of the Third Reich. In his diary for 14 June 1928 Count Kessler noted that at a lunch hosted by Hugo von Hofmannsthal, Strauss had made a complete fool of himself by venting his reactionary political views and calling for a dictatorship. With his patrician contempt for democracy and the Weimar Republic, he showed no concern over Nazi oppression and believed that Hitler's New

Order held promise of improving musical life in Germany. Not long after Hitler's rise to power, Bruno Walter was prevented by Nazi threats from conducting in Leipzig and Berlin, prompting Arturo Toscanini to quit Bayreuth as a result. Whatever his motivation, Strauss took over their engagements and thereby ingratiated himself with Hitler. In April 1933 he signed the notorious letter condemning Thomas Mann for his Wagner lecture.

When the Reich Music Chamber was established the following November Strauss was offered, and possibly sought, its presidency. He and Furtwängler were the most eminent cultural figures left in Germany and associating both of them with the Nazi state was a coup. The composer's acceptance was a bitter blow to the anti-Nazis inside Germany. 'Too bad about Strauss,' wrote Erich Ebermayer. 'The great, beloved master of *Salome*, *Elektra*, *Ariadne*, *Rosenkavalier*, who will be truly immortal through his music – did he really find this necessary? What can have moved him to give them his great, eternal name?' Strauss himself was exuberant. In his inaugural address to the Chamber the following February, he expressed 'the warmest thanks' to Hitler and Goebbels on behalf of 'the entire German music world' for creating a body that would reorganize German musical life and integrate 'the German nation with its music' as closely as it had been centuries earlier. With Hitler's advent to power, much had changed politically and culturally, he said, and the new government proved it would no longer allow music to languish but would 'give it new impetus'. To honour the great occasion the composer even wrote a song, 'Das Bächlein'. The piece was dedicated to Goebbels, but its concluding line – '. . . will be my Führer, my Führer, my Führer!' – was widely considered a respectful nod to someone else. Although his ardour eventually cooled, for some years he went on praising Hitler publicly and privately for his political accomplishments and his encouragement of the arts.

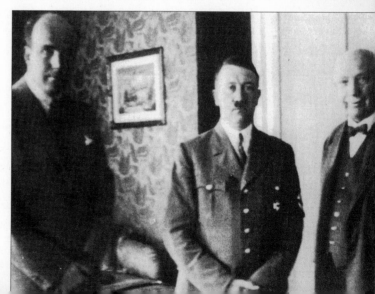

Richard Strauss and his son Franz with Hitler at Wahnfried in 1933. Although relations between the Wagner dynasty and Richard Strauss had long been strained, the composer was always a great friend of Bayreuth and used his meeting with Hitler to propose ways of aiding the Festival.

A few days after his speech to the Music Chamber Strauss convened a meeting of German musicians, and outdid himself in praise for the Nazi government and what it had already done for German music. He contrasted the indifference of the politicians of the Weimar Republic to 'the purposeful political work of Adolf Hitler'. To contribute his bit, Strauss announced a plan to reorganize concert and operatic programmes. First, he proposed to limit performances of music by foreign composers. As a rule only one-third of the operatic repertory should comprise works by non-Germans. Second, the Reich Music Chamber was to crack down on orchestras at health spas whose programmes comprised 'frightful trash'. A list was to be drawn up of 'respectable' entertainment music. Two-thirds of programmes were to be German and Austrian music, but 'Viennese operetta trash' was to be excluded and musical potpourris were to be totally banned. The playing by small bands of such major works as the 'Funeral March' from *Götterdämmerung* must be forbidden; a list of acceptable pieces was to be compiled and sent to spa orchestras to follow. Third, musicians themselves should be tested and classified, and those not meeting the qualifications were to be dropped from the profession. The composer also advocated a special 'culture tax', the distribution of which would 'be accompanied by strict admonitions about the role of an opera house in raising standards and banishing operetta from big houses. The foreign repertory would have to be limited to one-third ... and contemporary works encouraged.' Some smaller opera companies were to be closed down entirely.

Such a scheme was far more totalitarian than anything the dictator himself ever dreamed of. If Furtwängler longed to be the Führer of musical performance, Strauss wished to be Führer of what was performed. Like Hitler himself, he appeared intent on imposing his own standards and taste on the German public. The call for more 'contemporary works' and a reduction in performances of Verdi and Puccini as well as of operettas looked like a transparent attempt to promote his own compositions at the expense of others'. And his complaint that too much Wagner and too little music by living German composers was being performed abroad seemed like a blatant effort to force his own works on foreign audiences. Hitler would have none of it.

Strauss's relationship to Hitler was, roughly speaking, one of giving and asking for favours. In the summer of 1934 it was asking for one. While conducting at Bayreuth, Strauss met Hitler to discuss his newly completed opera, *Die schweigsame Frau*. Because its libretto had been written by Stefan Zweig, a Jew, he was uncertain whether Hitler would permit it to be performed. The composer had already raised the issue with Goebbels. 'I told him that I did not wish to embarrass Adolf Hitler and himself by performing my opera, and that I was willing to withdraw *Die schweigsame Frau* altogether and to forgo all showings at home and abroad,' Strauss subsequently recorded in a memorandum. 'In parting we agreed to submit the score to the Führer for a final decision.' After examining the libretto, Hitler responded that, though the work contravened the laws of the new Reich, it might be performed on an exceptional basis.

There was also accommodation. When Goebbels founded the so-called Permanent Council for the International Co-operation of Composers in 1934, Strauss agreed to be the head. The Propaganda Minister had dreamed up this organization to compete with the long-existing International Society for Contemporary Music whose members included Jews and Modernists. The Permanent Council was a Nazi-front organization with the purpose of exerting German influence in the international music world at the expense of Jews and atonalists. Strauss was also compliant when informed that his engagement at the Salzburg Festival that summer would be 'contrary to the Führer's policy towards Austria'. Although one of the founders of the festival, the composer agreed to stay away. Not long afterwards he signed the noted artists' proclamation supporting Hitler's elevation to chief of state in succession to President Hindenburg. It was such acts of osculation that prompted Thomas Mann to comment in his diary, 'He is stupid and miserable enough to place his fame at its disposal, and the Reich makes equally stupid and miserable use of it.'

By 1935 Hitler decided no longer to make miserable use of it. The relationship between the two men was never more than a marriage of convenience, hopeful on Strauss's part, but bound to end in tears. In character they could scarcely have been more unlike, with little in common beyond their compulsive pursuit of self-interest. Goebbels, who faithfully echoed his master's voice, rarely had anything good to say for the composer in his diaries and repeatedly spoke of him as being 'senile'. Strauss could be as malicious and wounding as he could be obsequious and craven, and his sarcastic remarks about the Nazi leaders undoubtedly got back to them. The composer's extensive Jewish connections – his Jewish daughter-in-law, his Jewish publisher, his part-Jewish librettist – and his resistance to anti-Semitic actions in the Reich Music Chamber fuelled their distrust. The dictator would have had sympathy for Strauss's proposals to foster serious music and suppress jazz and Modernist music, but the rest of his programme, particularly in its contempt for operetta, was bound to cause offence. And since he was no great lover of the composer's own operas, Hitler could not be expected to promote them. Strauss's animus against light entertainment music also clashed directly with Goebbels's policy of encouraging it.

What precipitated the conductor's downfall was a letter to Stefan Zweig in June 1935 in which Strauss wrote that he was using the Music Chamber for his own purposes, that neither anti-Semitism nor political ideology had any place in his work and, above all, that he wished to continue collaborating with his Jewish librettist. The letter was intercepted and passed on to Hitler who demanded Strauss's resignation. 'We'll do it without any fuss,' Goebbels commented. *Die schweigsame Frau*, which had premièred in Dresden twelve days earlier, was withdrawn after four performances and never again staged in the Third Reich. After resigning on health grounds, Strauss wrote a grovelling letter to Hitler maintaining that the offending letter, written in a moment of anger with Zweig, had been misunderstood – 'As if I had little sympathy for anti-Semitism or the concept of national unity or the significance of my position as head of the Reich Music Chamber!' Hitler, it is said, never forgave Strauss and shunned him to the extent possible.

Anxious for a reconciliation, the composer continued to place his prestige at the disposal of the government. In late March 1936, following the German march into the Rhineland, he was in Antwerp for a Strauss festival. So strong was anti-German feeling at that moment that the performances were nearly cancelled. As he wrote to his wife at the time, '. . . I have made this success a German one entirely on my own, through my work, my conducting and my personal presence here. The newspapers are raving. I'd like to see any other German artist do what I have done – at a time like this in a foreign country in a hostile mood. Really I deserve the goldest medal of the Propaganda Ministry.' Relations improved in the same year when the composer and the Führer met for a fifth time in Berlin where Strauss conducted his just completed 'Olympic Hymn', composed for the Berlin games. On this occasion Hitler, tactlessly but perhaps deliberately, gushed about Wagner's music, leaving Strauss to respond lamely that, yes indeed, it did represent the culmination of several thousand years of musical development. When the Reich Music Festival opened in 1938 – the counterpart to the notorious Degenerate Music Exhibition – Strauss was there to conduct. In 1940 he wrote another quasi-political piece, *Japanische Festmusik*, which commemorated the 2600th anniversary of the Japanese empire and which also coincided with the signature of an alliance between Germany, Japan and Italy. And in 1943 he composed *Festmusik* for the city of Vienna in celebration of the fifth anniversary of the annexation of Austria. To ingratiate himself with certain government leaders, he also composed works which he dedicated to them – Goebbels; Walter Funk, Economics Minister, and Hans Frank, the infamous Governor of Poland.

By 1938 Hitler's feelings towards Strauss had already improved to the point where he attended the Vienna première of his latest work, *Friedenstag*, and at a reception afterwards the Führer was said to have spoken warmly about the composer. In the same year Strauss found it necessary to write to him about the mistreatment at school of a half-Jewish grandson. As a result a directive was passed down that both grandsons were to be considered Aryan, though with certain civil liabilities. However, that fatal combination of indiscretion and sarcasm that precipitated his downfall in 1935 caused Strauss further trouble in his ceaseless ridicule – jealousy, perhaps – of Franz Lehár, whose works were so beloved of the Führer and even more popular with the German public than Strauss's own. Eventually, in February 1941, Goebbels summoned Strauss to Berlin and gave him a brutal dressing-down for referring to Lehár as a 'street musician'. 'Lehár,' he screamed, 'has the masses and you do not. . . . Tomorrow's art is different from yesterday's. You, Herr Strauss, belong to yesterday.'

Another tempest occurred in 1943 when the composer adamantly declined to house a number of evacuees, bombed out of their homes, on his own property. Hitler was enraged and Strauss's goose was saved only through the intervention of Hans Frank. But when Strauss again refused in early January 1944, Hitler personally gave instructions that a *dépendence* on the composer's estate should be confiscated. To smooth things over, a now frightened composer wrote to Hitler reminding him of the good old days. 'My accomplishments as composer and conductor are known to you, my Führer,' he remarked, 'certainly at Bayreuth where I had the honour to meet you for the first time at a *Parsifal* performance.' It did no good. Once again Goebbels no doubt expressed Hitler's feelings in giving vent to his own. 'To my pleasure I find that with Furtwängler the worse things go for us, the more he supports our regime – in contrast to Richard Strauss who earlier could not do enough for us in terms of declarations of devotion but today says things that qualify for a people's court. . . .' Although rejecting Goebbels's proposal to limit or ban Strauss's operas, Hitler decreed that important party officials should have nothing to do with him. 'The Führer does not want anything done to harm Richard Strauss. He was just terribly angry because he behaved so shabbily about accepting evacuees. Nonetheless his works should be performed without hindrance.'

On the occasion of Strauss's eightieth birthday in June of that year, Hitler had to balance his personal dislike of Strauss against the fact that the composer remained the country's most noted cultural figure. In the end he decreed that the event should be ignored to the extent possible. There were to be no major articles in the press; what was written should discuss the work rather than the person and no official should attend any celebration, though Schirach was permitted to be seen with him at a concert in Vienna. When the war was over, the man who had been content to live in Germany under the Nazis found life there too difficult under American occupation. Now at last he fled to Switzerland.

There was no other prominent artist whose views on culture and politics so closely corresponded to Hitler's own as Hans Pfitzner. A National Socialist *avant la lettre*, he embodied the standard traits of the arch-conservative – xenophobic and anti-Semitic in politics, and anti-Modernist and anti-Semitic in the arts. To him, as to Hitler, the ethos of the Weimar Republic was symptomatic of a broader spiritual degeneration of the German nation. But even before Hitler spoke of such matters, Pfitzner had already taken up arms. He let go in 1917 with an attack on Ferruccio Busoni, accusing him of the crime of 'musical radicalism'. He hurled his next thunderbolt three years later against Paul Bekker, an eminent Jewish music critic and friend of the avant-garde who, in Pfitzner's view, was an instrument of the 'Jewish-international spirit'. Bekker was guilty of doing in the cultural sphere what 'Russian-Jewish criminals' were doing in politics. Pfitzner was also a proponent of the stab-in-the-back legend of Germany's military defeat in 1918 and by extension saw German culture being similarly undermined from within. The composer was outraged by the slightest alteration in traditional operatic stage design and in 1926 went so far as to propose a law to forbid innovative staging.

Pfitzner 's hatred of Weimar culture bore such similarity to Hitler's own that the two men were assumed to be kindred souls. In anticipation of a dramatic and fruitful meeting of minds, friends brought them together in early 1923. The encounter took place in a hospital where Pfitzner lay ill. It went badly. After some talk of the German political situation and the question of the Jews, Hitler stalked out, disgusted with the way Pfitzner 'had lain before him with a beard that made him look like a rabbi'. Despite the affront, the composer's admiration never dimmed. Once Hitler came to power it was assumed that Pfitzner, though not a member of the Nazi party, would be made head of a state opera, music conservatory or other institution. In fact, he received only meagre recognition. In 1933 he was appointed to the governing council of the Reich Music Chamber and in 1936 was nominated to be a Reich culture senator. A worse blow fell when, to his shock, he was put in retirement from the Munich Academy of Music on his sixty-fifth birthday in 1934. He subsequently complained so insistently of being impoverished that Furtwängler appealed to Goebbels who, with Hitler's approval, authorized a sizeable monthly stipend. But when it eventually emerged that he had in fact a reasonable income, Hitler concluded that he was a swindler. Pfitzner also turned to Göring for help and, when this was unsuccessful, he sent the Marshal an insulting telegram which nearly earned him a one-way trip to a concentration camp.

Pfitzner was notoriously irascible and self-pitying. The kindly Bruno Walter once remarked that the composer 'made it extremely difficult to give him all the warmth one wishes'. But his nemesis was Hitler himself. He despised the composer, ostensibly because Pfitzner's 'rabbinical' appearance convinced him the composer was half Jewish. He also disliked his music. 'Only his best pieces should be played, insofar as it is possible in Pfitzner's case to speak of good pieces,' he commented. The two never met after 1923. Pfitzner, apparently sensing the coldness, made few efforts to see him. And Hitler snubbed the composer brutally and repeatedly. In 1934 he would not permit Pfitzner to conduct at the Nuremberg party rally and on another occasion even excluded him from a reception following a concert of his own music in Weimar. In 1937 Hitler rejected Goebbels's proposal to award him the National Prize for Art and Science. Pfitzner's invitations to Hitler to attend concerts he conducted were invariably rebuffed. The dictator permitted only a modest commemoration of his seventieth birthday in 1939. As Goebbels recorded, 'The Führer is in general very hostile to Pfitzner. He considers him a half-Jew, which documentation shows not to be the case.' Despite these slights, the composer seems never to have lost his admiration for his Führer and in 1943, though the war had turned irretrievably bad, he was still able to say, 'Today there is no one besides him with the strength of body, spirit or soul, him whom we have known as our German Führer for the past ten years.'

Of all the noted German composers of the Third Reich years the one who benefited most from Hitler was Werner Egk. His career typified the confusions in the music world in National Socialist Germany. Though his eclectic 1935 opera, *Die Zaubergeige*, contained elements of Modernism, it encountered little opposition from party authorities and went over well with the public. With his next great work, *Peer Gynt*, he sailed more perilously close to the wind. Some passages were stylistically similar to the music of Křenek, Weill and Schreker, at times approaching atonality. In fact there were rumours that the score had been ghosted by Křenek or Weill. The text, moreover, was potentially even more risky. Upon reading it, Tietjen foresaw possible political difficulties – it could be interpreted to cast the National Socialists in a bad light – but he ventured to stage the première at the Berlin State Opera.

The performance took place in November 1938 and was badly received by outright Nazi publications, such as Goebbels's *Angriff*. Worse still, it was reported to Göring that Egk claimed to have conceived the Troll as a fat general with a uniform covered with medals. When the Reich Marshal heard that Hitler had been advised to attend the opera, he telephoned Tietjen to say, 'I order you to inform the Führer that I would regret his going to that piece of shit.' As soon as this advice was conveyed to him, Hitler exploded, saying, 'I do not need to ask Göring whether I may go to the opera.' And so, on 31 January 1939, the Führer went, accompanied by Goebbels, who recorded in his diary, 'We both go with strong misgivings. . . .' In the event Hitler liked the work sufficiently to summon the composer to his box and say, 'Egk, I am pleased to make the acquaintance of a worthy successor to Richard Wagner!' Although the reference to Wagner must have been deeply insincere, he was sufficiently pleased that Goebbels could speak for both of them in describing the composer as 'a tremendous, original talent', 'a new discovery', 'a name to reckon with'.

Hitler's reaction gave rise to a good deal of consternation. It was argued that, as with Hindemith's *Mathis der Maler*, the initial criticism of the work had nothing to do with music but was connected to intrigues among party leaders. Then, when it turned out that the Führer liked the opera, it was assumed that he had associated the objectionable Modernist elements in the score – jazz and polytonality – with the wicked world of the Trolls and had identified the evil Trolls in the plot with Communists and Jews, not with Nazis. The fact is, however, he did not like the story. As Goebbels recorded a short time later, 'The Führer complains about Werner Egk, who always composes such weird librettos. Good writers generally do not consent to write librettos.'

Once Hitler had ostentatiously demonstrated his approval, *Peer Gynt* was praised as exemplary Nordic art. Egk himself was greeted as the great hope for Third Reich opera. Opera managers who had earlier declined to perform the work now rushed to put it on. Goebbels selected it for the 1939 Reich Music Festival in Düsseldorf, and it had thirty-eight performances in various cities during its first two seasons. It was performed in Prague in 1941 and twelve times in Paris in 1943. The composer went from strength to strength.

He was appointed head of the composer's section of the Reich Music Chamber in 1941 and made a delegate to a meeting of the Permanent Council for the International Co-operation of Composers a year later. By now Egk was not only fairly wealthy but had developed into a leading figure in the Nazi music establishment. He demonstrated his loyalty to the National Socialist state even as it was going up in flames, writing in February 1943 in the *Völkischer Beobachter* that he remained confident in the final victory of the world's greatest cultural power and looked forward, following 'the healing process' then under way, for a 'marriage between idealistic politics and realistic art'.

In 1947 the Munich denazification court issued a judgement on Werner Egk's record in the Third Reich which concluded with the remark, 'As National Socialist barbarism took over in 1933, it was deeply disappointing that the intellectual elite, instead of opposing, one by one collaborated with National Socialism. . . . Everyone who placed his talents and his name at the disposal of National Socialism has brought guilt upon himself.' It was a comment that could have applied to any and all of the others.

THE
MASTER BUILDER

18 IMMORTALITY THROUGH ARCHITECTURE

LORD OF THE WORLD. SUCH WAS WHAT Hitler dreamed of being. Through political and military means he hoped to achieve it. And through architecture he intended to manifest it. He began the moment he became chancellor in 1933, declaring on the very evening of his appointment that one of his priorities was to remodel the Reich chancellery. Some years later he unfolded his larger vision. A statesman coming to be received by him would arrive at a mammoth railroad station, go under a colossal Arch of Triumph, progress down a grand boulevard, pass a gigantic Soldiers' Hall and finally reach a Great Hall, the world's largest building. These sites alone 'would take his breath away'. Then the visitor would enter a newly constructed Reich chancellery and proceed through its vast and magnificent rooms. By the time he reached his destination – Hitler's study – he would be overwhelmed with 'the sense that he is standing before the lord of the world'.

For Hitler architecture had a variety of purposes – self-gratification, self-glorification, social indoctrination and nationalistic self-assertion. The impulse to create an ideal society – to remake the world – is no doubt the conscious or unconscious aspiration of every architect. And the desire to construct buildings that arouse admiration and fear is timeless and universal. But while there may be a bit of Hitler in every architect and patron, other architects and patrons have not been dictators with a desire to dominate the world. What inspired Hitler's building programmes was no different from what impelled his foreign policy or his military adventures. It is striking that his sketchbook of 1925 contains not only floor plans of museums and theatres, drawings of public buildings and stage designs but also sketches of tanks, artillery, warships and a gigantic triumphal arch.

Just as Hitler was the sole designer of Germany's political, diplomatic and military objectives, so was he the *primus motor* of the country's state architecture. The popular notion that Third Reich architecture was 'Speer's architecture' is a drastic misconception. It was first and last Hitler's

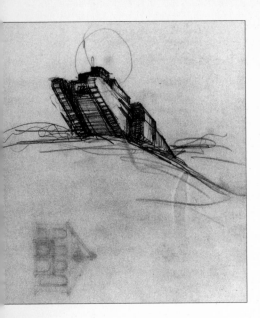

Like a schoolboy's notebook, Hitler's 1925 architectural sketchbook included drawings of battleships and tanks. Among his favourite books was the annual Jane's Fighting Ships.

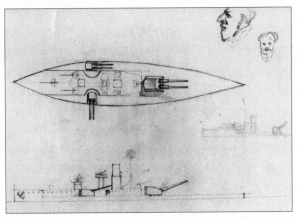

architecture. The wild inflation of Speer's role is traceable to Speer himself – survivors write the histories – and was subsequently perpetuated by his acolytes and certain architectural historians. In fact he was but one of a dozen architects working directly for Hitler, and most of his important projects were based on Hitler's sketches. In book after book Speer is identified as the architect of, for example, the proposed Berlin Arch of Triumph. Yet the original idea was completely and characteristically Hitler's as was the design and its location. Speer's intended role was little more than that of a contractor. So it was with most other state buildings throughout Germany. Hitler conceived them, determined their style and drew them in rude outline. He chose the sites, the architects, the building materials and date of completion. He approved the final plans, arranged the financing and directed the work as it progressed. Nothing was done without his knowledge and approval. To be sure, a few important state buildings were executed autonomously by other architects – chiefly, the Zeppelin Field spectator stands at Nuremberg and the new Reich Chancellery by Speer, the Ordensburg at Sonthofen by Giesler, Tempelhof airport by Sagebiel, the Olympic stadium by Werner March and the new Berlin museums by Wihelm Kreis. Even so, in both Nuremberg and Berlin, as indeed in cities throughout Germany, the most important were based on Hitler's ideas. In Linz as well the art gallery, the opera house, the planetarium, his parents' mausoleum, the bridges and so on followed his original designs.

Hitler's fascination with architecture can be traced to his childhood. He spent countless hours roaming the streets of Linz studying its buildings and thinking about how he would remodel the city. Even after moving to Vienna, he wrote several times to Kubizek about it. By now he had come to consider architecture, along with music, the queens of the arts, later writing in *Mein Kampf*, 'I was firmly convinced that I should some day make a name for myself as an architect.' No doubt this is what impelled the lad's naïve decision to participate in the competition announced in 1908 for a design of a new opera house in Linz. When city authorities then decided to remodel the existing structure rather than replace it, Hitler was furious. 'Their excellencies,' he grumbled to his friend, 'have as much idea of theatre construction as a hippopotamus has of playing a violin.'

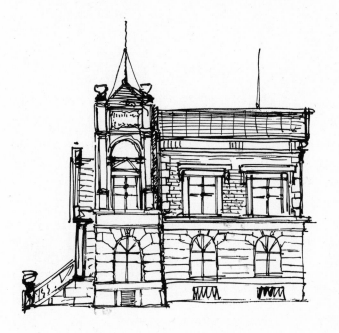
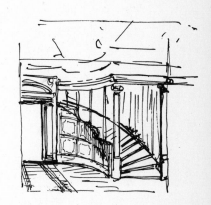

'On my eighteenth birthday, 3 August, 1906, my friend presented me with a sketch of a villa . . . in his favourite Italian Renaissance style. The ground plan reveals a well-thought-out arrangement of rooms, which are pleasantly grouped around the music room. The spiral staircase . . . is shown in a separate drawing. . . .'

(August Kubizek)

All that remains of his fantasies of that period are a few stray drawings that he gave Kubizek during their early years in Linz – two villas, the interior of the proposed opera house in Linz along with the watercolour of the restaurant at Pöstlingberg. Of those done later in Vienna and Munich, he commented:

> The architectural sketches which I did in those days were my most precious possession, the product of my brain, which I should never have given away as I did my paintings. No one should forget that all my current ideas, my architectural plans, go back to what I acquired in those days during my long nights of labour. If today I am able without any difficulty to sketch out the floor plan of a theatre, for example, it is not because I am in some sort of trance. It is simply the result of my study in those days. It is a terrible shame that most of those old drawings have been lost.

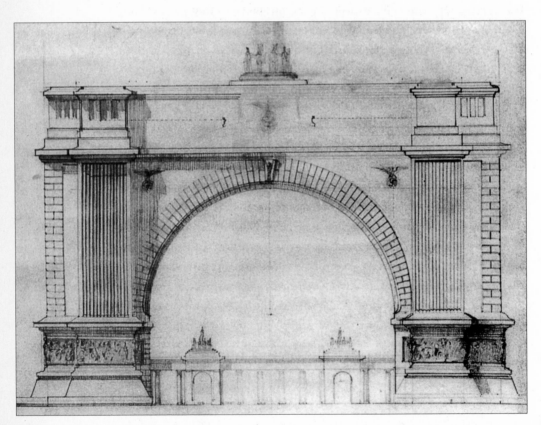

In 1925 Hitler sketched an Arch of Triumph for a grand Berlin boulevard that he dreamed of creating. It was to be decorated with seventy-five bas-reliefs and the names of the 1,800,000 Germans who fell in the First World War. At 386 feet high, 550 feet wide and 392 feet deep it dwarfed the Arc de Triomph in Paris at 164 feet high and 148 feet wide and miniaturized the nearby Brandenburg Gate at 65 feet high, 213 feet wide and 36 feet deep.

What had been a mere youthful dream developed into a serious interest after the war. And it did so at the same moment he took up a political career. From then on his political and architectural ambitions developed hand in hand. Not only were they linked in his own life, but they were also linked in his architectural philosophy – or, better perhaps, his architectural theology: great architecture is the outward sign of inward political greatness. This was a theme of one of his earliest speeches – at the Munich Hofbräuhaus in August 1920 – when he cited Athens, Rome, the Prussia of Frederick the Great and the France of Napoleon III as evidence. It is impossible to know whether this idea simply reflected Hitler's innate nationalism or was one he picked up from Arthur Moeller van den Bruck, whose 1916 essay, *The Prussian Style*, interpreted the monumentalist architecture of Schinkel and Gilly as an expression of Prussia's political and military successes. Certainly he admired Moeller and may have taken the term 'Third Reich' from the title of his 1923 book.

Since 'great nation–great architecture' or perhaps 'great architecture–great nation' was his premise, Hitler logically came to the conclusion that commercial considerations had no place in the equation. He made a big point of this in *Mein Kampf*, denouncing nineteenth-century market forces for transforming cities from cultural sites to urban wastelands dominated by business interests. The ancients did it better. 'The few still towering colossuses which we admire in the ruins and wreckage of the ancient world,' he wrote in a characteristic passage, 'are not former business palaces but temples and state structures – in other words, works belonging to the community.' This simple notion was the keystone of his later architectural projects, and he came back to it again in speeches and, later, in conversations with his architects. Indicative was an impassioned address in Munich in April 1929 in which he derided the meretricious values of the era. Germans had to adopt a wholly new way of thinking and a wholly new concept of the cultural role of the state. If there were to be a new Germany it had to be one known not for its department stores and factories, its skyscrapers and hotels but for 'documents of art and culture' that would last for centuries. The Parthenon, the Colosseum and medieval cathedrals were examples. They were not only an inspiration for the ages but had at the time engendered a sense of identity and communal unity. Contrast them, he said in disgust, with a Germany that had spent 60 to 80 million marks on a battleship lasting fifteen to twenty years rather than spending 10 to 12 million on a beautiful building lasting for centuries. The past was the way to the future.

Hitler looked on Rome not simply as a model community but also as an architectural inspiration. Everything about its ancient structures enthralled him. In *Mein Kampf* he referred admiringly to 'the overpowering sweep and force' of these 'towering colossuses' and 'the splendour of late Rome' which were still visible in the ruins of its 'temples and baths, stadiums, circuses, aqueducts, basilicas and so on. . . .' By the early 1920s, as is evident in drawings in the party's Hauptarchiv as well as his 1925 sketchbook, he had abandoned his youthful infatuation with the Vienna Ringstrasse style. Although he never lost his admiration for the achievements of such architects as Gottfried Semper, Theophil von Hansen and Karl von Hasenauer – whose works defined late nineteenth-century Viennese architecture – their complex, ornate and heavily encrusted façades and echoes of Renaissance features were a world away from his new-found neoclassicism. Whether it was the inspiration of such Prussian classicists as Gilly, Schinkel and Klenze that led him to Rome or views of Rome that led him to neoclassicism is impossible to know. Perhaps he was influenced by German architectural periodicals, which at the time were filled with photos and plans of contemporary neoclassicist structures stripped of ornament. This style, Hitler said years later, appealed to him because its simplicity, power and austerity were also the traits of his ideology. In any event he always insisted he was seeking not to develop a new style but to adapt what racially similar peoples – meaning the Greeks and Romans – had developed in the past. It was better, he contended, to imitate something good than to create something new but bad.

Other past styles held no attraction. He strongly disliked Romanesque; its darkness, he believed, had contributed to the mysticism of the era. In Gothic architecture he found something 'foreign and unnatural' and asked, 'Why suddenly break up a naturally beautiful arch and turn it into an unnecessary, absolutely useless pointed arch? And why all the pointed towers and pinnacles that are there only for the sake of appearance since they are walled up and make entry impossible?' For some unknown reason he made an exception of Strasbourg cathedral. After a brief visit there in June 1940, he pronounced it the most beautiful of Gothic edifices and declared his intention of converting it into a German national monument, possibly the site of Germany's unknown soldier. Baroque was also not to his taste, but he welcomed its development out of the counter-Reformation since it had moved architecture away from Gothic towards a style that he characterized as 'bright, open and light'.

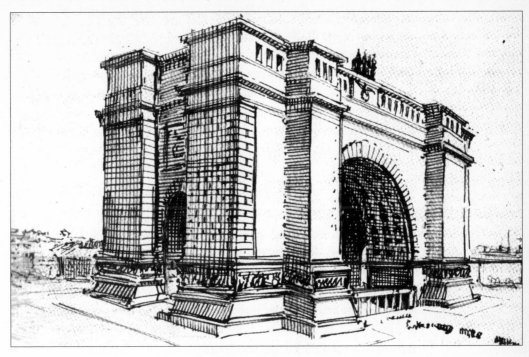

Hitler also did a perspective drawing of his Arch of Triumph; the great domed hall can be seen dimly in the distance.

Hitler's few surviving early architectural drawings are therefore more than historical curiosities. Although rude sketches, they show that he had freely selected and rejected various styles to develop something, albeit unoriginal, uniquely his own. It was neoclassical, Roman in particular, incorporating columned porticoes, domes and arches and displaying little or no decoration. Loath as he would have been to admit it, the style did not differ in its fundamentals from an international mode that influenced structures as various as the parliament building in Helsinki, the Musée d'Art Moderne in Paris, the Senate House of London University, the Supreme Court, National Archive and Federal Reserve buildings in Washington and in its way even Lutyens's Viceregal Lodge in New Delhi. Third Reich state architecture was Adolf Hitler's variant on this style, rooted in the concepts he developed in those early years.

The sketches are also interesting in demonstrating that Hitler regarded them in the same light as he viewed his political aspirations. With his sense of being a tool of destiny, only rarely did he doubt that he would some day achieve both his political and architectural ambitions even though at the time he was no more than one of a number of insignificant politicians with a minuscule following. He never drew industrial or commercial buildings, the sort of thing he might have aspired to design as an average architect. His designs were for state buildings, the types of structures that could only be realized if he were ruler of the country. Politics and architecture were therefore not competing but mutually reinforcing interests. Nothing could illustrate this better than a comment he made to Speer in 1936 when he handed him his two sketches of a triumphal arch to be erected in the centre of Berlin, 'I made these drawings ten years ago. I've always saved them because I never doubted that some day I would build these two edifices.' The statement is corroborated by an entry in Goebbels's diary in 1926, reporting that Hitler had been expatiating to him on 'his architectural picture of a future Germany'. The nearer he got to power the more he filled in the picture. By 1932 Goebbels was noting in his diary, 'In his free time the Führer occupies himself with designs for a new party building as well as a major reconstruction of the Reich capital. He has his projects completely prepared. . . .' It might be said that Hitler's political career can be extrapolated from his architectural plans.

In an address at the cultural session of the party rally in 1935 Hitler spoke at length about the principles governing these plans. He highlighted eight themes.

- Germany's cultural greatness was to be manifested in its architectural achievements
- no longer would Germany be 'a dumping ground for astute charlatans and morbid imbeciles' and 'stupid imitators of the past'
- private buildings and public ones should follow different styles; the latter should be monumental but not bombastic
- design and construction should be guided by the rule: maximum effect by minimum means
- the appearance of a structure had to be 'obviously and unambiguously' consistent with its purpose – a theatre should look like a theatre, not a farm building
- modern construction might require modern means; architects should therefore not shun modern building materials
- to exhibit their ideological pre-eminence, state and party buildings should be grander than other structures and as impressive as the great structures of the past
- it was 'an essential part of the cultural mission of National Socialism' to ignore commercial considerations in state and party buildings.

In a word, form was to follow function, with each type of building having its own appropriate style and materials. Neoclassicism offered the cold grandeur suitable for his state buildings. Structures for other purposes were to follow other modes. Social housing, Hitler Youth hostels, recreational facilities and the like could conform to local tradition; in such cases gabled and thatched roofs were permissible. Party schools and buildings grouped in so-called party forums were to be in the starkest, coldest functionalist style. Structures connected with modern technology, such as airports and railway stations, factories, the *Luftwaffe*'s buildings and autobahn service stations and bridges should be functional and Modernist. There was little room here for Paul Schultze-Naumburg and other 'stupid imitators of the past'. As Hitler said to Giesler: 'I will have nothing to do with Romantic eccentricity or anachronistic buildings – as, for example, a service station on a contemporary autobahn of all places that tries to give the impression, through half-timber and gables, of being part of the landscape. Instead they should be declaring, "Here autos are fuelled, not horses given water."'

So for all his reactionary taste in music and the visual arts, Hitler was an eclectic Functionalist when it came to state buildings. Contrary to his reputation, he was even at times receptive to Bauhaus ideas. He selected a few of Mies van der Rohe's sleek designs for autobahn service stations and approved a plan for the interior of a railway station for Linz that might have come straight out of Mies's studio. But he was opposed to the way he – however falsely – claimed Bauhaus architects put the structural cart before the stylistic horse. In time, however, he came to accept that modern technology and the use of steel, glass and reinforced concrete made possible new styles of buildings. As Speer wrote of a visit to the Hermann Göring Works outside Linz in 1943:

> When we left the big steel plant, Hitler expressed his appreciation of modern steel and glass architecture. 'Do you see this façade more than three hundred metres long? How fine are the proportions. What you have here are different requirements from those governing a party forum. There our Doric style is the expression of the New Order; here the technical solution is the appropriate thing. But if one of these so-called modern architects comes along and wants to build housing projects or town halls in the factory style, then I say: He does not understand a thing. That is not modern, it is tasteless. . . .'

Similarly, Hitler's views on skyscrapers shifted drastically in the course of the 1930s. Like many German architects, he initially criticized those in

America as an inhuman blight on the urban landscape. Believing, during his early years, that buildings should follow a horizontal plane, he thought the vertical thrust of skyscrapers defied harmonious proportions and produced 'a massive brutality'. He also detested their symbolism. As Freud had found the church domes of Rome symbolic of the *prepotenza* of a religion he scorned, so Hitler saw the skyscrapers of New York as emblems of commercialism – 'I think in general of Manhattan and specifically of that ill-conceived work, Rockefeller Center,' Giesler quotes him as commenting. 'That has nothing to do with urban development and nothing to do with proportions; it is a symbol of an ice-cold calculation of expenditure and profit, expressed in the erection of more than seventy floors of steel, concrete and glass.' By the late 1930s, however, he came to believe that such structures were, like the Eiffel Tower, symbols of technological advance and a nation's scientific prowess. Constructing them was therefore an architectural game that the Third Reich had to play. 'We will build these high rises in the future,' he averred. 'But these structures must be sensibly integrated into the specific urban environment.'

Hitler's passion for building, like his passion for Wagner's operas, exasperated party leaders. They decried it as a terrible waste of public funds and his own time. Even the ever-obsequious Goebbels could not forbear an occasional grunt of disapproval. In 1931 he commented bitterly to his diary about the new party headquarters in Munich, the so-called Brown House. 'All he thinks about: the party building. And at this very time. I don't like it. . . . Something must be done about it. That is what everyone thinks. That damned party building!' Ten years later Goebbels was still grumbling. 'Linz is costing us a pile of money. But it is so important to the Führer.' Hitler was no doubt aware of the discontent and made clear – by personal decree – that his architects were to work without any interference from political officials. Infringement of this rule was punished by removal. When the gauleiter of Augsburg, aghast at construction costs of Hitler's projects in his city, sent word that he wanted a written statement absolving him of financial responsibility, Hitler went into a rage. 'So he wants something in writing. All right, let him have it. This minute. His dismissal! . . . Here I am initiating a renaissance for Augsburg and these asses ask about costs.' He also fired the mayor of Berlin, Julius Lippert, though an old and active party member, after he had fallen foul of Speer.

Although architecture offered Hitler the main outlet for his aesthetic drive, it was also an important political instrument. Like other leaders in history, he used it as a means of developing national pride. 'Why put up these huge public buildings?' he asked in a speech to construction workers. 'I do this to restore to each individual German his self-respect. In a hundred areas I want to say to the individual: We are not inferior; on the contrary, we are the complete equals of every other nation.' This was a message he repeated over and over in his speeches. At the same time he wanted his buildings to be a medium of political intimidation. As he declared quite openly at the 1937 party rally,

> The greater the demands that a state makes on its citizens today, the more powerful must it appear. Our enemies will come to realize this, but even more our adherents must know that our buildings exist to strengthen our authority. . . . The buildings which you see rising in this city, the buildings already erected or under construction or planned in other places – such as Berlin, Munich, Hamburg – are to serve the interests of this authority.

It was in this sense that he referred to his architectural creations as '*Wort aus Stein*', word in stone – in short, ideology made manifest in buildings.

By 1939, with Germany self-confident, rearmed and ready for war, he lent his projects an even more aggressive intent. In a secret speech, indicatively given to *Wehrmacht* troop commanders in February 1939, he declared that Germans were by then the 'strongest people not only in Europe but . . . for all intents and purposes in the world' and he linked this fact directly to his building programme. His architecture was motivated not by a desire for ostentation, he said, but by 'the coldest calculation'. It had restored German self-assurance and 'had gradually brought the country to a recognition that it was not second-rate but equal to every other nation in the world, including America'. That was why Berlin was to be made the greatest city in the world, Munich the greatest cultural centre, Linz the greatest arts centre and Hamburg the greatest port. As for the autobahns, 'they are being built not just for transport alone but also in the conviction that it was necessary to restore to the German people the self-confidence they had lost and that a nation of 80 million people deserves and needs'.

Hitler's buildings and monuments had yet another purpose, the most important of all. Through them he would leave his visible mark on history. Not since the Roman emperors did any European leader plan to decorate his realm with such an array of monuments, buildings, forums, bridges, roads and whole new cities. And like the works of the ancients, his were to last for centuries. A repeated theme of his lectures at the cultural session of the party rallies was 'the timeless significance', the 'eternal value' and 'the millennial legacy' of his planned structures. He had chosen granite as a building material, he once explained, so that his buildings 'will still be standing unchanged in ten thousand years!' The remark was made at his field headquarters during the Russian campaign and, to drive the point home, he added, 'Military battles are eventually forgotten. Our buildings, however, will stand. The Colosseum in Rome lasted over the ages. . . .'

And that was what he envisaged. 'I want German buildings to be viewed in a thousand years as we view Greece and Rome,' he said. In his memoirs Speer claimed to have invented the means of achieving this sort of impression through 'a theory of ruin value'. In truth, the concept was far from original; it had a long history and was a European-wide Romantic fad. In the late eighteenth century the Landgraf of Kassel built a new ruined castle. In designing the Bank of England in the early nineteenth century, Sir John Soane presented the governors with three oil sketches of the building he planned; one illustrated it as new, another when weathered and a third after 1000 years as a ruin. But if the idea was not his, Speer was the only architect to employ it on a large scale. Using special materials and applying certain principles of statics, he claimed to have produced structures that in 1000 years would roughly resemble Roman ruins.

Obviously buildings to immortalize a great dictator had to be grandiose. It was Hitler's intention – and became a ruling passion – to cover Germany with the world's most monumental urban architecture. Every city of importance was included in his grand scheme and almost always he himself produced sketches of the main buildings. Berlin was to be the focus and, like Augustus who found Rome a city of brick and left it a city of marble, he was determined to turn Berlin into the world's most magnificent city. 'As capital of the world,' he boasted, 'Berlin will be comparable only to ancient Egypt, Babylon or Rome! What will London or Paris be in comparison!'

Rome was in fact the only city that he truly admired and that he felt challenged to surpass. Hitler rarely travelled abroad – a brief visit to Venice in 1934, a cruise along the Norwegian coast, a night in Prague and a quick tour of Warsaw in 1939, a few hours in Paris and Strasbourg as well as a meeting with Franco on the French–Spanish border in June 1940, a short visit to Finland to see Field Marshal Mannerheim in 1942 and several hours in Florence to see Mussolini in 1940. His six-day visit to Rome in May 1938, followed by excursions to Naples and Florence, was therefore his sole experience of foreign

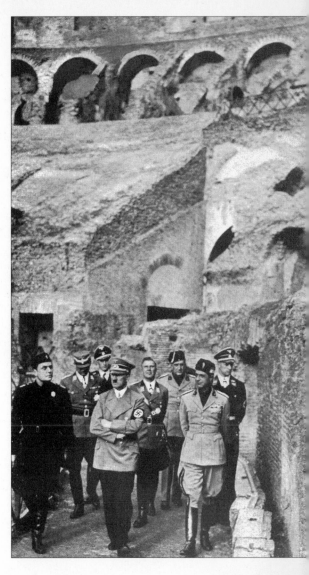

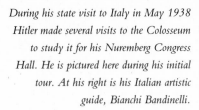

During his state visit to Italy in May 1938 Hitler made several visits to the Colosseum to study it for his Nuremberg Congress Hall. He is pictured here during his initial tour. At his right is his Italian artistic guide, Bianchi Bandinelli.

tourism and took place under the guise of a state visit. Mussolini was anxious to impress Hitler with his military strength and largely failed; the king and queen wanted to make Hitler feel vulgar and largely succeeded.

It was Virgil's eternal city that Hitler had above all looked forward to seeing and it did not disappoint. He revelled in its ancient sights – the Roman forum and the imperial forums, the Circus Maximus, the Servian wall, the Arch of Constantine, the Ara Pacis and the like. He spent a full day, without a break, visiting museums, galleries and monuments. Mussolini, who had prided himself on never having set foot in a museum or art gallery, accompanied him until overcome by boredom and exhaustion. So fascinated

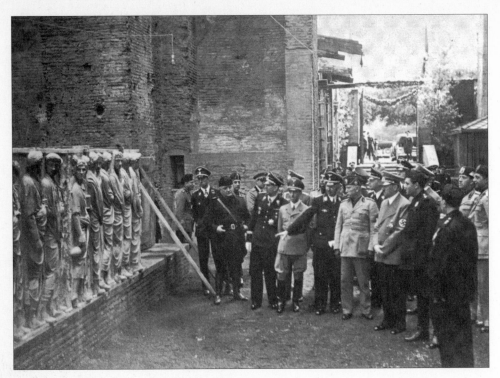

*Hitler's fascination with reliefs was fired by Greek and Roman examples. On 7 May 1938
he toured Diocletian's baths, which temporarily housed the famous Ara Pacis Augustae,
then being excavated. In attendance* (from left): *unidentified, Schaub, Goebbels, Himmler,
the Duce, the Führer and Bianchi Bandinelli.*

was Hitler by an exhibition celebrating Augustus's bimillennium that when
rain – mercifully from his point of view – forced the cancellation of a military
display, he was able to return a second time and go on to tour the Capitoline
Museums. Thrilled though he was by the Baths of Caracalla, the Colosseum
and Hadrian's tomb, it was above all the Pantheon that left him
overwhelmed. He had gone there formally, to pay respects at the tombs of
the House of Savoy, and then returned privately. He asked to visit it alone,
and when Bottai and Bianchi Bandinelli insisted on accompanying him, he
forbade them to speak and spent a quarter of an hour observing in silence.
He later termed the structure one of the most perfect ever built.

Hitler viewed these sites with the eye of an architect and a builder, picking
up ideas for his own monuments. Both the interior and exterior of the
Pantheon were a model for his Great Hall, and the Colosseum for the
Congress Hall in Nuremberg. According to Fritz Wiedemann, he spent

hours examining the Colosseum. 'One Sunday afternoon in Rome I had to accompany him there,' the adjutant recalled. 'He studied all the architectural details and the way they affected the overall impression; after our return from Rome he made changes in the design of his Congress Hall.' Needless to say, Hitler had to outdo the Flavian emperors. Their arena accommodated 50,000 spectators; his was to seat 60,000.

In comparison with Rome every other city was inferior. Even Paris. So anxious had he been to see the French capital after his military victory in 1940 that he could not even wait for the armistice to come into effect. Escorted not by generals or party leaders but by the three principals engaged in his building projects – Speer, Giesler and Breker – he spent four hours there on 23 June. Arriving before dawn, he went directly to the opera house. Acting almost as a tour guide, he led his small group through Charles Garnier's splendid building, commenting on the *belle époque* decoration and praising the proportions of the auditorium. 'He knew the ground plan of the opera perfectly, its precise dimensions and a thousand other details,' Breker later wrote. His fascination was boundless. After visiting the backstage

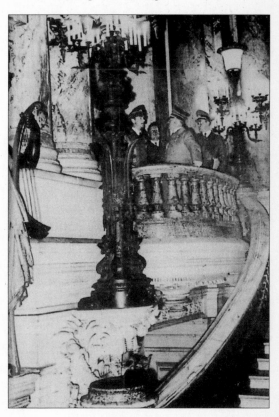

Hitler on the grand staircase of the Paris Opera. With him (left to right) are Arno Breker, the house concierge and Albert Speer.

machinery and the dance foyer, he asked to see the private entrance and reception salon for the head of state. The building attendant, completely nonplussed, denied that such a room existed until it finally dawned on him that, indeed, there had once been one, but it had been removed during a renovation many years before. 'There you see,' Speer quotes Hitler as saying proudly, 'how well I know my way about.' On exiting he had a long look at the exterior, now in full daylight, and went on to the Madeleine. Despite its classical façade, the church seemed to him coldly academic. Then, standing in the front of his car, he was driven slowly around the Place de la Concorde while he absorbed the prospect in every direction and proceeded up the Champs-Élysées. From there he admiringly observed the perspective down the avenue to the Tuileries. The Arch of Triumph itself and its reliefs, which he knew well from descriptions and photographs, he inspected with care. His enthusiasm, according to Breker, 'knew no bounds'.

The tour then moved on to the Trocadéro, with its view of the Eiffel Tower. This was just the sort of urban symbol he admired. Not beautiful, but a unique landmark, he said, and at the same time the hallmark of an epoch, embodying a new era in engineering techniques. After a brief visit to the

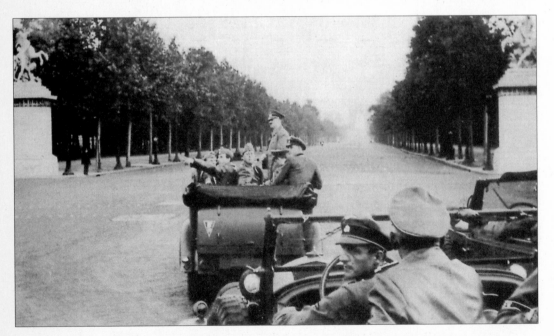

Paris around six in the morning on 23 June 1940: Hitler at the Place de la Concorde. Breker is pointing, Giesler looks straight back. Breker had spent many years in Paris; his Francophilia did not diminish his pleasure in showing Hitler around a defeated France.

École Militaire, the group entered the Invalides where the sight of Napoleon's tomb created, more than any other station of the tour, the deepest emotional impact. 'He stood,' Giesler recorded, 'long and earnestly, with bowed head, and stared motionless at Napoleon's sarcophagus. . . . Then he said softly to me, you will build my tomb, Giesler; we shall talk about this later.' The group progressed to the Panthéon which, contrary to Speer's account, Hitler disliked intensely – 'a huge disappointment'. 'By God,' Giesler quotes him saying, 'it does not deserve the name, when one thinks how the Roman Pantheon – with the classicism of the interior space and its uniquely beautiful light effect from open central oculus – combines dignity with solemnity. In contrast, this space . . . is dark, more than dark it is downright gloomy. Yet today is a bright summer day.' From there they drove past the Sorbonne, the Ile de la Cité, Notre Dame – all of which Hitler showed he knew well from photographs – to the Louvre, whose façades he praised, and on to the Place Vendôme. The tour ended at the Butte Montmartre so that Hitler could see, not the Sacré-Coeur, but the prospect of the city he had just inspected. Lost in thought, it is said, he returned to his aeroplane in silence. Once aboard, he instructed his pilot to fly over the city several times before heading back to his field headquarters. On arriving, he took Breker aside and said, 'Today I must tell you frankly that, like you, I would have studied in Paris had destiny not forced me into politics. My only ambition before the First World War was to be an artist. And Paris has been the place for artists since the nineteenth century.'

The visit was neither a touristic indulgence nor a celebration of conquest but a study tour to pick up ideas for his own urban plans. Most of what he had seen were nineteenth-century structures in a manner he found 'very decorative, naturally to some extent overdone, given the style and taste of the time', as he said to Giesler. Looking at the centre of Paris from Montmartre, he found that the great buildings and squares seemed to some extent swallowed up in the monotony of apartment houses and commercial buildings. Only the great axis from the Tuileries to the Arc de Triomphe, the Ile de la Cité and the Eiffel Tower stood out. Apart from the tower, the nineteenth-century buildings of Napoleon III and the Third Republic appeared to him undistinguished in the overall perspective. These impressions he carried away with him and took into account in his own building programmes.

'It was the dream of my life to be permitted to see Paris,' Speer quotes Hitler as saying after the trip. Yet later on, as he looked back, he was harshly critical. 'I have seen Rome and Paris and I must say that Paris, apart perhaps from the

Arc de Triomphe, has nothing great in the style of the Colosseum or Castel Sant'Angelo or St Peter's . . . . There is something bizarre about Paris buildings . . . whether the dormer windows, unhappy in their relationship to the overall structure, or a gable which overwhelms the façade or when I compare the original Pantheon with its Paris version, how badly the latter is constructed; and then the statues! What I saw of Paris left me cold. Rome moved me,' he said to his staff. At another time he said he had been impressed by the 'great perspective' achieved by the 'Concorde–Tuileries axis'. But, apart from the Eiffel Tower, he complained that the city had nothing as distinctive as the Colosseum. The Panthéon, with its sculptures 'like cancerous tumours', had been a 'horrible disappointment' and the Sacré-Coeur, 'ghastly!' Even Garnier's opera, that he had previously so esteemed, now seemed 'overdone' and less 'tasteful' than the houses in Dresden and Vienna. While he found the basic structure 'a work of genius', he considered its 'execution, from an artistic point of view, rather vulgar'. Still, for all his cavils, he regarded Paris as a 'cultural document' and, ever the big-hearted humanitarian, said he rejoiced that it had not proved necessary in the 1940 campaign to destroy it.

After his Paris visit he even thought better of Vienna, which he now decided was the 'more tasteful' of the two cities. But far and away the most beautiful city on the Danube was Budapest, and for that very reason Linz had to be developed so that it would surpass the Hungarian capital and demonstrate the superiority of the German creative spirit over that of the Magyars. No other city excited him. London, with few great vistas or eye-catching monuments, could not have had much appeal and met his silence. He did think highly of Sir Charles Barry's Houses of Parliament in Westminster, albeit as much for their historical ambience as their architecture. In *Mein Kampf* he wrote admiringly of Barry for delving into the history of the British Empire to find inspiration for the 'decorations of the twelve hundred niches, consoles and pillars of his magnificent edifice'. In that way a structure had been created that was 'the nation's hall of fame'. Hansen's Vienna parliament, by contrast, could not glorify Austrian history, since the multinational character of the empire deprived it of anything to glorify. The structure was therefore no more than an 'opera house of Western democracy' whose decorative quadrigae, he commented with some wit, fly from one another in all four directions, ironically symbolizing the activities that went on inside the building.

As statesman and architect Hitler was obsessed with outdoing every other statesman and architect of his time. Mussolini worried him a bit, however, and he instructed his architects publicly to play down the monumentality of his projects. Otherwise, he warned Goebbels, 'Mussolini will certainly imitate us.' What really disquieted him were developments in the Soviet Union and the United States. So aghast was he at the prospect of the tower of Stalin's proposed Palace of Soviets rising higher than the dome of his Great Hall in Berlin that he saw his attack on the Soviet Union as having an additional advantage. 'Now this will be the end of their building for good and all,' he remarked. Several years earlier, when Fritz Wiedemann had returned from a visit to the United States with thirty or so books on American architecture, he found his chief fascinated by what he saw. From then on Hitler was determined to overtake the Americans in every sphere. In the course of his pep talk to the *Wehrmacht* in February 1939, he defended his great projects by speaking of the need to be supreme:

> It is for this reason that I am going to have the biggest bridge built in Hamburg. Someone may ask, 'Why don't you build a tunnel?' Well, I do not consider it as practical. But even if I did think it was in fact practical, I would still build the biggest bridge in the world in Hamburg so that Germans, coming or going abroad and comparing Germany with overseas, will think, 'What is America with its bridges? We can do the same.' And that is why I am going to have skyscrapers built as tall as the tallest American ones.

He therefore resolved to have the widest streets and bridges, biggest stadium, biggest airport, biggest enclosed meeting place, biggest and fastest ships, most impressive highways, biggest and fastest trains and even the most powerful radio station in the world. A common trait of the despot, said Jacob Burckhardt, is 'a passion for the colossal'.

19 POLITICAL ARCHITECTURE

'*Bauen, bauen!*' – Build, build! So Goebbels recorded in his diary in September 1937 after the cornerstone of the massive German Stadium had been laid in Nuremberg. That year had been a relatively quiet one in both domestic and foreign affairs – 'the year of no surprises', as Hitler had promised the world in a speech to the Reichstag in January. It was also one when, his position now consolidated at home and abroad, he felt confident enough to begin moving towards the realization of two of his great ambitions – the military domination of Europe and the architectural remodelling of Germany. The former objective was promulgated to his military chiefs in November and recorded in the famous Hoßbach Memorandum. The latter was enshrined around the same time in a law giving him formal legal authority to seize any property and construct whatever he wished. With that began his urban projects. The two objectives, military expansion and urban construction, were to be pursued simultaneously and ultimately for a similar purpose. The link was spelled out in January of that year when, on appointing Speer to take charge of his Berlin architectural programmes, he said: 'We are going to create a huge Reich combining all Germanic people, starting in Norway and going down to northern Italy. . . . And your Berlin buildings will be the crowning achievement.'

Several months later Goebbels made the point even more bluntly:

The Führer really loves Berlin. The more he gets to know it the more attached he becomes. Discussions with Speer about building projects . . . Austria and Czechoslovakia. We must have both of these to round off our territory. And we will get them. When their citizens come to Germany, they are bowled over by our size and power. These little countries have a pathetic sense of their own greatness. But when their people come to Germany they are simply bowled over by the size and power of the Reich. We need to emphasize this more. It is the reason for the Führer's gigantic building projects.

After the war began, each addition to his empire left Hitler more excited about his architectural projects. Upon the fall of Norway, he told Goebbels he had 'great plans' for that country. Near Trondheim 'was to be built a great German city, probably named Nordstern [Polar Star]'. From there an autobahn would be constructed to Klagenfurt on the Austrian–Italian border – 'A line of communication straight through the Germanic Reich. In no time at all these countries will be completely Germanified.' Implicit in all these programmes, as Speer admitted, was Hitler's plan for world domination. That was why his building projects had to be completed in 1950. By then he would have achieved all his political and military goals. Final victory would be permanently manifested in stone. Berlin, now renamed 'Germania', would be inaugurated as capital of the world.

With his sense of destiny, he actually began making concrete plans even before coming to power. A grand party headquarters and two further large party buildings in Munich had already been completed by 1932. Then immediately upon his appointment as chancellor, he ordered the old Berlin chancellery to be thoroughly remodelled. Soon afterwards work began on the site for the party rally in Nuremberg and the renovation of the opera

Hitler, Speer and Ludwig Ruff studying designs for the Congress Hall
at the Nuremberg party rally site. Ruff, on Hitler's left, had done an initial design which
Hitler later altered and then, after visiting the Colosseum,
altered further. Parts of models lie in the foreground.

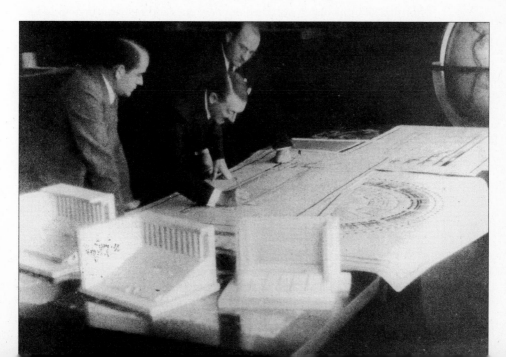

house in that city. In Munich he initiated the reconstruction of the great Königsplatz and laid the cornerstone for the House of German Art. Hitler's enthusiasm for building was the talk of a soirée at Goebbels's house in November of 1933. One of the guests, Prince Schaumburg-Lippe, noted in his diary that Hitler had arrived with photos of the models of his proposed projects in Munich. These he proudly showed around and to elucidate them, as the diary recorded,

> . . . he asks for a pencil and then goes at it. Bending over, he rapidly sketches the Munich street network with large, bold strokes and then puts in his buildings. Every now and then he sits back in his chair so as to be able to check the accuracy of the sketches from a greater distance. He is completely absorbed. Building after building arises for us to see. No carelessness – no, the dimensions are absolutely accurate. He has no ruler to work with. He sees only proportions. Everything has its proper place. Sheer perfection! The purest pleasure glows in his eyes as he looks around after finishing his sketch. And then he cites the essential statistics. He knows them all. He backs them up.

Despite the gush, the diary shows how swept up Hitler was in his building plans. At the very time he was doing away with democracy and civil liberties, establishing concentration camps, crushing trade unions, instituting anti-Semitic policies and so on, he never lacked time for the most detailed attention to these projects. Not long after the Goebbels's party he was shown proposals for statues to be erected on Königsplatz. They did not appeal to him and he immediately sketched out new ones and gave instructions to local officials to follow his drawings. 'The Führer played a decisive role in the choice of the style, execution and interior design. He determined the construction materials and completion date.' Such was a typical comment of the time – in this case in a memorandum of the committee overseeing the construction of the House of German Art.

In 1937 he set in motion the vast programme he had been dreaming of. This foresaw major projects in five favoured 'Führer cities' – Berlin, Hamburg, Nuremberg, Munich and Linz, a development so massive it entailed a drastic change in the face and character of entire urban centres. In addition a more modest redevelopment programme was to be carried out in no fewer than thirty-five – according to some accounts, fifty – other cities. Even that was far from the end of it. There were also projects elsewhere for museums and opera houses, autobahns and bridges, a wide-gauge railway line, war monuments and party schools. And these were only Hitler's projects. The three branches of the military, various party organizations and private industry all had their own construction plans.

As architect-builder Hitler was in his element. When Finance Minister

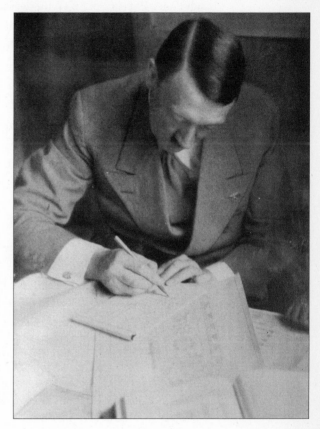

Hitler sketched the initial rough outline of important public buildings and gave these to one of his architects to work out. Their designs, which he invariably spent endless hours refining, were eventually translated into scale models, which he then further tinkered with. Reflecting his ideology, the overriding trait of Hitler's architecture was its uniformity: no expression of variety or individuality was tolerated.

Schwerin von Krosigk went to the chancellery in 1939 to discuss budget problems, he found the floor of Hitler's study littered with plans for the reconstruction of Berlin. With waxing ardour the Führer discussed how beautifully laid out the city had once been. After the unification of the country, however, the old design had been overlaid with a disorderly mélange of streets and structures. As he elaborated his ideas for creating a new urban order, he left Krosigk with the impression that the vision was taking shape before his very eyes as he spoke. 'One had the feeling that all this was the very centre of his existence.' In chatting with Speer while tramping around the prison yard at Spandau, Schirach complained about Hitler having ignored him and commented enviously, 'You were better off in that respect. He was absolutely obsessed with building.'

In developing his plans, Hitler could draw on an impressive range of personal knowledge. He had long been a voracious reader of books on architecture and, at least from the time he became chancellor, assembled a substantial collection. Since the war the Library of Congress has held some 3000 surviving items from his private library, presumably a fraction of the complete collection. These include designs of his Berlin projects; miscellaneous architectural drawings, blueprints and city maps; two albums with 610 photos of the construction of the House of German Art, 500 photos of architectural material on various European art museums and theatres as well as hundreds of photos of the interiors and decorations of his residences. 'Hitler's architectural knowledge was amazing. He knew by heart the size and ground plans of every significant building in the world,' Christa Schroeder remarked. 'I observed important architects and experts being absolutely dumbfounded by his ability and his unanticipated imagination.' Giesler recalled travelling with Hitler on his train from Munich to Berlin when he was treated to a long discourse which began with the evolution of Munich's urban formation and went on to ancient city walls and gates – the Lion Gate at Mycenae, the Gate of Ishtar at Babylon, the Propylaea of the Acropolis at Athens and the thirteenth-century gate of Frederick II at Capua. After gates, he spoke of representational entrances – Bernini's colonnades, the *cours d'honneur* of chateaux and the grand staircases of baroque palaces and residences. When Bormann interrupted his monologue to raise a political matter, Hitler curtly sent him away and went on to discuss how he planned to create a monumental entrance to Munich.

Speer was no less stinting in his praise of Hitler's competence. Hitler, he said, repeatedly demonstrated a professional understanding of designs and could easily combine a floor plan and renderings into a three-dimensional concept. Despite all his other responsibilities, he was able to keep track of the work on as many as fifteen projects in various cities. Whenever plans were again shown to him, even if months had passed, he immediately found his bearings and recalled exactly the changes he had asked for. 'Those who assumed that a request or a suggestion had long since been forgotten quickly learned otherwise,' Speer said. In working with his architects, Hitler almost invariably drew sketches to illustrate what he wanted, sometimes a well-executed one he had done overnight but more often a few hasty strokes made during a discussion. In these sketches he was able to draw outlines, cross sections and renderings to scale, demonstrating a good sense of architectural dynamics and proportions. These were, Speer testified, accurate in perspective even when casually tossed off. 'An architect could not have done better.' But he was never satisfied with initial drafts or plans, whether his own or one of his architect's, and revised them again and again. Sketches and models of his design of the party monument in Munich, for example, show how he fiddled endlessly until he got it just as he wanted. 'Even today,' Speer commented in his memoirs, 'these changes strike me as real improvements, providing better for the transition between the static elements of the base and the dynamic thrust of the column.'

So even though Hitler himself could not paint, compose or sculpt the great works he had hoped would characterize the Third Reich, he had both the minimal ability and the maximal power to construct the buildings he wanted. And what he wanted was monumental state structures – put another way, structures that were monuments – in neoclassical style. At various times Hitler identified the qualities he sought – 'greatness of conception', 'clarity of plan' and 'harmony of proportion'. While these were unexceptionable principles, the treatment he imposed on them – *germanische Tektonik*, he called it – produced a result that was brutal and cold.

He once remarked to Giesler that he had found Paris 'very decorative, to some extent overly elaborate in keeping with the mood and style of the time'. But that, he added, was not what he wanted. 'In *our* plans we shall strive for an architecture that is stronger and more austere, a classicism more in keeping with the simpler forms of our way of thinking.' And in keeping with his way of thinking, he and his architects used the language of classicism – portals, pillars, pediments, friezes, bas-reliefs, coffers – but translated it into bloated rectilinear structures with endless colonnades. Every design had strictly to conform to Hitler's stylistic imperatives. In their coldness, uniformity and size, the results were destructive of any sense of humanity or individualism. With their massiveness, solidity, deep-set windows and spare decoration, the buildings gave the impression of fortresses exuding the raw power of the National Socialist state. In narrow architectural terms, however, they had a strength and integrity lacking in Stalin's kitschy wedding-cake extravaganzas.

If Hitler wanted his buildings to be simple and austere, even more did he want them to knock people out. This was to be achieved through overbearing massiveness. He was far from the first person to seek to humble the world through giganticism. One thinks of Persepolis, the pyramids, Roman baths and basilicas, Gothic cathedrals, royal palaces, New York skyscrapers. But as his political and military successes mounted and his self-confidence became ever more bloated, size became an end in itself. His creations developed into a pastiche of historical references based on Roman examples that were often grotesquely blown up into ill-proportioned, crushingly huge structures. The overall effect – and, indeed, intent – was to aggrandize himself and to debase human beings into tiny objects, automatons as insensate as the stone of the building. Such was what they had been in his paintings and what they were in his political life.

This was also evident in a seemingly trivial but highly important, indeed requisite, feature of Third Reich buildings – the 'Führer balcony'. Far from being a mere embellishment, it was the visual manifestation of Hitler's

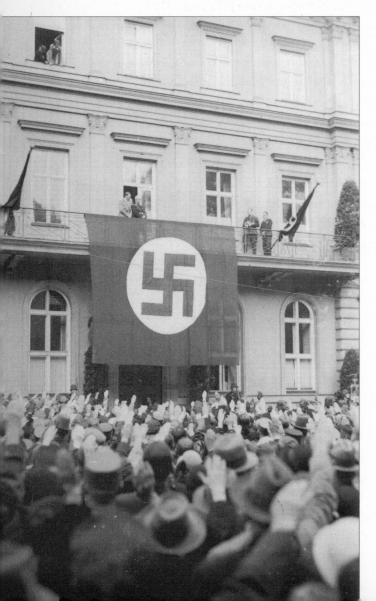

Another feature of Hitler's architectural stage settings was the Führer balcony, a structural accretion Hitler insisted on from the moment he took power. On this occasion, 9 November 1933, he is cheered by a crowd at the Brown House, commemorating the 1923 Putsch.

relationship to the German people as one of Führer to Volk. Balconies became a symbol of Hitler's rule and his appearance on them developed into an official fetish. Never before in history had so many balconies been stood upon so often by a political leader. No fewer than four of them were attached to the Führer Building and the party administrative headquarters in Munich. One of Hitler's first acts after achieving power was to have such a platform attached to the Reich chancellery. He himself designed it and ordered Speer to construct it 'in great haste'. From then on similar ones were included in the plans of every important state building. Even the existing ornamental balconies of hotels, theatres and opera houses were adapted for his use during his travels around Germany. Looking down upon the crowds, he demonstrated his Führer-ship while inviting popular adulation. In his absence as well, the ubiquitous balcony was a reminder of his status and omnipresence.

With the passage of time Hitler recognized that sculpture was another highly effective way of conveying his ideology. It was the 1936 Olympics that first brought this home to him and that at the same time acquainted him with the talent of Breker and Thorak to express it. No longer were sculptures to be confined to museums and interiors; from now on they were to be on streets, in squares and around his public buildings. The Olympic complex was the only completed example of his sculptural-architectural idea and merely hinted at what was to come.

Symbolism eventually prompted Hitler to modify his initial insistence on having state buildings constructed along a horizontal plane. By 1936 he was beginning to use vertical structures such as towers and tall monuments. He and the party were now solidly in power, even triumphant. These erections would transmit two messages – power within the party was strictly vertical and the party towered over all. He spelled out these principles to Speer, who recounted the conversation in his Spandau diaries. Discussing the construction of a party forum in Augsburg, Hitler suddenly asked the height of the tallest tower in the city. On hearing the answer, he

> . . . added twenty metres, saying that in any case the new tower must be higher than the tallest church steeple in the city. The bells in the forum tower were also to be bigger and louder than all the others. Just as in the Middle Ages the cathedrals had towered over the homes and warehouses of the burghers, so the party buildings must surpass modern office buildings. . . . We are the ones who will shape the new state; our state belongs to the party and not to the banks.

This notion gave rise to one of Hitler's most distinctive urban programmes, the construction of 'party forums' throughout Germany. The inspiration went back to his early years and was first mentioned in *Mein Kampf*. There he argued that while cities in the Roman Empire had been defined by a grouping of proud communal buildings, German towns had developed unplanned and without a distinctive core of public monuments – a claim that blatantly ignored the fine civic buildings that had been commissioned by various royal and ducal houses throughout the country. After becoming chancellor, he devised a plan to resurrect the classical forum, still as the central civic meeting place but now as the site of a National Socialist and Hitler cult. Every city and town of importance was to have one and they were to be essentially uniform. Arranged along a central axis, there was to be a broad avenue, an outdoor assembly area – for 60,000 in towns like Weimar to a half-million or more in the case of Berlin – and an indoor meeting hall, for anywhere from 15,000 to 180,000 people. Normally constructed away from the existing city centre, the forum was intended to emphasize the new direction in society. The effect, like the intent, was to replace a city's individual character with an optically uniform sacred cultic site.

Ideology necessarily guided the selection of construction materials. For the exterior of state buildings these had to be 'German' and 'natural' – granite, travertine, marble, limestone and other hard stone. Concrete, steel and glass were to be shunned, at least officially. In fact, concrete and steel were widely used but were in most cases concealed behind stone. Materials were not only to be hard and therefore durable but also hard and therefore intimidating. In the interiors of his buildings, Hitler aimed at similar effects. He helped to design imposing entrances, great lobbies, grand staircases and broad corridors. Marble was favoured along with wood, in particular German oak, a symbol in Teutonic folklore of Germanness, the equivalent of Roman laurel. The result was a combination of the sensuous, solemn and showy with the austere, cold and impersonal.

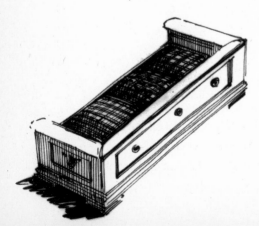

Hitler might have been an interior decorator. He designed not only sofas, tables, chests, lamps and lampshades but even cutlery and other household items. The objects were manufactured at Gerdy Troost's workshop.

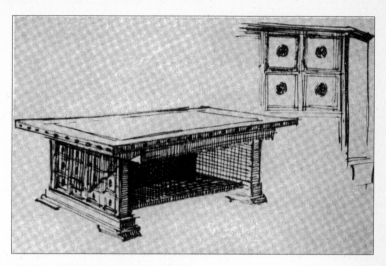

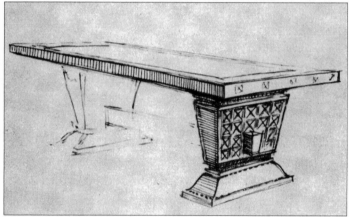

Such was also the case with Hitler's personal forays into interior design and furnishings. On the one hand he favoured 'a style that suits the times by being plain and simple and at the same time dignified' and even allowed himself to be photographed sitting contentedly in a Bauhaus tube chair. Among his surviving sketches are several of fireplace mantels, a sofa, a sideboard, a table lamp and shade, and large wooden tables with intricately carved legs, some of which were manufactured by his friend Gerdy Troost and her assistant Leonhard Gall. On the other hand Hitler was prey to his compulsive ostentatiousness, which Troost was only partially able to control. Her firm, the Vereinigte Werkstätten of Munich, provided the furnishings both for his residences and the new chancellery. Photographs show how these combined Troost's traditional Central European solid, middle-class style with Hitler's pretentiousness. What resulted was a bizarre mixing of rich oriental carpets, paintings and tapestries with slabs of marble, oak panelling and coffered ceilings. The overall effect was stilted, vulgar and cold – lavish kitsch.

The big question after 1933 was which architects or school of architecture Hitler would turn to in carrying out his grand projects. Generally speaking, the field was as polarized as music, painting and some of the other arts. The battle line was the familiar one, in this case with traditionalists, led by Schultze-Naumburg, Paul Schmitthenner and Alfred Rosenberg, himself an architect by training, pitted against such noted figures as Peter Behrens and Hans Poelzig as well as members of the Bauhaus, such as Walter Gropius and Mies van der Rohe. The differences were partly political, most Modernists being on the left or perceived as such, and most traditionalists very far to the right. But the main disagreement was over style, if sometimes just the symbols of style. The Modernists used flat roofs, modern technology, glass and metal, all of which they considered suitable for any type of building. The traditionalists held to the 'true Germanic tradition' of gabled roofs and old-fashioned design concepts and materials, and believed that style varied with function. Some noted architects, such as Wilhelm Kreis and Paul Bonatz, managed to find a position between the two camps. Others extricated themselves entirely. Erich Mendelsohn and the few other Jewish architects left in 1933; the leftists Bruno Taut and Ernst May had gone to the Soviet Union even earlier.

Once Hitler came to power the conservatives took for granted that their anti-technological, historicist, *Blut und Boden* Germanicism would be adopted as the official style. Modernists, however, hoped that their high-tech modernity and simplicity would appeal to a movement dedicated to a revolutionary New Order. Like Barlach and Nolde in painting and Hindemith and Schoenberg in music, Gropius and Mies believed that their style was *the* German style and would ensure German dominance in their field. They and their colleagues – the Bauhäusler – also imitated their counterparts in other fields by doing their best to ingratiate themselves with the new government, and Nazi authorities willingly let them try. They were offered contracts and they happily signed on – many of them for Göring's official and personal projects. Both Gropius and Mies unhesitatingly joined the visual arts section of the Reich Culture Chamber and participated in the Nazis' early architectural competitions. Although they never compromised their architectural principles, they compromised their politics. A number of sketches survive of their entries which show structures decorated with swastikas.

The first real sign of Hitler's intentions appeared shortly after the Nazis came to power. In a competition for an extension to the Reich Bank building in Berlin Gropius, Mies, Poelzig and twenty-seven others had contributed designs and, though Mies's was one of six to receive a prize, Hitler rejected them all and selected a banal, Functionalist one by Heinrich Wolff, whose proposal the jury had rejected. Mies's powerful Modernist design, though simple and sleek, had no traditional classical features and, worse still, was not of stone but of glass and steel. Although Mies achieved monumentality, he did so not by solid stone surfaces and columnar shams but by lightness, transparency and spatial rhythm. This was definitely not what Hitler had in mind for his state buildings.

In theory Mies and Hitler might have found common ground. Mies's remark that 'Architecture is the will of the epoch translated into space' was as good as identical to one Hitler made at a 1938 architecture exhibition. But in practice they disagreed on the way the will of the epoch was to be translated into space. For Hitler function determined style, for Mies style could suit just about any function. Mies, like Gropius, hoped against hope to be accepted in the New Order, participating in competitions and signing the artists' manifesto supporting Hitler's succession to Hindenburg. It all went for naught, however, and in 1938 an embittered Mies followed Gropius and a few other avant-garde architects into reluctant exile. Paradoxically, the traditionalists fared far worse. Not only was Hitler disappointed with Schultze-Naumburg's revamp of the Nuremberg opera house, but he was also appalled by his design of a party forum in Weimar. 'It looks like an oversized marketplace for a provincial town,' he said and threw it out. Thus ended Schultze-Naumburg's career as a state architect. From then on he had to rest content with empty awards.

In truth, the doctrinal disputes among architects did not interest Hitler. He commissioned works of importance from Kreis. He much admired Peter Behrens for his Modernist 1911 German embassy in St Petersburg and approved, over Rosenberg's objection, his design of a building on one of the new avenues in Berlin. In 1936 he appointed Behrens to be head of the architecture section of the Prussian Academy and in 1943 Kreis as president of the Reich Chamber of Visual Arts. Bonatz built ultra-Modernist bridges for the autobahns, and numerous other Modernists and semi-Modernists worked on his various projects. Having developed his ideological and stylistic desiderata, Hitler had no intention of allowing his architects any scope for originality. He wanted malleable men who were on the same stylistic wavelength and who would unquestioningly follow his directions. Typically, he did not select them on the basis of demonstrated skill but more or less by chance. In the end it made relatively little difference who these men were because he dictated the basic elements of every project – the sites, building style, the size and characteristics of the structure and the exterior and interior decoration. 'The fact is that Hitler worried over every aspect of his buildings, even the tiniest detail, so that Speer himself was not much more than an assistant who carried out Hitler's ideas,' Wiedemann observed. Heinz Linge said much the same. No major project could be undertaken without his authorization and only after he had personally examined the designs, altered and approved them. His final decisions even on technical matters had the character of a command and were to be carried out without reservation.

Hitler eventually engaged an army of architects. Some concentrated on major urban projects; others designed roads and bridges and still others were responsible for opera houses, theatres and a variety of special projects. Each had platoons of architectural assistants. In their way these men were as important to him as his generals. While there were few, if any, generals whom he liked, trusted or was close to, he respected and took pleasure in the company of most of his architects. He gave them financial and other privileges, and exempted many of them from military service after the war began. He endowed his favourites, such as Speer and Giesler, with the title of professor and gave Speer huge honorariums – 7 million marks for Berlin alone. In July 1937 Hitler purged the Prussian Academy of Arts and expelled, among others, Mies, Heinrich Tessenow, Schultze-Naumburg, Heinrich Wolff, Wilhelm Kreis and Peter Behrens. In their places he installed Speer, Giesler, Roderich Fick, Leonhard Gall and Ernst Sagebiel, all of them the Führer's creatures.

There were four principals. The first and least typical was Paul Ludwig Troost, a minor Munich architect and interior designer of neoclassical bent and modest ability. In 1910 he became the leading interior designer for passenger liners of Lloyds shipping lines. His chef-d'oeuvre was the *Europa*, and the heavy wood panelling and Gemütlichkeit of its fittings suited Hitler's taste. The two men met in 1929 when Hitler was looking for furnishings for his new Munich flat in Prinzregentenplatz and visited Troost's workshop. There Hitler admired the simplicity both of the furniture and the man himself, who also happened to be an early party member. The subject of architecture arose and Troost took the occasion to show Hitler his design – rejected by a jury – for an art museum to replace the Glass Palace. 'When I encountered him the first time, he was deeply frustrated, embittered and fed up with life,' Hitler commented years later.

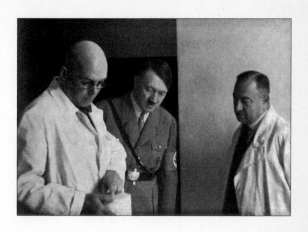

Hitler with Paul Ludwig Troost and Leonhard Gall. Gall managed Troost's studio and, after Troost's death, gained Hitler's confidence and was put in charge of Troost's outstanding projects. In 1940 Hitler commissioned him to design a great library at Linz.

Troost's simple neoclassical style coincided with Hitler's own and he decided to entrust the architect with the conversion of the Barlow-Palais, the former Italian Legation in Munich, into the party's national headquarters, the so-called Brown House. Work on this was scarcely finished when Hitler, not yet chancellor but now closer to power following elections which put big business money in his pockets and National Socialists into the Reichstag, collaborated with Troost on plans for two larger structures, an administrative headquarters for the party and offices for himself, known as the Führer Building. These were to tell the world that he and his party were firmly established and a factor to be reckoned with. Both were to be situated at the far side of the Königsplatz, which Hitler already had eye on for other purposes. And, indeed, as soon as he achieved power in 1933, he and Troost started converting the space into the most sacred site of the Nazi movement, with two 'temples of honour' as the focal point. In his youth Hitler had done watercolours of some of the structures on this square, and it was a dream come true that he now found it in his power to reshape the site exactly as he wished.

Even during the hectic months just after becoming chancellor, Hitler often visited Munich, not least of all to see Troost. According to Speer's account:

> In the train he would usually talk animatedly about which drawings 'the professor' would probably have ready. . . .
>
> On arrival . . . we would go up two flights of a dreary stairway that had not been painted for years. Troost, conscious of his standing, never came to meet Hitler on the stairs, nor ever accompanied him downstairs when he left. In the ante-room, Hitler would greet him: 'I can't wait Herr Professor. Is there anything new – let's see it!' And we would plunge right in – Hitler and I would stand in the studio itself while Troost, composed and quiet as always, spread out his plans and the sketches of his ideas.

It makes a nice story. Alas, Gerdy Troost insisted that Speer never met her husband and never set foot in his atelier while he was alive. Still, there is no reason to doubt the basic point, that with his architects Hitler behaved with uncharacteristic humility. Giesler was amazed at how amiable and relaxed he found him at their first meeting; it was, he said, as though they had known one another for ages. According to Speer whenever Hitler asked for changes in a design he did so in a friendly, professional manner. And in the face of disagreement he sometimes gave way. 'Yes, you're right, that's better,' Speer quotes the sort of comment he would make.

Troost's principal work was the House of German Art. It was the first public building Hitler commissioned and one of his few personal projects to be completed and to survive the war. Based on Troost's insipid entry in the Glass Palace competition, the design was a Modernist riff on standard neoclassicism. The structure's severe flat surfaces were emphasized by the lack of any ornamentation save the restrained cornices and pediments of the pillars. Its dominant feature was a 480-foot-long classical colonnade – inspired by Schinkel's Altes Museum in Berlin, much admired by Hitler – which in its Cubist forms and flat surfaces betrayed a Modernist bent. The building is of little architectural interest and no merit, its rank of twenty-two columns popularly derided even at the time as looking like a sausage stand. What *is* of interest is what it tells about Hitler's own early architectural concepts. A comparison of Troost's fatuous original with what was actually built suggests that the edifice was more Hitler than Troost.

Hitler delighted in the structure, describing it as 'the first beautiful building of the new Reich' when it opened in 1937. But at the laying of the cornerstone in October 1933, the hammer had broken in his hand and left him with a terrible foreboding. Three months later, Troost died after a brief illness. 'Now we know why the hammer broke. The architect was destined to die,' Hitler said. There was no other architect in whom he had such confidence. At the party rally following Troost's death, he praised him as 'Germany's greatest architect since Schinkel' and in 1937 posthumously awarded him the National Prize for Art and Science.

Following Troost's death, Hitler himself fashioned the basic scheme for the redevelopment of Munich. Only after long hesitation did he finally entrust its implementation to the thirty-six-year-old Hermann Giesler, an early and devout Nazi who to the end of his life revered his beloved Führer. The architect had designed the Ordensburg at Sonthofen in 1934. Two years later Hitler commissioned him to construct the party forum in Weimar and the year after that the forum in Augsburg. In the same year he won both a competition to erect a Nazi party school at Chiemsee and, like Speer, a grand prix at the Paris World's Fair. In 1938 he undertook the reconstruction of Haus Elefant, a 400-year-old Weimar inn. Bach had slept there, Thackeray had satirized it in *Vanity Fair* and Hitler loved it. Adopting Troost's steamship style, Giesler remodelled it to the Führer's great satisfaction. In December 1938 Hitler placed him in overall charge of the redevelopment of Munich and later instructed him to oversee the construction of various buildings at the Berghof. During the war Giesler was responsible for military construction in the Baltic states and northern Russia. But it was in 1940 that Hitler put him in charge of the project that by then meant most to him emotionally, the redevelopment of Linz.

'Your husband is going to erect buildings for me such as have not been created for four thousand years.' So Hitler to Margarete Speer, the architect's wife in the spring of 1934. Twenty-eight-year-old Albert Speer, who had joined the Nazi party and the SA in March 1931 and the SS in the following year, had studied under the noted Berlin architect Heinrich Tessenow. He came to Hitler's attention thanks to a series of minor party projects in Berlin. In reality Speer was an organizational wizard who happened to be an architect and it was his ability to get things done, as Hitler wanted them done and on time, that made him stand out. Given the drastic differences in their character and social background, Hitler must have regarded him at first with misprision. In fact, for years he was uncertain how far he could rely on Speer as an architect. First he tested him with the Zeppelin Field project at Nuremberg. But as late as June of 1935 he was on record as saying that he could not decide whom he could entrust with his greatest project, the redevelopment of Berlin. Not until 1936 did he make up his mind and only in January 1937 did he officially appoint him. Within three years, however, Speer's insatiable thirst for power drove him to ask Hitler to make him 'National Socialist Commissioner for Architecture and City Planning' – alias architectural czar of Germany. Hitler turned him down. The snub was a calamitous blow to his self-esteem and, though Speer mentioned it only *sotto voce* in his memoirs, at the time he admitted to Bormann that 'inside much of me went to pieces'. He then offered to resign his various party positions and when the Führer 'happily' concurred, the architect became more miserable still. A short time later Hitler salved the wound somewhat by placing him in charge of the Drontheim project.

Speer was extremely wary of anyone who threatened to intrude on his relationship with Hitler and was particularly suspicious of Giesler. Relishing such rivalries, Hitler made certain that the lots were evenly cast by balancing Speer's projects against Giesler's more numerous assignments. From 1938 on, Giesler and Speer were the best of enemies, engaged in a never-ending *braccio di ferro*. 'Speer was afraid of Giesler's competition,' Speer's biographer Gitta Sereny has written, 'and did what he could to undermine it.' By the same token Giesler was jealous of Speer's personal closeness to Hitler, which he reckoned he could never match. His projects were as important as Speer's and, as Speer commented, 'From 1943 on he probably did actually prefer my Munich rival to me.' Even so, the Führer took malicious pleasure in tormenting Giesler by occasionally discussing the Munich and Linz projects with Speer. The quarrelling went on after the war as well. Freud would have found it revealing that in his memoirs Speer seldom mentioned his rival's name and, when he did, always misspelled it. By contrast Giesler, far from subconsciously trying to erase his rival's existence, devoted a chapter of his memoirs to him. Like millions of other Germans, Giesler's main regret in 1945 was that Hitler had lost the war, and he detested Speer for later turning against the man whom he had served and who had trusted him. Giesler's own memoir, as Sereny remarks, was largely a monument to that hate.

How to characterize the intense relationship between Hitler and Speer? Sereny concluded that it was a non-erotic love affair. Speer had more qualities in common with Hitler than he cared to admit – high intelligence, a narrow range of emotion, brutality, egomania, vulgar taste, a penchant for showmanship and an insatiable craving for power among them. Speer was probably right in supposing that if Hitler had been capable of having a true friend, it would have been he. Hitler might have said the same of Speer. One thing is certain. Hitler considered Speer the only person in his inner circle who was intellectually and culturally on his own level. As Christa Schroeder commented:

> Of Speer, he once said, 'He is an artist and a kindred soul. I have the warmest human feelings towards him because I understand him so well. Like me he is a builder, intelligent and unassuming and no military blockhead. I did not believe that he would be able to master his great responsibilities so well. But he has great organizational talent and always measured up to the demands of the work. If I develop a project with Speer and give him an assignment, he will think it over for a while and then say, "Yes, my Führer, I think that is certainly doable", or he might say instead, "No, that is not really possible" in which case he will have his reasons down pat.'

Giesler, Breker and probably most of Speer's other colleagues were deeply angered by his post-war books. Unrepentant Nazis themselves, they had expected him to remain loyal to his old chief whom he had faithfully served up to the end. But although Speer's two books slid lightly over Hitler's atrocities and presented a portrait of the dictator that was often far from unflattering, they were an invaluable chronicle of the Third Reich years. When it came to architectural matters, however, Speer at times seriously distorted the record in an evident attempt to exaggerate his role and to diminish Hitler's. He completely misrepresented Hitler's architectural concepts, dismissing the sketchbook drawings, for example, as 'attempts at public buildings in the neo-baroque style of Vienna's Ringstrasse – products of the eighteen-nineties'. A few paragraphs later he maintained that Hitler was always drawn to 'inflated neo-baroque such as Kaiser Wilhelm II had also fostered' and then, egging the

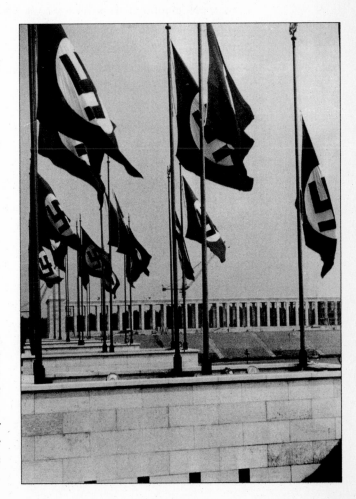

Flags are the most primitive of tribal totems, proclaiming the unity of the group ('patriotism') against outsiders ('the enemy'). 'United We Stand' is their xenophobic message; to drive it home, the Third Reich was festooned with flags.

pudding still further, defined this style as 'decadent neo-baroque, comparable to the style that accompanied the decline of the Roman Empire'. In one breath he proclaimed that 'it is ghastly to think what his architectural taste would have been like without Troost's influence' and in the next that Troost's 'influence upon Hitler remained marginal'. In summary, he argued that Hitler's style was 'only the neoclassicism transmitted by Troost' which was then 'multiplied, altered, exaggerated and sometimes distorted to the point of ludicrousness'.

But who did the multiplying, altering, exaggerating and distorting? Speer himself. At a time when Hitler was praising Troost's work on his chancellery residence for being 'bright, clear and simple', Speer was independently devising flamboyant decorations for the 1933 May Day celebration in Berlin. On showing Tessenow sketches of this open-air stagecraft, his old professor dismissed them with the comment, 'It's showy, that's all.' That was, of course, the whole point, and the novel display of gigantic banners, flags and searchlights left the Führer thrilled. He thereupon created the position of Chief of Artistic Production of Mass Demonstrations and appointed Speer to it. The dramaturge next displayed his talents at the first national harvest festival at Bückeburg and then went on to outdo himself at the 1933 Nuremberg rally when he festooned the site with forests of flags and bedazzled everyone with his great 'cathedral of light'. Although this massing of searchlight beams into the night sky was, despite Speer's claim, far from original – it had been widely used for many years at world's fairs – he was the first to use it on such a gigantic scale.

It was from these modest beginnings that Speer went on to design monumental structures for Nuremberg and Berlin. As much as his boss, he was a man of the theatre. An anecdote of Gerdy Troost's makes the point well. If Hitler had told her husband to design a building of a hundred metres, she said, he would have thought it over and replied that for structural and aesthetic reasons it could be merely ninety-six metres. But if Hitler had given a similar order to Speer, the latter's reply would have been, 'My Führer, two hundred metres!' She said she made the remark in the presence of Hitler, who roared with laughter. Similarly, Speer's biographer, Joachim Fest, observed that it was the architect, not Hitler, who inflated the size of some important buildings, at times provoking the Führer to poke fun at him. 'What a nice little victory gate,' he said of Speer's rendering of the gigantic Arch of Triumph. And when Speer insisted that the height of the Great Hall could not be less than 300 meters, Hitler responded, 'The same then as the altitude of the Obersalzberg over Berchtesgaden.' Only after Speer showed him a sketch of the Great Hall, on which he had drawn a few people in correct proportion, did Hitler really grasp the size of the structure, when he reacted at first with horror, fearing it was bound to collapse.

In interviews and private correspondence after his release from prison, Speer went to great lengths to argue that his style of spectacle and architecture was innocent of any ideological intent. He claimed he had not tried to create a Nazi style but to give an old style contemporary meaning. If Hitler used his buildings to glorify the state and party, and if party propagandists interpreted his works as nationalistic, that was not his fault; he was merely seeking to apply neoclassicism to a new era. Yet in his Spandau diaries he admitted, '. . . I cannot say he [Hitler] led me away from myself; on the contrary, through him I first found a heightened identity.' More damning still, he avowed in his memoirs that he wanted his work to 'spell out in architecture the political, military, and economic power of Germany'. As he said to Gitta Sereny: 'Of course I was perfectly aware that he sought world domination. . . . That was the whole point of my buildings. They would have looked grotesque if Hitler had sat still in Germany. All I *wanted* was for this great man to dominate the globe.'

Speer also tried to have it both ways about his professional role. He insisted on the one hand that Hitler was responsible for the 'baroque effects' and further extravagances of his buildings but on the other that Hitler had never interfered in his work. In fact, how independent was Speer in carrying out his projects? Repeatedly he maintained that he worked out his ideas on his own and presented them to Hitler who studied and accepted or altered them without discussion. According to other testimony, such as that of Hitler's adjutant Fritz Wiedemann and the ever-watchful Heinz Linge, Hitler played an active role in every aspect of a building's genesis and construction. Speer was undoubtedly far more than the mere executor of Hitler's architectural programmes, but there can be no doubt that all the important decisions were made by the Führer. Speer's talent lay in understanding

Early in 1934 Hitler charged Speer with the construction of viewer stands for the Zeppelin Field at Nuremberg. The stone structure, 1300 feet long and 80 feet high, was one of the most emblematic of Third Reich buildings.

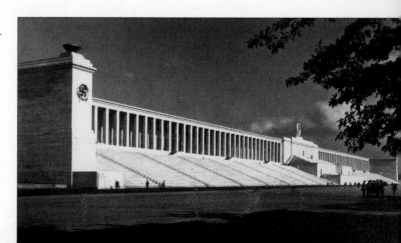

Hitler's ideas, embellishing them magnificently and driving his projects to successful completion. His first assignment was the Nuremberg rally site which he took over from Troost who had been working on it with Hitler even before 1933. It was because he carried this out with such flair and competence that Hitler eventually gave him the greatest architectural prize of all, the remodelling of Berlin.

Another of Hitler's architects was Wilhelm Kreis. Known before 1914 for his monuments and memorials – especially the 500 or so dedicated to Bismarck – he gained note in the 1920s for his 'Germanization of the skyscraper', which was to be the German answer to what was seen as mismanaged urban development in America. He also designed a great variety of other structures, employing at times Modernist ideas without abandoning traditional forms. Although he lost several institutional positions after Hitler came to power, he joined the Nazi party in early 1933 and thanks to Gerdy Troost entered and won a competition for an air force headquarters in Dresden. This initiated his rise to the top of his profession in the Third Reich. In 1938 Hitler put him in charge of designing a party forum in Dresden while at the same time Speer, who badly needed someone of proven competence, took him on for certain Berlin projects. Hitler also gave Kreis responsibility for the construction of war memorials, military cemeteries, *Totenburgen*, a memorial to Reinhard Heydrich as well as the gallery for arms and armour in Linz. Kreis was in effect the architect of death.

During the Third Reich, Kreis called himself 'Germany's architect', meaning that he felt several cuts above his colleagues. He was no different from the others, however, in providing his Führer not only with the sort of buildings that he wanted but also with professional cover for his architectural views. In articles and speeches he condemned 'anti-German and Jewish elements' in his field, praised 'the German style' and contrasted 'the austere beauty of Germanic-Nordic art' to the 'formless nihilism' of architectural Modernism and 'internationalism'. In return he received commissions, awards and prizes along with financial and other perquisites.

20 REMODELLING GERMANY

RETURNING FROM PARIS TO THE FARMHOUSE that was his field headquarters in June 1940, a euphoric Hitler sat down at a wooden table in the kitchen and dictated a memorandum to his architects:

> In consonance with our stupendous victory, Berlin must as soon as possible receive its new architectural form as capital of a strong new Reich.
>
> This is the most important construction project of the Reich, and I regard its implementation as the most important contribution to the final securing of our victory.
>
> I expect it to be completed by the year 1950.
>
> The same is true for the reconstruction of the cities of Munich, Linz, Hamburg and the party rally structures in Nuremberg.
>
> Every office of the Reich, the länder and cities as well as of the party are to offer the General Building Inspector for the capital of the Reich [Speer] any assistance that he asks for in carrying out his responsibilities.

As he later commented to Field Marshal von Kluge, 'At present Berlin is miserable, but one day it will be more beautiful than Paris.'

Hitler claimed that the original inspiration for his Berlin projects went back to his years in Vienna. So wretched had his life been, he said, that he compensated for it by dreaming about living in a palace and thinking of how to redevelop Berlin. Although he may well have fantasized about living in a palace, it is implausible that he gave thought to a city unknown to him at the time. While in Landsberg prison, however, he did begin thinking about its architectural redevelopment and followed discussions in the press about dealing with the central issue, the outmoded rail network in the centre which cut the city in two. A competition among urban planners prompted him to get hold of a map and draw a sketch of how he would replace the two large stations with a single one, opening up a large space for development. 'Thus my ideas for a reorganization of Berlin developed as early as that,' he told Giesler.

Berlin was not a city he genuinely liked. It was Prussian, Protestant and Social Democratic. It was experimental theatre and opera, cabarets and jazz, Jewish press and Jewish department stores. Architecturally as well it had little to commend it. During the war he even said it would be 'no loss' were it destroyed by British bombers. Naturally enough, he blamed the city's failings ultimately on race. The area had been settled by Saxons and Frisians, who lacked the south German Catholic's natural feeling for art. The last cultured Prussian monarch was Frederick William IV, who had reigned in the middle of the nineteenth century. His royal and political successors were hopeless. Similarly, the last great architects were Friedrich Gilly and Karl Friedrich Schinkel, and they had worked more than a century earlier.

Oddly, Speer made a point of denying that Hitler had admired the Prussian architects. Many times, he claimed in his memoirs, he and the Führer had driven past Schinkel's great works without Hitler's even seeming to notice them. He also said that during the war he presented Hitler with a book on Gilly – probably one just published by Alfred Rietdorf – and asserted that Hitler never mentioned having so much as looked at it. Whether or not he ignored Speer's gift, Hitler was familiar with the architect's work. In fact, his great Berlin Arch of Triumph took its inspiration from a monumental arched gate drawn by Gilly in 1794. And Schinkel he considered Troost's only great predecessor; after him there had been no one. For the great monument of the Bismarck era, Paul Wallot's Reichstag building, he had only disdain – Speer's assertion to the contrary notwithstanding. Julius Raschdorff's turn-of-the-century Berlin cathedral he openly derided. Otherwise the city's notable buildings were contemptible Jewish department stores and hotels for rich businessmen.

Berlin therefore needed what he labelled a massive 'facelift'. This was hardly a novel idea. With the unification of the country in 1871, the city had expanded too rapidly for much thought to have been given to urban order or beauty. After the turn of the century a number of leading architects had outlined projects to redevelop the metropolis – notably, Martin Mächler in 1917–19 and Hugo Häring in 1927. Key elements of their proposals included a north-south axis and a consolidation of railway stations to permit the redevelopment of the city centre. Hitler was clearly familiar with these proposals and his own ideas, which he had worked out in the course of the 1920s – his sketchbook included at least one element of them – followed similar lines. During the critical years before reaching political power, he found time to refine his concepts and the summer after becoming chancellor, he was bursting with enthusiasm about his projects. 'They will be grandiose,' Goebbels commented.

On returning to Berlin from vacation at the Berghof in September 1933 he was ready to move ahead. He realized he had to be cautious. He was new in office and the economy was still in deep depression. Construction programmes for prestige purposes could be revealed only little by little and had to commence with practical projects. His first step was to summon municipal and Reichsbahn officials to take up the unresolved problem of the rail network. In fact, he used the session less to settle the rail problem than to give city officials a hint of his broad schemes for Berlin and let them know that he, not they, would be in charge of carrying them out. A few months later he again met with city authorities and lifted the veil further. He said he wanted an entirely new stadium for the 1936 Olympics, a new Reich Bank building, two airports and two broad avenues that would intersect the city. Then, as before and in later years, he left no one in any doubt that he saw it as his personal mission to create a Berlin that would be the architectural and cultural equal of such cities as London, Paris and Vienna.

The next big meeting occurred in March 1934. Now his tone was different. No longer merely 'chancellor' but now 'Führer', his word was law. He informed city officials that he expected them to carry out four major projects. The first was to construct two axes of at least a hundred metres in width, one running east-west for fifty kilometres and the other extending north-south for thirty-eight kilometres. They were to intersect near the Brandenburg Gate in the heart of Berlin and terminate at a ring autobahn around the capital. Along the north-south axis he wanted a new railway station with a link to a new airport, new headquarters for the army, air force and navy and a gigantic Arch of Triumph. The second project foresaw a reorganization of the city's art collections and the construction of four new museums to house them. The main feature of the third was a new complex of university and research buildings. The final and the heart of it all was a gigantic meeting hall, intended for an audience of 250,000. Even in this rough and incomplete outline, Hitler's building programme vastly exceeded what had been carried out by Schinkel more than a century earlier and was matched only by the reconstruction projects of the 1990s.

Political and economic circumstances made it prudent to begin modestly, taking up schemes that had been planned before he came to office – the Reich Bank extension and the site for the Olympic games. Although Hitler initially had been opposed to the Olympics because they were open to Jews and blacks, once in sight of power at the end of 1932, he recognized their tremendous propaganda potential and informed the International Olympic Committee that he supported holding the games in Berlin. Some months later, now chancellor, he initiated the construction of a monumental sports complex to be adorned with Nazi imagery that he himself commissioned. He summarily increased the budget from the original 1.5 million marks to 28 million and was completely unfazed when construction costs eventually went three times over budget. Under Hitler's eagle eye, Werner March designed a highly impressive compound, comprising a stadium for 100,000 spectators, indoor and outdoor swimming pools, a large outdoor Greek theatre, facilities for various sports, a parade ground for 250,000 men and an Olympic village set in the Grunewald forest. Although the International Olympic Committee's guidelines provided for the contractor's complete independence, Hitler insisted on controlling the projects. Presented with a design for a stadium of steel, concrete and glass, he took such violent exception, according to Speer, that he threatened to cancel the games. Though this was doubtless a bluff, the Committee gave in. With his usual self-effacement, Speer claimed to have put matters right by ingeniously eliminating the glass and encasing the whole in stone. All in all the various structures were Functionalist and modern in design. They were embellished, however, with elements of blatant propaganda. The most provocative example was a monument to the volunteer army of 1914 which had fought on the Western front at Langemarck. 'The rhetoric of this ensemble, which lined up on one axis the bell tower inscribed with memorials to the dead, a trough of soil from the cemetery at Langemarck, Hitler's dais, the parade ground and the stadium,' it has been pointed out, 'made absolutely explicit the connection between sport and militarism.'

Linked in Hitler's mind to the Olympic games was another ostentatious project, the construction of an airport on the old jousting field of the Knights Templar not far from the centre of Berlin. Turning to Ernst Sagebiel, a factotum of the eminent Jewish architect Erich Mendelsohn, he directed him to construct 'the biggest and most beautiful civil airport in the entire world'. For its time, it probably was. Always intent on impressing arriving travellers, he was so determined to have it finished for the games that to finance it he even shifted funds earmarked for armaments. The structure, with its 2000 rooms, was built in eight months and opened in 1935. Although the architectural frame was criticized as being cold and monotonous, the hangars were admired as a model of modern technology. The more remote airport at Gatow was even more advanced.

★

Piece by piece, in meeting after meeting during those early years of the Third Reich, Hitler set his great projects in place. Nothing deterred him from indulging his obsession. At the end of March 1934, for example, embroiled though he was in disarmament negotiations with the British and the explosive crisis between the army and the Storm Troops that led three months later to the infamous Röhm purge, he held a long meeting with city and government officials and rendered a detailed critique of various plans, questioning this and approving that. A few days after the bloody purge he again took up these matters and gave them his full attention. By the end of the year construction was under way on the airports at Tempelhof and Gatow, the Olympic facilities and the Reich Bank as well as buildings for the Aviation Ministry, the so-called House of Pilots and exhibition halls at the Berlin radio tower.

In the summer of 1936, following his successful gamble in remilitarizing the Rhineland, Hitler was ready to move ahead with his larger programme. 'I tell you, Speer, these buildings are more important than anything else,' he said. City officials, now fully aware of the immensity of the projects and horrified by their cost, baulked at the prospect. As one of them said long after the war, 'I was appalled at the idea of rebuilding a whole metropolis; government and representational buildings, roads and even the railway system was one thing, but a whole city? It seemed mad to me.' For his part Hitler was so angered by what he considered parsimony and lack of imagination that he took his programmes out of the hands of city bureaucrats and turned them over to Speer. 'Berlin [authorities] are hopeless. From now on you make the plans,' he said. If officials still proved recalcitrant, he threatened to abandon Berlin and build a new capital to the north, in Mecklenburg. No doubt this was another of his bluffs, but it worked. Resistance collapsed and the city lost any role in deciding its future. It would pay, Hitler would design and Speer would build.

The models of his urban projects were revealing of Hitler's desire, typical of dictators, to reduce people and cities to playthings. Germany, if not the world, was to be his toy. In this model, an architectural assistant emplaces a military formation marching down the north-south axis.

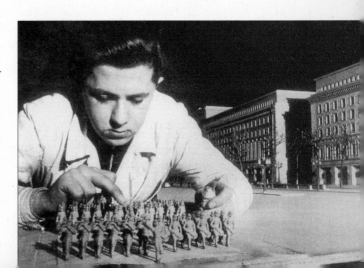

Whatever foreign policy and other issues were on his mind in the weeks and months that followed, Hitler never lacked time for his various building programmes. The extent of his interest can be judged from a few of the jottings that Goebbels, though himself entirely uninvolved, made in his diary in the early weeks of 1937:

5 January. The Führer discusses his construction plans with Speer . . . . The Führer explains to me his plans for the redevelopment of Berlin . . . . The projects are truly grandiose. They are of a scale that will last for the next 300 years. Berlin will be the world metropolis in terms of buildings as well.

9 January. Discuss with the Führer the reconstruction plans for Hamburg. Grandiose bridge construction and a huge skyscraper.

13 January. Führer agrees to new building for our ministry. . . . Speer has difficulties with [Prussian finance minister] Popitz. Führer intends to give him very broad authority.

25 January. The Führer once again outlines his construction plans. He wants to make Berlin the capital of Europe. Huge projects. With strong political connotations.

4 February. At lunch Hitler talks about his construction plans.

5 February. Construction plans. A new theatre for Zwickau.

8 February. At noon to the Führer. . . . He is occupied with construction plans for Berlin and Munich. . . . He is really deeply involved. An architectural idealist.

9 February. Reconstruction of Berlin discussed. An enormous number of problems arise that must be dealt with one by one.

16 February. With the Führer. . . . He talks about Munich and the new buildings.

22 February. Führer is at work on the restoration of the Reichstag building. It might be feasible. . . . He intends to disclose his intentions with regard to the [reconstruction of the] Schiller Theatre.

23 February. Restoration of the Reichstag. He was there and now has little hope for it. A huge pile of kitsch.

And so on it went.

Answerable only to Hitler and enjoying unrivalled authority and a staff of 1000 to help him carry out his Berlin projects, Speer moved ahead with typical efficiency. Despite a sense of omnicompetence, he was well aware, though, that he had neither the ability nor the time to do it all. He limited himself to designing a few key buildings and co-ordinating the overall programme. The other projects he delegated to architects who were senior in age and experience – Bonatz, Kreis, Behrens, German Bestelmeyer and even several of Gropius's Bauhaus associates such as Hanns Dustmann, Ernst Neufert and Herbert Rimpl. But you would know little or nothing about them from Speer, who wrote his memoirs in a way that kept the spotlight exclusively on himself.

Speer knew exactly how to play up to Hitler. By driving himself and his staff ruthlessly, in less than six months he developed a detailed plan. He then had cabinetmakers create a gigantic model showing the tiniest details and painted to simulate the actual materials to be used. Hitler was enchanted with his toy and often paid excited visits to Speer's studio, which he had installed in a building adjacent to the chancellery. Bending low over the model, he would envisage how the structures would look at ground level when completed in 1950. He loved to show it off to dinner guests. As Speer related, 'We would set out armed with flashlights and keys. In the empty halls spotlights illuminated the miniature replicas. There was no need for me to do the talking, for Hitler, with flashing eyes, explained every single detail to his companions.' So obsessed was Hitler with these projects that he made Göring swear that, in the event of his death, Speer would be retained and given whatever support was necessary for their completion.

Finally the day to start actual work arrived. 'Berlin's new construction programme will begin on 14 June [1938] at sixteen sites,' Goebbels noted in his diary. 'The most magnificent construction programme of all time,' he added. 'The Führer overcame all opposition. He is a genius.' The point of it

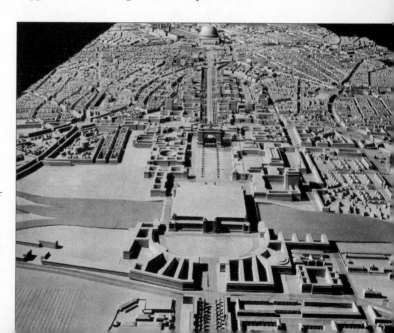

Highlights of this 1940 model of the north-south axis are the South Railway Station (foreground), *the Arch of Triumph* (centre) *and the Great Hall* (top).

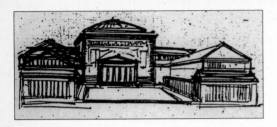

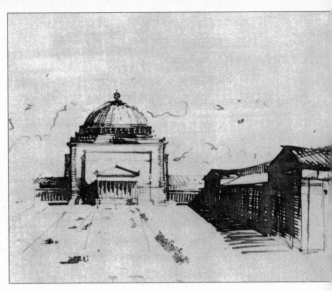

*Hitler's sketches of what became the Great
Hall (left, early 1920s, right 1925)
make clear that from the earliest stages
his model was the Pantheon. The later
models of the interior and exterior make the
similarity even more stark.*

all, as Speer summed it up, was to leave everyone 'overwhelmed or, rather, stunned' at the power and majesty of the Reich. The core was the north-south axis, the key features of which Hitler and Speer worked out together. The six-mile-long central section was to be, in the manner of the *sacra via* of the Roman Forum, a *via triumphalis*. It would begin at the world's largest railway station – adjacent to the world's largest airport – and lead immediately to an enormous plaza, 2300 feet long and 900 feet wide, lined with captured enemy ordnance. This would open to a great arch of triumph, the monument sketched by Hitler in the 1920s. It would easily eclipse, at 386 feet high, its Parisian counterpart, a mere 164-foot equivalent. In keeping with Hitler's view that the German army had been defeated not on the battlefield in 1918 but by a 'stab in the back' by the politicians, this monument was to honour the 'undefeated army of the World War'. On to the granite was to be inscribed the name of each of the 1.8 million Germans who fell in that war.

Then came the grandest stretch of the avenue, lined with uniformly designed structures housing party offices, ministries, the headquarters of industrial concerns as well as cinemas, theatres, hotels, restaurants, a Reich opera house, a philharmonic hall, a wine house, a beer house, a convention hall, a Roman bath modelled on the stupendous Baths of Caracalla and a cinema to seat 6000. This led to the Round Plaza, north of which lay the Soldiers' Hall, a huge hall of fame for future war victims, and finally, the jewel of it all, a gigantic domed meeting hall large enough to accommodate as many as 180,000 people standing. This behemoth, which also went back

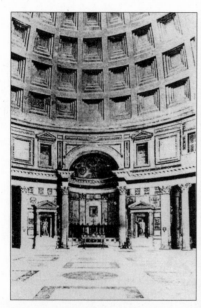
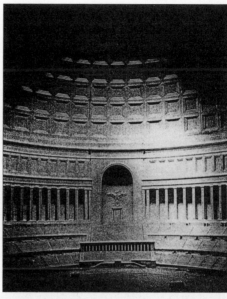
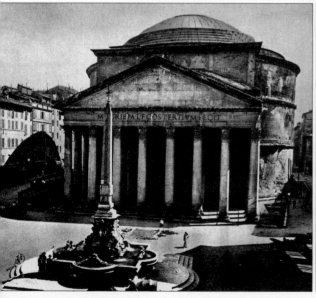
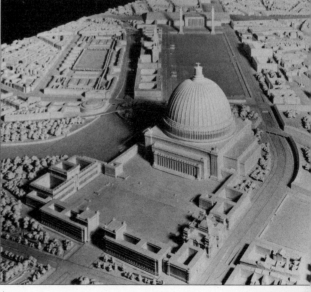

to one of the drawings in Hitler's old sketchbook, was to be the world's largest structure. It would be surrounded on three sides by water – a newly created lake formed by the Spree river – and face a granite-paved space large enough to hold a million people. The entrance of the Great Hall would be flanked by two 45-foot-high sculptures which Hitler commissioned from Arno Breker. On the left was to stand *Atlas*, holding the heavens, and on the right *Tellus*, holding the earth.

Rome figured in the structure both as an architectural model and as a historic challenge. Only with the construction of this building, Hitler once said, 'will we be in the position to put Rome, our only competitor, in the shade. The Great Hall will be such that St Peter's and the square in front will disappear inside it.' This was no exaggeration; the Roman basilica, as Speer commented, could have fitted inside several times over, as could the capitol building in Washington. If its size defied imagination, its purpose was scarcely less fantastic – to provide, according to its architect, a place to worship the Führer. A great bronze eagle with a swastika in its claws was to adorn the very top. But just before launching his war in 1939 Hitler said to Speer, 'That has to be changed. Instead of the swastika, the eagle must be perched above the globe.' This was to symbolize Hitler's status not as mere leader of National Socialism and Germany but as Lord of the World.

In addition to Speer's buildings on the north-south axis, there were two other projects of exceptional importance to Hitler and both were assigned to Wilhelm Kreis. One of these was appropriate to the architect's past. This was the design of a complex of buildings to include a headquarters of the army high command – to conduct wars – and the Soldiers' Hall – to honour those who would in the future be killed, an earthly Valhalla. A little further away he was to design a Weapons and Armour Museum – to display the means of death – and at a still further distance a 'cemetery of honour' – to inter the victims. For Hitler the centrepiece was the gigantic Soldiers' Hall. As early as October 1936 he had done a sketch of the front façade which was the model for Kreis's final design. The hall was a monster in every way. Physically huge – 750 feet long and 240 feet high – it was not only to be a resting place for military heroes, possibly including Frederick the Great, but also a museum of military booty, such as the railway car in which the 1918 and 1940 armistices with France had been signed. Adjacent to it was to be the army high command, a series of buildings at the centre of which stood a seventeen-floor structure topped by a gigantic statue of a warrior. Facing and balancing this was a tall obelisk mounted by a huge eagle.

It is revealing that from the beginning Hitler wanted to link the Soldiers' Hall with the army headquarters in a single complex – thus demonstrating that he was already planning a war that would produce dead heroes. The architectural and political were linked in another way. Physically at the heart of the new Berlin were to be structures dedicated to death – the Arch of Triumph, military headquarters, Soldiers' Hall, a weapons museum and a mausoleum. Moreover, as in Munich where the Temples of Honour were adjacent to the Führer Building, in Berlin these buildings were to be adjacent to the chancellery and a fabulous new residence for Hitler himself.

Kreis's other Berlin project was to design four museum buildings. Hitler's interest in the city's art galleries went back as far as 1917 when he had visited them during a brief leave from the front. Their architecture seems to have interested him at least as much as their contents, and the one that gained his particular attention was the Kaiser Friedrich Museum, situated on the tip of Museumsinsel, the small island in central Berlin which was the location of the city's principal galleries. On the back side of a picture postcard of the museum, which he sent to an army companion at the front, he wrote that he had 'studied' the structure. It is this building that he may have had in mind in designing the 'German Museum' that he envisaged in his 1925 sketchbook. In subsequent years he gained greater familiarity with the city's principal collections, then housed in four museums – the Old Museum-Pergamon Museum, the New Museum, the Kaiser Friedrich Museum and the National Gallery. These collections were now to be reorganized and four new buildings were to be constructed – a museum for Nineteenth-Century Art, a Germanic museum and a museum for Egyptian and Middle Eastern Art. A fourth structure was to be the new Weapons and Armour museum. A fifth building, to be designed by Hanns Dustmann, was to accommodate an expanded ethnology collection, which Speer proposed to turn into 'a type of race museum in keeping with the new ideological principles'. Hitler's aim was to heighten Berlin's reputation as a centre of the visual arts and ensure that its museums were collectively on a level with the greatest in the world. The fortress-like appearance of these structures and their domineering towers – in a style suggestive of such Babylonian architecture as the Gate of Ishtar – would have left no one in doubt that the Third Reich was an aggressive cultural power.

For years Hitler forbade any mention of these plans to the public and disclosed them only to the narrowest circle of officials. Not until 1939 was the overall scheme released to the press and even then only in generalities.

Still wary of public opinion, he was apprehensive of the reaction not only to the enormous funds being lavished on his showy projects at a time when consumer goods were becoming scarce but also to the extent of the destruction of what were in some cases much admired buildings and urban areas. So touchy was he that a noted cabaret artist who made fun of the projects was dispatched to a concentration camp. Speer himself admitted floating as a trial balloon a proposal to demolish the tower of Berlin's famous city hall. 'When angry protests from the populace poured in, I postponed the matter,' he wrote in his memoirs. But that was nothing compared with the extent of the demolition about to befall the city centre. Countless office buildings, shops, industrial concerns, embassies, even churches were to be razed. No fewer than 54,000 dwellings were to be sacrificed, 25,000 on the north-south axis alone. This gave rise to a joke that Hitler himself liked to tell about a Russian aircraft sent by Stalin to bomb Berlin. On his return the pilot reported that a raid was unnecessary since the city already lay in ruins. The first buildings to go were those belonging to Jews and Speer set up a special bureau for this purpose. 'How is the clearing of the 1000 Jewish residences coming along?' he asked in a 1940 memo. According to Speer's assistant Rudolf Wolters, 23,765 Jewish residences were eventually confiscated and their 75,000 occupants sent to concentration camps. Later, air raids destroyed the greater part of the area. 'For our new construction project 80,000 houses in Berlin alone would have had to be torn down,' Hitler commented nonchalantly to his architect in 1944. 'Unfortunately the British did not quite do the job according to your plans. Still, a beginning has been made.'

Strange to say, only one major building in Hitler's Berlin scheme was ever constructed. This was his pride and joy, the new Reich chancellery. Its purpose was political. At the turn of the year 1937–8 he had decided to 'solve the Austrian question' and would, as head of the new Greater German Reich, require more impressive offices. The story goes that he summoned Speer in January 1938 and complained that the existing chancellery was only 'fit for a soap company'. The charge was not unjust; the building was nothing more than a small, Functionalist structure erected a decade earlier as an annexe to the eighteenth-century Palais Radziwill, which had become the chancellor's residence in 1875. As Hitler explained, foreign policy considerations required a much grander building, 'one that would make an impression on people, especially the smaller dignitaries'. The work must infallibly be completed within one year. '. . . If it is possible to annex a country to the Reich in three or four days,' he commented with the impending seizure of Austria in mind, 'it must be possible to erect a building in one or two years.' This structure was to be ready for his annual diplomatic reception in January when he could vaunt his embellished status.

When the new chancellery was completed with forty-eight hours to spare, it was proclaimed a sensational triumph for the architect and the spirit of the new Reich. However, both Hitler and Speer deliberately distorted the facts. Discussions about the new building went back as far as March 1934 and preparatory work had begun as early as 1935. Speer had worked out costings by March 1936 and plans themselves were finished by mid-1937. Speer's insistence that Hitler allowed him to carry out his remit independently is also misleading. The dictator himself had in 1935 sketched out a rough ground plan of the structure, which set down basic features. To be sure, the final designs were Speer's and the construction in a twelve-month of such a substantial building with sumptuous interiors was an amazing accomplishment. With his tremendous organizational capacity, Speer was no doubt the only architect who could have achieved it. But it was done at a terrible cost. He drove himself and his workers mercilessly, keeping construction going in two shifts, twenty-four hours a day, seven days a week. The number of serious injuries resulting from the stress and the long hours was so great that a special clinic was set up to treat workers and get them back on the job as fast as possible. Morally far worse was the use of forced labour. Flossenbürg, Mauthausen and Sachsenhausen were some of the concentration camps where 'enemies of the Nazi state' were punished by having to quarry stone, make bricks and finish stone for these projects.

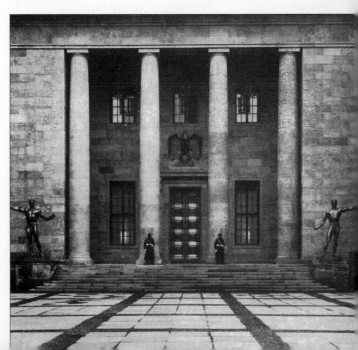

The grand entrance to the new chancellery opened into a court of honour of stark grey marble. On either side of the great bronze doors stood Breker's twin bronze sculptures, The Party (left) *and* The Military, *symbolizing the twin bases of Hitler's institutional power.*

What Hitler wanted and Speer gave him was 'an architectural stage set of imperial majesty', in the architect's phrase. If the cold exterior was intended to intimidate, the opulence of the interior was meant to bedazzle. Here the dictator, contrary to the abstemiousness of his personal life, indulged himself with Byzantine abandon in an attempt to outdo the later Roman emperors and overwhelm his guests. The building was designed so that visitors would enter through great bronze doors and find themselves in a long open courtyard,

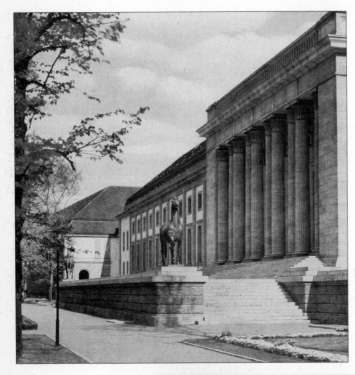

The garden façade of the new chancellery was less cold and intimidating than the rest of the structure. The gigantic bronze horses were sculpted by Thorak.

The interiors of Hitler's buildings were as much stage settings as their exteriors, as is evident in the mosaic hall in the new chancellery. This is the room — skylight shattered, walls stripped bare and floor covered with rubble — that appears in most post-war photos of the wrecked hulk of the building.

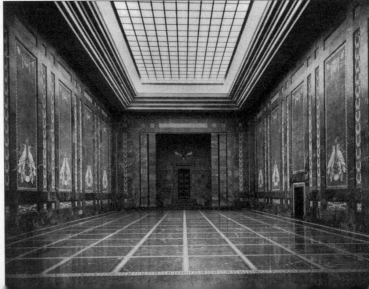

the court of honour, decorated solely with Breker's twin statues. They would proceed through a reception room, past double doors seventeen feet high and enter the mosaic hall, a windowless room with a glass roof and covered with red and brown mosaic panels that Breker described as 'permeated with the fire of political power'. From here they would traverse a round room with a domed glass ceiling and enter the great marble gallery, twice as long as the gallery of mirrors at Versailles. The decoration was done in a rich

The office, if not throne room, of the Lord of the World. Hitler's study sent differing signals to a visitor. The furniture group said, 'Please be my guest.' The writing table with its three panels – Gorgon, whose glance turns the beholder to stone; Mars, god of war with his sword and Minerva, goddess of war – said, 'I will destroy you, if I please.' The cartouche over the door – portraying a knight, with Hitler's face, being pursued by Death and the Devil – symbolizes fearlessness.

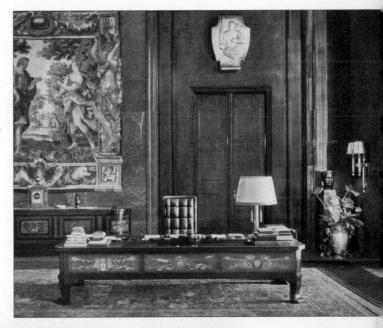

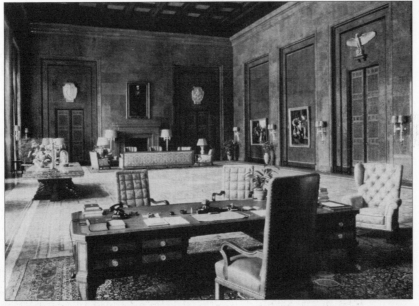

variety of colour combinations and materials – carpets, paintings, tapestries, mosaics, various kinds of marble, wooden panelling, gilt sconces and the like. At the far end was the formal reception hall. 'On the long walk from the entrance to the reception hall, they'll get a taste of the power and grandeur of the German Reich,' Speer quotes a delighted Hitler as saying on first seeing the finished space. When Speer said he was loath to carpet the slick marble floors, the Führer responded, 'That's exactly right; diplomats should have practice in moving on a slippery surface.'

It was his office that exhibited most clearly the way Hitler used interior design to demonstrate his political purposes. Here symbolism reached its zenith. On either side of the entrance were tapestries illustrating a triumphant Alexander the Great, conqueror of the world. Over the great doors was emplaced a cartouche with his initials. Similar in style to those of Napoleon and Albrecht Dürer, an architectural historian noted, the intent was 'to establish a clear link to the desired image of Hitler as both statesman and artist'. The room itself, ninety feet long and more than half as wide, was lined in dark-red Limbach marble and covered by a reddish-brown carpet decorated with a swastika design. The furnishings were to demonstrate not only Hitler's status as head of state and party and as commander-in-chief but also his position in German history. Portraits of Frederick the Great and Bismarck and a bust of Hindenburg implied not only his political legitimacy but also, in the case of the king and Iron Chancellor, his claim to have completed the work begun by those predecessors. Since few individuals were ever destined to observe all this at first hand, it fell to the press and illustrated journals to make the points to the public.

There were three focal points. At one end, ranged before a large mantel, also of Limbach marble, were six large chairs and a thirteen-foot-wide sofa. This was meant to suggest Hitler as the *bourgeois gentilhomme*, the friendly man of the people. To symbolize Hitler the military commander, a huge map table, made of a single piece of marble, stood at the midpoint of the room before a tall window. At the other end was Hitler's writing table, signifying his position as head of state. Here the message was one of threat and intimidation. Affixed to the front of this desk were three panels of marquetry inlay. One of these depicted a partly unsheathed sword. 'Good, good!' Hitler said of this. 'When the diplomats, who are sitting in front of me at this table, see that, they will learn what fear is.' The writing table and its accoutrements were all for show – the table, at fifteen feet, was pointlessly large, the telephone and table lamp were beyond reach and there was nothing on the table related to work. In truth, as his personal adjutant noted, Hitler never worked at a desk.

'The time of ambassadors is over; the century of the architect has begun,' commented a French architect who inspected the building shortly before the official opening. For Hitler architecture and diplomacy were mutually reinforcing. 'As Reich chancellor and Führer of the German nation, I want Germany to be able to present an image like any other state, indeed, better than others,' he said, in an effort to explain away his wanton extravagance. 'If others live in the Kremlin, in the Hradschin or in a castle, we want the representative of the Reich to be in a building of our own time. The moment someone is called upon to represent Germany, he is to be the equal of any king or emperor.' Speer's biographer, Joachim Fest, argued that the new chancellery was 'largely free of traces of megolomania' and certainly not on the same scale as Versailles or the palaces of Peter the Great. This misses the point, however, that it was not simply grandeur that Hitler demanded – for that he could simply have moved down the street to Schlüter's great Berlin Schloß – but a structure expressing his taste and ideology.

The new Reich chancellery was badly damaged by air raids in February 1945, following which Hitler moved into its subterranean bunker. After being further battered during the last days of the war, the building was largely intact but a burned-out hulk, a symbol of the denouement of the Third Reich itself. Just before the Potsdam Conference convened in July 1945, Churchill visited the site. He was met by a considerable crowd. In his war memoirs he recalled:

> When I got out of the car and walked among them, except for one old man who shook his head disapprovingly, they all began to cheer. My hate had died with their surrender, and I was much moved by their demonstrations, and also by their haggard looks and threadbare clothes. Then we entered the Chancellery, and for quite a long time walked through its shattered galleries and halls.

Four years later the building was demolished, and some of its marble used in the construction of the Karl-Marx-Platz underground station and a Russian war memorial.

Even before Speer had finished the new chancellery Hitler had begun quietly planning an even more fabulous office-residence, to be known as the Führer-Palais. No doubt his string of diplomatic successes, culminating in the crushing of Czechoslovakia, went to his head. After only a year in the new Reich chancellery, he complained about his cramped living accommodations. With his usual dog-like devotion, Goebbels commiserated: 'He lives like an impoverished backwoods nobleman. Yet he rules Europe and will make Berlin the centre of this part of the world.' Inspired by fortress-like Florentine palazzi, Speer designed a structure that was no longer a residence but a fortified palace. In splendour and size – the new 'diplomatic walk' would have extended for nearly half a mile – it would have exceeded even the notorious Golden House of Nero to which it has been compared. It was appropriate that the two egomaniacs should join hands across the ages. The Roman emperor also persecuted minorities, rebuilt his capital, murdered at will, was a great admirer of Greek culture, had ambitions to be a great artist and eventually came to be hated by his people. 'What an artist the world loses in me!' were supposed to have been his last words.

In Hitler's Germania the world would have seen an urban sight not witnessed since the height of imperial Rome – at every turn vast plazas, gigantic state buildings, great thoroughfares, columns, towers, statues, reliefs, arches, baths, theatres, forums, temples, memorials, bridges, palaces, museums, stadiums, tombs, fountains, galleries, obelisks. And all of it was to speak for its creator and memorialize him for 1000 years. In the end, despite the years of drafting plans and building models, little actual construction work on the grand projects ever got under way in the months between the defeat of France and the invasion of the Soviet Union. A part of the north-south axis – the Charlottenburger Chaussee – was widened and the foundation of the Great Hall was laid. But all that survived the war were a number of street lamps and a chair that Speer designed for the new Reich chancellery in a style that might be labelled Nazi Chippendale. Hitler had wanted architectural ruins and got urban rubble.

Hitler's ideas for Munich went back to the early 1920s and were initially inspired more by politics than by aesthetics. As he wrote in *Mein Kampf*, 'The geopolitical significance of one central focal point for a movement cannot be overestimated. Only the existence of such a place, exerting the magic spell of a Mecca or a Rome, can in the long run give a movement a force based on inner unity and a summit representing this unity.' Logically enough his Mecca-Rome was Munich, the birthplace of the National Socialist movement and its ideological centre. He made it the site not only of the party's administrative headquarters but also of its most sacred relics and the scene of the annual ritual honouring its 'martyrs'. It was also to be the centre of German culture or, in the words of a decree of May 1938, 'Capital of the Movement and Capital of German Art'.

During his time in Landsberg, while mulling over ideas about Berlin, Hitler was also thinking about the redevelopment of Munich and by 1927 had worked out a number of vague ideas. One of these envisaged a star-shaped plaza, with a great monument in the centre and broad avenues radiating from it – the Place de l'Étoile in Paris may have been an inspiration. Another addressed the problem, then in public discussion, of how to preserve the medieval character of inner cities in the face of rapid motorization. His own proposal foresaw a new railway station away from the city centre and an underground rail system. Already then, he told Giesler, he anticipated the time when Austria would be annexed to Germany and there would be a great increase in rail transport through Munich. Here, again, was visible the connection between his political and his architectural aspirations.

The beginnings were relatively modest – the Brown House, the Führer Building, the party's administrative headquarters, the Temples of Honour and the House of German Art. These were Hitler's first architectural ventures and he was exuberant as he watched them taking shape. 'Beautiful Königsplatz can no longer be recognized,' Goebbels commented with

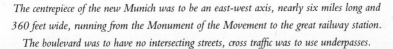

The centrepiece of the new Munich was to be an east-west axis, nearly six miles long and 360 feet wide, running from the Monument of the Movement to the great railway station. The boulevard was to have no intersecting streets, cross traffic was to use underpasses.

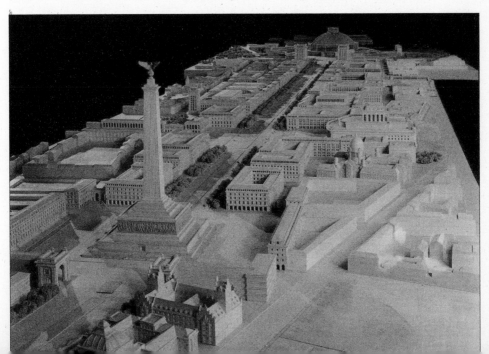

unintended irony. 'We are deeply moved by the monumentality of this site. Here the Führer has written his will in stone.' Going on to the skeletal party buildings, he noted, 'We climb around from the basement to the top . . . . The Führer is proud and happy.' Two months later, in November 1935, Hitler returned to Munich and again immediately headed for the Königsplatz. 'Absolutely unique. The very picture of the ancient world. . . . Monumental works of our creating. The Führer is absolutely delighted. . . . Whatever has to do with building leaves him content.'

Planning the city's broader redevelopment had begun soon after Troost's death in early 1934. Hitler admired Munich's basic design as it had evolved under Ludwig I in the early nineteenth century. But there were problems and these were to be corrected by laying out a grand east-west axis, similar to that in Berlin. At one end, as in Berlin, he wanted a gigantic railway station to be crowned with the world's biggest dome. The plans foresaw a structure occupying six times the space of St Peter's basilica *and* Bernini's square in front of it. The station was remarkable in another way. Not only did Hitler permit the structure to be designed by Paul Bonatz, a Modernist of Functionalist stamp, but he also agreed that the building should be constructed in Modernist steel and glass. In fact, he was downright thrilled by the prospect, declaring that the proposed building would be 'a monument to the technology of our century'.

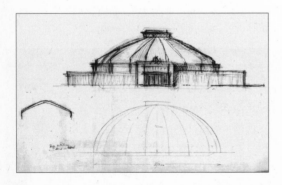

The initial design of a new central railway station for Munich was done by Bonatz and went through countless subsequent alterations by Hitler and Giesler. This sketch shows Hitler's changes.

At the other end of the axis was to stand a 700-foot column dedicated to the party. Hitler designed – and repeatedly redesigned – every detail of it. On top was to be an eagle with a 100-foot wingspan; the friezes at the base were to portray scenes of the party's early struggles. Needless to say, this 'Monument of the Movement' dwarfed the twin towers of Munich's most noted landmark, the Frauenkirche, which rose a mere 320 feet. It was his favourite monument, and a photograph caught him gazing at a model of it in deep satisfaction. Along

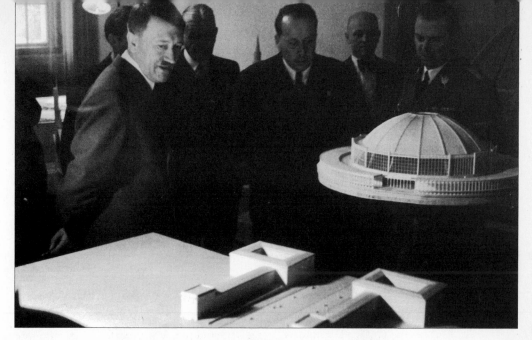

'The new central railway station will be a monument to the technology of our century,' Hitler declared. He envisaged it as a pendant to the party monument at the other end of the east-west axis.

the broad avenue between the station and the column were to be new theatres for opera and operetta, an opera hotel and an opera café, a huge Roman-style bath, a large cinema, a high-rise hotel and a corresponding structure for the party's publishing house. The culmination would be a Great Hall of the Party, which was to be connected by a bridge to Hitler's mausoleum, itself modelled on the Pantheon. The basic design of most of these structures Hitler himself drew – the mausoleum and the opera house as far back as 1937.

A critical element in the entire scheme was a fundamental reorganization of inner-city traffic. His solution was complex and costly, and posed great difficulties for his architects and engineers. No sooner had they been solved – it was now 1942 – than he introduced a new set of problems by conceiving the idea of a broad gauge railway line. This required widening the diameter of the dome of the station from 280 to 350 metres. Bonatz, who had at first been excited by the challenge of designing a gigantic dome but soon saw it as foolish, considered the notion of an even larger one as utterly mad. So, after producing a basic design, he resigned and took a post in Ankara. 'If I had one single reason for going abroad,' he wrote in his autobiography, 'it was to flee from this insanity.'

As always, Hitler guided every step in the development of these projects. Anyone who had the temerity to demur was sacked. As in the case of Berlin, he eventually became so dissatisfied with the attitude of local officials that by the end of 1938 he had placed the entire programme in the hands of Giesler, presumably

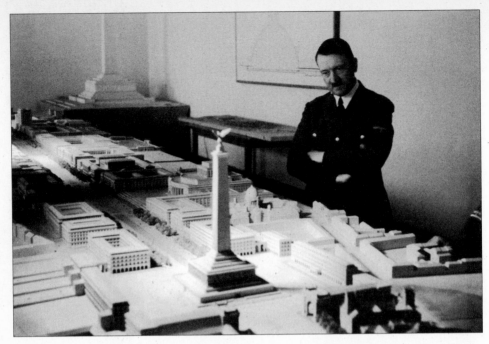

Probably no single monument meant so much to Hitler as the Monument of the Movement, a towering column dedicated to the National Socialist party and decorated with reliefs telling its history. Inspired by Trajan's column, he produced one detailed drawing after another, altering its proportions until it seemed right.

Hitler repeatedly altered the design and size of his Munich opera house. By mid-1940 he had what he wanted and intended it as a model for other opera theatres. Here Hitler discusses the final touch, the addition of a machine house, with Hermann Giesler.

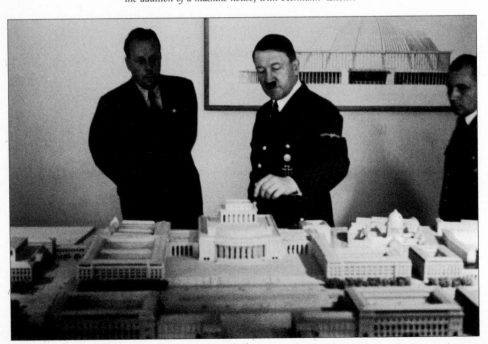

in recognition of the architect's demonstrated competence and servility. In his memoirs Giesler described the long and detailed conversations the two held as the projects evolved. Although the technical and engineering problems were vast, Giesler considered his main obstacle to be Speer. When Speer learned that the new Munich railway station was to be larger than his in Berlin and that its dome would exceed the size of the one he planned for his Great Hall in Berlin, he tried to bully his rival into scaling it down. He failed but in the end gained the upper hand. As the war dragged on Speer, now Armaments Minister, succeeded in strangling Giesler's projects by denying him necessary construction materials.

With its internationalist, north German, Protestant and cosmopolitan atmosphere, Hamburg was not a city that Hitler could ever have warmed to. But he recognized that it was Germany's principal gateway to overseas and as early as 1934 proposed several projects to impress arriving visitors – a tunnel under the Elbe and a suspension bridge over it. With the passage of time he wanted to build more ostentatious symbols of German power. These were to be the world's tallest building and the world's biggest bridge. Unlike most structures intended for other cities, they were to be Modernist in design and materials. 'There is something American about Hamburg,' Hitler once said in a remarkable statement to the Hamburg Senate, 'and it would be utterly wrong to construct buildings in, say, the manner of the Brown House. Munich must remain unique, like the new Nuremberg. By the same token Hamburg must develop its own new style.'

The Elbe bridge was his main interest and with every visit he pressed city officials to produce a plan. The models they eventually presented in 1936 were not to his liking, however, and the following year he himself sketched the sort of structure he had in mind. His supreme desideratum was that it must exceed the size of the Golden Gate Bridge. Since soil conditions made this impossible in length, only through total surface could it be achieved. 'There can be no doubt,' Speer later said, 'that Hitler attached very great importance to this bridge, which for him was one of the most important structural documents that he hoped to build in his lifetime. It was to outdo America . . . as Hamburg itself was intended to surpass American standards.' Although soil tests were made and trial piers laid, the project never reached the construction phase. The skyscraper failed even to reach the final planning stage. Hitler disliked the design and, unlike Manhattan, Hamburg did not rest on rock and could not support the weight of the planned structure. Although Hamburg was not to undergo the substantial reconstruction of the other

Führer cities, additional projects included hundreds of canal bridges, a ring road, an autobahn tunnel, museums, an opera house and the usual north-south axis on which was to sit an assembly hall for 50,000, government buildings, a parade ground and so on.

On a visit to Linz in April 1943, Hitler returned to the opera house for the first time since his youth. He was accompanied by Speer who later recalled:

> With visible emotion he showed us the cheap seat in the top gallery from which he had first seen Lohengrin, Rienzi and the other operas, and then indicated by a slight gesture that he wanted to be alone. For some time he gazed dreamily into space, his eyes absent, his features slack . . . . It must have been five minutes before Hitler returned to reality.

Not just the opera house but everything about his home town touched Hitler's deepest feelings. In the years that followed the annexation of Austria his interest steadily waxed, until at the end it transcended even his affection for Munich. He developed his ideas and sketched one by one the structures he envisaged – a suspension bridge, party headquarters, hotel, city hall, Hall of the Community, theatre, opera house, command headquarters, stadium, art gallery, library, weapons museum, exhibition hall, concert hall and two towers. To these he added a planetarium, a technical university and an institute of metallurgy and, again, sketched their basic outline. There was also to be a new railway station with a stately entrance opening into a starkly modern station hall entirely of steel and glass. His personal library, later found at Alt Aussee, included sheaves of detailed architectural renderings of these plans as they evolved. At the core was the European Cultural Centre concentrated around a large piazza, dominated by the great art gallery. The

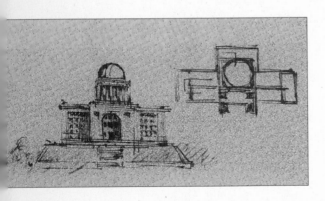

Despite a marked lack of interest in science, Hitler planned to establish technical universities in various areas of the Reich, even in Linz. He himself did a sketch of a planetarium and observatory.

library was to be across from it and on the eastern side was sited the opera house, flanked by an operetta house and a concert hall named after Bruckner. Inevitably there was an axis, in this case a broad avenue called In den Lauben, to extend from the Culture Centre to the new railway station. Completing the project, the Danube embankment was to be radically redeveloped. 'Everything was well thought through and everything had its rationale,' according to Giesler. 'Environment was taken into consideration, even how a building would look in the sunshine.'

From his remarks to Goebbels and others, it is apparent that Hitler had three objectives in mind. Linz was to replace Vienna as the cultural capital of Austria, it was to be one of the greatest arts centres in the world and it was to be the most imposing city on the Danube or, in his own words, 'a German Danubian city which vastly surpasses Budapest'. Linz was also to be a hub of trade and industry, with a steel plant, named the Hermann Göring Works,

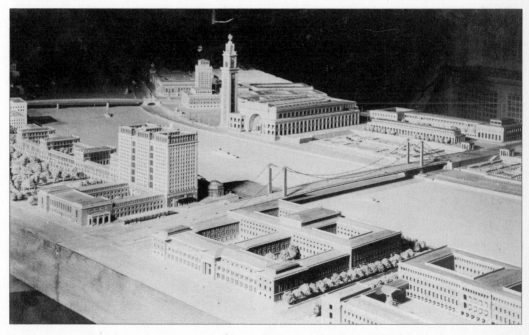

As Hitler's interest in Munich declined after 1940, his determination grew to make Linz a world arts centre and the most splendid city on the Danube. On the far side of the river in this model are visible the city hall, a tower with a carillon and a mausoleum for his parents, a communal hall and a park. On the opposite bank are situated the Strength through Joy Hotel, offices of the Hermann Göring Works and the Technical University.

which was eventually to be three times the size of the Krupp Works in the Ruhr. Hitler's architects, city officials and even the country's premier technical expert, Fritz Todt, strongly opposed the industrial development as aesthetically and ecologically incompatible with an arts centre. But Hitler had his reasons. As long as he was alive, he would give Linz whatever funds were necessary to operate its vast cultural infrastructure. But what of his successor? he would ask. The steel plant would provide the city with earnings and tax revenues. In this way he intended to put arrangements in place locking his successors into funding his great cultural institution. It is not surprising therefore that among his papers at Alt Aussee was a seventy-five-page bound volume, *The Future Economic Status of the City of Linz*.

Linz was to be Hitler's retirement home as well. There he wanted to spend his final years cultivating his garden – that is, tending his treasured museum collections. His residence, designed by Giesler, was to be situated on a hill overlooking the river and the new city centre. The city's dominant feature was to be a tower. Although a characteristic of every new city forum, this one would be unique. Inside its base was to be an octagonal groined vault which was to be a mausoleum for his parents. Speer's claim that Hitler once thought of the tower for his own final resting place was firmly denied by Giesler. The tower had to be shorter than the tower of the Ulm cathedral, at 172 metres the world's tallest Gothic spire. 'I do not want to hurt the feelings of the people of Ulm,' Hitler explained to Giesler, 'since they are rightly proud of the achievement of their forefathers.' Yet it had to be higher than that of St Stephen's in Vienna – another act of revenge against the hated city. He further instructed Giesler to design the tower so that it suited the Danube landscape and would catch the first rays of the sun in the morning and the last in the evening. 'In the tower I want a carillon to play – not every day but on special days – a theme from Bruckner's Fourth, the Romantic Symphony. It is suitable for a carillon, this odd melody, that moves me so strangely.'

When Goebbels visited Hitler's military headquarters on the Eastern front in March 1942, he found the Führer desperate for the smallest crumb of news about his Linz projects. As the war dragged on, Hitler occasionally summoned Giesler to his military headquarters where, between situation conferences on field operations, the two discussed the Linz plans. Occasionally Hitler visited Giesler in his Munich atelier to study a large model that had been constructed. In 1943 they visited Linz together for a last time. The official purpose of the trip was to tour the Nibelungen Works, the manufacturer of the new Tiger tank, which Hitler held crucial to victory in the Russian campaign. After

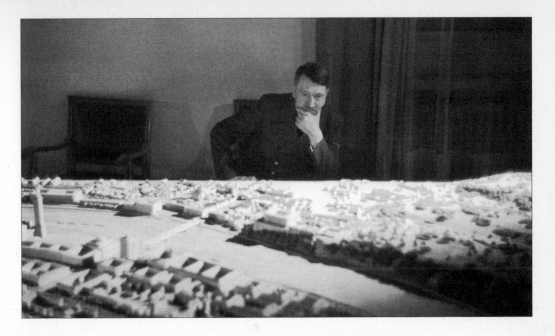

touring the plant, Hitler's mind turned entirely to his cultural projects. 'He was a different Hitler,' Speer recalled. 'The anxieties about tank production, which he had discussed with me the previous evening, seemed to be swept away.'

The closer military catastrophe approached, the more absorbed Hitler became in his Linz dream. The large model of the Linz-to-be was moved from Munich and installed in the bunker under the chancellery on 8 February 1945. It was a great event. 'I still see him before my eyes as I showed him the model [Giesler recalled]. I still wonder whether I provided him with his final pleasure or only deepened the pain that all his efforts for Germany and for the achievement of his aims and all the sacrifices were in vain.' Heinz Linge recorded in his appointment book that the Führer revisited the model – in the first week alone – at 4 a.m. on the ninth, 3 a.m. on the tenth and at 6.45 p.m. on the thirteenth. And so it went in the weeks that followed. Giesler observed: 'Whatever the time, whether day or night, when er he had the opportunity in those weeks, he sat in front of the model. . . . Before I could speak he waved me away as if nothing mattered and he did not want to be disturbed, his eyes remaining fixed on the model.'

It was a mark of special esteem for a visitor to be invited to view the model. When Ernst Kaltenbrunner, head of the Gestapo, ventured to the bunker on 13 February to attempt to persuade Hitler to negotiate a truce with the British and Americans, he found himself directed to it, where Hitler stood with Giesler and Linge. Before he could say a word, Hitler launched into a detailed description of his plans to transform Linz into Europe's great centre of culture. Bending low over the model as every detail was elaborated,

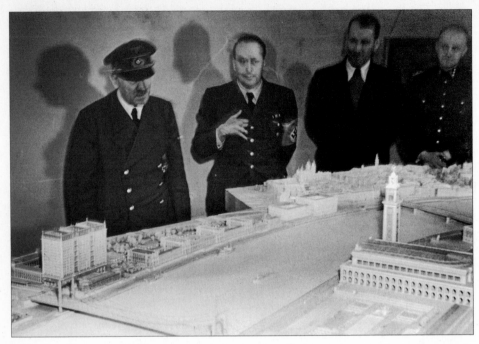

Hitler, Giesler, Kaltenbrunner, himself a Linz native,
and Heinz Linge in the Berlin bunker.

Kaltenbrunner was said to have been transfixed. Eventually the monologue stopped. 'I know, Kaltenbrunner, what you want to say to me,' Hitler remarked. 'But believe me, if I were not convinced that one day you and I will rebuild the city of Linz according to these plans, I would put a bullet through my head this very day. You need do nothing more than believe!' Kaltenbrunner went away believing, convinced that Hitler was not living in some escapist dreamworld but remained confident of final victory.

While none of his urban reconstruction programmes was ever realized, some progress was made with party forums. Although he initiated design competitions as early as 1935, it was not until October 1937 that legislation was enacted and the projects got under way. The dictator personally decided whether a city should be included in the programme, and every plan had to have his approval. To be approved carried with it not just the prestige of enjoying the Führer's interest but also commercial advantages, most directly through the injection of huge construction funds. Officials generally could not do enough to court Hitler's favour and were only too willing to sacrifice their city's historic character. The design, similar for every city, followed a rigid symmetry and a style which conformed to Hitler's neoclassical Functionalism. The buildings, aligned along a central axis, were identical – a large marching area, a People's Hall, an assembly area, a headquarters for the gauleiter, a bell tower and an avenue along which would be situated a theatre, opera house, hotel and administrative buildings. The key element was the tower, which had to be higher than any other in the city. No one ever divined Hitler's purpose better than Goebbels. 'The [community] halls are to have bell towers; they will be the churches of the future,' he confided to his diary. Thus was architecture to contribute to a new religion – Hitler worship.

Photos and descriptions survive of models of several forums. The earliest to take shape and the only one to be nearly completed was that for Weimar. Though that city had long been one of his favourites, Hitler disliked its original layout. 'The visitor comes to Weimar with high expectations; he expects classicism and finds shapelessness.' Giesler did the design which Hitler altered in a number of important ways. He moved the tower, dramatized the entrance to the gauleiter's office, placed a fountain near the tower so as to give the area more atmosphere and on the left side of the

Model of the Weimar party forum, designed by Giesler. Arranged around Adolf Hitler Platz (centre) are the People's Hall with a Bauhaus-style flat roof (left), party offices and the all-important bell tower. Begun in 1936, work on it continued until the end of the war. It stands today as a community centre.

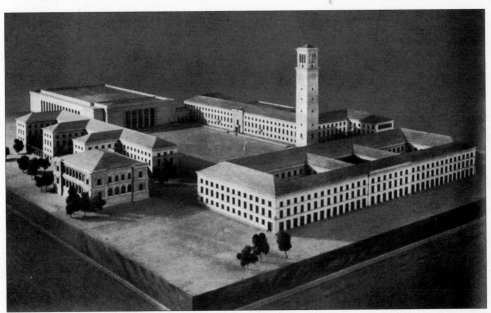

People's Hall – to pick up on Goethe's poem – emplaced a large statue of Prometheus. To avoid giving the gauleiter too visible an importance, he also insisted on moving his building off the middle axis of the square. The Weimar scheme was a template for the others. In its way it resembled the traditional forum of Roman towns, with the People's Hall significantly at the end of a long axis, in a position comparable to the main temple of an ancient city. These halls corresponded to the Great Hall in Berlin and were similarly to be a place of worship of the Führer.

In contrast to Hitler's personal projects, where much was planned but little ever built, a great deal of construction went on under the auspices of individual Nazi organizations. Although less social housing was built than in the Weimar era, much was made of 'Hitler villages' and rows of tiny houses for the lower classes. The Führer cared little for these and similar projects, and he allowed them to follow their own stylistic course. In contrast to industrial construction, which was generally Functionalist and used glass and steel, the preferred concept for Hitler Youth facilities, hostels and similar buildings was variations of old Teutonic, with wooden pillars, exposed oak beams, wrought iron, half-timbering, and thatched or gabled roofs and other archaic features. The design usually followed the stylistic tradition of the region, with chalet features in the south, half-timbering, gables and thatched roofs in the north. In its way this architecture was both functional and relatively humane.

Humane was the last trait of the party schools, known by such names as Adolf Hitler Schools, National Socialist Colleges, National Political Education Institutes and the so-called Ordensburgen, which were structures reminiscent of castles of the old knightly orders. The sites were carefully chosen for their symbolism. Situated on mountaintops or other high ground, the buildings seemed to dominate and menace the vast landscape. Hitler took great interest in their design, praising the 'austere rigour in the use of space' in the three Ordensburgen – Sonthofen in Bavaria, designed by Giesler, Vogelsang in the Rhineland and Falkenburg in Pomerania, designed by Clemens Klotz. In imitation of a medieval fortress, they were constructed of stone and timber in a style that was stern and rough – symbols of masculine power and the Nazi ideal of heroism. The architecture of party schools reached its grotesque apotheosis in Giesler's academy at Chiemsee. A detailed wooden model projected a building complex which, if sheer brutality was the aim, could scarcely have been bettered. Although one architectural

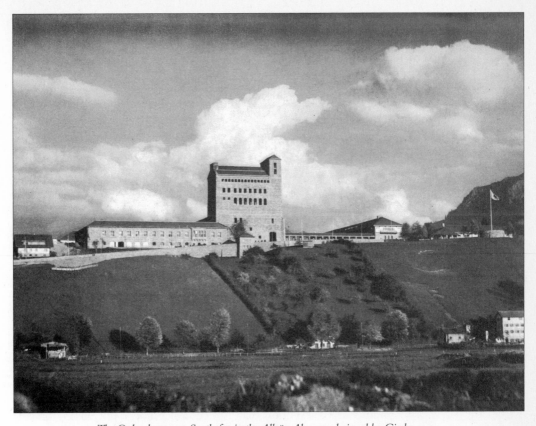

The Ordensburg near Sonthofen in the Allgäu Alps was designed by Giesler as a site where a select few were to undergo 'tough ideological and physical training' and then serve party and state. The structure, begun in 1934 and dedicated in 1937, was never completed.

historian characterized these schools as 'among the most aesthetically successful of the official buildings of the Nazi regime', they were oppressive in their dimensions, cold, impersonal and prison-like in appearance. Here, the buildings proclaimed, was where human beings were to be indoctrinated and converted into good National Socialists who, as Peter Gay remarked, 'thought with their blood, worshipped the charismatic leader, praised and practised murder, and hoped to stamp out reason – forever – in the drunken embrace of that life which is death'.

In the mood of intense euphoria that followed his victory in the West, Hitler could scarcely wait to get his building projects under way. 'During that wonderful hot summer,' Speer later told Gitta Sereny, 'it really sometimes seemed as if he had nothing else on his mind.' But even if he had not carried his war into the Soviet Union, completing all the building plans then on the drawing boards within the ten years he had set as a limit would have been impossible. The projects together amounted to the biggest construction programme in history. The practical and financial problems left his architects, ministerial officials, party leaders and mayors aghast. Hitler refused to deal with the problems and the officials. Goebbels's diaries and Speer's memoirs contain any number of comments about how he would not allow anything to stand in his way.

One of the most intractable problems was finance. To cite the sums today, even if they could be calculated, would have little meaning in light of the drastic change in the value of currency. But some impression can be gained from the fact that the cost of the projects in the Führer cities alone has been computed to be as much as 150 billion marks, while the entire 1938–9 Reich budget, heavy with armament spending, was a mere 38 billion. The figures terrified everyone except Hitler. Even before the projects got under way he waved aside monetary considerations. 'The Führer does not want to talk about money,' Goebbels noted. 'Somehow it will be paid for. Frederick the Great did not worry about money when he built Sans Souci.' And, as he had told Speer, buildings came before battleships. All his life Hitler had been contemptuous of the notion that a price tag could be put on anything of cultural value and, as in *Mein Kampf*, he would wax indignant over the fact that big corporations spent more on buildings than did governments. He had not let money stand in his way before he came to power, and he refused to do so after.

In his autobiography, Finance Minister Schwerin von Krosigk commented that Hitler left no doubt from the moment of their earliest meetings that anything to do with money was extremely distasteful to him. For a time he showed a certain understanding that public funds were not to be spent profligately but even then made plain that he would not permit any of his programmes to fail for lack of money. As time went on and financial problems became more acute, whenever the two men met the Führer would launch into a monologue that prevented the interjection of a single dissenting word. Discussing his building plans on one occasion, he read his minister's thoughts but, before the latter could raise objections, remarked, 'It was always more economical and practical to create something radical and lasting than to accept an interim solution that would have to be altered after one generation at most. A reconstructed Berlin will attract countless foreigners, and the money these tourists will bring to Germany will pay for the interest on the loans.' With that the meeting was concluded.

Hitler used the same line of argument with Speer: 'If only the Finance Minister could realize what a source of income to the state my buildings will be in fifty years! Remember what happened with Ludwig II. Everyone said he was mad because of the cost of his palaces. But today? Most tourists go to Upper Bavaria solely to see them. The entrance fees alone have long since paid for the building costs.' Speer came to share Hitler's cavalier attitude towards money, and Schwerin von Krosigk found him almost equally difficult to deal with. Like Hitler, Speer dismissed the minister as a philistine.

Nonetheless, since the money was coming out of the pockets of German taxpayers, Hitler went to great extremes to conceal the costs. He not only forbade any mention of them to the public, but he also even prohibited any calculation of them inside the government. Instead, what he insistently harped on to the German people was that great cultural works – he liked to cite the Parthenon as an example – were a one-time sacrifice for an achievement of millennia. In 1938, with military expenditures on the rise, Hitler dreamed up the extraordinary scheme of raising funds for his projects by, in effect, taxing his own government ministries and other agencies. Each was assessed a certain sum which went into an account – by 1942 it amounted to 300 million marks – that was administered by Speer to help cover costs. In the end, except in the case of the Führer cities, it was the municipalities themselves that had to bear most of the pain. Money for the Augsburg forum, for example, was found by stopping all public housing construction.

No less problematic were the practical problems of finding the necessary manpower and raw materials. Hitler's deadline for completing the projects by 1950 was never realistic. Speer reckoned that architects would need ten years just to work out the plans for the Führer cities. Given all the competing demands, including a staggering military construction programme, it was impossible to find workers and artisans in adequate numbers. The projects in Munich and Hamburg alone would have required 100,000 workers for the better part of a decade. Even before the war there was labour unrest in Nuremberg as a result of the exceptionally long hours labourers were being forced to work on the party rally buildings every day of the week. As early as 1937 the SS set up an organization to manage concentration camp inmates and, later, slave labourers to mine stone. It has been calculated that Hitler's projects were so vast they would have required the induction of 3 million forced labourers from Eastern Europe and the Soviet Union for the length of the ten-year period that Hitler allowed. Fritz Sauckel, in charge of rounding up foreign workers, was later hanged for the crime; Speer, who used them, was sentenced to twenty years.

Then there was the problem of finding adequate supplies of building materials. Wood, scarce in much of Europe for centuries, was in such demand that it had to be rationed from 1937 on. Granite and similar hard stone that Hitler insisted on was not readily available. Granite required just for Munich and Nuremberg amounted to four times the combined annual production of Denmark, France, Italy and Sweden. With the occupation of Norway another source became available, but then ports and a fleet of ships had to be built to handle transport from Scandinavian quarries. Procuring enough marble posed similar difficulties. Hitler was quick to see in the invasion of the Soviet Union promise of a solution, remarking to Speer, 'We'll be getting our granite and marble from there in any quantities we want.'

Although most projects were suspended following the attack on Poland, after the easy victory in the West, Hitler ordered work to be resumed. But Britain's decision to continue the war posed an infuriating distraction, and he complained that 'Churchill was robbing him of a third of his time that could have been devoted to his marvellous construction plans.' After the *Wehrmacht*'s disastrous first winter on the Russian front – when the transport system had nearly collapsed – Speer begged Hitler to let him shift half the construction force of 65,000 men from work on the Führer cities to repair the railway network. Hitler rejected that and similar appeals out of hand. Not until mid-1942 did he gird himself to accept the inevitable. 'With a heavy heart the Führer has taken leave of his construction projects,' Goebbels noted. 'No longer do they give him pleasure. . . .' Following the Stalingrad disaster, he finally permitted work to stop, though even then the rebuilding of bomb-damaged opera houses and some work in Führer cities went on fitfully almost to the end. From 1943 on the need was not for construction but reconstruction.

Hitler rarely let himself be seen in public after 1940 and, despite Goebbels's appeals, never visited any city that had been bombed. With his usual cold-bloodedness, he was indifferent to the horrific destruction of German cities. Not just indifferent, in fact, he welcomed it as a way of clearing out old urban centres in anticipation of his reconstruction programmes. On the day after a massive raid on Cologne in August 1942, Goebbels found him studying a map of the city which showed the bombed areas. 'In strict confidence he maintained that the British attacks on certain cities, horrible though they might be, had their favourable aspect. . . . Streets had been demolished that for the most part needed to be demolished and that could only have been cleared at the cost of extreme psychological difficulties for the population. In this respect the enemy did us good service.' Nearly a year later, following the heavy raids on the Ruhr when cities like Düsseldorf, Dortmund and Wuppertal were blasted, and towns like Barmen nearly wiped off the face of the earth, he remarked that these places were 'aesthetically not attractive' and in view of the anticipated increase in vehicular traffic after the war they would in any case need to be rebuilt.

Ever the architect-builder, by now he was giving thought to a massive programme of post-war urban reconstruction. Some of his ideas were relatively enlightened. In Berlin he decided that inner-city apartment blocks and tenements should not be reconstructed but the sites should instead be transformed into green areas. Mass housing was to be moved to the periphery and linked to the city centre by an expanded underground network. Even now, though, his projects were entirely impersonal and lacked any human element. Indeed, he did not even see firsthand the extent of the spreading devastation until he flew over Berlin on his return from the front in April 1944. What he then witnessed was such a shock that he realized the whole of the city would have to be reconstructed and commented that it would take twenty years.

21 Aesthetics and Transport

Hitler's autobahn network has been universally praised as his one innovative, successful and enlightened achievement. Even while under construction, these *Straßen des Führers* or *Straßen Adolf Hitlers* were heralded as one of the great manifestations of Hitler's genius, the vitality of National Socialism and the excellence of German technology. Their divided roadways, generous width, superb engineering, environmental sensitivity, harmony with the countryside, tasteful landscaping, cloverleaf entries and exits, sleek bridges and overpasses, Modernist service stations, restaurants and rest facilities were in advance of road systems anywhere else and presented a model for the world. Among their numerous foreign admirers was David Lloyd-George. The former prime minister travelled to the Berghof in September 1936 to pay his respects to Hitler and, among other topics, to discuss the motorways, which he had evidently inspected with care. He returned home greatly impressed by what he had observed and praised his host as 'a great man'.

What is not widely appreciated is that Hitler regarded these highways above all as aesthetic monuments. For the first time in history roads were to be not merely or even primarily a utilitarian mode of transportation but a lasting work of art, in his mind comparable to the pyramids. The visual element was central from the very beginning. He once commented how unbearably boring he found the highway between Bonn and Cologne. 'But when I go from Berlin to Munich, there is one beautiful sight after another. . . .' The autobahns were therefore intended not so much to facilitate cars going from one place to another as to show off the natural and architectural beauty of the country. Routes were chosen to go through attractive areas without disturbing the harmony of hills, valleys and forests. Lay-bys were created for travellers to stop and admire the panorama. In some cases the roadway itself made a detour, despite additional costs, to offer a particularly impressive view. Great effort went into construction so as to minimize damage to the environment. Landscape architects vetted the plans, directional signs were discreet and service

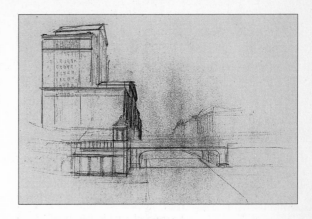

This drawing from Hitler's 1925 sketchbook shows that his notion of urban restructuring already foresaw unimpeded traffic on main avenues, with intersecting streets either elevated or underground. Hitler later insisted on this feature in all his major urban projects.

stations were made as inconspicuous as possible. Bridges and overpasses were designed and built not only to fit in with the landscape but also to be architectural achievements in themselves. Linked to beauty was sleekness. The roadways were to sweep through the countryside without intersections, a notion that was prefigured in a drawing in Hitler's 1925 sketchbook.

But if the means were aesthetic, the aim was another example of megalomaniac self-indulgence. Hitler was fascinated by roads, a curiosity that has been traced to his time at Landsberg. During the subsequent *Kampfzeit* – the period of 'political struggle' – when he was constantly on the move from one meeting to another, it was said that he crisscrossed Germany by car to the point that his 'journeys on the German country roads added up to twelve or fifteen times the circumference of the earth'. Small wonder, accounts concluded, that he commanded an 'astounding' knowledge of the German road network and so had come to be the prime mover behind the new motorways. Left unmentioned was that it mattered little to Hitler that railways were vastly more important to the population as a whole and, along with canals, to commerce and industry. Train travel he found boring, however, and, after an unhappy early experience, he developed a dislike of flying that he never lost. 'It is the automobile I love,' he once remarked. 'I really must say that it has given me some of the pleasantest hours of my life – seeing people, countryside, monuments.' That sentiment, more than a precocious insight that society was on the verge of mass motorization, was the underlying incentive.

The superhighway concept was anything but original with Hitler. In Germany it went as far back as 1911, and a small stretch of express roadway had been built in Berlin as early as 1921. It was in northern Italy a year later, however, that the first genuine prototype was laid down and in 1924 opened to traffic. A private German road association then developed a proposal for a similar roadway from Hamburg via Frankfurt to Basel and worked it out in such technical and financial detail that by 1932 it was ready to be carried out. The plan never got off the drawing board for a variety of reasons, including the strong opposition in the Reichstag of the Communists and National Socialists, who wanted to destroy the Weimar Republic, not make it work.

Within a fortnight of being appointed chancellor, Hitler spoke on two occasions – at his first cabinet meeting and at an international automobile show in Berlin – of his interest in a large-scale road-building programme. The horse and cart had its paths, the railway its tracks and now modern transport needed modern roads, he said at the car show. 'In the past a nation's standard of living was measured by the quality of its railway system, in the future it will be measured by the quality of its highways.' It is generally assumed that Hitler had been influenced by a report he was given in January 1933 by the party's adviser on transport, Fritz Todt. This proposed constructing 5000 to 6000 miles of roadway, in that way creating 600,000 jobs, facilitating commercial transport and making possible the rapid deployment of troops in wartime. Todt's report, combined with the existing technical groundwork on the Hamburg-Basel motorway, offered Hitler an eye-catching project ready to be put into action. It would not only appeal to the public, the construction industry and the unemployed, but would also create the impression of a decisive, dynamic and modernizing Nazi government in contrast to the dawdling Weimar regimes.

'Create the impression.' This was a vital element in Hitler's calculations. For the time and circumstances, a modernistic road network was not practical. In all, there were then merely 500,000 passenger cars and 160,000 lorries in Germany. Building an enormously complex and expensive highway system was an extravagance that would benefit few. Resources would more logically have been devoted to rail and such badly needed inland waterways as the Rhine-Main-Danube canal. Even though strongly held in the ranks of his own party, the objections were swept aside by Hitler. He would have his highways because that is what he personally wanted – one more monument to his own genius. Popular doubts were to be overcome by a massive propaganda campaign. In time the roads would be crowded with cars, he assured his critics, and he had an idea up his sleeve how to achieve that as well.

Hitler pressed ahead with such determination that by June 1933 he was able to promulgate a law authorizing the construction of an autobahn network. To carry it out he turned to Todt, chief executive of a major road construction firm and a convinced National Socialist. Like Speer, he was hugely efficient and, like the architect, he not only had an artistic sense but also grasped Hitler's ideals and put them into practical form with great skill. Together he and Hitler worked out the guidelines – road width, siting of routes and similar desiderata – which were announced in July. Todt was probably the only high official whom all other high officials spoke well of – a straight arrow, a man devoted to his job rather than self-promotion. But he was a devout Nazi and, when it came to the autobahns, more of an ideologue than his Führer. Like a good German, Todt conceived of the road not just as a physical object but as a philosophical concept and, like a good Nazi, he defined the concept in racist terms. The function of the autobahns was, he said in a speech entitled 'The Nordic Man and Travel', to unleash the spirit of adventure that was a hereditary impulse of the Nordic race. The roads on which the Nordic man would travel, he declared on another occasion, were to be German roads, reflecting the character of the German landscape and the 'German soul'. As for their construction, 'Concrete and steel are material things. . . . National Socialist technology endows their use with ideological content.' Fortunately when this malarkey was translated into practice the result was quite benign. It ultimately meant that aesthetic principles were controlling. Todt even employed a leading landscape architect, Alwin

Hitler opened the first stretch of the autobahn from Frankfurt am Main to Darmstadt on 19 May 1935. No mere superhighway, the autobahn told the world that dictatorship was more effective than democracy and that Nazi Germany had reconciled technology and aesthetics, machinery and nature, the past and the future.

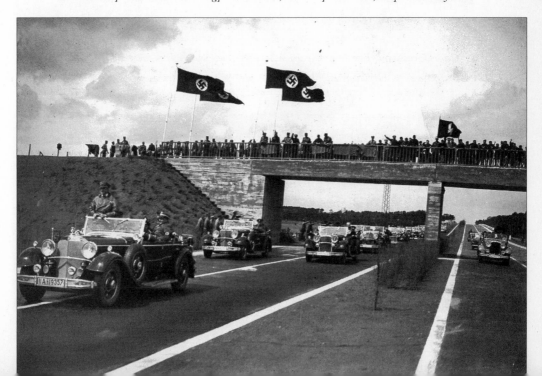

Seifert, to take charge of landscaping and endowed him with the baroque title, *Reichslandschaftsanwalt des Generalinspektors für das deutsche Strassenwesen.*

A mere eight months after becoming chancellor, on 23 September, Hitler turned over a spadeful of earth to inaugurate construction of the first leg of a Hamburg-to-Basel autobahn. Work went forward with the speed and competence of a successful military campaign. The initial stretch, from Frankfurt to Darmstadt, was opened less than two years later, in May 1935. Press and newsreels showed the Führer in his open Mercedes progressing down the highway on either side of which heiling masses saluted him and celebrated his road. In no time the autobahn caught the world's attention.

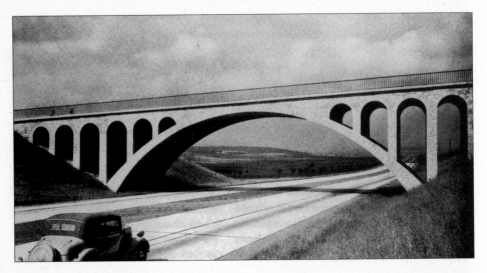

The stone bridge near Eisenberg in the Rhineland-Palatinate and the brick overpass near Münzheim were sleek, even Modernist examples of autobahn overpasses. Constructed to be compatible with their environment, these structures also signalled the transition from flat to hilly countryside.

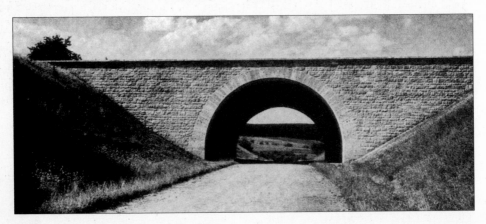

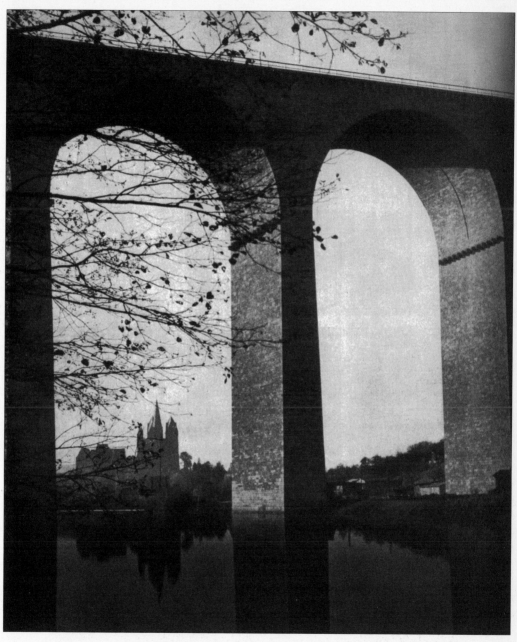

Bridges were a key element in the autobahn myth. Although Swiss and Italian bridge builders sometimes faced more challenging technical problems, their German counterparts surpassed everyone else in their aesthetic accomplishment. Paul Bonatz was the master; his bridge over the Lahn River at Limburg and another over a valley along the Stuttgart-Ulm autobahn are examples of how he harmoniously balanced monumentalism, care for the environment and technical skill to produce a stunning architectural work.

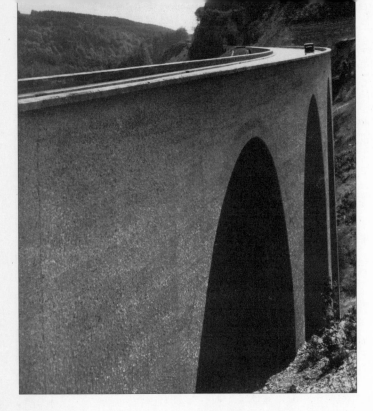

Indeed, it rapidly developed into one of Hitler's greatest propaganda windfalls. German media had a heyday, ballyhooing the road system as 'the greatest single masterpiece of all times and places', 'the sixth wonder of the world', 'greater than the Great Wall of China', 'more impressive than the pyramids', 'more imposing than the Acropolis', 'more splendid than the cathedrals of earlier times'. Needless to say, it was also trumpeted as evidence of the superiority of the National Socialist system over democratic government.

As with his buildings, Hitler carefully followed the work so as 'to ensure that it was done in accordance with his will . . . even down to the smallest detail', in Todt's words. Sometimes he suggested the choice of route and made the final selection in bridge competitions. When it came to his autobahns, Hitler was a Modernist, and his motorways were an outstanding example of up-to-date design and technology. He even insisted on selecting the design of service stations and in the early years these were so functional, simple and flat-roofed they might have come straight out of the Bauhaus. In fact, two of them did. Plans of them have been found that were submitted by Mies van der Rohe himself. In 1938 the concept changed. No longer were the autobahns to be punctuated by simple service stations for cars to tank up. Now they were to provide rest stops – with restaurants and recreation areas – and be situated in places of natural beauty or near sites of historic or other importance. The style of such buildings was to be consonant with the architectural tradition of the area and functionality gave way, it was said, to aesthetic effects.

For largely aesthetic reasons bridges and overpasses posed the challenge of reconciling technology with pastoral environment. It was a conundrum that fascinated Hitler. 'I don't know how many times I listened to him, holding forth on the theory and practice of bridge construction,' Heinrich Hoffmann commented after the war. But when the first few bridges turned out to be disappointing, Hitler and Todt decided that bridge design should be in the hands not of engineers but of architects with imagination and an aesthetic sense. To oversee the work Todt therefore called in Friedrich Tamms and Paul Bonatz, whose earlier bridges Hitler had admired. Bonatz later designed several bridges, and two in particular – the stone bridge at Limburg and the Cologne–Rodenkirchen suspension bridge – were Modernist works of art. Of the latter, Giesler quoted Hitler as commenting, '. . . It possesses a classicism that we should strive for in all our buildings; it has a validity that will last over time.' By the end of 1938 stone had become so scarce as a result of Hitler's other building projects that different materials had to be found. Design gradually fell prey to monumentalism – notably in the late projects of Friedrich Tamms – with the result that technology began overtaking nature. In all, 9000 bridges and overpasses were built between 1933 and 1941. They are generally reckoned to be the most notable aesthetic success of the autobahns and a key element in the autobahn myth.

Just as Hitler hoped that the public would share his feeling for his favourite paintings and operas, so he wanted travellers to enjoy the autobahn as did he – as an aesthetic adventure. And to help them, the media told them how to do so. The party's automobile journal, *Die Straße*, instructed them not to use the roads to hurry from one place to another but to 'experience' the beauties of the countryside. Road travel would provide, it promised, a consciousness of space and movement, of heights and depths, of narrow passes and great open spaces. However, for the vast mass of the carless population the experience had to be a vicarious one, enjoyed through film and photo. Still, the autobahn spoke for itself and nearly half a century later a German architectural historian could write, 'It was without a doubt the dictatorship's most popular construction project, far more appealing to the public than the forums and remodelled cities. . . .' Too popular, in a way. In the early post-

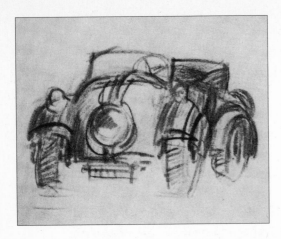

Of the various purported drawings by Hitler of what eventually became the Volkswagen, this is an authentic, though undated, one.

war years 'but at least the autobahn . . .' became a veritable refrain for unrepentant Nazis who wanted something good to say about Hitler.

As early as 1938 autobahn construction had begun winding down, as Hitler's thoughts turned to war and Todt's to building defence fortifications along the western border. By that summer 3000 kilometres of road had been completed and another 3500 or so were under way, of which around 500 were eventually finished. Although one of Todt's original arguments claimed the highways might be useful in war, Hitler was never taken with this notion. In fact the routes did not run to likely front lines, the surfaces were too thin to support tanks and so on. Far from being helpful to the *Wehrmacht*, the roads, with their shiny white surfaces, proved so useful to enemy aircraft by providing points of orientation that they had to be camouflaged with paint. This was a terrible blow to Hitler who complained

Porsche and Hitler discuss the mechanics of the Strength through Joy car (alias Volkswagen). The first prototype of the Volkswagen was ready in 1936 and tested the following year.

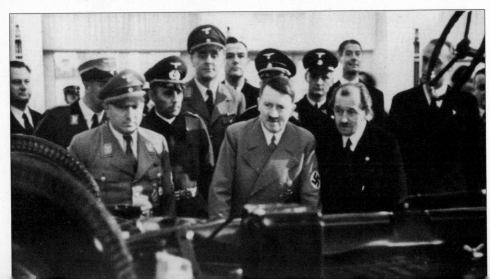

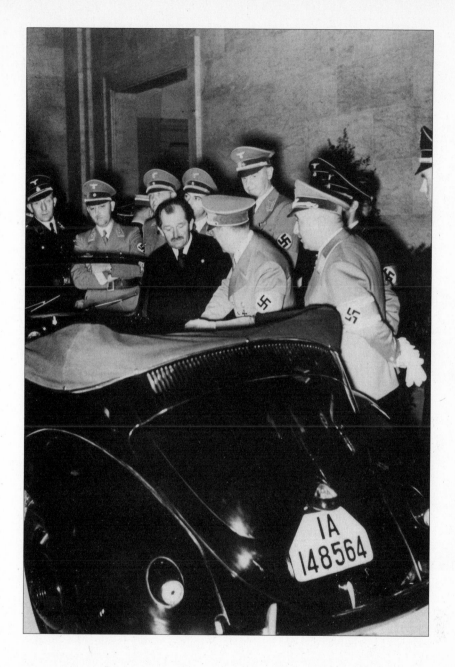

how much it pained him 'no longer to be able to drive along those beautiful wide white surfaces that had always given him the greatest of pleasure'. At Hitler's insistence some construction work went on until the exertions of the Russian campaign required it to be suspended in 1941. The Hamburg–Frankfurt–Basel autobahn, the original inspiration, was completed only in 1962.

★

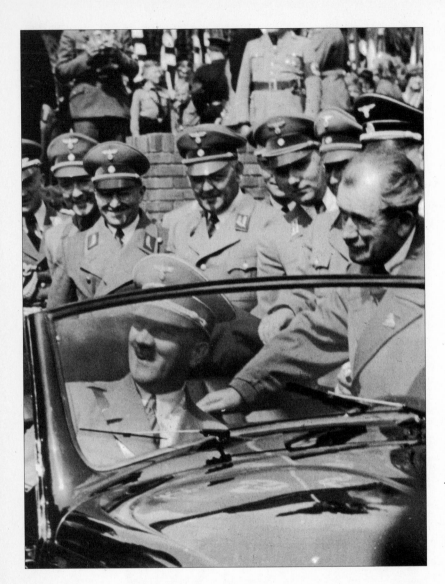

Following the ceremonial laying of the foundation stone of the Volkswagen factory at the newly-named Wolfsburg, a delighted Führer and a proud inventor take their places for a drive in a model car.

With the autobahns necessarily went a new type of car and here again Hitler played the decisive role. No longer was it to be a luxury product for the rich but one available to the mass population. A few years after Herbert Hoover invented the election slogan 'a chicken in every pot, a car in every garage', Hitler thought up a German equivalent, '*ein Volksauto und ein Volkseigenheim für Jedermann*' – for everyone a car and house of his own. The idea went back to the early 1920s when in Landsberg prison he read an article entitled 'Automobilisierung Deutschlands' (Automobilization of Germany), which raised the possibility of manufacturing, à la Henry Ford, a small, cheap car. In the following years, while driving to political meetings, he found an even greater fascination in cars, and as royalties from *Mein Kampf* accumulated he purchased a six-seater open Benz, similar to the Mercedes he was later often photographed in. It was not only automotive technology that fascinated him but the aesthetics of industrial design. Studying the sketches and models of streamlined cars that were appearing in automobile publications at the outset of the 1930s, he was much taken with the Czech Tatra. In 1932 he met a Daimler-Benz official, Jakob Werlin, and purportedly showed him his own rough sketch, similar to the Tatra, of the sort of small, inexpensive vehicle he wanted to promote. Such a car would not only permit the German public to enjoy driving around the countryside as he did but would also forestall discontent among the working classes.

Although the German car industry was largely sceptical about mass motorization, an engineer who had made a name manufacturing racing cars, Ferdinand Porsche, had been toying with the idea of a small car. Hitler had been introduced to Porsche in 1926 at an auto race and a month after Hitler came to power the two men met again. Porsche showed him designs of a small car and offered his services. By the end of that summer Hitler had worked out what he wanted and laid down his criteria – a simple vehicle for a German family with two or three children, economical to run and repair and to be sold for 1000 marks. Although gasping at the exiguous price, Porsche accepted the challenge. With funds confiscated from the old trade union movement, the project went forward. Workers were invited to contribute a sum from their wages and, once paid up, receive a voucher for a car. To make clear that the intent was pleasure rather than business, Hitler instructed that it should be distributed by the party's leisure organization. In May 1938 he formally christened the vehicle not 'Volkswagen' – people's car – but 'Kraft durch Freude-Wagen' – Strength through Joy Car. He could with justice have called it a 'Hitler'. No democratic politician could have pushed the project through and no other Nazi leader had any interest in the idea.

By the end of 1937, with Hitler watching like an anxious father over every stage of its gestation, Porsche had developed and tested a prototype. The dictator could not have been more pleased and presented one of the first to come off the production line to Eva Braun for her birthday in February 1939. 'The way these cars buzz up to the Obersalzberg and, like a bee, overtake and buzz past a Mercedes is really impressive,' he later commented. It was 'the car of the future', he declared, and for once he could not have

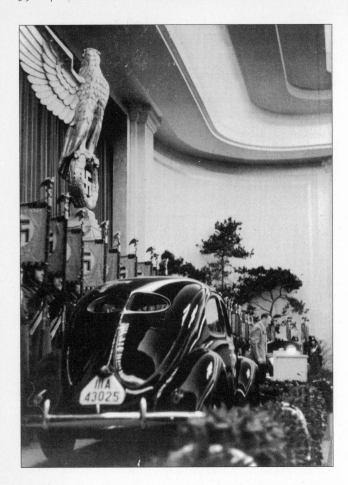

Hitler introduces his car to the world at the opening of the International Automobile Show in Berlin on 17 February 1939.

been more right. He wanted a million a year to be built. Before it could go into mass production, however, the war began and the factory switched to the manufacture of a variant of the car suitable for military purposes. Still, what developed after the war into 'the car of the century' went back to his concepts and reached fruition through his determination – and dictatorial authority.

In July 1941 Hitler uttered his last recorded words on his autobahns and the Strength through Joy car, commenting to his staff:

> More than the railway – which is rather impersonal – automobiles will link people to one another. What a step on the way to a new Europe! Just as the autobahns are dissolving the internal German borders, so will they surmount the borders of individual European countries.

Afterword

Hitler's prophetic words about how mass motorization and an elaborate web of superhighways would change the character of Europe and the way of life of its people were indicative of the sort of leap of imagination that made him at times so formidable in politics, diplomacy and war. But they were also typical in concealing an ulterior purpose. The autobahn and Volkswagen projects were the most visible examples of how the dictator combined aesthetics, technology, social engineering and a political vision with a determination to leave a personal mark for the world to see. Both the highways and the car were ultimately meant to be a material legacy lasting long after his death. Immortality through his monuments was what he ever more ardently sought as time passed.

It has been a trait of megalomaniacs throughout history to use the arts to control thought, gain respectability, bolster their power and memorialize themselves. The more absolutist the ruler, the more rigorously he pursued these objectives and the more grandiose the artistic monuments he left. The earliest surviving example, the pyramids apart, is Darius the Great's Persepolis. Of this, Lord Curzon wrote after visiting the site in 1889, 'Everything is devoted, with unashamed repetition, to a single, and that a symbolical, purpose, viz. the delineation of majesty in its most imperial guise, the pomp and panoply of him who was well styled the Great King.' All absolutist rulers – whether Darius or Augustus or Louis XIV or Stalin or Hitler – think and act alike. They manipulate art and seek to overwhelm by constructing gigantic buildings. They are motivated by self-assertion and self-worship, and they accept no limits on their extravagance. But Hitler went well beyond the others. He alone used aesthetics to help get and keep power. He alone defined and legitimized his rule in cultural terms.

Because his interest in the arts was also personal and genuine, and because – for all his railing against art for art's sake – he saw culture as the supreme value in itself, he was bound to act as Plato would have acted in controlling it. And therein lay the tragedy. Had he been, like Mussolini, a cretinous philistine without interest in the arts, he would have been less destructive. It is a further paradox that it was precisely the exceptional importance of culture in German life that afforded Hitler such great scope to use it for his own purposes. The pillars of state and society he left essentially intact – administration remained in the hands of the old Prussian civil service, industry in those of the old capitalist barons, agriculture in those of the Junkers, the army in those of the traditional Prussian aristocracy. The much vaunted 'National Socialist revolution' was therefore far less a social than a cultural revolution – or, rather, counterrevolution. In this sense a subtext of the whole sad story is one of a perverted form of cultural continuity. Hitler tried to obliterate the present to return to the past. Since the past could in the nature of things not be resurrected, the effect was to turn Hitler into a reverse King Midas, destroying whatever he touched without being able to replace it. Hence he ruined art while believing he promoted it and engaged in savagery while thinking he was creating a more beautiful world. He proved that culture and barbarism can exist side by side and have the same progenitor. 'There is never a moment of culture, without its being at the same time a document of barbarity.' The words on Walter Benjamin's tombstone are a fitting epitaph for Hitler's cultural legacy.

At the same time the record also shows that Hitler's destruction and corruption of the arts was possible only with the active collaboration not just of party apparatchiks such as Rosenberg and Goebbels but also of artists like Posse, Voss and Haberstock; Breker and the two Zieglers; Furtwängler, Strauss and Egk; Speer, Giesler and Todt and their like. They were not the political innocents they later claimed to be. They had eyes to see and ears to hear and knew by June 1933 that the Third Reich was an anti-Semitic totalitarian state, and, like thousands of others, they took advantage of that very situation to seek personal benefit. They were not corrupted by Hitler, they were eager volunteers in his cultural design without any regard for the moral consequences. More than anyone else they gave Hitler respectability at home and abroad, creating an aura of civilization in a society where inhumanity reigned. They bring to mind the concierge in Albert Camus' anecdote about two members of the Resistance in occupied Paris who were being tortured by the Gestapo. When the concierge arrived to clean up the mess around them, they appealed for her help. 'I don't get mixed up in the affairs of my residents,' she responded.

Hitler did not inject ideology into the arts. It was always there and, as philosophers from the time of Plato observed, it was always and necessarily there. This is why even in democratic societies today there are continuous threats against free artistic expression, justified with the same arguments Hitler used about corrupting the public mind. The most ironic of these threats, however, is one that stems from the very fear of Hitler himself and the way he used aesthetics in public life. Hitler's authority did not rest primarily on repression, violence and terror. But when in 1988 the president of the Bundestag, Philipp Jenninger, sought, however ineptly, to address an aspect of this question – why Hitler held such fascination for the German people – his words created a scandal, and he was forced to resign. The fear is equally evident in the way the art produced in the Third Reich has been hidden away or the public invited to mock it on the rare occasions when some of it has been shown – a precise replay, mutatis mutandis, of the 1937 degenerate art exhibit. An exhibition of Hitler's paintings – or an exhibition of Hitler's and Churchill's paintings that would show vividly the difference in character of the two statesmen – is unthinkable. In an argument submitted in the spring of 2001 to the Federal Appeals Court in Washington, the United States Justice Department maintained that the very brush strokes of Hitler's watercolours have such incendiary potential that they must be guarded from the gaze of all but screened experts. Similarly, the governments of Germany and a number of other countries have decided that their citizens should not be permitted to read *Mein Kampf* and have banned it. Who is afraid of Adolf Hitler? Just about everyone.

The artist creates his own world out of nothing. Hitler took the existing world and tried to turn it into his own. His dream was to create a culture-state in which Germans were to listen to music he liked, attend operas he loved, see paintings and sculptures he collected and admire the buildings he constructed. That was to be his legacy. He thought of himself as Prospero, wanting to give up statecraft for the arts, exchanging a dukedom for dedication to culture. And he also believed he was Prospero in thinking of himself as the all-powerful tool of destiny, not perhaps able to make water run uphill and reverse the seasons but to change human nature, the face of Europe and the course of history.

More than any other single person, Hitler made the twentieth century what it was and largely created the world we live in today. By the time of his suicide he had, in fact, created a new world by destroying the old one. Britain was no longer the supreme world power and the United States and the Soviet Union had become the two dominant superpowers. He ushered in the atomic age, decolonization and the cold war. Culturally as well as politically he finished Europe off as the centre of Western life. He left the world poorer by 60 million souls, including an incalculable number of artists in every field. It was supremely fitting that he should have claimed Rienzi as his model. Rienzi sought to create social order and restore the empire. But in the end he brought destruction upon his world and was consumed in the fiery ruins of the Roman Capitol. The opera did indeed foretell Hitler's destiny.

Who was he, then? A homicidal maniac, a gentle artist, a brutal artist, a tyrant, a weak dictator, a would-be Roman emperor, an artist-politician, a supreme actor, a revolutionary, a reactionary? He was each of them. Above all, he was a catastrophe. But that, as Thomas Mann said, is no reason not to find him interesting, as a character and as an event.

SOURCE NOTES

1 The Bohemian Aesthete

page 3 'Like it or not . . .' Thomas Mann in *Bruder Hitler, Gesammelte Werke*, Band XII, 845ff.; *Thomas Mann Essays*: vol.4, 305ff.

page 3 'not a fanatic . . .' Letter of 7 October 1923 in Hartmut Zelinsky, *Richard Wagner: Ein deutsches Thema*, 169.

page 3 Indeed, Hitler's most perceptive . . . Joachim Fest, *Hitler*, 86 and *passim*.

page 3 As the joy of a child . . . Letter of 17 October 1923 from Josef Stolzing-Cerny to Eva Chamberlain in Winfried Schüler, *Der Bayreuther Kreis*, 126–7.

page 3 'of rigid mind . . .' John W. Wheeler-Bennett, *The Nemesis of Power*, 449.

page 3 'that bohemian corporal' Fest, *Hitler*, 781.

page 4 According to his sister Paula . . . Interview with Paula Wolf, 5 June 1946, 2.

page 4 'For hours I could stand . . .' Adolf Hitler, *Mein Kampf*, 19.

page 5 the exterior and floor plan . . . August Kubizek, *Adolf Hitler, Mein Jugendfreund*, 45–6; Billy F. Price, *Adolf Hitler: The Unknown Artist*, figs 28, 29, 100.

page 5 an ink drawing . . . Kubizek, after 176; Price, fig. 59, 107; restaurant in Price, fig.27, 100; opera house in Kubizek, after 176 and 192; Price figs 57, 58, 107.

page 5 'This was the saddest period . . .' *Mein Kampf*, 21.

page 5 'kills all pity' *Mein Kampf*, 23.

page 5 At times he had to barter . . . Price, figs. 276, 152, 364, 172 (examples).

page 6 'art history, cultural history . . .' Letter of 29 November 1921 in Jäckel/Kuhn, eds, *Hitler: Sämtliche Aufzeichnungen, 1905–1924*, 525.

page 6 'I had but one pleasure . . .' *Mein Kampf*, 22.

page 6 Long afterwards his secretary . . . Christa Schroeder, *Er war mein Chef*, 75.

page 6 'the granite foundation . . .' *Mein Kampf*, 22.

page 6 'Babylon of races' *Mein Kampf*, 126.

page 6 'inner revulsion for the Habsburg state' Franz Jetzinger, *Hitler's Youth*, 157.

page 6 'This period before the war . . .' *Mein Kampf*, 126.

page 6 'I am more attached to this city . . .' *Mein Kampf*, 127.

page 7 'a release' *Mein Kampf*, 161.

page 7 'I, nameless as I was . . .' *Mein Kampf*, 207.

page 8 'by far the most difficult decision' Fest, *Hitler: Eine Biographie*, 124.

page 8 'I became a politician . . .' Werner Jochmann, ed., *Adolf Hitler: Monologe im Führerhauptquartier 1941–1944*, 235 (title hereafter referred to as *Monologe*).

page 8 'Oh, how I wish . . .' Carl J. Burckhardt, *Meine Danziger Mission*, 344.

page 8 'Among the various points . . .' Sir Nevile Henderson to Viscount Halifax, 25 August 1939 in Great Britain. Foreign Office: *Documents concerning German–Polish Relations* (Cmd. 6106), 123; also Otto Dietrich, *Hitler*, 72.

page 8 'How I would like to stay here . . .' *Architecture of Doom* (film).

page 9 'All I wished then . . .' *Monologe*, 21–2 July 1941, 44.

page 9   'When he spoke this way . . .'   Ranuccio Bianchi Bandinelli: *Dal diario di un borghese e altri scritti*, 184.

page 9   Over the years Hitler . . .   Schroeder, 219; Elke Frölich, ed., *Die Tagebücher von Joseph Goebbels*, 23 January 1943, 10 May 1943 (title hereafter referred to as Goebbels diaries).

page 9   Speer said he had . . .   Albert Speer, *Inside the Third Reich*, 80.

page 10   Sitting in his cell . . .   Albert Speer, *Spandau: The Secret Diaries*, 399.

page 10   Hitler was, he said . . .   Harold Nicholson, *Diaries and Letters 1939–1945*, 39.

page 10   All totalitarian leaders . . .   David Elliott, 'The Battle for Art' in Dawn Ades et al., *Art and Power*, 33.

page 10   'The process within a nation . . .'   Speech of 18 January 1928 at Neustadt, in Hitler, *Reden, Schriften, Anordnungen: Februar 1925 bis Januar 1933*, Band II, Teil 2, 627 (title hereafter referred to as Hitler, *Reden*)

page 11   whose five-volume collected works   *Monologe*, 19 May 1944, 411.

page 11   'the sinister artist . . .'   quoted in H. G. Schenk, *The Mind of the Romantics*, xvii.

page 11   Christa Schroeder noted that . . .   Schroeder, 226 and *passim*.

page 11   'I cannot enumerate . . .'   Goebbels diaries, 10 August 1943.

page 12   'The intensity of the Führer's longing . . .'   Goebbels diaries, 20 January 1942.

page 12   Four months later . . .   Goebbels diaries, 30 May 1942.

page 12   'despite the gravity of the situation . . .'   Goebbels diaries, 23 January 1943.

page 13   'a variety of cultural . . .'   Goebbels diaries, 11 May 1943.

page 13   'complete failures in the field . . .'   Goebbels diaries, 10 May 1943.

page 13   'He looks forward . . .'   Goebbels diaries, 10 May 1943.

page 13   A scarcely less remarkable . . .   Goebbels diaries, 23 September 1943.

page 14   'We talked about problems of the theatre . . .'   Goebbels diaries, 6 June 1944.

page 14   'Cultural life of course . . .'   Goebbels diaries, 2 December 1944.

page 14   Ever since he had launched . . .   *Monologe*, 14 October 1941, 81.

page 14   'I am glad you seek me out . . .'   Schroeder, 107.

page 15   'an escape . . .'   Norman H. Baynes, ed., *The Speeches of Adolf Hitler*, 573.

page 15   'the eternal, magic . . .'   Baynes, 593.

page 15   Thinking back on those years . . .   Schwerin von Krosigk, *Es geschah in Deutschland*, 200.

2   A Philosophy of Culture

page 16   'he was a genius of dilettantism'   Speer, *Spandau*, 347.

page 16   Significantly, Hitler's theories on race . . .   'Warum sind wir Antisemiten?', 13 August 1920, Jäckel/Kuhn, 184-204.

page 17   'All great art is national'   Jäckel/Kuhn, 779.

page 17   A 'moral plague' . . .   *Mein Kampf*, 254.

page 18   'into the arms of . . .'   *Mein Kampf*, 259.

page 18   'lunatics or criminals'   *Mein Kampf*, 262.

page 18   'Theatre, art, literature . . .'   *Mein Kampf*, 255.

page 18   A further symptom of . . .   *Mein Kampf*, 263.

page 18   'If the fate of Rome . . .'   *Mein Kampf*, 265.

page 18   'artistic state of mind'   *Mein Kampf*, 279.

page 18   'All mingling of Aryan blood . . .'   *Mein Kampf*, 286.

page 18   'All human culture . . .'   *Mein Kampf*, 290.

page 19   'the basis on which . . .'   *Mein Kampf*, 302.

page 19   'the Jewish people . . .'   *Mein Kampf*, 302.

page 19 'What they do accomplish . . .' *Mein Kampf*, 303.

page 19 'the Jew . . . is always . . .' *Mein Kampf*, 304.

page 19 '. . . he contaminates art . . .' *Mein Kampf*, 326.

page 19 'nine-tenths of all . . .' *Mein Kampf*, 58.

page 19 One of these . . . 'Nationalsozialismus und Kunstpolitik', 26 January 1928 in Hitler, *Reden*, Band II, Teil 2, 652ff.

page 19 'major oratorical flights' Albert Speer, *Inside the Third Reich*, 60.

page 20 What he saw in their culture . . . *Mein Kampf*, 423.

page 20 'What makes the Greek concept . . .' *Mein Kampf*, 408.

page 21 'May you all then realize . . .' Max Domarus, ed., *Hitler: Speeches and Proclamations*, vol.2, 1127.

page 21 'the excellence of their . . .' *Monologe*, 25-6 January 1942, 232.

page 21 'We would not be in any danger . . .' *Monologe*, 11 November 1941, 135.

page 21 'You need only look at . . .' *Monologe*, 25–6 January 1942, 232; also, Goebbels diaries, 8 April 1941.

page 21 'Perhaps there is still . . .' Goebbels diaries, 8 April 1941.

page 21 'sad that he considered it at all necessary . . .' Goebbels diaries, 30 April 1941.

page 21 He admired their 'grandeur' . . . Speech of 6 September 1938, Baynes, 596.

page 21 The age of Augustus . . . Goebbels diaries, 8 April 1941.

page 21 'Ancient Rome was . . .' *Monologe*, 7 January 1942, 184.

page 21 'Rome moved me.' *Monologe*, 21–2 July 1941, 44.

page 22 'Rome was broken . . .' *Monologe*, 27 January 1942, 236.

page 22 'Rarely has the Jewish . . .' Henry Picker, ed., *Hitlers Tischgespräche*, 5 July 1942, 422.

page 22 'Why do we . . .' Speer, *Inside*, 94; also, Domarus, vol. 2, 1145; Mosse, *The Nationalization of the Masses*, 117, 118.

page 23 'one eternal art . . .' Hitler to Otto Strasser, 21 May 1930 in Baynes, 567.

page 23 'The Teuton must go . . .' *Monologe*, 4 February 1942, 263–4.

page 23 'He expressed, in a crude . . .' Henry Grosshans, *Hitler and the Artists*, 122.

page 23 'anti-social vermin' George Hersey, *The Evolution of Allure*, 144.

page 24 'A life-and-death struggle . . .' Bertold Hinz, *Art in the Third Reich*, 45.

page 24 'When a conductor . . .' *Weltbühne*, 21 April 1931, in Eckhard John, *Musikbolschewismus*, 108.

page 25 Hitler spelled this out . . . 'Art and Politics' in *Liberty, Art, Nationhood: Three Addresses Delivered at the Seventh National Socialist Congress*, Nuremberg, 1935; also, Baynes, 569ff.

3   The Grand Paradox

page 28 'For me politics . . .' *Monologe*, 25–6 January 1942, 234.

page 28 'I am convinced . . .' *Mein Kampf*, 387.

page 28 The old Reich . . . Speech at opening of House of German Art, July 1939, in Baynes, 606ff.

page 28 'Wilhlem I had no taste . . .' *Monologe*, 21–2 October 1941, 101.

page 28 When his friend . . . Heinrich Hoffmann, *Hitler Was My Friend*, 184.

page 29 'The world will come . . .' Speech of 14 June 1938 in Baynes, 610.

page 29 'the armament of a nation . . .' Baynes, 594.

page 29 'That is less than two battleships . . .' Speer, *Inside*, 68.

page 29 'It is a pity that . . .' Picker, 21 March 1942, 128.

page 29 'By the time of the War . . .' *Monologe*, 21–2 October 1941, 101–2.

page 30 The intention had been . . . *Mein Kampf*, 255.

page 30   'Simultaneously with the . . .'   Baynes, 568.

page 30   'All important posts . . .'   Goebbels diaries, 17 May 1933.

page 30   Around 250 notable writers . . .   Fest, *Hitler: Eine Biographie*, 583.

page 31   Already by the end of . . .   Erik Levi, *Music in the Third Reich*, 175.

page 31   By December 1933 more than . . .   Fest, *Hitler*, 424.

page 31   'Ridding Jews from the Chamber . . .'   Goebbels diaries, 5 May 1937.

page 31   'Führer decrees: nothing.'   Goebbels diaries, 27 July 1938.

page 31   Roughly 3000 . . .   Berguslaw Drewniak, *Das Theater im NS-Staat*, 163.

page 32   He railed against it . . .   Jäckel/Kuhn, 126, 178, 197; also speech of 26 January 1928 in Hitler, *Reden,* 655; speech at opening of 1939 Great German Art Exhibition in *Die Kunst im Dritten Reich*, August 1939, 240ff.

page 32   'The filthy Jews labelled . . .'   *Monologe*, 3 September 1942, 386.

page 32   'Only reporting is permissible.'   Goebbels diaries, 22 October 1936.

page 33   including the 40,000 works of art . . .   Wolfgang Michal, 'Der Fall Bernsteinzimmer' in *Geo*, 1996.

page 33   Hitler himself chose the specific site . . .   *Monologe*, 15–16 January 1942, 201; also 456–7.

page 33   His intention was to deprive it . . .   Walter Thomas, *Bis der Vorhang fiel*, 200–1; Speer, *Spandau*, 96.

page 34   Schirach affected an American accent . . .   Goebbels diaries, 9 May 1943; 8 August 1943 and *passim*.

page 34   The barbs of course . . .   Speer, *Inside*, 261, 276; Goebbels diaries, 2 April 1943 and *passim*.

page 34   Entries in Goebbels's diaries show . . .   Goebbels diaries, 13 and 19 March, 6 April, 17 May, 22 November 1941; 23, 24, 30, 31 May 1942 and *passim*.

page 34   The animosity eventually became . . .   Goebbels diaries, 6 April, 16 December 1941; 24, 30, 31 May, 23 June 1942.

page 34   On a visit to the Berghof . . .   William L. Shirer, *The Rise and Fall of the Third Reich*, 348.

page 34   On taking over . . .   Oliver Rathkolp, *Führertreu und Gottbegnadet*, 69 ff.

page 34   A large part of the attraction . . .   Thomas, 202–3, 213 ff.

page 34   This was one reason why . . .   Norman del Mar, *Richard Strauss*, vol.3, 242 and 400.

page 34   Goebbels recorded a meeting . . .   Goebbels diaries, 30 May 1942.

page 35   As soon as Hitler heard of it . . .   Goebbels diaries, 15 October 1941.

page 35   Despite a dressing down . . .   Rathkolb, 73f.

page 35   An outraged Hitler . . .   Baldur von Schirach, *Ich glaubte an Hitler*, 288–94.

page 35   'I am certainly not prejudiced . . .'   *Monologe*, 25 June 1943, 403–6.

page 36   Hitler never really forgave . . .   Goebbels diaries, 9, 10 May, 25 June, 10, 21 August 1943.

page 36   Hitler responded that . . .   Fest, *Hitler*, 56–7.

page 36   'his last message . . .'   Henriette von Schirach, *Der Preis der Heerlichkeit*, 17.

page 36   'racially completely worthless'   Henriette von Schirach, 227.

page 36   'I remember Strength through Joy weekends . . .'   Alfred Rosenberg, *Memoirs of Alfred Rosenberg*, 158.

page 37   'The artist does not create for . . .'   Baynes, 591.

page 37   It was to be expected . . .   Baynes, 607.

page 37   In part Hitler feared . . .   Goebbels diaries, 27 July 1941.

page 37   In addition he wanted . . .   Goebbels diaries, 16 January 1942, 19 May 1942, 3 June 1942; Klaus Backes, *Hitler und die bildenden Künste*, 82–3.

page 38   'It must be our principle . . .'   26 November 1941.

page 38   'It was heartbreaking . . .'   Howard K. Smith, *Last Train from Berlin*, 38.

page 38   'Cultural life is an effective way . . .'   Goebbels diaries, 26 November 1941.

page 38   The worse the military situation . . .   Goebbels diaries, 29 May 1943.

page 38   'under all circumstances . . .'   Goebbels diaries, 27 April 1942.

page 38   'He is of the opinion . . .'   Goebbels diaries, 7 July 1944.

page 39   '[Bormann] calls for a total . . .'   Goebbels diaries, 24 August 1944.

page 39   'I can easily foresee . . .'   Goebbels diaries, 2 December 1944.

4   The Artist as Politician

page 43   'His creativity is that of . . .'   Fest, *Hitler*, 446.

page 43   Political leadership, he said . . .   Jäckel/Kuhn, 1190.

page 43   'You cannot educate for politics . . .'   'Volksrepublik oder Judenstaat', 17 February 1922 in Jäckel/Kuhn, 574.

page 43   General Ludendorff had botched . . .   Rosenberg, 252.

page 43   'the greatest actor in Europe'   Schwerin von Krosigk, *Es geschah*, 220.

page 43   'agitators led by demagogues'   *Mein Kampf*, 475.

page 43   As George Orwell . . .   Sonia Orwell and Ian Angus, *The Collected Essays*, vol.2, 29.

page 44   'psychological masterpieces in the art . . .'   *Mein Kampf*, 476–7.

page 44   'hate-fomenting oratorical activity'   *Mein Kampf*, 475.

page 44   'I spoke for thirty minutes . . .'   *Mein Kampf*, 355.

page 44   'That was what drew me . . .'   John Toland, *Adolf Hitler*, 102.

page 44   'My critical faculty . . .'   Kurt G.W. Ludecke, *I Knew Hitler*, 13–14.

page 45   And on hearing him . . . Leni Riefenstahl, *Leni Riefenstahl: A Memoir*, 101.

page 45   'gift of a rare magnetic power . . .'   Schroeder, 283.

page 45   After seeing him in action . . .   André François-Poncet, *Souvenire d'une ambassade à Berlin*, 354.

page 47   Ernst Hanfstaengl, one of his . . .   Toland, 129.

page 47   According to Goebbels, he rehearsed . . .   Karlheinz Schmeer, *Die Regie des Öffentlichen Lebens im Dritten Reich*, 123.

page 47   'All these histrionic elements . . .'   Fest, *Hitler*, 150.

page 47   'Hitler was not an emotional . . .'   William Sheridan Allen, ed., *The Memoirs of Ex-Gauleiter Albert Krebs 1923–1933*, 152.

page 47   'He spoke very proudly of . . .'   Goebbels diaries, 27 April 1944.

page 48   For all his occasional shrillness . . .   Domarus, vol.1, 65.

page 49   'Not a single one . . .'   Dietrich, 141.

page 49   'Like the woman whose psychic state . . .'   Quinn, 163.

page 49   'They reminded me . . .'   Shirer, *Berlin Diary*, 15.

page 49   'What he learned from Wagner . . .'   Günter Scholdt *Autoren über Hitler*, 291.

page 50   Colour, an art critic . . .   John Russell, *The Meanings of Modern Art*, 43.

page 50   'In *red* we see . . .'   *Mein Kampf*, 496–7.

page 51   'An uncanny power . . .'; 'psychological magic'   Konrad Heiden, *Der Führer*, 144; Fest, *Hitler*, 128.

page 51   'had the effect . . .'   *Mein Kampf*, 496.

page 51   Such was the importance . . .   Fest, *Hitler*, 128.

page 52   He then asked a jeweller . . .   Schmeer, 14; Price fig. 486, 201; fig. 495, 202 (Related sketches in Price are forgeries.).

page 53   not only supremely violent . . .   Susan Sontag, 'Fascinating Fascism' in Brandon Taylor and Wilfried van der Will, *The Nazification of Art*, 215.

page 53   He personally rehearsed it . . .   Schmeer, 14–5.

page 53   'The same lecture . . .'   *Mein Kampf*, 474.

page 53   'the quintessentially Romantic glorification . . .'   'Leiden und Größe Richard Wagners' in Erika Mann, ed., *Wagner und unsere Zeit*, 96.

page 54   'Never before,' it has . . .   Sontag, 218.

page 54   'the marriage has been consummated . . .'   John W. Wheeler-Bennett, *Wooden Titan*, 445.

page 55   'Dead warlord . . .'   Fest, *Hitler*, 176; Domarus, 447f.

page 56   'I went to the ceremony . . .'   Shirer, *Rise and Fall*, 284.

page 56   'Hitler was one of the first great . . .'   Scholdt, 339.

page 56   Even those who despised him . . .   Scholdt, 348 ff.

page 56   '*Politik des Bluffs* . . .'   Scholdt, 350–1.

page 56   '. . . his virtuoso use of lighting . . .'   Scholdt, 348–9.

page 57   'all this fulfilled the German . . .'   Scholdt, 350.

page 58   the 'mysterious magic' . . .   *Mein Kampf*, 474.

page 58   His intent, he declared . . .   *Mein Kampf*, 474–5.

page 59   In planning his mass meetings . . .   Schmeer, 127f.

page 60   'The same purpose, after all . . .'   *Mein Kampf*, 475.

page 60   'I'm beginning to comprehend . . .'   Shirer, *Berlin Diary*, 15, 19.

page 60   'With its boundless mystical magic . . .'   Goebbels diaries, 13 September 1937.

page 60   'an eclectic conglomeration of ideas . . .'   Karl Dietrich Bracher, *Die deutsche Diktatur*, 48.

page 61   On examining one of Hitler's . . .   J. P. Stern, *Hitler,* 90; Scholdt, 126.

page 61   Hitler himself once remarked . . .   Schmeer, 115.

page 61   'all these formations, processions . . .'   Speer, *Spandau*, 262.

page 61   'from artist to "God-man"'   Domarus, vol.1, 24.

page 62   Some 500 trains . . .   Hamilton T. Burden, *The Nuremberg Party Rallies*, 115.

page 62   a surviving sketch in his own hand . . .   Weihsmann, *Bauen unterm Hakenkreuz*, 697.

page 62   'the most German of all German cities . . .'   Yvonne Karow, *Deutsches Opfer*, 22.

page 62   He regarded it, he said . . .   Speech of 2 August 1929, in Hitler, *Reden*, Band 3, Teil 2, 334.

page 62   'more than half a millennium . . .'   Domarus, vol.2, 1160.

page 62   'It is as though the Third Reich . . .'   Karow, 213.

page 63   'magical half-darkness'   Karow, 21.

page 64   'sealed their loyalty to the Führer . . .'   Karow, 215.

page 64   'The German people know . . .'   Karow, 216.

page 64   These occasions were of such importance . . .   Price, figs 608–10, 227; Speer, *Inside*, 69.

page 65   'The fulfilment of duty . . .'   Burden, 125.

page 66   After sundown 110,000 men . . .   Schmeer, 111–2; Karow, 25; Burden, 127–8.

page 66   More vividly, the British ambassador . . .   Nevile Henderson, *Failure of a Mission*, 72.

page 66   'a great tide of crimson . . .'   12 September 1936, quoted in Stern, 89.

page 66   'I had spent six years in St Petersburg . . .'   Henderson, 66–7.

page 66   'I swear by God this sacred oath . . .'   Karow, 250ff.

page 67   'With a raised right hand . . .'   Karow, 265.

page 67   Older military officers are said . . .   Wiedemann, *Der Mann der Feldherr werden wollte*, 106.

page 67   By the end of each rally . . .   *Monologe*, 225.

page 69   'many returned home seduced . . .'   François-Poncet, 268.

page 69   'Like the *Ring* [*des Nibelungen*] . . .'   Franz Schulze, *Philip Johnson*, 133–4.

page 69   Hitler oversaw each aspect . . .   Speer, *Der Spiegel* 46 (1966), 54; Karow, 73ff.

page 69   'The eye-to-eye position . . .'   Peter Adam, *Art of the Third Reich*, 242.

page 71   The complex, covering more than . . .   Speer, *Inside*, 67; Hildegard Brenner, *Die Kunstpolitik des Nationalsozialismus*, 121.

page 71   'by far the largest such site . . .'   Karow, 56.

page 71   Each of the major structures . . .   Jost Dülffer, Jochen Thies and Josef Henke, *Hitlers Städte: Baupolitik im Dritten Reich*, 212–13.

page 71   'the power and greatness of . . .'   Karow, 51.

page 71   Hitler had begun thinking . . .   Burden, 56 ff.

page 71   Hitler's initial rough sketches . . .   Price, figs 608–10, 227; figs 626–9, 231.

page 72   'a monumental backdrop'   Speer, *Inside*, 62.

page 72   Hitler used a good deal of legerdemain . . .   Karow, 73; Speer, *Inside*, 68.

page 72   'I can still see him in Nuremberg . . .'   Wiedemann, 87–8.

5   The Politician as Artist

page 73   'He talks about the future . . .'   Goebbels diaries, 25 July 1926.

page 73   And the year after that . . .   Goebbels diaries, 3 February 1932.

page 73   'He was deeply excited and agitated . . .'   Walter Görlitz and A. H. Quint, *Adolf Hitler*, 367; Fest, *Hitler*, 369.

page 73   Upon its completion in 1937 . . .   Speech of 19 July 1937 in Domarus, vol.2, 913.

page 74   'stuff nobody can understand'   Speer, *Inside*, 96.

page 74   'the narrow-minded Balt'   Speer, *Inside*, 96.

page 74   'He sharply criticizes Rosenberg . . .'   Goebbels diaries, 28 July 1933.

page 75   Rosenberg himself described . . .   Rosenberg, 165.

page 75   But he had, as one of . . .   Viktor Reimann, *Dr Joseph Goebbels*, 185.

page 75   'Goebbels never spoke a single . . .'   Rosenberg, 167.

page 75   'Hitler knew very well . . .'   Rosenberg, 165.

page 76   'Cultural leadership clearly lies . . .'   Goebbels diaries, 17 November 1935.

page 76   By 1939 even Goebbels was moved . . .   Goebbels diaries, 9 December 1939.

page 76   'I have few friends in the party . . .'   Goebbels diaries, 10 June 1931.

page 77   'Despite the large number of . . .'   Heinz Boberach, ed., *Meldungen aus dem Reich*, vol.2, 80.

page 78   'nothing more than to be . . .'   Brenner, 54.

page 78   'During the early months . . .'   Fest, *Hitler*, 426.

page 79   Painters volunteered a statement . . .   Brenner, 172.

page 79   'The artists and musicians of the . . .'   Adam, 116.

page 79   'If German artists knew what I intend . . .'   Joseph Wulf, ed., *Musik im Dritten Reich*, 127.

page 79   'My artists should live . . .'   Arno Breker, *Im Stahlungsfeld der Ereignisse*, 100.

page 79   And like princes . . .   Backes, 83–8.

page 79   Conductors like Furtwängler . . .   Drewniak, 149–55.

page 80   In 1938 Hitler approved . . .   Rathkolb, 166ff; Drewniak, 149–55; Goebbels diaries, 15 December 1937.

page 80   Hitler further arranged . . .   Picker, 222.

page 80   Gerdy Troost, the widow . . .   Backes, 83–8.

page 80   'The Führer gives me an explicit . . .'   Goebbels diaries, 30 May 1942.

page 80   As late as the end of 1944 . . .   Rathkolp, 75.

page 80   'No royal patron was ever . . .'   Goebbels diaries, 19 November 1936; Backes, 71.

page 80   It also gave Hitler pleasure . . .   Drewniak, 155f.

page 81   'a bandage for a wound . . .'   Goebbels diaries, 3 September 1937.

page 81   In practice, a Cultural Senator's . . .   Drewniak, 158.

page 81   'excess of unrestrained spending'   Goebbels diaries, 8 February 1939.

page 81   1.5 to 2 million marks annually . . .   Wulf C. Schwarzwäller, *Hitlers Geld*, 160, 194.

page 81   Hitler earmarked these monies . . .   Backes, 89.

page 81   no less than 75 million marks . . .   Backes, 89.

page 82   Estimates of this ever-replenished . . .   Backes, 89; Schwarzwäller, 197–8.

page 82   These monies largely went . . .   Backes, 89.

page 82   'Only at times like this . . .'   Hans-Jürgen Eitner, *Der Führer*, 94.

page 82   'he felt, with his whole heart . . .'   Albert Zoller (pseud. Christa Schroeder), *Hitler Privat*, 138.

page 83   'undoubtedly the most light-hearted . . .'   Wiedemann, 203.

page 83   'beautiful and gifted artists . . .'   Rosenberg, 165.

page 83   The esteemed bass died . . .   Dietrich, 148–9, 211, 217.

page 84   'He spoke favourably of such . . .'   Goebbels diaries, 22 December 1940.

page 85   'The man is an artist . . .'   Wiedemann, 75.

page 85   Convinced that it was rampant . . .   Goebbels diaries, 19 August 1941.

page 86   'Churchill will live comfortably . . .'   Henriette von Schirach, 238.

page 86   According to Speer . . .   Speer, *Inside*, 167.

page 86   Those on list A were . . .   Reimann, 215–18.

page 86   In all, there were at least 20,000 . . .   Goebbels diaries, 24 March 1942; 24 June 1942.

page 86   an additional 800,000 men . . .   B. H. Liddell Hart, *History of the Second World War*, 243.

page 86   'If we gradually wind down . . .'   Goebbels diaries, 20 January 1942.

page 86   'What is served by sending . . .'   *Monologe*, 24 February 1942, 295.

page 87   'Instead he took the position . . .'   Goebbels diaries, 8 February 1943; also, 11, 12 February 1943; 21 March 1943.

page 87   Three months later he forbade . . .   Goebbels diaries, 10 May 1943.

page 87   'a list of the so-called "divine" . . .'   Goebbels diaries, 26 August 1944.

page 87   It was near the end that . . .   Joachim Fest, *Speer: Eine Biographie*, 355.

page 87   Similarly, on learning that . . .   Goebbels diaries, 10 May 1943.

page 87   In revenge Hitler revoked . . .   Helmut and Beatrice Heiber, *Die*

Rückseite des Hakenkreuzes, 260–1; Goebbels diaries, 25 June 1943; Otto Thomae, *Die Propaganda-Maschinerie*, 256–7.

page 88 'too unsettled, too independent . . .' Hoffmann, *Hitler wie ich ihn sah*, 65.

page 88 'He regarded them one and . . .' Speer, *Spandau*, 261.

page 88 'I have no intention of forcing . . .' *Monologe*, 2 August 1941, 53.

page 88 'Oh, you know I don't . . .' Speer, *Spandau*, 261.

page 88 Convinced by the summer . . . Hoffmann, *Hitler wie ich*, 218–19.

page 88 'Ziegler is not only a . . .' Goebbels diaries, 21 August 1943.

page 88 artists are 'like children' . . . Backes, 85–6.

page 89 Göring's 'concept of painting' . . . Goebbels diaries, 23 September 1943.

page 89 gauleiters were 'complete failures . . .' Goebbels diaries, 10 May 1943.

page 89 To arrange a tête-à-tête . . . Speer, *Inside*, 128.

page 89 'My entourage is certainly . . .' Pierre Galante and Eugene Silianoff, *Voices from the Bunker*, 72.

page 89 'from this moment on . . .' Nicolaus von Below, *Als Hitlers Adjutant*, 23.

page 89 'criticism, especially of a man's . . .' Speer, *Inside*, 137.

page 90 After seeing Hess's newly . . . Dietrich, 189.

page 90 'totally inartistic' and swore 'never . . .' Speer, *Inside*, 137; Dietrich, 89.

page 90 Considering Göring unreliable and . . . Speer, *Inside*, 276; Fest, *Hitler*, 382, 744 and *passim*.

page 90 'He is an artist; we are . . .' Schroeder, 132.

page 90 'If something happens to me . . .' Schroeder, 209.

page 91 'The Führer has no guarantee . . .' Goebbels diaries, 23 June 1942.

page 91 By June of 1942 Hitler decided . . . Goebbels diaries, 23 June 1942.

page 91 'Hitler himself works too little . . .' Goebbels diaries, 29 January 1930.

page 91 A year later . . . Goebbels diaries, 29 February 1931.

page 91 'That was the end of . . .' Dietrich, 237.

page 91 He might spend days . . . Fest, *Hitler*, 535.

page 92 'the greatest confusion that . . .' Dietrich, 113.

page 92 On occasion his staff found . . . Wiedemann, 68ff.

page 92 And always there was time to see . . . Speer, *Spandau*, 102f; Rathkolb, 112; Dietrich, 138, 145.

page 92 'In the bohemian manner . . .' Speer, *Inside*, 88.

page 92 'Act! Not look and . . .' Goebbels diaries, 26 February 1931.

page 92 'The genius has a right . . .' Goebbels diaries, 22 November 1929.

page 92 'By nature Hitler was . . .' Dietrich, 136.

page 92 Even the uncritical Below . . . Below, 76.

page 92 'problems resolve themselves' Wiedemann, 68–9.

page 93 'The surer Hitler felt . . .' Fest, *Hitler*, 445.

page 93 'recall statistical data about . . .' Schwerin von Krosigk, *Es geschah*, 199.

page 93 'an ice-cold realist . . .' François-Poncet, 354.

page 94 In such a world, he . . . Dietrich, 104, 108.

page 94 The amazing blitzkrieg . . . Liddell Hart, 66 and 68.

page 94 'His ability to gauge the . . .' Alan Clark, *Barbarossa*, 99.

6   The New Germany and the New German

page 98 By 1936 Goebbels could claim . . . Backes, 71.

page 98 'to convince the nation of . . .' 'Art and Politics' in *Liberty, Art, Nationhood*; also, Baynes, 575.

page 99 24,000 square feet of . . . Adam, 233.

page 99   'uniformly designed so that . . .'   Albert Speer, *Neue Deutsche Baukunst*, 13.
page 99   'It is precisely these buildings . . .'   Baynes, 594.
page 100   'Perhaps future leaders of the . . .'   Speer, *Spandau*, 262.
page 101   'the unity of the people based . . .'   Schmeer, 72.
page 101   'Germans and foreigners with the . . .'   François-Poncet, 113.
page 101   The principal event took place . . .   Goebbels diaries, 4 October 1937.
page 101   Even the opera houses were . . .   Thomas Mathieu, *Kunstauffassung und Kulturpolitik*, 79–80.
page 102   Obeisance reached its zenith . . .   *Völkischer Beobachter*, 21 April 1939; Below, 160–1; Schroeder, 92–4; Arno Breker, *Paris, Hitler et moi*, 83.
page 102   'pretty much a collection of kitsch'   Speer, *Inside*, 149.
page 102   The model and the other gifts . . .   Anton Joachimsthaler, *The Last Days of Hitler*, 108–9.
page 104   A 'Bureau for 8–9 November' . . .   Schmeer, 101 ff.
page 104   'What a great moment!'   Goebbels diaries, 9 November 1935.
page 104   'An overpowering display . . .'   Goebbels diaries, 10 November 1936.
page 105   'I am in Stalingrad . . .'   Dietrich, 95.
page 105   The vocabulary of the speeches . . .   Schmeer, 104; Speer, *Spandau*, 262.
page 106   'People are no longer a mass of . . .'   Werner Hager, 'Bauwerke im Dritten Reich' in *Das innere Reich*, 1937, vol.1, 7.
page 107   'We therefore have no cultic . . .'   Domarus, vol.2, 1145–6.
page 107   It was the 'brutality' of . . .   *Mein Kampf*, 144.
page 107   'Nonetheless', as he hastened . . .   *Monologe*, 7 January 1942, 184.
page 107   'upsurging American continent'   *Mein Kampf*, 638.
page 107   'The German Reich has 270 . . .'   *Monologe*, 1 August 1942, 321.
page 107   Unable to 'see beyond the waves . . .'   *Monologe*, 13 June 1943, 398.
page 109   'To the Japanese we have no . . .'   *Monologe*, 7 January 1942, 184.
page 109   'forcing the white man into . . .'   Goebbels diaries, 20 March 1942.
page 109   'is more than a religion . . .'   Fest, 533.
page 109   'slender and supple, swift . . .'   Domarus, vol.2, 701.
page 109   'the sanctity of beauty'   Picker, 260.
page 110   'We see a new type of man . . .'   Adam, 177.
page 110   After that, as leader of . . .   Jochen Thies, *Architekt der Weltherrschaft*, 91.
page 111   When it was pointed out . . . .   Speer, *Inside*, 70.
page 111   The formal invitation to . . .   George Mosse, *The Fascist Revolution*, xvi.
page 111   'It is surprising', a writer on . . .   Adam, 179.
page 111   'If he emphasized the contrast . . .'   George Mosse, 'Beauty without Sensuality' in Stephanie Barron, ed., *Degenerate Art*, 30.
page 111   'His private life does not interest . . .'   Hoffmann, *Hitler wie ich*, 70.
page 111   'purely in the private sphere'   Ian Kershaw, *Hitler*, 348; Fest, *Hitler*, 294.
page 111   'Hitler pays too little attention . . .'   Goebbels diaries, 27 February 1931.
page 111   'There is a virile male voluptuousness . . .'   Mosse, 178.
page 112   illustrations 'of Nordic racial types' . . .   Wilfried van der Will, 'The Body and the Body Politic . . .' in Taylor and van der Will, 42–3.
page 112   By 1942 homosexual acts in the SS . . .   Goebbels diary, 25 February 1942.

7   Purification by Death

page 113   'purificatory in intention . . .'   James George Frazer, *Golden Bough*, 642.
page 113   On one occasion, as his . . .   Hans Frank, *Im Angesicht des Galgens*, 211–12.
page 113   would unhesitatingly say that . . .   Speer, *Spandau*, 80.

page 113 'Above all he was deeply impressed . . .' Goebbels diaries, 4 December 1940.

page 113 'skyscrapers being turned into . . .' Speer, *Spandau*, 80.

page 114 'baptismal water . . .' Schmeer, 104.

page 114 'Looks like a great deal of blood . . .' Speer, *Inside*, 162.

page 114 'The hero says, what is . . .' Speech of 4 August 1929 in Hitler, *Reden*, Band II, Teil 2, 350.

page 114 The music he wished to hear . . . Schroeder, 189–90.

page 115 Orwell saw it as . . . Orwell and Angus, 29.

page 116 To adapt a phrase of Walter Benjamin . . . Walter Benjamin, *Illuminations*, 244.

page 118 'Each palazzo in Florence . . .' *Monologe*, 21–2 July 1941, 44.

page 118 'Florence is too beautiful a . . .' David Tutaev, *The Consul of Florence*, 94.

page 118 'I can imagine that some people . . .' *Monologe*, 25–6 September 1941, 71.

page 118 'To save the old city of culture . . .' *Monologe*, 17–18 October 1941, 93.

page 119 '. . . Mankind has a natural . . .' *Monologe*, 1–2 December 1941, 149.

page 119 'Really outstanding geniuses' . . . *Mein Kampf*, 449.

page 119 'If a million children were born . . .' Hitler, *Reden*, Band III, 2, 348–9, 354.

page 120 'Wars come and go . . .' *Monologe*, 15–16 January 1942, 201; 25–6 January 1942, 234.

page 120 '*wahre Gesicht*' . . . Schroeder, 9.

page 120 '*Es gibt ein Reich* . . .' *Ariadne auf Naxos*.

8 The Struggling Watercolourist

page 123 'How it happened . . .' *Mein Kampf*, 9.

page 123 'I wanted to become a . . .' *Mein Kampf*, 17.

page 123 a 'sound thrashing . . .' Interview with Paula Wolf, 2.

page 123 'He spent his days doing . . .' 'Hitler in Urfahr', Hauptarchiv der NSDAP, Reel 1, folder 17a.

page 123 went to Munich for several months . . . Konrad Heiden, *Der Führer*, 51.

page 123 'I set out with a pile of . . .' *Mein Kampf*, 19.

page 124 To prepare himself he . . . Letter of 4 February 1908 from Magdalena Hanisch to Johanna Motloch, Institut für Zeitgeschichte, Munich.

page 124 In this time a candidate was . . . Werner Maser, *Hitler*, 78; sketches in Price, figs 40–5, 103 are forgeries.

page 124 The examiners found . . . Document reproduced in Price, 8.

page 124 'I was so convinced that I . . .' *Mein Kampf*, 20; drawings in Price, figs 60–2, 107 are forgeries.

page 124 Then he maintained that he had . . . *Mein Kampf*, 20.

page 124 'The professor asked me what . . .' Picker, 31 October 1941.

page 124 'Makart and Rubens also worked their . . .' 'Hitler in Urfahr' in Hauptarchiv der NSDAP, Reel 1, folder 17a.

page 124 not as 'artist' but as 'student' Bradley F. Smith, *Adolf Hitler*, 122.

page 125 'the sons of poor parents . . .' Zoller, 54.

page 125 'I owe it to that period that . . .' *Mein Kampf*, 21.

page 125 'I paint what people want.' Price, 9.

page 126 Some of these paintings can be . . . Schütz in *Kunst dem Volk*, January/February 1944; von Alt in Price, figs 210, 210a, 139.

page 127 'As a rule he did one painting . . .' 'Wie ich im Jahre 1913 Adolf Hitler kennen lernte', dated 31 May 1939, Hauptarchiv der NSDAP, Reel 1, folder 17.

page 127   Years later Hitler estimated . . .   Price, 15.

page 127   Some scenes he painted so often . . .   Maser, *Hitler*, 100.

page 127   'These were the cheapest things . . .'   Hamann, 236.

page 127   a series of landscapes . . .   Price, figs 98–110, 115–17.

page 127   more than three or four krone . . .   Bradley F. Smith, 141 ff.

page 127   It is said he sometimes bartered . . .   Price, fig. 276, 152; fig. 564, 172 (examples).

page 127   But claims that he was reduced to . . .   Price, figs 318–320, 161 (examples of alleged graphics).

page 128   In testimony to the Vienna police . . .   Report of interview of Otto Kallir by Vienna Police, 23 and 24 November 1936, Hauptarchiv der NSDAP, Reel 86, file 1741.

page 128   'I had the impression that he . . .'   Statement to police by Jakob Altenberg on 19 November 1936 in Hauptarchiv der NSDAP, Reel 86, file 1741.

page 128   Hitler went to the police, claiming he . . .   Police report of 5 August 1910 in Jäckel/Kuhn, 52.

page 128   'Morgenstern was the first person . . .'   Hamann, 507.

page 128   'Morgenstern's shop was at that time . . .'   Price, 15.

page 129   Following the *Anschluß*, Feingold . . .   Hamann, 508–12, 606, 628.

page 129   Indeed, his sister Paula . . .   Interview with Paula Wolf, 7; Kubizek, 'Reminiscences', 23; *Mein Kampf*, 57–9.

page 129   'Hitler's works had an architectural . . .'   Memorandum of police interview with Karl Leidenroth of 20 November 1936 in Hauptarchiv der NSDAP, Reel 86, file 1741.

page 129   'I believe that Hitler was . . .'   'Wie ich im Jahre 1913 Adolf Hitler kennen lernte', 31 May 1939, Hauptarchiv der NSDAP, Reel 1, file 17.

page 130   According to people who knew . . .   Joachimsthaler, *Adolf Hitler*, 78, 82.

page 130   'Around eight o'clock I noticed . . .'   Hans Schirmer, Niederschrift in Hauptarchiv der NSDAP, Reel 2, file 30.

page 130   *Evening*   Price, fig. 342, 166.

page 130   two further small oils . . .   Price, figs 343 and 344, 167.

page 130   an oil painting for the dining room . . .   Price, fig. 311, 67, 159.

page 130   odd jobs to earn a little money . . .   Joachimsthaler, *Adolf Hitler*, 81.

page 130   'The fact is I earn my living . . .'   Jetzinger, *Hitlers Jugend*, 262–4.

page 131   Some considered the works . . .   Testimonies in Hauptarchiv der NSDAP, Reel 2, file 40.

page 131   'I liked the picture'   Josef Attenberger, Hauptarchiv der NSDAP, Reel 2, file 40.

page 131   'I just wanted to help the young man . . .'   Joachimsthaler, *Adolf Hitler*, 89.

page 131   One customer, a jeweller . . .   Alfred Detig, report of 10 November 1937, Hauptarchiv der NSDAP, Reel 2, file 31.

page 131   Gradually he found . . .   Hauptarchiv der NSDAP, Reel 2, files 24 and 40.

page 131   'I looked at two of his paintings . . .'   Josef Würbser, Hauptarchiv der NSDAP, Reel 2, file 40; Price, fig. 382, 177 (Old Residenz) and fig. 392, 179 (City Hall and Marienplatz).

page 131   he could do it in his sleep . . .   Price, figs 393–6, 180.

page 131   To Hoffmann's daughter . . .   Price, caption to fig.380, 177.

page 131   Even if he sold only ten . . .   Josef Würbser, Hauptarchiv der NSDAP, Reel 2, file 40; Joachimsthaler, *Adolf Hitler*, 85–90.

page 132   he was painting to live . . .   *Mein Kampf*, 126.

page 132   a battlefield scene survives   Price, fig. 411, 184.

page 132   a number of works . . .   Price, figs 421–7, 187–8.

page 132   In all, at least a dozen watercolours . . .   Price, figs 411 and 412, 184; figs 413–15, 185; figs 421–9, 188; fig. 433, 189; figs 438–42, 191; figs 446 and 447, 192; figs 449, 451 and 452, 193; figs 457–9, 195; fig. 464, 196; figs 466–470, 197; figs 478 and 479, 199 appear genuine; Joachimsthaler, *Adolf Hitler*, 136–40.

page 133   'On calm days at the front . . .'   Hauptarchiv der NSDAP, Reel 2, folder 47.

page 133   On the two occasions when . . .   *Monologe*, 21–2 October 1941, 100.

page 133   'At last I have an opportunity . . .'   Postcard of Kaiser Friedrich Museum to Ernst Schmidt in Hauptarchiv der NSDAP, Reel 1, folder 17a; text in Jäckel/Kuhn, 82.

page 134   After the armistice . . .   Maser, *Hitler*, 110.

page 134   his watercolour sketchbook . . .   Ada Petrova and Peter Watson, *The Death of Hitler*.

page 134   Works such as *Weissenkirchen* . . .   Price, figs 151, 41; 172, 43; 353, 76; 458, 86; 459, 87.

page 134   Alfred Rosenberg . . .   acknowledged finding . . .   Rosenberg, 249.

page 135   A packet of twenty paintings . . .   Hermann Weiß, 'Gli acquerelli attribuiti a Hitler dell'eredità Siviero'; *Corriere della Sera*, 25 October 1993.

page 137   Christa Schroeder walked off with . . .   Schroeder, 134.

page 137   Zoller returned only fifty . . .   Schroeder, 20, 134.

9   Forgers and Collectors

page 138   'a total failure'   Heiden, *Der Führer*, 54.

page 138   'crude little pictures'   Shirer, *The Rise*, 19.

page 138   'modest postcard copyist'   Fest, *Hitler*, 59.

page 139   'drawings'   Alan Bullock, *Hitler*, 34.

page 139   'by now half forgotten'   Heiden, *Der Führer*, 46.

page 139   'that phenomenon of early rigidity'   Fest, *Hitler*, 529.

page 139   'empty and pompous theatricality'   Adam, 109.

page 139   the watercolour sketchbook of his youth   Petrova and Watson, 150–1.

page 139   When, as chancellor, he wished . . .   Speer, *Inside*, 115.

page 139   '*kleiner Maler*'   *Mein Kampf*, 21.

page 140   After becoming chancellor . . .   Thomae, 160–1.

page 140   When Martin Bormann informed Hitler . . .   Memorandum of 29 March 1939 in Hauptarchiv der NSDAP, Reel 2, folder 24.

page 140   Altenberg still held two . . .   St Ruprecht's in Price, fig. 264, 150; Ober St Veit may be Price, fig. 219, 140.

page 140   Hanisch therefore took the direct . . .   Report of 29 November 1936 by Bundes-Polizeidirektion in Vienna, Hauptarchiv der NSDAP, Reel 89, folder 1741.

page 140   Dubious about the work's authenticity . . .   Joachimsthaler, *Adolf Hitler*, 65–6.

page 141   Although police files . . .   Composite Report of 29 November 1936 by the Bundes-Polizeidirektion in Vienna, Hauptarchiv der NSDAP, Reel 86, folder 1741.

page 141   'pursued him with implacable hatred'   Vienna Criminal Police document of 1 December 1936, 48/5, Hauptarchiv der NSDAP, Reel 86, folder 1741.

page 141   They were also the basis of . . .   Vienna Criminal Police document of 1 December 1936, 48/5, Hauptarchiv der NSDAP, Reel 86, folder 1741.

page 141   'I Was Hitler's Buddy' *New Republic*, 5 April, 239–42; 12 April, 270–2; 19 April, 297–300.

page 141   With the help of a middleman . . .   Report by Bundes-Polizeidirektion in Wien of 29 November 1936, Hauptarchiv der NSDAP, Reel 86, folder 1741.

page 141   'Hitler's fear of appearing foolish'   Schroeder, 363; also, Hoffmann, *Hitler wie ich*, 196–8.

page 142   'were made confidentially aware' . . .   Undated memorandum of Bundes-Polizeidirektion in Wien, Hauptarchiv der NSDAP, Reel 86, folder 1741.

page 142   declared 'with absolute certainty'   Police memorandum of 19 November 1936, Hauptarchiv der NSDAP, Reel 86, folder 1741.

page 142   He testified that Hanisch . . .   Testimony of Otto Kallir, in police memoranda of 23 and 24 November and 11 December 1936 in Hauptarchiv der NSDAP, Reel 86, folder 1741.

page 142   'suddenly died in . . .'   Document SB 17105/36, Hauptarchiv der NSDAP, Reel 86, folder 1741.

page 142   Hitler 'had Hanisch tracked down . . .'   Fest, *Hitler*, 46.

page 142   However, the case against . . .   Bradley F. Smith, *Adolf Hitler*, 164.

page 142   'Hanisch hanged himself . . .'   Memorandum dated 22 February 1944, Hauptarchiv der NSDAP, Reel 3, folder 64.

page 143   Before 1938 it was a responsibility . . .   Hauptarchiv der NSDAP, Reel 86, folder 1741.

page 143   Within days of the *Anschluß* . . .   Reports of 19 and 20 March 1938 by the Kriminalbeamtenreferat of Bundes-Polizeidirektion in Vienna; Report of 23 March 1938 by the Bundes-Polizeidirektion in Vienna, Hauptarchiv der NSDAP, Reel 86, folder 1741.

page 143   'As a member of the party . . .'   Testimony of Paul Kerber, cited in Joachimsthaler, *Adolf Hitler*, 87, 273.

page 143   Eventually the Hauptarchiv had to pay . . .   '*Aquarelle des Führers*', undated report, Hauptarchiv der NSDAP, Reel 2, folder 37.

page 143   'These things should not go for . . .'   Memorandum of 12 March 1944, in Schroeder, 133–4.

page 143   fewer than fifty paintings . . .   Hauptarchiv der NSDAP, Reel 2, folders 22–43.

page 143   But up to the end of the Third Reich . . .   Amtsbestätigung of 19 July 1939, Hauptarchiv der NSDAP, Reel 86, folder 1741.

page 144   As late as 1942 . . .   Hauptarchiv der NSDAP, Reel 2, folder 36.

page 144   But the chief culprit was . . .   Günther Picker, *Der Fall Kujau*; Charles Hamilton, *The Hitler Diaries*, 7ff; Jäckel/Kuhn, 'Neue Erkenntnisse zur Fälschung von Hitler-Dokumenten' in *Vierteljahreshefte für Zeitgeschichte*, January 1984; Joachimsthaler, *Hitler*, 62.

page 145   For Hitler-the-struggling . . .   Price, 184–99 passim.

page 146   'I was often a guest here . . .'   Price, fig. 599, 224.

page 146   To add interest to the exhibit . . .   Price, figs 551, 552, 214.

page 146   'I extend my best wishes . . .'   Price, fig. 552, 214.

10   The Modernist Enemy

page 151   It was the era, as he said . . .   Speech opening the Great German Art Exhibition in 1937, quoted in Backes, 90–1; also, Domarus, vol.2, 911; Below, 168; Speer, *Inside* 44.

page 151   'Up to 1910 we displayed an . . .'   Picker, 146.

page 151   'In or about December . . .'   'Mrs Bennet and Mrs Brown' in Andrew McNeillie, ed., *Virginia Woolf Essays*, vol.3, 421.

page 152   'stands in inverse relation to the length . . .'   *Völkischer Beobachter*, 3 January 1921 in Jäckel/Kuhn, 286.

page 152   'the products of spiritual degenerates . . .'   *Mein Kampf*, 258, 262.

page 153   twenty in 1933 alone . . .   Paul Ortwin Rave, *Kunstdiktatur*, 24 ff; Brenner, 40; Barron, 9.

page 153   Yet, attesting to the muddle . . .   Marion-Andreas von Lüttichau, 'Entartete Kunst, Munich 1937: A Reconstruction' in Barron, 63; Andreas Hüneke, 'On the Trail of Missing Masterpieces' in Barron, 122.

page 153   Noted dealers in various cities . . .   Brenner, 77.

page 153   'Europe's last great artistic . . .'   Brenner, 74.

page 155   An entry in August 1924 . . .   Goebbels diaries, 29 August 1924.

page 155   His taste for the latter . . .   Hoffmann, *Hitler wie ich*, 149.

page 155   'The pictures have to go at once'   Speer, *Inside*, 27.

page 156   'We must not permit . . .'   Lüttichau, in Barron, 53.

page 156   The party, he said, faced . . .   Brenner, 82–3; Hinz, 10, 35; Rave, 44.

page 156   'So, today, they propose railway stations . . .'   Brenner, 83; also, Heiber, 224–5.

page 156   Hitler was suitably outraged . . .   Rave, 32; Annegrat Janda in Barron, 107, 116; Brenner, 255.

page 156   Schardt made his choices . . .   Rave, 33–4; Brenner, 71–2.

page 156   Still adamant, museum officials . . .   Rave, 40; Franz Roh, *'Entartete'* *Kunst*, 91–2.

page 158   He winced but said nothing.   Rave, 41.

page 158   'cleaning out all that rubbish'   Goebbels diaries, 15 December 1935.

page 158   'It is not the function of art . . .'   Baynes, 579.

page 158   'There really are men who . . .'   Baynes, 590.

page 158   'It is either impudent effrontery . . .'   Baynes, 589–90.

page 158   'Theirs is a small art . . .'   Baynes, 586.

page 158   'Just as in fashions one must . . .'   Baynes, 585–6.

page 158   '. . . Art was said to be "an . . .'   Baynes, 585.

page 158   'An art which cannot count . . .'   Baynes, 591–2.

page 159   'To every age, its own art'   Russell, 331.

page 160   '*Deutsch sein heißt klar sein*' . . .   Brenner, 84; Domarus, 910–11.

page 160   'another Gunpowder Plot . . .'   Malcolm Bull, 'Cézanne and the housemaid', *Times Literary Supplement*, 5 April 1996.

page 160   'Art is not art if it transgresses . . .'   Russell, 80.

page 160   In 1897 Berlin's National Gallery . . .   Barron, 15.

page 160   the director of the Tate said . . .   'The Tate celebrates its centenary', *Financial Times*, May 1997.

page 161   German museums were steadily . . .   Rave, 9–11.

page 161   Of nearly a thousand painters . . .   Hinz, 14; Rave, 11.

page 161   His speeches condemned not Jewish . . .   Baynes, 585.

page 161   He once explained . . .   Schroeder, 217.

page 161   'What is so remarkable'   Picker, 27 March 1942, 146.

page 161   'manufacturers of this nuisance'   Baynes, 578.

page 162   'In the name of the German people . . .'   Baynes, 590–1.

page 162   In delivering this speech . . .   Rave, 55–6.

page 162   So it was not until October . . .   Rave, 50; Janda in Barron, 107ff.

page 162   Goebbels feared being outflanked . . .   Backes, 73–4; Ralf Georg Reuth, *Goebbels*, 366–7.

page 163   By holding the exhibition in . . .   Backes, 73; Goebbels diaries, 19 and 30 June 1937.

page 163   'German degenerate art since 1910 . . .'   Hinz, 38.

page 163   Degenerate art was defined . . .   Barron, 19.

page 163   'five ignorant fanatics'   Hinz, 39.

page 163   'Opposition on all sides'   Goebbels diaries, 5 and 12 June 1937.

page 163   'In the face of all the animosity . . .'   Goebbels diaries, 24 July 1937.

page 163   Actually, the Führer wavered . . .   Goebbels diaries, 15 July 1937.

page 163   In a mere two weeks . . .   Barron, 45, 87; Rave, 63; list of confiscated works, 82–3.

page 163   The show opened on 19 July . . .   Stuttgart, *Bildzyklen* and Backes, 73 (730 works); Barron, 112 and Adam, 32 (more than 650); Rave, 67 (730).

page 163   '. . . The end of madness in German art . . .'   Brenner, 203; Domarus, 915.

page 165   Ensuring that no one could have . . .   Christoph Zuschlag, 'An "Educational Exhibition"' in Barron, 89.

page 165   One million people went . . .   Goebbels diaries, 1 September 1937.

page 165   Another million or so . . .   Zuschlag in Barron, 90.

page 165   'It became increasingly obvious . . .'   Peter Guenther, 'Three Days in Munich' in Barron, 38.

page 165   A Boston art critic . . .   Lynn Nicholas, *The Rape of Europa*, 7.

page 165   The Führer was enormously pleased . . .   Goebbels diaries, 1 August 1937.

page 165   a pamphlet with illustrations . . .   *Entartete Kunst: Ausstellungsführer;* Goebbels diaries, 1 August 1937.

page 166   'In this hour I affirm . . .'   Barron, 382; Domarus, 914.

page 166   Within the week he issued . . .   Führer's order of 27 July in Barron, 124.

page 166   'between the months of August . . .'   Hüneke, 'On the Trail of Missing Masterpieces', Barron,124; Lüttichau in Barron, 47.

page 166   By the time the confiscation committees . . .   Rave, 82–90; Hüneke in Barron, 124; Hinz, 39–40.

page 167   In the summer of 1938 Herbert Read . . .   Rave, 61–2.

page 167   A few weeks afterwards at the annual . . .   Karow, 221.

page 167   'Naturally it is not important . . .'   Baynes, 598.

page 167   'The result is devastating.'   Goebbels diaries, 14 January 1938.

page 168   'We hope to be able to earn . . .'   Goebbels diaries, 29 July 1938.

page 168   'was royally pleased to have . . .'   Picker, 12 April 1942, 222.

page 168   Göring grabbed . . .   Hüneke in Barron, 125; Jonathan Petropoulos, *Art as Politics*, 79.

page 168   Even though earning foreign . . .   Nicholas, 25.

page 168   paintings 'were being sold by the kilo . . .'   Goebbels diaries, 5 May 1944.

page 168   Much of the total residue . . .   Rave, 68; Roh, 53.

page 168   In his final report to Hitler . . .   Backes, 77.

page 168   'Degenerate art has brought us . . .'   Goebbels diaries, 4 November 1939.

page 168   Some sales and trades . . .   Petropoulos, 80.

11   The Failure of National Socialist Realism

page 169   'When we celebrated the laying . . .'   Hinz, 2.

page 169   'When people pass through . . .'   Baynes, 591.

page 171   The response was staggering . . .   Hinz, 9.

page 171   Of the many descriptions . . .   Hoffmann, *Hitler wie ich*, 143ff; Rave, 54f.

page 171   'The sculptures are all right . . .'   Goebbels diaries, 6 June 1937.

page 171   'These are grey.'   Toland, 415.

page 172   So disappointed and humiliated . . .   Goebbels diaries, 7 June 1937.

page 172   'These paintings demonstrate'   Hoffmann, *Hitler wie ich*, 143.

page 172   'But I don't like any sloppy . . .'   Hoffmann, 144.

page 172   Hoffmann made his choices . . .   Rave, 55.

page 172   'But . . . I knew Hitler's wishes . . .'   Hoffmann, *Hitler wie ich*, 144.

page 172   left Gerdy Troost 'in tears'   Goebbels diaries, 19 July 1937.

page 172   But his disillusionment was so great . . .   Dietrich, 190.

page 172   By the time of the following year's . . .   Baynes, 605.

page 172   'In the case of many pictures . . .'   Hinz, 10.

page 172   As for painters . . .   Baynes, 605.

page 172   His disappointment was such . . .   Picker, 147.

page 173   'Hitler, going the rounds . . .'   Dietrich, 190–1.

page 173   'Day of German Art'   Robert S. Wistrich, *Weekend in Munich*, 70ff; *Good Morning Mr Hitler!* (documentary film).

page 173   It was held every summer . . .   Hinz, 1–2; Backes, 82.

page 173   and every year he bought . . .   Backes, 82; *Architecture of Doom* (documentary film).

page 173   He usually ignored paintings glorifying . . .   Rolf Bothe and Thomas Föhl, *Aufstieg und Fall der Moderne*, 406–7; Speer, *Spandau*, 400.

page 174   'He did not really care for . . .'   Schroeder, 217.

page 174   'I am convinced that . . .'   'Art and Politics' in *Liberty, Art, Nationhood*, 44.

page 174   'I have no doubt you will be moved . . .'   Domarus, vol.2, 1127.

page 174   'You cannot manufacture an artist'   Goebbels diaries, 16 June 1936.

page 174   'It is always easier . . .'   Brenner, 42.

page 176   'The National Socialist state must . . .'   Brenner, 83.

page 176   Roughly eighty per cent . . .   Bothe and Föhl, 312.

page 176   At the first exhibition . . .   Hinz, 17.

page 177   'clean out the Munich crowd'   Goebbels diaries, 25 August 1943.

page 177   'Munich-school kitsch'   Goebbels diaries, 21 September 1943.

page 177   'By standing foursquare . . .'   Picker, 479f.

page 177   These figures, a German scholar . . .   Backes, 84.

page 178   In 1938 alone there were . . .   Taylor and van der Will, 12.

page 178   Arno Breker, who happened to attend . . .   Goebbels diaries, 20, 23, 25 February 1943; 18, 21 March 1943.

page 178   'I remembered the dinner . . .'   Speer, *Spandau*, 312.

page 178   *liberalistische Schweinerei*   Thomas, 217.

page 179   Most works were purchased by state . . .   Angele Schönberger, *Die neue Reichskanzlei*, 43.

page 179   'This nation has works . . .'   'Art and Politics' in *Liberty, Art, Nationhood*, 48.

page 180   six landscapes . . .   Reproductions in *Die Kunst im Dritten Reich*, July 1939, 219ff.

page 180   Of the 5000 or so . . .   S. Lane Faison, Consolidated Interrogation Report No.4, 78.

page 180   And these, a German scholar . . .   Backes, 92.

page 180   When the art purges . . .   Rave, 79–90.

page 181   'ever greater and more significant'   Picker, 30 May 1942, 341.

page 183   'The iconography was always . . .'   Adam, 188.

page 184   'Thorak is our strongest . . .'   Goebbels diaries, 11 February 1937.

page 185   'among the most beautiful . . .'   Backes, 97.

page 185   'The Führer highly praises . . .'   Goebbels diaries, 23 February 1940.

page 185   Breker's starting point was . . .   Volker G. Probst, *Der Bildhauer Arno Breker*, 28f, 33.

page 185   'Each muscle, each tendon . . .'   Adam, 179.

12   The Art Collector

page 187   He explained, as Posse recorded . . .   Posse diaries, entry of 21 June 1939.

page 187   Six days after this meeting . . .   Text in Faison, Consolidated Interrogation Report No.4, attachment 1; reproduction of text in Günther Haase, *Kunstraub und Kunstschutz*; also, Posse diaries, 28 June 1939.

page 189   'He never stopped expressing . . .'   Schroeder, 217.

page 189   So deeply, in fact, did he . . .   Tutaev, 12.

page 189   As early as 1919 Posse . . .   Birgit Schwarz, 'Hans Posse, Hitlers Sonderbeauftragter für Linz' in *Frankfurter Allgemeine*, 19 May 2000; Anja Heuss, *Kunst- und Kulturgutraub*, 47–9.

page 190   He promptly closed the museum's . . .   Ruth and Max Seydewitz, *Das Dresdener Galeriebuch*, 109.

page 190   In May 1933 he applied . . .   NSDAP Zentralkartei-Karte, Federal Archive, Berlin.

page 191   'Through him, my husband . . .'   Ernst Kubin, *Sonderauftrag Linz*, 17.

page 191   he was Posse's preferred agent . . .   Faison, 47.

page 192   Charged with 'cosmopolitan . . .'   Faison, DIR No.12, Hermann Voss.

page 192   a memorandum was found . . .   Memorandum of 17 February 1943 to Lammers in Faison, Attachment 83.

page 192   'a particularly vicious Nazi'   James S. Plaut, 'Hitler's Capital', *Atlantic Monthly*, October 1946.

page 193   'He's even worse than . . .'   Faison, DIR No.12, Hermann Voss.

page 193   Voss could not forbear . . .   Faison, attachment 19.

page 193   When interrogated by American . . .   Faison, CIR, 18; Faison, Detailed Report No.12; Hermann Voss, 10.

page 193   Not until April 1943 . . .   'Kunstwerke für die neue Galerie in Linz' in *Kunst dem Volk*, Sonderheft zum 20 April 1943.

page 194   With Hoffmann as his agent . . .   Werner Maser, *Adolf Hitler*, 107; *Monologe*, September 1942, 387.

page 194   'He . . . takes great pleasure . . .'   Goebbels diaries, 5 August 1940.

page 194   Many hung in his . . .   Hoffmann, *Hitler wie ich ihn,*152, 169; Friedelind Wagner, 128; Backes, 90; Faison, 66.

page 195   'The walls around the room . . .'   Dietrich, 215.

page 195   In the dining room of . . .   Backes, 90; Hoffmann, *Hitler was My Friend*, 198.

page 195   In the reception room . . .   Schönberger, 142.

page 196   'The Führer is a great admirer . . .'   Goebbels diaries, 25 June 1943.

page 196   'Yesterday morning at the National . . .'   Goebbels diaries, 14 January 1929.

page 196   Even Troost and Rosenberg . . .   Rosenberg, *Memoirs*, 249, 250.

page 196   'Hitler went on about his favourite . . .'   Speer, *Inside*, 179.

page 197   This is the saga of . . .   *Financial Times*, 20 November 1999.

page 197   'As we entered we almost . . .'   William L. Shirer, *Berlin Diary*, 189.

page 197   the Gestapo went on to seize some 10,000 . . .   Faison, attachment 72; Kubin, 21.

page 198   After a further visit in October . . .   Faison, CIR No.4, 15 December 1945, attachment 72.

page 198   'Vienna already has enough works . . .'   Letter of 16 May 1940 in Faison, attachment 4.

page 198   Through Haberstock, Posse also obtained . . .   Bredius, *Rembrandt Paintings, Self-portrait*, No.44; *Portrait of Hendrickje Stoffels*, No.115.

page 199   They had been put up . . .   Faison, attachment 74; Kubin, 53.

page 199   'plundering expeditions that are reducing . . .'   Faison, 76.

page 199   Hitler's contempt went so far . . .   David Roxan and Ken Wanstall, *The Jackdaw of Linz*, 37.

page 200   One of his most important bags . . .   Faison, attachment 68.

page 200   'nine panels of the Hohenfurth . . .'   Faison, attachment 70.

page 200   Nonetheless a catalogue . . .   Brenner, 157.

page 200   These gave him such pleasure . . .   Faison, 6.

page 200   'Meeting with the Führer . . .'   diary entry of 9 April 1940.

page 200   'The acquisition of riches . . .'   Gibbon, vol.3, 136.

page 201   Pieter de Boer . . .   Nicholas, 108.

page 201   Nathan Katz . . .   Nicholas, 109.

page 201   'the most elaborate purchasing expedition . . .'   Faison, Art Looting Investigation Unit, Detailed Interrogation Report No.12, 15 September 1945: Hermann Voss, 21.

page 202   'no reason to forgo the enormous profits . . .'   Nicholas, 101.

page 202   'the big Jewish art dealers'   telegram, 7 August 1940 in Faison, attachment 10a.

page 202   'a very beautiful Momper . . .'   Kubin, 39.

page 202   'I took the best . . .'   Faison, attachment 59a.

page 202   These included Brueghel's *Carrying* . . .   Faison, CIR No.4, attachment 58, part I.

page 202   'Buy! Buy!'   Kubin, 60.

page 202   From his old crony Hoffmann . . .   Faison, CIR, No.44.

page 202   Another source was . . .   Faison, 44.

page 203   obtained no fewer than 270 paintings . . .   Faison, 49.

page 203   She was admonished . . .   Faison, attachment 52.

page 203   One unwilling donor . . .   Faison, CIR, attachment 58, part II.

page 203   Franz Koenigs's collection of Old Master drawings . . .   Nicholas, 110; Faison, attachment 60.

page 203   Posse took 527 . . .   Nicolas, 111; Faison, 63 and attachment 60.

page 203   The biggest prize . . .   Nicholas, 113.

page 203   The Dutch portion . . .   Faison, attachment 35b.

page 204   In July 1940, one year after . . .   Faison, attachment 73.

page 204   In a striking resurrection . . .   Faison, attachment 2.

page 205   To forestall any transfer . . .   quoted in Kubin, 26.

page 205   Hitler gave Rosenberg . . .   Faison, attachment 6.

page 205   'Truckload after truckload . . .'   Nicholas, 133.

page 206   In toto the Einsatzstab . . .   Kubin, 36; Roxan and Wanstall, 56–7, 175.

page 206   A partial list of his acquisitions . . .   Faison, attachment 57.

page 206   Haberstock also procured Watteau's . . .   Faison, supplement, 8; attachments 74 and 76.

page 206   Out of a total of 320 works . . .   Haase, 51.

page 206   Through Hildebrandt Gurlitt . . .   Faison, Supplement, 9.

page 207   fifty-three masterpieces for Linz . . .   Faison, attachment 56 (parts I and II).

page 207   A serendipitous purchase . . .   Edward Craig, *Gordon Craig*, 346.

page 207   The archive included . . .   L. M. Newman, *Gordon Craig Archives*, 60.

page 207   A significant acquisition . . .   Faison, CIR No.4, 29; Nicholas, 172; Hector Feliciano, *The Lost Museum*, 96.

page 207   To drive the point home . . .   Faison, attachment 19.

page 208   In all, the Linz museum acquired . . .   Heuss, 63–4.

page 209   Two weeks after that Foreign Minister . . .   Mario Ursino, ed., *L'arte e il Nazismo*, 20.

page 209   A month later, when Hitler . . .   Tutaev, 22.

page 210   '. . . I was in Rome (twice) . . .'   Letter of 23 March 1941 in Faison, attachment 67.

page 210   In no time Posse and Prince Philipp . . .   Faison, attachment 65.

page 210   'I have little faith . . .'   Hugh Gibson, ed., *The Ciano Diaries*, 374.

page 210   'Where art is concerned . . .'   Hoffmann, *Hitler Was My Friend*, 88.

page 211   Following lunch with Ciano . . .   Giordano Bruno Guerri, ed., *Diario*, 274.

page 211   Reporting to Hitler in March 1941 . . .   Posse to Bormann, 23 March 1942 in Faison CIR No.4, attachment 67.

page 212   The Guttmann collection   Faison, 74.

page 212   He was a ruthless despoiler . . .   Faison, 74.

page 212   On first seeing the holdings . . .   Faison, CIR, 20.

page 212   His main victims were . . .   Faison, CIR, 20.

page 214   'Not by the widest stretch . . .'   James S. Plaut, 'Hitler's Capital' in *Atlantic Monthly*, October 1946.

page 215   In the chaos just before . . .   Faison, CIR, 23.

page 216   The highest accession number . . .   Faison, CIR, 18.

page 216   'Summary of deposits . . .'   Kubin, 68.

page 216   Obviously this inventory also excluded . . .   Kubin, 30.

page 216   Only one painting was . . .   Heuss, 68.

page 217   Moreover, the claim . . .   Faison, CIR No.4, 26.

page 217   'Hitler had spent all his money . . .'   Speer, *Spandau*, 105.

page 217   The most striking feature . . .   Faison, 70; Kubin 68.

page 218   'Anyone who wants to study . . .'   Picker, 12 April 1942, 221.

page 218   '. . . We must once again . . .'   Faison, CIR, attachment 46.

page 219   'The Linz museum was one . . .'   Schroeder, 218.

page 219   'admiring, even if he did not . . .'   Bianchi Bandinelli, 183.

13 Hitler's Wagner or Wagner's Hitler?

page 223   In that first week of February . . .   Johanna Motloch to Alfred Roller, 5 February 1908; Roller to Motloch, 6 February 1908, F 19/19, Institut für Zeitgeschichte, Munich.

page 223   The young man was overjoyed . . .   Alfred E. Frauenfeld, *Der Weg zur Bühne*, 290; also, Toland, 31, 929; Heiber, 43.

page 224   'Without a recommendation . . .'   *Monologe*, 15–16 January 1942, 200.

page 224   When Winifred Wagner decided in 1933 . . .   Winifred Wagner, television interview with Hans Jürgen Syberberg; Manfred Wagner, *Alfred Roller in seiner Zeit*, 308.

page 224   'I was captivated at once'   *Mein Kampf*, 17.

page 224   'Tomorrow I am going . . .'   Postcard, 7 May 1906, Jäckel/Kuhn, 44; reproduction in Kubizek, facing 193.

page 225   'The interior of the edifice . . .'   Postcard, 7 May 1906, Jäckel/Kuhn, 44; reproduction in Kubizek, facing 193.

page 225   He sang in a church choir . . .   Percy E. Schramm, *Hitler*, 68.

page 225   On leaving school . . .   '*Der Klavierlehrer des Führers*', undated document in Hauptarchiv der NSDAP, Reel 1, folder 17a; other spellings of the name include Prewatsky (document of 8 December 1938 in Hauptarchiv der NSDAP, Reel 1, folder 17a); Prewratzky (Kubizek); Prevratski (Jetzinger).

page 225   He soon quit . . .   Bradley F. Smith, 105.

page 225   However, his sister Paula . . .   Interview, 3.

page 225   In later years . . .   Winifred Wagner interview with David Irving, 13 March 1971, ZS 2242, Institut für Zeitgeschichte, Munich.

page 225   Kubizek's 1954 book . . .   Kubizek, 251–2.

page 225   The assertion that Hitler read Wagner's prose . . .   Jetzinger, 120.

page 226   'transported into that extraordinary . . .'   Kubizek, 143.

page 226   'Eventually there was produced . . .'   Kubizek, 'Reminiscences', 44, 46.

page 226   At that time Kubizek said . . .   Hauptarchiv der NSDAP, Notizen für Kartei, dated 8 December 1938; 'Bericht über meinen Besuch bei Herrn Kubizek', undated, Reel 1, folder 17a.

page 226   'Mobile Reichs Orchestra'   Kubizek, 203ff; 'Reminiscences', 34–9.

page 226   By far the best known . . .   Kubizek, 98–101.

page 227   is a rare case . . .   Kubizek, 'Reminiscenses', 39; letter to Jetzinger, 19 June 1949.

page 227   'Listening to this blessed music . . .'   Speer, *Spandau*, 88.

page 227   'I believe it was God's will . . .'   Shirer, *Rise and Fall*, 349.

page 227   Wilhelm Furtwängler learned this . . .   Curt Riess, *Furtwängler*, 163–4.

page 228   'He would then sit back . . .' Schroeder, 130.

page 228   'Before long . . .'   Speer, *Inside*, 91.

page 228   Unlike the others, however . . .   David B. Dennis, *Beethoven in German Politics*, *passim*.

page 228   an 'artistic Führer'   Dennis, 150.

page 228   And played he was . . .   Dennis, 161–2, 236–7.

page 228   His works, above all . . .   Dennis, 162–3, 167–9.

page 230   Brahms he did not like . . .   Goebbels diaries, 27 February 1940.

page 230   'Well, Furtwängler is *such* . . .'   Ziegler, 71–2.

page 230   The story that Hitler begged money . . .   Schramm, 59; Schramm in *Der Spiegel*, 6/1964, 49; Kurt Wilhelm, *Richard Strauss*, 102; Maser, 101.

page 230   Even so, when once attending . . .   Below, 22.

page 230   According to Heinrich Hoffmann . . .   Hoffmann, *Hitler wie ich ihn*, 162.

page 230   Hoffmann did not so much as mention . . .   Hoffmann, *Hitler was my Friend*, 189–90.

page 230   Even after becoming chancellor . . .   Speer, *Inside*, 130.

page 232   'I do not really like . . .'   Goebbels diaries, 20 November 1944.

page 232   'We should promote him . . .'   Goebbels diaries, 7 June 1937.

page 232   Even then he did not take . . .   Levi, 217.

page 232   Speculation has ranged . . .   Picker, 336; Brian Gilliam, *Musical Quarterly*, 78, 1994.

page 232   But suddenly in 1940 . . .   Goebbels diaries, 23 January, 27 February, 6 April 1940.

page 232   'He told me . . .'   Goebbels diaries, 23 January 1940.

page 232   By 1942 he placed Bruckner . . .   Goebbels diaries, 20 August 1942.

page 232   '[Those are] pure popular melodies . . .'   *Monologe*, 13–14 January 1942, 198.

page 233   'He wants to establish . . .'   Goebbels diaries, 13 March 1941.

page 233   He even designed a monument . . .   Price, figs 721, 722.

page 233   he singled out *The Merry Widow* . . .   'Warum sind wir Antisemiten?' 31 August 1920; 'Positiver Antisemitimus', 4 November 1922 in Jäckel/Kuhn, 197, 718.

page 233   He never missed a new production . . .   Speer, *Inside*, 130.

page 234   Eventually Hitler came to revere . . .   Stefan Frey, *Franz Lehár oder das schlechte Gewissen der leichten Musik*, 138; Wulf, *Musik*, 62.

page 234   So thrilled was he . . .   Speer, *Spandau*, 106; Frey, 142.

page 234   Making a tremendous to-do . . .   Speer, *Spandau*, 59.

page 234   'He showed an astonishing array . . .'   Wilhelm, 242.

page 234   While confirming the story . . .   Hotter, letter of 25 September 1996.

page 234   'could not stop raving . . .'   Lieslotte Schmidt, letter of 27 July 1938.

page 234   In the same vein . . .   Michael Karbaum, *Studien zur Geschichte der Bayreuther Festspiele*, part 2, 111–12.

page 235   'In all my life . . .'   Schirach, 28.

page 235   'showed sheet after sheet . . .'   Speer, *Spandau*, 105.

page 235   Despite the poverty of his Vienna years . . .   *Monologe*, 22–3 February 1942, 294; Fest, 520, 712.

page 235   he knew *Die Meistersinger* . . .   Dietrich, 151.

page 235   'In Bayreuth, whenever the citadel . . .'   Fest, *Hitler: Eine Biographie*, 712.

page 235   'Well, *Tristan* was his greatest . . .'   *Monologe*, 24–5 January 1942, 224.

page 235   According to Christa Schroeder . . .   Schroeder, 189.

page 235   'dreamed of *Tristan*'   Letter of 10 January 1924 to Vogel, Jäckel/Kuhn, 1060.

page 235   'He is overjoyed at each . . .'   Liselotte Schmidt, 27 July 1938.

page 235   At some point in the 1930s . . .   Ziegler, 176.

page 236   'Out of *Parsifal* I shall . . .'   Frank, 213.

page 236   After the war he declared . . .   Goebbels diaries, 22 November 1941.

page 236   Managers were informed that . . .   Thomas Mathieu, *Kunstauffassungen und Kulturpolitik*, 79–80.

page 236   'When I hear Wagner it seems . . .'   *Monologe*, 25–26 January 1942, 234.

page 237   'Wagner's musical language sounded . . .'   Schroeder, 189–90.

page 237   'exaltation and liberation from all . . .'   'Warum sind wir Antisemiten?' 31 August 1920 in Jäckel/Kuhn, 197.

page 237   'He was familiar with . . .'   Schirach, 26ff; Speer, *Spandau*, 102.

page 237   He was insistent that . . .   Ziegler, 64.

page 237   Although a drawing of Siegfried . . .   Price, figs 539–42, 212.

page 237   This interest in stage design . . .   Speer, *Inside*, 128.

page 239   'At the chancellery Hitler . . .'   Speer, *Spandau*, 103; Ziegler, op.cit., 70.

page 239   His setting for the second act . . .   *Die Kunst im Dritten Reich*, February 1939.

page 239   went into ecstasies . . .   Speer, *Spandau*, 103.

page 240   'I must be frank to say . . .'   Ziegler, 125.

page 240   'The Führer talks to me . . .'   Goebbels diaries 27 July 1937; Backes 44.

page 240   'When I stood at Wagner's grave . . .'   Jäckel/Kuhn, 1210.

page 240   'Of all German creative figures . . .'   Scholdt, 291.

page 241   '*stärkstes, bestimmendes Erlebnis*'   Erika Mann, 7.

page 241   At one point he insisted that . . .   Letter of 14 September 1911 to Julius Bab, in Erika Mann, 30; 'Richard Wagner und *Der Ring des Nibelungen*', in Erika Mann, 131.

page 241   'I can write about him today . . .'   Letter of 18 February 1942 to Agnes Meyer, Erika Mann, 161.

page 242 'Wagnerian, albeit in a perverted way . . .'   *Bruder Hitler* in *Thomas Mann Essays*, Band 4, 307.

page 242 'elements of a frighteningly Hitleresque . . .'   entry of 13 October in *Thomas Mann: Diaries 1918–1939*.

page 242 *'furchtbare Hitlerei'*   diary entry of 4 September 1937; Scholdt, 293.

page 243 'I find an element of Nazism . . .'   *Common Sense*, January 1940.

page 243 'There is, in Wagner's bragging . . .'   Letter to Emil Preetorius, 6 December 1949, Erika Mann, 167ff.

page 243 'a splendid work, a festival drama . . .'   Letter of 25 August 1951 to Friedrich Schramm in Erika Mann, 181–2.

page 243 'succumbed to the music . . .'   Fest, *Hitler,* 22.

page 243 'Hitler himself in fact later . . .'   Fest, *Hitler,* 49.

page 244 'The style of public ceremonies . . .'   Fest, *Hitler,* 50.

page 244 'For the Master of Bayreuth . . .'   Fest, *Hitler,* 56.

page 244 It was 'Wagner's Hitler'   Joachim Köhler, *Wagners Hitler.*

page 244 In a speech in 1923 . . .   Speech of 14 October 1923, Jäckel/Kuhn, 1032, 1034.

page 246 But Kubizek himself contradicted . . .   Kubizek, *Adolf Hitler,* 101.

14 'Führer of the Bayreuth Republic'

page 247 To attend the Festival . . .   Letter of 5 May 1924 in Jäckel/Kuhn, 1233; Kubizek letter to Hitler, 21 July 1939 in Heiber, 72.

page 247 'as the answer to his doubts . . .'   Fest, *Hitler,* 259.

page 247 On his arrival the Wagners . . .   Ebermayer, *Magisches Bayreuth,*174.

page 247 twenty years later he was still . . .   *Monologe,* 24–5 January 1942, 224.

page 248 He promised that if he ever . . .   Ebermayer, *Magisches,* 174.

page 248 According to a story . . .   Friedelind Wagner and Page Cooper, *Heritage of Fire,* 16–17.

page 248 Nothing could have given him . . .   Letter of 5 May 1924 in Jäckel/Kuhn, 1231–3.

page 248 'It was not just the others . . .'   *Monologe,* 24–5 January 1942, 224.

page 249 'I did not really want to go . . .'   *Monologe,* 28 February–1 March 1942, 307f.

page 249 'It was a sunny time . . .'   *Monologe,* 3–4 February 1942, 259.

page 249 'culturally pre-eminent little town . . .'   Speer, *Spandau,* 104.

page 249 'Then for years . . .'   *Monologe,* 28 February–1 March 1942, 308.

page 250 Hitler was entirely untroubled . . .   Goebbels diaries, 30 May 1942.

page 250 it 'radiates life'   *Monologe,* 17 February 1942, 281.

page 250 'Sometimes Hitler's car . . .'   Friedelind Wagner, 31.

page 250 'We used the familiar . . .'   *Monologe,* 24–5 January 1941, 225.

page 250 'With no other family . . .'   Below, 23.

page 250 Hitler revelled in his role . . .   Below, 23; Dietrich, 151; Schroeder, 276; Hoffmann, *Hitler wie ich,* 139–40.

page 251 'On these festival days . . .'   Speer, *Inside,* 149–50.

page 251 'The ten Bayreuth days . . .'   *Monologe,* 24–5 January 1942, 225.

page 252 'He did not so much speak . . .'   Heiber, *Die Rückseite,* 42–3.

page 252 Hitler, she said, could . . .   Friedelind Wagner, 101–2.

page 252 'My dear Wini . . .'   Hitler, *Reden,* Band II, 587.

page 252 'These have been very sad days . . .'   Wolfgang Wagner, ed., *Das Festspielbuch 1997,* 24.

page 253 'For weeks I have been bogged . . .'   Wolfgang Wagner, 24.

page 253   Whatever her feelings . . .   Hoffmann, *Hitler wie ich*, 139; Friedelind Wagner, 70–1.

page 253   The relationship cooled . . .   Ebermayer, *Magisches*, 216–17.

page 253   'destroyed and exterminated'   Friedelind Wagner, 224.

page 253   notations in her diary . . .   Letters of 14 January and 29 February 1940; diary entries of 9, 10, 11 February 1940 in Wolfgang Wagner, *Bayreuther Festspiele 1997*, 25–6.

page 253   'The fat, little Wagner . . .'   Goebbels diaries, 4 May 1940; also, 10 May 1940.

page 255   high treason   Goebbels diaries, 12 May 1940.

page 255   'The Führer has told Wieland . . .'   Goebbels diaries, 5 May 1940.

page 255   'He is deeply shaken by . . .'   Goebbels diaries, 6 June 1940.

page 255   He showered him with favours . . .   Geoffrey Skelton, *Wieland Wagner*, 46; Berndt Wessling, *Wieland Wagner*, 114.

page 255   'After coming to power . . .'   Breker, *Paris*, 123.

page 256   Hitler placed the institution . . .   Drewniak, 287.

page 256   At Winifred Wagner's instigation . . .   Hans Jürgen Syberberg in *Zeit Magazin*, 30 April 1976; Köhler, 422.

page 256   Hitler's passion for Wagner . . .   Ziegler, 132.

page 256   'Most leading National Socialist figures . . .'   Karbaum, 2/115.

page 256   'In reality leading party officials . . .'   Karbaum, 2/112–13; Ebermayer, *Magisches*, 188.

page 257   In 1930 he had offered . . .   Karbaum, 2/111.

page 257   'smoke out that international . . .'   Ebermayer, *Magisches*, 197.

page 257   A frightened Winifred . . .   Ebermayer, *Magisches*, 197.

page 257   He said he could best . . .   Ebermayer, *Magisches*, 196–8; Karbaum, 2/77–8.

page 257   He had once maintained he could imagine . . .   *Monologe*, 20–1 February 1942, 287–8.

page 258   He came to detest Winifred . . .   Goebbels diaries 23 October 1937; also, 26 July 1937; 26 July 1938.

page 258   'With a woman in charge . . .'   Goebbels diaries, 3 November 1937.

page 258   '. . . You know that nothing happens . . .'   Letter of 9 June 1935, Richard Strauss Archive, Garmisch.

page 259   'Hitler never interfered . . .'   Undated memorandum, supplementing oral testimony given on 31 August 1945, Richard Wagner Museum.

page 259   'The Führer told my dad . . .'   Letter of 16 December 1933 from Franz Strauss to Daniela Thode, in Karbaum, 2/96.

page 259   According to Friedelind Wagner . . .   Friedelind Wagner, 143, 144.

page 260   But while he more or less imposed . . .   Liselotte Schmidt, 8 October 1937.

page 261   'she pretended not to know . . .'   Speer, *Spandau*, 103.

page 261   'Hitler himself never expressed . . .'   Karbaum, 2/112.

page 261   After enduring one act . . .   Hoffmann, *Hitler wie ich*, 139–40.

page 262   'Führer of the Bayreuth Republic'   Scholdt, 275.

page 262   'I consider it a particular joy . . .'   *Monologe*, 24–5 January 1942, 225.

page 263   So enamoured was Hitler . . .   Schroeder, 190.

page 263   The final and most curious . . .   Schroeder, 130.

15   The Rape of Euterpe

page 267   'the result is not . . .'   Speech of 2 November 1922 in Jäckel/Kuhn, 718.

page 267   'cultural poisoners . . .'   Speech of 27 November 1927 in Weimar, in Hitler, *Reden*, 560.

page 267 'a single German military march . . .' Speech of 26 January 1928 in Munich, in Hitler, *Reden*, 654.

page 269 Others who were removed . . . Prieberg, *Musik*, 44–5; Levi, 171; Rothkalb, 15; Geissmar, 66ff.

page 269 Racially or politically unacceptable . . . Juan Allende-Blin, ed., *Musiktradition im Exil*, 24; Levi, 44–5.

page 269 'It really is a shame . . .' *Monologe*, 19–20 February 1942, 285.

page 270 'the most appalling kitsch' 'Warum sind wir Antisemiten?' in Jäckel/Kuhn, 197.

page 270 'the complete judification of music' Speech on 3 May 1921, 'Erzberger und Genossen' in Jäckel/Kuhn, 374.

page 270 unable to accomplish anything original . . . 'Warum sind wir Antisemiten?' in Jäckel/Kuhn, 189.

page 270 The public did not want . . . Speech of 26 January 1928 in Munich in Hitler, *Reden*, 652–4.

page 271 The scope for political intervention . . . Levi, 175, 195; Michael Meyer, *The Politics of Music,* 13.

page 272 Of 110 players . . . Prieberg, *Musik*, 74.

page 272 of the entire staff of the Berlin . . . Rathkolb, 90.

page 272 Hitler could therefore pursue . . . Prieberg, *Musik*, 19, 264–72; Levi, 35.

page 272 Occasionally he laid down the law . . . Levi, 35; Karow, 214; Heiber, op.cit., 207.

page 273 'We do not intend to tell a conductor . . .' Heiber, ed., *Goebbels-Reden*, 227–8.

page 273 An investigation by Rosenberg's office . . . Frey, 138; Wulf, 360, 437f.

page 274 'I forbid that this should come . . .' Goebbels diaries, 5 June 1938.

page 274 Also troublesome were . . . Heiber, *Die Rückseite*, 258; Goebbels diaries, 26 June 1942.

page 274 'Only a person lacking respect . . .' Drewniak, 284.

page 275 'It is a great Mozart *revue*' Goebbels diaries, 22 November 1941; also, 22 March 1943.

page 275 'This belongs . . .' Goebbels diaries, 22 March 1943.

page 275 'They arise from a primitive . . .' Heiber, *Die Rückseite,* 258.

page 275 Foreign policy considerations . . . Prieberg, *Musik*, 372–4.

page 275 'The Finns ask us to . . .' Goebbels diaries, 12 March 1942.

page 276 Under the circumstances . . . Levi, 218.

page 276 Several months later a list . . . Michael Walter, *Hitler in der Oper*, 232–3.

page 276 That was followed by a blacklist . . . Rathkolb, 25ff.

page 276 In reality the show was less . . . Levi, 96.

16 The Music Patron

page 277 In 1933 alone, fifty-eight works . . . Levi, 256.

page 277 by 1935 the Führer . . . Kater, *The Twisted Muse*, 13.

page 277 Among the more notable . . . Prieberg, *Musik*, 174; Heister-Klein, 120–1.

page 277 Three years later Hitler . . . Goebbels diaries, 17 April 1937; Prieberg, *Musik*, 236.

page 277 The occasion was . . . Goebbels diaries, 2 May 1937.

page 277 But a choral work . . . Goebbels diaries, 27 April 1944; 4 May 1944.

page 278 'The Führer does not like . . .' Goebbels diaries, 26 July 1937; Speer, *Spandau*, 88.

page 278   'Music as an absolute art . . .'   Walter, 155–7.

page 280   Verdi replaced him . . .   Levi, 192.

page 280   As time passed . . .   Walter, 233; Levi, 216ff.

page 280   'An opera house is . . .'   Speer, *Spandau*, 92.

page 281   the drawings show that he was . . .   Kubizek, sketches between 126 and 127.

page 281   '. . . I would enter . . .'   *Monologe*, 29 October 1941, 115.

page 282   Edwin Sachs's classic . . .   Joachimsthaler, *Adolf Hitler*, 263.

page 282   he was familiar with . . .   Speer, *Inside* and *Spandau*, *passim*; Dietrich, 174; Schroeder, 218–19.

page 282   'The theatre there . . .'   Ziegler, 89.

page 282   Similarly, on once encountering . . .   Percy Schramm, *Hitler: The Man and the Military*, 59.

page 282   When Hugh Trevor-Roper . . .   Hugh Trevor-Roper, *The Last Days of Hitler*, 104.

page 282   'a maniacal passion'   Speer, *Spandau*, 92, 95; Goebbels diaries, 3 February 1939.

page 282   'various theatre construction plans . . .'   Goebbels diaries, 3 February 1939.

page 283   'Big enough for a mass public . . .'   Goebbels diaries, 6 December 1936.

page 283   The funds Hitler was prepared . . .   Backes, 184–5.

page 283   opera houses 'must also be . . .'   Backes, 181; Speer, *Spandau*, 95.

page 283   They had been proved wrong . . .   Speer, *Spandau*, 95.

page 284   'the best and most beautiful imaginable'   Goebbels diaries, 31 August 1940.

page 285   The very first project . . .   Goebbels diaries, 19 August 1935; Backes, 184.

page 285   Although he sketched rough plans . . .   Ziegler, 188; Backes, 184.

page 285   'Examined plans for new Munich . . .'   Goebbels diaries, 8 March 1937.

page 286   'a gift of the Führer'   Joachim Petsch, *Baukunst und Stadtplannung im Dritten Reich*, 119.

page 286   'The bombing of an opera house . . .'   Speer, *Spandau*, 104.

page 287   '. . . the theatre is not merely . . .'   Goebbels diaries, 4 October 1942.

page 287   'fought tooth and nail'   Goebbels diaries, 20 October 1943.

page 287   However, Goebbels had to record . . .   Goebbels diaries, 27 October 1943.

page 287   He undoubtedly had an excellent ear . . .   *Monologe*, 19–20 February 1942, 285; Speer, *Spandau*, 104.

page 288   He also watched over . . .   Goebbels diaries, 30 May 1942.

page 288   'We'll probably have to get him . . .'   Goebbels diaries, 30 May 1942.

17   Conductors and Composers

page 289   Instead of an exchange . . .   Prieberg, *Trial of Strength*, 32.

page 289   Furtwängler found himself under pressure . . .   Prieberg, *Trial*, 106.

page 289   'If the battle against Jews . . .'   Wulf, *Musik*, 86–7.

page 290   'norms of the state'   Wulf, *Musik*, 88–9.

page 290   a politically compliant conductor . . .   Thomas, 124–30; Prieberg, *Trial*, 225.

page 290   The conductor's views . . .   Prieberg, *Trial*, 100f.

page 290   Furtwängler set down a list . . .   Prieberg, *Trial*, 106.

page 290   'shouted at each other . . .'   Berta Geissmar, *The Baton and the Jackboot*, 103.

page 291   Prior to the meeting . . .   Levi, 113; Kater, *Composers of the Nazi Era*, 38.

page 291   'The Führer is furious . . .'   Prieberg, *Musik*, 393f.

page 292   The two agreed on a . . .   Prieberg, *Trial*, 172–3.

page 292   Even Berta Geissmar . . .   Geissmar, 158.

page 292   'I feel despondent . . .'   Ebermayer, *Denn heute gehört uns Deutschland*, 505.

page 292   'A great moral success . . .'   Goebbels diaries, 2 March 1935.

page 293   Not until April did Hitler . . .   Wiedemann, 206–7.

page 293   'He is now entirely on our side . . .'   Goebbels diaries, 11 December 1936; also, 27 July 1936.

page 293   And being in line . . .   Prieberg, *Trial*, 210.

page 293   'He is one of the . . .'   Wulf, *Musik*, 86.

page 293   'be booted out'   Lieselotte Schmidt, 8 October 1937.

page 293   He had wanted to use Bayreuth . . .   Prieberg, *Trial*, 221.

page 293   To this, Hitler responded . . .   Lieselotte Schmidt, 25 November 1937.

page 294   'the clockwork regularity . . .'   Prieberg, *Trial*, 225.

page 294   'to avoid even the shadow . . .'   Prieberg, *Trial*, 230.

page 294   'We can use him . . .'   Goebbels diaries, 9 January 1940.

page 294   'He is very willing . . .'   Goebbels diaries, 5 October 1940.

page 294   'Once again he has done . . .'   Goebbels diaries, 22 November 1941.

page 294   'We can certainly use him . . .'   Goebbels diaries, 9 January 1940.

page 294   Hitler was 'particularly pleased . . .'   Goebbels diaries, 21 March 1940.

page 295   'He has become an out-and-out . . .'   Goebbels diaries, 20 June 1940.

page 295   'practically bursting with . . .'   Goebbels diaries, 28 February 1942.

page 295   'I am pleased that I succeeded . . .'   Goebbels diaries, 28 November 1941.

page 296   'would never be forgotten . . .'   Goebbels diaries, 25 January 1944.

page 296   'The Führer has the highest . . .'   Goebbels diaries, 4 March 1944.

page 296   'Czechoslovakia was not actually . . .'   Berlin Denazification Board for Artists: Second day of hearing of the case of Wilhelm Furtwängler, 17 December 1946, 103–4.

page 296   He gave him and his artists . . .   Goebbels diaries, 23 September 1943; Rathkolb, 108–12.

page 296   Again the answer . . .   Thomas, 132–4.

page 296   'any number of jerky . . .'   Ziegler, 169.

page 296   The dictator certainly did not . . .   Speer, *Spandau*, 104.

page 297   'I try to break a lance . . .'   Goebbels diaries, 27 April 1944.

page 297   Böhm he termed . . .   Thomas, 131.

page 298   'Exactly like Knappertsbusch . . .'   Goebbels diaries, 22 November 1941.

page 298   'That was extremely inconsiderate . . .'   Speer, *Spandau*, 104.

page 298   Karajan himself later told . . .   Rathkolb, 215.

page 298   'He has a very derogatory . . .'   Goebbels diaries, 2 November 1940; also Ziegler, 178.

page 299   'Too bad about Strauss . . .'   Ebermayer, *Denn heute*, 205.

page 299   In his inaugural address . . .   Wulf, *Musik*, 194–5.

page 299   The piece was dedicated . . .   Norman Del Mar, *Richard Strauss*, vol.3, 396.

page 300   He contrasted the indifference . . .   Gerhard Splitt, *Richard Strauss 1933–1935*, 120ff; Wilhelm, 220–3.

page 300   'I told him that I did not wish . . .'   Wilhelm, 226.

page 301   'contrary to the Führer's policy . . .'   Splitt, 63.

page 301   'He is stupid and miserable enough . . .'   *Thomas Mann Diaries*, 2 May 1934.

page 301   spoke of him as being 'senile'.   Goebbels diaries, 23 and 24 July 1933 and *passim*.

page 302   'We'll do it without . . .'   Goebbels diaries, 5 July 1935.

page 302   'As if I had little sympathy for . . .'   Wulf, *Musik*, 198–9.

page 302   Hitler, it is said . . .   Thomas, 260; Kater, *Composers*, 248.

page 302   'I have made this success . . .'   Wilhelm, 239.

page 303   Goebbels summoned Strauss . . .   Wilhelm, 255.

page 303   'My accomplishments as . . .'   Splitt, 244.

page 303   'To my pleasure I find . . .'   Goebbels diaries, 13 January 1944.

page 303   'The Führer does not want . . .'   Goebbels diaries, 4 March 1944.

page 303   On the occasion of . . .   Drewniak, 297; Rathkolb, 190ff; Thomas, 262.

page 304   He hurled his next thunderbolt . . .   John, 58ff.

page 304   The encounter took place . . .   Johann Peter Vogel, *Hans Pfitzner*, 106; Kater, *Composers*, 150–1.

page 305   He despised the composer . . .   Goebbels diaries, 10 June 1943.

page 305   'Only his best pieces . . .'   Drewniak, 300.

page 305   And Hitler snubbed . . .   Vogel, 106–7; Kater, 218.

page 305   In 1937 Hitler rejected . . .   Goebbels diaries, 24 June 1937.

page 305   'The Führer is in general . . .'   Goebbels diaries, 9 June 1943.

page 305   'Today there is no one besides him . . .'   Kater, 219.

page 305   His career typified . . .   Prieberg, *Musik*, 320ff; Walter, 178ff.

page 306   'I order you to inform the Führer . . .'   Walter, 175; Prieberg, *Musik*, 320.

page 306   'We both go with strong . . .'   Goebbels diaries, 1 February 1939.

page 306   In the event Hitler . . .   Prieberg, *Musik*, 320; Kater, *Composers*, 10.

page 306   'a tremendous, original talent'   Goebbels diaries, 1 February 1939.

page 306   It was argued that . . .   Walter, 189, 198ff.

page 306   'The Führer complains . . .'   Goebbels diaries, 22 February 1940.

page 306   Opera managers who had earlier . . .   Prieberg, *Musik*, 321.

page 307   'the healing process'   Prieberg, *Musik*, 324.

page 307   'As National Socialist barbarism . . .'   Prieberg, *Musik*, 25.

18   Immortality through Architecture

page 311   'would take his breath away'   *Monologe*, 21–2 October 1941, 101.

page 313   Hitler's fascination . . .   Speer, *Spandau*, 173.

page 313   he wrote several times . . .   Jäckel/Kuhn, 49–51.

page 313   'I was firmly convinced . . .'   *Mein Kampf*, 35.

page 313   'Their excellencies . . .'   Letter of 17 August 1908 in Jäckel/Kuhn, 50–1.

page 314   'The architectural sketches . . .'   Schroeder, 134.

page 315   'This was a theme of one . . .'   'Warum sind wir Antisemiten?' 13 August 1920 in Jäckel/Kuhn, 184–204.

page 315   'The few still towering . . .'   *Mein Kampf*, 265.

page 315   If there were to be a new . . .   Speech of 9 April 1929 in Hitler, *Reden*, 192.

page 316   'the overpowering sweep and force'   *Mein Kampf*, 265.

page 316   By the early 1920s . . .   Hauptarchiv der NSDAP, Reel 3, folder 64; also, Price, fig. 491, 202; figs 525–8, 209; figs 531–4, 210; Backes, 29, 32, 39.

page 316   'foreign and unnatural'   Schroeder, 95; also Goebbels diaries, 8 April 1941.

page 316   After a brief visit there . . .   Goebbels diaries, 7 August 1940.

page 316   Baroque was also not to his taste . . .   Speer, *Spandau*, 15; *Monologe*, 21–2 July 1941, 42; Goebbels diaries, 8 April 1941.

page 318   'I made these drawings . . .'   Speer, *Inside*, 74.

page 318   'his architectural picture . . .'   Goebbels diaries, 25 July 1926.

page 318   'In his free time the Führer occupies . . .'   Goebbels diaries, 3 February 1932.

page 318   In an address at the cultural session . . .   'Art and Politics' in *Liberty, Art, Nationhood: Three Addresses Delivered at the Seventh National Socialist Congress,* Nuremberg, 1935.

page 319   Social housing, Hitler Youth . . .   Hermann Giesler, *Ein anderer Hitler*, 202.

page 319   'I will have nothing to do . . .'   Giesler, 210.

page 319   He selected a few of Mies . . .   Gudrun Brockhaus, *Schauder und Idylle*, 95; Weihsmann, 962.

page 319   'When we left the big . . .'   Speer, *Spandau*, 174–5.

page 320   Similarly, Hitler's views on skyscrapers . . .   Giesler, 202–3.

page 320   'All he thinks about . . .'   Goebbels diaries, 26 February 1931; also, 25 March 1931.

page 320   'Linz is costing us a pile . . .'   Goebbels diaries, 17 May 1941.

page 320   Infringement of this rule . . .   Decree of 25 June 1940 in Dülffer, Thies, Henke, 36.

page 320   'So he wants something in writing . . .'   Speer, *Spandau*, 96.

page 321   'Why put up these huge public buildings?'   Speer, *Inside*, 69.

page 321   'The greater the demands . . .'   Baynes, 592.

page 321   In a secret speech . . .   Thies, 79–80.

page 322   'the timeless significance'   Baynes, 584.

page 322   He had chosen granite . . .   *Monologe*, 21–2 October 1941, 101–2.

page 322   'I want German buildings to be viewed . . .'   Ziegler, 123.

page 322   'As capital of the world . . .'   *Monologe*, 11–12 March 1942, 318.

page 323   Mussolini was anxious to impress . . .   Wiedemann, 34–44; also Below, 100.

page 324   He asked to visit it alone . . .   Bianchi Bandinelli, 181; Schramm, 62.

page 325   'One Sunday afternoon in Rome . . .'   Wiedemann, 87–8.

page 325   his was to seat 60,000.   Dülffer, Thies, Hencke, 212.

page 325   So anxious had he been . . .   *Monologe*, 29 October 1941, 115–16; Giesler, 386–96; Speer, *Inside*, 171–3; Breker, *Paris*, 99–113.

page 325   'He knew the ground plan . . .'   Breker, *Paris*,100.

page 326   'There you see . . .'   Speer, *Inside*, 171.

page 326   After a brief visit to the École Militaire . . .   Giesler, 390; Hoffmann, *Hitler Was My Friend*, 123.

page 327   'a huge disappointment' . . .   *Monologe*, 29 October 1941, 116.

page 327   'By God,' Giesler quotes him . . .   Giesler, 391.

page 327   'Today I must tell you frankly . . .'   Breker, *Paris*, 112.

page 327   Most of what he had seen . . .   Giesler, 391.

page 327   'It was the dream of my life . . .'   Speer, *Inside*, 172.

page 327   'I have seen Rome and Paris . . .'   *Monologe*, 21–2 July 1941, 44; also Goebbels diaries, 3 July 1940.

page 328   At another time he said . . .   *Monologe*, 25–6 September 1941, 75.

page 328   The Panthéon, with its sculptures . . .   *Monologe*, 29 October 1941, 115.

page 328   Even Garnier's opera . . .   *Monologe*, 13 June 1943, 400.

page 328   a 'cultural document' . . .   *Monologe*, 29 October 1941, 115.

page 328   After his Paris visit he even . . .   *Monologe*, 29 October 1941, 115.

page 328   But far and away the most beautiful city . . .   Picker, 26 April 1942, 245; Goebbels diaries, 22 November 1941.

page 328   'decorations of the twelve hundred niches . . .'   *Mein Kampf*, 75.

page 328   an 'opera house of Western democracy'   *Mein Kampf*, 75.

page 329   'Mussolini will certainly imitate us.'   Goebbels diaries, 15 June 1938.

page 329   'Now this will be the end . . .'   Speer, *Inside*, 155.

page 329 thirty or so books on American architecture . . . Wiedemann, 220–1.

page 329 'It is for this reason . . .' Thies, 79–80.

19 Political Architecture

page 330 '*Bauen, bauen!*' Goebbels diaries, 10 September 1937.

page 330 The latter was enshrined . . . Backes, 117.

page 330 'We are going to create . . .' Gitta Sereny, *Albert Speer*, 185.

page 330 'The Führer really loves Berlin . . .' Goebbels diaries, 14 March 1937.

page 331 Upon the fall of Norway . . . Goebbels diaries, 9 July 1940.

page 331 Implicit in all these programmes . . . Speer, *Inside*, 69.

page 332 'he asks for a pencil . . .' Friedrich Christian Prinz zu Schaumburg-Lippe, *Als die goldene Abendsonne*, 30.

page 332 They did not appeal to him . . . Backes, 152.

page 332 'The Führer played a decisive role . . .' Backes, 153.

page 332 In addition a more modest . . . Backes, 120; Thies, 99.

page 333 'One had the feeling that all this . . .' Schwerin von Krosigk, *Es geschah*, 200.

page 333 'You were better off in that respect.' Speer, *Spandau*, 312.

page 334 Since the war the Library of Congress . . . Library of Congress, Washington, item 347, Hitler Collection.

page 334 'Hitler's architectural knowledge was amazing.' Schroeder, 219.

page 334 Giesler recalled travelling with Hitler . . . Giesler, 182ff.

page 334 Speer was no less stinting . . . Speer, *Inside*, 79; Sereny, 138.

page 335 'An architect could not have done better.' Speer, *Inside*, 143.

page 335 He once remarked to Giesler . . . Giesler, 391.

page 337 One of Hitler's first acts . . . Speer, *Inside* 34; Price, fig. 613, 228.

page 337 '. . . added twenty metres, saying . . .' Speer, *Spandau*, 93–94.

page 338 There he argued that while cities . . . *Mein Kampf*, 263–5.

page 339 sitting contentedly in a Bauhaus tube chair. Winfried Nerdinger, ed., *Bauhaus-Moderne im Nationalsozialismus*, 20, 86.

page 339 Among his surviving sketches . . . Price, fig. 606, 226; fig. 611, 228; fig. 672, 240; figs 633–6, 232; figs N633.1, N633.2 and N634.1, 257.

page 339 Her firm, the Vereinigte Werkstätten . . . Schönberger, 116–19.

page 340 A number of sketches survive . . . Nerdinger, *Bauhaus-Moderne*, 155–7.

page 341 In a competition for an extension . . . Philip Johnson, *Mies van der Rohe*, 96; Wolfgang Schäche, '1933–1945: Bauen im Nationalsozialismus', in Josef Paul Kleihues, ed., *750 Jahre Architektur*, 187.

page 341 Mies's remark that 'Architecture . . .' Johnson, 186; Barbara Miller Lane, *Architecture and Politics in Germany*, 189.

page 341 'It looks like an oversized marketplace . . .' Speer, *Inside*, 64.

page 342 'The fact is that Hitler worried . . .' Wiedemann, 204.

page 342 Heinz Linge said much the same. Linge, 46.

page 342 While there were few, if any, generals . . . Wiedemann, 202.

page 342 He gave them financial and other privileges . . . Backes, 84.

page 342 The two men met in 1929 . . . Schroeder, 176–7; Picker, 128; Schönberger, 126.

page 342 'When I encountered him the first time . . .' *Monologe*, 13–14 January 1942, 198.

page 343 In his youth Hitler had done watercolours . . . Price, fig. 383, 177.

page 343 'In the train he would usually talk animatedly . . .' Speer, *Inside*, 39.

page 344 Alas, Gerdy Troost insisted . . . Toland, 414.

page 344   Giesler was amazed at how amiable . . .   Giesler, 122.

page 344   'Yes, you're right, that's better.'   Speer, *Inside*, 79.

page 344   Based on Troost's insipid entry . . .   Entry design reproduced in *Die Kunst im Dritten Reich*, July 1937.

page 344   'the first beautiful building of the new Reich'   *Die Kunst im Dritten Reich*, August 1937.

page 344   'Now we know why the hammer broke.' Speer, *Inside*, 49.

page 345   'Your husband is going to erect . . .'   Speer, *Inside*, 58.

page 345   But as late as June of 1935 . . .   Thies, 85.

page 345   The snub was a calamitous blow . . .   Fest, *Speer*, 122.

page 346   'Speer was afraid of Giesler's competition . . .'   Sereny, 236.

page 346   'From 1943 on he probably did actually prefer . . .'   Speer, *Spandau*, 140.

page 346   Even so, the Führer took malicious pleasure . . .   Picker, 245.

page 346   'Of Speer, he once said . . .'   Schroeder, 132.

page 347   'attempts at public buildings in the neo-baroque . . .'   Speer, *Inside*, 41–2.

page 348   'bright, clear and simple'   Speer, *Inside*, 37.

page 348   'It's showy, that's all.'   Speer, *Inside*, 27.

page 348   An anecdote of Gerdy Troost's . . .   Toland, 414–15.

page 348   Similarly, Speer's biographer . . .   Fest, *Speer*, 489–90.

page 349   Yet in his Spandau diaries . . .   Speer, *Spandau*, 141–2.

page 349   More damning still . . .   Speer, *Inside*, 138.

page 349   'Of course I was perfectly aware . . .'   Sereny, 186.

page 349   According to other testimony . . .   Thies, 76; Linge, 46.

page 350   'Germanization of the skyscraper'   'Wilhelm Kreis – Repräsentant der deutschen Architektur des 20 Jahrhunderts' in Nerdinger/Mai, *Wilhelm Kreis: Architekt*, 17.

page 350   Although he lost several institutional positions . . .   Nerdinger/Mai, 25–6.

page 350   In articles and speeches he condemned . . .   Nerdinger/Mai, 15.

20   Remodelling Germany

page 351   'In consonance with our stupendous victory . . .'   Dülffer, 36.

page 351   'At present Berlin is miserable . . .'   *Monologe*, 29 October 1941, 115.

page 351   Hitler claimed that the original inspiration . . .   *Monologe*, 27–8 September 1941, 72.

page 351   'Thus my ideas for a reorganization . . .'   Giesler, 153, 203–4.

page 352   it would be 'no loss' were it destroyed . . .   *Monologe*, 21 July 1941, 44.

page 352   The area had been settled by Saxons . . .   *Monologe*, 21–2 October 1941, 100–1.

page 352   He also said that during the war . . .   Speer, Spandau, 112; Alfred Rietdorf: *Gilly: Wiedergeburt der Architektur*.

page 352   In fact, his great Berlin Arch of Triumph . . .   Rietdorf, 36, 60.

page 352   For the great monument of the Bismarck era . . .   *Mein Kampf*, 266; *Monologe*, 13 June 1943, 400; Speer, *Inside*, 151; Goebbels diaries, 22 February 1937.

page 352   Key elements of their proposals . . .   E. M. Hajo and L. Zahn: *Berliner Architektur der Nachkriegszeit*, vii–xiii; Wolters, *Stadtmitte Berlin*, 203.

page 353   'They will be grandiose'   Goebbels diaries, 23 August 1933.

page 353   He said he wanted an entirely new stadium . . .   Dülffer, Thies, Henke, 94–5.

page 353   The next big meeting occurred in March . . .   Dülffer, Thies, Henke, 86, 97–100.

page 353   Although Hitler initially had been opposed . . .   Peter Reichel, *Der schöne Schein des Dritten Reiches*, 263–4.

page 354   He summarily increased the budget . . .   Picker, 216–17.

page 354   With his usual self-effacement . . .   Speer, *Inside*, 80.

page 354   'The rhetoric of this ensemble . . .'   Dawn Ades, et al., eds., *Art and Power*, 265.

page 354   'the biggest and most beautiful civil airport . . .'   Dülffer, Thies, Henke, 109.

page 354   he even shifted funds earmarked . . .   Backes, 125.

page 355   'I tell you, Speer, these buildings are . . .'   Speer, *Spandau*, 16.

page 355   'I was appalled at the idea . . .'   Sereny, 156.

page 355   'Berlin [authorities] are hopeless'   Speer, *Inside*, 74.

page 357   'We would set out armed with flashlights . . .'   Speer, *Inside*, 132.

page 357   'Berlin's new construction programme . . .'   Goebbels diaries, 4 June 1938.

page 358   'overwhelmed or, rather, stunned'   Speer, *Inside*, 134–5.

page 358   the 'undefeated army of the World War'   Memorandum of 29 March 1934 in Dülffer, 97.

page 360   Only with the construction of this building . . .   *Monologe*, 21–2 October 1941, 101.

page 360   This was no exaggeration . . .   Speer, *Inside*, 74, 154.

page 360   'That has to be changed.'   Speer, *Inside*, 160; also *Spandau*, 164.

page 361   On the back side of a picture . . .   Postcard to Ernst Schmidt in Hauptarchiv der NSDAP, Reel 1 File, 17a; text in Jäckel/Kuhn, 82.

page 361   'a type of race museum . . .'   Karl Arndt, 'Großaufträge in Berlin . . .', in Nerdlinger/Mai, 176.

page 362   So touchy was he that a noted cabaret artist . . .   Speer, *Inside*, 139.

page 362   'When angry protests from the populace . . .'   Speer, *Inside*, 139.

page 362   Countless office buildings . . .   Schäche, '1933–1945: Bauen . . .' in Kleihues, 197.

page 362   This gave rise to a joke that Hitler . . .   Wiedemann, 201.

page 362   'How is the clearing of the 1000 . . .'   Schäche, '1933–1945: . . .' in Kleihues, 202.

page 362   23,765 Jewish residences were . . .   Schmidt, *Albert Speer*, 20; Sereny, 225.

page 362   'For our new construction project . . .'   Schäche, 211.

page 362   only 'fit for a soap company'   Speer, *Inside*, 102.

page 362   As Hitler explained . . .   Speer, *Inside*, 107.

page 363   Discussions about the new building . . .   Schönberger, 37–44.

page 363   The dictator himself had in 1935 . . .   Schönberger, plan 24: *Grundrißskizze* (no page number).

page 363   He drove himself and his workers . . .   Schönberger, 60, 63.

page 363   Morally far worse . . .   Paul B. Jascot, *The Architecture of Oppression, passim*.

page 364   'an architectural stage set . . .'   Speer, *Inside*, 102.

page 365   'permeated with the fire of political power'   Alex Scobie, *Hitler's State Architecture*, 103.

page 366   'On the long walk from the entrance . . .'   Speer, *Inside*, 103.

page 366   'That's exactly right; diplomats should . . .'   Speer, *Inside*, 113.

page 366   'to establish a clear link . . .'   Schönberger, 112.

page 366   The room itself . . .   Schönberger, 104–5.

page 366   'When the diplomats . . .'   Speer, *Inside*, 113–14.

page 367   'The time of ambassadors is over . . .'   Georg Krawietz, *Peter Behrens im Dritten Reich*, 68.

page 367   'As Reich chancellor and Führer . . .'   Schönberger, 111.

page 367   The new Reich chancellery was . . .   Anton Joachimsthaler, *The Last Days of Hitler*, 81–2.

page 367   'When I got out of the car . . .'   Winston Churchill, *Triumph and Tragedy*, 630–1.

page 368   'He lives like an impoverished . . .'   Goebbels diaries, 6 August 1940.

page 368   In splendour and size . . .   Scobie, 98, 107.

page 368   'The geopolitical significance . . .'   *Mein Kampf*, 347.

page 369   One of these envisaged a star-shaped plaza . . .   Backes, 146.

page 369   Already then, he told Giesler, he anticipated . . .   Giesler, 153.

page 369   'Beautiful Königsplatz . . .'   Goebbels diaries, 19 August 1935.

page 370   'Absolutely unique. The very picture . . .'   Goebbels diaries, 3 and 5 November 1935.

page 370   Hitler admired Munich's basic design . . .   *Mein Kampf*, 264, 576; *Monologe*, 25 September 1941, 69; 15–16 January 1942, 201; 13 June 1943, 400.

page 370   'a monument to the technology of our century'   Giesler, 169.

page 371   This required widening the diameter . . .   Paul Bonatz, *Leben und Bauen*, 179–80.

page 371   'If I had one single reason . . .'   Bonatz, 180.

page 373   As the war dragged on . . .   Sereny, 236.

page 373   'There is something American . . .'   Heinrich Breloer and Horst Königstein: *Blutgeld*, 116.

page 373   he himself sketched the sort of structure . . .   Helmut and Beatrice Heiber: *Die Rückseite des Hackenkreuzes*, 83; Price, figs 621–4, 230.

page 373   His supreme desideratum was that . . .   Breloer, Königstein, 116; Backes, 140.

page 373   'There can be no doubt,' Speer later said . . .   Breloer, 116.

page 374   'With visible emotion he showed us . . .'   Speer, *Spandau*, 173.

page 374   His personal library, found at Alt Aussee . . .   Dülffer, 253–4, 258–62; Backes, 143–5; Faison, Consolidated Interrogation Report No.4, 1.

page 375   'Everything was well thought through . . .'   Giesler, 213.

page 375   Linz was to replace Vienna . . .   Goebbels diaries, 13 March, 5 April, 17 May 1941; 29 March, 24 April, 30 May 1942; 10 May 1943.

page 376   Speer's claim that Hitler once . . .   Speer, *Spandau*, 172; Giesler, 216.

page 376   'I do not want to hurt the feelings . . .'   Giesler, 216.

page 376   Yet it had to be higher than that of St Stephen's . . .   Speer, *Spandau*, 171–2.

page 376   'In the tower I want a carillon . . .'   Giesler, 216.

page 376   When Goebbels visited . . .   Goebbels diaries, 20 March 1942.

page 377   'He was a different Hitler'   Speer, *Spandau*, 170.

page 377   The large model of the Linz-to-be . . .   Joachimsthaler, *The Last Days of Hitler*, 37.

page 377   'I still see him before my eyes . . .'   Giesler, 96.

page 377   Heinz Linge recorded . . .   Heinz Linge, 'Hitlers Terminkalender vom 14.10. 1944–28.2.1945', Institut für Zeitgeschichte, Munich.

page 378   'I know, Kaltenbrunner, what you want'   Peter R. Black, *Ernst Kaltenbrunner*, 238; Giesler, 21–2; Schwerin von Krosigk, *Es geschah*, 221.

page 379   'The [community] halls are to have . . .'   Goebbels diaries, 17 April 1937.

page 379   'The visitor comes to Weimar . . .'   Giesler, 121.

page 380   the 'austere rigour in the use of space'   Giesler, 117.

page 380   Although one architectural historian . . .   Miller Lane, 197.

SOURCE NOTES | 435

page 381 'thought with their blood, worshipped . . .' Peter Gay, *Weimar Culture*, 82.

page 381 'During that wonderful hot summer . . .' Sereny, 217.

page 382 the cost of the projects . . . Dülffer, 18.

page 382 'The Führer does not want to talk . . .' Goebbels diaries, 10 September 1937.

page 382 In his autobiography, Finance Minister . . . Schwerin von Krosigk, *Staatsbankrott*, 189–91.

page 382 'It was always more economical . . .' Schwerin von Krosigk, *Staatsbankrott*, 200–1.

page 383 'If only the Finance Minister could realize . . .' Speer, *Inside*, 140–1.

page 383 He not only forbade any mention to the public . . . Thies, 100.

page 383 Each was assessed a certain sum . . . Schwerin von Krosigk, *Staatsbankrott*, 346.

page 383 Money for the Augsburg forum . . . Speer, *Spandau*, 97.

page 383 Speer reckoned that architects . . . Dülffer, 16.

page 383 The projects in Munich and Hamburg alone . . . Dülffer, 17.

page 383 Even before the war there was labour . . . Thies, 100.

page 383 As early as 1937 the SS set up . . . Thies, 101.

page 383 3 million forced labourers . . . Scobie, 130.

page 384 Wood, scarce in much of Europe . . . Schönberger, 134.

page 384 Granite required just for Munich . . . Dülffer, 17.

page 384 'We'll be getting our granite . . .' Speer, *Inside*, 180.

page 384 'Churchill was robbing him . . .' Fest, *Speer*, 495.

page 384 'With a heavy heart . . .' Goebbels diaries, 31 May 1942.

page 384 'In strict confidence he maintained . . .' Goebbels diaries, 20 August 1942.

page 385 Nearly a year later . . . Goebbels diaries 25 June 1943; also 14 March 1944.

page 385 What he then witnessed was . . . Goebbels diaries, 27 April 1944.

21 Aesthetics and Transport

page 386 The former prime minister . . . Picker, 442.

page 386 'But when I go from Berlin to Munich . . .' *Monologe*, 9–10 January 1942, 192.

page 387 Hitler was fascinated by roads . . . Fritz Todt, 'Adolf Hitler and his Roads' in Goebbels, et al., *Adolf Hitler: Pictures from the Life of the Führer*, 88; Giesler, 203–4; Hoffmann, *Hitler wie ich*, 214; Hans Kallenbach, *Mit Adolf Hitler auf Festung Landsberg*, 61–2.

page 387 During the subsequent *Kampfzeit* . . . Todt, 'Adolf Hitler and his Roads' in Goebbels, et al., *Adolf Hitler:Pictures*, 89.

page 387 'It is the automobile I love . . .' *Monologe*, 9–10 January 1942, 192.

page 387 A private German road association . . . Martin Kornrumpf, *HAFRABA e.V.: Deutsche Autobahn Planung*, 22ff; Stommer, ed., *Reichsautobahn*, 24–5.

page 388 'In the past a nation's standard of living . . .' Speech of 11 February 1933 in Todt, 89; Domarus, 250–2.

page 388 In all, there were then merely 500,000 . . . Karl Ludvigsen, *Battle for the Beetle*, 18; Weihsmann, *Bauen unterm Hakenkreuz*, 126.

page 389 Todt was probably the only . . . Schwerin von Krosigk, *Es geschah*, 296–300; Speer, *Inside*, 193.

page 389 The function of the autobahns was . . . Angela Schumacher, 'Vor uns die endlosen Straßen, vor uns die lockende, erredende Ferne . . .' in Stommer, ed., 77.

page 389 The roads on which the Nordic . . . Angela Schumacher, 77; Claudia Gabriele Philipp, 'Die schöne Straße im Bau und unter Verkehr' in Stommer, ed., 112.

page 392   As with his buildings, Hitler . . .   Todt, 93.

page 392   In fact, two of them did.   Gudrun Brockhaus, *Schauder und Idylle*, 95; Hochmann, 210, 228.

page 393   'I don't know how many times . . .'   Hoffmann, *Hitler Was My Friend*, 188.

page 393   '. . . It possesses a classicism . . .'   Giesler, 206.

page 393   In all, 9000 bridges . . .   Stommer, 'Triumph der Technik' in Stommer, ed., 75–6.

page 393   The party's automobile journal . . .   Weihsmann, 132.

page 393   'It was without a doubt the dictatorship's . . .'   Wolfgang Pehnt, quoted in Weihsmann, 124.

page 394   'but at least the autobahn . . .'   Brockhaus, 68.

page 394   By that summer 3000 kilometres . . .   Stommer, 'Geschichte der Reichsautobahn' in Stommer, ed., 30–1.

page 394   This was a terrible blow to Hitler . . .   Picker, 18 July 1942, 443.

page 396   '*ein Volksauto und ein Volkseigenheim für Jedermann*'   Picker, 49.

page 396   The idea went back to . . .   Hans Mommsen and Manfred Grieger, *Das Volkswagenwerk*, 59.

page 397   purportedly showed him his own . . .   *Die Welt*, 2 May 1981.

page 397   Hitler had been introduced to Porsche . . .   Karl Ludvigsen, *Battle for the Beetle*, 8.

page 397   By the end of that summer . . .   Mommsen, Grieger, 76–80.

page 397   'The way these cars buzz up . . .'   Picker, 22 June 1942, 374.

page 398   He wanted a million . . .   Speer, *Spandau*, 157.

page 398   More than the railway . . .   *Monologe*, 5–6 July 1941, 39.

Afterword

page 399   Of this, Lord Curzon wrote . . .   George N. Curzon, *Persia and the Persian Question*, 195.

page 400   'There is never a moment . . .'   Benjamin, 258.

page 401   In an argument submitted . . .   *New York Times*, 8 May 2001.

Books Cited in Text

Adam, Peter: *Art of the Third Reich* (1992).

Ades, Dawn et al.: *Art and Power: Europe under the Dictators 1930–45* (1995).

Alford, Kenneth D.: *The Spoils of World War II: The American Military's Role in the Stealing of Europe's Treasures* (1994).

Allen, William Sheridan, ed.: *The Memoirs of Ex-Gauleiter Albert Krebs 1923–1933* (1976).

Allende-Blin, Juan, ed.: *Musiktradition im Exil* (1993).

Arent, Benno von: *Das deutsche Bühnenbild 1933–1936* (1938).

Backes, Klaus: *Hitler und die bildenden Künste: Kulturverständnis und Kunstpolitik im Dritten Reich* (1988).

Baird, J. W.: *To Die for Germany: Heroes in the Nazi Pantheon* (1990).

Barron, Stephanie, ed.: *Degenerate Art; The Fate of the Avant-Garde in Nazi Germany* (1991).

Bartetzko, Dieter: *Illusionen in Stein: Stimmungsarchitektur im deutschen Faschismus* (1985).

Baynes, Norman H.: *The Speeches of Adolf Hitler April 1922–August 1939* (1942).

Below, Nicolaus von: *Als Hitlers Adjutant 1937–45* (1980).

Benjamin, Walter: *Illuminations: Essays and Reflections* (1970).

Bianchi Bandinelli, Ranuccio: *Dal diario di un borghese e altri scritti* (1948).

Bielefelder Kunstverein: *Totalitäre Kunst – Kunst im Totalitarismus? Beispiele aus dem NS-Staat und der DDR* (1997).

Birken, Lawrence: *Hitler as Philosophe: Remnants of the Enlightenment in National Socialism* (1995).

Black, Peter R.: *Ernst Kaltenbrunner: Ideological Soldier of the Third Reich* (1984).

Boberach, Heinz, ed.: *Meldungen aus dem Reich. Die geheimen Lageberichte des Sicherheitsdienstes der SS 1938–1945*, 17 vols (1984).

Bollmus, Reinhard: *Das Amt Rosenberg und seine Gegner: Zum Machtkampf im nationalsozialistischen Herrschaftssystem* (1970).

Bonatz, Paul: *Leben und Bauen* (1950).

Bothe, Rolf and Thomas Föhl: *Aufstieg und Fall der Moderne* (1999).

Bracher, Karl Dietrich: *Die deutsche Diktatur: Entstehung, Struktur, Folgen des Nationalsozialismus*.

Bredius, A.: *Rembrandt Paintings* (1937).

Breker, Arno: *Paris, Hitler et moi* (1970).

———: *Im Stahlungsfeld der Ereignisse* (1972).

Breloer, Heinrich and Horst Königstein: *Blutgeld: Materialen zu einer deutschen Geschichte* (1982).

Brenner, Helmut: *Musik als Waffe?* (1992).

Brenner, Hildegard: *Die Kunstpolitik des Nationalsozialismus* (1963).

Brockhaus, Gudrun: *Schauder und Idylle: Faschismus als Erlebnisangebot* (1997).

Bullock, Alan: *Hitler, A Study in Tyranny* (1962).

Burckhardt, Carl J.: *Meine Danziger Mission 1937–1939* (1960).

Burden, Hamilton T.: *The Nuremberg Party Rallies: 1923–39* (1967).

Carr, William: *Hitler: A Study in Personality and Politics* (1978).

Cecil, Robert: *The Myth of the Master Race: Alfred Rosenberg and Nazi Ideology* (1972).

Chamberlin, Russell: *Loot: The Heritage of Plunder* (1983).

Churchill, Winston S.: *Triumph and Tragedy* (1953).

Clark, Alan: *Barbarossa: The Russian-German Conflict 1941–45* (1965).

Craig, Edward: *Gordon Craig: The Story of his Life* (1969).

Curzon, George N.: *Persia and the Persian Question* (1892).

Dambacher, Eva: *Literatur- und Kulturpreise 1859–1949: Eine Dokumentation* (1996).

De Felice, Renzo and Luigi Goglia: *Storia fotografica del fascismo* (1981).

Del Mar, Norman: *Richard Strauss*, vol.3 (1986).

Dennis, David B.: *Beethoven in German Politics: 1870–1989* (1996).

Dietrich, Otto: *Hitler* (1955).

Drewniak, Berguslaw: *Das Theater im NS-Staat: Szenarium deutscher Zeitgeschichte 1933–1945* (1983).

Dülffer, Jost, Jochen Thies and Josef Henke: *Hitlers Städte: Baupolitik im Dritten Reich: Eine Dokumentation* (1978).

Du Moulin Eckart, Richard: *Cosima Wagner: Ein Lebens- und Charakterbild* (2 vols 1929 and 1931).

Ebermayer, Erich: *Magisches Bayreuth: Legende und Wirklichkeit* (1951).

———: *Denn heute gehört uns Deutschland: Persönliches und politisches Tagebuch* (1959).

Eitner, Hans-Jürgen: *'Der Führer': Hitlers Persönlichkeit und Charakter* (1981).

Feliciano, Hector: *The Lost Museum: The Nazi Conspiracy to Steal the World's Greatest Works of Art* (1997).

Fest, Joachim: *Hitler: Eine Biographie* (1973).

———: *Hitler* (1975).

———: *Speer: Eine Biographie* (1999).

François-Poncet, André: *Souvenire d'une ambassade à Berlin, Septembre 1931–Octobre 1938* (1946).

Frank, Hans: *Im Angesicht des Galgens* (1953).

Frauenfeld, A. E.: *Der Weg zur Bühne* (4th ed., 1943).

Frazer, James George: *The Golden Bough: A Study in Comparative Religion* (1922).

Frey, Stefan: *Franz Lehár oder das schlechte Gewissen der leichten Musik* (1995).

Galante, Pierre and Eugene Silianoff: *Voices from the Bunker* (1989).

Gay, Peter: *Weimar Culture: The Outsider as Insider* (1968).

Geissmar, Berta: *The Baton and the Jackboot* (1944).

Gibson, Hugh, ed.: *The Ciano Diaries 1939–1943* (1945).

Giesler, Hermann: *Ein anderer Hitler: Bericht seines Architekten* (1978).

Goebbels, Joseph: *Goebbels-Reden*, Helmut Heiber, ed., 2 vols (1971).

———: *Die Tagebücher: Sämtliche Fragmente*, Elke Frölich, ed., 19 vols (1987–1996).

Goebbels, Joseph et al.: *Adolf Hitler: Pictures from the Life of the Führer* (1978).

Görlitz, Walter and H. A. Quint: *Adolf Hitler: Eine Biographie* (1952).

Golomstock, Igor: *Totalitarian Art in the Soviet Union, the Third Reich, Fascist Italy and the People's Republic of China* (1990).

Great Britain. Foreign Office: *Documents Concerning German–Polish Relations* (Cmd. 6106) (1939).

Gregor-Dellin, Martin and Michael von Soden: *Richard Wagner: Leben, Werk, Wirkung* (1983).

Grosshans, Henry: *Hitler and the Artists* (1983).

Guerri, Giordano Bruno, ed.: *Diario, 1935–1944: Giuseppe Bottai* (1982).

Haase, Günther: *Kunstraub und Kunstschutz: Eine Dokumentation* (1991).

Hajo, H. M. and L. Zahn: *Berliner Architektur der Nachkriegszeit* (1928).

Hamann, Brigitte: *Hitlers Wien: Lehrjahre eines Diktators* (1996).

Hamilton, Charles: *The Hitler Diaries* (1991).

Harpprecht, Klaus: *Thomas Mann: Eine Biographie* (1995).

Hartung, Ulrike: *Raubzüge in der Sowjetunion: Das Sonderkommando Künsberg 1941–1943* (1997).

Heiber, Helmut, ed.: *Goebbels-Reden* (1971).

Heiber, Helmut and Beatrice: *Die Rückseite des Hakenkreuzes: Absonderliches aus den Akten des Dritten Reiches* (1993).

Heiden, Konrad: *Hitler: A Biography* (1936).

———: *Der Führer* (1944).

Heister, Hanns-Werner and Hans-Günter Klein: *Musik und Musikpolitik im faschistischen Deutschland* (1984).

Henderson, Nevile: *Failure of a Mission: Berlin 1937–1939* (1940).

Hersey, George: *The Evolution of Allure* (1996).

Heuss, Anja: *Kunst- und Kulturgutraub* (2000).

Hinz, Berthold: *Art in the Third Reich* (1979).

Hitler, Adolf: *Mein Kampf*, trans. Ralph Manheim (1971).

———: *Monologe im Führerhauptquartier 1941–1944*, Werner Jochmann ed. (1980).

———: *Tischgespräche im Führerhauptquartier*, ed. Henry Picker (1976).

———: *Le Testament politique de Hitler*, ed. Martin Bormann (1959).

———: *Sämtliche Aufzeichnungen 1905–1924*, Eberhard Jäckel and Axel Kuhn, eds (1980).

———: *Reden Schriften Anordnungen: Februar 1925 bis Januar 1933*, 5 vols (1992–1998).

———: *Liberty, Art, Nationhood: Three Addresses Delivered at the Seventh National Socialist Congress, Nuremberg, 1935* (1935).

———: *The Speeches of Adolf Hitler April 1922–August 1939*, Norman H. Baynes, ed., 2 vols (1969).

———: *Speeches and Proclamations 1932–1945*, Max Domarus, ed., 3 vols (1962)

———: *Gli acquerelli di Hitler: L'opera ritrovata: Omaggio a Rodolfo Siviero* (1984).

Hobsbawm, E. J. and Terence Ranger: *The Invention of Tradition* (1983).

Hochmann, Elaine S.: *Architects of Fortune: Mies van der Rohe and the Third Reich* (1989).

Hoffmann, Heinrich: *Hitler wie ich ihn sah: Aufzeichnungen seines Leibfotografen* (1974).

———: *Hitler Was My Friend* (1955).

Jäckel, Eberhard and Axel Kuhn: *Hitler: Sämtliche Aufzeichnungen, 1905–1924* (1980).

Jascot, Paul B.: *The Architecture of Oppression: The SS, Forced Labour and the Nazi Monumental Building Economy* (2000).

Jay, Martin: *The Dialectical Imagination: A History of the Frankfurt School and the Institute of Social Research, 1923–1950* (1973).

Jetzinger, Franz: *Hitlers Jugend: Phantasien, Lügen – und die Wahrheit* (1956).

———: *Hitler's Youth* (1958).

Joachimsthaler, Anton: *The Last Days of Hitler: The Legends, the Evidence, the Truth* (1996).

————: *Adolf Hitler 1908–1920: Korrektur einer Biographie* (1989).

Jochmann, Werner, ed.: *Adolf Hitler: Monologe im Führer Hauptquartier 1941–1944: Die Aufzeichnungen Heinrich Heims* (1980).

John, Eckhard: *Musikbolschewismus: Die Politisierung der Musik in Deutschland 1918–1938* (1994).

Johnson, Philip: *Mies van der Rohe* (1978).

Kallenbach, Hans: *Mit Adolf Hitler auf Festung Landsberg* (1939).

Karbaum, Michael: *Studien zur Geschichte der Bayreuther Festspiele* (1976).

Karow, Yvonne: *Deutsches Opfer: Kultische Selbstauslöschung auf den Reichparteitagen der NSDAP* (1997).

Kater, Michael H.: *The Twisted Muse: Musicians and their Music in the Third Reich* (1997).

————: *Composers of the Nazi Era* (2000).

Kershaw, Ian: *Hitler 1889–1936* (1998).

Kleihues, Josef Paul, ed.: *750 Jahre Architektur und Städtebau in Berlin: Die Internationale Bauausstellung im Kontext der Baugeschichte Berlins* (1988).

Köhler, Joachim: *Wagners Hitler: Der Prophet und sein Vollstrecker* (1997).

Kornrumpf, Martin: *HAFRABA e.V.: Deutsche Autobahn Planung 1926–1934* (1990).

Krawietz, Georg: *Peter Behrens im Dritten Reich* (1995).

Krosigk, Lutz Graf Schwerin von: *Es geschah in Deutschland* (1952).

————: *Staatsbankrott: Die Geschichte der Finanzpolitik des Deutschen Reiches von 1920 bis 1945* (1974).

Kubin, Ernst: *Sonderauftrag Linz: Die Kunstsammlung Adolf Hitler. Aufbau, Vernichtungsplan, Rettung* (1989).

Kubizek, August: *Adolf Hitler Mein Jugendfreund* (1953).

————: *Young Hitler: The Story of Our Friendship* (1955).

Kurz, Jakob: *Kunstraub in Europa 1938–1945* (1989).

Levi, Erik: *Music in the Third Reich* (1994).

Liddell Hart, B. H.: *History of the Second World War* (1970).

Linge, Heinz: *Bis zum Untergang: Als Chef des persönlichen Dienstes bei Hitler* (1980).

Ludecke [Lüdecke] Kurt G.W.: *I Knew Hitler* (1937).

Lutvigsen, Karl: *Battle for the Beetle* (1999).

Mann, Erika, ed.: *Thomas Mann: Wagner und unsere Zeit: Aufsätze, Betrachtungen, Briefe* (1983).

Mann, Thomas: *Gesammelte Werke*, 20 vols (1980–1986).

————: *Essays*, 6 vols.

————: *Letters of Thomas Mann, 1942–1955*, 2 vols (1970).

————: *Diaries 1918–1939* (1982).

Maser, Werner: *Adolf Hitler: Legende, Mythos, Wirklichkeit* (1971).

Mathieu, Thomas: *Kunstauffassungen und Kulturpolitik im Nationalsozialismus. Studien zu Adolf Hitler – Joseph Goebbels – Alfred Rosenberg – Baldur von Schirach – Heinrich Himmler – Albert Speer – Wilhelm Frick* (1997).

Merker, Reinhard: *Die bildenden Künste im Nationalsozialismus: Kulturideologie, Kulturpolitik, Kulturproduktion* (1983).

Meyer, Michael: *The Politics of Music in the Third Reich* (1991).

Miller Lane, Barbara: *Architecture and Politics in Germany 1918–1945* (1968).

Mommsen, Hans: *Der Nationalsozialismus und die deutsche Gesellschaft* (1991).

Mommsen, Hans and Manfred Grieger: *Das Volkswagenwerk und seine Arbeiter im Dritten Reich* (1997).

Mosse, George L.: *The Nationalization of the Masses* (1975).

———: *Nazi Culture: Intellectual, Cultural and Social Life in the Third Reich* (1966).

Müllern-Schönhausen, Johannes von: *Die Lösung des Rätsels Adolf Hitler: Der Versuch einer Deutung der geheimnisvollsten Erscheinung der Weltgeschichte* (1959).

Nerdinger, Winfried, ed.: *Bauen im Nationalsozialismus: Bayern 1933–1945* (1993).

———, ed.: *Bauhaus-Moderne im Nationalsozialismus: Zwischen Anbiederung und Verfolgung* (1993).

Nerdinger, Winfried and Ekkehard Mai, eds: *Wilhelm Kreis: Architekt zwischen Kaiserreich und Demokratie, 1873–1955* (1994).

Newman, L. M.: *Gordon Craig Archives* (1976).

Nicholas, Lynn H.: *The Rape of Europa: The Fate of Europe's Treasures in the Third Reich and the Second World War* (1995).

Nicolson, Harold: *Diaries and Letters 1939–1945* (1967).

Noakes, Jeremy and Geoffrey Pridham: *Documents on Nazism, 1919–1945* (1974).

Olden, Rudolf: *Hitler the Pawn* (1936).

Orwell, Sonia and Ian Angus: *The Collected Essays, Journalism and Letters of George Orwell*, vol.2 (1970).

Petropoulos, Jonathan: *Art as Politics in the Third Reich* (1996).

———: *The Faustian Bargain: The Art World in Nazi Germany* (2000).

Petrova, Ada and Peter Watson: *The Death of Hitler: The Full Story with New Evidence from Secret Russian Archives* (1995).

Petsch, Joachim: *Baukunst und Stadtplanung im Dritten Reich* (1976).

Picker, Günther: *Der Fall Kujau: Chronik eines Fälschungsskandals* (1992).

Price, Billy F.: *Adolf Hitler als Maler und Zeichner* (1983).

———: *Adolf Hitler: The Unknown Artist* (1984).

Prieberg, Fred K.: *Musik im NS-Staat* (1982).

———: *Trial of Strength: Wilhelm Furtwängler and the Third Reich* (1991).

Probst, Volker G.: *Der Bildhauer Arno Breker: Eine Untersuchung* (1978).

Raith, Frank-Bertolt: *Der heroische Stil: Studien zur Architektur am Ende der Weimarer Republik* (1997).

Rasp, Hans-Peter: *Eine Stadt für tausend Jahre: München – Bauten und Projekte für die Hauptstadt der Bewegung* (1981).

Rathkolb, Oliver: *Führertreu und Gottbegnadet: Künstlereliten im Dritten Reich* (1991).

Rave, Paul Ortwin: *Kunstdiktatur im Dritten Reich* (1949).

Reich, Simon: *The Fruits of Fascism* (1990).

Reichel, Peter: *Der schöne Schein des Dritten Reiches: Faszination und Gewalt des Faschismus* (1991).

Reichhardt, Hans J. and Wolfgang Schäche: *Von Berlin nach Germania* (1984).

Reif, Adalbert: *Albert Speer: Kontroversen um ein deutsches Phänomen* (1978).

Reimann, Viktor: *Dr Joseph Goebbels* (1971).

Reuth, Ralf Georg: *Goebbels* (1990).

Riess, Curt: *Furtwängler: Musik und Politik* (1953).

Rietdorf, Alfred: *Gilly: Wiedergeburt der Architektur* (1940).

Roh, Franz: *'Entartete' Kunst: Kunstbarbarei im Dritten Reich* (1962).

Rosenberg, Alfred: *Memoirs of Alfred Rosenberg* (1949).

Roxan, David and Ken Wanstall: *The Jackdaw of Linz: The Story of Hitler's Art Thefts* (1964).

Russell, John: *The Meanings of Modern Art* (1981).

Schaumburg-Lippe, Friedrich Christian Prinz zu: *Als die goldne Abendsonne: Aus meinen Tagebüchern der Jahre 1933–1937* (1971).

Schirach, Baldur von: *Ich glaubte an Hitler* (1967).

Schirach, Henriette von: *Der Preis der Heerlichkeit* (1956).

Schmeer, Karlheinz: *Die Regie des öffentlichen Lebens im Dritten Reich* (1956).

Schmidt, Matthias: *Albert Speer: The End of a Myth* (1984).

Schneede, Uwe M., ed.: *Paul Ortwin Rave: Kunstdikatur im Dritten Reich* (1987).

Schönberger, Angele: *Die neue Reichskanzlei von Albert Speer: Zum Zusammenhang von nationalsozialistischer Ideologie und Architektur* (1981).

Scholdt, Günter: *Autoren über Hitler: Deutschsprachige Schriftsteller 1919–1945 und ihr Bild vom 'Führer'* (1993).

Schramm, Percy E: *Hitler: The Man and the Military Leader* (1971).

Schroeder, Christa: *Er war mein Chef: Aus dem Nachlaß der Sekretärin von Adolf Hitler* (1985).

Schuh, Willi: *Richard Strauss-Stefan Zweig: Briefwechsel* (1957).

Schüler, Winfried: *Der Bayreuther Kreis von seiner Entstehung bis zum Ausgang der wilhelminischen Ära: Wagnerkult und Kultusreform im Geiste völkischer Weltanschauung* (1971).

Schulze, Franz: *Philip Johnson: Life and Work* (1994).

Schenk, H. G.: *The Mind of the Romantics: An Essay in Cultural History* (1966).

Schwarzwäller, Wulf C.: *Hitlers Geld: vom armen Kunstmaler zum millionschweren Führer* (1998).

Scobie, Alex: *Hitler's State Architecture: The Impact of Classical Antiquity* (1990).

Sereny, Gitta: *Albert Speer: His Battle with Truth* (1995).

Seydewitz, Ruth and Max: *Das Dresdener Galeriebuch: Vierhundert Jahre Dresdener Gemäldegalerie* (1964).

Shirer, William L.: *The Rise and Fall of the Third Reich* (1959).

———: *Berlin Diary 1934–1941* (1941).

Skelton, Geoffrey: *Wieland Wagner: The Positive Sceptic* (1971).

Smith, Bradley F.: *Adolf Hitler: His Family, Childhood and Youth* (1967).

Smith, Howard K.: *Last Train from Berlin* (1942).

Speer, Albert: *Inside the Third Reich* (1970).

———: *Spandau: the Secret Diaries* (1976).

———: *Neue deutsche Baukunst* (1943).

Splitt, Gerhard: *Richard Strauss 1933–1935: Ästhetik und Musikpolitik zu Beginn der nationalsozialistischen Herrschaft* (1987).

Stommer, Rainer, ed.: *Reichsautobahn: Pyramiden des Dritten Reiches* (1982).

Stuttgart: Staatsgalerie Stuttgart. *Bildzyklen: Zeugnisse verfemter Kunst in Deutschland 1933–1945* (1987).

Taylor, Brandon and Wilfried van der Will, eds: *The Nazification of Art: Art, Design, Music, Architecture and Film in the Third Reich* (1990).

Taylor, Robert R.: *The Word in Stone* (1974).

Thies, Jochen: *Architekt der Weltherrschaft: Die 'Endziele' Hitlers* (1976).

Thomae, Otto: *Die Propaganda-Maschinerie: Bildende Kunst und Öffentlichkeitsarbeit im Dritten Reich* (1978).

Thomas, Walter (alias W. Th. Anderman): *Bis der Vorhang fiel* (1947).

Toland, John: *Adolf Hitler* (1976).

Trevor-Roper, Hugh: *The Last Days of Hitler* (1947).

Troost, Gerdy: *Das Bauen im neuen Reich*, 2 vols (1942).

Tutaev, David: *The Consul of Florence* (1966).

Ursino, Mario (ed.): *Rodolfo Siviero: L'arte e il Nazismo: Esodo e ritorno delle opere d'arte italiane 1938–1963* (1984).

Vogel, Johann Peter: *Hans Pfitzner: Leben, Werke, Dokumente* (1999).

Voss, Hermann: *Der Ursprung des Donaustils* (1907).

———: *Albrech Altdorfer und Wolf Huber* (1910).

———: *Die Malerei der Spätrenaissance in Rom und Florenz* (1920).

———: *Die Malerei des Barock in Rom* (1926).

Wagner, Friedelind: *Heritage of Fire: The Story of Richard Wagner's Granddaughter* (1945).

Wagner, Manfred: *Alfred Roller in seiner Zeit* (1996).

Wagner, Wolfgang, ed.: *Das Festspielbuch 1997* (1997).

———: *Acts: The Autobiography of Wolfgang Wagner* (1994).

Walter, Michael: *Hitler in der Oper: Deutsches Musikleben 1919–1945* (1995).

Warlimont, Walter: *Im Hauptquartier der Wehrmacht 1939–1945* (1964).

Weihsmann, Helmut: *Bauen unterm Hakenkreuz: Architektur des Untergangs* (1998).

Wessling, Berndt: *Wieland Wagner: Der Enkel* (1997).

Wheeler-Bennett, John W.: *The Nemesis of Power: The German Army in Politics 1918–1945* (1961).

———: *Wooden Titan: Hindenburg in Twenty Years of German History 1914–1934* (1936).

Wiedemann, Fritz: *Der Mann der Feldherr werden wollte* (1964).

Wilhelm, Kurt: *Richard Strauss: An Intimate Portrait* (1989).

Windsor, Alan: *Peter Behrens: Architect and Designer* (1981).

Wistrich, Robert S.: *Weekend in Munich: Art, Propaganda and Terror in the Third Reich* (1995).

Wolters, Rudolf: *Stadtmitte Berlin: Stadtbauliche Entwicklungsphasen von den Anfängen bis zur Gegenwart* (1978).

Wulf, Joseph, ed.: *Musik im Dritten Reich: Eine Dokumentation* (1963).

Zavrel, B. John: *Arno Breker: His Art and Life* (1985).

Zelinsky, Hartmut: *Richard Wagner: Ein deutsches Thema: Eine Dokumentation zur Wirkungsgeschichte Richard Wagners 1876–1976* (1983).

Ziegler, Hans Severus: *Hitler aus dem Leben dargestellt* (1964).

Zoller, Albert (pseudonym: Christa Schroeder): *Hitler Privat: Erlebnisbericht seiner Geheimsekretärin* (1949).

Index

NB: page numbers in italics indicate illustrations

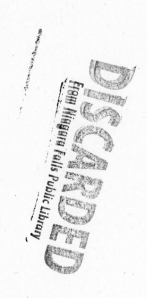